Southern Biography Series
Bertram Wyatt-Brown, Editor

George Henry White

George Henry White

An Even Chance in the Race of Life

Benjamin R. Justesen

Louisiana State University Press
Baton Rouge

Copyright © 2001 by Louisiana State University Press

All rights reserved

Manufactured in the United States of America

First printing

10   09   08   07   06   05   04   03   02   01

5   4   3   2   1

Designer: Amanda McDonald Scallan

Typeface: Goudy

Typesetter: Crane Composition, Inc.

Printer and binder: Thomson-Shore, Inc.

Library of Congress Cataloging-in-Publication Data

Justesen, Benjamin R., 1949–

 George Henry White : an even chance in the race of life / Benjamin R. Justesen.

        p. cm. — (Southern biography series)

Includes bibliographical references and index.

 ISBN 0-8071-2586-5 (alk. paper)   1. White, George H. (George Henry), 1852–1918. 2. Afro-American
legislators—Biography. 3. Legislators—United States—Biography. 4. United States. Congress. House—
Biography. 5. Afro-Americans—Politics and government—19th century. I. Title. II. Series.

 E664.W593 J87 2000

 328.73'092—dc21

                                                                                00-010079

The paper in this book meets the guidelines for permanence and durability of the Committee on Production
Guidelines for Book Longevity of the Council on Library Resources. ♾

Portions of chapters 10 and 11 appeared in different form in "George Henry White, Josephus Daniels, and the
Showdown over Disfranchisement, 1900," *North Carolina Historical Review* (January 2000).

To Elizabeth, Fredrika, and Margaret
with love and respect

Mr. Speaker, my plea is not for special privileges for my people, but what we want and have a right to expect is . . . all the privileges of an American citizen. We will be content with nothing less. . . . An even chance in the race of life is all that we ask, and then if we can not reach the goal, let the devil take the hindmost one!

—George Henry White in the U.S. House of
Representatives, 7 March 1898

Contents

Acknowledgments | xv
Introduction | xix
Abbreviations | xxiii

1
From the Turpentine Woods | 1

2
A New Home for an Adopted Son | 37

3
Into the Public Arena | 63

4
The Next Political Campaigns | 94

5
"The only colored solicitor in America" | 124

6
The Siren's Call of the Black Second | 151

7
The Long Road to Congress | 179

8
Into Congress: The First Term, 1897 | 201

9

Facing the Lions: Reelection to a Second Term | 228

10

The Second Term in Congress | 256

11

The Showdown over Disfranchisement | 276

12

Life after Congress: Testing the Currents, 1901 | 312

13

Dueling Editors and a "Winged Statesman" | 331

14

The Dream of Whitesboro | 356

15

Leaving Washington Behind | 385

16

Philadelphia and the Final Years | 400

Epilogue: Eden at Last | 423

Appendix | 429
Bibliography | 443
Index | 459

Illustrations

following page 200

George Henry White in his congressional years

Reverend Robert Owen Spaulding's house, Columbus County

Town of New Bern

William John Clarke

William Edwards Clarke

John Campbell Dancy

Ebenezer Presbyterian Church, New Bern

George White after election as solicitor

Craven County Courthouse

James Hunter Young

George White residence, New Bern

Henry Plummer Cheatham

Della White's graduating class, Scotia Seminary

Josephus Daniels

Cartoon: "He Doesn't Like to Let Go."

Advertisement for George H. White Land and Improvement Company

Jeter Conley Pritchard

People's Savings Bank, Philadelphia

George White in later years

Acknowledgments

It is always a challenge, as well as a risk, to begin listing those who have contributed to the production of a biography requiring such extensive research as this one, over such a lengthy period; the fear is that someone will be overlooked. I begin, therefore, by expressing my deep and abiding appreciation to three people who encouraged me to continue the project through a particularly difficult period, when my enthusiasm and stamina were waning. They are, in no special order, Bill Powell, professor emeritus at the University of North Carolina at Chapel Hill, whose wise words and gentle manner helped renew my flagging dedication; Bert Wyatt-Brown, professor at the University of Florida, whose sharp editorial eye, humorous spirit, and thoughtful consideration of the manuscript weathered months of inconsistent production; and Sylvia Frank, acquisitions editor at Louisiana State University Press, whose discerning style and encouraging manner I have come to cherish. Their friendship has been my unexpected gain.

I owe debts of gratitude to the reference librarians at a number of institutions of higher learning, including those of Lincoln University, Oberlin College, Case Western Reserve University, and the University of Pennsylvania, who enabled me to dig deeply into their archives. The reference staff in the rare book room at the Moorland-Spingarn Library, Howard University, were especially gracious and helpful during my several visits there. The staffs of two special collections at the University of North Carolina at Chapel Hill—the Southern Historical Collection and the North Carolina

Collection—were unfailingly creative in their ability and willingness to help on short notice.

My research would never have been completed without the ongoing assistance of the capable and experienced staff at the Library of Congress, particularly in the Manuscript Reading Room and the Periodicals Reading Room, where I spent weeks poring over old microfilm; the Local History and Genealogy Reading Room and the Microform Reading Room, where I spent many days; and above all, the patient, polite staff in the Main Reading Room, who never failed to help me locate the dusty volumes I needed to check one more fact.

The staff of the National Archives, both on Pennsylvania Avenue and in College Park, made my research at both locations rewarding and far less complicated than I had feared. In like manner, the unusually helpful staff at the North Carolina Division of Archives and History in Raleigh were a pleasure to work with. For his expert and gracious assistance in helping locate so many of the photographs used here, I single out Stephen Massengill of the Archival Services Branch. For similar kindnesses, I express my appreciation to the staffs of the Library of Congress Photo Duplication Service and the University of Chicago.

To friends Angella Reid and James O'Connor, who volunteered to read the manuscript and offer constructive suggestions at various times, I offer both affection and gratitude for their critical skills and the hope that the book will read far better the second time. For Odessa Spaulding, whose memories of Whitesboro and her family proved invaluable, and Rudolph Knight, whose thoughtful advice on aspects of Tarboro's history facilitated my efforts to reconstruct George White's life there, I offer my repeated thanks.

Finally, to my manuscript editor, Sara Anderson, whose wise counsel, sharp eyes, and steady touch polished and shaped the manuscript into its final form, goes my deepest appreciation for a job well done. I could not have finished the project without her gentle and wise assistance.

Last, I owe this book in no small part to the encouragement offered by the three women with the greatest influence on my life: my mother, Elizabeth, whose sense of adventure led her to take research trips with me; my wife, Margaret, whose love and untiring efforts made my unorthodox sabbatical possible; and my daughter, Fredrika, whose own academic commitment restored my sense of perspective. To them, I dedicate this work, with much love and respect.

Note Regarding Birth Dates and Spellings of Names

I have made every effort to standardize the spellings of all proper names used in this book, using the spelling most likely to be correct and noting any major variant(s). In each case, I based my choice on what from my research seemed to be the most authoritative sources.

For instance, George White's third wife, Cora Cherry, generally used only her first name and a middle initial—"Cora L."—in her writings. Her name appears elsewhere variously as "Cora Lena," "Cora Lina," and even "Coraline." Although almost all historians have tended to use "Cora Lina," my research indicates "Cora Lena" is correct, based on four sources: her gravestone in New Bern; her 1905 obituaries in the *Washington Post* and *Washington Evening Star*, obviously provided by the family; and her daughter's unmistakably clear handwriting in a 1939 Social Security application.

In some cases of family names, there were few sources to compare. I chose to spell Fannie Randolph White's first name as "Fannie" based on her gravestone and the 1880 census, although it often appears as "Fanny," including in her marriage license application. In the case of Nancy Scott White, the spelling on her gravestone—"Nancey"—appears to be an aberration; there is no marriage license available for comparison, but her name in state normal-school records is always "Nancy." White's daughter Mamie rarely used her full name, but wrote it as "Mary Adelyne" in 1908, the form I selected; she changed this in 1939 to "Mary Adelaide," and it appears elsewhere as "Mary Adlyne." Even her nickname is often spelled differently—as "Mayme," "Maymie," and "Mammie"—but I preferred the simplest, most frequent spelling.

Outside the White and Cherry families, I have simply used the most common spellings of Christian names and surnames found in contemporary documents.

Selecting birth years and computing ages was often problematic, since birth certificates from the period 1850–1900 are rarely available. In most instances, the best sources for ages are the family's U.S. census entries, but these entries are sometimes incomplete or inaccurate, and not available at all for 1890. Even marriage license applications from the period can be misleading, since they rarely specify birth years for either spouse and sometimes contain ages of questionable accuracy.

When several sources provided conflicting information for the age of a White family member, particularly a child born before 1900, I chose the most plausible birth year based on the best evidence available—usually either the gravestone, a newspaper article announcing a recent birth, or a document signed by the person.

Introduction

He would live to become the best-recognized political leader of his race during the last decade of the nineteenth century, yet today George Henry White is among the least remembered of that group. From poor rural beginnings in North Carolina's turpentine belt, he became arguably the most powerful African American speaker of his day, a towering figure whose well-reasoned arguments and rhetorical flourishes drew applause from audiences in Canada as well as in the United States, yet to most he remains only a footnote in an era dimly remembered, even by those who followed in his wake. He was at once the most acclaimed and most reviled symbol of the freed slaves whose cause he took up on the floor of the U.S. Congress, yet both his origin and his end now lie shrouded in obscurity. The 1901 departure of this last African American to serve in Congress in the post-Reconstruction period left a void unfilled for nearly three decades, yet only paragraphs of his stirring farewell speech are now recalled, rather than the details of its creator's life.

George Henry White was a public servant who lived under the unremitting glare of public scrutiny. But he remained a complex, intensely private man whose public roles masked his inner turmoil. A privileged individual of mixed race forced by circumstance to wage an unpopular war for racial justice, he stood virtually alone in an era of public apathy and civic scorn. He forfeited fame and retired to comparative oblivion while still relatively young, his death two decades later barely noted by the media that had once paid him such close attention. By his life's end, however, as a teacher, principal, prosecutor, banker, and civic and religious leader, he had for decades touched the lives of thousands of his fellow citizens with compassion and fairness, embodying a sense of integrity that few could match.

A widely known figure as the nation's only black congressman, George White sought to stave off the effective reenslavement of the African American masses by a nation weary of domestic problems and unable to resolve its most painful social dilemma. In so doing, he became a prisoner of his own inflexible conscience, in a world that demanded compromise at any cost and punished those who disobeyed with marginalization and banishment.

Like many other self-made men of the nineteenth century, George White was a farm boy who parlayed an inquiring mind and an ambitious nature into a career far removed from his native soil. Little is known with certainty about his childhood since much of what has been written about him tends upon closer examination to fall away as legend, either false, inaccurate, or misleading. Imaginative chroniclers are partly to blame for thus filling in gaps left by White's reticence regarding his upbringing. Journalists who addressed the subject often depended on a single interview, with no documentary research; later historians frequently repeated and compounded the contemporaries' errors. White's reticence, whether intentional or involuntary, may have concealed inner discomfort about his past, for much of what he did tell others about his early life seems to have been incomplete at best, and is not always supported by the few facts available.

In a sense, then, it is best to begin by saying what this man was not, before describing him in any positive way. George White was neither "black" in skin color nor in pure heritage; he was of mixed race, perhaps half Negro and part American Indian, the balance white, probably of Irish extraction. He seems not to have been born a slave, although this cannot be proven with any certainty; it seems definite in any event that he was not freed by the Emancipation Proclamation of 1863. Nor were either of the parents he claimed as his own ever slaves. The woman he called his mother was almost certainly not his natural parent, although she apparently raised him as her child; he was probably born out of wedlock, and perhaps not under the name he took as an adult, to avoid a difficult legal dilemma. He did not grow up in abject poverty, but in a reasonably secure agricultural setting, as part of a large, well-known, respected family of moderate means. His earliest education came in private subscription schools paid for by his family, not the postwar public schools as was later claimed. An exceptionally bright and well-read man, he was neither a high-school nor university graduate, in the modern sense, nor did he attend law school. Yet he received quite a bit more education than the average student, including college-level training as a teacher, and he read the law under a sympathetic and distinguished white attorney, a popular tradition at the time.

White did not leave politics completely in 1901, but attempted to return to Congress in 1912, although his campaign was brief and unsuccessful. As an adult, he was married not twice, as most often reported, but four times, and widowed three times. Two of his four children survived him, one daughter living for more than fifty years after his death, but in the same kind of quiet obscurity that had marked her father's later life. White was not permanently estranged from his own father, as was hinted when he entered Congress, but resided with him while a student and brought him back to North Carolina to live until his death in 1893.

George White was not a militant who demanded total civil and social equality for the millions he represented—as antagonistic white Democrats charged—but rather a thoughtful, philosophical shepherd of his race. He passionately loved his nation's democratic traditions, and his plea was always for simple justice. He was outspoken in his challenge to racial injustice, yet preferred a gradual preparation of his followers for equality in their maturity. A conservative in philosophy, he was a dedicated Republican to the end, but reserved special disdain for those of his party who had seduced his race as political pawns and abandoned them when they became liabilities. In the end, he was an enigma: a proud and private man whose principles cost him his public acclaim and consigned his memory to the shadows.

I first encountered George Henry White while working as a journalist in North Carolina in 1975. Although we were born within a hundred miles and a century of each other, I had never heard of him before a museum press release crossed my desk that summer and piqued my interest. Over the next two decades, through my years in graduate school and more than a decade in the Foreign Service, I became increasingly fascinated by his life, carrying my notes around the world in a footlocker, literally, before deciding to write his story. My portrait of him is necessarily incomplete; two years of steady research shed much light on his life, but left many questions unanswered. Unable to locate his personal papers or any living descendants, I was forced to reconstruct his life from a wide variety of sources, including a heavy reliance on contemporary journalistic accounts.

To find the truth about George Henry White, I had to sift through a century of legend for even the most basic facts. To understand him, I had to shed both the flattering misconceptions of his admirers and the shrill hyperbole of his detractors. To present a complete portrait of him to others, I had to begin, simply and straightforwardly, at the beginning.

Alexandria, Virginia, 1999

Abbreviations

BTWP   Booker T. Washington Papers, Library of Congress, Washington, D.C.

DNCB   *Dictionary of North Carolina Biography* (ed. William S. Powell)

NCG   *North Carolina Government, 1585–1979* (Office of the North Carolina Secretary of State)

RN&O   *Raleigh (N.C.) News and Observer*

SHC   Southern Historical Collection, Wilson Library, University of North Carolina at Chapel Hill

WCA   *Washington (D.C.) Colored American*

George Henry White

1

From the Turpentine Woods

The village of Rosindale is today little more than a rural highway crossing in North Carolina's Bladen County, some fifty miles from the Atlantic Ocean. With few homes visible from the road and no community buildings of note, its only distinction is an abandoned railroad stop a block from the state highway that passes through the village. In 1852, the settlement had not even been named; that event would come only a decade later, after the war-ravaged economy of North Carolina's turpentine belt had begun to rebuild. Then as now, there was little to suggest the isolated Rosindale as the birthplace of a successful political leader. But it was here, in a log cabin near the banks of Richland Branch, that George Henry White was born in December 1852.[1]

It was a week before Christmas, and the small pine cabin offered little defense against the cold winter winds from nearby Slap Swamp. The newborn boy seems, fortunately, to have been large and healthy; although his mother's

1. William S. Powell, *The North Carolina Gazetteer: A Dictionary of Tar Heel Places* (Chapel Hill: University of North Carolina Press, 1968), 259; "Hon. George H. White, LL.D." in Daniel W. Culp, ed., *Twentieth Century Negro Literature, or a Cyclopedia of Thought on Vital Topics Relating to the American Negro* (Napierville, Ill.: J. L. Nichols, 1902), 224. Rosindale was "settled in 1866 by George C. McDougald, who produced turpentine and rosin (from which the name was taken)"; a post office was located at Rosindale from 1869 to 1947, according to U.S. postal records. Culp's biographical sketch, obviously written with White's assistance, listed White's birth date as December 18, 1852, and his birthplace as "at the confluence of 'Richland Branch' and 'Slop Swamp,' near the Columbus County line." (According to Powell, the correct spelling of the second body of water is "Slap Swamp.")

labor may have been a long and difficult one, there was no physician to attend her in this remote setting. Perhaps a neighbor or a midwife, assisted by an older son, brought forth the infant; the father, an itinerant turpentine hand on a farm in nearby Columbus County, was probably not allowed to witness his son's birth, if indeed he was even present.

In the state capital of Raleigh, a hundred miles to the northwest, a young Democratic lawyer was poring over the state's treasury records, unaware of the arrival of his future protégé. Despite his 1849 defeat for Congress, thirty-three-year-old William John Clarke was quickly gaining stature in the Democratic Party; a decorated veteran of the Mexican War, he had been elected state comptroller in the 1850 election. A few blocks away, Clarke's longtime friend William Woods Holden, thirty-four, was preparing for battle as editor of the *North Carolina Standard*, attacking his former fellow Whigs in advance of the upcoming legislative session. Both men were progressive Democrats, committed to their party, and neither could have foreseen the emergence of a powerful third national party—the antislavery Republicans—in just four years. For neither would it have been even conceivable that they would eventually help bring those Republicans to power in North Carolina; Holden, the emerging firebrand of state politics, would publicly prefer secession to the election of a Republican president in 1856, and would be an unsuccessful Democratic candidate for governor in 1858 before becoming a leader in the antiwar movement.[2]

Nor could either man have envisioned the turbulent changes of the next decade, which would shake their world and thrust them into leading roles within the new party: Abraham Lincoln's election to the presidency, the outbreak of civil war, the emancipation of slaves, and the bitterness of Reconstruction. Neither man could have dreamed that the little boy from Rosindale would grow up to have a deep impact on their new party, or that he would surpass them both in fame and power. For this particular child, the usual obstacles of poverty and circumstance were augmented by a legal barrier likely to be lifted in only the most radically different of futures.

This peculiarly southern barrier was the color of his skin. George Henry White's race was mixed: part Negro, part white, part Indian. His father, a free

2. Hugh T. Lefler and Albert R. Newsome, *North Carolina: The History of a Southern State*, 3d ed. (Chapel Hill: University of North Carolina Press, 1973), 376–8; "William John Clarke," *DNCB*, 1:381–2; "William Woods Holden," *DNCB*, 3:169–71.

mulatto, could not even vote; his natural mother—by some accounts a slave—had even less standing in the white-dominated society. No matter how bright and ambitious their child might be, his future was a legally limited one, with political power an almost impossible hope in this last decade before the war.[3] Yet he would confound the odds and become the most powerful political leader of his race in the state and, for a short time, the nation.

The forces shaping George White's destiny began in southeastern North Carolina's vast turpentine belt of primeval pine forests, from which much of the state's colonial and early federal wealth had come and to which Bladen County owed much of its prewar prosperity. There were other cash crops—cotton, wheat, corn, even tobacco—but it was the lucrative turpentine that spawned several of the finest riverfront plantations in historic Bladen. Columbus County, where White grew up, was still largely a raw frontier of swamps in 1850, but was already beginning to follow the vigorous lead of its mother county to the north. The pine tree, unlike man, knew no artificial borders, and its rosin was like liquid gold.

The two thinly populated counties reflected the region's rural character. Barely sixteen thousand people lived on their eighteen hundred square miles of mostly swamps and forest stretching north and east from the South Carolina border. Bladen had been settled first, thanks to the presence of the Cape Fear River, that early hub of transportation inland from the Atlantic below Wilmington. Bladen's fertile soil and promise of agricultural wealth had pulled nearly as many African slaves into thrall as free whites; by 1850, its population was split almost evenly between the races, with a handful of indigenous Indians still present. The Cape Fear bisected the heart of the county in a northwesterly direction; steamships like the *Henrietta* and riverboats like the *Wilmington* passed between Fayetteville and Wilmington once a week or more, stopping to let off passengers or pick up freight at plantation docks as the workers stopped and stared.[4]

3. Blacks were excluded from the North Carolina political arena between 1835 and 1868; free black males, who never accounted for more than 3 percent of the state's prewar population, lost the right to vote in 1835 but retained most economic rights. Slaves were considered property, with no individual political rights.

4. "Bladen," in Bill Sharpe, *A New Geography of North Carolina* (Raleigh: Sharpe, 1954–65), 3:1137–60. Population density figures, derived here from the 1850 census, show that Columbus had six residents per square mile and Bladen about twelve; the statewide average was eighteen.

In contrast, Columbus County had far fewer large plantations and only a third as many slaves at midcentury as Bladen, although their white populations were nearly the same; Columbus had been formed only in 1808, whereas Bladen dated back nearly a century earlier. But like Bladen and other rural counties of the period, Columbus boasted a significant subgroup of free blacks, as much as three percent of the total population. Most were not of pure African descent but were mulattoes, usually the offspring of white farmers by slave women; many had bought their own freedom, some had been given it by their fathers. Most free blacks were at least minimally literate, in an era when educating slaves was strongly discouraged. Several of these freed slaves even owned slaves of their own, although their motives were as often benevolent as financial; manumitted slaves of the period frequently purchased their relatives out of slavery, but were later unable or unwilling to convince the legislature or the courts to grant them total freedom. Bladen's Gooden Bowen, for instance, owned forty-four slaves at the height of his prosperity in 1830; he was one of nearly two hundred free blacks in North Carolina who owned slaves, according to that year's census.[5]

The coming of the railroad to southern Bladen County in the 1860s would begin to transform its river-oriented culture, spurring the growth of small settlements like Abbottsburg and Rosindale and forever changing the way residents looked at the outside world. The new railroad ran along the Bladen-Columbus line, thus helping also to catalyze the growth of Columbus County, and it was here that a freed slave named Benjamin Spaulding, the patriarch of George White's family, established himself in the early years of the nineteenth century.

Benjamin Spaulding had been one of the first large landowners in northern Columbus, gradually acquiring more than twenty-three hundred acres of cheap forest and fertile farmland in the Welches Creek area from his neighbors, adding to that obtained from his white father, a plantation owner in Bladen. In turn he parceled that land out to his many children and their families, and with it, the prospects of relative prosperity. The thinly populated

5. John Hope Franklin, *The Free Negro in North Carolina, 1790–1860* (Chapel Hill: University of North Carolina Press, 1995), 156–61. Most such slaves were held by free blacks for benevolent purposes, according to Franklin; by 1860, the incidence of this slaveholding had rapidly declined, to where only eight free blacks owned slaves, totaling only twenty-five for the state.

Columbus County, which had been created from Bladen and neighboring Brunswick only after citizens complained about the distances to their respective courthouses in Elizabeth Town and Smithville, was where George White would spend much of his youth.[6]

Like Bladen, the new county of Columbus contained vast forests of profitable pine and oak trees for naval stores and sawmills, the Spaulding clan's two specialties; oak-staved casks for turpentine and other products were among their most prized products. In 1850 just 725 barrels of turpentine were produced in Columbus—a small fraction of Bladen's output—but Columbus soon developed its own lumber and naval-store industries, as a second new railroad pushed westward from Wilmington to Whiteville and the South Carolina line in the 1860s.[7]

Before the days of the railroad, hardy men like Spaulding had defied distance and geography by rolling heavy barrels of tar to river ports like White Hall. It was a grueling task, as was much of the work associated with production of naval stores. Only slaves could be forced to perform the hard physical labor required to milk the pine trees of precious rosin by "blazing" each tree—cutting diagonal gashes into the bark—and, twice a month or more, collecting the turpentine from wooden bowls built around the bases into barrels for the distillers. One slave was expected to collect as many as fifteen to twenty barrels each day, working up to six months out of the year; the rosin was later distilled, producing both oil of turpentine and a thick residue that could be dried to powder form. It was monotonous, exhausting work, and few free men were willing to work that hard for someone else's profit.[8]

---

6. "Columbus County," in Sharpe, *A New Geography*, 2:737–60; Louis D. Mitchell, *A Story of the Descendants of Benjamin Spaulding (1773–1862), with Genealogy by John A. Spaulding* (Greensboro, N.C.: Deal Printing Company, 1989), 112 (Appendix I). Whiteville became the new county's seat; the other towns are now known as Elizabethtown and Southport. The three counties are among the state's largest in area, with Columbus covering 937 square miles, Bladen 875, and Brunswick 855. Dr. Mitchell's 1989 account of his ancestor's life is the basis for much of the description here. The turpentine figures come from the U.S. Census Columbus County, N.C., 1850 (manuscript on microfilm).

7. John F. Stover, *The Railroads of the South, 1865–1900: A Study in Finance and Control* (Chapel Hill: University of North Carolina Press, 1955), 264. The second railroad was the Wilmington, Columbia and Augusta Railway, with a depot at Vineland, just outside Whiteville.

8. "The Spaulding Family," in *Columbus County, North Carolina, Recollections and Records*, edited by Ann Courtney Ward Little (Whiteville, N.C.: Fisher-Harrison, 1980), 98–9; Marvin

Perhaps because he had himself been born a slave, Benjamin Spaulding knew the meaning of hard work better than many, and it was a personal ethic he drilled into every member of his family. There was no time for laziness in the Spaulding household, a harsh but secure environment that produced a remarkable string of successful descendants capable of beating the odds in almost any situation. "Old Ben" Spaulding had set the legendary example as a young man defying his plantation-owner father to gain his freedom before the turn of the nineteenth century; the persistent oral tradition that Samuel Swindell Sr. actually threw an ax handle at him and "sent Ben sprawling" before deciding to free him seems unlikely, yet he was thereafter known as Ben Sprawling.[9]

When Swindell died around 1808, he had apparently not completed the legal action required to make the manumission official; only the 1825 intervention of Ben's white half brother, Samuel Jr., accomplished the necessary technical maneuvers. In April 1825, young Swindell (also spelled Swindale), successfully petitioned the superior court of Columbus County "to liberate and set free a certain slave named Ben & that sd Slave hereafter be known & called by the name of Benjamin Sprawling & that he be entitled to all the rights & priviledges of a free born Negro." Now that Ben was completely free, the spelling of his name gradually began to change; the U.S. census records it as Sprauldin in 1820, Spraldin in 1830, Spalding in 1840, and finally Spaulding in 1850.[10]

The details of Benjamin Spaulding's adult life are now obscure, since family accounts vary. One persistent tale describes him as permanently crippled by his father's brutal beating, but his long and virile life belies that story. Documentation of his personal life is limited, but the year of his death and his age are inscribed on his gravestone as 1862 and eighty-nine. The U.S. census lists his place of birth as neighboring Duplin County. Various legal dealings,

L. Michael Kay and Lorin Lee Cary, *Slavery in North Carolina, 1748–1755* (Chapel Hill: University of North Carolina Press, 1995), 44–5.

9. Mitchell, *A Story*, 28–9; Little, *Recollections*, 108–9. Little cites a separate work by J. H. Moore (*Noble Ancestry*) whose accuracy Mitchell disputes; the anecdote about Ben Spaulding's crippling injuries is probably fanciful, says Mitchell.

10. Mitchell, *A Story*, 28–9. Mitchell surmises that the elder Samuel Swindell had previously "freed Ben without making it official"; according to the census, Swindell still owned eleven slaves in 1800, and left four slaves to his wife in an 1807 document that served in lieu of a will.

including his will, list the names of his wife and some of his children, his possessions, and the boundaries of his homestead.[11]

It is clear that Benjamin Spaulding lived a long and productive life after his inauspicious beginnings as a house slave on a Bladen County plantation. He functioned as a free man for many years before his brother's petition, indicating that those around him perceived him as already free; he was even listed as a free man of color in the 1820 census. Sometime after 1800 he married Edith Delphia Jacobs, of Indian descent, and sired nine sons and one daughter, all of whom for generations lived around the family's center at Sandy Plains in Welches Creek Township. Although the Spaulding patriarch apparently never learned to sign his name—instead affixing his "X" to the many deeds and grants legalizing his growing real-estate holdings—he nonetheless encouraged his children and grandchildren to learn to read and write. In time, many of his descendants would become schoolteachers, perhaps in homage to an ancestor's forceful personality and to their own strict upbringing.[12]

How Old Ben felt about the institution of slavery is a paradoxical matter. Freed himself as a young man, Ben Spaulding declined to own slaves afterward, although he evidently never forbade his family to do so; at least three of his sons owned slaves, perhaps as investments, more likely for benevolent purposes. Whatever the reason, Emmanuel and David Spaulding owned slaves as late as the eve of the Civil War—seven and three, respectively, according to the 1860 census. These sons lived on property adjoining their father's lands, where the presence of their slaves was a visible reminder of the old days. Another son, Iver, who owned a fourteen-year-old female slave in 1850, lived across the line in Bladen County.[13]

With their large families and demanding agricultural routines, it would have been difficult for the Spauldings to function without some type of help,

11. Benjamin and Edith Spaulding, who died a decade later, are buried in a family cemetery called Mitchell Field, located near their Columbus County home. Spaulding's will appears as Appendix II in Mitchell, *A Story*, 113.

12. U.S. Census, manuscript on microfilm, Columbus County, N.C., 1850 and 1860. Ben Spaulding, eighty-three, was listed as owning $1,500 in real estate and $600 in personal property in 1860; he was also listed as unable to read or write. Several of his children were listed as illiterate in 1850, but almost all his grandchildren could read and write, according to later censuses.

13. Mitchell, *A Story*, 17; U.S. Census, manuscript on microfilm, Bladen County, N.C., 1850, Slave Schedules. The census notes Iver Spaulding's ownership of one slave.

whether slave, servant, or hired contractor. Edy Spaulding bore ten living children over the course of two decades, beginning with William in 1810 and Emmanuel and Armstrong in 1813. These three may have been born near Rosindale, perhaps on land given or sold to Ben by his father; by 1817, however, the Spaulding family had established itself permanently across the Columbus border in Sandy Plains, when Ben's property near Slade Swamp was first noted in an unrelated deed as the boundary of a property transaction. In that year, Ben and Edy had a total of five sons, now including Armstead and John; over the next fourteen years, the Spaulding household would grow to include four more sons—Iver, Benjamin Jr., David, and Henry—and their only daughter, Ann Eliza.[14]

By 1837 Emmanuel, sometimes called Manual, was married and working in the family's sawmill business, set off on a seven-acre plot described in Ben Spaulding's 1862 will. Emmanuel Spaulding had saved enough to buy 140 acres of adjacent land for seventy-five dollars from his father in March of 1837; his wife was Susannah Gumby, also called Susan, who may have been of Indian descent. The couple would continue the Spaulding tradition of large families, with at least nine children of their own; Sarah Jane and Mary Anna arrived in 1838 and 1840, followed by first son Benjamin McLean Spaulding in 1844. Then came Anna E., Madalaine, Amanda, Laney, William Chavis, and finally Andrew in 1859. Emmanuel also had a son, Guy, from a purported liaison with a slave predating his marriage by several years; Guy was born in 1831 but never listed by name as a household member.[15]

Though never wealthy, Emmanuel Spaulding gradually achieved comparative prosperity as a farmer and sawmill operator. His lands were valued at

14. Mitchell, A *Story*, 43; Powell, *N.C. Gazetteer*, 457. The birth years of Benjamin and Edith Spaulding's children were as follows: William, 1810; Emmanuel and Armstrong (possibly twins), 1813; Armstead, 1814; John, 1817; Iver, 1819; Ann Eliza, 1822; Benjamin Jr., 1824; David, 1829; and Henry, 1831. Henry inherited his father's house and remaining lands at his father's death in 1862. Slade, or Slades, Swamp is separate from Slap Swamp, according to Powell.

15. U.S. Census, Columbus County, 1840, 1850, 1860, and 1870; Mitchell, A *Story*, 50–5. The names and birth years of Emmanuel and Susannah Spaulding's children are taken from the censuses and from Spaulding's genealogy in Mitchell. Madalaine's name is sometimes spelled Madaline. Laney Spaulding, whose name appears in the censuses of 1850 and 1860, is not mentioned by John Spaulding, but he does list Guy as Emmanuel's apparent son by Joanna Swindell. Neither Joanna nor Guy is listed by name in either census, presumably because they remained slaves until after Emancipation.

$500 in the 1850 census and at $2,200 a decade later; in 1853 alone he purchased another two hundred acres from his father. His $5,000 in "other property" in 1860 almost certainly included the value of his slaves, who would, of course, be freed at the end of the war; in the June 1870 census—the last taken before Emmanuel Spaulding's death, and the first taken after Emancipation— his personal property had dwindled in value to $450, with his real estate remaining at almost the same level as a decade earlier.[16]

Other changes in Emmanuel Spaulding's household during the 1850s were the marriages of his two oldest daughters, each at age seventeen. Sarah Jane married John W. Freeman in December 1855, later bearing him eight children. Mary Anna followed suit on April 16, 1857, marrying Wiley Franklin White, a Pitt County native who had moved to Columbus County a decade earlier. Wiley and Mary Anna White would raise a smaller family, including Wiley's two sons from earlier relationships; one of those sons would later become known as George Henry White, and he would always consider Mary Anna his natural mother.[17]

Mary Anna's home township, Welches Creek, was an insular community of swamps and forests, hardly appealing to most outsiders. Largely white, the population nevertheless contained numerous slaves, a few free blacks, and many more mulattoes; all lived alongside each other in a peaceful fashion, often mixing in working situations but rarely in social settings. Noticeably absent was any sign of the racial tension that would inflame the state in decades to come. This seems to have been due in part to the frontierlike mentality of the farmers and in part to the rather rigid social structure of the mulattoes themselves. Families like the Spauldings, the Freemans, the Jacobses, the Mitchells, and the Moores tended to keep to themselves, often intermarrying generation after generation. First and second cousins would become husband

16. U.S. Census, Columbus County, 1840, 1850, 1860, and 1870. Emmanuel owned no slaves in 1840, the first for which he and his brothers William and Strong (Armstrong) are listed by name; he owned seven slaves in 1860.

17. *Marriage Records, Columbus County, Whiteville, N.C.*, vol. 1 (Whiteville, N.C.: Barfield & Duncan Genealogy Service, 1984); *Who's Who in America, 1906–1907* (Chicago: A.N. Marquis, 1907), 1924. Mary Anna White was the only woman George White ever claimed as his mother, although her name appeared in print for the first time only in George White's biographical entry for *Who's Who* in 1907. White never mentioned any of his siblings by name, although Mary Anna White had at least two children of her own and Wiley White had at least one other son, perhaps as many as three.

and wife, their choices dictated by the limited stock of available partners of acceptable ancestry. These families were bound together tightly by blood and common belief, from their dedication to hard work to the education of their children to their habit of caring for the least fortunate among them. Raising orphans or castoffs was a way of life, with some locals assuming legal obligations for relatives' children.[18]

The lure of turpentine seems to have drawn Wiley White to the closed circle of Sandy Plains during the 1840s from his native Pitt County, some hundred miles to the north. He appears for the first time in Columbus records in the 1850 census as a free twenty-seven-year-old turpentine worker on the Columbus County farm of William and Mary Sessions, a prominent white family in the Welches Creek area. A mulatto, Wiley White was now too old to be an apprentice, but may have been a wage worker or bound by contract.[19] He had apparently lived in the area since about 1845, when he would have been in his early-to-mid twenties; his oldest known son, John W. White, was born there in 1846.

The name of John White's mother is not recorded, and it is unlikely that she and Wiley White were ever married; possibly a slave, she may also have been the mother of Wiley's second son, born in December 1852. If so, her children would also have been slaves, under prevailing state law, and Wiley White may have been forced to purchase them from the mother's owner; this may have been expedited, however, by his marriage into the Spaulding family.

Wiley White's ability to read and write indicate a free upbringing; his very mobility during that era suggests at least the possibility of family connections, money, or influence. But little else is known about his background before he came to Columbus County, where he spent a quarter century before abruptly departing for Washington, D.C., never to return. Years after Wiley White's death, son George described his father's racial ancestry as part Irish, part Negro; his paternal grandmother, he said, was a full-blooded white woman, presumably from his father's Pitt County home. His paternal grandfather was probably a mulatto, or perhaps of pure Negro ancestry; the man's legal status is

18. Mitchell, *A Story*, 31.

19. U.S. Census, Columbus County, 1850. White's first name was spelled "Willie" and his age given as 27. Other records show he was born between 1820 and 1823; his age is variously listed as 39 in the 1860 census, as 49 in the 1870 census, as 55 in an 1875 U.S. Treasury personnel document, but as only 70 at his death in his 1893 newspaper obituary.

not known. But since marriage between whites and nonwhites of any status was legally discouraged in North Carolina even before 1830 when it was completely outlawed, it is unlikely that Wiley White's parents were ever married to each other.[20]

The first detailed glimpse of Wiley White comes from the 1860 census, taken three years after his marriage to Mary Anna Spaulding. Their farm household in Welches Creek included real estate worth $250, probably purchased from a Spaulding family member, and personal property valued at another $300, perhaps even including a slave. Their nearest neighbors were Mary Anna's grandparents, still active farmers despite their advanced age; her uncle Benjamin Spaulding Jr. and his wife, Mariah, with their five children; and her father and mother, along with Mary Anna's four younger sisters and two brothers. Three children already lived in the White household: John W. White, fourteen; seven-year-old W. F. White, doubtless named for his father; and W. S. Freeman, also aged seven and probably a nephew of Mrs. White's. There were as yet no daughters listed, although two may already have been born; they would appear for the first time in the next census, aged eleven and thirteen.[21]

The Whites' life was reasonably secure in 1860, if not prosperous. Although North Carolina's free mulattoes lacked the same political rights as their white neighbors, their civil and economic rights were more protected here than in many southern states. For instance, free persons of color could own, inherit, and transfer real property, even passing on that property to heirs; they also retained the rights of habeas corpus and trial by jury. There were

20. Franklin, *The Free Negro*, 136; Culp, *Twentieth Century Negro Literature*, 224–5. Since Wiley White was literate, he must have either come from a well-to-do home or been apprenticed out in a trade as a child, when masters were strongly encouraged to teach their free black apprentices to read and write. North Carolina law restricted the movement of free blacks by requiring them to prove their lack of debt, and free blacks could not legally move into the state at all after 1835. As for Wiley White's choice of work, free black turpentine hands earned as much as $200 per year in the 1850s, according to Franklin. George White described his father's mother as "Irish, full blood," in the 1902 Culp sketch. In 1897, George White had described himself as "one-third Irish, some Indian and the balance Negro." For this to be true, his father Wiley White would necessarily have been two-thirds Irish, and Wiley's father therefore at least part Irish— and thus part white.

21. Lefler and Newsome, *North Carolina*, 422–3. For an in-depth discussion of the status, rights, and accomplishments of free mulattoes in North Carolina before 1860, see Franklin, *The Free Negro*.

some unreasonable restrictions on their behavior—men like Wiley White could not testify against a white man in court, nor could they legally force a white debtor to pay his debts to them—but they could farm or practice almost any normal business or trade. Their marriage options were limited to free partners of similar race, but their children would be legally free; interracial marriage, on the other hand, would remain forbidden for another century. As public sentiment turned against them on the eve of the war, some free blacks preferred to return to slavery rather than endure the uncertainties of their half-free status.[22] But others, like Wiley White, were determined to retain their freedom at almost any price.

The structure that had guided their lives for generations began to crumble in the 1860s, strained first by war, then by its aftermath. The wartime economy played havoc with local food supplies and the labor market; higher taxes on property, ruinous inflation, and near-worthless Confederate currency reduced many townspeople in nearby Whiteville to the poverty level. Wiley White and his family weathered the period with gritty determination, but even the self-sufficient farmers of Welches Creek were nearly bankrupted by severe wartime weather; heavy rains and flooding ruined county grain crops in 1863, and most residents came to depend on the barter system to survive.

Yet the long war did spare Columbus County direct blows, with no major battles fought in the isolated setting. And while almost every white male of age in the county was called up for duty as a soldier, the free blacks and mulattoes of Welches Creek were generally exempted from such duty during the first years of the conflict. The advance of Sherman's Union marauders after the fall of Wilmington in February 1865 brought looting and destruction to Whiteville, but the outlying homes of former slaves and free blacks were apparently spared from plunder for political reasons.[23]

Curiously, the Civil War may even have served to bolster Wiley White's prosperity by pushing up demand for turpentine and lumber and the wooden casks that his family had recently begun to manufacture. His overall position

---

22. U.S. Census, Columbus County, 1860. Mary Anna's natural children by Wiley White appear to include two daughters, Flora and Penelope, according to the next census (1870); because of their ages, the two sons with the White surname must have predated the marriage.

23. Little, *Recollections*, 18–22. According to local accounts, only ingenious methods saved family heirlooms and foodstuffs from the Union invaders; many items of value were reportedly hidden in the swamps outside Whiteville.

in 1870 was certainly no worse than that of a decade earlier; the 1870 census showed him owning $800 worth of real estate and $500 in personal property, probably livestock. The same year's census also recorded the increased size of his household, listing five or six children between the ages of eleven and nineteen. And for the first time in his life, forty-nine-year-old Wiley White was now recorded as a voter, thanks to the state's new constitution of 1868. He was undoubtedly registered as a Republican and could have cast his first vote in the fall of 1868 to help elect the new Republican governor, William W. Holden—who had served as North Carolina's appointed military governor in 1865—and the Third District's new Republican congressman, Oliver H. Dockery. He had also gained a new stature within the community, becoming one of the first justices of the peace in postwar Columbus.[24]

But the 1870 census also raises some perplexing questions. None of the children listed in Wiley White's household bore any of the names listed ten years earlier. Three teenaged males now carried the surname of White— Wesley, nineteen; "White," also nineteen; and Jackson, seventeen—as did two daughters: Flora, thirteen (listed twice), and Penelope, eleven.[25] But where were the two sons of 1860, John and W. F. White? Why had two adolescent daughters suddenly appeared? Where was George Henry White, later to become the best known of the family?

Simple explanations are possible, of course. The son called "White" White could easily be 1860's W. F. White, nicknamed to distinguish him from his father; Wesley could be W. S. Freeman from 1860, now adopted. The appearance of Jackson is more difficult to explain, but he may have been a slave son, now freed; all three youths might have been "outside" sons, even freed slaves. As for the daughters, perhaps they had lived elsewhere in 1860. The absence of John W. White remains a mystery until the census of 1880, when he reappears as a separate householder nearby. He seems to have married as early as 1870; in 1880 John, now thirty-four, and wife Mary had three children, ages four to ten, including son Wiley F. White, surely named for his grandfather.

John White would live on until the 1920s, fathering at least four more

24. U.S. Census, Columbus County, 1870; Columbus County Officials' Bonds, 1868–1881, in N.C. Division of Archives and History. W. F. White and S. W. Smith were the only justices of the peace bonded in Columbus County in 1868.

25. U.S. Census, Columbus County, 1870. Flora was listed at the bottom of one census page and again at the top of the next page, an apparent error by the census taker.

children and taking a second wife after Mary's death; his children and grand-children would remain in Columbus County for generations to come, but they constitute the last remnants of Wiley White's lineage in the local census records. By 1880, Wiley White vanishes from the scene, along with every other identifiable member of his immediate family.[26]

Whatever the reason for his sudden departure from Welches Creek, Wiley White reappears in Washington, D.C., in early 1872. Despite little formal education and few skills outside the farm world, he received an appointment in January of that year as a laborer in the U.S. Department of the Treasury, where he worked until his retirement in 1886. His application had been catalyzed by the third auditor of the Treasury, Allan Rutherford, formerly a Freedmen's Bureau official in Wilmington. Despite the suddenness of his departure from Sandy Plains, Wiley White would remain on good terms with son George—with whom he later lived in both Washington and New Bern—and would remain married to his wife for years after his departure, according to Treasury records; they were never divorced, and Mary Anna's date of death is uncertain. But nowhere is there any indication of his return to Columbus County, or of any direct contact with other family members.[27]

Why had he deserted them? There is no way to be sure, but two anecdotes may hold indirect clues to that mystery and perhaps even to the origin of George Henry White's name. In 1897, after his election to Congress, George

26. U.S. Census, Columbus County, N.C., 1880, 1900, 1910, and 1920. John White died shortly after the 1920 census, when he and his second wife, Ella, 43, and one son were listed. According to the 1900 census, White and his first wife, Mary, had by then been married for thirty years; in addition to the children listed in 1880, they had at least four more children, including two sons and two daughters. Ellen White, 19, was a student in 1900 at Concord's Scotia Seminary, where her cousin Della White taught briefly; Ellen later married a Dr. Whitted, according to Mitchell. In 1910, Ellen's brother Wiley, age 47, lived in Columbus County with his wife, Berthe, and at least five children, including a daughter named Mary Ann, perhaps named after her step-grandmother.

27. *Official Register of the United States, Treasury Department, Year Ending September 30, 1873* (Washington, D.C.: GPO, 1874), 52. Wiley White's 1875 application for reappointment to his job in Rutherford's office, on file in the National Archives, gives his original appointment date as January 28, 1872. All records listed his marital status as "married." White remained in Washington until 1892, according to city directories for the next two decades; his Treasury appointment was terminated in April 1886, presumably for reasons of age. Although neither her burial place nor her exact date of death is known, Mary Anna White appears to have been alive as late as 1905, when she apparently visited Whitesboro with the family.

White told a Washington, D.C., newspaper that he had remained in Welches Creek after 1872 as part of a contract with his father. The deal promised George a year's profits from the family farm and cask-making business to stay and manage them for that period; he claimed to have saved nearly a thousand dollars during the year. Congressman White said little else about his father, by then deceased, except that he had "moved to Washington a year before he [George] went to Howard . . . and stood ready and willing to help" his son. George White used his savings toward tuition at Howard, but said it was the last financial assistance he ever took from his father.[28]

More than a century after Wiley White moved to Washington, a great-grandnephew recounted a more puzzling episode, allegedly involving George. The Reverend C. H. C. White related the tale in 1974 to George Reid, a Howard University graduate student preparing a dissertation on George White; the minister claimed his famous relative had fled vigilante justice during his "courting age," after a brawl in which a white youth was severely injured. In order to escape lynching, George White first eluded capture by moving to New Bern, then attempted to conceal his identity by changing the name of his birthplace from Roseville, in Franklin County, to Rosindale, in Bladen.[29]

The story sounds more allegorical than true; as with many family legends, it fits neither the known facts nor the chronology of George White's life, and raises more questions than it answers. Changing his birthplace, for instance, would hardly have disguised George White's background for long, and could not alter his distinctive appearance—certainly a stronger clue for vigilantes on his trail. And while George White did live in New Bern for nearly two decades, he moved there only in 1877, when he took his first job as a school principal. That he was later able to travel freely across all parts of North Carolina for nearly three decades afterward, as a lawyer, prosecutor, and congressman—without fear of recognition or apprehension or violence—hardly seems the course of a fugitive.

28. "Hon. George H. White, LL.D.," article from the *Washington Colored American*, reprinted by *Raleigh Gazette*, 12 June 1897. An earlier article on George White's successful passage of the North Carolina bar exam, printed in the *Wilmington Post* in January 1879, mentions his father's name as "Wiley F. F. White."

29. George W. Reid, "A Biography of George H. White, 1852–1918" (Ph.D. dissertation, Howard University, 1974), 41. The Reverend C. H. C. White told Reid that the incident had occurred in Franklin County, near Louisburg.

Yet even if distorted by time and retelling, the tale retains broader historical accuracy. The event described could have happened to any vigorous young man in the postwar period; for black men of any age who ran afoul of the law, self-imposed exile was not a rare occurrence. And there were possible White family connections to Franklin County, including black residents of Franklin County in the 1870s with the same surname: young Franklinton men named Wiley and George White, for instance. Although born in Pitt County, Wiley could easily have had relatives in Franklin County, or may even have lived there as a youth; until at least the 1890s, the populations of both Pitt and Franklin were predominantly black. By 1880, a young mulatto man named Wesley White also lived in Franklin, at twenty-five very close in age to Wiley's other son of that name from the 1870 census.[30]

No other evidence links George White to the alleged brawl; a large, robust man of admirable strength, he was certainly capable of defending himself, though never known for losing his temper as an adult. The incident likely happened to someone else, possibly even another family member; at least one member of the White family did flee North Carolina in the early 1870s, though the man was not young and his reasons for moving are unknown. He apparently never returned to his former home, and he did eventually move to New Bern, if only to die as an old man in the home of his son.

That man was, of course, Wiley Franklin White himself. An unlikely coincidence, perhaps, but consider the quandary faced by such a fugitive's grown son carrying his father's name: W. F. White, or almost certainly, Wiley F. White Jr., possibly the "White" White noted by the census in 1870. Forced to remain behind on a disgraced father's farm for a long year and more, ever watchful of avengers with long memories, not wishing to endanger his family by carrying so public a resemblance to a wanted man—could an ambitious youth be blamed for permanently discarding his father's name? George Henry White appears under that name only at age twenty-one, when he entered Howard University. And what better Christian names to adopt than two appearing with such frequency in his stepmother's family: George and Henry?[31]

30. U.S. Census, manuscript on microfilm, Franklin County, N.C., 1870. Both men lived in Franklinton. Nor was either name uncommon in the state; at least two other Wiley Whites and fourteen George Whites, all of whom were black, were listed in various counties by the same census.

31. "Scholastic Record of George H. White," Office of the Registrar, Howard University, Washington, D.C., as provided to the author by the university from its archives; Mitchell,

George White rarely spoke of his childhood in later years, except to emphasize the hardships of his rural upbringing and his limited early education.
He told Daniel Culp in 1902 that his "early boyhood was a struggle for bread
and a very little butter, his schooling being necessarily neglected"; he had usually attended school "two or three months a year" at most. In an 1897 newspaper interview, White had described the struggle as "having to work at manual labor on farms and in the forests, gathering naval stores"; in an 1899
speech to Howard University law students, White said he had been "born in a
log cabin [and] found himself ushered into the world surrounded by many obstacles." This included "several years at hard labor on a farm from early morn
till late at night . . . in the turpentine forest that surrounded his rural home,"
resulting in "very meagre" educational opportunities. Only by the good fortune of "having parents able to educate him" had he been able to succeed, he
told a Brooklyn, N.Y., newspaper in 1901.[32]

His parents' determination aside, George White's educational options as a
farm child in Columbus County would have been limited at best, even had he
been born of the dominant race. North Carolina's "common" (public) schools
of the prewar era were closed to blacks, and even to white children offered
only four years of primary education, four months a term, mostly in towns and
not at all in isolated areas. The few black children in school before 1869
mostly attended special night classes, mainly in a few urban areas. While free
black parents were allowed to educate their children privately before the war,
they were required by state law after 1835 to hire white teachers to do so. As
for slaves, their education was technically all but forbidden, although neither
law nor custom was often invoked to prevent an owner from providing private
tutoring for his brightest slaves.[33]

A Story, 43–84. The name George Henry White first appears in print in January 1874, on the
records at Howard. Among close family members, Mary Anna White had one uncle named
Henry Spaulding, two first cousins named George Spaulding, and two first cousins named Henry
Spaulding, according to John Spaulding's genealogy. At least four of her first cousins also had
sons named either George or Henry, although no male relative bore both names.

32. Culp, Twentieth Century Negro Literature, 224–5; "Hon. George H. White, LL.D.,"
Raleigh Gazette, 12 June 1897; "Cong. Geo. H. White Speaks, The Students and Faculty of
Howard Law School Entertained by the Eloquent North Carolinian," WCA, 18 March 1899;
"Negro Representative's Last Speech in Congress," Brooklyn Daily Eagle, 3 February 1901.

33. Franklin, The Free Negro, 169. A total of 217 black children were listed as attending
school in the 1850 census, compared to more than 100,000 whites. Three-fourths of the black

It is unclear how much early education George White actually received, or at what age he went to school, but the matter is closely related to the unresolved question of his legal status at birth. If born a slave, his only opportunity for education would have depended on the unlikely generosity of his owner in those last troubled years before the war. Such education would certainly have been limited to rudimentary subjects like reading and writing, in order to prepare him for effective use as a house servant. If born free, George's opportunities would have depended on the ability and willingness of his family to hire a private teacher for a "subscription" or "old field" school; even the white children of Welches Creek lacked a county-run common school. The other private option was a tuition academy, one chartered by the General Assembly; these academies were open up to ten months a year, but were not only beyond the reach of farmers of moderate means but also impractical, since children were needed for farm work in all but winter months.[34]

Undeniably bright and determined, George White was also ambitious, even as a child; he "early determined to lay a foundation for his future life [and] finally resolved to store his mind with knowledge that would serve him in years to come."[35] It seems certain that he received some type of formal classroom education before 1869, if only in a one-teacher subscription school attended by his siblings, cousins, and the children of mixed-race neighbors in the Welches Creek area. And if he could attend the neighborhood school only two or three months each year, as he said in 1901, he must have studied relentlessly on his own, for George White completed the equivalent of a modern middle-school education in just three years—between 1869 and 1872—exhibiting a strong background in reading and basic subjects.

In an 1897 interview, George White recalled the names of his first two schoolteachers. The first was W. B. Duncan, a white man who operated a sub-

students came from just three North Carolina counties: Wake (Raleigh), Craven (New Bern), and Robeson (Lumberton).

34. Ibid., 164–74; also Lefler and Newsome, *North Carolina*, 403–5, 422–6. Free Negro adults had a remarkably high level of literacy that year; 43 percent could read and write, Franklin says.

35. Lefler and Newsome, *North Carolina*, 404–5. Subscription schools were most common in thinly populated rural areas, where large schools were not feasible; in some areas, parents who opposed government-sponsored education ran their own private facilities. Tuition academies, chartered by the General Assembly, typically prepared children for university studies. About 10 percent of prewar schoolchildren attended nonpublic schools.

scription school in Sandy Plains before 1869; Duncan's school may have been located on the Rehobeth Church site, which, according to county records, housed a series of such schools. But itinerant teachers like Duncan were paid only about twenty-five dollars a month, and rarely stayed in one area for long; Duncan, about whom little is known, soon moved on. Somewhat more is known about George's next teacher, a black woman who opened the first public school near his home in 1869; the 1870 census lists Mrs. Fanny Jackson of Wilmington as a twenty-three-year-old schoolteacher, carpenter's wife, and mother of a three-year-old son. She seems to have returned to Wilmington after just one term in Welches Creek.[36]

George White may also have attended classes at the new Freedmen's Bureau school that operated in the Welches Creek area at least from August 1869 until January 1870. The Rehobeth Freedmen's School was open under the supervision of John W. Spaulding of Rosindale, probably Mary Anna White's cousin, who was later to become an active Republican leader in Bladen County. According to his 1869 report to the Wilmington Bureau office, Spaulding taught thirty-five black students that term, all but one under sixteen years of age and two-thirds of them male, but none of their names were listed. George White would have been nearly seventeen that fall, and was perhaps too advanced in age and previous education to participate. His strong presence was certainly needed on the family farm, but if he did attend these classes, he may well have met the man who would soon change his father's life: Captain Allan Rutherford, who often visited the schools under his charge as regional subassistant commissioner for the Wilmington district.[37]

Rutherford, a New York native, had entered the Freedmen's Bureau in 1867 after an 1862 medical discharge from the Union Army left him free to study law; he later established legal offices in both Wilmington and Washington, D.C. In April 1870, he would be appointed third auditor of the U.S. Treasury in Washington, where he would remain until 1877. There is no di-

36. "Cong. Geo. H. White Speaks"; "Hon. George H. White, LL.D."; Little, *Recollections*, 109; U.S. Census, manuscript on microfilm, New Hanover County, N.C., 1870.

37. "Monthly Report, Rehobeth School, September 1869," in *Records of the Bureau of Refugees, Freedmen and Abandoned Lands, North Carolina, Wilmington Sub-District* (microfilm, National Archives, Washington, D.C.) Allen Rutherford (1840–1900) and his new bride, Della, still lived in Wilmington in the early 1880s but soon moved to Washington, where he practiced law until his death; his widow ran the law firm for another decade until her own death in 1911.

rect evidence that he met Wiley White before January 1872, but the likelihood of an existing acquaintance is nonetheless great, since nearly two years
after departing the area, Rutherford would enthusiastically recommend White
for the Treasury laborer's position in Washington. If Allan Rutherford took no
immediate notice of the potential of Wiley's son George in 1869, however,
another mentor was waiting to do so, the first well-educated black man the
youth may ever have encountered in his formative years.

In 1870, David P. Allen succeeded Mrs. Jackson at the Welches Creek
school, becoming the single strongest influence on George White's early education. In subsequent official biographical sketches of George White, Allen's
name would often appear alone, even to the exclusion of White's parents.
After a brief stay in Columbus, the Virginia native opened a private school for
training teachers in nearby Lumberton, quickly rising to become one of the
most noted black professional educators in the state. By 1882, "Professor"
Allen was a leader in North Carolina's new association of black teachers; by
1888, his Whitin (or Whitten) Normal School was among those praised by
the U.S. Bureau of Education for "its important work in the State in supplying
[black] communities . . . with a higher order of instruction than would ordinarily come to them."[38]

D. P. Allen operated the Whitin School for the next three decades with
help from his large family; at least five of his nine children had also become
teachers by 1900. The boarding school was not free of charge, a fact George
White himself noted in 1902; only "by dint of toil, and saving a few dollars"
was he "able to secure training under Prof. Allen," according to Culp's biographical sketch. A dozen black students boarded with the Allens in 1900;
like them, George White must have lived with the Allens for at least a year,
from about 1871 to 1872, when Wiley White left for Washington.[39]

38. *Who's Who in America, 1906–1907*, 1924; "The Colored Teachers: Formation of Their
State Association," *RN&O*, 25 November 1882; "Robeson County Colored Teacher's Institute,"
North Carolina Educational Journal, November 1882; Prof. G. S. Adkins, "History and Status of
Education among the Colored People," in *The History of Education in North Carolina* (Washington: U.S. Bureau of Education, 1888). D. P. Allen's name figures prominently in almost every
biographical sketch, interview, and directory entry printed about George White after 1886; both
parents' names appeared for the first time only in the 1907 *Who's Who* entry.

39. U. S. Census, Robeson County, N.C., 1880 and 1900. Born in 1844, D. P. Allen was still
active as late as 1907; wife Sarah and daughter Susan had both died by 1900, according to the
Raleigh Gazette. His daughters Laura (born 1865), Letitia (1874), Susan (1878), and Nancy (1879),
and son Thomas (1876) were all schoolteachers.

No more than forty miles separated Sandy Plains from Lumberton, but the social and cultural differences must have been startling to a young man who had never left his family's farm. The small town of Lumberton was already a bustling commercial center on the railroad between Wilmington and Charlotte, as well as a river port and the Robeson County seat. But its vigor belied its size; even though founded nearly a century earlier, it was not yet even the largest town in the county, and would reach a population of one thousand only in the twentieth century. Other towns scattered across the sprawling agricultural countryside included the popular mineral-springs resort town of Red Springs; the college town of Maxton, then home to the South's oldest school for women, Floral College; and the swamp settlement called Scuffletown, now known as Pembroke, center of Robeson's proud community of Indians.[40]

These Indians were probably not related to the Cape Fear and Waccamaw Indians from whom Ben Spaulding's descendants drew part of their ancestry. Indeed, while Robeson's Indians were also of mixed blood, they laid claim to a much older history of intermarriage, often bearing children with blue eyes and traditional English names; their bloodline was traced by many to the oldest English settlement in the New World, the fabled "Lost Colony" of North Carolina's Outer Banks. They were called Croatoans or Croatans, named for the single mysterious word found carved on a tree near the site of the vanished settlement on Roanoke Island three centuries earlier.

The first European settlers along the Lumber River had encountered these aboriginals around 1730, noting that they spoke broken English. Legend held that the Hatteras Indians had assimilated the Roanoke colony before moving south to farm the fertile soil of western Bladen; the mystery was never solved, although Robeson's Indians willingly embraced the name and the legend until the twentieth century, when they adopted the tribal name of Lumbee.[41] For

40. "Robeson," in Sharpe, *A New Geography*, 1:386–410. Lumberton was founded on the Lumber (Lumbee) River in 1787, but incorporated only in 1852. Red Springs (1775) took its name from its famous mineral springs; a popular hotel had been built there in 1852. Floral College—the first women's college in the South—operated in Maxton from 1841 to 1878. Scuffletown (1789) was renamed Pembroke in 1895; the University of North Carolina at Pembroke is now located there.

41. Ibid., 1:394–6. One small irony: the English governor of the "Lost Colony" was John White, presumably no relation to Wiley White. John White's granddaughter was Virginia Dare, the first child born of English settlers in the New World.

all their unique history, the Croatans generally kept to themselves, farming and trading in the swamps around their main settlement, although they emulated their new white peers before the war by owning black slaves. But the truce between them and the Europeans was not always peaceful, as evidenced by the outbreak of violence George White witnessed from close range, when Scuffletown held sway over Lumberton in the early 1870s.

What began as a family vendetta grew into an eight-year guerrilla war. Swamp outlaw Henry Berry Lowry, a man of mixed Portuguese and Indian ancestry, led a gang of relatives and friends to seek vengeance for the 1864 executions of his father and a brother; they repeatedly attacked Lumberton and murdered, one by one, those white citizens responsible for the lynchings. Captured twice and tried once, Lowry always escaped, once while in handcuffs; his gang eventually killed all but one of the "court-martial" committee, including a former Robeson sheriff. The eight-year spree came to an end with Lowry's accidental shooting death in 1872, but not before his men had managed to steal the sheriff's safe from the Lumberton courthouse that same year, apparently in broad daylight.[42]

Even with assistance from state and federal authorities, the county was unable to maintain law and order against the onslaught. The chronic tension was broken only by occasional news of the capture or death of a Lowry gang member, which was often cause for public celebration. Yet even during this crisis, Lumberton remained a proud, almost elegant setting, a largely white enclave in a county divided more or less equally between the races.[43] D. P. Allen's school, located on the outskirts, offered its local and boarding students a quiet, pleasant learning environment; in addition to academic training, students were able to observe classrooms and assist trained teachers in the black and Indian public schools of the county. By the time George White graduated from the Whitin School, probably in the spring of 1872, he had begun learning Latin, a subject he would continue studying at Howard University. An excellent student, he was now qualified to teach in those same schools he had recently attended as an observer.

42. Ibid., 1:400–1. Lowry's gang members were gradually hunted down by local posses, with periodic help from state and federal authorities.

43. *Compendium of the Ninth U.S. Census, 1870*, Robeson County, N.C., Table VIII, 78–9. Robeson's population of 16,262 contained 8,892 whites and 7,370 "colored" residents, which included Indians, mulattoes, and blacks.

The sudden departure of his father from Welches Creek seems to have kept George White from becoming a teacher immediately after completing his studies at Whitin. But an equally powerful factor must have been his own ambition to become a lawyer, a desire undoubtedly sharpened by close-range observation of the state's judicial workings during the Lowry gang's reign of terror. Superior court proceedings in Robeson were reportedly interrupted on one occasion by an unnamed judge who chose to praise a white posse's successful slaying of a Lowry gang member. While state judges of the era were unabashedly partisan and outspoken, it was nonetheless an imprudent move for any jurist to praise vigilantes; it was certainly not characteristic of the five Republicans elected to the superior court during Reconstruction, especially Judge William John Clarke of Craven.[44]

The former Democratic state comptroller and Confederate war hero was an iconoclast; often outspoken but never erratic, he had undergone a political transformation after the war, becoming an ardent Republican. He had been held prisoner in Delaware for six months in 1865 before walking the four hundred miles to his home; three years later he would emerge as an avid supporter of the presidential candidacy of General Ulysses S. Grant, former commander of the very Union forces who had imprisoned him. Clarke was no stranger to controversy, on or off the bench; just weeks before his appointment as judge, he had led an all-black militia regiment from Wilmington to Raleigh for Governor Holden's protection in the notorious "Kirk-Holden War," during a period of intense racial unrest in parts of North Carolina. Clarke was then elected to the state senate, but resigned before the legislature convened to accept Holden's judicial appointment. His lifelong friendship with Holden did little for Clarke's popularity, especially after Holden was impeached and removed from office in early 1871 by a Democratic-controlled legislature, of which Clarke was no longer a member.

Clarke retired from elective office in 1874 and returned to a law practice with his son in New Bern, but his penchant for controversy did not end. He began publishing a Republican newspaper in Raleigh, the *Signal*, in 1879, the

---

44. The state's judges "traveled the circuits," including their own districts. Clarke served on the superior court bench from Craven County until 1874; other prominent Reconstruction judges included Daniel L. Russell of Brunswick (1868–1874), Ralph P. Buxton of Fayetteville (1868–1880), Albion W. Tourgée of Greensboro (1868–1874), and Samuel W. Watts of Edgecombe (1868–1877).

same year that his legal apprentice, a young black schoolteacher named George White, passed the state's bar examination.

Whether their paths actually first crossed in Lumberton is not known, but if not, their meeting was only a matter of time, since George White was regularly exposed to active politics on all fronts during this period. Although he could not register to vote before his twenty-first birthday in December 1873, he had an early interest in politics, including the intricate interplay of the state's Republican and Conservative (Democratic) parties during the boisterous Reconstruction era. The backdrop was one of rearguard guerrilla warfare; William Holden's Union League had actively recruited blacks as Republican voters in 1868, while the white Ku Klux Klan had used intimidation and terror to discourage them from turning out at the polls. In part, Holden's impeachment had grown out of his stubborn efforts to break the Klan's spirit by arresting dozens of its sympathizers; in the main, it was partisan enmity by Democrats, who had just won control of the General Assembly.[45]

What first turned George White's interests toward the law is not clear, but his fervor was certainly not dampened by early observations of such events, nor by the obvious shortage of black attorneys in the state. By 1873, there were just three: Wilmington's George L. Mabson and Fayetteville's John S. Leary, both former state legislators and fresh graduates of the new law school at Howard University in Washington, and Enfield's James O'Hara, who had studied there but not graduated.[46] Howard was still the only nearby option for George White and other black students who wished to study law; although his decision meant leaving his home state indefinitely, he soon began to believe that he could "best serve his race and himself as an advocate of justice," in Culp's words, and not simply as a teacher.[47] It was a fateful decision, one that would eventually

45. Lefler and Newsome, *North Carolina*, 498–9. Holden was convicted on six of eight impeachment charges, including illegal arrests of 105 citizens in three counties and refusal to obey judicial orders to release them. In the fall of 1871, a federal grand jury in Raleigh indicted nearly one thousand North Carolinians for Ku Klux Klan activities, though just thirty-seven were convicted.

46. All three were freeborn mulattoes. Mabson and Leary graduated from Howard in 1871 and 1873, respectively; both had previously served in the North Carolina General Assembly. O'Hara studied law at Howard before reading the law under a white attorney in Halifax County; he was elected to Congress in 1882.

47. Culp, *Twentieth Century Negro Literature*, 224–5; Hugh Victor Brown, *A History of the Education of Negroes in North Carolina* (Goldsboro, N.C.: Irving-Swain Press, 1961), 67. Raleigh's Shaw University, a Baptist denominational school, opened its law department in the 1880s; it

catapult George White into the national spotlight, first as the nation's only elected black prosecutor, later as the only black member of Congress.

By early 1874, George White had fulfilled the contract with his father and was ready to depart the turpentine woods of Columbus County for the urban setting of the nation's capital. He was already an imposing figure, nearly six feet tall and weighing well over two hundred pounds, with a complexion of "rich saffron," according to one close acquaintance; the years of heavy farm labor had given him a powerful physique and great physical strength.[48] The train ride to Washington, D.C., would have required nearly two days' travel, including stops, giving him ample time to read, perhaps even to ponder the uncertainty of his future as he passed through the flat countryside of eastern North Carolina and on through Virginia. Armed with transcripts from the Whitin School and D. P. Allen's personal recommendation, he intended to enroll in winter quarter classes at Howard University, the first public, biracial, coeducational institution of higher learning in the nation.

At twenty-one he was slightly older than the average entering student at Howard, at least in the preparatory and normal departments, where students ranged in age from thirteen to thirty; on January 5, 1874, he entered the two programs simultaneously. The normal department for training of teachers offered the equivalent of a two-year high school program, largely practical in nature; the separate preparatory department offered a full four-year program, steeped in classical liberal arts education for students intending to enter baccalaureate programs. George White must have wished to keep his academic options open; neither degree seems to have been required for admission to the Howard law department, but the school's medical department did require extensive knowledge of mathematics, Latin, and Greek.[49]

---

later opened the state's first medical school for the training of black physicians, according to Brown.

48. "Color of Congressmen in Recent Days," editorial, *Philadelphia Tribune*, 8 January 1916. T. Thomas Fortune, a contributing editor for the *Tribune* in 1916, responded here to a recent article in *World's Work* by Burton J. Hendrick, who had described North Carolina congressman Claude Kitchin's predecessor as "an exceedingly black man named White." Said Fortune: "Now George H. White is not 'an exceedingly black man' at all; he is a rich saffron color, and not much darker than his grandfather, who was very white." (The reference was probably to George White's Irish grandmother, the only ancestor he ever described as being "white.")

49. "Scholastic Record of George H. White."

The Howard campus was still new, and rather small; open only since 1867, the school had managed to construct just three brick-and-stone academic buildings so far, including Freedmen's (Teaching) Hospital, in addition to its original leased property—a red frame building reportedly once used as a beer saloon and dance hall—on nearby Seventh Street (now Georgia Avenue, NW). Two dormitories, one for each sex, housed boarding students; the new residence of General Oliver O. Howard, the school's first president, completed the list of campus structures. The school's pastoral setting gave little hint of its recent history; located inside Washington County but outside the smaller municipal limits of the city of Washington, the Howard tract had until 1862 been a 150-acre farm on the city's northern edge, perhaps even a slave plantation. Now residential neighborhoods were springing up on all sides, built on lots sold off by the university to finance its own precarious development; still within the 50-acre campus were a "romantic grove . . . a Hill" and a series of large, gushing springs of sparkling water, features observed by Washington's *Evening Star* in 1867.[50]

The university had barely survived the national panic of 1873, saved from bankruptcy only by the austerity program forced upon the board of trustees by its secretary-treasurer; salaries were cut in half, and the professional departments were forced to become self-supporting. And while Howard's large enrollment already surpassed the expectations of its founders—surpassing five hundred students of both genders and races, as well as a handful of foreign students—the school was largely dependent upon tuition from students and private contributions when George White arrived. Its patron agency, the Freedmen's Bureau, had been abolished by Congress in 1872, yet Howard still received no regular appropriations from the U.S. government; public arguments raged over the efficacy of providing higher education at public expense to ill-prepared black students. Howard's future was uncertain, and George White's savings would finance his education and living expenses for little

50. Rayford W. Logan, *Howard University: The First Hundred Years* (New York: New York University Press, 1969), 27; Walter Dyson, *Howard University, The Capstone of Negro Education: A History, 1867–1940* (Washington, D.C.: Howard University, 1941), 222. The city and county of Washington had merged and became coterminous with the boundaries of the District of Columbia by the end of the nineteenth century. Dyson says the immediate area around Howard was rather unsavory, due to the presence of a large amusement park and many German beer gardens.

more than a year, if the school remained open that long. He was forced to work—at least during the summers, when he would return to North Carolina to teach—and to move in with his father to save on living expenses. This was an obstacle in itself, since his father lived two miles from the campus; daily travels by foot or horse-drawn trolley would be time-consuming during good weather and difficult during Washington's treacherous winters. Yet living with his father was probably no worse than the hazards of living in a campus dormitory, where individual coal stoves heated two- and three-person rooms and frozen water pipes were a constant winter problem.[51]

Whatever logistical problems he faced, it was still a rare opportunity for a young farmer determined to gain admission to one of the Howard professional departments. Under the direction of Dean John Mercer Langston, the law department had the most flexible approach of the three professional divisions; many law students worked as government clerks by day, attending classes only at night, when part-time law professors were free from their own daytime jobs. Perhaps for that reason, law courses had proved more popular than the medical or theological offerings; by spring 1874, a total of forty-eight students had completed the school's legal curriculum—including the first woman to receive a law degree in the United States—compared to just twenty-five medical graduates, two of them women, and seven theology graduates, all male. For his part, George White had no interest in becoming a minister, preferring to pursue either medicine or the law; he would later tell an interviewer that he "was matriculated for medicine, but finding it not congenial to his taste, he abandoned it" in favor of law. Confirming his account is difficult, since school records show he apparently never enrolled formally in medical courses at Howard; he did take four quarters of "rhetoricals," apparently the legal department's evening course in rhetorical exercises, and seems to have studied Blackstone, either on his own or perhaps under a benevolent tutor.[52]

51. According to the 1875 City Directory for Washington, D.C., Wiley White lived at 1149 16th Street, NW, near the future site of the Soviet Union's embassy. Transportation between the campus and the government sector was indirect and limited to "uncertain horse-drawn street cars" only as far north as Florida Avenue, leaving a considerable distance to walk over "unpaved and unlighted streets," according to Dyson, *Howard University: The Capstone*, 22.

52. Logan, *Howard University*, 48–50; *Alumni Catalogue of Howard University, 1867–1896* (Washington, D.C.: Howard University, 1896), 15, 26–7; "Hon. George H. White, LL.D."; "Scholastic Record of George H. White"; Reid, "A Biography," 42. White's transcript shows no

Before he could apply to either department, however, George White needed to establish a firm academic record at Howard. His Whitin preparation had been limited primarily to those courses needed for teaching in rural schools; Howard advisers must have suggested he enroll first in basic refresher courses in reading, spelling, and mental arithmetic, all of which he passed his first two quarters. That fall, perhaps because of a late return from his summer teaching job, his next courses would prove more challenging; he received high grades in arithmetic and spelling and a perfect score in his first Latin course, but failing grades in grammar and history, two courses he was apparently forced to repeat.[53]

George White would later recall that his summer job had interfered with his schoolwork, requiring him to make special arrangements in certain courses, including "weekly directions from his professors" in what may have been quasi-correspondence courses. His performance, even if inconsistent, must have satisfied the school's requirements, for in his sixth quarter, he finally entered the full preparatory phase of his Howard education. From then on George White received essentially the same training as students in the college department, which remained under the practical control of the school's "United Faculties" from all three departments. His performance would soon stabilize at an above-average level, with no grade below 70 during the next four quarters, and his performance was judged excellent (93 or higher) in four upper-level high school courses: history, physical geography, physiology, and geometry. His lowest grade came in his second course of rhetoricals, during the spring quarter of 1876; it was a 70—barely passing— an omen, perhaps, of his own uncertain future.[54]

---

courses taken in the medical department, and there were no "premedical" courses in Howard's preparatory or collegiate programs; its high tuition and annual fees ($155) and rigorous entry requirements made it unlikely White could have afforded to enter or remain in the medical school. A later dean of the law school, A. Mercer Daniel, told George Reid flatly in 1973 that White was never enrolled in the law school. His four "rhetoricals" courses in 1876 and 1877 were apparently standard law department courses; he may have received special permission to take these courses in addition to his regular course load.

53. "Scholastic Record of George H. White." The school's passing grade was listed as 70; White received grades of 60 in grammar and 45 in history. Both courses were again listed for the next two quarters, along with arithmetic/reading, algebra, and Latin, but no grades were recorded for any of these courses in the winter quarter.

54. "Hon. George H. White, LL.D."; "Scholastic Record of George H. White." He received grades of 77 in both chemistry and his first rhetoricals course and 75 in grammar; in seven other

In the spring of 1876, George White would make an important interim decision concerning his career, choosing to accept a summer internship with the U.S. Coast Survey at the upcoming Centennial Exposition in Philadelphia rather than return to summer teaching in North Carolina. He may have been despondent over his prospects for entering the law department at Howard, which was under financial pressure and criticisms of its lenient admission policies and which would shortly close its doors to new students; its handful of 1876 graduates would be the last for five years. Salary may have been another consideration; he could certainly earn at least twice as much in Philadelphia as he could by teaching. How he obtained the appointment is unknown, but it was presumably a political patronage job, and the U.S. Coast Survey was within the Treasury Department, where his father still worked and where Allan Rutherford still served as third auditor in 1876.[55] There was no guarantee of a permanent job, but it was an opening to the future, and the opportunity to live in one of the nation's largest cities must have been enticing.

Although George White could not have known it in 1876, Philadelphia was to become a key city in his life; as an adult, he would live there for his last twelve years, as a successful banker, lawyer, and real estate developer. In 1876, Philadelphia was home to one of the oldest, largest, and most prosperous urban black communities in the nation; more than twenty thousand blacks lived in Philadelphia in 1870, and their ranks would triple by the end of the century. The city's concern for education was obvious; the Institute for Colored Youth, open since 1842, was a renowned private school, offering courses on the secondary level and producing a steady stream of highly qualified black teachers. The oldest black college in the nation stood nearby: Lincoln University, known as the "Black Princeton." Philadelphia was a city of seemingly unlimited promise for ambitious blacks from the South, who would begin migrating there in large numbers by the 1890s.[56]

In 1876, Philadelphia also played host to the first U.S. international exposition, held in honor of the centennial of the nation's founding. Nearly ten

---

courses, he received grades of 82 or higher. No final grade was recorded for three other courses he took in the 1875 autumn quarter, perhaps due to his late return from summer teaching in North Carolina.

55. Rutherford remained third auditor until 1877; Wiley White worked at Treasury in various menial capacities until 1886.

56. Philadelphia contained the nation's fourth-largest urban black population in 1900, after Washington, D.C., Baltimore, and New Orleans.

million visitors attended the exposition, which featured more than thirty
thousand exhibitors from thirty-eight states and fifty foreign countries during
its five-month run in the city's Fairmount Park.[57] The U.S. Coast Survey exhibit in the U.S. Government Building at the Centennial was just a small part
of the gigantic fair, and George White's duties as assistant-in-charge must
have been largely administrative, much like that of a booth attendant at a
modern trade fair; although his course in bookkeeping at Howard may have
helped him fulfill his duties, much of his work was doubtless far more menial.
Yet it offered the opportunity to meet both foreign dignitaries and important
people from all walks of American life; while manning the exhibit, George
White would have informally encountered many of the nation's current and
future leaders, including statesmen, businessmen, educators, and scientific
leaders. He must have met many of the rising leaders of his race, including
Fanny Jackson (later Coppin), head of the girls' department at the Institute
for Colored Youth, and Ebenezer Bassett, that school's illustrious principal
and the outgoing U.S. minister to Haiti; White already knew the renowned
orator Frederick Douglass, the Howard trustee who addressed opening ceremonies at the exposition.

At least one black office holder and religious leader from North Carolina
visited the exposition: the Reverend Adam M. Barrett of Raleigh, who would
have been delighted to meet such an accomplished young man from his native state at the faraway fair. George White may even have crossed paths with
a teenaged black waiter from Tennessee, temporarily in Philadelphia for the
event: Edward Elder Cooper, who would one day play a key role in White's
congressional career.[58]

It was an exhilarating time for ambitious, educated young blacks in America, with job opportunities unparalleled in the nation's history. Just eleven
years after the end of the war, the nation's economy was moving into high

57. Eric Foner and John A. Garraty, *The Reader's Companion to American History* (Boston:
Houghton Mifflin, 1991), 106; *Philadelphia Inquirer*, 11 May 1876. The Centennial Exposition
opened May 10, 1876, with an address by President Ulysses S. Grant before hundreds of U.S.
government representatives and foreign dignitaries, including the Emperor of Brazil.

58. Henry L. Suggs, ed., *The Black Press in the Middle West* (Westport, Conn.: Greenwood
Press, 1996), 54; W. H. Quick, *Negro Stars in All Ages of the World* (Henderson, N.C.: D. E.
Aycock, Printer, 1890), 221. Suggs called Cooper "a man of ability and enterprise, but unscrupulous"; Cooper moved to Indianapolis after the Centennial, then to Washington, D.C., eventually founding that city's *Colored American* and becoming White's friend and indefatigable publi-
cist after 1898. Barrett's trip to Philadelphia is noted by Quick.

gear, with industries and an increasingly urbanized population luring large numbers of rural residents to the cities of the North and East. If the opportunities open to blacks were not yet equal to those offered whites, prosperous black professors, lawyers, and physicians were nonetheless on the verge of bright futures in Philadelphia and other northern and midwestern cities. But as his five months in Philadelphia came to an end, George White was not yet dreaming of a future in any sprawling metropolis, tempting as that might have been; he was convinced that his destiny lay in the South, where most members of his race still resided and where the need for strong teachers was greatest. He was now planning to return to his home state as a teacher, with his dream of practicing law on hold; he would resign from the Coast Survey at the close of the fair in October to return to Howard and complete his formal education.

George White was a lifelong student of society, as much as any academic subject; while a student, he was learning as much outside the classroom as within it. He could easily attend lectures or speeches by outstanding African American speakers in Washington, such as Frederick Douglass, who spoke there on several occasions during White's student years. In addition, no fewer than eleven blacks served in Congress during his three years in Washington; it would have been a simple matter to attend legislative proceedings at the U.S. Capitol, perhaps to hear one of his race address the House or the Senate.[59]

Given George White's later interest in politics and his proximity to the event, he must surely have attended the inauguration in early March 1877 of the new Republican president, Rutherford B. Hayes of Ohio. The outcome of the 1876 election had been officially in doubt for nearly four months, and the interest level among Washington residents was higher than usual. The electoral commission issued its decision barely in time for the inauguration to take place on March 5; curious crowds of onlookers watched Hayes formally assume office just three days after the commission had given him its dubious endorsement.[60]

The nation's black leaders rushed to embrace the new chief executive,

59. Douglass had escaped from slavery as a youth to become an ardent abolitionist and illustrious orator; the fourth black member named to Howard's board of trustees, he held various official capacities within the federal government before his death in 1895. U.S. senator Blanche K. Bruce (R-Louisiana) served one term from 1875–1881; ten blacks also served as U.S. House members between 1874 and 1877, including North Carolina's John A. Hyman (1875–1877).

60. The actual announcement of Hayes's victory came on March 2, four months after the election and just two days before the constitutional deadline. Because March 4 fell on Sunday in

meeting with him four days after his inauguration, as Reconstruction began drawing to its inexorable close in the South. A "large body of colored ministers [and] other colored citizens" congratulated Hayes, and "the President gave them an attentive and patient hearing," wrote Washington's *Evening Star* on March 9. The delegation appeared gratified at his "words of encouragement and sympathy expressed to them and for their race." If Hayes was not noted for a particular interest in civil rights or in expanding the number of federal positions given to blacks, he did continue to appoint prominent blacks to a few selected posts. Among his earliest appointments were Howard University's former acting president Langston as minister to Haiti in September 1877; Langston had resigned from his Howard position in mid-1875, although he had remained in Washington. He also served as the first charge d'affaires for neighboring Santo Domingo; his selection for both posts was a popular one among blacks, many still disgruntled that he had been denied the Howard presidency in 1875.[61]

A month after being sworn in, during George White's final quarter of classes, President Hayes did recommend a black Ohio educator, Dr. Peter H. Clark, for the Howard presidency, in what must have been welcome news on campus. A spirited contest between trustees supporting Clark and those in favor of another black candidate, Francis L. Cardozo of South Carolina, gave Clark four and Cardozo two of fourteen votes on an informal ballot on April 25, but Clark's name was then withdrawn from consideration. Frederick Douglass, one of four black trustees, argued unsuccessfully that "it was due to the colored race to elect a colored man to the [Howard] Presidency because all the students were colored except a few in the Medical Department," but Howard's stubbornly independent trustees instead selected a white Chicago professor, Dr. William W. Patton.[62]

1877, the inauguration was set for Monday, March 5; Hayes took the oath of office privately, however, at 7 P.M. on Saturday, March 3.

61. "A Delegation of Colored Ministers at the White House," *Washington Evening Star*, 9 March 1877. Those attending were mostly members of the Ministers' Aid Association; A. M. Green and the Reverend R. S. Laws of the First Baptist Church, South Washington, spoke at the meeting. President Hayes appointed Langston minister to Haiti in September 1877, as well as Frederick Douglass U.S. marshal for the District of Columbia in 1877 and John H. Smyth of North Carolina minister to Liberia in 1878.

62. "The Contest for the Presidency of Howard University," *Washington Evening Star*, 26 April 1877.

Although disappointing, the outcome did not mean that all doors were closed to black advancement in Washington, where George White had already been exposed to his first black-owned and black-oriented newspaper, the local *People's Advocate*. Under the editorship of lawyer and teacher John W. Cromwell, the *Advocate* published its first issue in April 1876, carrying an eclectic mixture of items of interest to educated blacks. George White's fellow Howard classmate Timothy Thomas Fortune soon left his preparatory classes to become a full-time printer and journalist for Cromwell, who described the newspaper as "in the interests of the whole people, advocating the principles of Republicanism without descending to low personal abuse."[63]

The *People's Advocate* carried both national and local news, clearly seeking to appeal particularly to those associated with Howard. One 1876 story dealt with the organization of an "alumni association of the Normal Department of the Howard University," and the election of its first officers; another noted a falling-out between the trustees of the private Miner Fund, which had long supported the university's Normal School, and the trustees of the school itself. The issues also contained more cosmopolitan stories, including one front page devoted to the "Great Exhibition" in Philadelphia—with engravings of the Main Exhibition Building, descriptions of the exhibits and tips for prospective travelers—days before George White departed for the exposition.[64]

When White returned to Howard five months later, he no longer intended to apply formally to the law department. Along with regular course work in the normal and preparatory departments, he took two more quarters of rhetoricals, but the legal department soon fell victim to federal funding problems and declining enrollment. The law department had just fifteen students during John Mercer Langston's final year as dean (1874–1875) and only four graduates in 1876, far too few to cover its costs as a self-sufficient program. It thus closed, temporarily, in 1877, and upon its reopening in 1878–1879, the reorganized department had significantly tightened its criteria for admission,

63. *Washington People's Advocate*, 17 June 1876. Fortune (1856–1928) entered Howard around 1876; he left after a year to work for Cromwell, and did not return to Howard. By 1880 he had moved to New York City, where he became one of the nation's premier black journalists.

64. Untitled editorial and "Local Department," both in *People's Advocate*, 6 May 1876; also "The Great Exhibition," covering the issue's front page. "A week's expenses to a single person inclined to live economically in Philadelphia need not exceed . . . $25.00," the *Advocate* wrote, describing the availability of "lodgings . . . in a good location for $6.00 per week, and good board in restaurants for $1.25 per day."

in response to widespread criticism of its previous requirements. There were no new law graduates until 1881.[65]

George White concentrated on scientific courses during his final year, taking physics (then called natural philosophy), geography, astronomy, geology, and botany, although his highest grades came in moral philosophy and English history. He passed his third course in rhetoricals, but failed his final course in that subject with a grade of 62, a bitter denouement to his academic career. Still, at the end of the spring quarter in May 1877, he received his normal certificate and prepared to return to North Carolina for good, this time as a public-school principal in New Bern.[66]

It was a decision he claimed he never regretted. Years later, in a speech to Howard law students, White recalled being offered "a position as messenger in one of the Departments, but I refused to accept. Why? Because I knew it was far better to go out into life and carve out my own destiny without the aid or assistance of Uncle Sam." Some of his classmates, who had accepted similar offers, "are here to-day, still paying rent and cannot get away if they wanted to." Even at the turn of the century, new graduates should beware the false security, he warned; it "may be tempting to enter some governmental department, but my advice to you is to refuse. . . . I believe it is the duty of every student . . . to go out into the world to battle with mankind for a livelihood."[67]

White's year of Latin and his heavy concentration in science—nine courses in all—indicate that he had considered obtaining a preparatory certificate. But apparently the prospect of devoting more years and more of his hard-earned funds to his studies was daunting. Such a certificate would likely have required at least another full year of courses, and as many as four additional years might have been required for a bachelor's degree. And he had, of course, experienced some difficulty in certain areas; later reports that he grad-

65. Varying treatments of the Howard law department's situation are found in both Logan, *Howard University*, 78–97, and Dyson, *Howard University: The Capstone*, 219–26. Other accounts claim the law department closed in 1876, although the university continued in 1877 to have two law faculty members, Dean W. F. Bascom and instructor John H. Cook, a later dean; Logan says twenty-three students were still enrolled in law courses during 1875–1876.

66. "Scholastic Record of George H. White." White received grades of 95 in moral philosophy and 90 in English history; his science course grades ranged from 75 in geography to an apparent 95 in astronomy. He failed one other course, geometry, with a grade of 63.

67. "Cong. Geo. H. White Speaks," *WCA*, 18 March 1899.

uated with honors were an exaggeration, possibly based on his high grades in certain subjects.[68]

In contrast to previous years, the Howard class of 1877 was small; there were only about thirty graduates, including five other normal students, two men and three women: Carey P. Thompson, Charles S. Waring, Alice D. Johnson, Victoria D. Shaw, and Anna L. Smallwood. Waring was a simultaneous graduate of the preparatory program, from which another ten students took certificates; this dual degree was what White had originally hoped to receive. On the collegiate side, at least four bachelor's degrees were awarded in 1877, along with at least three doctorates of medicine. But however few their numbers, the class of 1877 included many notable students. Perhaps the best remembered was preparatory graduate George William Cook, who continued to study at Howard and went on to become principal of the Normal Department and have a men's dormitory named in his honor. At least one of White's colleagues in the normal course, Alice D. Johnson, would also become famous, if largely for her later marriage to one of the nation's most highly regarded black physicians, Dr. Daniel Hale Williams, reputed to have performed the world's first open-heart surgery.[69]

George White eventually surpassed all his classmates in both prominence and political power, and over time his academic record would be elevated to mythical proportions. Although his successful completion of the Howard course was an admirable achievement in itself and needed no embellishment,

68. Logan, *Howard University*, 34–8; "Hon. George H. White," in William J. Simmons, *Men of Mark: Eminent, Progressive and Rising* (Chicago: Johnson, 1970), 536–7; "Lawyer and Legislator," *New York Freeman*, 9 February 1887; "George H. White, LL.D.," *Raleigh Gazette*, 12 June 1897. The Simmons sketch mentions White's "excellence in science and mathematics" in the "elective" course. The *Freeman* reported that White "excelled in mathematics and the sciences and captured distinguished honors for his unusual record in both" at Howard, adding that he graduated "from the eclectic course" in 1877. The *Gazette* said White "graduated with honors from the electic [sic] department," but offered no further details.

69. Howard University Union Alumni Association, *Alumni Catalogue of Howard University, with List of Alumni, 1870–1896* (Washington, D.C.: Howard University, 1896); "Williams Performs Heart Surgery," in Charles M. Christian, *Black Saga: The African American Experience* (Boston: Houghton Mifflin, 1995), 278. According to the directory, there were a total of ten preparatory graduates in 1877: George Wm. Cook, James C. Delphy, Richard L. Gaines, Jesse Lawson, Temple Robinson, George Sewall, James E. Simpson, Charles S. Waring, James H. N. Waring, and Henry S. Washington.

it was almost inevitable that others would exaggerate his accomplishments, particularly after his election to Congress. Few normal school graduates, after all, would receive honorary master's and doctoral degrees, as he did after 1896. That he was able to pass the North Carolina bar exam so soon after leaving Howard led many to conclude that he had actually been enrolled in the law department; even the university's own publication, *The Record*, erroneously listed him as a graduate of the Howard "Law School"—which had technically not even existed in 1877—in printing his obituary four decades later.[70]

The normal certificate from Howard remained George White's only earned degree, fittingly epitomizing his commitment to education as a tool for raising his race up from poverty. He became a successful teacher and principal, and even after leaving the profession continued to be an advocate of schools and the training of teachers. Yet he quickly recognized the limits of teaching as a career, both financially and professionally. Teachers' salaries were low and employment was sporadic, causing teaching to become largely a woman's profession by the end of the century.

Money was important, if not preeminently so, to George White, and there was little of it in teaching. But there was another, equally powerful driving force within White: the quest for professional fulfillment, which would soon occupy his energies and begin to produce remarkable results.

70. *Howard University Record*, January 1919, 35.

2

A New Home for an Adopted Son

New Bern was isolated and quite small by most demographic standards of the 1870s, but its size disguised a surprisingly cosmopolitan atmosphere. In the words of a later historian, North Carolina's second-oldest town was nothing less than an "urban oasis in a rural desert."[1] Founded by Swiss and German settlers at the turn of the eighteenth century as a river port, almost within sight of the fabled Outer Banks, it was about as far from the rest of the future state as one could go. The port that became a convenient location for Atlantic shipping traffic to enter the Trent and Neuse rivers via the Pamlico Sound, however, would long remain the only town of any size in the colony's northeast region, although its early political significance as the colony's last royal seat and first wartime capital during the Revolution would quickly decline when the legislature sought a more central location far inland. Yet the loss of political power had diminished neither its stature as a port and commercial center nor its sense of history in the century; like the ruins of Governor Tryon's Palace, later rebuilt into a splendid tourist attraction, New Bern would proudly persevere. Its population had matched its growing prosperity, keeping it the state's largest town until the eve of the Civil War, when it was finally overtaken by upstart Wilmington to the south. Only its occupation by Union troops in early 1862 had interrupted its near-idyllic existence, ending its usefulness as a Confederate port and changing its future dramatically into a long-term haven for both fugitive slaves and freedmen.

1. Alan D. Watson, *A History of New Bern and Craven County* (New Bern, N.C.: Tryon Palace Commission, 1987), 548.

In many ways, New Bern's location defined its character: proud, isolated, almost stubbornly progressive, defying the geographical odds of its narrow peninsula, the early Indian wars that had nearly destroyed the first settlement, and the British rage that had resulted in its being burned down in the waning days of the Revolution. Some might attribute this dogged persistence to the town's Swiss founder, Baron de Graffenried, who escaped the wrath of Indians to return to his native Bern. Even the radical trauma of its lengthy occupation during the recent war had only redefined New Bern's spirit, not broken it. Yet the changes wrought by that experience were readily apparent. A traveler returning in 1877 after a long absence would have been stunned by the metamorphosis from a courtly old bastion of southern civility into a daring symbol of the Reconstructed South, where former slaves now formed an overwhelming majority of the town's residents; if not in control of the new Republican government, they were far more influential than any prophet of the 1850s could have dreamed. African Americans had finally arrived at the seat of local power, and with it, went forth as ambassadors to the outside world.

When George White arrived at New Bern in 1877, the political transformation was nearly complete. Black citizens had recently been elected to the town's board of aldermen and to the Craven County commission, at least until an indignant Democratic majority in the state's General Assembly rescinded the right of Craven voters to choose many of their own officials. Even as Reconstruction ground to a halt with the election of Rutherford Hayes to the presidency, the local black citizenry retained significant influence, defiantly sending at least one black legislator to Raleigh each session for another decade and more, in lockstep with other black-majority counties throughout the northeast. More surprising, perhaps, had been 1874's larger regional act of defiance: the election of North Carolina's first black congressman, John A. Hyman, who had swept Craven and seven other counties in the newly created district that came to be known as the Black Second. In seeking to neutralize the enemy by confining its voters to one district, the party known at that time as the Democracy had instead galvanized the Grand Old Party into victory; only two Democrats would be able to break that hold over the next quarter century.

The town that was to be George White's home for nearly two decades offered him opportunity on every conceivable level, whether social, professional, religious, or political. His determination to succeed would be the single strongest factor in his many careers, yet his initial goals were characteristically cautious ones; his first permanent job was as principal of a small black public school, and in his spare time he worked to complete his legal studies under a sympathetic white attorney. At first this seemed enough for the twenty-four-year-old farmer's son from Welches Creek. His fascination with public service would propel him into office far sooner than he might have expected, and his popularity would keep him there for much of the next generation, but for now, at least, his dreams were far more mundane ones.

In the spring of 1877, White began a professional cycle to be repeated many times over the next four decades: a significant opportunity, followed by initial success, then unexpected failure, often compounded by personal tragedy, yet followed almost inevitably by new opportunity. The grand times of George White's life began with his law study under William John Clarke, now fifty-eight and retired from the bench. This former Confederate officer and his bright black protégé, working side by side, perhaps made for an unusual sight, but one hardly out of character for Judge Clarke, who had always taken a strong interest in education, first as a teacher and principal and later as a proud proponent of equal education for all.

Clarke's brilliance was unquestioned, although his maverick behavior had cost him political success, and his new Republican philosophy mandated an interest in the betterment of the lives of blacks, so that the opportunity to lure George White to New Bern was doubtless irresistible. Taking on a bright young legal apprentice of African heritage was both a philanthropic and strategic venture for Clarke, who ran a small New Bern law firm with his oldest son, William Edwards Clarke, a former teacher of disabled students and a recent law graduate of New York's Columbia College.

For White, moving to New Bern was like coming home, since the town lay roughly a hundred miles northeast of Welches Creek. But his decision to move there had more to do with New Bern's black majority than its proximity to his home. Its six thousand residents made it the state's second-largest urban area after Wilmington, and it boasted the largest relative population of black voters of any state municipality. Moreover, its treatment of its new citizens was generous and egalitarian; notably, few other North Carolina towns had gone so far as to fund such a progressive school system as New Bern's. And while its public schools were segregated by race, thanks to state law, neither race had seriously objected to that arrangement. Little else in the community was noticeably segregated. Some of its churches had members of both races, blacks lived in almost every neighborhood of the city, juries were mixed by race, and blacks had served on both the municipal and county governing boards.[2] As the Craven County seat, New Bern was the site of all county offices as well as regional state and federal offices, and though Reconstruction was now legally over, the national Republican administration still showed favoritism to its party in the South in regional appointments.

Simply put, the area was an enigma to visitors from other parts of the South, and even to some northerners; to George White, it offered a radically new version of the South in which he had grown up. Columbus County, where he had matured, had been two-thirds white; his home township of Welches Creek had held a slight majority of mulatto and black residents in 1870, but it accounted for only a tenth of the county's total residents and held little political power. Lumberton had been predominantly white, although Robeson County had been split almost equally between its white and nonwhite populations. Even Washington, D.C., home to one of the nation's largest urban concentration of African American residents, had been overwhelmingly white and rigidly segregated when White had lived there.

New Bern, in contrast, had enjoyed a long tradition of comparative racial harmony, dating back almost to its founding in the early 1700s. Even during the days of slavery, free blacks had lived and prospered here, with little open hostility from the white majority; one wealthy free black, John Stanly, had owned some of the town's most desirable land and at least eighteen slaves in 1830. Stanly had been a particularly benevolent slave master, using some slaves to "increase his own wealth" but regularly emancipating others, freeing at least seven slaves during one prewar year alone; his wife, herself a freed slave, had been one of the original members of the biracial First Presbyterian Church. Other free Craven County blacks had apparently purchased spouses and family members in order to emancipate them afterwards, as Thomas Newton had done in 1811.[3]

2. Ibid., 469–76. Republicans were effectively barred from the county commission in Craven after the Democratic General Assembly began appointing all commissioners in 1877, but at least two previous Craven commissioners, Robert G. Mosely and Jesse Brooks, had been black. After 1877, Brooks, Willis D. Pettipher, and Edward R. Dudley were appointed justices of the peace, serving as late as 1883. When White arrived in 1877, Virgil A. Crawford was a black member of the elected New Bern council, and at least three other blacks served on the town council by 1888.

3. John Hope Franklin, "The Free Negro in the Economic Life of Ante-Bellum North Carolina," in *Free Blacks in America, 1800–1860*, edited by John H. Bracey Jr. et al. (Belmont,

If war and its aftermath had transformed the racial balance of New Bern significantly, neither the town's occupation by Union forces after 1862 nor a decade of Reconstruction had permanently altered the orderly fashion in which both races lived. A temporary upsurge in local crime during the late 1860s, attributed to blacks employed by white syndicates for both political and criminal mischief, was an aberration. After blacks began to assume responsible posts in the local government, peer pressure and self-policing helped return the rates of murder and arson to more normal levels. The local white population adjusted to the new political reality of Republican and black dominance, if somewhat grudgingly so, and civil peace was soon restored.[4]

New Bern may have lacked the worldly glamor of the nation's capital, but its vigor and openness were nonetheless appealing to George White. His previous home remained a strictly segregated southern city, where wealthy light-skinned blacks kept to themselves or mixed infrequently with selected progressive whites, generally avoiding contact with lower-class blacks and often bemoaning their influx. The city's housing had been particularly segregated; only a few mixed-race residents whose skin color allowed them to pass for white were able to negotiate purchases of homes in fashionable quarters outside the poorer black neighborhoods. The first middle-class community for free blacks had grown up around the campus of Howard University, developed on lots sold off by the school to finance its operations.[5]

Money was not necessarily a prerequisite for acceptance in the upwardly mobile postwar society of the capital city, but it certainly helped. Poorer blacks with acceptable family histories— read free before the war—were generally accepted into the lower echelons of the black aristocracy as long as they behaved properly. Few poor schoolteachers would have felt at home in the rather snobbish environment of the nation's so-called "capital of the colored aristocracy." George White remained true instead to his rural roots, a proud but poor southerner whose dreams of success lay much closer to the land of his birth. His private belief in social equality had kept him from being entirely comfortable in the aristocracy's rarefied atmosphere; New Bern, offering up-

Calif.: Wadsworth, 1971), 47–56; Lachlan C. Vass, A History of the Presbyterian Church in New Bern, N.C., with a Resume of Early Ecclesiastical Affairs in Eastern North Carolina and a Sketch of the Early Days of New Bern, N.C. (Richmond, Va.: Whittet and Shepperson, 1886), 183. According to Franklin, Stanly emancipated a slave woman, her five children, and a slave man in 1815.

4. Watson, History of New Bern, 468.

5. Logan, Howard University, 27–8, 63.

ward mobility to energetic black immigrants without their having to endure the starchy lifestyle of the favored few, proved a more manageable milieu for the ambitious young schoolteacher.[6]

Beyond its psychological advantages, New Bern was also a pleasant sight to view. A compact, appealing port city at the confluence of the Neuse and the Trent, it lay just west of the Pamlico Sound and the Atlantic. Having been named after the Swiss capital, it still thought of itself as an important place long after Raleigh displaced it as a political center. New Bern's vigorous commercial sector catered to both agricultural and retail interests and contained ten of the state's eighty black-owned businesses in 1880. It was also a marketing center for agricultural products from the rich soil of the surrounding counties, with soaring outputs of rice and cotton in the late 1870s and early 1880s. As the county seat of Craven County and site of the region's federal courthouse, it held appeal for a growing cadre of lawyers, although so far all of them were white.[7]

George White quickly did his part to rectify that imbalance. While he had come to New Bern specifically to serve as principal of the city's black schools, his professional ambitions remained focused on the law, which he pursued with his reading under former judge Clarke. There were soon two black schools in New Bern, one a public graded system operated by the city and the second a parochial school funded by the local Presbyterian church; White served both schools for the next five years or so, presumably drawing a separate salary from each. Still, neither job was full time, since public schools were open less than six months a year—thus easily affording him the time he needed to complete his legal studies.[8]

6. Willard B. Gatewood, "Washington: Capital of the Colored Aristocracy," in his *Aristocrats of Color: The Black Elite, 1880–1920* (Bloomington: Indiana University Press, 1990), 39–68. Gatewood provides an incisive analysis of social attitudes among the black upper class; several wealthy black families were members of Washington's "Elite List" of socialites in the 1880s, but homes in respectable neighborhoods were rarely available to most blacks. Gatewood cites the 1881 complaint of a local black newspaper concerning "the shortage of 'houses for our people,'" especially the "official class" (65).

7. Watson, *History of New Bern*, 519–21, 548. Other Craven crops included sweet potatoes, corn, wheat, oats, and tobacco. Based on a letter printed in the *Raleigh News and Observer* on 1 March 1885, at least eighteen attorneys were then practicing law in New Bern: the fifteen members of the New Bern bar who signed the letter plus three others—George White, Leonidas J. Moore, and William E. Clarke. Only White was black.

8. *Historical and Descriptive Review of the State of North Carolina*, vol. 2 (Charleston, S.C.: Empire, 1885), 96. According to this biographical sketch, White headed the New Bern public

Reading for the law was a time-honored practice in the South. An increasing number of lawyers were obtaining their educations in the nation's law schools, but private study under an experienced attorney was still an accepted route. Many law students in larger cities, particularly Washington and New York, worked at full-time day jobs as clerks to support themselves, taking law classes at night or on weekends; others combined both methods, starting in law school and completing their studies under established attorneys, as had James O'Hara. As long as a prospective lawyer learned enough to pass a state's bar examination, it made little difference how his education had been accomplished.[9]

The Clarke family themselves had used both methods. After graduating from the University of North Carolina with highest honors in 1841 and returning for a master's degree, Judge Clarke had read law under attorney Henry Watkins Miller of Raleigh, decades before law schools had become prevalent. A generation later, Clarke's son William Edwards Clarke graduated from the law department of New York's Columbia College and immediately began practicing law in New Bern, where, as former teachers and active Republicans, both he and his father continued to take a strong interest in public education.[10]

How or when George White met William John Clarke is not clear, although Clarke may have helped recruit White for the public-school job. The retired judge may well have decided to seal the deal by offering a legal apprenticeship on the side; an active proponent of education for blacks, he was

---

school for five years. He may have continued to work in the parochial school until he ran for solicitor in 1886, since he continued to be active in the black state teachers' association until at least 1885.

9. For southern blacks who wished to be trained as lawyers, the choices of schools were still few; Howard University's law school was closed during in the late 1870s due to funding problems, and Shaw University's law school was not yet open in 1877.

10. "William John Clarke," *DNCB*, 1:381–2; "William E. Clarke," in Samuel A. Ashe, *Cyclopedia of Eminent and Representative Men of the Carolinas of the Nineteenth Century*, vol 2: *North Carolina* (Madison, Wis.: Brant & Fuller, 1892), 126–7. Although a man of substantial intellectual prowess, Judge Clarke had little experience in the private practice of law until the mid-1870s. He was a railroad president in Texas and a businessman in Raleigh and New Bern before becoming superior court judge in 1870. William E. Clarke taught at New Bern Academy for two years and at a New York asylum for deaf children for three years before attending law school at Columbia.

certainly determined to persuade the talented Howard student to move there. However it came to happen, George White's eighteen months of law study under Clarke allowed him to prepare for the N.C. Supreme Court's examination while working as an educator.[11]

The local schools for blacks in New Bern were successors of the Freedmen's Bureau schools of the late 1860s; the Bureau had operated the first regular schools for freed blacks in New Bern until about 1870, shortly before its offices there closed in 1871. The newer public school for blacks had opened after that, when the General Assembly had first authorized a new system to replace the common schools closed in 1865. The New Bern system, like other local units, was funded by Peabody Fund contributions, which were matched by local revenues. The new statewide system was segregated by race, but was otherwise notably progressive, using a four-month term and local taxation to supplement state revenues, although financial limitations and political problems prevented effective implementation of the plan until after 1877.[12]

George White served in his dual principalship in New Bern for about five years after 1877. He probably took the public-school position first, then gradually assumed control of the parochial school, which may have been instituted under the auspices of the all-black Ebenezer Presbyterian Church he himself helped to found in 1878.[13] It is also possible that the parochial school

11. Watson, *History of New Bern*, 476. Clarke was appointed superior court clerk in 1879, serving until the next election in 1880, only after the Democratic board of commissioners refused to accept the bond of the winning Republican in late 1878. Superior court judge Augustus S. Seymour (a Republican who defeated Clarke in 1874) selected Clarke, who was forced to wait two months to be sworn in while Democrats debated his fiscal solvency. Clarke also edited a newspaper in Raleigh until mid-1880. Because of his declining health, it is likely that his son performed much of the firm's legal work.

12. Lefler and Newsome, *North Carolina*, 531, 535. The state's interim conservative government effectively closed the school system after the war's end by abolishing the office of state superintendent of common schools, refusing to appropriate funds for schools, and throwing all responsibility upon local resources; this period of educational stagnation lasted until 1869, when the Republican General Assembly began to revive public education. In principle, the new North Carolina system was among the most progressive in the nation, but state funding was largely withheld until the state constitution was amended in 1876. Supplementary local taxes were only rarely approved by local voters; as a result, only a few progressive areas operated adequate school systems during this era.

13. Vass, *New Bern Presbyterian Church*, 183. Reverend Vass (1831–1896) wrote this in 1886; he served First Presbyterian from 1866 until 1890. Nowhere does he mention the parochial

predated the public system as a charitable adjunct of First Presbyterian Church, which had a number of black members, but it is unlikely that the church school could have afforded to hire White as principal on its own.

There was a demonstrable need for schools to serve the city's sizable black population; like other towns in North Carolina's Union-occupied northeastern sector, New Bern had attracted large numbers of fugitive slaves between 1862 and 1865, including an all-black settlement of "squatters" across the river in James City. More than ten thousand fleeing slaves had crowded into the area around New Bern after 1862, and many of them stayed on after the war's end. Craven County's population had been more than 53 percent white on the eve of the war; by 1870, about 60 percent of the county's 20,516 residents were black, a figure that climbed to 66 percent a decade later.[14]

The short-lived Freedmen's Bureau regional office in New Bern had opened around 1867 and helped establish the city's first permanent public schools for black children under the statewide leadership of H. C. Vogell, the bureau's superintendent of education for North Carolina. At least four bureau staff members worked in New Bern in September 1867, including an assistant surgeon and three clerks; two years later, the office included just one regional agent, a clerk, and a messenger, and by 1871, it had closed completely, just before the bureau itself was abolished by Congress.[15]

However brief its presence, the Freedmen's Bureau had energized the city's black community, and New Bern's middle-class blacks soon became a potent force within the local Republican Party. When George White arrived in 1877, black citizens served on the town council, worked as policemen, and served as notably active Republican politicians, regularly representing Craven County in the lower house of the General Assembly.[16] White Republicans, however,

---

school; had it been started by First Presbyterian, the fastidious minister would certainly have said so in discussing Ebenezer's founding.

14. An extremely useful history of James City and the area is Joe A. Mobley's *James City: A Black Community in North Carolina, 1863–1900* (Raleigh: N.C. Department of Cultural Resources, 1981).

15. U.S. Census, manuscript on microfilm, Craven County, N.C., 1860, 1870, and 1880. New Bern had 6,443 residents in 1880, of which at least 60 percent were black; the only larger city in the state before 1890 was Wilmington, which also had a black majority.

16. Watson, *History of New Bern*, 548; *Records of the Freedmen's Bureau, North Carolina, Wilmington Sub-District*.

held a large share of the party's power in Craven, two of the most influential being Judge Clarke and his son.

The elder Clarke had been an active Democrat until just after the war, when he had moved from Raleigh to New Bern. A colonel in the Fourteenth North Carolina Regiment, Clarke had been recommended for promotion to general, although the promotion was never carried out. His wartime experiences having changed his political outlook radically, he joined the new Republican Party in 1868 and campaigned diligently for presidential candidate Ulysses S. Grant despite heavy pressure from the state's Democratic and Conservative leaders.

Two years later, in August 1870, Clarke was elected to represent Craven County in the state senate, but resigned before taking his seat. The catalyst was apparently the separate election to Congress of fellow Republican Charles R. Thomas, who had thus resigned his superior court seat. The vacancy left the choice of a successor to Clarke's longtime friend and fellow lawyer, Republican governor William W. Holden, who appointed Clarke to the judgeship, which the latter held until the end of 1874.[17]

Judge Clarke was an iconoclast, both in his personal beliefs and in his avocations. In addition to being a dedicated Republican public servant, he was also a published poet, teacher, and newspaper editor. But Clarke's penchant for unorthodox public activity was not always popular, even with leaders of his new party. Despite a strong record as superior court judge, he failed to receive his district's Republican nomination for reelection in 1874, and his unsuccessful independent candidacy that year was his last try for political office. He nevertheless remained faithful to the party, continuing to actively support Republican candidates and editing his Raleigh-based newspaper, the *Signal*, from 1879–1880.[18]

Clarke's wife, Mary Bayard Devereux of Raleigh, was a widely respected

17. "Clarke," *DNCB*, 1:381–2; *NCG*, 558, 594. Granted the rank of captain in the Confederate army, Clarke had chosen to serve as a colonel in the 14th N.C. Regiment, later designated the 24th; Confederate president Jefferson Davis refused to promote Clarke to brigadier general, a bitter disappointment to the proud soldier. Wounded in an 1864 battle, Clarke was sent home to recuperate, but on his way to rejoin his unit, was ambushed, captured, and imprisoned by Union forces. Clarke resigned his senate seat on September 22, 1870, and was appointed to the superior court bench on September 27, the day Thomas resigned.

18. Clarke's action had no direct bearing on the outcome of the Kirk-Holden "war," but his personal and political connections to the unpopular Holden—the only North Carolina governor ever removed from office—does not seem to have helped his standing in 1874.

poet and former teacher at New Bern Academy; the academy was one of the oldest schools in the state, and the judge had served it as a trustee after 1868 and briefly as its principal in 1869. The couple's son William taught handicapped students in New York City schools before entering law school there. William was also successful politically, serving a total of four terms in the General Assembly before age thirty-five. He apparently mastered the difficult art of compromise in an often-divided party, at least more capably than his stubbornly independent father.[19]

And it was a difficult political environment to navigate, despite the Republican Party's regional majority. Craven and the adjacent counties to the north and west formed the "Black Second" Congressional District, a heavily Republican outpost in the otherwise largely Democratic state. Black residents outnumbered whites nearly two to one in the district's ten counties in 1880, and since almost all black males were registered as Republican voters, along with a small minority of whites, the district's Republicans outnumbered Democrats by roughly the same margin. The Black Second had been created by the state's General Assembly during statewide reapportionment in 1872, when Democrats had first attempted to isolate and neutralize the eastern core of their Republican opposition.[20]

So far the attempt had backfired. By 1877, no Democrat had come close to winning in the congressional race, and the district had astounded many by actually electing a black Republican in 1874, John Adams Hyman of Warrenton. The Republican ascendancy would finally change in 1878, when Democrat William H. "Buck" Kitchin took advantage of a split in Republican ranks to defeat black candidate James E. O'Hara.[21] Kitchin served just one term,

19. William E. Clarke served in the North Carolina General Assembly from 1877 until 1883; he was appointed postmaster of New Bern by President Harrison in 1889.

20. Democrats apparently underestimated both the numbers and the tenacity of black voters in the ten counties, or perhaps they expected Democratic postelection techniques to overcome any obstacles.

21. Eric Anderson, *Race and Politics in North Carolina, 1872–1901: The Black Second* (Baton Rouge: Louisiana State University Press, 1981), 10 (Table I). Hyman (1840–1891) had served as a state senator from Warren County for three terms when nominated for Congress in 1874. He was overwhelmingly elected in November 1874 over Democrat George Blount and independent black Republican Garland H. White, but because Blount challenged the results, the U.S. House only affirmed Hyman's election in August 1876. Hyman was not renominated in 1876. In 1878, Kitchin defeated two black opponents: regular GOP nominee James O'Hara and independent reformer James H. Harris. By 1880, the Second District's overall population was 56.4 percent

however, and Republicans easily won four of the next five elections. All but two of the district's ten counties had black majorities in 1880, though the percentage varied considerably from county to county. Craven's proportion mirrored the district's that year, with its black population hovering around the 66 percent level. The counties of Jones, Lenoir, and Greene—those closest to Craven—each had populations around 55 percent black in 1880.

Geographically, however, the Second District left much to be desired. On its northern tier, the counties of Halifax, Northampton, Edgecombe, and Warren—those nearest to Virginia—contained just under half the district's total population; these counties were far more heavily populated by blacks, averaging 68 percent in 1880. The "bridge counties" of Wayne and Wilson, located in the center of the district, were the only two with white majorities, Wayne with 51 percent and Wilson with 54. In 1882 the legislature moved Wayne out of the district, in exchange for Bertie County and the newly created Vance, but returned it to the Second District after the 1891 statewide reapportionment.[22]

Concentrating Republican-voting blacks in one district had theoretically strengthened the Democratic chances of carrying other adjacent districts, particularly the First and Third, during the 1870s. The 1883 reapportionment made the Black Second even more Republican, all but guaranteeing a black congressman. The Democrats had not given up completely on the district—their occasional victories in congressional races (1878, 1886) proved that—but they seemed content, for the 1870s and 1880s at least, to tolerate Republican dominance on certain levels in the Second District.[23]

Yet the state's Democrats refused to leave the district's Republican politics entirely alone, especially at the local level. Angered at the alleged extravagant actions of Republican county commissioners, which included many blacks during Reconstruction, in 1875 the Democrats had drafted amendments to the 1868 state constitution, creating an ingenious new system that statewide voters approved the next year. After 1876, local magistrates chosen

black. About three-fifths of the blacks lived in four counties: Edgecombe, Halifax, Northampton, and Warren. Bertie County's population was 58.4 percent black, while Vance was about 64 percent black at the time of its formation in 1881.

22. After 1883, the redrawn Second District held about 195,000 residents, but its population was now 62 percent black, due to the loss of predominantly white Wayne County.

23. Lefler and Newsome, *North Carolina*, 500.

by the General Assembly in turn selected each county's board of commissioners, without resort to popular vote. Thus, even in Republican areas, decisions
on taxation and expenditures were now made by appointed Democratic commissioners. The policy was not universally popular even with Democrats, but
was rigidly enforced to doubters with dark reminders of the excesses of "radical" days.[24]

In this way, Democrats expected to ensure their party's permanent dominance at the state and local levels. They could tolerate Republicans in office
so long as the Republicans held no effective power. The system seemed relatively harmless, if patently unfair; over time, however, the inevitable effects of
this Democratic hegemony would be political explosions and deadly racial
hostility, as George White and other black leaders would learn in the 1890s.[25]

Before White could hope to become an active politician, he needed to become a lawyer. That quest was nearing its end in early 1879, as the young apprentice prepared to undergo the state's rigorous oral bar exam, administered
annually by the justices of the North Carolina Supreme Court. Before 1879,
only a handful of black attorneys had been admitted to practice in the state,
and almost all had attended law school at Howard before passing the bar, although not all had graduated. But White had studied relentlessly under Judge
Clarke's guidance, and on January 5, 1879, White was the only black applicant among at least thirty-one aspiring attorneys to sit for the exam, which
was required for all attorneys wishing to be licensed.[26]

"The class was an unusually intelligent one," wrote Raleigh's News and
Observer in listing the successful applicants, "and more gentlemanly well con-
trived young men we have never met." The exam itself was described as "severe and exhaustive," part of the high court's intention to "increase the strict-
ness of each recurring examination until they shall become tests of legal
scholarship and proficiency instead of being prosey, idle expensive farces."
White and thirty others were listed by the newspaper as having passed the

24. Ibid.
25. Although appeals to "white supremacy" marked all elections beginning in 1888, the return of Republicans to power after 1894 during the "fusion" era intensified the racial overtones of
succeeding elections, leading to Wilmington's racial riot in late 1898 and the disfranchisement
of blacks after 1900.
26. "The City," RN&O, 7–8 January 1879. Due to illness, only two of the three members of
the supreme court were present for the examination.

two-day exam, which "covered the whole course" of state legal matters. Most applicants came from the western half of the state. George White was the only applicant from Craven County, although three others came from counties within the Second District: Jacob Thomas Barron of Edgecombe, Benjamin Stancell Gay of Northampton, and James Bryan Martin of Bertie. All were licensed to practice law in the courts of their native state on January 6, 1879.[27]

It was the middle of a very cold winter, the coldest on record since before the war. The Trent River froze as far east as New Bern, where ice skaters were reported in record numbers. A large contingent of black workers from New Bern passed through Raleigh by train, en route to the turpentine orchards of Georgia and away from the suddenly frigid Tar Heel state. In his moment of triumph, George White probably noticed neither event; barely twenty-six, the former turpentine cask maker from Columbus had just become the newest black attorney in North Carolina. Five days earlier, he had been recognized as one of the state's aspiring black leaders at an Emancipation Day ceremony in Beaufort; now he had joined a select group of other blacks who had passed previous exams, including O'Hara, Mabson, Leary, and the state's only black solicitor—John Henry Collins, elected just four months earlier. Their ranks would not grow rapidly; even by 1890, North Carolina was home to just over a dozen black lawyers.[28]

White seems clearly to have loved both his new profession and the status that came with it. "The lawyers in every community are the leading lights, the moulders of public sentiment. This is true in the common councils of the cities, and also abundantly true in the management of state affairs," he told Howard law students two decades later. Lawyers tended to become legislators,

27. Ibid. At least one other candidate, Benjamin S. Gay, became an active politician in the Second District; a Democrat, Gay served in both houses of the General Assembly after 1900.

28. Ibid.; Paul Escott, *Many Excellent People: Power and Privilege in North Carolina, 1850–1900* (Chapel Hill: University of North Carolina Press, 1985), 199; "The Emancipation Anniversary," *Wilmington Post,* 19 January 1879. The Cape Fear River at Wilmington was also frozen over, for the first time in twenty-two years. There were 132 turpentine workers from New Bern and Beaufort on the train. In addition to O'Hara, Mabson, and Leary, at least four other black lawyers were practicing in the state: Charles B. Warrick and John H. Smyth, praised by the *Monthly Elevator* in March 1876; John H. Collins of Enfield, licensed in 1874; and George T. Wassom of Goldsboro, licensed before 1879. The census states that there were fourteen black lawyers in North Carolina in 1890.

he added, partly because of their training, but also because of their desire to serve the community. A lawyer was a "useful, intelligent and industrious citizen, [who] in order to succeed permanently, must be an honest and admirable man; must deal fairly and squarely with his clients," said White, perhaps describing his mentor, William J. Clarke.[29]

Sadly, he admitted, this was not the public's prevailing view of lawyers. "The average man throughout the country looks up on lawyers as liars, and it has almost become a common belief that they are unscrupulous and untrustworthy," although White himself had "never found anything in the profession that prevented a successful lawyer from being an honest, dignified, truthful, Christian gentleman." He cautioned his listeners to be "courageous, . . . manly, . . . honest, undaunted in the right, flinching from the wrong, moulders of public sentiment, doers of good and honoring the profession."[30]

George White's own reputation for public and personal probity was remarkably solid. Although he prospered quickly, and became one of the largest black landowners in New Bern in less than a decade—he reputedly owned more than fifteen thousand dollars' worth of property by the time he was elected to Congress—his record contains not a hint of greed or shady dealings. He specialized in civil law, including real-estate conveyances, and handled a strong caseload over the next seven years, apparently counting more than a few whites among his list of satisfied clients. His ability was widely respected, and his courtroom strengths quickly became legendary among his white adversaries.[31]

White's strong beliefs about public service and honorable behavior were rooted in his religious philosophy, and his single most enduring commitment as an adult was to the church. It was hardly surprising, therefore, that one of his first acts after moving to New Bern was to seek out a church to attend. While there is no record of his previous religious affiliation, he would have felt a natural affinity for one of several higher-status denominations—Episcopalian, Presbyterian, or Congregational—whose churches either accepted black members or whose leadership encouraged separate black congregations within their denomination. In New Bern, an obvious choice would have been First

29. "Cong. Geo. H. White Speaks," *WCA*, 18 March 1899.

30. Ibid.

31. White's advertisement in the *New Bern People's Advocate*, 31 July 1886, also listed "Prompt Attention Given to Collection of Claims" as a feature of his practice.

Presbyterian Church, which had accepted black members since its origin and offered both separate and combined services for its white and black members.[32]

The social strains of serving both races, however, presumably pleased neither race in the church, and it was perhaps inevitable that a black parish would split off. Within a year of his arrival, George White spearheaded a drive to establish the Ebenezer congregation from within the ranks of First Presbyterian communicants. With such a large pool of local black residents to work with, the project flourished, assisted by members of the locally prominent Randolph family. Planning for the new congregation began in May 1878 under the direction of the session of First Presbyterian, in the Congregational School House located at the nearby corner of Johnson and Middle Streets. Benjamin Boswell Palmer, a thirty-three-year-old black graduate of Lincoln University in Pennsylvania, former teacher, and licentiate of the regional Orange Presbytery, was chosen as the interim pastor for Ebenezer Presbyterian Church. Ebenezer Church was formally organized by an Orange Presbytery committee on November 24, 1878.[33]

Ebenezer's founding members were George White and ten other black Presbyterians, including three Randolph family males. White, John Randolph Sr., and Junius Willis were elected as ruling elders, responsible for overseeing Ebenezer's affairs, including construction of the first building and recruitment of a permanent pastor. Meanwhile, temporary services continued in the Congregational School House. Assisted by First Presbyterian's Rev. Lachlan C. Vass, licentiate Palmer served only until February 1879; he was succeeded in May 1879 by the Reverend Allen A. Scott, a native of South Carolina.[34]

White was now preparing for the bar exam, and was doubtless preoccupied also with his duties as school principal. But he nevertheless found time in his busy schedule for his first recorded romantic involvement, one which would help cement his ties to the church and the New Bern community. He began to

32. Vass, *New Bern Presbyterian Church*, 183. According to Vass, "Mrs. Stanley, an emancipated slave, was one of the original members. As far back as 1832 I have records of special separate services held for them. . . . After the war we were still, during the present pastorate, receiving colored members, and at times separate services were conducted for them, though they attended the regular ministrations of the sanctuary."

33. Ibid., 184. Palmer (1845–1915) remained at Ebenezer only a few months.

34. Scott served Ebenezer Church until 1887 and died in 1889.

court Fannie B. Randolph, the twenty-year-old daughter of his fellow Presbyterian John Randolph Jr. In late February, just six weeks after he passed the bar, George and Fannie were married. The February 27, 1879, service was performed at First Presbyterian Church by the Reverend D. J. Sanders, apparently an interim minister at Ebenezer. Witnesses to the marriage included Edward R. Dudley, W. H. Burton, and Junius B. Willis, according to the Craven County marriage register.[35]

Fannie Randolph, barely twenty-one, seems to have been a trained schoolteacher, as were her uncle, Henry Randolph, and several cousins. The new Mrs. White may have continued to work briefly after her marriage to the city's newest lawyer, but because she became pregnant almost immediately, she probably did not work again after the summer of 1879. She was most likely well educated, given George White's propensity for associating with socially prominent and prosperous members of his race. Like her new husband, Fannie Randolph White was a mulatto, as was her father, a fifty-year-old New Bern mail agent and former painter; her mother's name and racial ancestry are unknown. Little else is known about the first Mrs. White, except that she had two older brothers, William and John, and one younger brother, Lewis.[36]

The June 1880 census indicates that she and George lived on New Bern's Pasteur Street, near the site of Ebenezer Church, where she kept house and cared for their infant daughter, Della, who had been born in January 1880. Their neighbors on Pasteur Street were a varied group of middle-class blacks, including Gilbert Moye, 35, a mulatto grocer who served on the Ebenezer Church board with White, his wife, Caroline, 34, and their two children. Other neighbors were Sylvester Mackie, a 40-year-old mulatto undertaker, his wife, Susan, 40, and daughter Laura, 16; "Gen" Jones, 55, a black fisherman, his wife, Phoebe, 46, their three children and five other relatives; and Joseph Mann, 40, a black Baptist elder, his wife, Harriet, 38, and their five children.[37]

Fannie's family lived just a block away on Queen Street. Her father and his second wife, Kate Green Randolph, thirty-one, lived there with two children:

35. Marriage Register, Craven County, N.C., 1879, microfilm, N.C. Division of Archives and History. Mrs. White's name is spelled "Fanny" here.
36. U.S. Census, manuscript on microfilm, entry for the family of John Randolph Jr., in New Bern and Craven County, N.C., 1870.
37. U.S. Census, manuscript on microfilm, entries for Pasteur Street, New Bern, and Craven County, N.C., 1880.

Fannie's brother Lewis, about eighteen at the time, and a second child identified as a niece, Aliona Pegrim. Fannie's two older brothers had moved out of
the family home by 1880, but remained in New Bern, where her extended
family included her grandfather, her uncle Henry, another uncle, one aunt,
and several cousins.[38]

The marriage was tragically brief. The 1880 census is the last mention we
have of Fannie Randolph White alive; less than four months later, during the
last week of September, she died of an unspecified illness at age twenty-two
and was buried in New Bern's Greenwood Cemetery. Her death may have
come as the result of consumption (tuberculosis), or perhaps of tetanus, the
two leading killers of New Bern's black residents that year; outbreaks of smallpox and yellow fever had also swept New Bern in recent years, often felling
black residents at twice the rate of whites.[39] Whatever the cause, Fannie's
death was a tremendous shock to the young widower, and his only consolation
was young Della. His ongoing political campaign spared him little time for active grief, a mixed blessing for a private man on public display.

Fannie White's death would be poignantly remembered during the dedication ceremony for the new Ebenezer Presbyterian Church building, held just
five weeks after her funeral. George and Fannie had been among the first
church members to be married, and she had almost certainly been the youngest adult to pass away, if not the first.

The young widower quickly returned to his professional routines. He continued to serve as principal of both black schools, although his new law prac-

38. U.S. Census, 1880, Randolph family entry; Beverly Tetterton, ed., *North Carolina
Freedman's Savings & Trust Company Records* (Raleigh: N.C. Genealogical Society, 1992). John
Randolph's brother Henry, a New Bern schoolteacher, listed their birthplace as Washington in
his application for a Freedmen's savings account in 1871; their mother, Harriet Randolph, and
one brother, Lewis, were listed as deceased. Della's grandfather John Randolph Sr., her uncle
William O. Randolph, and her aunt, Fannie B. Randolph McLean, also lived in New Bern at the
time, according to the 1880 census. Fannie's stepmother, Kate Randolph, claimed to have been
raised in Memphis, Tennessee; Kate's father lived in Warrenton and her mother in Tarboro, according to Kate Randolph's 1871 Freedmen's account application. She also listed one sister,
Fanny Green, residence unknown.

39. North Carolina Graves Index, N.C. Division of Archives and History; Vass, *New Bern
Presbyterian Church*, 183. Fannie B. Randolph was born on January 27, 1858, according to her
gravestone. Della lived until 1916. Ebenezer Church had grown from eleven members in 1878 to
seventy-four in 1886.

tice gradually provided an increasing proportion of his income. His entry into politics, which had consumed much of his free time during the fall of 1880, would also transform his educational career in an unexpected way; during the summer of 1881, he would become principal of one of the state's new "normal" schools for the training of black teachers, chartered by the 1881 General Assembly, in which he had served. The school principal at Plymouth, another of the new schools, was a legislative colleague, Alexander Hicks Jr. The four new schools complemented the one earlier established in Fayetteville; all were subsidized by the Peabody Fund, as well as by the state.[40]

George White remained principal of the New Bern normal school for its first two years, until the beginning of 1883. The school's first term lasted about half a year, opening in July and closing in early December 1881, and White bore the teaching burden alone for the first three weeks, afterward being assisted by teachers William J. Herritage of Washington, North Carolina, and Nancy J. Scott of Columbia, South Carolina. Occasional faculty members included Rev. Allen A. Scott, George White's pastor at Ebenezer Presbyterian, and George D. Jammison. Salaries were adequate, if not exceptional: White earned an annual salary of $258, Herritage $161, and Miss Scott $162 for the first term ending on December 5, 1881, according to White's first annual report to the state superintendent of public instruction.[41]

In that same report, White noted that about two-thirds of the graduates were expected to teach in the next school term. His students were divided into three sections (Middle, Junior, and Sub-Junior) plus an "unclassified" level for those who entered late in the term. Courses for experienced teachers included spelling, geography, higher arithmetic, higher grammar, elocution, bookkeeping, algebra, physiology, and penmanship, while lower classes took essentially the same courses as the senior students—except for algebra and physiology—but used elementary-level texts in grammar and arithmetic. A period of literary exhibition and three days of public examinations, both oral and written, demonstrated students' accomplishments at the term's end.

40. *1883 Principal's Report, Plymouth (Colored) Normal School*, in the 1885 report of the superintendent of public instruction to the General Assembly. Henry Cheatham succeeded Hicks on the latter's death in January 1883.

41. *1881 Principal's Report, New Berne Normal Colored School*, in the 1883 report of the superintendent of public instruction to the General Assembly. One of the teachers listed in the school's junior class was Henry T. Randolph, Fannie White's uncle.

Nearly all of the students were from Craven County, and about half were hired to teach there and thus received county teaching certificates from the county's new superintendent, John S. Long, according to White's report; the other students came from adjacent eastern counties.[42]

New Bern's sizable black population made it an ideal site for a regional normal school; James City, just across the Neuse River, offered a largely female population of perhaps eleven hundred from which to draw. Hoping to bolster a request to expand his school, George White later described New Bern as "an exceptionally favorable point for extensive educational work among this race. " In 1881, White recommended that the next legislature loosen the "rigid" entry requirements, since so many worthy applicants had been rejected on grounds of age or previous academic achievement.[43]

During the 1882 term, George White again taught classes, again assisted by Herritage and the former Miss Scott, who had recently become White's second wife.[44] Their students included a total of 98 men and women from twelve eastern counties, 68 of them from New Bern itself. Applicants were required to be at least fifteen years of age and "proficient in Spelling, Reading, Writing, and the four fundamental rules of Arithmetic." Tuition was free, while board could "be had at low rates," according to an advertisement placed in a state teacher's journal in May 1882 by the school's board of directors.[45]

About half the students had previously worked as public-school teachers in North Carolina, according to White's 1882 report. The 1882 term began on May 29 and ended October 20, during which White received a salary of $262.50. Nancy Scott White received $113.75, while Herritage received $165, or slightly more than the state's average salary for teachers, then about $22 per month. Herritage may have earned more than Mrs. White did this

42. Ibid. Long, appointed in 1881, was the Methodist bishop of New Bern. Other counties from which students came were Bertie, Carteret, Hyde, Lenoir, and Pamlico.

43. Ibid.; also *1882 Principal's Report, New Berne Normal Colored School*, in the 1883 report of the superintendent of public instruction to the General Assembly.

44. *Descriptive Review*, 96; *Assembly Sketch Book, Session 1885: North Carolina* (Raleigh, N.C.: Edwards, Broughton, 1885). George White and Miss Scott were probably married in February 1882; neither account lists a date for the marriage, but the legislative sketch says the marriage lasted only ten months. The marriage apparently took place outside New Bern, since Craven records do not mention it.

45. Advertisement, *N.C. Educational Journal* 2 (May 1882). The directors were Rev. Lachlan C. Vass, George T. Fisher, and George Allen, all of whom were white.

term only because he taught more of the term; Nancy White apparently became pregnant or ill and stopped teaching before the session ended.[46]

A total of thirty students received "fresh certificates" in 1882, and about fifty would resume teaching after the normal school term ended, according to the directors' report. W. R. Moore, the only student listed as a senior, drew a small salary for teaching during the final three months of the term, perhaps as a replacement for the absent Nancy White. Other occasional instructors included at least seven community leaders who delivered their lectures in local churches, such as Rev. Lachlan Vass of First Presbyterian.[47]

The setting for most normal classes was a "handsome and commodious school house" built by the local public-school committee; it was dedicated for seasonal use as the normal school and featured a small library. The courses taught "embrace[d] all that is required to be taught in the public schools of the State, and in addition to that we teach Natural Philosophy, Physiology, Chemistry, Rhetoric, Algebra, Book-keeping &c," George White wrote in 1882, adding that vocal and instrumental music were also offered as extra courses.[48] He did not say which courses he taught personally, and he may well have left much of the teaching to his assistants and community lecturers, since he was quite busy with political campaigning during this period.

By the time White left the normal school's principalship in 1883, the curriculum had been expanded to include such courses as reading, calisthenics, physics, and hygiene; the latter two would be taught by lecturer Eustace E. Green, who joined the staff in 1885. Green, who graduated from Howard University's medical school in 1886, went on to establish a successful practice as a physician and pharmacist in Macon, Georgia. Green and his wife, Georgianna, eventually assumed key roles in the former principal's personal life.[49]

46. *1882 Principal's Report, New Bern.* Nanc(e)y Scott White died on December 20, 1882, according to the N.C. Graves Index, N.C. Department of Archives and History. She was buried in New Bern's Greenwood Cemetery, near Fannie White's grave.

47. *1882 Principal's Report, New Bern.*

48. Ibid.

49. *1885 Principal's Report, New Berne Normal Colored School,* and *1886 Principal's Report, New Berne Normal Colored School,* both in the 1887 report of the superintendent of public instruction to the General Assembly. Eustace Edward Green (1845–1923?), a native of Wilmington, graduated from Lincoln University in 1872 and taught school for several years before marrying Georgianna Cherry on July 2, 1879. Her younger half-sister, Cora Lena, became George White's third wife in March 1887.

White apparently continued to serve as principal of both the graded school for blacks and the Presbyterian parochial school during his tenure as head of the normal school. The state's public schools were open just four months a year, and for practical reasons would have been closed during the summer sessions of the normal school. But White's active role as a teacher and principal at the normal school ended before July 1883, when a new principal, Ella W. Somerville of Washington, D.C., began work two weeks into the term, after a period of vacancy during which three of the school's teachers had acted in turn as principal.[50]

George White's departure from educational work coincided with a unique political development that may have influenced his decision. New Bern had officially implemented graded school systems for both races in 1882, combining a half-dozen white schools into one operated in the New Bern Academy building; it was free to local students and available by tuition payment to others. The black schools continued to operate in the building used by the normal school. Funding, however, for both schools remained uncertain, largely dependent upon the inadequate county school fund, which supported as many as fifty small township schools.

The 1883 General Assembly passed the Dortch Act, which authorized a "segregated school system for New Bern, patterned after that of Goldsboro and Durham," in which each race would support its graded schools by its own designated tax collections, subject to approval by city voters at a special referendum. The Dortch Act allowed voters of either race to call for an election, in which only that race could vote, a feature to which most black leaders were understandably and strongly opposed. The New Bern city election, however, was open to voters of both races.[51]

Voters in black-majority Tarboro, presented with the choice earlier in 1883, had overwhelmingly rejected the concept of race-based funding. New

50. *1883 Principal's Report, New Berne Normal Colored School,* in the 1885 report of the superintendent of public instruction to the General Assembly. Normal school sessions were held in the late spring through early fall, when teachers were not working; the state's schools were open during the winter and early spring, to accommodate seasonal work needs of agricultural families. Miss Somerville became principal at New Bern in July 1883, and was assisted by teachers Lewis T. Christmas, J. A. Savage, and Rev. M. A. Hopkins, who had jointly directed the school since its opening in late June. Somerville later returned to Washington, and the next year married former congressman John R. Lynch of Mississippi.

51. Watson, *History of New Bern,* 571–2.

Bern's black majority was clearly expected to follow Tarboro's example, until a countywide meeting of black teachers in early May unexpectedly urged otherwise, calling on black voters to "depend upon themselves" and work to "become a powerful race" by paying for their own schools. This was a curious move for Craven's black teachers, since their statewide association of teachers had vehemently opposed the Dortch bill and "denounc[ed] the ingratitude of white people" for proposing an inherently unfair system of tax division.[52]

The referendum passed two days later, apparently with much black support, yet New Bern's black leaders soon discovered the sad truth about self-reliance. The special twenty-cent property tax and fifty-cent poll tax were intended to benefit both systems, but the disparity in tax bases was alarming; New Bern's annual taxes produced less than two hundred dollars in revenue for its black schools in 1884, compared to fourteen times as much in tax revenue for white schools. The meager amount would not pay a principal's salary, let alone that of teachers, in the black school. The Dortch Act authorizing discriminatory funding was ruled unconstitutional in 1886 by the North Carolina Supreme Court, following a lengthy battle by opponents of the 1883 law. New Bern's voters later refused to approve a similar funding effort.[53]

George White certainly favored self-reliance for his race, and may have favored the general thrust of the Dortch Act, even if he was skeptical of the wisdom of total self-reliance for funding black schools as a practical matter. In any event, he did not openly oppose the local referendum in May 1883. After five years as principal of the local black school, he was ready to pursue both a full-time law practice and his own political career. There were now qualified, experienced black teachers available to succeed him, and he no longer needed the relatively small income from his position as principal; by 1882 his outside income had gradually stabilized, both from his legal fees and his shrewd investments in local real estate.

52. Jeffrey J. Crow, Paul D. Escott, and Flora J. Hatley, *A History of African Americans in North Carolina* (Raleigh: N.C. Division of Archives and History, 1994), 111–2. The authors describe the opposition of the black state teachers' association to the Dortch Act. Senator William T. Dortch (1824–1889) of Wayne County was the author of the bill; a former member of the Confederate senate, he served in the North Carolina General Assembly from 1852 to 1854, 1858 to 1861, and 1879 to 1885.

53. Watson, *History of New Bern,* 571–2. Watson cites reports of the plea by Craven teachers to the voters in the *New Bern Daily Journal,* 6–8 May 1883.

By the mid-1880s, White had become one of the wealthiest blacks in New Bern, and later in the eastern part of the state. His acquisitions would eventually include an impressive house at 519 Johnson Street, which he constructed in 1890; the two-story, twelve-room house is still standing, and has recently been restored. He eventually purchased a second home in Tarboro, where he would move his family by early 1894; he apparently maintained homes in both towns for a time, even after moving to Washington, D.C.

But he did not confine his attention solely to business or the law. In addition to his profound interest in religious affairs, he also found time for civic affairs. He was active in as many as five social fraternities in New Bern—the Good Samaritans, Knights of Gideon, Royal Knights of King David, Knights of Pythias, and the Odd Fellows Lodge—as well as a member of a Raleigh fraternal order. As his public stature increased, White went on to serve six consecutive terms as North Carolina grand master of black Masons, leaving this role only after his first election to Congress in 1896.[54]

He had other interests as well, both social and professional. In 1880, George White had become coeditor of the *Good Samaritan*, a new fraternal newspaper, along with his colleague and fellow Republican activist Israel Braddock Abbott. Abbott was White's closest friend during the early New Bern era, beginning soon after White's arrival in 1877. The older man's flamboyant style and near-mythical status as a fugitive from his Confederate employer made him a popular speaker and debater; a free employee, he had written himself a pass and fled through Union lines to New Bern in 1862. Although lacking the polish of formal schooling, Abbott was literate and widely respected, even among Democrats, for his shrewdness and the strength of his administrative skills, including his performance as cofounder of an early lobbying group for black education, the Young Men's Intelligent and Enterprising Association. He had served one term in the North Carolina house of representatives from 1872–1874, but was unable to win regional office again after

---

54. Reid, "A Biography," 43, 97–8; *Descriptive Review*, 96. Reid cites records in the Craven County register of deeds for this claim. After Craven County was removed from the Second District, White moved to his wife's hometown of Tarboro in February 1894 in order to qualify for the district congressional nomination. White also served as district grand master of New Bern's King Solomon Lodge No. 1. Reid contends, based on his review of state Masonic records, that White served fewer than six terms, but because the six-term claim is repeated so widely in other contemporary sketches after 1896, I have allowed it to stand here.

1874. He remained active in party politics, serving one term on the New Bern board of aldermen in the mid-1870s, but that was his last successful election. He also served as statewide head of the Grand Lodge of Good Samaritans in 1881.[55]

The short, stocky, dark-skinned carpenter and the tall, distinguished lawyer of mixed race made an unlikely pair of friends. Abbott often described himself as "pure African" and proud of it, openly scorning light-skinned opportunists like James O'Hara, whom he passionately detested. White, of course, had a far lighter complexion than Abbott and made no secret of his mixed racial heritage. Yet unlike O'Hara, White maintained close relationships with darker-skinned blacks, and both Abbott and White believed fervently in the power of education and diligence to raise up their race. Abbott's candor and his plain lifestyle reflected a deep-seated belief in hard work and integrity, helping to develop a shared bond between these two men of unshakable principle. Both were devoted family men, as well; Abbott and his wife, Susan, had seven children by 1880, including a son Della's age, and his older daughters Ann and Hannah undoubtedly took a special interest in the infant Della.[56]

Israel Abbott quickly became the trusted older brother George White had always seemed to need, but up to now, had never found. Though both men were committed to the Republican Party, they did not always agree politically; Abbott tended to be more hotheaded and spontaneous, and resigned his last elected post in anger. In a prolonged fit of pique, he even ran as an independent Republican against his personal nemesis, O'Hara, in 1886. The stoical White endured political storms with aplomb and persistence, and, as a result, was far more successful than his friend. Although Abbott and White took somewhat different approaches to politics, both condemned the reported

55. *Washington People's Advocate*, 27 March 1880; "Israel B. Abbott," in Eric Foner, *Freedom's Lawmakers: A Directory of Black Officeholders during Reconstruction*, rev. ed. (New York: Oxford University Press, 1995), 1. The *People's Advocate* welcomed the "appearance of the 'Good Samaritan,' published weekly at New Berne, N.C. in the interests of the colored people of the South." The freeborn Abbott (1840–1887) had been a Confederate officer's servant when he escaped to New Bern in 1861; he resigned in protest from the New Bern city council in 1876, then served as a delegate to the 1880 Republican National Convention and an alternate delegate to the 1884 convention.

56. U.S. Census, Craven County, 1870 and 1880. In 1880 the Abbotts are listed as having seven children, ranging in age from one to sixteen years.

growing corruption among black party leaders, particularly outside Craven County. Both dealt effectively with the largely white leadership of the Craven party, which carefully parceled out nominations to qualified candidates of both races and preserved the two-term tradition.

Like George White, Israel Abbott was also a blunt and honest man. He believed in "bolting"—running as an independent if a candidate lost the regular nomination—but only under special circumstances when one sincerely believed the nominee to be corrupt or detrimental to the party, such as in the O'Hara case. George White's one unsuccessful attempt at bolting the party, in 1882, had stemmed from a purely factional dispute, and he publicly refused to consider running as an independent thereafter. Yet he never condemned "conscience bolters" like Abbott, instead cautioning that the practice was potentially harmful to party stability.

White may have privately supported Abbott against O'Hara in 1886, but White's practical nature would have prevented him from risking his own race by publicly endorsing his friend's bold, doomed gesture. And while Abbott's penchant for unorthodox and unpopular moves such as labor organizing may have diminished his chances of electoral success, his personal standing in the party remained high. In 1884, for instance, he served as chairman of the Second District Republican convention, possibly because he now declined to oppose O'Hara's renomination; for once, he seemed to be heeding the advice of his more prudent friends.

Abbott went on to seek the same nomination in 1886; although unable to win it himself, he helped defeat O'Hara that year, while assuring his status as provisional front-runner in 1888. Meanwhile, his best friend served as the district's elected prosecutor. Sadly, high office was a dream never to be fulfilled for Abbott, who died suddenly in May 1887.[57] By then, George White was well on his own way to the pinnacle of political success in the Black Second, after two terms in the General Assembly and election as district solicitor, but the loss of his friend and trusted confidant would be a blow to his inner confidence. For all his later success, the intensely private White would never again form such an enduring friendship.

---

57. Obituary for Israel B. Abbott, *New Bern Daily Journal*, 7 May 1887. The *Daily Journal* praised his "unexcelled" ability as "presiding officer of a body of colored representatives disposed to be unruly."

3

Into the Public Arena

George White seemed to have a natural affinity for politics; his impressive stature and booming voice, combined with his sound education and a subtle flair for drama, made him a popular speaker, as evidenced by the reaction to his first recorded speech at Beaufort, North Carolina, on Emancipation Day in 1879. His "very eloquent and telling speech" on January 1 had drawn "loud applause" and easily dissuaded any listeners considering imminent departure from the state, according to S. A. Blount's account in the *Wilmington Post*. "His very appearance seemed to beam for the rhetorical magnitude, and we were all edified" at his words, which came just days before his successful bar examination. Black lawyers were still at a premium, and Blount seemed to speak for the appreciative crowd, who "wish[ed] him every imaginable success attending those of his profession."[1]

Joining White on the speaker's rostrum that day was another budding politician, twenty-two-year-old John Campbell Dancy, whose potential Blount saw as equally unlimited. The two prospective public servants were similar in several ways: both were unquestionably bright and ambitious, both were teachers, and both shared a deep interest in religion and fraternal affairs. But while White would follow a natural path from law into elective politics, Dancy's route would be less direct; for one, his ambitions leaned more toward the literary than did those of his colleague. Dancy spent a decade as a journal-

1. "The Emancipation Anniversary," letter from S. A. Blount, *Wilmington Post*, 19 January 1879. Blount, a Republican, also lived in Beaufort; parade participants gathered at his house.

ist, eventually becoming the editor of the state's leading black newspaper, Salisbury's *Star of Zion*, in 1885, and later served more than a decade in two important federal patronage positions; he went on to achieve national recognition as a leader in the black ranks of the Republican Party.[2]

The careers of the two men were separate but complementary. Though their paths would frequently cross, these fellow North Carolinians always maintained a polite, formal distance from each other; they were cordial colleagues, never friends. Despite their shared passion for the truth and determination to uplift their race, their methods, like their expressions of religion, were distinct. Dancy, son of a freed slave from Edgecombe County, was a member of the African Methodist Episcopal Zion Church, one of the two purely black Methodist denominations; White's Presbyterianism, while equally devout, was more closely identified with the white denomination from which it had sprung. Dancy was cool, cerebral, and polished, capable of playing two contradictory roles at once: detached observer and highly political player. By contrast, George White was direct, almost alarmingly outspoken in his bluntness, yet almost naive in his determination to eschew secrecy, even as he sought to master the rough-and-tumble world of elective politics. Dancy would receive an unending flow of offices, honors, and appointments, propelled by administrative deftness and an unerring sense of timing, as well as his well-tended ties to other Republicans; White would be more often disappointed, if only for his greater idealism and thinner skin, and his sometimes exasperating streak of independence.

Both men entered public service in the same year, 1880, although Dancy would soon forsake elective politics for appointive office; his first defeat, in 1884, would be his last. For White, the entry into public service would only whet his enormous appetite for political success. The first year of decision would be his doorway into decades of challenge, with occasional defeats accepted as the inevitable side effects of his relentless drive to the top.

The year 1880 proved momentous for White. The young lawyer and his wife enjoyed the birth of a daughter, Della, in late January, just before their first anniversary; in the same month that he began his second year as a li-

2. Ibid.; "John Campbell Dancy, Jr.," *DNCB* 2:7–8. Dancy served as U.S. collector of customs at the port in Wilmington from 1891 to 1893 and as recorder of deeds for the District of Columbia from 1902 to 1910, both presidential appointments. Dancy appears to have been named for his father, John C. Dancy, but did not use Jr. and named his own son John C. Dancy Jr.

censed lawyer, with a growing practice and reputation. In May, White was selected as a delegate to his new party's upcoming state convention, a signal
honor for a young member; he was later nominated by the Republicans to run
for a seat in the General Assembly, more proof of his growing stature among
party elders. In June, he entered his fourth year as principal of the city's graded
school for blacks, having built a strong following in his community.[3]

By year's end, three more events had made indelible imprints on George
White's memory. Two of them, in November, would normally have been
happy occasions: his November 2 election to the state house of representatives, and just five days later, the dedication of the new building for Ebenezer
Presbyterian Church, which he now served as church school superintendent
as well as a ruling elder. Both were overshadowed, however, by the sudden
death of his young wife Fannie in late September, as previously noted.[4]

His private grief, like almost all his emotions, was publicly controlled;
shaken but resilient, White went on to win his seat in the house from Craven
County, joined in victory by George Green Jr., son of a former state senator
and prominent white Republican leader. It was the first test of either man's
political skills, and served both well. White had lived in New Bern for less
than four years, but over the next decade became one of the most experienced
and respected public servants in his new home; Green, a New Bern native,
went on to serve two terms in the state senate.[5]

The race factor played its traditional role in the county's selections; only
once since 1868 had all Republican legislative nominees been of the same
race, when all were black in the 1874 contest. White had been nominated by
county Republicans for the house to succeed a fellow black, Willis D. Petti-

3. Joseph E. Elmore, "North Carolina Negro Congressmen" (Master's thesis, University of
North Carolina, 1964), 151. Della White was born in January, according to the 1880 census.
The Craven County Republican convention, at which White was nominated, was held May 20,
according to the *Newbernian*, 22 May 1880, cited in Elmore.

4. Vass, *New Bern Presbyterian Church*, 184; Watson, *History of New Bern*, 509–10. Ebenezer
Presbyterian Church was dedicated on Sunday, November 7, 1880, five days after the fall election. While public health improvements were gradually being made in New Bern, epidemics of
disease still struck with alarming regularity; Watson describes the incidence of disease among
New Bernians in the late 1870s and early 1880s.

5. George Green Sr. (1823–1900?) served as state senator from 1876 to 1877 and later as
Craven County attorney before being elected clerk of the superior court. His son, George Jr., was
elected to the state senate in 1886 and 1888.

pher; Green was chosen to succeed veteran William E. Clarke, who was moving up to the senate after two terms in the lower body. As usual, the Republican nomination was tantamount to election, for no Democrat had won a legislative seat from Craven since the end of the war fifteen years earlier.[6]

The 1880 election was in most respects a routine one in Craven, although it was the first to combine statewide and national elections on one November ticket. The presidential and gubernatorial elections stirred considerable interest, primarily among county Republicans, but much local interest also focused on the contests for Congress and county office, including the choice of a successor to outgoing sheriff Orlando Hubbs, now the Republican nominee for Congress. The party's trio of legislative nominees faced an uncomplicated course, easily defeating their Democratic opponents with only limited campaigning—a fortuitous break for the grief-stricken young widower George White.

The Republican Party scored impressive wins across the Second District, electing Hubbs to the U.S. House and a total of eleven legislators from counties within the district. Only Halifax, Wayne, and Wilson Counties sent Democrats to the 1881 General Assembly. In addition to White, Republican winners included five other black house candidates: William W. Watson and Clinton W. Battle from Edgecombe; Paul F. Hayley from Northampton; and Daniel R. Johnson and George H. King from Warren. Senator-elect Hawkins W. Carter of Warren completed that county's all-black delegation to the General Assembly, matching Northampton's effort in that respect; Samuel G. Newsom, Republican of Margarettsville, was the only other black elected to the senate from within the Second District. Edgecombe and Craven each elected at least one black to the lower chamber but chose white senators.[7]

Such split results were not uncommon in the quixotic Black Second. The

6. Pettipher, a Craven deputy sheriff, former county commissioner, and justice of the peace, served one term in the house in 1879. As senator, William E. Clarke succeeded Rev. Edward W. Bull, who returned for a second term in 1891. The delegation elected in 1874 consisted of Senator Richard Tucker and Representatives John R. Goode and Edward H. Hill, all black. The county had previously elected three black representatives in August 1870—Edward R. Dudley, Richard Tucker, and George B. Willis—but had also elected two white men senators in September 1870, Leonidas J. Moore and R. F. Lehman.

7. NCG, 560. Edgecombe County voters elected Walter P. Williamson to the North Carolina senate in 1880; he resigned the office on May 16, 1882. Craven sent sixteen and Edgecombe eighteen black legislators to Raleigh between 1868 and 1888.

district's counties shared many characteristics, including rural lifestyles, agricultural dependency, and a large black population, but the Second was hardly
monolithic; its voting patterns were inconsistent, usually staunchly Republican but varying widely from county to county and year to year. At one end of
the spectrum were Wayne and Wilson Counties, the only two with white majorities; neither elected a black legislator between 1868 and 1898, and Wilson
usually went Democratic, while Wayne elected white Republicans with some
regularity. At the other end were Craven and Edgecombe, whose heavily
black populations regularly produced straight Republican tickets and black
legislators in significant numbers.[8]

Warren County sent Republican delegations, mostly black, to Raleigh for
twenty straight years after 1868, but remained something of an anomaly, even
in the unpredictable Black Second; under a special arrangement with Democrats there, black Republicans in Warren regularly voted for white Democrats
for all but one county office. Largest of the district's counties was James
O'Hara's home of Halifax, which despite a population 70 percent black and
overwhelmingly Republican, still tended to alternate politically, electing
black Republicans and white Democrats to both houses in roughly equal numbers. Covert deals and large-scale fraud were the likely reasons there, as well as
in Greene, Jones, and Lenoir Counties, which all had black majorities but
elected only white Republicans to the legislature. Northampton, by contrast,
tended to alternate by race in selecting its Republican nominees, occasionally
electing a white Democrat as well.[9]

The situation in Craven County was unique: blacks accounted for more
than three-fourths of the Republican Party membership but did not control
the party apparatus. A small number of influential white Republicans controlled the nomination process in consultation with black leaders, parceling
out house seats to selected black members but reserving the senate seat almost
exclusively for white party members. The results were not always systematic;

8. Anderson, *Race and Politics*, 249; NCG, 1157–8. Of 41 separate elections between 1868
and 1888, 26 were won by blacks and 15 by white Republicans from Warren. Only one black
Republican was elected to a county office during this same period: Mansfield Thornton, the
perennial register of deeds in Warren. Between 1868 and 1896, Halifax elected 13 black
Republicans and 13 white Democrats to the house, usually in alternating elections, although the
1868 and 1870 delegations contained both.

9. NCG, 1221–2.

party elders had chosen White in place of Pettipher, who had served just one term, even though they had previously allowed William E. Clarke to run for two consecutive terms in the house. So far, the results had been generally satisfactory to both sides, but that would change; as the black GOP leadership matured, they were less likely to be satisfied with anything less than a fair share of all offices.[10]

The key factor in the selection process appears to have been a subjective one: the assessed effectiveness of one's past or potential performance in office. With a far smaller pool of white party members to choose from, white candidates were more likely to "earn" the right to be renominated, based on their greater effectiveness in dealing with white Democratic leaders in Raleigh. Conversely, with so many black candidates to consider, renominating one black meant depriving another of a chance at office. Unlike Republicans in other counties, however, the Craven party hierarchy generally enforced a two-term rule of fairness; in most cases, no Craven man of either race could serve more than two terms in the General Assembly, and in any case, never more than two terms in the same house.

The arrangement was flawed but flexible, and seemed to fit Craven County's peculiar needs. It tended to ward off factional splits, defuse personal disagreements, and preserve both the Republicans' dominance on most levels and a countywide consensus, a rare enough occurrence in the Second District. Few blacks challenged the Craven arrangement, which did favor the smaller white wing of the party but which most black party members accepted as a reasonable cost of long-term stability. Those blacks who did not support party nominees were not likely to gain a later nomination; running as an independent candidate was strongly discouraged, if rarely punished.[11]

10. For instance, the house seat won by White in 1880 would be held by a black Republican for twelve years, until a white Republican won the seat in 1892. But White was the only black senator from Craven during the period, and the last one Craven ever elected; Craven merged with adjacent mostly white counties to form a multisenator district after 1891.

11. By the time White ran as a "reform" candidate in 1882, the stricture against bolting had all but disappeared in Craven County. Israel Abbott refused to support James O'Hara's nomination in 1878 and campaigned instead for independent James H. Harris; Abbott was named chairman of the district convention in 1884 after seeking the congressional nomination in 1882, and later ran as a reform nominee in 1886.

George White's initiation into elective politics was part of a carefully structured ritual that demanded stability, valued service, and rewarded loyalty. The ritualized selection of candidates reinforced the system in the fledgling Craven party, which had achieved power suddenly in the late 1860s and was determined to avoid the pitfalls of corruption and factionalism. Indeed, there were few major intraparty factional feuds here, like those that plagued the less stable parties in Edgecombe, Halifax, and Warren. Craven never produced the stream of disruptive competing delegations that other counties regularly sent to district conventions, often producing chaos during the credentials process.[12]

White had now taken his place in the hierarchical structure, for gradual advancement as the party judged him ready. He was the tenth and youngest black so far to serve as a state house member from Craven; the next were his close friend Israel B. Abbott, twenty-nine, who had served one term from 1872–74, and Willis Pettipher, thirty-one, whom he replaced. The average age of all black house members until now had been forty. Other blacks elected from the New Bern area between 1868 and 1880 included Benjamin W. Morris (1868), Edward Richard Dudley (1870, 1872), George B. Willis (1870), Richard Tucker (1870), John R. Goode (1874), Edward H. Hill (1874), and Henry H. Simmons (1876).[13]

Its racial imbalance aside, the Craven Republican Party faced difficult external political problems. After Democrats had reclaimed the General Assembly in 1876, local Republican winners were often denied office on legal technicalities, such as refusal to accept performance bonds. The situation began to destabilize after 1881, when Craven lost its second house seat to reapportionment, and was further clouded by a feud between two white party candidates for sheriff in 1882. The party structure had all but collapsed in 1886, when the "mongrel coalition" with Democrats sought to mirror the

12. Factions in other counties often held separate meetings to choose their own delegates, then challenged the "regular" delegation at the district convention, leaving the decision to hopelessly partial credentials committees. This happened most often in Edgecombe, but delegations from almost all Black Second counties were challenged at both district and state levels during the 1880s.

13. When first elected, Richard Tucker (1817–1881) was 53 years old, Goode (1819–1880) 55, Abbott and Dudley, 29, and Pettipher 31.

Warren arrangement. But at its peak in 1880, when George White prepared to take office, the Craven system was the most stable and predictable one in the district.[14]

The year's combination of statewide and national elections produced a concentrated political effort at all levels during the fall. This was the first presidential election since the end of Reconstruction, effected during the administration of outgoing Republican president Rutherford B. Hayes, and Democrats had strong hopes to reclaim the nation's top office after twenty years. Democrats had controlled the U.S. House since 1875, and badly wanted to control the executive branch as well; to do so, they needed to carry all the southern states plus several large northern states, including New York.[15]

The 1880 Democratic national ticket pitted preelection favorite General Winfield Scott Hancock and Indiana banker William English against Republican congressman James A. Garfield of Ohio and his running mate, lawyer Chester Alan Arthur of New York. The contest was complicated by the presence of a third-party candidate, General James B. Weaver of Iowa, who represented the Greenback Party and drew more than 300,000 votes, mostly from disaffected Republicans expected to vote Democratic. Garfield won the popular vote by the narrowest of margins: 7,000 votes out of 9.2 million, the closest race to date in U.S. history.[16]

Winfield Hancock swept the solid South, including North Carolina, and carried New Jersey and two western states; had he won New York as well, he would have become president. But his unexpected loss in the Empire State cost him the electoral college. Nationally, the Democrats were distraught. For the second time in a row, they had come within a handful of votes of winning

14. The turbulent 1882 race for sheriff pitted incumbent Mayer Hahn against Daniel Stimson; Hahn won the election, but the split within the party deepened, setting the stage for the "mongrel coalition" battle four years later. Stimson initially won the 1886 sheriff's race with Democratic support, but Hahn was awarded the seat by court action a year later.

15. David M. Jordan, *Winfield Scott Hancock: A Soldier's Life* (Bloomington: Indiana University Press, 1996), 298–305. The Democrats had carried all but the three "stolen" states of Florida, Louisiana, and South Carolina in 1876. In 1880, Hancock hoped to carry his native Pennsylvania, the South, several western states, New Jersey, and New York to seal the victory; losing New York's thirty-five electoral votes cost him the election.

16. General Weaver won no states in 1880; in 1892 he ran again as the Populist nominee, drawing more than a million votes in his second losing cause.

the presidency, but now they had lost not only that race but control of the U.S. House as well.[17]

Like the rest of the South, North Carolina gave its electoral votes to Hancock, by a margin of about nine thousand popular votes; he became the second Democrat in a row to capture the Tar Heel State in the presidential race. On the other hand, Craven County had gone heavily for Garfield, and Republicans across the state charged the Democrats with election fraud. Senator-elect William Clarke, a member of the state elections board, supplied graphic details of the fraud he had observed in a December 1880 letter to president-elect Garfield, whom he believed should have carried the state. Clarke charged that Democrats had deprived Garfield of ten thousand votes by refusing to register Republican voters in the eastern part of the state, by keeping Republican voters in line until the polls had closed, and by allowing challenged voters to cast ballots only to turn around and disallow entire precincts on the basis of those "illegal votes."[18]

In North Carolina, however, the national race was, for both parties, secondary in importance to the governor's race, which pitted Democratic incumbent Thomas J. Jarvis against Republican Ralph P. Buxton, a former superior court judge. Jarvis had been appointed governor to succeed Zebulon B. Vance, who had been elected to the U.S. Senate by the General Assembly in 1878. Although sometimes labeled a white supremacist, Jarvis sporadically sought to draw blacks into the Democratic Party, arguing after 1885 that blacks' rights were secure and they should now eschew blind Republican loyalties. But Jarvis did little during the 1880 campaign to appeal actively to black voters, and most blacks voted for Buxton. In the Second District, for instance, Jarvis won no counties with a majority of black voters, while Buxton carried all but Wayne and Wilson Counties.[19]

17. In 1876, Republican Rutherford B. Hayes had won the disputed electoral college by one vote, 185 to 184. Democrat Samuel Tilden had a plurality of more than 250,000 popular votes, and most historians agree that the election was stolen from Democrats when southern leaders obtained Hayes's pledge to end Reconstruction.

18. William E. Clarke to James A. Garfield, 2 December 1880, in Garfield Papers (microfilm), Library of Congress; NCG, 1333. Garfield received 115,879 votes to Hancock's 124,746 in North Carolina; Hancock polled about 1,000 fewer votes than had Tilden in 1876, while Garfield received about 7,500 more than Hayes had received in 1876.

19. NCG, 1404–5. In the black-majority counties, Buxton's average victory margin was 16 percent. Even Wayne barely went Democratic, by 51 to 49 percent.

Craven's voters overwhelmingly favored Buxton, but to no avail, as Governor Jarvis managed to hold the office by a narrow statewide margin of six thousand votes. It was yet another contest that Republicans believed had been stolen from them, and was certainly the party's closest loss of the century. After taking office, Jarvis made overtures to black members of the General Assembly, meeting with a black delegation at the request of George White and others in early March to discuss matters of interest to them, including education. White would become a public supporter of Jarvis in years to come, even recommending Jarvis to President Grover Cleveland for a U.S. cabinet post in 1885, although Jarvis proved to have a short memory, betraying White's confidence by joining the white supremacists in 1898.[20]

The congressional race in the Black Second proved even more intriguing. Despite its overwhelming Republican registration, the Second District had been represented in Congress since 1879 by Democrat William H. Kitchin. In 1878, Kitchin had defeated two black Republican opponents, James E. O'Hara and independent James H. Harris, but his victory had been tainted by charges of blatant fraud, postelection lawsuits, and O'Hara's futile appeal to Congress itself. O'Hara's exotic parentage, alleged bigamy, and doubtful American citizenship, among other things, had not endeared him to all members of his race or his party, and his controversial nomination had prompted Harris to split the Republican vote by running independently.[21]

In 1880, Second District Republicans had chosen Craven County sheriff Orlando Hubbs, the only white carpetbagger ever nominated there, to face Kitchin, thus denying renomination to former congressman and governor Curtis H. Brogden, who grumpily refused to concede the loss for months. Hubbs, a New York native, had moved to New Bern in 1865 and been elected sheriff in 1870; his brother Ethelbert was the city's postmaster and a former newspaper editor. Sheriff Hubbs was a consensus choice in Craven, but faced

20. Ibid. Craven went to Buxton by a margin of better than 2.5 to 1, Jarvis receiving just 1,190 votes to Buxton's 2,819. The state total was Buxton 115,559, Jarvis 121,837.

21. Anderson, *Race and Politics*, 62–4. O'Hara was born either in New York City or the Danish West Indies; his parents were an Irish seaman and a West Indian woman, who were not married, and he variously claimed American citizenship through his father's citizenship, his own birth, and naturalization. O'Hara claimed he had divorced his first wife in the District of Columbia, though she was unaware of it, and he fathered at least one child out of wedlock while still married to her.

a less enthusiastic reception outside the county, primarily because of Brogden's stubborn opposition. His support among black party members, however, was generally quite strong.

Still, the racial lines were neither obvious nor very effective. One avid Hubbs supporter was George T. Wassom of Goldsboro, a black attorney who had succeeded Hubbs as chairman of the district executive committee and who was also the brother-in-law of defeated 1878 nominee James O'Hara. O'Hara himself strongly disliked Hubbs, petulantly blaming him for the 1878 defeat. Meanwhile, Col. Lotte W. Humphrey, a white leader defeated by O'Hara for the nomination in 1878, now joined forces with O'Hara to oppose Hubbs well into the fall. It was a free-for-all, confusing and frequently hostile, as alliances shifted and re-formed. Despite the tension, Hubbs defeated Kitchin by five thousand votes, restoring the house seat to the GOP column. But his success was short-lived; Hubbs was forced to withdraw from the next race, in 1882, in the face of an all-out challenge by James O'Hara.[22]

The 1880 Hubbs campaign had little direct effect on the county's local elections, except perhaps to increase Republican turnout. That in itself was a boon to newcomer George White, who carefully avoided needless involvement in regional rivalries. Having just turned twenty-eight, he entered the 1881 General Assembly as the youngest member of a youthful Craven delegation; his house colleague George Green Jr. was twenty-nine, while Senator William E. Clarke was the seasoned veteran at thirty. Despite White's youth, his superior debating skills and legal training quickly made him a floor leader among the largely inexperienced black contingent in the house. Of the dozen blacks elected in 1880, only two—John Newell of Bladen and Clinton W. Battle of Edgecombe—had any previous legislative experience.[23]

Black newcomers to the house from beyond the Second District included John Hays of Granville; Alexander B. Hicks Jr. of Washington; Augustus Robbins of Bertie; and William H. Waddell of New Hanover. They were joined in the senate by Hawkins W. Carter, who had served two terms in the lower chamber, and Samuel G. Newsom of Northampton, a newcomer to the legislature. There was no formal caucus of blacks in the 120-member lower

22. *RN&O*, 15 October 1882. Hubbs withdrew from the race on October 10, 1882.

23. Clarke was born in Raleigh in 1850, Green in New Bern in 1851. Newell was serving his third house term in 1881 and Battle, his second.

house, although black members did tend to vote as a group, sometimes joined by a very few white colleagues.[24]

When the house convened in Raleigh on January 5, 1881, Craven's two Georges, White and Green, were among the first group of one hundred representatives to be sworn in. Their first duty came during the vote for house speaker. Democrats outnumbered Republicans almost two to one, but Green and White dutifully cast their losing ballots for Republican colleague Jacob W. Bowman, who lost to Charles M. Cooke in a straight party vote, 68-32. A second vote for assistant doorkeeper then saw White and six black colleagues split their votes among three losing candidates.[25]

One day later, White joined a smaller group to vote for the losing candidate for reading clerk, Aaron Owen; the black resident of Warren County received twelve votes, including those of White and seven other black members. On the next vote, for the office of engrossing clerk, the losing candidate received seventeen votes, including those of White and eight other black members. Both candidates had been nominated by black members, Owen by Daniel Johnson of Warrenton and engrossing-clerk nominee W. Price by Paul Hayley of Jackson. The two votes were largely symbolic; black candidates for General Assembly offices were only occasionally successful, and experienced house members had surely cautioned their freshman colleagues not to expect to win such races. Afterwards, the black members generally joined their Republican colleagues in partisan votes, as in the election for speaker.[26]

On January 9, George White received his session's committee assignments, Education and Military Affairs. Within a week he introduced his first four bills, two of which were fairly controversial: one to provide for the pay of

24. Black house members met with the state Republican caucus. The race of Senator Henry Ephraim Scott of New Hanover is difficult to determine; he may have been white, although some historians have described him as black.

25. In the house, Democrats numbered 76, Republicans 44. Not all representatives showed up to be sworn in the first day; as candidates, Cooke and Bowman did not vote. White and members Battle, King, and Waddell voted for Charles Guyer; member Johnson voted for a third candidate, Carter, while members Hicks and Robbins voted for a fourth candidate, Pugh. The winner was J. P. Norton of McDowell, who received the votes of 84 members, including almost all Republicans.

26. *1881 House Journal*, 12–3. Even had all Republicans joined their black colleagues, they could not muster a simple majority in the house without significant Democratic support, which was unlikely for any black nominee.

state jurors, another to make seduction an indictable offense. Both were referred to committees on which he did not serve, and in which each bill died: the jurors' pay bill to the Committee on Salaries and Fees, the seduction bill to the Judiciary Committee.[27]

A third bill of interest to New Bern constituents sought to amend the charter of the city and was referred to an unspecified committee. House Bill 154 was reported unfavorably by the committee on January 27, and White would argue "at considerable length," though unsuccessfully, that the house should override the adverse report. White's fourth bill, to amend a private law of 1879 relating to the Independent Order of Good Samaritans and Daughters of Samaria of New Bern, was referred to the Committee on Common Corporations. It passed the house on January 27.[28]

On January 15, Representative White presented the first of numerous petitions from Second District residents, asking for prohibition of the sale of alcoholic beverages across the state. This particular petition was from the residents of Woodbridge, a small community in Craven County, and was referred to the Committee on Prohibition. Prohibition was to be the single most politically charged issue of the 1881 assembly, which argued the matter regularly but could reach no satisfactory resolution; the body eventually deferred the final decision to voters by authorizing a statewide referendum to be held later in the year.[29]

George White's most provocative bill, however, dealt with mandatory public education in the state. It was the first of many efforts on his part to influence public thinking on notable educational issues, and was obviously a subject close to his professional heart as a teacher and principal. The bill he introduced on January 26 sought to compel attendance in state public schools by all children between the ages of six and eighteen years for a minimum of sixteen months, or four school years, unless they were educated privately. Its call for mandatory education of all students stood very little chance of pas-

27. Daily house proceedings for 1881, Day 8 (January 13) and Day 21 (January 27), as reported in the *Raleigh News and Observer*. White introduced the juror-pay and seduction bills on January 13.

28. Ibid., Day 9 (January 14) and Day 21 (January 27); Reid, "A Biography," 60.

29. *RN&O*, 1881 house proceedings, Day 10 (January 15). Petitions were also introduced by three other representatives, including William H. Day of Halifax. The prohibition bill's final version was described by the *RN&O*, 20 March 1881.

sage, for it echoed an unpopular provision in the state's "radical" 1868 constitution, which had been gutted by amendments in 1875; even the public-school law of 1869, which contained a similar provision, had never been fully implemented. Representative White's bill was referred to his education committee, where he argued his case for a week, until it was reported out unfavorably on February 1.

On that day, White rose to address the house, pleading for the bill in strong fashion and asking the chamber to pass it without regard for the report and independently of other bills being considered by the committee. Despite his efforts, the bill was tabled without a vote being taken. It is possible that the house refusal was related to a separate resolution, introduced by William Watson of Edgecombe but drafted by White, that sought to clarify state law regarding local supervision of school districts. This bill sought a report on the need for separate boards of committeemen for segregated local school districts, rather than one local board for both. White's earlier bill would have empowered the separate boards of committeemen to enforce his mandatory-attendance law.[30]

The Watson maneuver, if approved, would inevitably have led to calls for mandatory black membership on local boards of committeemen for the black schools, and the Democratic assembly was in no mood to consider such a controversial question. Watson's resolution was also given an unfavorable report by the Education Committee, another blow to White's educational agenda. While the 1881 General Assembly passed several notable amendments to the public-school law, any significant expansion of the state's school system would have to be performed gradually; funding the universal system anticipated by White and other Republicans was still an expensive dream for the next century.[31]

Nevertheless, George White continued to demonstrate his deep concern

30. *RN&O*, 1881 house proceedings, Day 20 (January 26) and Day 25 (February 1); Reid, "A Biography," 61. The idealistic 1869 public-school law had authorized local taxes and, as a fallback, state funding; despite support by then-governor Holden, it never achieved its goal, since few localities could provide adequate funding and the General Assembly refused to assist, even after Holden was removed from office. Reid says the draft of the Watson resolution was in White's handwriting.

31. A lengthy, positive account of the bill's provisions appeared on the editorial page of the *Raleigh News and Observer* on 16 March 1881, mentioning the bill's $4,000 appropriation for the expansion of normal schools for black and white teachers.

for education, particularly for the training of teachers, and on his next attempt, he was successful. Establishing new state normal schools for the preparation of black teachers was an absolute necessity, in White's view. Four years
earlier, the General Assembly had created one such school for teachers of
each race: for white teachers at Chapel Hill, under the auspices of the
University of North Carolina, and another for blacks at Fayetteville, which
absorbed the private Howard normal school opened during Reconstruction.
The Chapel Hill normal school was actually a summer-long institute administered by the university to improve the instructional methods used by existing
teachers, while the Fayetteville normal school was intended as a freestanding
operation aimed at recruiting and training black males for the profession, with
eight months of classes offered each year. Annual appropriations amounted to
two thousand dollars for each school.[32]

The Fayetteville school was intended to provide three years of basic training to prospective black teachers, who were then expected to teach for at least
three more years. It was a pitifully small step toward resolving the shortage of
qualified black teachers, barely supplementing the similar efforts at private
black universities like Shaw and Biddle and at private normal schools like the
Whitin School at Lumberton, which White himself had once attended. The
task faced by the Fayetteville normal school was clearly daunting, for across
the state, there were perhaps two hundred thousand black children of school
age, with about half that number attending classes in 1880. With at least one
teacher needed for every forty to fifty students, this meant at least 2,000 new
teachers would be needed if all black students were to be enrolled. But by
1879, only 114 student teachers had received training at Fayetteville; about a
third were women, admitted only with special permission, even though the
majority of elementary schoolteachers at the time were female. Fayetteville
principal Robert Harris said he had found it difficult to induce young black
men to enter the normal school and recommended immediate expansion of
admission to include both sexes.[33]

32. Marcus C. S. Noble, A History of the Public Schools of North Carolina (Chapel Hill:
University of North Carolina Press, 1930), 421–5. The law specified male schoolteachers, but
the state board of education gave special permission for women to receive training at each site.

33. Brown, Education of Negroes, 35–84; Lefler and Newsome, North Carolina, 535; James A.
Padgett, "From Slavery to Prominence in North Carolina," Journal of Negro History 22 (October
1937); Noble, Public Schools, 424. Shaw University, a Baptist school in Raleigh, had been train-

Having served as a grade-school principal for the past four years, George White was certainly familiar with the problems faced by local black schools. Recruiting qualified black schoolteachers was somewhat easier in New Bern, with its relatively well-educated black population, than in many other areas. Retaining them was still difficult, however, due to low pay; the state's average wage for teachers was less than twenty-five dollars per month, for an average annual term of two to three months. And while schoolteachers generally worked longer and were paid better in New Bern's white schools each year than the state average, the city's black system was not quite so fortunate. Tuition was charged at the white school, but the city's far larger population of poorer blacks could rarely afford such a supplemental payment, even a modest one.[34]

Since the late 1860s, the private Peabody Fund of Boston had awarded matching grants to local school systems in the state, both white and black, who were willing to operate for ten months a year; black schools generally received two-thirds the amount that white schools received. Even while New Bern participated temporarily in the philanthropic Peabody procedure, the local need remained greater than the available resources, especially for salaries. For its part, the public school committee of New Bern had by 1882 constructed a large two-story building for use as a black school, capable of holding between three and four hundred students, although the black student population was considerably larger. It was used seasonally by the normal school

---

ing teachers since 1865. Presbyterians founded Biddle Institute in Charlotte in 1867 and Scotia Seminary for women in Concord in 1870; other denominational schools included Livingstone College, Saint Augustine's, and Bennett College. Private normal schools included Albion Academy, Gregory Institute, and the Thompson Institute at Lumberton; Brown does not mention D. P. Allen's Whitin School. The average teacher's salary was $22 per month and the average school term about nine weeks a year in 1880, according to Lefler and Newsome; about 40 percent of the state's black children were enrolled in 1874, compared with nearly 60 percent a decade later. Harris made the statement in his first annual report to the state superintendent of public instruction; the 1879 legislature then amended the law to authorize training of both sexes.

34. Brown, *Education of Negroes*, 34. New Bern and Greensboro charged $10 per pupil in 1885. At least one system charged more (Wilson, $11.05) but most charged less; Goldsboro's system was free. New Bern's white teachers earned $35 per month, less than most of the other city systems; Raleigh paid its white teachers $53 per month, its black teachers $40. No figures are available for the salaries of New Bern's black teachers.

as well; George White described the schoolhouse as "large and commodious," and the rent was free.[35]

As a member of the house's Education Committee, White was in a strategic position to influence the content of draft bills regarding educational appropriations; whether he was the actual author of the 1881 provision to create additional normal schools for training black teachers is not clear, although a biography printed some sixteen years later in the *Raleigh Gazette* claimed that distinction for him. More likely, White took strategic advantage of his presence at committee deliberations to amend a proposed bill—one doubtlessly offered by a member of the Democratic majority—to include funds for new normal schools for both races, as claimed by the *New York Freeman* in 1887.[36]

According to the *Freeman's* account, White "caught some of the Democratic members with their suspenders down and hitched on a bill providing for normal schools for the colored people as a rider to the University bill." Even this may have been an exaggeration, since Democrats had supported the concept since 1877 and needed little prodding; still, the precise relationship between the normal schools and the university was a tenuous one, since only the white summer school at Chapel Hill was attached to the university or held on a college campus. The Fayetteville normal school was administered by the state board of education and the state superintendent of public instruction, and the new schools were to be run in the same fashion; the two-thousand-dollar appropriation for 1881 may have been part of the same bill funding the university, but the new schools were not intended as part of the university's structure. In any event, the additional appropriations were extremely small, just five hundred dollars per school per year, but these amounts were initially supplemented by Peabody grants.

35. Lefler and Newsome, *North Carolina*, 538; *1882 Principal's Report, New Bern*. The Peabody Fund contributed a total of $87,000 to various school systems in North Carolina by 1877, mostly to towns with schools already among the state's best, which were also the only systems able to raise sufficient funds from local resources.

36. "Hon. Geo. H. White, LL.D," *Raleigh Gazette*, 12 June 1897; "Lawyer and Legislator," *New York Freeman*, 5 February 1887. The *Gazette* says White "introduced the bill (of which he is the author) creating four of the present State Normal Schools, and was three years principal of the one located in Newbern." This account of White's life, one of the longest published during his lifetime, was reprinted from an out-of-state source; it contained numerous minor errors. White's tenure as normal school principal, for instance, was less than two years.

By 1880, the Peabody Fund had begun recommending freestanding normal schools for both races, rather than departments within existing schools,
and the General Assembly's action may well have been influenced by this as a
source of extra funding; it ratified the omnibus public school revisions bill on
March 9, 1881.[37] Clearly, one normal school could not train enough teachers
quickly enough to meet the state's growing needs. So the bill, which was cod-
ified in Section Five of Chapter 141 of the Laws of 1881, authorized the appropriation of $4,000 "for other normal schools, $2,000 for white teachers and
$2,000 for colored teachers, providing that not less than four schools for each
color shall be established." The state board of education was given control
over the location, organization, and management of the new schools, and by
late April had begun the task of selecting the new sites.

Arguments on behalf of at least nine towns and cities seeking the new
normal schools for blacks were presented on April 29, and one day later, the
board picked its first two sites: New Bern and Franklinton.[38] Having in-
vested much energy in the process during the General Assembly session just
ended, George White made certain to attend the April 29 hearing to press
for New Bern's selection, if not for his own selection as principal. Both he
and Senator Clarke did present oral arguments on behalf of New Bern that
first day, and the board members agreed on April 30 by selecting New Bern
as one site. The board further authorized Superintendent Scarborough to
hire staff and make necessary arrangements for an expeditious opening of
the first two schools, and White, having suitably impressed Scarborough, was
hired shortly afterward. Rather than extend the selection hearings, the board
then authorized Scarborough to use his best judgment to select either Tarboro

37. "Lawyer and Legislator"; Brown, *Education of Negroes*, 32; *RN&O*, 19 March 1881. The
Freeman noted that "under the matchless pilotage of Mr. White the bill went through like a
breeze"; White, however, was careful to point out that many Democratic leaders, including U.S.
senator Zebulon B. Vance, had helped push the concept of normal schools for blacks, and he had
depended on Democrats for their cooperation. During the first year, New Bern and other black
schools received $205 each from the Peabody Fund.
38. Untitled editorial, *RN&O*, 16 March 1881; Noble, *Public Schools*, 425. The towns of
Wilson and Monroe were passed over, along with Tarboro, Charlotte, and Greensboro.
Scarborough chose Plymouth for the site of the third school and Salisbury for the fourth. The
four new schools together received only the same appropriation as the Fayetteville school—a
"pitifully small sum," according to Noble.

or Plymouth for the third school site and either Charlotte, Salisbury, or Greensboro for fourth.[39]

The New Bern normal school for black teachers opened for its first five-month term on July 11, 1881, with George White as the principal and sole teacher. Its mission, like that of all the new schools for blacks, would be similar to but narrower in scope than that of the Fayetteville normal school, where students received financial aid from the state for transportation and were expected to attend for three years. Students at New Bern and the other new schools were drawn only from adjacent counties, and paid all their own expenses, although tuition was free. For all its limitations, the system was a distinct improvement, and White was clearly committed in both principle and practice to the task at hand.[40]

Thus education had been a primary concern for White during the legislative session, and both he and his city had profited from his diligence. The enhancement of the teacher-training programs was certainly an important step for the state in its quest to regain its prewar stature as an educational leader. Yet educational issues had often taken second place to more politically important matters, such as well-publicized debates on home rule for counties and the statewide prohibition of alcoholic beverages. These were practical matters, of interest at home, and White paid attention to them as well, tailoring his perspective to the wants and needs of his constituents.

For instance, he spoke at some length on January 28 during discussion of House Bill 37, which sought to restore to counties the right to elect their own officers, including magistrates and county commissioners. At one point, he criticized the General Assembly for hypocrisy in electing "one of the blackest and one of the meanest men in his county [as] a justice of the peace." White and two black colleagues, Paul Hayley and Alexander Hicks, "had much to say about a Democratic legislature appointing negro magistrates in the east, while the pretense for electing magistrates by the people was to protect the east from negro rule," according to a newspaper account.[41]

Representatives White and Hicks were infuriated by one western repre-

39. "State Board of Education," *RN&O*, 30 April–1 May 1881; *1881 Principal's Report, New Bern*, 107–9.

40. Noble, *Public Schools*, 423–6.

41. *RN&O*, 1881 house proceedings, Day 22 (January 28).

sentative's argument against the bill, following its unfavorable report out of committee. Buncombe County Democratic legislator M. E. Carter had quoted former Reconstruction leader Albion Tourgée's comment about the Republican Party and its black majority, that "ignorance, poverty and inexperience were its chief characteristics." Rising to respond, White sarcastically suggested that Carter "look among the poor people of the west [where] he would find as much ignorance as among the stinking negroes of the east."[42]

Hicks, ever the diplomat, echoed White's sentiments in a subtler tone, noting that "if a comparison were made between the poor whites of the west and the negroes of the east, it would be found that the negroes had the advantage." The bill failed to pass on its second reading, but only by a surprisingly narrow margin. Supporters came within victory by a mere handful of votes, failing by fifty to forty-two; a shift of just five votes would have at least compelled a third and final reading.[43]

On another legislative front, meanwhile, the prohibition movement was gaining momentum across the "Old North State." Petitions from both individuals and groups of citizens, all favoring an absolute ban on sales and manufacture of liquor, had been presented by the hundreds to their legislators in 1881. George White submitted at least five such petitions, including one on February 16 from the North Carolina Colored Conference with seventy names, and petitions from Craven constituents on February 21 and 28. On several occasions, White introduced petitions from citizens in counties other than Craven, probably at the request of a fellow member of the house who could not attend, or perhaps because the citizens in question were black.[44]

The public record gives no clear signal of White's personal feelings on the issue, although as an active Presbyterian, he was probably expected to favor prohibition on religious grounds. He certainly received strong pressure from his constituents, particularly ministers and church groups. The debate would drag on until the last week of the session, with at least one black legislator fre-

42. Ibid. Tourgée's comment is noted in Lefler and Newsome, North Carolina, 488.

43. RN&O, 1881 house proceedings, Day 22 (January 28).

44. Reid, "A Biography," 68; RN&O, 1881 house proceedings, Day 38 (February 16). The Colored Conference was a statewide organization based in Craven and apparently headed by the Reverend Joseph C. Price; this was the only organizational petition White presented. According to Reid, White introduced petitions from Pender and Duplin Counties on February 8; he also introduced a petition from Northampton County, with eighty-eight names.

quently expressing strong opposition to the concept of prohibition; the blunt and demonstrative Daniel R. Johnson of Warren said he "wanted more whisky, better whisky and cheaper whisky" instead. The house version of the bill, for which White voted on its second reading on February 28, pleased few in the ranks of black legislators; although admitting the bill was imperfect, White had argued during debate that since "the state was not in a condition to receive an absolute prohibition by law, he would willingly and heartily vote for the bill." By the next day, however, he had apparently begun to have second thoughts, for he now became the first member listed as arguing against the bill, although he was not recorded as voting at the end of the night.[45]

Because the amended bill had become a strict regulation of the sale of liquor—rather than an absolute prohibition of its sale, as many preferred—the debate threatened at times to descend into chaos as members argued about specific provisions, including one making it a criminal offense to sell liquor to habitual drunkards and a second to allow county commissioners to impose a heavy tax. As the vote neared, even note takers became confused; one reporter misidentified Alexander Hicks, who was explaining his vote against the bill, as George White, who seems to have been absent at the time. The bill passed by a narrow margin, with all black members and most Republicans present opposing it; neither White nor Daniel Johnson, however, was recorded as voting on the final reading.[46]

George White rose "to a question of personal privilege" on March 2, 1881, in regard to the *News and Observer*'s incorrect attribution to him of the previous day's remarks. While he had agreed that the people of the state seemed to prefer an absolute prohibition bill, he had never declared himself willing to vote only in favor of such a bill, he said now. (Hicks, in fact, had made that

45. *RN&O*, 18 May 1881; *RN&O*, 24 September 1886; *RN&O*, 1881 house proceedings, Day 48 (February 28) and Day 49 (March 1). Republicans in Craven County tended to favor prohibition personally, although the party did not support it. A large group of prohibition supporters meeting at the New Bern courthouse in mid-May included about two hundred persons of both races, including Rev. Lachlan C. Vass, Rev. Edward H. Bull, Rev. Joseph C. Price, Congressman Orlando Hubbs, and former state legislator Edward R. Dudley. Many of those present had attended the recent state prohibition convention in Raleigh. Johnson was later described as "making a violent harangue against [local option], holding the holy Bible in one hand and a bottle of whisky in the other, telling the negroes that whisky had been here as long as the Bible and they must vote to keep it here."

46. *RN&O*, 1881 house proceedings, Day 49 (March 1).

statement.) The newspaper corrected this error and others in its next report. But the debate raged on, as Republicans now charged that Democrats favored prohibition and Democrats countered that the referendum allowed the state's voters to choose prohibition in a nonpartisan election, if that was what they wanted.[47]

In response to petitions, however, the assembly did allow bans on sales of hard liquor in certain localities in the state, the house acting on March 2 and the senate on March 12. Sale of liquor was prohibited within a mile of "a great number of places," according to the *News and Observer;* hundreds of localities would request similar bans over the next two decades, as absolute prohibition drew nearer and nearer.[48]

Not all of George White's political actions involved such heady statewide issues. One of the private bills he sponsored contained his own name, as an elder of Ebenezer Presbyterian Church, now seeking incorporation. After White introduced the bill on February 2, it was referred to the Committee on Corporations, from which it was reported out favorably and passed by the assembly three weeks later. The bill listed all members of the church board, including White, the church's minister, and both White's father-in-law and brother-in-law. Incorporating churches and Masonic organizations was a fairly routine affair, but White doubtless took personal pride in lending substantial public recognition to the church he had helped found. Yet he overlooked minor typographical errors in the final version of the bill: incorrect middle initials for himself and the Reverend Allen Scott, soon to become part of his own extended family.[49]

47. Ibid. The Raleigh newspaper had also incorrectly attributed remarks made by Republican Cowan of Pender to Democrat Cowell of Currituck and recorded Democrat Worthington of Martin as voting for the bill when he had actually voted against it.

48. *1881 House Journal,* 586; *RN&O,* 1881 house proceedings, Day 50 (March 2). The bill, eventually passed by both houses, allowed the new regulations—still far from a complete ban on the sale of liquor—to take effect in October 1881, unless rejected by the voters first. North Carolinians resoundingly rejected the new law in August. Localized bans on liquor sales were increasingly enacted in decades to come, however, and state voters eventually authorized prohibition in North Carolina in a 1908 referendum.

49. Chapter 27, *1881 Private Laws,* "An Act to Incorporate Ebenezer Presbyterian Church of New Berne," 683. Rev. Allen A. Scott was listed as "Allen H. Scott" on the first line of the bill, followed by "George M. White"; White's middle name, of course, was Henry. Within a year, White married Scott's younger sister Nancy J. Scott.

White's absence from the General Assembly in early March 1881 may well have been due to "sickness in the family," as he had specified when requesting an "indefinite leave" in late February, although there is no documentation of his travels. He was definitely absent from the legislative floor between March 2 and 8, when he neither spoke nor voted, and missed at least one important roll-call vote; he was forced to seek special permission to record his vote against a bill passed by the house in his absence, which incorporated the New Bern Board of Trade. The next day he introduced an amendment to that bill, clarifying the powers of the new board, and it quickly passed both houses.[50]

But his absence could have been owing to other reasons, perhaps even a return to Washington, D.C. During the same period, the state's Republican leadership traveled north to Washington in early March to attend festivities marking the inauguration of president-elect James A. Garfield. The presidential oath was administered on Friday, March 4, 1881, and three days later, the new chief executive received the North Carolina delegation at the White House in one of several afternoon receptions. Led by state Republican chairman Tom Cooper, more than a hundred men from North Carolina filled the reception room at the executive mansion, while William P. Canaday acted as the delegation's master of ceremonies. (Canaday, editor of the *Wilmington Post*, apparently fulfilled his introductions to the president so well that the waiting delegation from Colorado prevailed upon him to perform the same task for them.)[51]

One mission probably undertaken by the group included a request that Garfield consider former judge William J. Clarke for a "diplomatic or legal appointment" in the new administration. A letter dated March 7, 1881, and signed by twenty-five Republican members of the General Assembly—including both George White and Clarke's son—was to be delivered to Garfield by

50. *RN&O*, 1881 house proceedings, Day 56 (March 9) and Day 57 (March 10); *1881 Private Laws*, 1882, cited in Reid, "A Biography," 72. Rep. E. R. Page of Jones had introduced the New Bern Board of Trade bill on March 7, indicating that both White and Rep. Green of New Bern were absent that day. The bill passed the house quickly, and was passed by the senate on March 10. White's amendment, as part of the new law, provided that the board could not pass any regulation that conflicted with either state or city laws.

51. "North Carolina Republicans in Washington," *RN&O*, 10 March 1881. Canaday was the only white Republican to endorse the black leaders' convention two months later, drawing a resolution of thanks from the assembled participants, according to the *News and Observer*, 19 May 1881.

the group. Senator Clarke had previously corresponded with Garfield following the election, and may well have chosen to deliver this letter in person; George White, whose ties to Judge Clarke were less familial but equally strong, would doubtless have considered it an honor to be among that delegation. The names of those who did meet Garfield are not recorded, but both Clarke and White were absent from the General Assembly that day, indicating that both may have been in the White House instead.[52]

Garfield was courteous and cordial, at times even effusive; one awestruck delegate from Pasquotank County told the News and Observer that the president "merely said 'howd'ye do' to the others, but to me he said, 'I'm glad to meet you.'"[53] But while the delegation was basking in Washington's postinaugural limelight, trouble was brewing back home for the party in the shape of personal scandal.

George White arrived back in Raleigh on March 9, just in time to witness a "trial" on forgery charges of his friend and associate, Tarboro's William Watson, with the maximum penalty being expulsion from the General Assembly. There could hardly have been a more embarrassing incident for the state's black Republicans in 1881 than Watson's public ordeal, which involved the apparent theft and forgery of another house member's expense voucher; the scandal and its aftermath were carried in no small detail by the News and Observer. While White had no connection to the inquiry or to Watson's actions, he had worked closely with him on the recent education bill, and he and Watson had jointly requested a meeting with Governor Jarvis to discuss issues of importance to the race in late February, although White had left Raleigh by the time Jarvis granted the request and could not attend the meeting.[54]

52. Letter, dated March 7, 1881, to "His Excellency, The President of the United States," from "the undersigned Republican members of the General Assembly of North Carolina," William John Clarke Papers, SHC. A total of ten senators and fifteen representatives signed the letter; one noticeable absentee was William W. Watson, whose expulsion hearing was scheduled in the house later the same week.

53. "North Carolina Republicans in Washington."

54. W. Buck Yearns, ed., The Papers of Thomas J. Jarvis: Volume I, 1869–1882 (Raleigh: N.C. Department of Archives and History, 1969), 369. The request for a meeting was contained in an undated letter from White and Watson to the governor; Jarvis accepted it in a March 3 reply, saying, "I will be glad to see them at the Executive office at 4:30 P.M. to-day." Jarvis addressed his letter only to Watson; White was apparently out of Raleigh by the time Watson received it.

White's reappearance came just after the March 7 presentation of a report on the Watson affair, compiled by a special committee of inquiry. He made no public comment during the daylong hearing four days later, but he was certainly chagrined at the details of his friend's erratic behavior; at least three black house members and at least one black employee of the house were involved in the case, and one black observer said he felt "the standing of the whole negro race would be affected by this." The bipartisan committee found Watson's actions worthy of dismissal from the house, even if not been proven guilty of a crime; "on the facts of the case, as presented in this report and finding of the committee, the Edgecombe darkey has perpetrated a forgery. Such is the unanimous voice of the committee," wrote a Raleigh onlooker.[55]

The case involved a state per diem voucher, or warrant, issued in February to veteran black house member John Newell of Bladen. The $16 warrant had been cashed, yet Newell claimed he had never received it or the money, and had learned about it only after applying for a separate voucher. Poor bookkeeping procedures had aggravated the situation, since house members were apparently not required to collect their payments in person. The special committee of inquiry held hearings and compiled its evidence before distributing the printed version to house members.[56]

Among those testifying before the full house on March 11 were Newell, Watson, state capitol employee Solomon Geer, and three house pages. The written details of the incident were confusing enough, but several house witnesses contradicted both each other and, in Watson's case, his own previous testimony to the committee. Newell claimed that he had asked Watson to endorse only a different warrant, for $100, on January 29, and claimed he had never discussed the smaller warrant with Watson; although Newell never explained why he asked for help in endorsing the warrant, it may have been be-

55. RN&O, 7 March 1881. The three Democrats on the special committee were Representatives McClure, Grainger, and Rowland; the trio "gives us an assurance of the utmost impartiality. [The Democrats] are just as fair and impartial in such a matter as any other gentlemen could be. Mr. Blaisdell is a Northerner, a man of unusual intelligence, and like Mr. Holton . . . is a leader of the Republican party in the House."

56. "The Per Diem Forgery," RN&O, 10 March 1881. As the paper later acknowledged, this report seems to have been less convincing than many had expected; the newspaper withdrew its earlier call for Watson's expulsion and criminal trial, and suggested the house give him a fair hearing.

cause he could not write his own name, and was too proud to put an "X" on the line.

In any event, Newell's public memory was somewhat selective; in his earlier deposition, he had told the committee that both Watson and Clinton W. Battle of Edgecombe were present at the time, that he had asked both to endorse the $100 warrant, and that he could not remember which one had agreed. Battle quickly verified his presence elsewhere on that date and told the committee he remembered only a February 2 incident, when he saw Watson endorse Newell's warrant as requested; the only warrant with that date was for $16. Other house members and one senate member, all black, witnessed the February 2 endorsement and corroborated Battle's account to the committee, thus exonerating him.[57]

Newell's testimony implicated black employee Geer, who apparently told different versions of his story to different people. According to Newell, Geer approached him to report Watson's forgery, calling Watson "a low, degraded man" who had taken Newell's money; after Newell and Watson examined the forged warrant, Newell was convinced someone else had committed the forgery, since the signatures were quite different. Geer, however, testified that Newell had both given him the warrant, already signed by Watson, and taken the money from Geer; other witnesses recalled contradictory accounts from Geer, who told one witness that "some colored person in the House" had the money, although he was not sure which one.[58]

The situation had become low comedy, humorous despite the shameful nature of its core issue. With so much finger pointing and so little actual evidence, the house was probably quite close to dismissing the case when the central figure suddenly changed his story. Watson had told the committee, not once but three times, that he had not signed the $16 warrant, but had signed only the earlier $100 warrant, then filled out an application for a post-office order the same day. But he seems to have been unnerved by having to testify before the full house, for he reversed himself completely, now claiming that he had been "mistaken" in his committee testimony.[59]

Though he seemed oblivious to the implications of changing his story, Watson had now publicly confessed to forgery—since Newell denied asking

57. Ibid.; *RN&O*, 1881 house proceedings, Day 58 (March 11).

58. *RN&O*, 1881 house proceedings, Day 58 (March 11).

59. Ibid.

him to endorse the $16 warrant—and worse, to virtual perjury before the committee, which already believed him guilty of forgery. Testimony was quickly concluded; a motion to expel Watson was made, and closing arguments were offered by both sides. Democrat William H. Day of Halifax defended Watson, citing "a dozen conclusions as probable as the one the committee arrived at . . . the evidence was fully as strong against Newell as against Watson."[60] But it was painfully clear that Newell's "good character," however weakened by the full testimony, was still the more widely respected and Newell's version of the story easily more accepted than that of Watson, who inspired little confidence in any quarter.

The final roll call produced 25 Democratic votes to expel Watson, but this was not enough. Astonishingly, 44 members of both parties voted against the expulsion; many apparently felt sorry for Watson, who had foolishly risked so much over so little. Half the "no" voters were Democrats, joined by all 22 Republicans present, including George White and at least nine other black members. He thus went home unpunished, if in disgrace. The hapless Solomon Geer, publicly branded as a possible thief, was fired.[61] Twenty house members rose afterwards to explain their votes; of these, only three who had voted to expel Watson thought it necessary to explain why. Many of the others said that because they were not certain of his guilt, they had had to vote no.

The four black members who spoke revealed a subtle split among the ranks of the black community, at least on the question of disciplining an errant member. Clinton W. Battle said Watson had signed the warrant as Newell requested, and was therefore innocent. John Hays of Granville claimed to be "satisfied that Mr. Watson was innocent," a statement with which George King of Warren agreed. But Washington County's Alexander Hicks provided clues to the divisions behind the united racial front. "Mr. Hicks could recall no occasion on which he felt more humiliated than the present; this was not because the character of one man was implicated, but because the standing of the whole negro race would be affected by this," he was quoted as saying. "He wished it understood that if he believed Watson was guilty, no man would vote more cheerfully for his expulsion; but not being satisfied on this point, he voted no."[62]

60. Ibid.
61. Ibid.
62. Ibid.

This was as close as Hicks could come to chastising Watson for embarrassing the race. Neither Hicks nor anyone else was willing to defend Watson's character, probably because he was widely known to be corrupt. Hicks, an educator with a reputation for honesty and frankness, almost certainly spoke for George White here. Both men strongly believed in the importance of developing strong character among the ranks of freed slaves; setting a good example by prudent and honest behavior was in their opinion the obligation of all black leaders.

The Watson ordeal was now over, but the season of scandal was not. Outside the legislative halls, the criminal trial of Republican house member Joshua Simpson now took center stage in the Raleigh mayor's court. This trial was more sensational than Watson's, but almost anticlimactic, as Simpson was charged with extensive larceny of property from hotel boarders, including other legislators. The *New York Times* dubbed the affair "a cowardly revenge" on Simpson, a "conspiracy growing out of his opposition to certain measures before the Legislature." The *News and Observer* had initially reported both Simpson's arrest and his subsequent arraignment, calling it "a Republican melee from beginning to end," but the newspaper staunchly defended Capt. E. R. Page, the Jones County Republican on whom Simpson blamed his troubles.[63]

Simpson, a Dare County representative in the 1881 house, had allegedly stolen a "great quantity and variety" of property from boarders at the National Hotel, ranging from personal clothing and smoking tobacco to silverware and other items belonging to the National and a second hotel. The list included, "strangest of all, a set of iron bed casters." Police had searched Simpson's room on March 13 and found the missing items; the *News and Observer* labeled him a kleptomaniac, claiming he had been taking items since early January. Simpson was arraigned before Raleigh mayor B. C. Manly on March 14, the day of the General Assembly's adjournment.[64]

Simpson angrily claimed it was a "put up job"; he had been framed, he said, by both Page and Dare politician W. C. Ethridge, who had brought the actual charges against him. After an "exhaustive trial . . . lasting a portion of two days," Simpson's attorney, fellow house Republican J. E. Bledsoe of Raleigh, apparently "proved his character to the satisfaction of the court."

63. "A Cowardly Revenge," *New York Times*, reprinted in untitled editorial, *RN&O*, 18 March 1881.

64. "Serious Charges Against a Republican Member of the House," *RN&O*, 15 March 1881.

Mayor Manly dismissed the case for insufficient evidence on March 15, warning that the legislature itself might choose to reopen the investigation at an expected special session later that year; the body never reconvened, however, and no further investigation was carried out.[65]

The *New York Times* observed that Simpson "suffered the great indignity put upon him without the evidence being conclusive beyond a doubt," and blamed a partisan conspiracy perpetrated by Simpson's enemies, without specifying either's political affiliation. The Democratic *News and Observer*, sensitive to implications advanced by its New York counterpart—and perhaps, as well, to the political leanings of the correspondent—responded that all involved had been Republicans and its only concern was the damage to the reputation of Mr. Page, "a man of fine feeling, generous impulse and utterly incapable of" such a conspiracy.[66]

If George White attended the trial of his Republican colleague on March 14 and 15, his presence was not noted, but neither local newspaper saw fit to list the names of onlookers in the Mayor's crowded court. Legislators of both parties were understandably anxious to depart Raleigh; the simultaneous adjournment of the General Assembly had found only forty-one house members of either party remaining to answer the final roll call. Yet White's absence from the adjournment roll call on March 14 is worth noting, since at least six of his black colleagues—even the now-notorious William Watson—made sure they remained at the capitol until the very end. Incidentally, the National Hotel, for all its venerable history, would suffer no more such scandals, having recently been purchased by the state for use as an office building.[67]

For those involved in the scandals of 1881, the effects varied. John Newell won reelection to the 1883 General Assembly, his fourth and final term; E. R. Page was also reelected in 1882. But William Watson never ran for office again, and Joshua Simpson never won another legislative contest. Alexander Hicks, the public conscience of his race, retired from politics to become a

65. "Mr. Simpson's Trial," ibid., 16 March 1881.

66. Untitled editorial, ibid., 18 March 1881. The unnamed *New York Times* correspondent was probably perennial gadfly J. C. L. Harris.

67. The fifty-room hotel was adjacent to Capitol Square; the funds to purchase it had been appropriated by the General Assembly late in the session, and it housed both the supreme court and the department of agriculture.

normal-school principal; later in 1881, he served as temporary chairman of the state's first convention of black political leaders, but died unexpectedly in January 1883, as the next legislature was just getting under way. Both William H. Day, the white Democrat who defended Watson, and J. E. Bledsoe, the white Republican who defended Simpson, retired from the legislature but remained active in politics and the law for years to come.[68]

George White's record was not tainted by his professional relationship with Watson, with whom he would continue to deal on matters political during the next two decades. Indeed, if White's silence on the issue of Watson's guilt was noted at all, it was probably taken as a sign of stubborn party loyalty: "never speak ill of another Republican." He would be guided by this credo for the next decade and more, as he began his ascent into the upper ranks of Second District leadership.

Soon after the 1881 assembly ended, White joined James O'Hara and forty-seven others in signing a call for the statewide convention of black leaders, whose purpose was to push for better political opportunities and more offices for blacks, although White does not appear to have attended the actual convention.[69] Many of North Carolina's black Republicans were actively pressing claims for appointments upon the new Garfield administration, making at least two trips to Washington that spring to visit the White House. In a March 17 visit, a delegation headed by George W. Price of Wilmington pressed its request for the appointment of James H. Harris as Raleigh's postmaster, displacing William W. Holden, the impeached ex-governor, from that position; meanwhile, white Republicans, led by Craven's Lotte W. Humphrey, vigorously supported Holden. Two months later, a delegation of fifteen led by Price returned to the White House, this time expressing the sentiments of those attending the May convention, "relative to the wrongs we have suffered and are still suffering at the hands of certain white men now in office."[70]

---

68. "Colored Republican Council," *RN&O*, 18 May 1881. Rev. Joseph C. Price of New Bern was elected permanent chairman; the object of the convention was to "find out why the negro was not recognized in the distribution of offices," Price said.

69. Ibid. Seventeen of the signers were from New Hanover County alone. The *Wilmington Post* of 24 April 1881 published the letter, signed by White, O'Hara, and many others, including Israel Abbott and John Randolph Jr. of New Bern and White's kinsman John W. Spaulding of Columbus. White was not selected as a Craven delegate.

70. "A Probability that Gov. Holden will Lose His Place," *RN&O*, 20 March 1881; "The Colored State Convention," *RN&O*, 19 May 1881.

George White's absence from the May convention may have been intentional. He would have been hard pressed to endorse the wording of the memorial, for instance, having no wish to offend the new Republican president with such unseemly persistence. He was certainly busy enough with other pursuits at the time to plead the demands of work; in addition to his law practice, he was heavily involved in preparations for the opening of the new normal school. This part-time responsibility involved helping to mold the lives and skills of young black men and women, many away from home for the first time; this was undoubtedly a deep concern to the young widower, already burdened by his own family demands and by year's end considering remarriage.

Still, thoughts of his political future were never far from his mind. By the summer of 1882, White again attended the Republican state convention as a respected Craven delegate, this time described by a Wilmington newspaper in its convention account as being among "the very best colored men in the state."[71] He was ready for advancement, if and when Republicans in his county and district agreed.

71. *Wilmington Post,* 18 June 1882, cited in Elmore, "North Carolina Negro Congressmen," 155.

4

The Next Political Campaigns

Buoyed by his 1880 success at the polls and his strong 1881 legislative record, George White was ready for new challenges as 1882 opened. His tenure as principal of the New Bern normal school through its first term had upgraded his credentials as both a public servant and an administrator, while his law practice was progressing comfortably. His remarriage in February would subtly reinforce his image as a devoted family man. If any unresolved question marred his personal agenda, it had to be the choice of an appropriate office to seek; having served one term as a state representative, he could easily seek reelection if county GOP leaders agreed. Or, depending on the direction of the political winds, he might choose to aim slightly higher, to the senate or even some regional position.

While remaining in the house held some appeal for White, his appetite for public service impelled him toward more rapid advancement. For the moment, at least, seeking the senate seat was not the preferred option, as incumbent William E. Clarke seemed comfortable there. The best course seemed to lie outside the legislature, and it seems likely that other Republicans must have encouraged him to consider the office of Second District solicitor. The incumbent was John Henry Collins, a black lawyer from Halifax, now completing his first four-year term but not highly regarded by either Republican leaders or lawyers in general. Democratic critics roundly savaged his courtroom performance, painting dark images of Svengali-like "handling" of Collins by J. C. L. Harris, a former solicitor.[1] Republican lawyers must have been trou-

---

1. *Kinston Journal*, 16 June 1881; *Wilmington Post*, 19 January 1879. Democratic newspapers like the *Journal* rarely minced words in ridiculing Collins: "The colored solicitor is not a compe-

bled by the young solicitor's mediocrity; even Craven Superior Court clerk and former judge William J. Clarke may have quietly suggested that White consider a challenge.

Collins was bright, well-educated, and ambitious, but alarmingly inefficient; moreover, public pressure and constant criticism had taken their toll on his pride. He had considered leaving the post early, unsuccessfully seeking appointment by President James Garfield as U.S. minister to Haiti in the spring of 1881. If Raleigh newspaper accounts are accurate, many Republicans had encouraged Collins in this unlikely quest.[2] Garfield's reappointment of John Mercer Langston had ended that unlikely dream; the shooting of the President in July, followed by his gradual decline and death in September, had precluded further overtures by Collins. Shrugging off the barrage of partisan barbs, he dug in his heels as solicitor; as a result, only the voters would be able to dislodge him at the polls, and only if the Republicans could find the right substitute candidate.

Convincing George White to take on the responsibility required little effort. In March, White had been one of several black leaders to address a statewide black convention on the subject of black political participation; according to the *Wilmington Post*, the convention dealt specifically with the problem of exclusion of blacks from local juries, but ended by encouraging more blacks to seek nominations for office in North Carolina as a partial remedy. Seeking nominations for district solicitor was a logical next step for lawyers White and George T. Wassom of Goldsboro, another convention speaker; Wassom went on to win the Republican nomination in the adjacent Third District but lost the fall election.[3]

---

tent prosecutor. He is slow and inaccurate, and not able to compete either in scholarship or piney woods sense." The Republican *Post* was more sympathetic, saying "he shows much ability in drawing out the bottom facts in the examination of witnesses," and noting that Collins had studied law under Halifax attorney W. P. Solomon after graduating from Toronto College in Canada. But J. C. L. Harris was generally seen as the "real" solicitor.

2. "The City," *RN&O*, 16 March 1881. "His recommendation for the high place he seeks, we understand, is signed by many of the leading Republicans in the State and many leading Democrats," wrote the newspaper. "We would be happy to see him appointed."

3. "Colored State Convention," *Wilmington Post*, 2 April 1882; *RN&O*, 8 December 1882. John Dancy and Edward R. Dudley were also speakers at the March 29 Goldsboro convention, a follow-up to the May 1881 convention in Raleigh; both meetings were strongly encouraged by *Post* editor William P. Canaday, one of the few white Republicans to do so. George Wassom lost the solicitor's race to Swift Galloway by a vote of 18,985 to 16,472.

For the first time, George White's confidence seemed to overextend his reach. Whatever his level of support in Craven County and other parts of the district, the New Bern lawyer could not wrest the nomination from Collins, who was renominated for solicitor over White and another Republican legislator, Walter Williamson, at a district convention in Tarboro on June 12, 1882. The reduction of Craven's convention delegate strength from four votes to two, based on the 1881 state reapportionment of legislators, was a critical and controversial factor in White's loss, as well as a source of hard feelings between geographical wings of the district party.[4]

Each county's delegation to the judicial convention was traditionally based on how many legislators it elected; three of the district's seven counties were thus affected by upcoming changes in the size of their delegations. Craven and Warren Counties were each slated to drop from two representatives to one in the 1883 General Assembly, while Northampton was to double its house delegation, from one to two. The Second District was not required to use the new figures until its next convention in 1884, after the reapportionment had actually gone into effect, but a majority of delegates voted to use them right away, despite pleas for a delay from Warren and Craven. Craven party members were angered by this slight, arguing at length to reverse the decision at the Republican state convention two days later; such a move would, of course, be to their benefit at the congressional nominating convention in July.[5]

Their strategy was successful, but the state convention's decision came two days too late to help George White. Whether White might have been able to defeat Collins with four votes from Craven—rather than the two he did receive—is not immediately clear, but Collins's position had certainly been enhanced by the increase in Northampton's votes and the reduction of those from Craven and Warren. Wake County, largest in the district, was still for

4. Anderson, *Race and Politics*, 100; NCG, 560. Williamson, a white Republican, resigned his seat in the North Carolina senate on May 16, 1882, apparently to devote his full energies to the solicitor's race; he was appointed Tarboro's postmaster in 1883.

5. Anderson, *Race and Politics*, 101. The first election using the new apportionment was set for November. The state convention argued the merits of Craven's issue at length before delegates overruled the chairman. Using the system in place at that time would have deprived the new counties of Vance and Durham of any representation, but the convention voted separately to grant them two delegates each.

Collins, as were Northampton and Halifax. The convention's obvious favoritism toward the Halifax-Northampton wing had certainly rankled leaders in Craven and Warren; relations between the two groups were still visibly strained at the first congressional nominating convention in July, which adjourned without a consensus decision. The hard feelings contributed to the holding of a second "rump" convention in August.[6]

Clearly disappointed by the setback in the solicitor's race, White was undaunted, but his immediate options were limited. Craven now elected just one seat in the house, and by choosing to seek the nomination for solicitor, White had all but relinquished his chance at renomination for his seat in the lower chamber. Redistricting meant that one less slot was available in Craven for interested black candidates, and the house nomination had by now been promised to fellow black party member William H. Johnson, a teacher and longtime deputy sheriff in Craven, who had no intention of stepping aside for White after the latter's June 12 defeat.

White next turned his hopes to the Craven seat in the state senate. There he hoped to succeed the county's most experienced incumbent, William E. Clarke, but Clarke was no more amenable than Johnson to the idea of stepping down. Even in his quest for an unprecedented fourth term in the legislature, Clarke retained consensus support, and the party's white wing was unwilling to give up its share of the nominations. All regular party doors thus seemed closed to White in 1882, despite his proven popularity; his only option was to run as an independent, a course he steadfastly refused to take.

White found that he had to bide his time and wait for the next election, two years hence. In an ordinary year, that would have been the end of the story. But 1882 was no ordinary year, as the fractious waves of district politics—long lapping at Craven's doorstep—would now wash over the county line, bringing George White back to the front lines of the fall election amid a curious turn of events. It began with the congressional nominating conven-

6. Ibid., 100–1, 108. The move had increased Collins's lead by at least six delegates: two from Northampton, two fewer votes for White from Craven, and two fewer votes from Warren available to either challenger. Whether Warren might have given White its two lost votes is speculation; Edgecombe's four votes probably went to the third challenger, Williamson. At the first convention in Wilson, Craven and Northampton drew four delegate votes each, although this required an increase in total delegates. A second congressional convention in August formally renominated incumbent Orlando Hubbs.

tions, as Craven's vaunted Republican equilibrium began to splinter, and ended with a badly fragmented party fighting to regain its past glory.

At the core of the struggle was Congressman Orlando Hubbs, whose support had begun to dwindle midway through his term. Hubbs had been a popular sheriff in Craven, but only marginally effective in the U.S. House; despite a creditable record on black appointments, he was unable to master the intricate maneuvers required of a white congressman in a largely black district. Most Craven County Republicans, black and white, continued to support him, but in the rest of the district the momentum seemed to be gradually shifting toward James O'Hara, the defeated black nominee from 1878.

O'Hara was most popular in his home stronghold of Halifax and Northampton, where an increasing number of black voters were convinced that the district ought to have a black congressman. He had little support in Craven, especially among black voters, many of whom distrusted him intensely. Neither his record as Halifax County chairman, which had led to criminal charges of corruption, nor his imprudent personal lifestyle recommended O'Hara to Israel Abbott, for instance; O'Hara had married his second wife without notifying his first wife of the divorce, a curious oversight for a future lawyer, while the legal uncertainty of his status as a U.S. citizen puzzled many onlookers. Craven party delegates to the first nominating convention in July were appalled at the events that took place; expecting an easy renomination for their own favorite son Hubbs, they had been treated instead to a spectacle of chaos, as Lotte Humphrey withdrew from the race and James O'Hara claimed a dubious victory, based solely on support from Humphrey's committed delegates. No vote took place; the convention simply adjourned in confusion, with its chairman claiming O'Hara was nominated.

Orlando Hubbs was renominated by acclamation, albeit by a smaller audience, at the second congressional convention, held just nine weeks before the 1882 general election. Hubbs's support was strong at home, and his renomination should have helped calm the forces of disunity, at least in Craven, but chaos was suddenly king; white leaders in Craven, like Leonidas J. Moore, actively began campaigning for O'Hara.[7] The county's party convention a week later was anything but placid, as a feud between two candidates for sheriff, in-

7. Eric Anderson, "James O'Hara of North Carolina: Black Leadership and Local Government," in *Southern Black Leaders of the Reconstruction Era*, edited by Howard N. Rabinowitz (Urbana: University of Illinois Press, 1972), 101–25.

cumbent Mayer Hahn and wealthy white opponent Daniel Stimson, now erupted with full force. Angry Stimson supporters, feeling cheated of the nomination, bolted the convention and nominated their own separate ticket for three offices in the fall election, including sheriff, in a room just doors away.

The *Newbernian's* account of the September 2 county convention painted a grim picture of party infighting. "It was a rehash of the disgraceful scenes that characterized the Wilson Congressional Convention," the newspaper wrote on September 9. "The delegates favoring the nomination of Mr. Stimson, feeling they had been unfairly treated, and with reason too we think, then withdrew from the courtroom, and under the lead of Mr. Robert Lehman, organized another convention in the grand jury room; in this room we counted 31 delegates, said-to-be, in the other convention, there were 39 delegates, said-to-be."

Neither gathering could claim to represent the true wishes of the Craven party, however, since there were now more delegates overall than had originally been chosen, and dispersed between the two rooms; only fifty-seven of the seventy delegates had originally been authorized to attend the single convention. "So now we had two Conventions going all under the same roof, and one as legitimate as the other," concluded the *Newbernian*. The Mayer convention chose William E. Clarke and William H. Johnson, the preconvention favorites for the legislature, one from each race. In response, the Stimson convention chose its own matched set: white lawyer W. W. Clark for the house and black lawyer George H. White for the senate. For the first time since the Republican Party had gained power in Craven in 1868, there would be multiple Republican candidates on the local legislative ballot.

The petulant behavior of the convention delegates did not extend further than the three offices, however; the split was far from total, and there appeared to be little personal hostility between the sides. Though in open disagreement on major offices, the party members were able to come together for the second tier; the two conventions did agree on joint nominees for four local offices, including previous winners for superior court clerk, county coroner, county treasurer, and register of deeds.[8] W. W. Clark was later replaced in

8. *Newbernian*, 9 September 1882. Two of the joint nominees—E. W. Carpenter for court clerk and David Kilburn for treasurer—had won those offices in 1878, but their bonds had been rejected by the county board of commissioners, all appointed by the Democratic General Assembly. Lawson, a black Craven County farmer, replaced W. W. Clark after Clark withdrew.

the house race, for reasons not altogether clear, by Isaac Lawson, a black farmer.

County Democrats had yet to hold their own convention; they may have scented victory in the air, for a change, but the Craven political spectrum seemed uniquely flexible. In any other county, such a fratricidal spat would almost certainly have produced a Democratic victory in the fall, but this was not true in Craven, where Republicans far outnumbered Democrats. Only direct intervention by the General Assembly had allowed any Democrats to hold office in the county since the end of Reconstruction. When Craven Democrats met in October to select their own nominees, their choices were two well-known faces: Henry R. Bryan for the senate and William B. Lane for the house. Both had bright political futures in their party; Bryan, a local attorney, later served for nearly two decades as a superior court judge, while Lane served eight years as the county's appointed sheriff.[9]

The local field was even more crowded than normal, as the new Greenback Party offered its own candidates for the legislature. Neither candidate— J. F. Heath for the senate, Major Dixon for the house—was widely known, and the third party was not expected to have much effect on the races. But each new name meant a longer and more confusing local ticket. Meanwhile, the setting itself was turbulent, clouded by the continuing statewide controversy over prohibition. Despite its overwhelming defeat by voters in August 1881, the issue simply refused to die. State Republican Party leaders had previously attempted to tie the issue squarely to the Democrats, despite the objections of a strong minority of Republicans who favored prohibition.

A fourth political movement now emerged to muddle the picture in the legislative elections: the Liberal Anti-Prohibition Party. It fielded no local candidates, and in fact hardly qualified as a "party"; it was more of a temporary movement peopled by disgruntled Democrats, unhappy with their own conservative state leaders. But its presence was unmistakable, and its appeal was curiously general. The state's Republican leadership quickly endorsed the handful of statewide Liberal candidates, in hopes of splitting the vote.[10]

9. *New Bern Daily Journal,* 10 November 1882. Lane also ran again for the house in 1886, but his victory in that race was overturned by a court judgment; he was next appointed sheriff in 1888 by the county's Democratic commissioners, after the Republican victor was denied the office on technical grounds.

10. Lefler and Newsome, *North Carolina,* 544.

The three-way Republican battle over the Second District's congressional nomination now became a furious one. Both Orlando Hubbs, a confirmed tee-totaler, and James O'Hara, now a spokesman for the statewide Anti-Prohibition Association, claimed to be the "true" nominee. Lotte W. Humphrey, who opposed the Liberal coalition and who had very nearly defeated Hubbs for the nomination two years earlier, endorsed O'Hara, along with influential white district leaders Hiram L. Grant and John T. Sharpe. Not to be outdone, perhaps, many black leaders openly campaigned for Hubbs, including former congressman John Hyman.

Hubbs stubbornly remained in the race as long as he could in the face of O'Hara's relentless attack; the congressman had been forced to remain in Washington for official business until after the first convention, losing valuable ground. By early October, it was apparent to all observers that his campaign was hopelessly behind, even in the once-solid black camp, and O'Hara was pulling away. The Democrats declined to nominate a candidate at all, hoping to encourage a duel to the death between the two Republicans, and apparently planning to trade votes in other races. Hubbs, feeling discouraged and betrayed, withdrew shortly after the middle of the month; whether he had been promised a patronage appointment after the election is not clear, and in any case, he did not receive one. He simply told supporters he knew he could not win with James O'Hara in the race.[11]

For George White, the Hubbs-O'Hara confrontation was less important than his own immediate future. Running against Senator Clarke, his ostensible ally, was a curiously uncharacteristic move for the freshman legislator. But White was committed to making some sort of race in 1882, and he could hardly afford to run for his own seat; losing it to a newcomer would have been humiliating. The Stimson ticket offered him one last semiofficial chance. It was not without risks—his dalliance with the Stimson "reformers" chanced angering the majority wing—but running as a nonparty independent candidate would have alienated both wings. White had little chance of winning the

11. Anderson, *Race and Politics*, 102–6. A Republican only since 1876, Humphrey was making his fourth attempt at the congressional nomination. He had helped defeat incumbent Curtis H. Brogden for renomination in 1878 before losing the nomination to O'Hara, then attempting to take the "reform" Republican nomination, claimed by James H. Harris. In 1880, he had lost the nomination to Hubbs by one convention vote. Hubbs's final political campaign, in 1886, was for county register of deeds. The other 1882 candidate was former Wilson legislator George W. Stanton.

Eighth District Senate seat this year, but undoubtedly hoped to win enough votes to score a moral victory: convincing GOP leaders that an all-black Republican legislative ticket could win in the future.

The only alternative—running as an independent, or "Liberal" Republican—was a different matter entirely, one that threatened to upset the balance of power in the party by siphoning off black votes from a white Republican nominee. It was a dangerous precedent; amid the confusion created by the coalition between Republicans and Liberals that year, the most feared outcome in Craven was a Democratic victory. The Liberals, mostly disgruntled Democrats, were campaigning largely on the antiprohibition issue; endorsing the antiprohibition move would have been personally problematic for George White, whose Presbyterian principles counseled temperance and favored prohibition. Worse for White, perhaps, was his partisan loyalty; he was not prepared to align himself with any predominantly white Democratic faction, even when his state party leadership was so inclined

George White preferred to campaign as a loyal black Republican, setting a strong example for other blacks in the party, perhaps even hoping for a surge in black votes with James O'Hara as the congressional nominee. Yet White's strategy was not enough to tip the balance. More than 3,000 voters turned out to cast ballots in the two Craven races on November 7, giving bare majorities to Clarke and Johnson, according to the *New Bern Daily Journal's* account. William E. Clarke won with 50.1 percent of the total; White came in a creditable but distant second, winning about 26 percent of the vote, but he did have the distinction of drawing 147 more votes than his Democratic opponent, Henry Bryan. White also outpolled Isaac Lawson, his Stimson-wing counterpart in the house race, by 45 votes.

In the congressional race, the unopposed James O'Hara drew more than 18,000 votes across the Black Second, but his reception in Craven was lukewarm; only 1,100 Craven voters bothered to include his name on their ballots. O'Hara's courtship of the Liberal vote had left a sour taste in the mouths of many Craven voters; if anyone benefitted from O'Hara's presence on the ballot in the county, it was almost certainly John Collins. The incumbent Republican solicitor was reelected by a 2-to-1 margin over his Democratic opponent, Duncan C. Winston; Collins carried Craven and the six other counties in the Second District.[12]

---

12. "Official Vote for Craven," *New Bern Daily Journal*, 10 November 1882. The two

In an eerie reversal of the events surrounding his 1880 victory, George White's loss in November was followed by another personal tragedy just six weeks later. His second wife, Nancy, died suddenly from unspecified causes just before Christmas 1882. It was another profound shock for White; he and Nancy had been married just ten months. Nancy White was only twenty years old when she died; no cause of death is known, but she may have contracted smallpox during a local epidemic, the second such epidemic in a decade. Her brother Allen, pastor of Ebenezer Church, was probably with her when she died, and certainly officiated at her funeral; again, young Della was apparently not affected by the disease that claimed her stepmother's life. Fannie's death two years earlier had been an equally sad blow, but Della had been White's consolation during his bereavement; this time, there was no child of their own to carry forward his second wife's memory.[13]

Nancy White's death was a depressing reminder of the brevity of life and love. Twice widowed before age thirty, George White was now at seemingly the lowest psychological point of his adult existence. Nancy's death had dashed his hopes of a new, larger family and a secure environment for Della. Not yet even three years old, Della had already lost both her mother and a stepmother; she may have gone back to live with her grandparents, John and Kate Randolph, for a time, although she would remain in New Bern, close to her bereaved father.

George White now immersed himself in his legal work for a time, hoping to restore a sense of purpose to his foundering personal life despite the failure of his political aspirations. His once-promising political standing had taken an abrupt, albeit temporary, downturn rendering his legal practice a natural outlet for the intensely private man; happily, his efforts during the next three years would be both professionally and financially rewarding. A comprehensive directory of Eastern North Carolina's "leading men" described his practice as "steadily growing" in 1885. "He gives faithful attention to work submitted to him, and makes a specialty of conveyancing," said the writers, who

---

Greenback candidates drew 101 votes each. Democrats had declined to nominate a candidate for Congress against O'Hara. Collins defeated Duncan C. Winston of Bertie by a vote of 18,558 to 9,547; another 427 votes were cast for John "A." Collins. The judicial district included Wake, Bertie, Edgecombe, Halifax, Northampton, and Warren Counties.

13. *Descriptive Review*, 96; N.C. Graves Index, N.C. Division of Archives and History; Watson, *History of New Bern*, 510. The smallpox epidemic of the winter of 1882–1883 is described by Watson.

also mentioned his "good library of law books," adding that "he makes good use of them."[14]

Twice thwarted as he was in his attempts at office during the year of Nancy's death, George White may have momentarily considered giving up politics altogether. Yet his dream of public service persisted, and it would not be long before the call of political office overcame any lingering reservations on his part. By 1884, he would resurface as a strong contender for the senate seat he had lost in 1882; William E. Clarke was now retiring to devote more time to his law practice, as his own father's health continued to fail. If any hard feelings within the party had resulted from George White's alternate-ticket race in 1882, there was no public sign of such feelings now.

Having served his fourth term in the 1883 General Assembly, Clarke retired undefeated from active politics; by the end of the decade he was appointed New Bern's postmaster, a job he would hold for many years. George White had little trouble gaining the Craven party's nomination for the senate in April 1884, his temporary aberration of 1882 now forgiven and apparently forgotten.[15] But the political ground was shifting; by 1883, the Second District had begun a significant metamorphosis, as race-based gerrymandering continued to play a strong role in the makeup of the General Assembly. The state's Democratic leadership had been unnerved by the strong showing of many Republican candidates for Congress in the eastern districts in 1882, and now sought to minimize the likelihood of a repeat in 1884.

The Democrats could not yet neutralize the Black Second, but hoped at least to reduce Republican potential in the adjacent First, Third, and Fourth Districts, where Republicans had very nearly scored congressional upsets. The results of the 1880 census had not been announced in time for the 1881 General Assembly to take action, and Democrats had decided not to call a special session; instead, action was deferred until spring 1883. The new reapportionment plan brought two black-majority jurisdictions—Bertie County and the newly created Vance County—into the Black Second to replace white-majority Wayne County, which was moved to the adjacent Third District. There may have been an element of punitive intent for Wayne County, since Wayne's voters had stubbornly voted for Republican legislative candidates; moving

14. *Descriptive Review*, 96.

15. *New Bern Weekly Journal*, 1 May 1884, cited in Elmore, "North Carolina Negro Congressmen," 156.

Wayne out of the Second District would isolate Wayne's Republicans and per-haps inspire the county's Democrats to more effective campaigns. Detaching Bertie County from the adjacent First District would also enhance the strength of a narrow Democratic majority there.[16]

The effect of the reapportionment spoke louder than any speculation about the General Assembly's intentions, however, for the new Black Second was now more Republican and more heavily black than in its first decade. Even as the internal structures of the party were beginning to strain under the pressures of factional strife, its potential for victory in the Second District was stronger than ever, at least for the moment.[17] And George White would begin to tap that potential as his quest for higher office, stalled by the 1882 defeats, resumed its inevitable course in the mid-1880s.

The general election of November 1884 featured a showdown in the gov-ernor's race between two incumbent congressmen, Democrat Alfred M. Scales of Rockingham County and Republican Tyre York of Wilkes County. York had run for Congress in 1882 as the state's only successful Liberal (Anti-Prohibition) candidate, but the third party had ceased to exist in 1884. The former Democrat and state legislator was now unable to generate a strong fol-lowing among liberal Democrats, however; his showing was so poor that he got several thousand fewer votes than even the Republican presidential nom-inee, James G. Blaine. York carried just thirty of the state's ninety-six coun-ties, losing the governor's race to Scales by twenty thousand votes, more than three times the margin of the 1880 race.[18]

Grover Cleveland became the first Democrat to claim the U.S. presidency in more than two decades, winning North Carolina by a healthy margin by

16. *RN&O*, 8 December 1882. William P. Canaday, editor of the *Wilmington Post*, had come within 500 votes of winning in the Third District, of about 32,000 votes cast. The Republican candidate in the First District, Latham, had come within 600 votes of winning, of about 28,000 cast. In the Fourth District, from which Vance was now being detached, the margin was equally close: Republican J. T. Devereux lost by 700 votes of 31,000 cast. Had Vance votes been counted, he would have lost by just 300 votes.

17. The population of the redrawn Second District was slightly over 195,000, using actual 1880 census figures for nine of the counties and prorated estimates for Warren and Vance; the same formula shows more than 121,000 of these residents were black. The old Second District's ten counties had totaled about 193,000 residents, with several thousand fewer blacks (approxi-mately 118,000) for a black population of 61.2 percent.

18. *NCG*, 1332–33.

carrying eight of nine congressional districts and winning more than 53 percent of the vote. Only the Black Second went Republican, voting nearly three to two for York and Blaine, behind an overwhelming reelection margin for James O'Hara. But the ominous signs of a breakdown in party loyalty were evident even in the heavily Republican counties of the Second, where factional splits and vote trading led to Democratic sweeps in Halifax and Northampton Counties, even as O'Hara carried them by huge margins over Democrat Frederick Woodard. In all, Democrats carried the legislative tickets in five of the Second District's eleven counties.[19]

Comparatively few bright spots appeared for Republicans that fall. The Second District party's legislative strength was cut almost in half; only nine Republicans, eight of them black, won seats in the senate and house, compared with fifteen in 1882. Three of the district's senate seats went to blacks, including George White; in all, six house seats were taken by Republicans, all but one of them black, including New Bern grocer and boardinghouse owner John E. Hussey. It was the first time in a decade that Craven had sent a single-race delegation to Raleigh, proof of the long-term effectiveness of George White's losing campaign in 1882. At thirty-three, White had swept back from defeat to become co-dean of the Second District delegation; he and Jacob Montgomery of Warren were the only district winners that year who could boast victories in elections to both houses of the General Assembly.[20]

After his successful campaign, George White was sworn in as senator from the Eighth North Carolina District on January 8, 1885, the second day of the session, by president *pro tempore* E. T. Boykin of Sampson County. White and a Democratic colleague, Senator John S. Johnston of Rockingham County, had been absent on the opening day, when the remaining forty-eight members had been sworn in and had elected Boykin to preside. White was one of just

19. Ibid., 1332–3, 1404–5.

20. Ibid., 464–5; also *RN&O*, 3 January 1883. Hussey, thirty-five, was elected to the first of three consecutive terms in this post. Jacob H. Montgomery of Warren and Robert S. Taylor of Edgecombe were also elected to the senate in 1884. House winners were Leslie Roulhac of Bertie, Bryant W. Thorpe of Edgecombe, J. W. Grant of Northampton, Harry B. Eaton of Vance, and Richard C. Ward of Warren. Former senator Napoleon D. Bellamy of Edgecombe was the only white among seventeen Republicans elected in the Second District. Montgomery had served a term in the house in 1883; Eaton and Grant were each elected to second terms in the house in 1882.

seven Republican senators, but he drew important committee assignments, including choice seats on the standing committees Judiciary and Insurance. Only two other senators were so honored, both Democrats: Robert W. Winston of Granville County and J. W. Todd of Ashe. George White declined his announced appointment to a third committee, Insane Asylums.[21]

Senator White immediately plunged into legislative tasks with his customary vigor by introducing a resolution calling on the state's U.S. senators and congressmen "to use their influence in favor of national aid for public education." Senate Bill 7 was placed on the senate calendar, and later referred to the Committee on Education; though it eventually passed its second reading, it was not enacted into law. White also took part in the elections for doorkeeper and assistant doorkeeper, voting for the unopposed candidate from Wake for the higher office. In the second election, however, White joined four other Republican senators in voting for a black candidate, I. L. Smith of Edgecombe, who lost to a Forsyth County Democrat.[22]

White's strong interest in educational matters continued during the 1885 session, in which on January 26 he introduced a mandatory-attendance bill similar to the one he had unsuccessfully pushed in 1881. Four days later he also sponsored a separate bill to establish and maintain a "home of refuge and correction," or reformatory, for black youths. Both bills were initially referred to the Committee on Education, although neither bill passed the senate, perhaps owing in part to White's absence from the committee's deliberations. The reformatory bill was reported favorably by the Finance Committee but was killed by parliamentary maneuvers on March 5. The mandatory-attendance bill was reported unfavorably late in the session, and the committee's report was accepted, the same fate White's earlier bill had met.[23]

George White's most outspoken comments on education during the session occurred during a protest lodged by the senate's three black members

21. *1885 Senate Journal*, 6, 20, 24. Winston was elected superior court judge in 1890 and presided over sessions between 1891 and 1894, when White was serving as Second District solicitor.

22. Ibid., 7–10. Joining White in voting for Smith were Montgomery, Taylor, Chadbourn of New Hanover, and Swain of Brunswick. A total of forty-two senators voted for James E. Oaks, including at least one Republican, P. C. Thomas of Davidson; another Republican, J. A. Franklin of Surry, did not vote.

23. Ibid., 99, 133, 244, 491, 529.

against sections of the biennial public-school law. On March 3, White, Jacob Montgomery, and Robert Taylor argued that two specific sections of the bill were unfair to North Carolina's black citizens. The trio viewed as unconstitutional and wasteful of limited funds a provision designed to regulate the selection of school administrators by allowing appointed county boards of education to hire all personnel, including new positions of arguable merit. This controversy was part of the larger home-rule battle, as well as a longstanding point of contention for Republicans, since the legislature invariably appointed Democratic board members. While Republicans could not hope to reverse that decade-old trend, White and his colleagues insisted on calling public attention to Democrats for violating the spirit, if not the letter, of the state constitution.[24]

A second offending section authorized a discriminatory division of state revenues for public schools that clearly favored facilities for white students over those for blacks, according to the three senators. This "proscriptive" method of funding was generally "injurious to the public, but more especially to the colored people," for it continued and expanded the trend, begun in the hated 1883 Dortch Act, toward limiting revenues available for operating black schools by equalizing school facilities without regard to race. In black-majority counties, this meant that white schools would receive as much for capital expenditures as black schools, even though the latter had substantially more students.[25]

Despite the trio's articulate protest, the public-school bill passed unchanged. It was a protest of principle, not practicality; none had expected it to succeed. George White almost certainly drafted the protest, which was phrased in his familiar legalistic style, a voice far less likely to belong to Taylor, a teacher who had immigrated from Jamaica in 1866, or to Montgomery, a farmer and merchant.

In a separate action concerning one of North Carolina's newest private colleges for blacks, White encountered a curiously myopic attitude among his fellow senators on the subject of education. White had introduced an innocuous bill aimed at incorporating Zion Wesley College, the AME Zion denomination's school for teachers and ministers; founded in Concord in 1870 as

24. Ibid., 520–1.
25. Ibid.

Zion Wesley Institute, the school had moved to Salisbury in 1882 under the leadership of its new president, the Reverend Joseph C. Price of New Bern. White's bill was the senate counterpart to a house bill sponsored by popular Democrat Lee Overman of Rowan County, and was expected to pass easily.[26] The Committee on Corporations had reported it favorably, and it had passed its second reading with ease.

Yet when White called up the Zion Wesley College bill for its third and final reading on February 3, the bill unexpectedly "provoked considerable discussion, as it appeared to be thought that the institution would confer degrees on some prominent white men, it being a colored institution." Unlikely as such risks must have seemed to black observers, and harmless at best, the thought triggered a predicably complicated series of parliamentary maneuvers. First, the senate voted to amend the bill to prohibit the granting of such degrees; this led to a temporary standoff with the house, which refused on February 12 to accept the amendment. Next, the senate reconsidered its earlier action, rescinding its amendment and sending the bill to a joint committee as a compromise measure; White may have been a conferee, although his name was not specified in the record. An acceptable conference report was produced, and the senate approved the final bill, using carefully drawn language to avoid the divisive issue entirely.[27]

George White had long believed that politics was the science of the possible, one always amenable to reason and steeped in compromise. He was well aware of the intransigence of many white Democrats—and even of some white Republicans, for that matter—on the issue of integrated education, but he had carefully cooperated in advance with Democrats on this bill, if to little apparent avail. Having attended a predominantly black public university from which more than a few white students had graduated, he could hardly have anticipated such a wasteful and time-consuming reaction. In any event, integrating higher education was not the issue here; this involved no use of public funds, and few whites would be interested in attending Zion Wesley. The hidden issue was white supremacy, and as such, it was impervious to reasonable

26. Brown, *Education of Negroes*, 76–7. The 1887 General Assembly renamed the institution Livingstone College, in memory of the son of prominent white missionary David Livingstone.

27. Daily senate proceedings for 1885, Day 24 (February 3), as reported in *Raleigh News and Observer*; *1885 Senate Journal*, 138, 141, 248; also Reid, "A Biography," 78. Contrary to Reid's assertion, both houses approved the conference report and the bill.

argument. What White was now witnessing was the absurd underbelly of his chosen avocation, an ominous indicator of days yet to come.

Not all of White's activities as state senator were so politically intricate. Even as a faithful Republican, he was willing to eschew partisan loyalty on occasion by supporting a Democratic candidate for national office, if he felt strongly enough about the man. Toward the end of the first month of the session, he found such an occasion to pay exceedingly warm tribute to one of the state's most illustrious Democrats, retiring governor Thomas J. Jarvis. Rising to address the senate on January 22, White endorsed a resolution recommending Jarvis to president-elect Grover Cleveland as a member of the next U.S. Cabinet:

> Ordinarily I should oppose a resolution of this kind, but I regard this as extraordinary. There are times when all party differences should disappear, and I should feel that I was derelict to one of the most sacred duties imposed upon me by those who sent me here, were I not to give my vote in support of this resolution. Gov. Jarvis has been the Governor of the whole people, and while my people differ from his race, and in politics, yet he has done more for them than anyone who ever graced the Governor's chair. I feel that this resolution should meet the hearty support of every member of the General Assembly; and I call upon every member of my race in both branches of the legislature to give it his earnest favor.[28]

At least one other black legislator agreed: Senator Robert Taylor, who echoed White's sentiments in a shorter speech later in the day. The resolution passed the senate unanimously, as expected; although Jarvis was not appointed to the Cabinet, President Cleveland did see fit by the end of March to appoint him minister to Brazil. Jarvis served in that capacity until the inauguration of President Benjamin Harrison in 1889; he also served briefly as U.S. senator in 1894–1895, completing the term of the late Zebulon B. Vance. It was poetic justice, after a fashion, since Vance's election as senator in 1879 had elevated then–lieutenant governor Jarvis to the state's highest office.[29]

Two days after his endorsement of Jarvis, Senator White took part in a somewhat more partisan debate with racial overtones, regarding a relatively

28. *RN&O*, 1885 senate proceedings, Day 14 (January 22).
29. *RN&O*, 31 March 1885.

minor bill to reduce the state's price of marriage licenses. Characterized as a "lively little debate" by the *News and Observer*, the discussion had featured unflattering remarks by one unnamed senator "supposed to be reflecting on the people of another district"—apparently black residents of eastern counties. The price of marriage licenses had been set by a Republican legislature in 1868, and raised a disproportionate share of its revenue from the white majority; Democrats now sought to cut the price. The Finance Committee had reported the bill unfavorably, but Democrats in the full senate were prepared to reverse their findings. White argued that the committee's analysis was correct, and that the bill "ought to be considered on its merits," rather than degenerate into a quarrel over the irrelevant racial issue. "We ought to leave party bickerings [aside]," he told the chamber on January 24. "The color of a man's skin, the texture of his hair and the thickness of his nose ought not to be taken into consideration." His sensible observations restored a measure of dignity to the discussion, allowing the debate to end "pleasantly," according to the newspaper account. Still, the vote to sustain the committee failed fourteen to eighteen, with White and Taylor among the minority. White was later recorded as moving—graciously, under the circumstances—that the senate adjourn for the day.[30]

Of all the issues considered in 1885 by the senate's Judiciary Committee, none could have been more personally relevant to George White than the proposed redrawing of the state's judicial districts. Both he and his fellow New Bern lawyers had a vested professional interest in the outcome of such redistricting, although White's interest may have been as much personal as professional. The Democratic measure before the 1885 General Assembly intended to add three new districts across the state, as the court system expanded to handle a growing number of cases in the postwar era. Because geographic contiguity had yet to emerge as a hard-and-fast rule in nineteenth-century North Carolina, however, the proposed alignment did nothing to rectify a longstanding complaint from New Bern's legal profession: their town's isolation from adjacent counties in the judicial circuit.[31]

Craven County's situation seemed historically absurd. As the seat of the second largest urban center in eastern North Carolina, its nearest neighbor in

30. *RN&O*, 1885 senate proceedings, Day 16 (January 24).
31. "Memorial to the General Assembly," dated February 27, 1885, printed in *RN&O*, 1 March 1885.

the new district lay "by the usual route of travel, more than one hundred miles distant" from New Bern. So, at least, the city's bar association argued in its late February memorial to the legislature; in a day when such distances might require a day's travel or more, both the people of the area and its lawyers suffered as a result. Lawyers in New Bern were already "in a district the people of which we have no business relations with," which placed an unfair professional burden on them. "Our interests and constitutional rights have been disregarded and sacrificed," said the fifteen signatories, who decried "the spectacle of three judicial districts within a dozen miles of the City of New Berne."[32]

The New Bern lawyers were a powerful lot, including one past congressman, another future congressman and U.S. senator, and one former superior court judge and clerk of the court. These prominent politicians from both parties sought nothing more than parity with the rest of the state, and their request seemed eminently sensible,[33] but it was only noted politely before being discarded. The reason was related neither to efficiency or cost, but instead to partisan obstacles: Craven County was regularly represented by Republican legislators, who had not controlled the General Assembly in more than a decade. When it came to redistricting, the Democrats preferred to isolate Republican opponents by concentrating the bulk of them in one district, as they had done in the Black Second. Since most decisions of this nature were made in party caucus rather than open debate, electing Democratic legislators would have been Craven's only sure way to address the issue of the judicial district's boundaries. Such a solution was years away, at best.[34]

Meanwhile, the new, smaller Second Judicial District in which Craven remained was no more convenient than before for New Bern's lawyers. No counties in the redrawn district were any closer than before. Democrats had left Craven in an overwhelmingly Republican zone, but had purposefully and carefully insulated Raleigh, the capital city, from the perceived embarrass-

32. Ibid. The memorial's signers included former Second District Republican congressman Charles R. Thomas (1870–1875) and Furnifold M. Simmons, elected to Congress in 1886 and the U.S. Senate in 1901.

33. Ibid.

34. This may have been a secondary factor in the unsuccessful 1886 coalition effort, by which two Democrats were to be sent to the General Assembly in exchange for Democratic support of local reform Republican candidates in Craven. The Democrats controlled the General Assembly until 1895, when Republicans and Populists fused.

ment of having a black elected solicitor. Wake County, where John Collins's presence had irritated the legal hierarchy for more than six years, was moved to the adjacent, and somewhat more Democratic, Fourth Judicial District.[35]

Craven County had been portrayed—if incorrectly—as the only noncontiguous "island" in the state's judicial realm when Collins was first elected in 1878, according to the *New York Times*; "it is the only district in the state that is not contiguous. Edgecombe and Craven do not touch at any point," wrote the correspondent, neglecting to mention that Wake touched none of the other counties either. Nearly a decade later, Craven had actually become the state's only such island, adjacent now to five counties in three different districts—Beaufort and Pamlico in the First, Pitt in the Third, Jones and Lenoir in the Sixth—but legally divorced from them all in the eyes of the state.[36]

How significant a role White played in this redistricting effort is not clear. He dutifully relayed the memorial of his hometown bar to the Judiciary Committee, on which he served, but made no comments in the public record during open debate on March 4. What he said during committee deliberations is not recorded, but his arguments undoubtedly made a favorable impression on committee chairman Robert W. Winston, who later expressed admiration for White's legal talents and methodical performance as a solicitor in Winston's court.[37]

George White was understandably philosophical about the situation; since statewide redistricting took place only every ten years, in mid-decade, no new action was likely before 1895. Like his fellow New Bern attorneys, he knew that geographic equity was probably impossible as long as the issue was mired in partisan politics. Like his fellow black legislators, whose frequent attempts

35. Collins, of course, was from Halifax County, not affected by the redistricting move. He attempted to use this scare tactic in his 1886 bid for renomination, claiming that the General Assembly intended to move Craven County out of the Second Judicial District. His claim was unlikely but not implausible, based on the previous removal of Martin and Wake Counties; in any case, it was not borne out by subsequent events.

36. "The Color Line in North Carolina." "Democrats are perfectly furious over the nomination," a result of the party's "gerrymandering" of large Republican counties in 1876, wrote the *New York Times* correspondent. Only eight counties were listed by the *Times* in the Second Judicial District in 1878: Wake, Warren, Halifax, Northampton, Martin, Bertie, Edgecombe, and Craven.

37. Robert W. Winston, *It's a Far Cry* (New York: Henry Holt, 1937), 234. Winston (1860–1944) published his autobiography almost two decades after White's death.

to exclude their home counties from new criminal judicial districts were generally unsuccessful, White could protest but do little else. As a minority within a minority party, black legislators had extremely limited negotiating leverage; changing that would require a virtual revolution by state voters.[38]

Such a revolution was not inconceivable, but was unlikely in the foreseeable future; the number of Republicans in the General Assembly had been reduced sharply by the 1884 election. There were just 7 Republican senators and 23 representatives in the 1885 legislature, compared to a total of 66 in the previous one. Across the counties of the Second District, just nine Republicans had been elected in 1884, due largely to splits within the party, but the election of at least one regional Democrat—Senator Thomas Mason of the Third District, which comprised Bertie and Northampton Counties—had generated a serious challenge afterward by the Republican loser, James W. Newsom of Northampton County. Newsom had received a majority of the votes cast in the 1884 election, but the disqualification of several hundred Northampton ballots by election judges had permitted Mason to win.[39]

As a devout believer in legal fairness and electoral justice, White took a special interest in Newsom's contest; White believed the candidate with the final majority of votes was entitled to victory, absent provable fraud. He may have had a personal interest as well, since Democrats had apparently attempted to use the same "device" argument to deprive him of votes in the election, but with little effect on his final victory margin. Republican colleague Robert Taylor of Edgecombe, with whom White shared lodgings in Raleigh that winter, served on the Committee on Privileges and Elections; White certainly discussed the case with Taylor, and probably helped him prepare the brief minority report.[40] Taylor's committee had taken testimony on the case in late January, but the committee's Democratic majority had upheld

38. The next assembly chose not to pursue the matter, even though Republicans and disaffected Democrats formed a potential majority in 1887. By then, George White was district solicitor, a fact complicating any plans to move Craven to another district.

39. Day 26 (February 5), 1885 *Senate Journal*, 251.

40. Elmore, "North Carolina Negro Congressmen," 156; "The City Addresses of the Members of the Legislature," *RN&O*, 28 February 1885. Elmore cites a report to this effect from the *New Bern Daily Journal* of 6 November 1884; White's final margin was large enough to offset the loss of the challenged votes. During the 1885 General Assembly, White and Taylor lodged at the Raleigh residence of Dr. W. H. Moore, as did two other black legislators, Edgecombe's Bryant W. Thorpe and New Hanover's Luke Grady.

Mason's victory, recommending that Mason be allowed to keep the seat he had held since the first day of the session, while Taylor and Democrat J. W. Todd of Ashe County had filed a minority report favoring Newsom's challenge.

The central issue was the inclusion of the phrase "House of Representatives, Northampton County" on the disqualified Newsom ballots. Under state law, any "device" enabling illiterates to "distinguish ballots without reading them," and which was intended to accomplish this, was sufficient to invalidate a ballot. Democratic election judges in North Carolina's Republican precincts were increasingly likely to utilize this method in close elections, whenever the opportunity to produce a Democratic victory was within legal reach. The house or senate itself was empowered to make a final decision, under existing court rulings that had upheld both the law and any reasonable interpretation of the term "device."[41] Either chamber could seat any candidate, or even order a new election if it desired, and few challenges by Republican contestants were successful, except in cases of demonstrable fraud or clear error by the original judges.

In the Newsom-Mason case, the outcome was predictable. The presentation of the two reports on February 5 led to a second victory for Senator Mason; senate members rejected the minority report by a 29-7 margin, then voted 28-7 to uphold the committee's majority report. Each time, George White was in the minority, joining five other Republicans and one Democrat (W. C. Troy of Fayetteville) in voting for Newsom; only one Republican senator did not vote on either report, announcing that he had previously agreed to "pair" his vote with an absent Democratic colleague voting the other way. Among Democrats present but not voting, Senator Todd—the coauthor of the minority report—was himself paired with Democrat J. L. King of Guilford; their votes, if counted, would also have negated each other.[42]

---

41. Day 26 (February 5), *1885 Senate Journal*, 251–3. The committee dealt only with the applicability of the state law to "Northampton County"; because the senatorial district included two counties, the ballot should have read "Third Senatorial District." Election judges used the entire phrase to throw out Newsom's ballots, arguing that the race was for the senate, not the house. The record does not indicate the wording on Mason's ballots.

42. Ibid., 253–4. Republican senator W. H. Chadbourn of New Hanover announced after the vote that he was paired with absent Democrat J. T. Kennedy of Wayne, both for the minority report and against the majority report. Newsom eventually received a $50 state reimbursement for his transportation costs to Raleigh.

Apparently concerned by the precedent being established, George White immediately asked that the report of the committee be printed, to preserve it for future reference, and his request was granted. He further introduced a resolution in Newsom's favor, S.R. 501, which was placed on the calendar. Previous experience had taught him that the election process was flawed, and that simple justice was not always possible. In any event, it was a more subdued performance than White had given four years earlier, when he had vocally denounced fraud in two contested election cases from Halifax County. Two 1880 Republican candidates had then been the obvious victims of widespread fraud, but neither contestant had been able to claim a house seat despite White's eloquent arguments on their behalf in 1881.[43]

As Craven County's representative in the senate, White now handled the introduction of local bills during the 1885 General Assembly. His submissions included a bill to revise the county boundary line established two years earlier between Craven and Carteret Counties; the bill, which passed on February 12, was less notable for its actual content than for White's unsuccessful attempt to have an appointed conference committee comprise representatives from the two counties, before the bill's actual referral to the senate's grievance committee. His next bill, to regulate oyster catching, was given a favorable report by the Fish and Oyster Committee, but apparently never came to a final vote; White had argued that his county's constituents needed protection that the bill would have provided. White also offered a successful minor amendment to Senate Bill 360, which authorized the issuance of bonds for New Bern city improvements, a week before its final passage.[44]

In other action, White introduced several bills calling for changes in state law, only one of which was enacted. The successful bill authorized state courts to order the name changes of minors; it was enacted on March 11, after gaining approval from White's own Judiciary Committee. Although critical to passage, the committee's approval was not always sufficient, however; his earlier bill, to extend the time for registration of grants, deeds, and other conveyances, was tabled during open debate despite the committee's stamp of approval.[45]

On January 21, White introduced a bill to amend Section 725 of the

43. Ibid., 254.

44. *RN&O*, 1885 house proceedings, Day 57 (March 10); *RN&O*, 1885 senate proceedings, Day 8 (January 15), Day 9 (January 16); Anderson, *Race and Politics*, 93; Reid, "A Biography," 79–80.

45. Reid, "A Biography," 77, 79.

North Carolina Code, relating to statements of clerks and justices of the peace, but the senate's action on the bill is not apparent from public records; White apparently later withdrew his draft of Senate Bill 160 for modification and referral to a new committee. Although he seems to have reintroduced the revised bill on January 31, there is no record of any debate on it or of its final disposition.[46]

When the 1885 General Assembly adjourned on March 11, George White ended his service as a state legislator with a commendable record of achievement. Although successful in enacting only a few notable bills, he had established a strong reputation as an intelligent and analytical representative committed to fair and thoughtful public service. He also displayed a significant independent streak, voting on at least one occasion as the only opponent, on principle, of a popular measure; his willingness to condemn racial discrimination in state laws was both courageous and politically risky, as Democratic opponents began to realize the strength of his potential appeal in campaigns beyond the confines of Craven County.[47]

White was now a seasoned veteran of three legislative campaigns, two of which he had won handily. He was also an accomplished and prosperous lawyer with a strong record of civic and religious service to his credit, and his previous record as a teacher, principal, and educational leader was the equal of any other black in the state. Having developed useful working relationships with black Republican leaders in neighboring counties, he was now prepared to broaden his political horizons, taking aim at the job that had eluded him three years earlier: district solicitor.

In the late spring of 1886, White took his first successful political step outside the secure confines of his adopted county, once again seeking his party's nomination for district solicitor. It remained a calculated risk, for White's name and face were still relatively unfamiliar to the voters in the district's outlying counties. He could have chosen to seek a safe reelection as state senator, having earned the right to a traditional second term in that job. But it was a question of timing, and the practical politician saw an irresistible opportunity to advance himself.

46. Ibid.
47. Ibid., 80. White was the only senator to vote against the incorporation of the Mount Holly and Denver Railroad. Reid says White's joint protest against the education bill undoubtedly raised his level of visibility among state Democratic leaders, already troubled by the continuing success of James O'Hara and John Collins.

White's hometown's newest newspaper agreed wholeheartedly with his decision. "It certainly gives us pleasure to bear testimony to the worth and high standing of our fellow townsman, George White," wrote the New Bern People's Advocate in a June editorial endorsing his candidacy, continuing with this praise:

> Would that we had more such professional colored gentlemen in our community, for the times demand that none but the very best should be chosen or elected to administer the affairs of the government. . . . Few young men of our race have made such rapid progress in their chosen profession. . . . We believe that we but voice the sentiment of at least eight-tenths of all true Republicans when we say that Mr. White will be elected our next Solicitor by an increased majority.[48]

White had lost the same quest four years earlier to incumbent John Henry Collins, partly for technical reasons, after legislative reapportionment cut the size of Craven's voting delegation to district conventions in half. But Collins had won then by appealing to the party's sense of fairness: always reward the winner with a second opportunity. A third term for Collins would not carry the same resonance with voters, since he had now served for eight years. Since 1882, both the post of solicitor and that of congressman had been held by two black men from the same county. Second District leaders outside Halifax were understandably inclined to spread the region's major electoral opportunities around.

In its obvious zeal for White, the Advocate did not bother to compare the two men; indeed, the newspaper chose not to mention John Collins at all in its editorial. The odds were clearly in White's favor this year, in a much smaller district, and the newspaper predicted an increased majority, both in Craven and beyond, if White became the nominee. The Advocate gave subtle hints, however, of its feelings toward Collins and his patron, Congressman James O'Hara, in describing George White's virtues. "[He] is the true type of a gentleman, as well as a consistent Christian, and would carry to the office of the Solicitor those noble qualities so very necessary to the faithful discharge of the important duties," the paper noted, calling White "the leading colored lawyer in this section [and] indeed, an honor to his race, both as a citizen and as a lawyer."[49]

48. "George H. White: A Leading Colored Lawyer of North Carolina," editorial, New Bern People's Advocate, undated, reprinted in New York Freeman, 26 June 1886.
49. Ibid.

One could hardly say the same for O'Hara, or for Collins, for that matter. As even the most casual observer knew, O'Hara was a dashing figure, but hardly a "noble" one; a tirelessly flamboyant and seemingly corrupt politician, he was now seeking his third term in Congress and his fourth nomination for the office. His protégé Collins was regarded as a well-meaning if barely competent and less-than-energetic lawyer; he was a devout Episcopalian, a devoted family man, and did not drink, and was therefore at least respectable. But by emulating O'Hara in clinging to office beyond two terms, Collins had unwittingly revealed his own arrogance and apparent disregard for common-sense political rules.

It would have been difficult to find a better, or more eager, replacement for Collins in eastern North Carolina than George White. At thirty-three, White was a rising star within the party, obviously ready for the challenge of a more demanding public office. He had worked hard at lesser jobs, shown prudence in his personal life, and achieved a comfortable, middle-class prominence. He was also twice widowed, with a young daughter to support; the solicitor's job offered both personal fulfillment and a higher income, depending on how hard he was willing to work. But the bottom line was that he was simply the best man for the job, as the *Advocate* put it that summer:

> Mr. White deserves the suffrage of every constituent in the District, not because he is a negro, not because he is a lawyer, not on account of his mental acquisitions, but because the structures on which these qualities or attributes rest are the broad principles of justice, equality and humanity.[50]

The position of solicitor now appealed even more strongly to White than previously; he had not brooded over his 1882 loss, but had patiently waited for a better opportunity. Much had changed for him professionally: with seven years of practical legal work to his credit and a growing reputation as an effective attorney, he was now far more experienced and widely known. He was also a more seasoned politician, with successful terms in both houses of the General Assembly and workmanlike service within the local Republican Party. And while public service was important to White, another goal was slowly taking shape in the back of his mind, that of national office. To reach this goal required exposure of his talents on a broader public scale. The next

50. Untitled editorial, *New Bern People's Advocate*, 31 July 1886.

election for solicitor would be in 1890, and for George White, that was much too long to wait.

The solicitor's position was a demanding and difficult one, requiring energy and organizational skills beyond the experience level of most ordinary young lawyers. Critics of John Collins had predicted disaster in 1878 because of his lack of significant practical experience, after just four years of legal work and no notable cases.[51] By contrast, George White's experience could not be faulted; he had appeared in both state and federal courts in a wide variety of civil and criminal cases since entering the bar in 1879, regularly defeating a host of skilled attorneys. He specialized in civil cases and conveyances, according to his 1886 advertisement in the *Advocate,* and represented clients before the superior court in New Bern and U.S. federal courts in New Bern and Raleigh.

White's recent career accomplishments were certainly worth noting, as summarized by a Washington, D.C., journalist the next year. "His management of the famous ferry case involving the interests and rights of the 2,000 colored people of James City, a settlement across the river from Newberne, was indeed masterly, and has long since passed into a proverb," wrote Edward L. Thornton. "He won the case against eight of the ablest white lawyers in Newberne. He now has twelve cases pending in the Superior Court against the Old Dominion Steamship Co., which involve damages to colored people, and beside these 35 general cases to be tried at the next term of the court. His practice covers an area of ten counties and yields an annual revenue of from $1,000 to $2,000."[52]

The solicitor's duties were equivalent to those of a prosecuting attorney in other states: handling prosecution of criminal cases and maintaining an exhausting travel schedule to follow the circuit of the state's superior court judges. An elected superior court judge held court for one or two weeks at a time in each of the six counties, rotating seasonally in the spring and fall sessions. The five-month spring term for 1887, for instance, ran from January 10 to June 18, with but one week off in late February.[53]

51. "The Color Line in North Carolina."

52. "Lawyer and Legislator."

53. *RN&O,* 6 January 1887. The Craven superior court was scheduled to meet in New Bern for two weeks in February and for another two weeks beginning May 30, according to the spring term schedule published here.

For George White, with just four weeks a term in Craven's courts, such a schedule would mean 18 of 23 weeks away from his home and his young daughter, but the position was still a lucrative prize, arguably the highest-paid elective position in the state. Its potential income ranged from $1,500 to $5,000 annually, according to observers; how much a solicitor earned depended in part on how quickly he mastered the vagaries of the highly politicized court system.[54]

Simply traveling by horseback or carriage from one courtroom to the next required significant stamina during winter months, since even in good weather, the distances between the district's courthouses were daunting. Although regular trains connected the area's larger cities of New Bern and Tarboro, the more isolated towns lay within reach only by horse and buggy, over hundreds of miles of poorly maintained rural dirt roads, often nearly impassable in winter. White, a tall and well-built man, was nothing if not vigorous and healthy; he was rarely sick during his adult life. Collins, on the other hand, was described as being of "small stature," weighing barely a hundred pounds; a nervously active man, he had apparently suffered unspecified wounds as a teenaged Union seaman at the Battle of Fort Fisher.[55]

While John Collins was generally well-liked personally in 1886, even by the white establishment, he had not been a notable success as solicitor. Several of the region's Democratic newspapers had openly ridiculed his poor managerial skills, although Republican newspapers like Wilmington's *Post* tended to be less critical of him. Much more important to his survival were his skills as a politician, however, and they would be sorely tested this time by the far more energetic legislative veteran. George White had spent much of 1885 quietly building a political base in Edgecombe, Bertie, Northampton, and Warren Counties. Craven, of course, was expected to be an easy win for White,

54. J. C. L. Harris to Albion W. Tourgée, 13 February 1875, cited in Anderson, *Race and Politics,* 65; *New York Age,* 22 November 1890. Only estimated ranges of the solicitor's income are available. Sixth District solicitor J. C. L. Harris estimated the potential annual income at $3,000 to $5,000 in 1875. Edward L. Thornton gave a lower estimate of $1,500 to $4,000 in an 1890 story on White's reelection.

55. "Our Raleigh Correspondent," *Wilmington Post,* 18 January 1879; Anderson, *Race and Politics,* 318. The newspaper writer described Collins's appearance at court in Raleigh as "quite a novel spectacle to see a negro solicitor prosecuting the high-toned wealth and intelligence in the Superior Court of Wake"; the same column noted George White's licensing by the North Carolina Supreme Court.

who had also established potential family ties in Edgecombe, and had made strong inroads in Warren and Northampton. He might write off Halifax to Collins, but no other county seemed beyond his reach.[56]

To White's distinct advantage in this election as well was the more compact size of the new Second Judicial District. The unwieldy old district had once included nine counties in three distinct locations, stretching from the coast to the state capital in Raleigh and covering about six thousand square miles of territory. Wake County had been a particularly strong base of support for John Collins in 1878 and 1882, and now it had been moved to an adjacent district.[57]

That move had been part of a wider Democratic strategy aimed at eliminating the possibility of another black solicitor in Raleigh's courts by transferring the strongly Republican but barely-white-majority Wake out of the Black Second. Collins's nomination and first election in 1878 had infuriated white Democrats at the state level, and even white Republicans in the district had scoffed at the nomination of an inexperienced rural black lawyer as "disastrous" for the party's image.[58]

Many Republicans had therefore encouraged Collins's futile effort to be appointed minister to Haiti in 1881, in hopes of removing him both from the courts of Raleigh and from the political arena of the Second District. But the Toronto College graduate had persevered, growing into the job at least well enough to win a second term in 1882, while defeating opponents White and Walter P. Williamson along the way. Much of Collins's support had come from Halifax and Wake, the Second District's largest counties.

But larger political forces beyond Collins's control had intervened to thwart his career. The 1885 redistricting plan had expanded the state's nine districts to twelve. George White had said nothing publicly about the wisdom of the plan, which had failed to answer vocal complaints by Craven attorneys of geographical hardship. As a member of the Judiciary Committee charged

56. *RN&O*, 20 January 1883. The Second District had shifted in both shape and overall size since Collins's first election; Martin and Beaufort Counties had moved to the First District. Collins lived in Enfield, where his patron, James O'Hara, had lived and worked since the early 1870s.

57. John A. Moore to William E. Clarke, 26 June 1878, cited in Anderson, *Race and Politics*, 64.

58. *Tarboro Southerner*, 15 June 1882.

with crafting the new arrangement, however, he had ample opportunity to air his opinion in off-the-record deliberations. Whatever he may have felt about the General Assembly's treatment of Craven, he could only be intrigued by the practical result. If a new, smaller Second District did nothing to resolve the simmering debate in Craven over logistics and fairness, it did have one compelling advantage: John Collins had lost his nucleus of Republican support in Wake County.

Like many courtroom attorneys, White saw Collins as a slow, mediocre prosecutor who had demonstrated ambition but little substance during eight years as solicitor; if not for the help of former solicitor J. C. L. Harris, some said, Collins would have been overwhelmed by the task. Collins was both intelligent and clearly dedicated to his job, but a prisoner nonetheless of circumstance; dominated by the brilliant, abrasive Harris, he never managed to emerge from the older man's shadow.[59]

As in any political situation, perception was crucial; George White clearly held the advantage of a stronger image. With his unblemished record of independence and the respect of white lawyers and political leaders, White was now the rising star of the black Republicans in eastern North Carolina.

---

59. "John Cebern Logan Harris," *DNCB*, 3:53–4; Anderson, *Race and Politics*, 318. Harris (1847–1918) practiced law in North Carolina for almost half a century after his admission to the bar in 1868, and was widely regarded as a brilliant attorney and legal "guide"; Collins "makes the bills and Mr. Harris does the pleading," one Raleigh observer said in 1880. Harris edited the *Raleigh Signal* from 1884 to 1894, then served as adviser to Gov. Daniel Russell after 1897.

5

"The only colored solicitor in America"

Eager for a rematch with John Collins, George White was certain he would win the 1886 showdown. He had laid his groundwork carefully, building a solid core of support in each county across the Second Judicial District. In contrast to Collins, who had little support among white voters, White fully expected support from white Republicans, especially in Craven County. As principal of the New Bern normal school, White had taught dozens of the region's black schoolteachers, and counted on strong support from his former pupils. The new district also had an increased majority of black voters, including a number of blacks too young to have voted four years earlier; its population was now two-thirds black, up from 62 percent in the former seven counties. Since only adult males could register, voter registration percentages did not always correlate closely to overall population, but there was no doubt that the Second District remained heavily Republican at election time. And the presence of black candidates, of course, tended to ensure a high turnout among black voters.[1]

Still, there were obstacles, and the nomination would not come easily to

1. U.S. Census, 1880; also, Anderson, *Race and Politics*, 345–6 (Tables 12, 14). According to the 1880 census, the seven counties had a population of about 183,000, of which 114,000, or 62 percent, were black; the redrawn district contained 135,000 residents, more than 90,000 of them black. Anderson's tables show that 16,029 Republicans voted for O'Hara in the congressional race in 1884 in the five counties of Craven, Edgecombe, Halifax, Northampton, and Warren, compared to 12,662 four years earlier, when Orlando Hubbs had run. Votes each year for the Democratic challenger were about the same: just under 8,000.

George White, who faced not only a stubborn adversary in John Collins but also a deteriorating situation among the ranks of black Republicans in general. The always fractious black leadership of the Second Judicial District, like that of the larger Second Congressional District, was already split down the middle in 1886 over candidates in the congressional race.[2] Some black leaders, particularly those in Collins's home county of Halifax, continued to back him, while others were attracted by the powerful speaking skills of his charismatic challenger.

At least some white Republicans, however, believed the time was right for one of their own, and pushed Francis D. Winston of Windsor as an alternative. Winston was still a Republican at this point, although he would later bolt the party to become an architect of white supremacy for the Democrats and, eventually, the state's lieutenant governor. The three candidates differed in style and background, yet had one common characteristic: their relative youth. John Collins was the oldest at thirty-six; George White was thirty-three during the campaign, and just before the November election Francis Winston turned twenty-nine.[3]

The judicial district's nominating convention was scheduled for the middle of August. Delegates were to be chosen at county Republican conventions, which were attended by the candidates and scores of both party members and interested onlookers. Even by the lax standards of the nineteenth century, these meetings were hardly models of party decorum; they were memorable instead for long, angry debates and frequent bouts of public name-calling, and were often plagued by competing hostile slates of delegates who each claimed victory. It was not unusual for a local convention to adjourn without reaching a consensus, leaving it to district conventions to decide which of several county delegations to seat. Worse for party unity, the county executive committees often disintegrated into feuding factions. Such factions were led in 1886 by supporters of Congressman James O'Hara and his determined opponents, including Israel Abbott, George White's friend and political colleague.

2. Anderson, *Race and Politics*, 130–4.

3. U.S. Census, manuscript on microfilm, Halifax and Bertie Counties, N.C., 1880; "Francis Donnell Winston," *DNCB* 6:244. John Henry Collins was thirty in 1880, married with five children. Francis Winston, still single, was born in 1857; he had previously served as Bertie's clerk of court.

The red-haired, mixed-race O'Hara was the product of an Irish father and West Indian mother, and had grown up outside the United States, adapting only incompletely to his adopted home's political structure after moving to North Carolina after the war. Never a strong leader or a source of party unity despite his apparent appeal to rank-and-file voters, O'Hara seemed instead to breed chaos around him. His disorganizing effect on the district dated from his first unsuccessful congressional attempt in 1878, when he had won the nomination but lost the election in a bitter contest marred by personal scandals, complicated by the presence of two independent candidates, and concluded only amid charges of widespread fraud finally dismissed by the U.S. House itself.[4]

O'Hara had unsuccessfully contested his loss before that body throughout 1879 and into 1880 before coming home to face prosecution on unrelated charges of malfeasance in office in Halifax. Although he was never convicted, most observers and party leaders assumed his political career was over, until O'Hara surprised almost everyone by returning to gain the nomination again in 1882. Charges of bigamy and a questionable claim of American citizenship, which had previously clouded the political air around O'Hara, were now seemingly forgotten by the party at large.[5]

One individual who had not forgotten, however, was O'Hara's nemesis, former state legislator and perennial gadfly Israel Abbott. The stocky, irrepressible carpenter detested O'Hara, and said so publicly on many occasions; he had stubbornly supported O'Hara's independent Republican opponent, "spoiler" James H. Harris, in the 1878 general election before unsuccessfully seeking the nomination himself in 1882. Abbott's antipathy was rooted partly in his abundant dislike for O'Hara's methods and corrupt associates, but there

4. Other Republican candidates in 1878 were James H. Harris (1832–1891), a black journalist, and Joseph Williams Thorne of Warren County, an eccentric white politician whose atheism and unorthodox lifestyle never failed to excite the derision of Democrats. The two drew more than 4,600 votes from O'Hara. Fraud was an undeniable factor in the counting of ballots in 1878, but O'Hara could never prove it cost him the election.

5. Anderson, "James O'Hara," 101–25. Although O'Hara was never convicted on any of the fifteen charges of malfeasance, he did plead *nolo contendere* to some of them; the charges were relatively minor, including "double-dipping" by being paid to act as county attorney while serving as chairman of the county board. O'Hara's often disreputable associates, combined with the cozy dealings of Halifax County politics, made him a suspicious figure to outsiders and opponents alike.

were curious racial overtones to his crusade as well. The pure-black Abbott saw the half-white O'Hara as both a carpetbagger and an unscrupulous hypocrite, an opportunist who cared nothing for fellow blacks and who set the worst possible example for the race.[6]

O'Hara's second nomination in 1882 had badly fragmented the district GOP, his defeat of incumbent Orlando Hubbs having incorporated both questionable convention tactics and a controversial alliance of sorts with the Liberal Anti-Prohibition Party. O'Hara had then run unopposed for Congress on the 1882 ballot, amid much grumbling by party regulars on both sides of the spectrum. By 1884, he had mended some if not all of the fences; engineering Abbott's selection as district convention chairman was a particularly shrewd cooptive move, though district Democrats did manage to field a candidate to oppose O'Hara that year. Wilson attorney Frederick A. Woodard posted the largest numerical Democratic vote in the district's history, establishing himself as a strong future contender.[7]

Yet O'Hara's sweeping reelection victory backfired on his ill-fated party, which lost badly at the local and county levels. This included the loss of previously secure legislative seats to Democrats in Northampton and Halifax Counties, doomed by the presence of rival slates on the ballots—encouraged, some said, by the Democrats and tacitly approved by O'Hara himself. As a result, the state house lost more than half its previous black membership in one election. This had little effect on the separate Craven senate race, which George White had won rather easily, but produced all-Democratic delegations in the Republican strongholds of Halifax and Northampton Counties.[8]

In 1884, therefore, James O'Hara was at the peak of his political career, but he was also perched on the edge of an unseen abyss. The statewide election debacle undermined the relatively new but now-accepted theory that the

6. Anderson, *Race and Politics*, 135. He cites reports in the *Salisbury Star of Zion*, *Raleigh News and Observer*, *New Bern Daily Journal*, and *Washington Bee*, all during September and October 1886.

7. Frederick Woodard went on to serve as Second District congressman from 1893 to 1897, twice defeating Henry Cheatham; in turn, White defeated Woodard in 1896.

8. Only nine blacks—six house members and three senators—were elected in 1884, seven of them from the Black Second. New Hanover and Pasquotank Counties also elected black legislators. In 1882, a total of nineteen blacks had won seats in the General Assembly, twelve of them from Black Second counties.

Black Second should be represented in Congress by a black man. During his second term in office, O'Hara would come to be seen by many as a party albatross, one who could win himself but who helped no one else, even after gaining office. Led by Israel Abbott, the vocal reform-minded minority within the district party now demanded James O'Hara's red-haired scalp in 1886, setting the stage for even worse losses as the Republican Party threatened to disintegrate into squabbling miniparties with no hope of success.[9]

Republican leaders also faced a peculiar dilemma as the Second District opened its congressional nominating convention in August. Since 1874, the party had regularly alternated the race of its nominees every two or four years, although this process did not always guarantee victory. In 1884, O'Hara had been the first incumbent to be renominated in more than a decade, and white Republicans were anxious to deny him a third term, in order to maintain some semblance of the biracial tradition. Col. Robert E. ("Q") Young, a white leader from Vance County, reportedly had enough delegate commitments to win the nomination, prompting threats from O'Hara to run as an independent if he lost the nomination to Young or any other white challenger.[10]

O'Hara supporters attempted to rig the convention by ordering all delegates off the floor as soon as it opened, a futile gesture by executive committee chairman William W. Watson, no longer in the legislature but still active in regional politics. Abbott's reformers then brought about their own brand of chaos by literally usurping the chair and nominating Abbott while ignoring O'Hara supporters completely and abruptly adjourning. A separate convention of "regulars" met immediately afterward in the same room to renominate O'Hara, while "Q" Young, furious at the bedlam, refused even to allow his name to be placed in nomination.[11]

Even though formally nominated by his faction, Israel Abbott did not expect to win the race. His goal was to defeat the man he described as "unfit for public office." Abbott's presence on the ballot would eventually siphon off 5,020 Republican votes, more than enough to tip the election away from

9. Editorial, *Salisbury Star of Zion*, 6 August 1886. Editor John C. Dancy said O'Hara had no one but himself to blame: if he "had only proved half so true to his friends, who risked everything in his support, as he has to his enemies, who have spared no opportunity to stab and destroy him, he would not now find them indifferent and careless."

10. *RN&O*, July–August 1886.

11. "A Double-Barreled Ticket," ibid., 26 August 1886.

O'Hara to Democratic challenger Furnifold Simmons. Abbott was even briefly listed as the winner of the race by the *New York Times*, based on fragmentary returns, although the newspaper quickly corrected its error. But the feisty reformer would not enjoy the fruits of his "victory" for long. Finally the front-runner for his party's 1888 congressional nomination, he collapsed and died suddenly in the spring of 1887, when he was only forty-four.[12]

Abbott's untimely death was just one confusing factor in the larger political landscape after 1886. The state Republican Party itself was split, threatening to compound the losses of 1884 into a disastrous landslide of defeat. Even as he weakened the party structure within his own district, O'Hara's growing personal power within the statewide GOP was apparently infecting the structure at higher levels. The renewed struggle between the party's old-line faction and the Craven reformers would become an important chapter in the long-term unraveling of black solidarity and Republican dominance in northeastern North Carolina, the party's stronghold.[13]

In Craven County, the personal feud between white Republican sheriff Mayer Hahn and his wealthy white opponent Daniel Stimson erupted with renewed force, producing a bizarre coalition between Craven County Democrats and those Republicans backing Stimson, both black and white. The coalition's goals were to elect Stimson and former congressman Hubbs, now seeking the office of county register of deeds, on the one hand, and Democratic candidates for the North Carolina house and senate, on the other.[14]

Such a volatile situation might have frightened away a less determined candidate, but George White pursued his own goal tenaciously. He remained the clear choice of "reform" Republicans in his own county, and his virtues were trumpeted weekly by the *People's Advocate*, which backed the anti-O'Hara challenge but not the "Coalition Mongrel" ticket between reformers and Democrats. Democrats outside the county races, including Furnifold

12. *New York Times*, 5 November 1886; *New Bern Daily Journal*, 7 May 1887. The *Times* corrected its error one day later. Abbott died May 6, 1887.

13. Although Craven was not the largest county in the district, its unified leadership had long helped the Republican Party maintain its relative strength in the Black Second, both by supplying strong candidates and by its consistent voting results. This steadying influence declined after the failure of the 1886 coalition, but the county's reassignment to the Third District was a distinct disadvantage to the Second's GOP during the 1890s.

14. Anderson, *Race and Politics*, 136–8. Anderson gives a detailed account of the coalition's aims and reasoning.

Simmons, eagerly supported the coalition, since it seemed to promise much at little political cost to them. Simmons, for instance, expected to gain a significant share of the votes cast by Craven's black majority; he did gain some of those votes, but most still went to O'Hara in the end. The reformers' standard bearer, however, fared badly; Abbott carried just two counties, Edgecombe and Warren.[15]

Even more Byzantine were the frequent charges of Democratic payoffs to either O'Hara or Abbott or both, depending on the scenario, for the purpose of keeping them in the race. Simmons's former father-in-law, Col. Lotte W. Humphrey, was the reputed source of the cash, though few Craven Republicans believed the tale and even fewer cared. Humphrey was a disaffected former Democrat, still influential, but his eccentric behavior bordered on the comical; the most plausible theory was that Humphrey and others coaxed Abbott into staying on the ticket by fueling his intense dislike for O'Hara, knowing the only way to ensure Simmons's election was to split the black vote. O'Hara was the more likely recipient of any cash payoffs, although both he and Abbott may have accepted Humphrey's assistance.[16]

By the end of July, George White had gained five of the eleven votes he needed to win the nomination for solicitor in August, through his careful attention to detail and relentless courting of black leaders in the five other counties. A total of twenty votes would be cast at the nominating convention, set for the middle of August in Jackson. Northampton, for instance, had delivered three of its four delegates to White at its own county convention in Jackson July 23, despite an all-out effort there by Collins—"the ablest effort of

15. Ibid., 347 (Table 15). The *People's Advocate* supported Leonidas J. Moore for the congressional nomination, with Abbott its fallback choice; the *New Bern Republican* supported the coalition. Both disappeared after the 1886 election. New Bern's Democratic *Journal* strongly supported Simmons and the coalition both for partisan and pragmatic reasons: Democratic legislators were viewed as more sensible for Craven. As many as 42 percent of Abbott's 5,020 votes came from Edgecombe, with 30 percent from Warren; Abbott received fewer than 300 votes in Craven, barely enough to tip Craven to Simmons, and only 42 votes in Jones, Lenoir, and Greene Counties combined.

16. Josephus Daniels, *Tar Heel Editor* (Westport Conn.: Greenwood Press, 1974), 499–500. In these memoirs, first published in 1939, Daniels alleged that Humphrey had paid the campaign expenses of both Abbott and O'Hara; the Abbott camp claimed at the time that O'Hara helped Democratic candidates to repay Humphrey's generosity. As Anderson points out, Humphrey did not create the Republican divisions, but made good use of them; see *Race and Politics,* 137.

his life," according to one Craven newspaper. The solicitor had warned delegates there of the General Assembly's alleged plans to remove Craven County
from the Second District entirely, making it useless to choose anyone from
Craven for the post. If White were elected solicitor, this would trigger an
eventual vacancy in the post, allowing the governor to appoint a Democrat in
his place, or so the scenario went.[17]

Few believed in the merits of Collins's political charge, which was improbable at best; it was a desperate ruse doubtless inspired by the far cleverer J. C. L.
Harris, to hold onto office for Collins by attempting to disqualify his opponent
in advance, if only in the minds of the voters. Even the Democratic leadership
would be loath to tinker with its own redistricting plan, lest the once-a-
decade tradition be abandoned by future legislatures. And declaring a vacancy
in an elected position was unlikely to succeed, since all the affected solicitor
need do was move his residence to any other district county before the new
law took effect.[18]

Craven County had previously promised its two votes to its favorite son,
George White. Bertie had apparently split its two votes between Collins and
challenger Francis Winston. White now had five votes, and realistically expected to win four more delegates on July 31 from Warren County, based on
discussions with his senate colleague Jacob H. Montgomery and Richard
Ward, Warren's member of the 1885 house. So the magic number for White in
late July was reduced to two votes of the eight left uncommitted. These would
be decided during the first week of August at county conventions in
Edgecombe and Halifax.[19]

Since Halifax was sure to support its own favorite son Collins with at least

17. "Judicial District Convention," notice, and "Craven Co. to be taken out of the district,"
editorial, both in *New Bern People's Advocate*, 31 July 1886. The notice from Second District
chairman J. B. Willis of New Bern listed the number of delegates from each county to the upcoming judicial convention. The editorial analyzed Collins's charge and found it unsound, since
the state constitution guaranteed a four-year term to every elected solicitor. Although the
General Assembly was free to redistrict the state at will, the newspaper claimed (inaccurately)
that the legislature could not act on one county alone.

18. Ibid. The *People's Advocate* briskly dismissed the claim, suggesting district voters reward
Collins with "a prize to stay at home for the next four years for his effort. . . . Any man who . . .
call[s] himself a lawyer ought to know better than to proclaim such a false doctrine."

19. Ibid. The newspaper expected White to win endorsements from both Edgecombe and
Halifax, but there is no other indication of his success in the Halifax convention.

three of its four votes, White was forced to cultivate votes from Edgecombe. This was a delicate move, since Edgecombe executive committee chairman William W. Watson supported Congressman O'Hara, whose main opponent happened to be Israel Abbott, George White's close friend. White had sensibly avoided involvement in the intraparty congressional fracas, although he almost certainly favored Abbott's challenge privately. The O'Hara spectacle had long been a source of private embarrassment for White, who could only have frowned upon the well-publicized excesses of O'Hara's personal and political life. Since opposing O'Hara publicly would hardly help him gain votes, White concentrated instead on his own positive ties to Tarboro's elder statesman, former two-term legislator Henry Cherry; White was already contemplating his third marriage, this time to Cherry's youngest daughter, Cora Lena.[20]

Through the good offices of his future father-in-law, George White shrewdly reminded both Watson and Clinton W. Battle of his support for them during the forged-voucher scandal five years earlier. Watson had faced expulsion from the house, and Battle, also a house member, had been briefly implicated in the affair. White had not been linked to the scandal, but had witnessed the hearing in the closing days of the General Assembly. The final vote had been relatively close, but Watson managed to escape expulsion; he was weak, gullible, and perhaps even dishonest, yet the evidence was inconclusive. In the end White had voted against expelling Watson; he may have been privately indignant that any fellow black leader could risk humiliating his race in so foolish a fashion, but he did not choose to criticize Watson publicly. For one thing, they had worked together closely on educational issues; for another, for any fellow black to speak out against him would have been deadly to Watson's chances at the time, as both surely knew.[21]

Watson, Battle, and other Edgecombe leaders agreed to withhold support from Collins for solicitor in observance of the two-term rule, and Edgecombe awarded its four votes to White. Whatever the outcome in Halifax, the nomination now seemed to belong to George White, once it was ratified by the

20. Cora Lena Cherry, twenty-one, apparently worked as a schoolteacher in Tarboro at the time. Her father had served in the General Assembly from 1868 through 1870.

21. The Watson affair was regularly recounted by the *Raleigh News and Observer* during the first half of March 1881. As many Democrats as Republicans voted to acquit Watson; at least one (white) Republican house member said that the evidence had "greatly shaken" his belief in Watson's innocence, but he still voted no.

district convention. Collins could continue to make his sensational predictions for the Second District if he wished; it should make no difference now, under ordinary circumstances. But as White was soon to discover, nothing in the Second was ever settled for long; the district's delegates did convene in Jackson on August 18, as scheduled, but never managed to take a vote on the nomination for solicitor.

Instead, the convention "broke up in a row" without formally nominating anyone, although White was clearly entitled to the endorsement. John Collins immediately claimed in a printed circular that he had been "fairly and honestly nominated" and intended to remain in the race, a common tactic among losing candidates of the period. Collins may have been persuaded to make such a move by O'Hara, but he probably received equally strong encouragement from Democratic leaders, who had chosen attorney William A. Dunn of Halifax as their standard bearer in the fall race. Meanwhile, candidate Francis Winston denounced the convention's "mob rule," denying that anyone had been nominated but removing himself from the solicitor's race; he went on to accept a nomination for the state senate seat shared by Northampton and Bertie, last held by Democrat Thomas Mason.[22]

Now it would be left up to the voters of the Second District to decide who should be their next solicitor. And while accounts of the campaign are scarce, one report from Warrenton in late September indicates that rallies were lively affairs, particularly when they involved joint appearances by the various claimants to be the "regular nominees of the Republican party." During a recess court proceedings, "these colored candidates began their harangues, O'Hara and Collins holding forth in the courthouse and the other parties [including Abbott] out-doors. . . . These speakers proceeded to 'lambaste' the opposition . . . each declaring his determination to expose the frauds by which the other obtained his so-called nomination," wrote the *News and Observer*.[23]

22. Anderson, *Race and Politics*, 134. The *Salisbury Star of Zion* claimed on 27 August 1886 that White would have been nominated had a vote been taken, but the *New Bern Daily Journal* of 25 September 1886 seemed to prefer Collins's version of the events. The *Raleigh News and Observer* summarized Collins's circular on 25 August 1886 and publicized Francis Winston's charges a week after the convention. Winston won his senate race but switched to the Democrats in the 1890s and became an architect of the white-supremacy campaigns.

23. "Politics," *RN&O*, 24 September 1886. White had served with Daniel R. Johnson in the 1881 house. At this rally, Johnson was vituperative but relatively restrained; during an earlier

Collins was appearing in his official capacity as district solicitor at the Warren County courthouse; George White was invited to the rally but did not attend, being represented by former state legislator Daniel R. Johnson of Warrenton. Johnson spoke in what was billed as a debate, and "for more than an hour indulged in the most indecent, dirty, profane language we ever heard from the lips of any man," according to the Raleigh correspondent. Johnson's "whole tirade of abuse was leveled at Collins for the gratification of his personal animosity . . . Collins replied to Johnson, but before he got through telling of Johnson's iniquities, etc., Johnson's strikers made such a fuss that he was compelled to stop."[24]

Solicitor Collins managed to win that "debate," in the reporter's estimation, but it made little difference in the outcome at the polls. George White went on to win the November 2 general election by a solid and surprisingly large plurality, carrying five of the six counties in the district. His young Democratic challenger, William Dunn, did manage to prevent a clean sweep by winning his own Halifax County, but two-term incumbent Collins came in a distant third in all six counties.[25]

White had survived the Democratic "triangular contest" trap, which defeated Congressman O'Hara that same year, by receiving at least 49 percent of the vote in his own three-way race. His name drew the approval of more than 10,000 voters, out of about 21,000 votes tallied; his respective margins over opponents Dunn and Collins were about 2,000 and 8,500 votes, according to one journalistic account. Dunn continued to have a promising future in the Democratic Party, but Collins's political career was now essentially over.[26]

---

antiprohibition drive, he had reportedly paraded through Warrenton with "the holy Bible in one hand and a bottle of whisky in the other, telling the negroes that whisky had been here as long as the Bible and they must vote to keep it here."

24. Ibid.

25. *RN&O*, 2 October 1886. William A. Dunn made at least one joint campaign appearance with Furnifold Simmons at Vanceboro in Craven County on October 2, but Dunn received little newspaper coverage.

26. "Official Canvass," ibid., 28 November 1886; *New Bern Daily Journal*, 5 November 1886. White's victory margin fell just short of an absolute majority, at 49.6 percent; the official statewide canvass gave White 10,584 votes, Dunn 8,639, and Collins 2,100. White's official margin over Dunn was 1,945 votes; over Collins, 8,484 votes. Ironically, the closeness of the Craven race was a crucial factor. White won a close plurality there, just 73 votes ahead of Dunn; since White won the rest of the district by more than 50 percent, even with his sizable loss in Halifax,

George White carried his home county of Craven by only a slight plurality, fewer than one hundred votes ahead of Dunn, but the separate efforts there of the mongrel coalition did not fare nearly as well. Although Daniel Stimson did not poll the largest number of votes, he was initially awarded the Craven sheriff's post after a county canvass threw out a significant number of Mayer Hahn's ballots, but the challenger's victory was short-lived. Less than a year into his term, the North Carolina Supreme Court overturned the Craven canvass, reinstated Hahn's disqualified ballots, and awarded him the victory. The coalition's two Democratic legislative contenders had even shorter celebrations; both were soon stripped of their own victories by the General Assembly and the "regular" Republicans seated in the house and senate, respectively, although they served less than full terms in the brief legislative session.[27]

Whatever confusion the mongrel coalition might have caused in other races, it had no effect on White's victory or the strength of his new mandate. Even New Bern's partisan *Daily Journal*, which had vigorously backed Dunn in the race, was forced to admit that the new solicitor was "a pretty fair lawyer and a man of good character." In an editorial printed a week after the election, the newspaper urged its readers to "make the best of the situation and sustain him when he is right and condemn him when he is wrong. . . . We have heard of but one complaint against him, or rather fears entertained that he would be disagreeable to members of the bar and others connected with the court, but he assures us that many will be disappointed in this respect. We hope it may be so."[28]

The *Journal* was not the only observer with a positive reaction to White's victory. The black community of the nation was also watching this race closely. The *New York Freeman*, the most widely read contemporary black newspaper in America, had publicized White's candidacy as early as June, in a

Collins's apparent alliance with the coalition in Craven may have alienated enough voters to make the difference. Collins ran unsuccessfully for the North Carolina house from Halifax in 1894, his last race.

27. *RN&O*, 19 February 1887. The Democratic "winners" were Senator Charles C. Clark and Representative William B. Lane. Republicans George Green Jr. (senate) and John E. Hussey (house) were awarded the seats by their respective legislative bodies, Hussey on January 26 and Green on February 18.

28. "What Darkened the Hole," editorial, *New Bern Daily Journal*, 9 November 1886; "George H. White," *New Bern People's Advocate*, undated.

front-page reprint of the effusive *People's Advocate* editorial endorsing White's candidacy.[29] White may not have been aware of the reprint, for when he wrote to *Freeman* editor T. Thomas Fortune—his old Howard classmate—two months after the election to praise Fortune's literary work, he mentioned his new office only as an apparent afterthought.

With a typical journalist's appreciation of the news value of White's letter, Fortune reprinted it in the *Freeman*. "I have been duly commissioned by the Governor of the State [in December] and have qualified as Solicitor of the Second Judicial District, and now enter upon a term of four years," White said in closing, after praising both the newspaper ("a constant and welcome visitor") and Fortune's two recent books. White had exceptionally strong praise for the books, which he said he had recently received. "I have never seen a book that I read with more . . . trust than I did yours. Both brim full of truth—too much truth for the politician," White wrote. "If the present generation does not fully realize the good work you are doing, the time will, yes, very soon come, when your efforts for the race will be properly appreciated. You and your works, like truth, 'crushed to earth, shall rise again.'"[30]

Fortune and White may have met only fleetingly while students at Howard in 1876, but their enduring friendship was now assured. Almost like clockwork, a detailed and flattering sketch of George White—one of the longest printed during his lifetime—appeared just three weeks later on the front page of the *Freeman*, along with a portrait of the new solicitor. The article was written by Edward Lofton Thornton, Washington-based correspondent for the New York weekly, and it described White's legal prowess in glowing terms: "The highest achievements of this distinguished leader have been made in the field of his chosen profession, where he has appeared in almost every conceivable case known to the criminal law." The new solicitor would "realize from three to four thousand dollars a year" from his "snug position," Thornton estimated.[31]

Despite his recent success, however, White was no "mere politician, but a lawyer devoted purely to the peculiar offices of the law and making a high and

29. Letter to the editor from George H. White, dated January 3, 1887, *New York Freeman*, 15 January 1887.

30. Ibid.; also "Lawyer and Legislator."

31. *New York Freeman*, 5 February 1887. This flowery compliment was also a subtle dig at O'Hara and Collins.

honorable station for himself and the race." Thus began the first term of the "only colored solicitor and prosecuting attorney in America," as Thornton dubbed him. The *Freeman* and its successor, the *New York Age*, would continue to track White's career, along with the *Washington Bee* and other black weeklies. By year's end, he would also be featured as one of the outstanding black men in America in the first of many such compilations, this one written by fellow Howard graduate William J. Simmons. George White's future on the national stage was becoming more and more a vital possibility.[32]

If there was a sad note to White's victory, it was the absence from the political scene of the one lawyer to whom he had seemingly dedicated his legal career. William J. Clarke, his former law tutor and longtime adviser, did not live to see his protégé gain the office of solicitor, much less his later success at the congressional level. After a lengthy period of declining health, Clarke had died in January 1886, just ten months before the election. His legacy—independence and integrity above all—would now be practiced as a fitting tribute by his most illustrious pupil.[33]

Clarke's death further narrowed White's inner circle of emotional support. There were new political friendships, of course, but few of any personal depth; above all, the lawyer needed a supportive home environment. White had been a widower for more than four years when the *New York Freeman* printed its lengthy biographical sketch of him; correspondent Thornton described White's young daughter Della as a "precocious little miss of seven years," but made no mention of White's plans to marry again that winter. Thornton may not have known, of course, even though the ceremony took place less than six weeks later. On March 16, 1887, White wed Cora Lena Cherry, now a twenty-two-year-old schoolteacher, in a ceremony later described in a neighboring newspaper as "the event in high colored society in Tarboro last week."[34]

32. Simmons, *Men of Mark*, 536–7. Simmons, an 1873 graduate of Howard, printed sketches of nearly two hundred notable black men, ranging from contemporary politicians like Blanche K. Bruce and educators like Booker T. Washington to legendary figures like Toussaint L'Ouverture of Haiti and slave rebellion leader Denmark Veazie. White was one of four North Carolinians listed; the others were John S. Leary, Joseph C. Price, and John C. Dancy.

33. "Circular to the Freemen of the Sixth Congressional District of North Carolina," broadside, William John Clarke Papers, SHC; "Clarke," *DNCB*. Clarke himself had run for Congress from the old Sixth District (Raleigh) in 1849, when he was still a Democrat. Clarke was sixty-six when he died; his wife, always in frail health, died two months later.

34. *Wilson Advance*, 27 March 1887.

Miss Cherry was described by the newspaper as "a very handsome quadroon," indicating that both her parents were of mixed race. Just how George White became acquainted with Cora Lena Cherry is not known, but a meeting could easily have been arranged by one or both of her older sisters, both of whom lived near New Bern and were married to prominent black professionals. Half-sister Georgianna Cherry Green lived in Wilmington after 1879; she may have spent time in New Bern in the mid-1880s with her husband, former state legislator Eustace E. Green, who served on the normal school faculty there in 1884 and 1885. Louisa S. Cherry Cheatham, Cora Lena's only full sister, lived in nearby Plymouth, where she and Cora Lena had both taught music at the state normal school; Louisa's husband, future congressman Henry Plummer Cheatham, was the Plymouth school's principal from 1883–1885. As prominent educators, Henry Cheatham and George White were already acquainted by 1885, when both had served on the educational executive committee of the black state teachers' association; soon enough, their friendly competition would turn to serious political rivalry.[35]

The Cherry family was a large and prosperous one. Patriarch Henry Cherry was a carpenter and merchant with an active political streak; he had served as a delegate to the state's 1868 constitutional convention before being elected to the General Assembly from Edgecombe County. He also served at least one term as an Edgecombe County commissioner, and was a member of the county's black public school committee in 1883. His wife, Mary Ann Jones Cherry, was a well-known figure in her own right as a noted religious leader and the owner of valuable local real estate.[36]

35. Ibid.; author's telephone interview with Rudolph Knight, 30 March 1998; Edward B. Reuter, *The Mulatto in the United States* (New York: Haskell House, 1969). *Quadroon* was generally defined as the offspring of a white parent and a mulatto parent; a mulatto was the offspring of a white parent and a Negro parent. *Quadroon* was more often used informally to designate the presence of one-quarter Negro blood. Tarboro historian Knight says *handsome* was applied to Miss Cherry in lieu of terms like pretty, which were reserved by white newspapers for describing white women. Georgianna Green spent much of her adult life in Macon, where she and her husband moved in the late 1880s. Louisa Cherry appears to have met Henry Cheatham while he was a student at Shaw University in Raleigh.

36. Foner, *Freedom's Lawmakers*, 44; U.S. Census, manuscript on microfilm, Edgecombe County, N.C., 1860; Robert Kenzer, *Enterprising Southerners: Black Economic Success in North Carolina, 1865–1915* (Charlottesville: University Press of Virginia, 1997), 86. Henry Cherry was born a slave in the 1830s but was living as a free man in Edgecombe County by 1860.

The couple had wed in March 1861, indicating that both had been free before the war, since their marriage would not have been registered otherwise. Cherry is said to have been born a slave, but had been freed and had moved to Edgecombe County by 1860, where he was lodging with another family, according to that year's census. His wife appears to have been born free; she was certainly free by the late 1850s, when she gave birth to her first two children, from a liaison with a white Edgecombe County plantation owner named Henry Lloyd.[37]

Lloyd died in Philadelphia, Pennsylvania, in early 1860, bequeathing Miss Jones a reputed total of fifteen to twenty thousand dollars in cash and real estate, in addition to sizable cash legacies for her two children. According to one local historian, the union of Mary Ann Jones and Henry Cherry was one of both love and good fortune, since the bride was "quite well off" at the time of the wedding. Her two daughters by Lloyd received $2,500 bequests from their father, to be held in trust until their twenty-first birthdays. Georgianna, born in 1857, was apparently adopted by Henry Cherry and lived in the Cherry household in 1870; she went on to attend the new Saint Augustine's College for blacks and become a schoolteacher before her marriage to Eustace Green in 1879. Less is known about her sister, Mary Ann, who evidently lived elsewhere in 1870; at her death in 1880, she named her husband, Mark Parker, as beneficiary of her estate, with "the children of my sister Louisa Cherry" named as contingent heirs.[38]

37. Interview with Rudolph Knight; U.S. Census, Edgecombe County, 1860. Mary Ann Jones was born free on or near the Lloyd plantation and lived there until Lloyd's death; her mother, Charity, a mulatto whose precise racial ancestry is not known, was also free. The will of John Lloyd was probated in Edgecombe County; he reputedly left $10,000 to each of his daughters by Miss Jones. She had $500 in real estate and $5,000 in personal property in 1860.

38. The wills of Henry Lloyd (probated in February 1860) and Mary Ann Parker (probated in April 1880) are on file at the office of the Edgecombe County Clerk of Superior Court, Tarboro. In addition to the cash bequests for her daughters, Lloyd left Mary Ann Jones her house and additional land, along with a $100 annual stipend for the next ten years; excepting some land given to a third illegitimate daughter in Martin County, the rest of the estate went to Lloyd's aunt and other relatives. Mary Ann Parker's age is uncertain; she appears to have been born in 1859, according to the 1860 census, but was already married when her will was drawn up in 1873. Her will specifies that if her husband died without issue, then the land would revert in equal portions to sister Louisa's children—as yet unborn—and to the children of three other persons, apparently her husband's relatives.

Over the next two decades, Henry and Mary Ann Cherry had eight children of their own, including three born during the war: son Henry H., born
1862; and daughters Louisa S., born 1863, and Cora Lena, born on Christmas
Day in 1864. Five more sons followed: Charles C., born in 1867; William,
born in 1871; Earnest A., born in 1874; Clarence E., born in 1876; and Claude,
born in 1882.[39]

Henry Cherry lived in Tarboro until the late 1890s, running both his car-
pentry business and a combination grocery-liquor store in town. About 1895
he entered a business partnership with York D. Garrett, a transplanted merchant and politician, but the partnership was dissolved in 1898 when Cherry
and Garrett had a political quarrel. Henry Cherry died shortly afterward, in
his early to mid-sixties. His widow lived alone, according to the 1900 Tarboro
census; both her mother, Charity Jones, and five of her ten children had also
died by that time. Mrs. Cherry lived on until at least her eightieth year; at her
death in 1917, she had outlived all but three of her children.[40]

During the eight years following his marriage to Cora Lena, much of
George White's time would be spent on the road, traversing the Second District and winning the admiration, often grudging but unmistakable, of both
the white judges and white lawyers before whom he now performed his official
duties. His "animated and almost florid" speaking style and his undeniable
eloquence made him an extremely convincing and effective prosecutor.
White's dedication to the job was obvious, for he handled as many as forty
cases per court day.[41] He also made no secret of his utter disdain for lawbreakers, regardless of their race.

39. Ibid.; Kenzer, *Enterprising Southerners*, 86; U.S. Census, manuscript on microfilm,
Edgecombe County and Tarboro, N.C., 1870, 1880, and 1900. The names and birth years of all
but one of the Cherry children are taken from the Cherry household entries for 1880; Claude,
the youngest, is listed separately in the 1900 census. Charity Jones lived with Mary Ann Jones in
1860, then with the Cherry family in both 1870 and 1880. According to Kenzer, Cherry refused
to support Garrett in an 1898 legislative race; Garrett lost, and never took on another business
partner afterward.

40. U.S. Census, Edgecombe County, 1900; interview with Rudolph Knight. Mary Ann
Jones was born in April 1837 and died about twelve years after her daughter Cora Lena, who died
in January 1905.

41. Reid, "A Biography," 87; "Hon. George H. White, State Solicitor of the Second Judicial
District of North Carolina." According to Thornton, "The Solicitor is an eloquent public
speaker . . . his style is animated and almost florid, but he has the necessary elements of eloquence."

One jurist, a former legislative colleague familiar with White's work, later described him in a fascinating vignette of the period:

Sweating and roaring, the big yellow fellow [White] would rush at the jury exclaiming, "Guilty? Yes, gentlemen, of course he's guilty. Why, just watch his capers. He waits twell [*sic*] the moon goes down, then he puts guano sacks under his shoes to hide his tracks, and he slips up to the back of the hog pen and cuts that pig's throat, so he can't squeal, and he runs. *Now wa'n't that just like a nigger?*" (emphasis in original)[42]

This plea for the conviction of a Negro before a white jury was vintage White theatrics: amusing, pointed, and deadly effective. The writer was re-tired superior court judge Robert W. Winston, a former senate colleague who praised White's vigor, noting "he was always on the job," since his salary as prosecutor depended on the number of convictions he obtained. White was not always the single prosecutor, but was assisted in specific cases by privately hired attorneys, as Winston also recalled. One such Northampton case, in which two disreputable but apparently innocent blacks charged with arson had hired the "strongest all-around lawyer" in the area, was a prime example; it produced not one but two assistant prosecutors for the plaintiff, the power-ful U.S. senator Matt W. Ransom, who was obviously determined to have the pair convicted, despite the slim evidence against them.[43]

The biracial trio of prosecutors succeeded in convincing the jury, but sharp words between the white defense attorney and one of the two white prosecu-tors nearly led to an old-fashioned duel in court just before the jury reached its guilty verdict. Judge Winston stepped in to defuse the situation; the trial had convinced him that neither defendant was guilty, but he was reluctant to set the verdict aside lest they be lynched once they left the courthouse. So Winston called all four attorneys into his chambers to suggest his strategy: set the prisoners free without punishment, ordering them to leave the county and

42. Winston, *It's a Far Cry*, 210. Winston (1860–1944), a Democrat, came from a remark-ably influential family; one older brother was the redoubtable Francis D. Winston (1857–1941), who had opposed White and Collins for solicitor in 1886. Another brother, George T. Winston (1852–1932), was president of the University of North Carolina, and a kinsman was Duncan C. Winston, whom John Collins defeated for solicitor in 1882.

43. Matthew Whitaker Ransom (1826–1904) was a U.S. senator from 1872 to 1895; he later served as U.S. minister to Mexico under Presidents McKinley and Roosevelt.

never return for their own safety. The attorneys agreed, and the plan was implemented: the defendants were discharged, safely escorted out of the county, and no lynching occurred. The two combatant attorneys settled their differences peacefully, and White presumably received his salary in the case, even though no one went to jail.[44]

George White's no-nonsense actions as a prosecutor won him respect in all quarters, from both other judges and lawyers whom he regularly defeated in court. He was described by one Raleigh newspaper as a "terror to evildoers," by another as "having more ability than any other negro in the state. [He] makes a first-rate speech." Yet White was unfailingly fair in his courtroom performances, full of righteous wrath for the obvious wrongdoer, regardless of race, while equally determined that lawful, fair punishments be administered and nothing more.[45]

White's reputation for courtroom impartiality and "great native ability" remained universal, even after his death. Nevertheless, two local historians hastened to remind white readers that White's "downfall" had been caused by "his desire for social equality." His increasingly vocal opposition to lynching became another factor in this reversal of public attitude; he would later emphasize this in thundering speeches before Congress. While his feelings against vigilante justice may have stemmed from his childhood, his experience as a prosecutor could only sharpen his widely unpopular but principled drive to make lynching a federal crime.[46]

44. Winston, *It's a Far Cry*, 210–1. Robert Burton was the defense attorney. The private solicitors were William H. Day, who had assisted O'Hara in his 1878 legal actions to reverse his election loss, and Fabius H. Busbee.

45. *Raleigh Signal*, 29 March 1888, cited in Joseph Elmore, "North Carolina Negro Congressmen," 161; "Jackson Notes," *RN&O*, 4 October 1890; Josephus Daniels, *Editor in Politics* (Chapel Hill: University of North Carolina Press, 1941), 363. A *News and Observer* correspondent in Jackson described White's performance during a superior court session during his reelection campaign. Presiding was Judge Spier Whitaker, a former state Democratic chairman, who "loses less time and is more systematic in all the business of this court than any judge I have yet seen on the bench." Whitaker, a close associate of onetime congressman W. H. "Buck" Kitchin, had proudly told Daniels in 1888 of perfecting his "system" of suppressing the black vote in the Second District.

46. J. Kelly Turner and John L. Bridgers Jr., *History of Edgecombe County, North Carolina* (Raleigh, N.C.: Edwards and Broughton, 1920), 287. White was described as a "man of great native ability, and had the reputation of being impartial in his prosecutions. . . . His greatest weak-

George White rarely laid aside his principles, although his pragmatic approach to prosecution may have occasionally trapped him in uncomfortable positions. Such was the case with juries and their racial composition. While White was equally effective before juries of either race, he was practical: all evidence notwithstanding, when a defendant was black, a white jury would be more likely to convict him. All black lawyers learned this early on, and even black editors acknowledged it. Often, it had less to do with the defendant than with the race of the lawyer; the subtler side effects of racial tension, such as the perverse hostility of many less affluent black jurors to black lawyers, sometimes worked against a defendant with a black attorney. As a black prosecutor, White was especially sensitive to this; he had spoken at a statewide convention of black leaders in 1882 on this subject, just before his first unsuccessful campaign for solicitor.[47]

But even in the black-majority counties of the Second Judicial District, it was fairly easy to obtain an all-white jury, for most jurors called to serve in all counties were white men. Registering to vote alone did not guarantee jury service; property ownership and payment of one's taxes were the guiding factors in most locations. In Craven County, for instance, black citizens accounted for two-thirds of the population through the 1890s, but never for more than a quarter of jury panels, usually no more than "a scattering." Under these circumstances, obtaining an all-white jury was certainly not difficult. In any event, it was hardly hypocritical for a prosecutor to act in the best interests of the state which he served; yet, mindful of the interests of his own race, George White continued to support the cause of black participation in the jury system.[48]

Across the Black Second and beyond, the situation was little different from that in Craven, even in those few counties with higher percentages of

---

ness was his desire for social equality, which eventually resulted in his rejection by not only the white people of the county, but also by his race."

47. See the *Washington Bee*, 11 May 1901, for the opinion of lawyer-editor W. Calvin Chase, as well as a similar view from a black newspaper in Charleston, South Carolina.

48. Watson, *History of New Bern*, 549. "During the 1870s and the fusion years, a scattering of blacks sat on [Craven] juries, sometimes composing as much as twenty-five percent of the panels," according to Watson; juries of mixed race were apparently acceptable in Craven in those years, if not elsewhere. White continued to encourage black participation in the system, even after disfranchisement of black voters in the South.

black residents. Jury lists for superior court could be virtually all white, as in Northampton County in 1892, when only 1 of the 54 jurors called was black. In Warren County in 1893, only 4 of 29 inferior-court jurors were black. Both counties had populations more than 70 percent black at the time. The participation level of blacks as jurors had declined markedly since the end of Reconstruction and North Carolina's return to Democratic control. The level had been significantly higher in many areas during the Reconstruction period; at least one Edgecombe County grand jury was five-eighths black in 1874, a height never reached there again.[49]

Yet while low in comparison to the race's actual percentage of the population, the level of black jury service remained quite high in the Second District, if judged by standards prevailing in the rest of the South, or even in other parts of North Carolina. Some counties in the state with significant black minorities, such as Carteret, never had a single black juror during Reconstruction. The level of black participation would go up once again briefly during the "fusion" era after 1894, at least in the black-majority counties, when control of the legislature passed temporarily into Populist-Republican hands. Black magistrates, who heard minor civil and criminal cases, also reappeared in many areas during this era.[50]

By the time of George White's reelection bid in 1890, his popularity had increased enough to ensure no serious opposition, at least within the ranks of his own party. Even Raleigh's *News and Observer*, later to become his scathing public critic during his congressional career, still printed favorable descriptions of him during this period. But not all white observers were so quick to agree. The *Wilson Advance*, for one, was rankled by the distasteful spectacle of White's questioning of white female witnesses in court and repelled by these apparent excesses of what it termed "Negro rule." That newspaper's editor, Josephus Daniels, went on to describe White during the 1888 campaign as the most "presumptuous, disgustingly would-be familiar negro [in] North Carolina."[51]

49. Anderson, *Race and Politics*, 318–9.

50. Ibid.; Watson, *History of New Bern*, 490; "Forty Negro Magistrates," *Wilmington Morning Star*, 20 August 1897. Watson says there were twenty-seven black magistrates in Craven alone in 1898, quoting a letter from Furnifold Simmons to U.S. senator Jeter C. Pritchard. The *Morning Star* claimed there were forty black magistrates in Wilmington in 1897.

51. *Wilson Advance*, 25 October 1888, cited in Anderson, *Race and Politics*, 207.

It is unlikely that White's behavior was actually offensive by any but the most narrow-minded standards; white judges would have intervened or reprimanded him if he had insulted a female witness, for instance, and there is no record that any judge felt rebukes necessary. It was more the idea that it could happen at all that seemed to offend Daniels, the outspoken young editor of the *Advance*; Daniels would later raise his criticism of White, whom he ardently disliked, to a level of biting racial caricature and ridicule. As White's stature in the Republican Party grew, his status as a partisan target also grew, particularly in Daniels's sight. As the highest black elected official in the state, and one of the two highest elected Republicans, George White was already highly visible. As an outspoken black Republican, he gradually became a symbol of all that seemed to be wrong with his party, despite his consistently superior performance as a solicitor and his own impeccable personal reputation. His insistence on being treated as an equal in the courtroom seemed to be the primary reason for Daniels's animosity towards him; the powerful journalist had kinder words for other, less abrasive black leaders, such as Henry Cheatham and John H. Williamson of Franklin County, whom Daniels counted as a personal friend.[52]

During the period between his two elections as solicitor, White had witnessed the disturbing growth of systemic corruption within his own political party, as well as the accompanying decline of success for the party's ticket across the Black Second. He had no responsibility for either process, for he had set a rare example of success without falling victim to greed or personal scandal. Yet his innate ambition and enviable accomplishments were taken by his critics as proof, however unfair or fallacious, that he must be capable of corruption, if not already corrupted; that he could not be bought off seems only to have infuriated such critics.

White's family ties to Henry Cheatham also threw an increasing shadow across his political path, as Cheatham became one of the Second District's premier party powers while serving as the nation's only black congressman. White's gradual rise to power might be explained by his intellect, hard work, and good luck, but Cheatham's sudden, dizzying ascent could not be ac-

52. Daniels, *Editor in Politics*, 336. Daniels used the larger forum of his *Raleigh News and Observer* to attack White with increasing viciousness after the latter's election to Congress in 1896. Daniels became secretary of the navy under President Woodrow Wilson, and later served as U.S. ambassador to Mexico.

counted for so easily. Cheatham was almost certainly in league with the most corrupt forces of his party, and no one close to him could be above suspicion. Cheatham's appearance on the scene coincided with a startling collapse of party unity in the face of North Carolina's first white-supremacy campaign in 1888. Disunity bred blame, even within the party; George White could do little to unite his party except serve as an example of integrity and perseverance. This he did relentlessly, publicly ignoring the dark rumors spread about him by Daniels and others, however painful they might be to him personally.

The proof was in the same success that others used to pillory him. George White benefitted greatly from the respect of white Republicans, many of whom were convinced that since no white contender could be nominated, White could have the job with their blessings. White was one of only a few blacks to earn even a small amount of consistent white support; he was, after all, a more effective lawyer and prosecutor than were the majority of his white colleagues. He had also become a prosperous landowner, including among his assets a large home on New Bern's Johnson Street, construction of which he completed during 1890. But his success was a mixed blessing, of course, since it did nothing to dispel rumors of susceptibility to corruption.[53]

In 1888 White purchased a large lot behind one of New Bern's most distinguished homes, the Palmer-Tisdale house, and within two years had constructed a large, late-Victorian style home on the property, incorporating the structure of a much older one-story cottage into a plain but impressive two-story residence. The new house featured interior-end chimneys, five bays, a full-length front porch, and a one-story rear ell; its lot adjoined the Palmer-Tisdale house to the west and the elegant New Bern Academy building to the south. White's growing family quickly filled the new home, which he would continue to own until 1903 and which stood several blocks and several social classes away from his earlier home on Pasteur Street.[54]

George White had now arrived as both a citizen of substance and a solid political player. Thus even in the face of both a Republican disaster and false accusations about his own behavior, White easily defeated his Democratic opponent, James M. Grizzard of Halifax, by more than 2,500 votes in the general election of 1890. White received almost 56 percent of the vote, again carrying

53. Peter B. Sandbeck, *The Historic Architecture of New Bern and Craven County* (New Bern, N.C.: Tryon Palace Commission, 1988), 285–6.

54. Ibid.

five of the district's counties; it was a virtual landslide, and the fourth straight election of a black to the post of district solicitor. It would not be the last time a black man sought the office, but it would be the last successful race by a black lawyer for a long time to come.[55]

The 1890 election was a painful experience, however, for North Carolina's Republican Party, both in the Second District and across the state. Besides White, only one other Republican was elected to a solicitor's post: future congressman Thomas Settle in the Ninth Judicial District, another party stronghold in the Winston area. Closer to home, only a handful of black legislators were elected, less than half as many as two years earlier. Only three blacks were able to win seats from Second District counties—Craven, Vance, and Warren—compared to totals of ten four years earlier and six in 1888. The Democratic rallying cry of "Negro rule" was slowly decimating their ranks.[56]

Henry Cheatham won reelection but was the lone Republican to carry a North Carolina congressional district that year. Cheatham's narrow victory over a last-minute substitute opponent had surprised many by its very closeness, although he did run ahead of Republican legislative candidates and even outpolled White by 350 votes in the six counties in which they both ran. That difference, said Cheatham's detractors, was the result of the congressman's desperate vote trading with Democrats, not of his greater popularity. If true, it would also serve as proof of White's refusal to trade votes, a fact few observers seemed to notice at the time.[57]

But even as the postelection dust settled, the political landscape was shifting beneath the feet of both candidates. The Farmers Alliance had emerged as a potent political force within the Democratic Party, sweeping aside conserv-

55. Black Republican Robert W. Williamson of Caswell was nominated for solicitor in the Second District in 1894 and 1898, but lost both races to Democrats by narrow margins.

56. Both Settle and White were reelected in 1890. Three incumbent Republican solicitors were not reelected: Thomas Munro Argo in the Fourth District, J. R. Strayhorne in the Fifth, and James M. Moody in the Twelfth. Blacks elected to the house in 1890 included Hugh Cale (Pasquotank County), John Chapman (Craven County), and James M. Watson (Vance County), a two-term veteran; Albert L. Alston of Warren was elected to the senate in 1890. A fifth black, John H. Wright of Warren, also won but was unseated after a house contest.

57. Anderson, *Race and Politics*, 184, 348 (Table 17). Cheatham received 12,467 votes for Congress in 1890 in the district's six counties, to 9,072 for Mewboorne. A larger vote total was actually tallied in the solicitor's race—21,705, of which White received 12,119 and Grizzard 9,586.

ative Democrats and upsetting the precarious balance within party leadership. As the precursor of the Populist Party in North Carolina, the Alliance would make a number of startling reforms in the General Assembly of 1891, albeit under the titular control of Democrats. By 1892, the idea of "fusion" with the Populists would seem a godsend for despairing Republicans, whose defeat in 1890 was their lowest point in decades. It was a temporary nadir, as later elections would prove, but still an omen of worse things to come if the Republican Party did not develop a way to attract more white North Carolinians as voting members.[58]

On the job, of course, George White gave little thought to politics; he seems to have been capable of a high degree of compartmentalization in his professional and personal lives, able to ignore the political implications of cases. As a result, he compiled a highly creditable record during his first term as the state's prosecutor in his district. His heavy workload included cases stemming from a wide variety of criminal acts, ranging from disorderly conduct, fraud, and larceny to arson, rape and murder; roughly two-thirds of his cases involved prosecution of black defendants. He was well prepared and methodical, bringing more than 80 percent of cases to trial and boasting an exceptionally high record for convictions upheld on appeal, with just one reversal noted in his first four years.[59]

That case had ominous racial overtones. *State of North Carolina v. Van Johnson* involved the alleged rape of Dilsey Ann Hyman, a fourteen-year-old black girl, by a man whose race was not noted (and presumed, therefore, to be white). White had argued successfully in Edgecombe Superior Court that no minor was legally capable of consenting to a mature man's physical advances, and that Van Johnson was therefore guilty of committing rape. On appeal, however, the North Carolina Supreme Court ruled that the age of the defendant was irrelevant if there was consent given; since the young woman had consented, no act of rape resulted. The Edgecombe conviction was reversed on a writ of error, and Johnson was freed in 1888.[60]

George White's personal reputation for fairness and impartiality continued

---

58. The Republicans temporarily enjoyed greater success in the 1890s, particularly after fusion with the Populists in 1894; North Carolina voters elected a Republican governor in 1896. After 1898, however, GOP prospects were decimated in the East by the loss of black votes and did not recover for nearly a century.

59. Reid, "A Biography," 86–7.

60. Ibid.

to grow during his second term as solicitor. But it was his diplomatic rather than his prosecutorial skills that proved particularly useful during a difficult incident in his home county in the early spring of 1893. White and a handful of other prominent black leaders were asked by state officials to help defuse a potentially deadly situation in James City, where residents had refused to be evicted from their homes despite a court order. A group of longtime residents of the all-black town appealed to Governor Elias Carr to stop their evictions from their homes, many established by fugitive slaves there during Union occupation of the county, but Carr instead promised to use military force if necessary to carry out the court-ordered evictions based on nonpayment of rent to the land's legal owner.[61]

More than a thousand blacks lived in the James City area, most of them descended from the runaway slaves settled there after 1862 by the Union Army. It was also a heavily Republican area, with its own school, several churches, and a police station in 1888, but little else of municipal conse-quence, according to the *New York Times*. Most of its residents worked across the river in New Bern as laborers or servants, and many used private boats or ferries to get to work; their short-lived strike for higher wages in 1881, led by Israel Abbott, had failed, mainly due to lack of support from neighboring New Bern's black population. But the attempt established an image of recalcitrance among James City residents that surprised few when it resurfaced twelve years later. Few whites, and no Democrats, dared set foot in the town without an invitation.[62]

As a private lawyer, George White had represented many local residents in successful lawsuits against the James City Ferry Company in the mid-1880s, defeating a number of better-known white attorneys in the process. Along with former congressman James O'Hara and Dr. Ezra E. Smith, the former U.S. minister to Liberia, White was among those who now intervened to me-diate the dispute, after James City residents vowed to fight rather than give up

61. Watson, *History of New Bern*, 516–8. Watson gives a brief account of the dispute; Mobley, in *James City*, deals at greater length with the complicated situation. The James City "Committee of Twelve" who appealed to Carr admitted that "the land is not ours, but the houses and the property on the land belongs to us," according to Mobley (80); the North Carolina Supreme Court dismissed that related claim. The dispute had dragged on for more than twelve years since Mary Bryan purchased the land from Evans's heirs; no rent had been paid, in many cases, since 1867.

62. Mobley, *James City*, 80; also, "No White Men Need Apply: A Town Tenanted Only By Colored People," *New York Times*, 8 April 1888.

their homes. The land underneath the homes of the "squatters" belonged legally to a wealthy white New Bern family, who had purchased it from the original owner years after it was returned to him by Union forces, according to the ruling by the state's supreme court. The current owner had refused to sell the land to the residents, but had proposed a compromise with them through short-term leases and reduced rent, an offer that residents had so far refused to consider. Sheriff William B. Lane and his deputies had attempted unsuccessfully to evict the residents after the owner obtained an eviction order in Craven Superior Court, thus provoking the residents' threats to "fight to the death."[63]

The mayor of New Bern was alarmed at the prospect, however faint, of a sympathetic uprising among his own black citizens; Matthias Manly therefore pleaded with Governor Carr on April 19 to send the First Regiment of North Carolina Militia to New Bern. Carr complied, but personally accompanied the soldiers to the scene by train, along with journalists and a committee of black leaders from Goldsboro. The governor then met with James City representatives and the mediators at the local Good Samaritan Lodge. Calmer heads eventually prevailed, under the patient arbitration of White, O'Hara, and Smith, and the community finally agreed to accept the landlord's counteroffer of three-year leases.[64]

It was a difficult moment for George White, who knew the settlers well and probably sympathized with their plight. As a prosecutor, however, he was sworn to uphold the decision of the courts, and as a leader of his race, he was determined to prevent bloodshed at all costs. His proven skills as a legislative leader and mediator were instrumental in accomplishing both tasks. That he was asked to assist at all was a sure sign of his growing stature among fearful white leaders, and the peaceful settlement of the dispute only strengthened his reputation for effectiveness under pressure.

No longer just a good lawyer who happened to be black, George White was now a good man to depend on in almost any situation. He was a seasoned and accomplished politician, a veteran public servant. And his dreams were no longer bound by the cautious limits of his youth; at forty-one, he had come of age, and his political future seemed boundless.

63. Watson, *History of New Bern*, 517–8.

64. Ibid., 518. O'Hara currently practiced law in New Bern. Smith, a respected educator from Goldsboro, had served as U.S. minister to Liberia under the first administration of Democrat Grover Cleveland and as head of the Fayetteville normal school for blacks.

6

The Siren's Call of the Black Second

George White had certainly entertained thoughts of higher office since the mid-1880s, when he had revived his political career with a successful term in the North Carolina senate. His election as Second District solicitor in 1886 had encouraged him to consider another step upward, to the U.S. Congress. James O'Hara's defeat by a Democrat that year had left the seat open to any Republican newcomer who could win the nomination and unite the district's majority party, after the sudden death in 1887 of Israel Abbott had removed the most likely experienced competitor in the district field. The path seemed unexpectedly clear for Abbott's closest friend, yet distinct disadvantages remained. Always practical, White knew he would need a solid record as solicitor before attempting to convince district voters to elevate him further. The solicitor's duties would require an enormous amount of his time, and he would be hard pressed to campaign for another office while holding down the job. His income had to be considered, as well; White's decision to remarry in March 1887 had been based in part on his expectation of steady income from his new position.

Any hopes White might have entertained for the congressional seat in 1888, however, went on hold after the sudden emergence of the man determined to become the Second District's next house member: Henry Plummer Cheatham, White's new brother-in-law. The challenge could hardly have come from a more unexpected source; Cheatham had just been reelected as Vance County register of deeds in 1886, and had little political visibility outside his home county. But his early success convinced White to wait for his own chance later on, after Cheatham was defeated or stepped down. As it turned out, White's earliest opportunity came six years later, in 1894, as Cheatham ran successfully for reelection in 1890 and easily gained renomination in 1892.

Henry Cheatham was a determined man, well read and articulate, but he was also young, just twenty-eight when he gained the nomination in the rambunctious district convention of May 1888. He was barely six years out of college, having spent much of his life in the classroom, either as a student or a teacher, until becoming register of deeds in 1884. Cheatham also faced a skilled Democratic opponent in Congressman Furnifold Simmons, who had been running for reelection since the day after his "triangular" victory in 1886. By most accounts, Simmons had charted a shrewd, low-key course through the political minefield of the Black Second, and was almost assured of reelection if the Republicans remained divided.[1]

Henry Cheatham seemed an unlikely choice for the task, after just two terms as an obscure county official. Hardly known in the Second District outside Vance County, Cheatham surprised almost all onlookers by winning the congressional nomination quickly in a crowded field, which included the veteran O'Hara. Like many observers from both parties, George White had been shocked at the ease with which his brother-in-law claimed the nomination. Most doubted that such a novice could pull off an even more daunting task: defeating a popular, well-financed incumbent who boasted support from both parties and, to a lesser extent, from both races.

Conventional wisdom saw many obstacles for Cheatham, beginning with the sorry state of the district's Republican Party. Republicans had remained badly fragmented since the 1886 election, and few leaders believed Cheatham capable of uniting the various factions. After all, he was not a rousing campaigner; although he was able to speak convincingly before large audiences, his early performances seemed out of character to those few who knew him well. He appeared more comfortable in small groups, behaving correctly but stiffly in public appearances; the quiet, well-mannered diplomat preferred to operate behind the scenes, and was not prone to making spontaneous stump speeches or handshaking. His few major speeches during the campaign were

1. Anderson, *Race and Politics*, 148. Anderson offers a concise description of Simmons's conciliatory actions during 1887 and 1888.

well rehearsed and delivered with vigor, yet for the most part lacked memorable phrases or ringing conviction.

George White was accustomed to speaking directly and consistently with all comers, and must have found Henry Cheatham's sudden political success puzzling. But like many politicians, Cheatham seemed to have two distinct personalities, one for the public and another for his circle of advisers. No one had expected to find a demagogue behind the smooth, reserved exterior, yet Cheatham could publicly accuse the Democrats of planning to reenslave blacks if they were victorious, then deal cozily with the opposing party on practical issues behind closed doors.[2]

Such behavior was anathema to the candid George White, who rarely said anything in private that he would not repeat in public. Still, he was willing to give his brother-in-law the benefit of the doubt; Henry Cheatham was young, relatively inexperienced, and understandably insecure. Cheatham's attitude toward whites betrayed an ambivalence born of his days as a house slave, a trait certainly not unique among postbellum black politicians.

Raised by free parents before the war, White was more confident in his dealings with the white power structure. If he perceived racial hostility toward himself, he refused to acknowledge it, and his brisk familiarity was legendary in the Second District. He trusted his own instincts, generally bearing no grudges and tending to treat whites in both parties as equals, to the frequent annoyance of Democrats. Furnifold Simmons was no ordinary Democrat, however, and even White sensed the difference there. As a congressman, Simmons had refused to "draw the color line," despite the urging of many fellow Democrats. He had carefully courted black voters without alienating whites, by such measures as reintroducing O'Hara's bills from the previous Congress. While admitting that he did not consider black rule acceptable in the state or in the nation, he nonetheless pleaded with his white listeners to "treat [blacks] fairly, justly and considerately and recognize their rights."[3]

Simmons often pointed out that he was a white man and a loyal Demo-

2. Ibid. Cheatham dealt effectively with Democrats during his time in Congress, with no apparent repercussions from his 1888 campaign. During the 1890 campaign, he was widely suspected of trading votes with district Democrats to win reelection.

3. Ibid., 153, 318. An account of Simmons's speech to this effect, given in Weldon in early June, was printed in the *Weldon News*.

crat, but nonetheless represented his Republican and black constituents just as well as those in his own party. Such a stance may well have cost him the votes of extreme whites, who vocally despised such accommodationist tactics, but so far Simmons had found it a risk worth taking. Any whites who might stay home on election day—where else could they go, after all?—were likely to be replaced by thoughtful black voters who admired his sensible and gentlemanly conduct. Many blacks seemed disenchanted with the less admirable and increasingly corrupt behavior of their own previous leaders like O'Hara, who could draw no crowds at all for his attempts at speeches in 1888.[4]

It was difficult to fault Simmons for this approach, since no Democrat had seriously attempted it before. Badly outnumbered in the Second District, the party had been able to win previous elections only by dividing the black vote. Republican registration, largely black, outnumbered Democrats by about two to one across the Black Second, and in many precincts the Grand Old Party was almost completely black.[5] In the face of such a moderate, cautious campaign by Simmons, the Republicans could not afford to have two candidates in the race again, but instead needed a unifying force. For once, they may have been prescient to choose a relative unknown like Henry Cheatham, whose pliable nature seemed adaptive to the peculiar nature of this campaign.

Yet it did not begin that way in 1888. At least eleven candidates, black and white, crowded onto the list of springtime hopefuls, including a potential spoiler, George Allen Mebane of Bertie County. A former slave who had previously served two terms in the state senate, Mebane now edited a black newspaper in Raleigh; he seemed to be Cheatham's strongest opponent, although at least two white candidates also had solid followings: future state senator Charles A. Cook of Warren and New Bern attorney Leonidas J. Moore. Moore, who had unsuccessfully challenged O'Hara for the nomina-

4. Ibid., 152. At one Enfield rally, O'Hara could not draw a crowd, even with the aid of a brass band, according to the *Raleigh Signal* of 12 July 1888.

5. Exact figures for district Republican Party registration levels are not available, but the Second's population was 62 percent black in 1880, easily the state's highest; many precincts in Edgecombe, Halifax, and Warren Counties were almost all black and all Republican. About 90 percent of black North Carolina voters registered as Republicans, and blacks certainly formed a majority of statewide GOP ranks, perhaps two-thirds at peak. A reliable 1882 estimate by a Wilmington journalist put the state's GOP membership at 120,000 and its black party membership at 70,000, or about three-fifths; using a ratio of one male voter to seven residents, this is plausible, since about 530,000 blacks lived in North Carolina in 1880.

tion in 1886, was the more highly rated candidate, with ten delegates committed to him.[6]

The wounds from the bitter Abbott-O'Hara feud had barely begun healing when Cheatham's campaign reopened them. His victory at the convention was sealed by a disputed credentials committee report that seated a pro-Cheatham delegation from Edgecombe County over one favoring Edgecombe sheriff Joseph Cobb with the dubious assistance of William W. Watson, despite strenuous objections and even defying recent party precedent. This effectively guaranteed Cheatham the nomination, and Mebane's supporters abruptly left the convention, after delaying the vote as long as they could.

In the end, only one other candidate was even nominated—Charles Cook, who lost to Cheatham on the first ballot by a vote of sixteen to two—but the new nominee was clearly not the convention's unanimous choice. Eight delegates, mostly supporters of Leonidas Moore, angrily abstained from voting, even on the motion to endorse Cheatham unanimously. George Mebane remained in the race long after the convention, apparently hoping to gain the nomination himself at a new convention; he even wrote Cheatham and requested his agreement to a new, fair vote, a suggestion Cheatham declined. Mebane dropped out of the race only in late September, amid the usual charges of being a Democratic puppet and a Cheatham stooge, bought off in the end by those who feared his presence on the ballot would tip the race to Simmons.[7]

Henry Cheatham's dizzying record spoke for itself, and the effects of his hasty ascent would become painfully clear down the road. To win the nomination, Cheatham had seemingly already allied himself with some of the most corrupt forces in the district party, including William W. Watson and others.

6. Anderson, *Race and Politics*, 149. Other candidates included former congressmen John A. Hyman and James E. O'Hara and Edgecombe sheriff Joseph Cobb, according to the *Weldon News*. Charles A. Cook was elected instead to the senate from Warren County; Colonel "Q" Young, who had lost the nomination three times, supported Cheatham.

7. Anderson, *Race and Politics*, 150–1, 156–7. Initially, ten pro-Moore delegates abstained, angered by the pro-Cheatham credentials report; Cook's delegates and two others then changed their votes to Cheatham, who was nominated by a vote of 20 to 0. Cheatham's supporters said Mebane was hired by Democrats to stay in the race; the price quoted by one Raleigh newspaper was $4,000. Critics in both parties alleged the GOP gave Mebane $2,500 more to drop out; this was confirmed in 1889 by an out-of-state campaign worker. One black Republican, Edward R. Dudley of Craven, denounced the second payoff and endorsed Democrat Simmons.

Was it naïveté, overriding ambition, or worse, on Cheatham's behalf? Did he understand the risks involved? Did he believe he could control the party bosses, or was he already under their control?

Henry Plummer Cheatham came from an unlikely background to have ended up as a politician in such a rough setting. He had been born a slave just four years before the war, although in a relatively genteel environment; his mother was a house maid on a plantation near Henderson, his father apparently the plantation's owner. After the war, Cheatham had received a sound public education and had graduated from the private Shaw University in Raleigh before studying law on his own. Yet he had only briefly considered becoming a lawyer before first settling on the teaching profession, serving as principal of the state normal school at Plymouth for two years.[8]

Henry Cheatham showed little affinity for that vocation and soon decided to enter politics instead. Shortly after Vance County was created in 1881, he became its second register of deeds, easily winning reelection in 1886. With his charming manners, his lovely, educated wife, and a growing family, Cheatham seemed destined for higher office. But not, perhaps, so high so soon, George White may well have thought to himself in 1888.[9]

By all rights, the two men should have been good friends. They had met as early as 1885, when both served on a state committee of the black teachers' association, and had become brothers-in-law two years later, when White married Cora Lena Cherry. Both were students of the law, and both had worked to train black schoolteachers; both were well-educated, ambitious and upwardly mobile mulattoes, whose social graces, racial heritage, and skin color would later allow them to move in the highest black social circles of Washington and other northern cities.[10] The parallels between their lives were not

8. Samuel Denny Smith, *The Negro in Congress* (Chapel Hill: University of North Carolina Press, 1940), 125; "Henry Plummer Cheatham," *DNCB*, 1:359. Cheatham was "treated with favor" by his white father, and "experienced few of the physical hardships of slavery"; after Cheatham's father died, another white man, Robert A. Jenkins, "took an interest in him and was largely responsible for providing him the opportunity to attend Shaw," where he obtained both bachelor's and master's degrees.

9. Louisa Cherry and her sister Cora Lena both taught at the Plymouth campus in the early 1880s. The Cheathams were married by the end of February 1884; their children were born between 1886 and 1891.

10. Escott, *Many Excellent People*, 180. Both Cheatham and White attended the fourth annual convention of the North Carolina State Teachers Association in Raleigh in 1885, serving

complete, however. White had come from a proud family of free farmers, fiercely independent and unerringly honest. He had been educated in a cosmopolitan setting in Washington, entering politics just after Reconstruction under the wise counsel of the maverick William J. Clarke and a relatively small circle of blacks in New Bern, who dealt with whites almost as social equals. He was accustomed to running on the same ticket with white nominees, and enjoyed their respect for his legal skills.

Henry Cheatham, on the other hand, dealt almost exclusively with other blacks within the party, except for a small circle of white advisers. As a former slave, he may well have had mixed feelings about whites and about his own mixed racial heritage. Having never lived outside the state, he had been exposed to few broadening influences, and had no significant white mentors. The politics of his native Vance County, dominated largely by black Republicans, had only reinforced his narrow upbringing.[11]

Their personality differences aside, the ideologies of the two men gradually pushed them to opposite ends of the political spectrum. White believed in total social and civil equality, but demanded that blacks behave according to the rules of the larger white society; to him, education was the key, and educated black men had every right to hold any position they could earn, without fear of discrimination or violence. Black citizens deserved the opportunity to prove their worth and earn equality, which they were now guaranteed by the U.S. Constitution. Black lawbreakers were to be punished as swiftly, but just as fairly, as whites.[12] Perhaps as a result of his slave upbringing, Henry Cheatham had a far more ambivalent, gradualist approach to the role of blacks in a

---

together on the executive educational committee. According to later descriptions, each man's skin color was lighter than the typical dark-brown or "black" of full-blooded Negroes; Cheatham was variously described as "fair skinned" and a "bright mulatto," while White was described by observers as having a "reddish-tan," "yellow," or "brown" complexion.

11. When Henry Cheatham was born in 1857, Henderson was still part of Granville County; the 1881 General Assembly created the predominantly black Vance County from parts of Granville, Warren, and Franklin Counties and named it in honor of U.S. senator Zebulon B. Vance, a former North Carolina governor. Cheatham formed a temporary political alliance in 1888 with a few white Republican leaders in Henderson, including "Q" Young.

12. White rarely vocalized this philosophy before entering Congress in 1897. While he was district solicitor, his belief in the swiftness and fairness of punishment for black lawbreakers was applauded by most whites, although few southern whites supported his later call for a federal antilynching law.

white society. He seemed to believe that only a few talented or ambitious blacks should expect to be rewarded by the inherently unequal American system. These limited "tokens," like Cheatham, should serve as models for the rest of the race—as ambassadors, in effect, to the white society. Black citizens should not aspire to mix in white society, but should form their own separate social institutions, like churches.

Such a social scheme did not promise equality to blacks, but rather a permanent inferiority for most of the race. It was a social model later to be perfected by educator Booker T. Washington, as the nation prepared to force and enforce "separate but equal" lives on its black citizens, along with second-class civil status. Cheatham, like Washington, was acceptable to whites as long as he did not demand equality. Both were politically inclined, but unlike Cheatham, Washington never sought elective office, although he was widely respected for his broader principles.

One seemingly minor difference, that of religious affiliation, may explain much about the different outlooks of George White and Henry Cheatham. Cheatham was a Baptist, White a Presbyterian. Generally speaking, with some notable exceptions, black Baptists in the 1880s represented only the middle and lower classes of blacks, and they ridiculed the standoffish "book religion" of the status-seeking black Presbyterians, Episcopalians, and Congregationalists. These denominations were often seen as beyond the pale of the so-called black church, where Bible-thumping preachers and emotionalism reigned, and their members were dismissed as "high-toned" blacks, the wayward imitators of a white society to which they could never belong no matter how hard they tried.[13]

As one might expect, the feelings were mutual. The often-strained relations between blacks of different denominations were based on perceptual differences as well as socioeconomic indicators. Educated, affluent blacks groaned at the churchly antics of their Baptist cousins, for instance, seeing this as an obstacle to advancement of black civilization and a throwback to slave days. Anything drawing the ridicule of whites was repugnant to the black upper class, who resented discrimination against them and frequently blamed lower-class blacks for causing white hostility. As black society gradually matured, the mutual resentment would fade, but the differences between the "black aristocracy" and the lower classes remained a nettlesome wall of disdain.

Such a wall gradually rose between the opportunistic Henry Cheatham

13. Gatewood, *Aristocrats of Color*, 273–4.

and his "proper" brother-in-law, whose disapproval could only grow as he witnessed Cheatham in action. Like the excesses of the Baptist services, such political behavior was in George White's eyes the worst kind of example a black leader could give to his followers: right and wrong were distinct, and Cheatham should have known the difference. Henry Cheatham, however, apparently viewed the political world as a predatory arena where simplistic rules were suspended. His native ability, courteous manners, and shrewdness were simply not enough to win in the notoriously corrupt substrata of the Black Second. Far more devious—and frequently dishonest—methods were necessary, including payment for votes and unspecified "ways that are dark and tricks that are vain," according to one insightful black editor, not coincidentally a political player himself.[14]

White's feelings about his brother-in-law were mixed. He was accustomed to the unpleasant necessity of dealing with corrupt and greedy blacks, for he was a practical politician, not a simpleminded one. But his own integrity was unquestioned, even among his detractors, and he would never trade his independence for success, nor would he bargain away matters of principle. He soon began to suspect the opposite about Cheatham, who was emerging as something of a political chameleon: wily and manipulative, perhaps not dishonest, but certainly not straightforward either. He was simply not to be trusted in important matters.

Ironically, many of those white leaders who later came to dislike George White most intensely and denounce him most vocally had nothing but kind words for his seemingly benign brother-in-law. These included the redoubtable Josephus Daniels of Wilson, not yet editor of North Carolina's largest newspaper but already a power to be contended with in the Democratic Party.[15] White prudently kept his own counsel during the campaign and

14. Henry Lewis Suggs and Bernadine Moses Duncan, "North Carolina," in Henry Lewis Suggs, ed., *The Black Press in the South, 1865–1979* (Westport, Conn; Greenwood Press, 1983), 263. John Dancy, a veteran politician, edited the AME Zion Church's weekly *Star of Zion* after 1882; it was considered the most accurate black newspaper in the state and among the best in the nation. At age twenty, Josephus Daniels owned the *Kinston Free Press* with his brother Charles. In 1882, Josephus Daniels bought the *Wilson Advance* and quickly transformed it into a rabid exponent of Democratic politics; after acquiring the *Raleigh News and Observer* in 1894, he became arguably the most powerful journalist ever in North Carolina.

15. Grover Cleveland was busily courting black voters in the North, to the dismay of some southern party leaders. Occasionally ambitious North Carolina blacks, such as educator James E.

afterward, during Henry Cheatham's entire term in Congress; to do otherwise was pointless since he might need Cheatham's future support or at least his neutrality whatever White's personal opinion of the man. It would also have risked unnecessary domestic friction, since their wives were almost the same age and remained close friends.

Furnifold Simmons may have drawn a sigh of relief when his opponent's name was first announced, having anticipated a more effective orator or, worse, a rabble-rouser. George Mebane, for instance, would have been a far more troublesome foe, as an outspoken and independent journalist and an experienced politician. As Simmons, other Democrats, and even his Republican detractors were soon to discover, however, Henry Cheatham was no pushover, but a surprisingly skilled, even ruthless campaigner.

Regardless of the expectations of others, Henry Cheatham did not shy away from the hot-button issues of the day, including the so-called hidden agenda of the Democrats. In power nationally only since 1884, the party was seemingly on the verge of consolidating its gains, with Grover Cleveland's reelection almost a certainty and North Carolina securely in the hands of its Democratic power brokers. Furnifold Simmons, for one, "was astounded at the ease with which Cheatham's demagoguery won Negro support," according to a later biographer of the black leader, who apparently "told the Negroes that President Cleveland and Simmons would put them back in slavery because it was too expensive to furnish Negroes with both work and wages." Whether Cheatham actually believed this is not known, but as a former slave, he may well have feared it instinctively.[16]

George White must have shaken his head at another report, stemming from an "inflammatory" Cheatham speech in Kinston. The candidate was said to have "raised his eyes toward Heaven and swore that he wished God would strike him dead if he didn't honestly believe" that the Democrats planned to reinstitute slavery; moreover, any black who voted Democratic was a "scoundrel," and nothing less. Judging by the source—a vehemently Democratic newspaper—the account was almost certainly exaggerated, but

Shepard, would join the Democratic Party but black Democratic voters were reportedly assaulted in public by groups of black women, and Shepard soon returned to the GOP.

16. "Henry Plummer Cheatham," in *Dictionary of American Negro Biography*, ed. Rayford W. Logan and Michael R. Winston (New York: W. W. Norton, 1982), 102.

White must have wondered what Henry Cheatham wouldn't say, or do, to win.[17]

Meanwhile, George Mebane's withdrawal from the campaign meant that the Democrats would face a single Republican candidate on the ballot, for just the third time in a decade. Chances for a Democratic victory now required depressing the black turnout, stirring up antiblack feelings among prospective white voters, and, if all else failed, sabotaging the actual counting of the votes by disqualifying as many ballots in Republican precincts as possible.

Furnifold Simmons did not agree personally with such tactics, for he continued to take the high road, conciliating blacks with an evenhanded campaign. His party, however, was deadly serious about winning at almost any cost, and the ensuing campaign was later dubbed the "first white supremacy campaign" in the state's history. Though pale beside the highly vitriolic race of a decade later, the 1888 campaign was certainly among the least rational and most negative of the century thus far, functioning as an ill omen of the future.

North Carolina Democrats were now feuding among themselves, disenchanted with President Cleveland's economic policies and overtures to black voters in the North and confused by the growing power of the fledgling national prohibition movement. They were openly afraid of the Farmers Alliance, to which the very popular Republican gubernatorial nominee, Oliver Dockery, belonged. Democrats remembered how close the opposition had come to controlling the General Assembly just two years before, in a surprisingly strong showing after a fitful and unimpressive campaign.[18]

A modicum of racial rhetoric was a given in any North Carolina cam-

17. Anderson, *Race and Politics*, 156. Accounts of Cheatham's 1888 speeches tend to vary widely. The *Kinston Free Press* called Cheatham's speech to supporters in Kinston in early September "inflammatory," but the *Henderson Gold Leaf* called his speech later that month in Vance County a "much more sensible and conservative talk than some of the papers in the lower half of the district credit him with having made." Anderson, who cites both, believes the *Free Press* account was exaggerated for partisan effect.

18. Lefler and Newsome, *North Carolina*, 546–7. The nationwide Farmers Alliance established its presence in North Carolina in 1887 as a primarily educational association concerned with farmers' social and economic problems. In 1888, Republican nominee Dockery benefitted greatly from his Alliance membership, though it took no active role in his campaign. Beginning in 1890, the Alliance took temporary control of the party, but split into two factions in 1892, one loyal to the Democratic Party and another to the new Populist Party.

paign, but the level of invective unleashed now became almost deafening. The Republicans were painted as the black party, ready to reimpose the horrors of Reconstruction on a local scale; even the party's white candidates were called "politically black," having supported black office seekers in the past and undoubtedly conspiring to produce more once they controlled the state. White voters were exhorted to turn back this "threat to white supremacy" by defeating all Republicans at all levels.[19]

There was no violence associated with this campaign; rhetoric was sufficient to meet Democratic needs. "Negro rule" had long since lost its visible presence, since few blacks held office outside the black counties. In 1888, the threat was less real than theoretical—what would happen *if* Republicans won?—and the mixed results were reflective of the tactics: confusing but mostly favorable for the Democrats and damaging to the long-term prospects for the Republican Party, but not a true landslide.

On election day, Henry Cheatham managed to defeat Furnifold Simmons by the narrowest margin in the history of the Black Second, less than seven hundred votes out of thirty-three thousand cast. Widespread fraud was believed to have been committed by Democratic canvassers; indeed, had disputed Cheatham votes not been thrown out by the thousands in several counties, he would likely have produced a handsome victory. This was according to the later trial records of election-law violation charges in Warren County, where no fraud was ever proved but solid evidence was readily available.[20]

Still, Henry Cheatham fared better than many candidates from his party that year. Fewer than a dozen black legislators were elected in 1888, all from the black-majority counties in the Second Congressional District. But not all the Second District's counties followed tradition; the Republican bastion of Halifax elected Democrats to both the legislature and local offices for the first

19. Anderson, *Race and Politics*, 154–5. Among those newspapers exhorting "white supremacy" were the *Wilson Advance*, the *Kinston Free Press*, the *Tarboro Southerner*, and the *Warrenton Gazette*.

20. Anderson, *Race and Politics*, 160–1. Charles A. Cook, now the U.S. attorney for eastern North Carolina, sought indictments in twenty-seven "perfectly plain" cases of election-law violations in Warren and Northampton Counties; Daniel Russell, who helped Cook prosecute, claimed that Cheatham lost five thousand votes to fraud. Tried in 1891, the Warren case drew a not-guilty verdict from a largely Democratic jury.

time in nearly a generation. Even some of the black Republicans who won elections were denied office by local authorities, who refused to accept their obligatory performance bonds and selected Democratic occupants instead.

Elsewhere, Democrats swept the Tar Heel state, winning the governorship and leaving Cheatham the sole Republican congressman from North Carolina. Meanwhile, the upset election of Republican Benjamin Harrison as president over incumbent Democrat Grover Cleveland convinced the state's conservative Democrats they were following the right course. Although Cleveland had carried the state, many Democrats still grumbled loudly at his courting of black voters. Now there would be no more such racial pressure from the national party. The conservative Democratic Party now held the upper hand in North Carolina.

The new Democratic dominance seemed enduring. Two years later, Henry Cheatham's narrow reelection against a last-minute Democratic opponent would prove one of the few bright spots in the Republican disaster of 1890; another was the strong showing by his brother-in-law, George White, in his own reelection effort as solicitor. But there were few others. Black legislators won just four seats in the 1891 General Assembly, by far the fewest since their first victories in 1868. Two counties with overwhelming black Republican majorities, Warren and Edgecombe, actually elected white Democrats instead for the first time in twenty-two years, following Northampton's example of 1888.[21]

Much of the blame was immediately assigned to Cheatham, whose alleged willingness to trade votes with the Democratic power brokers—in effect, offering them legislative seats in exchange for his own reelection—had betrayed his own party. One Democratic newspaper altered the spelling of his name to "Cheat'em."[22] The fact was, however, that Cheatham's victory in 1890 was it-

21. *Brief for Contestee: In the House of Representatives, Fifty-Fourth Congress, Henry P. Cheatham (Contestant) vs. Frederick A. Woodard (Contestee), from the Second Congressional District of North Carolina* (Wilson, N.C.: Landmark Steam Printing House, 1895), 53–4. Those elected in 1890 included W. W. Long of Warrenton and Dr. R. H. Speight of Edgecombe. Speight's defeat of George Lloyd, the regular GOP nominee, still rankled many Edgecombe blacks; in 1895, Frank L. Battle of Tarboro claimed he had been coerced into running as an independent against both Speight and Lloyd, and blamed his boss, Rocky Mount postmaster W. Lee Person, and Cheatham, "who had absolute control of him [Person]."

22. *Tarboro Southerner*, 2 October 1890, cited by Anderson, *Race and Politics*, 182.

self a fluke, due more to the baffling inability of the Democrats to field an effective opponent than to the dismal prospects of his fellow candidates, "cheated" or not. Former congressman Simmons, waiting for an enthusiastic draft, had made only a halfhearted attempt at the nomination, which went to a lesser-known "farmer nominee," William J. Rogers of Northampton.

Rogers, always in poor health, was unable even to campaign; he withdrew at almost the last moment, leaving Democrats in complete disarray. Desperate for a replacement, a week before the election they selected James M. Mewboorne of Lenoir, a Farmers Alliance agent with highly suspect credentials; he was openly accused of having voted for Republicans in the past, a charge he denied but never completely escaped. Rejected as the original nominee and now resurrected but distrusted, Mewboorne received the subliminal message; two years later, he jettisoned the Democrats for the new Populist Party.[23]

Cheatham won the 1890 election by just 1,200 votes, barely carrying Northampton and actually running behind the novice Mewboorne in Greene County, which no Republican had lost in twenty years. Mewboorne posted the second highest vote total ever for a Democrat, just 300 votes behind Simmons's number two years earlier. Cheatham's narrow margin, meanwhile, was attributable to crossover votes and a depressed turnout among district blacks, many of whom felt their congressman had failed to deliver on his promise to appoint more blacks to federal positions.

Henry Cheatham had actually obtained a significant number of postmasterships for blacks in the Second District, although the more lucrative district appointments by President Harrison had gone to white Republicans, such as veteran state legislator William E. Clarke, now postmaster at New Bern.[24] The growing disenchantment with Cheatham among black voters in the Second

23. Anderson, *Race and Politics*, 180–92, 196. He discusses both Rogers and Mewboorne at length, including Mewboorne's defection to the Populists in 1892. Mewboorne was elected to the state senate as a Populist in 1894.

24. Anderson, *Race and Politics*, 169. Other new white postmasters included Joseph J. Martin at Tarboro and Mrs. Ada Hunter at Kinston. In addition, Charles A. Cook became U.S. attorney. Cheatham failed to have "Q" Young appointed collector of internal revenue for the eastern part of the state. Cheatham appointed at least nine blacks to district postmasterships, including W. Lee Person at Rocky Mount, Samuel H. Vick at Wilson, and Augustus Robbins at Windsor, although three of his other appointees were removed for reasons of fraud or embezzlement.

District was palpable, however, and George White sensed a growing desire for a change at the top of the ticket—if not in 1892, then at least in 1894.

With Henry Cheatham's reelection in 1890, George White had begun to suspect that his brother-in-law would ignore the two-term rule when the next election rolled around in 1892. But this would not have been an optimal year for White, since he would have been in the middle of his own second term and unable to campaign effectively without resigning. So 1894 seemed to be the more appropriate target for his congressional hopes; with luck, Cheatham would no longer be a factor by then.

George White was an astute political observer, and in 1890 he knew several basic facts about the upcoming campaign. First, Cheatham was no longer a unifying force; he could barely win himself, and had no political coattails at all. Without a unifying nominee, the Republican Party's chances would continue to deteriorate. Second, the overall number of blacks in the Second District was already declining, due to noticeable emigration to the North and Midwest; congressional reapportionment, based on the 1890 census, would almost certainly decrease the voter base. And third, the Democrats were likely to continue their antiblack campaigns, marshaling white support and using any means possible to undermine black solidarity. The Democracy was desperately searching for its own unifying force.

White thus expected Cheatham to run again in 1892 and quite possibly to lose. Fewer blacks would vote for him, if his downward trend continued, and the Democrats would undoubtedly choose a stronger candidate than Mewborne. Their chances of victory would still depend on their luck in splitting the opposition; encouraging a second black candidate to run would be the surest way to divide and conquer, but George White would never again agree to bolt his party.

In addition, 1892 would be both a presidential and gubernatorial election year, with a higher turnout expected among whites than in 1890. No Republican could be sure of winning in the Second District against such odds in 1892. So George White began planning his own run for Congress for the 1894 election.

If Cheatham ran and lost in 1892, his effectiveness as an opponent would be greatly diminished, or so White believed. So his own choice of 1894 held several practical advantages: as an off-year for major races, as the end of his own term as solicitor, and, with luck, holding the attractive prospect of his brother-in-law's being permanently relegated to the sidelines. With his solid base of support in Craven, Warren, and Edgecombe Counties, his unsullied political background, and his freedom from debt to any of the major factions in his party, he could easily win the nomination.

What White could not foresee in 1890 was the precise action of the next General Assembly, aimed squarely at the Second District and at Republican hopefuls in general: the continuing reapportionment of the Black Second. Nor was he likely to foresee an even more curious development—the emergence of a full-fledged new political party, which would particularly muddle Second District politics until the end of the century.

On a personal level, neither could White foresee the tragedy that would befall his family during the next year. Cora Lena had given birth to his second daughter in late 1887, just nine months after their wedding. Mary Adelyne (or Adelaide), nicknamed "Mamie," was just three years old when her mother gave birth again in August 1891 to a sister, Beatrice Odessa; George White now had three daughters, including eleven-year-old Della. Little Odessa lived just five months, however, dying of an unknown illness in early January 1892. She was laid to rest in the family plot at Greenwood Cemetery, beside the graves of her father's first two wives, eventually to be joined by her grandfather and her own mother.[25]

Although White never spoke publicly about the loss of his youngest daughter, his tender devotion to his other children indicated that he must have suffered greatly. Cora Lena became pregnant again by the end of 1892, bearing their only son, George Jr., on July 1, 1893, and assuaging the sadness of Odessa's death in a small way, at least.

One sad irony of this year for George White was that it came in the middle of an elected term, when he was not actually running for office as he had been in 1880 and 1882 when his first two wives had died. There was no frenzy of political activity now to distract him, as there might have been if he had been a candidate for Congress; as it was, his full schedule as solicitor served the same immediate purpose. During his free time, he was busy, as always, with both religious and fraternal activities, although he found time to participate in Republican Party affairs, including the state convention in April 1892.[26]

25. N.C. Graves Index, N.C. Department of Archives and History. White later named his Whitesboro, N.J., hotel the "Odessa Inn" in memory of his youngest daughter.

26. White continued to be an elder at Ebenezer Presbyterian Church, which he also served as Sunday School superintendent. Either in 1890 or soon afterward, he was elected state grand mason, a post he seems to have held until 1896.

In retrospect, it was probably for the best that White had not made plans to run in 1892, based on the General Assembly's drastic redesign of the Second District in March 1891. Instead, Henry Cheatham's reelection plans were severely buffeted. Democrats announced that they intended to make the state's nine congressional districts more "compact" and, whenever possible, all Democratic, in the words of one candid senator.[27] The Second Congressional District, which had elected only two Democrats in ten elections, was finally to be neutered.

The General Assembly voted to remove three black-majority counties—Jones, Vance, and Craven—from the Second District and redistribute them to politically safer adjacent districts. Vance County was Henry Cheatham's home, and Craven, of course, was that of George White; both men were now politically homeless in terms of congressional aspirations. Neither could hope to run in their new, majority-white districts; both looked to the Black Second as their only hope. Replacing the black-majority counties in the new Second District was heavily white Wayne County, returning after a decade away.

The district's black population, 115,000 in 1880, dropped now to just over 101,000, a loss of one-eighth of its previous total. But the most significant news lay in the number of voting-age males, now almost equally divided between black and white. Black men now held only a slim majority of 400 over whites, in a district where more than 30,000 men could be expected to vote.[28]

Long known for its overwhelming Republican turnout on voting days, the Second District had suddenly become a virtual toss-up. If Democrats could spur their adherents to register and vote, while discouraging blacks from doing either, no Republican candidate for Congress could expect to win in the Second District perhaps ever again, or so the state's Democrats hoped. But the Democratic strategy had yet another wrinkle. The Second Judicial District, a smaller version of the congressional district, had been a constant source of irritation to Democrats since 1878, especially since the district's Republican voters had chosen a black solicitor in four straight elections. Removing Wake County in 1885 had not changed the outcome, so the General Assembly de-

27. *Raleigh Daily State Chronicle*, 7 March 1891, cited by Anderson, *Race and Politics*, 186.
28. Ibid.; also, *Brief for Contestee*, 2. According to the 1890 census, "if all black men met voting requirements the Negro majority was little more than 400." By 1894, however, the district showed a white majority of more than 1,500 voters, thanks to the addition of Wayne County, where white voters outnumbered blacks by 3,795 to 2,216.

cided to resolve the problem once and for all by changing the way state solicitors were selected.

Rather than each district holding its own election, voters would now
choose solicitors on a statewide basis, much the same way in which superior
court judges were now elected. This procedure had virtually ensured that all
state judges would be Democrats, since the majority of North Carolina's registered voters were Democrats. Just two of the current solicitors—George White
and Thomas Settle—were Republicans; if North Carolina voters approved a
constitutional amendment implementing the change, White and Settle
would be the last Republican solicitors for decades to come.[29]

In 1892, Henry Cheatham faced a pressing political and personal dilemma: he had to choose between retiring from Congress and cutting his ties
to his childhood home. He could no longer run in the Black Second—still the
only district in the state in which a black candidate could hope to win a congressional race—unless he actually lived there. But by moving away from his
home county of Vance, he would lose the security and solid base of black votes
he enjoyed there. Desperate to remain in Congress, he chose to move, but
now faced a new decision: where should he relocate his political base?[30]

Cheatham's native county had been on the far western edge of the old
Second District, so he looked for a town closer to the center of the new one,
yet not too far away from Henderson. His pragmatic choice was Littleton, a
small town in the easternmost part of Warren County, on its border with
Halifax; not coincidentally, it was to be the site of the Republicans' district
nominating convention in April 1892, to be held earlier in the year than
usual. It should have augured well for his first major test in the redrawn district.

And the convention did go well for Henry Cheatham, at least at first. It
was well planned and quite orderly, for a change; Cheatham was renominated
by acclamation, in a large and well-publicized affair attended by six hundred
people. Only the defection of a minority of delegates to a rump convention

29. The state's voters rejected the constitutional change in a special summer election in
August 1892, but no more Republicans were elected solicitor in the Second Judicial District after
White retired in 1894.

30. Mrs. Cheatham was expecting their third child in the late fall of 1891, further complicating the decision. The Cheathams might well have moved to Tarboro, where Louisa's mother
and family members still lived, but settled instead in Littleton.

held almost immediately afterward kept the congressman's transition from being completely smooth. The rumblings from the separate convention were ominous, as both Cheatham and other party bosses were loudly denounced for corrupt policies. Many of the delegates were black, including a Warren County delegation refused seating at the regular convention; rump conventioneers took the unprecedented step of nominating a young white Democratic legislator, W. W. Long from Warren, as Cheatham's opponent, with highly visible black support.[31]

This new split within the Republican ranks was only one of Cheatham's problems, however. A surprisingly strong broadside against corruption in black Republican ranks, written by three of the state's leading white Republicans and aimed squarely at Cheatham, appeared in a Raleigh newspaper the same week he was nominated. The actions of "corrupt and venal upstarts"— including Cheatham's recommended appointments of "completely unqualified" blacks to federal positions—had all but driven whites from the GOP in eastern counties, according to the "address to Tarheel Republicans."[32]

Led by Brunswick County lawyer and former Third District congressman Daniel Russell, the group urged the Republican Party to sit out the 1892 contest, giving the Democratic Party incentive to remain split as well as time to implode. The address was signed by twenty-three white Republicans, none of whom resided in the black-majority counties, although at least two did live in the Second District. It was a virtual declaration of war on GOP state chairman John B. Eaves, and on Henry Cheatham and his cronies, in advance of the upcoming state convention in April.[33]

George White continued to support Eaves. In a vigorous speech at the April convention, he had publicly endorsed Eaves's position, warning Democrats who predicted the death of the Republican Party to beware of the "liveli-

31. Cheatham supporters charged the rump Republicans with selling out to the Democrats, although Long was a popular leader with significant black support.

32. Anderson, *Race and Politics*, 190. The "address" was published in the April 7 issue of the *Raleigh Signal*, and followed a conference of "leading white Republicans" from eastern and southern parts of the state. Anderson argues that the authors simply failed to understand the changes in black leadership since Reconstruction.

33. Ibid., 191. Former congressional aspirant George W. Stanton was among the signers; former state party chairman John J. Mott had helped persuade the U.S. Senate to reject Eaves as internal revenue collector. Mott, Russell, and Harris all opposed the "revenue gang" led by Eaves, who backed Cheatham and seemed to be courting the black vote.

est corpse they ever saw." He was struck, he said then, "by the appearance of the delegates, black and white[,] and by the determination he saw in their faces." The Democrats were disorganized but resilient, and this "was no time for 'milk and water' business. What the Republicans must do is *not to yield an inch*." Fusion with the Populists was still an unacceptable option, according to White, especially for "colored members of the party [who] would be given no privileges."[34]

Despite his popularity and visibility at the convention, White fared poorly in winning party favors. He was one of six candidates for three delegate-at-large slots to the national Republican convention in Minneapolis; the first slot had gone by acclamation to Cheatham, as the state's highest-ranking black, and White, as the only other black holding an elected office, seemed likely to be chosen as well. But the convention selected the only other black nominated: John C. Dancy, currently the appointed collector of U.S. customs in Wilmington. Dancy drew more than twice as many votes as White, who came in fifth, a further embarrassment. The at-large delegation was equally divided between the races; the two white delegates were internal revenue collector Elihu White and future senator Jeter C. Pritchard.

Stung, White and another loser, Oscar Spears, withdrew from the separate race for presidential elector. White framed the decision in sardonic terms. "He said he had encountered Uncle Sam's Boys (meaning the Revenue Ring) and had been defeated, and that he did not care to be slaughtered a second time," wrote the *Raleigh Signal*.[35] White had little affection for the Revenue Ring, a name given the group of Republicans, white and black, who ran the party in the Wilmington region. Powerful Ring member James H. Young, still a Cheatham crony at this point, was a special customs inspector at Wilmington, and was named alternate delegate to Minneapolis. It would be a long four years before Young and White became allies, and even then, the defection would incense Henry Cheatham.

As usual, rivalries and intraparty divisions were swept under the rug as the convention closed. Of far greater significance, both to the statewide party and to Henry Cheatham personally, was the advent in mid-June of another opponent on the congressional ballot. This time it was the nominee of the brand-

34. "Republican State Convention," *Raleigh Signal*, 14 April 1892.
35. Ibid.

new Populist Party, Edward Alston Thorne of Warren County, formerly a Democrat and boasting the support of a sizable number of "honest" black voters. Democrats were angry at the defections of their faithful to the new Populist camp, and some even predicted Cheatham's reelection was now a certainty, whomever their party selected to run. But Republicans were troubled on two fronts: disenchanted Democrats might not stay home now, and Cheatham could not afford to lose any more black votes.[36]

The Democratic congressional nominee for 1892 was the last to be selected, named only in July 1892, but he was no stranger to the race: Frederick A. Woodard of Wilson, the party's sacrificial lamb against an unbeatable James O'Hara in 1884. Lawyer Woodard had been just thirty during his first campaign, but had managed to run a creditable race. He had still never held elective office, but this time managed to defeat four major contenders—two former congressmen, another former nominee, and the "rump Republican" choice—for the party's 1892 nomination. The district Democrats were divided, but Woodard hoped to unify them and achieve victory this time.[37]

Woodard's hope was not entirely unrealistic. By the time the Republican state nominating convention opened in September, the prospects for both Henry Cheatham and his fellow party members were declining rapidly, despite their valiant attempts to put the best face on the situation. Squabbles among party leadership and personal allegations against Cheatham by a rising party power punctuated the heavy air, while Cheatham struggled to hold on to what he hoped was a lead in the three-way battle for his district's seat in the U.S. House.

John B. Eaves, successor to John Mott and a strong opponent of Daniel Russell, presided over the turbulent state GOP convention in Raleigh, at which George White took an active part, according to newspaper accounts.

36. *Windsor Ledger*, 7 September 1892, cited in Anderson, *Race and Politics*, 199. Further complications included defections by two leading white Republicans: John T. Gregory of Halifax and William Lyon of Bertie, who charged that "ignorant, incompetent and corrupt negroes have taken complete control of the political machinery" of the eastern party.

37. Anderson, *Race and Politics*, 195. Woodard defeated Furnifold Simmons and W. H. "Buck" Kitchin, each of whom had served one term in Congress; 1890 nominee William J. Rogers, now apparently restored to health; and Long, the rump Republican nominee. Long nearly won the nomination on the eighth ballot, when he trailed Woodard by twenty-three votes of more than three hundred cast.

The main question was whether to field a full party ticket in statewide elections. Eaves and his so-called revenue gang had pushed for a full ticket since the year's first Republican state convention in April. Eaves had promised blacks "absolute freedom and equality" with whites within the party, although he made no commitments about specific public offices. Eaves's opponents by then had included Russell, former chairman John J. Mott, and John C. L. Harris, a Raleigh newspaper editor, Russell adviser, former district solicitor, and onetime handler of John Collins.[38]

In his vigorous speech at the April convention, George White had taken Eaves's side. But by September, White's views had changed significantly, although he continued to oppose "fusion" with the new Populist Party; he now found himself in the same crowded camp with Russell, Mott, Harris, and James O'Hara, and somewhat uncomfortably so. The huge, outspoken Russell was given to making exaggerated statements, interpreted by some as opposing black political participation; in fairness to Russell, he did not oppose black participation or office holding, but criticized the corruption of those who controlled the party in the east.[39] In any event, allying himself with Russell was at best an unsettling prospect for White.

Yet the question was a matter of principle for White, who saw the risks involved in a statewide campaign and who did not want the issue of race to become a red flag for his party. He felt he had no choice. White had participated in a preconvention caucus in Raleigh, where he had argued strongly against a statewide ticket, along with two white leaders: Oscar J. Spears of Harnett County and *Signal* editor Harris, now an increasingly harsh critic of Eaves's leadership. White's arguments were sensible, according to the *New York Times*, but few blacks within the party agreed with him.[40] Most black dele-

38. Harris edited the *Raleigh Signal*, once the property of William J. Clarke but taken over by the state Republican committee in mid-1880, according to Powell, *North Carolina Gazetteer*, 382.

39. "An Address." Russell and his coauthors wrote, "Many of the best Federal offices have been given to colored men. Of this we do not complain. It is perhaps simple justice . . . but now the tendency is towards the elevation of the most corrupt elements to the control of the party in the black counties . . . the party became in eastern North Carolina simply a negro party."

40. "They May Name A Ticket," *New York Times*, 7 September 1892. Few black Republicans favored fusion with the Populists in 1892. White's shift on the question of a statewide ticket was a pragmatic one; by sitting out the state election, Republicans could concentrate on rebuilding their organization for 1894 and 1896. If the Populists replaced the Democrats as the main opposition party, so much the better.

gates appeared to favor fielding a ticket, regardless of its potential ill effects on the overall election; they believed the lack of a statewide ticket would depress turnout among black voters and damage the chances of black Republican candidates in local and legislative races.

Long before the question of fielding a ticket could be resolved, however, a showdown over a credentials committee report very nearly halted the proceedings in a physical brawl. George White attempted to act as mediator, pleading with the full convention to hear both sides of a factional dispute over the composition of the New Hanover County delegation. Both sides deserved fairness, he said, before reportedly rambling uncharacteristically at one point and being "called to order" by another delegate.[41]

Not all delegates were interested in hearing both sides. White took no part in the ensuing personal exchanges, which quickly heated up and almost led to blows on the floor between two New Hanover party members, one on the delegation recommended for seating and a second not chosen but openly goaded by James O'Hara. The disagreement threatened to break open the convention; even temporary chairman John Schenck, an elderly and respected black delegate from Mecklenburg County, was unable to resolve it amicably, being drawn himself at one point into the increasingly angry exchange.[42] Parliamentary procedures were finally employed to halt the public quarrel and break the deadlock, and the convention then voted overwhelmingly to seat the recommended delegation. But the fissures within the party were painfully obvious as the convention approached its crucial question regarding the fielding of a full state ticket.

Cheatham, White, and O'Hara were among those opposing the naming of a state ticket, arguing in the face of "a majority of negro delegates [who] were clamorous for a ticket," according to the *New York Times* account.[43] It was a

41. "Eaves' State Convention: Republican Machine Politics Yesterday," *RN&O*, 8 September 1892. "White continued to talk in a rambling strain," wrote the reporter, perhaps mistaking his identity; White had already ceded the floor to New Hanover delegate George W. Price Jr., who was arguing with the convention chairman at the time.

42. Ibid. Schenck "retorted in words to the effect that the chair did not care a continental for what [J. C. L.] Harris said," after Harris accused the chair of attempting to "run over this convention." Schenck, crippled from a earlier accident, walked to the podium "with the aid of a crutch"; he died two years later at age seventy.

43. "Named a State Ticket, North Carolina Republicans in the Political Field," *New York*

rare moment of agreement for the three men—the past, present, and future of black congressional hopes—and the last time the three would appear together in a public show of agreement. White and O'Hara were Second District delegates, although Cheatham was apparently not a delegate; in the end, their voices were all ignored. A full ticket was named for the fall election, despite their warnings that it risked handing the election to the Democrats.

George White took the defeat in stride, addressing the convention's final ratification session calmly and confidently. He had hoped to persuade the party otherwise, but accepted its decision with grace and loyalty. In taking a principled stand against naming the full ticket, however, White had risked more than a simple philosophical loss. He had alienated Chairman Eaves and had lost his apparent chance to be the first black Republican nominated for a statewide office, that of attorney general.

The Republican convention selected nominees for a range of offices, including former judge David Furches for governor, and others for members of the governor's cabinet. Thomas R. Purnell, a white Republican from Raleigh, became the nominee for attorney general by acclamation, facing only one opponent, and then only momentarily; the name of Northampton County's Willis Bagley was withdrawn almost immediately by his sponsor, Charles A. Cook of Warren County.[44]

Just days before the convention, however, George White's name had begun circulating as a possible alternate nominee for attorney general, although he denied any interest in the post. His growing reputation as a prosecutor, the respect with which even Democrats treated him, and his undeniable political stature all made him a favorite in certain circles, mostly editorial, outside his own district. At least one convention delegate publicly expressed interest in nominating him, although the nomination was never made.

The idea was an intriguing one. No black had ever been nominated by ei-

---

Times, 8 September 1892. Cheatham, O'Hara, White, and John S. Leary opposed naming a ticket. The *Times* wrote, "A large number of negroes will not vote for it because they feel they have been betrayed into the hands of the Bourbon Democrats. Twenty-five thousand white Republicans have gone to the People's Party, and when the voting begins these men will go over to the Democratic Party."

44. "Eaves' State Convention." Black delegate John H. Williamson of Franklin seconded Purnell's nomination; Cook then withdrew Bagley's name and called for Purnell by acclamation.

ther party for a statewide office in North Carolina. Yet blacks had long been active in the state Republican Party, serving in several high capacities, and deservedly so. North Carolina blacks had long formed the largest single voting bloc within the party, probably even forming a majority of its registered members, although not the exaggerated proportion popularly reported in Democratic newspapers. But few blacks had ever run for any office outside the Black Second and other eastern counties with voting majorities of blacks.[45]

Perhaps 1892 was the year to float the possibility of a black statewide nominee for office. If so, who would be more ideal than George H. White? Indeed, even the Democratic *New Bern Journal* had broached the question the day the Republican convention opened, including White's denial of interest in its brief story on the subject.[46] The possibility was not discussed publicly at the convention, however, and two weeks later, the *Raleigh Signal* wondered aloud why the opportunity had so quickly vanished:

> Will some one please tell us why Eaves and his revenue gang did not have George H. White nominated for Attorney-General? Was it because Mr. White is a Negro? Shame upon Eaves and his crew if this is so. Mr. White has been solicitor for six years, and he has made an acceptable public officer. He is a good lawyer, a man of good character, and deserved the nomination. . . . Mr. White is equally as good a lawyer as Mr. Purnell, and his character has never been questioned.[47]

According to the *Signal*, Eaves had vetoed the idea because "it would hurt the ticket." New Hanover delegate F. B. Rice had intended to nominate White but was requested by Eaves's associates not to do so. Rice, incidentally, was the delegate involved in the near-brawl with fellow delegate C. P. Lockey; Lockey and delegation head James H. Young had successfully opposed Rice's plan to seat his own alternate delegation. Whether Rice was even eligible to make such a nomination was not mentioned; his convention status was not

45. Both metropolitan areas contained large black populations; the cities of Raleigh and Charlotte elected a number of black aldermen during and after Reconstruction, and Wake County elected a number of black legislators. But only a handful of blacks were ever nominated for Congress or district solicitor outside the Black Second, and no black was ever elected to a statewide office during Reconstruction in North Carolina.

46. *New Bern Weekly Journal*, 8 September 1892.

47. "Against the colored leaders," editorial, *Raleigh Signal*, 22 September 1892.

clear, although he may have been a member of the Young-Lockey delegation.[48]

The *Signal* further charged that Eaves was a false friend to party blacks, "simply baiting the negroes [and] using them to accomplish his own purpose" when "by one word [he] could have nominated George H. White . . . for Attorney-General."[49] While Eaves may well have intervened to prevent White's nomination, it was probably for a far more practical reason: to avoid handing the race issue openly to the Democrats. Having nominated a ticket against the wishes of its own articulate white minority, and against those of a few equally articulate blacks, the party could hardly afford to risk its new ticket by advancing such an untested idea. Better, surely, to wait until it had won at least one statewide election before tackling so sensitive a matter as a black statewide candidate, Eaves could have well argued.

The *Signal*, wrapped up in its Russell-Mott-Eaves tangle, had no such thoughts, nor did it ask the even more obvious question: how could George White have accepted such a nomination, after arguing so eloquently against the need for a statewide ticket? It seems far more likely that White, not Eaves, had asked Rice not to make the nomination; otherwise White would appear to be a simple opportunist, one whose principles changed with the political winds. There were already enough of those in his party, and White had no desire to emulate them. As a purely practical matter, he might also be forced to resign as solicitor, or at least to forgo much of his regular income by taking a leave of absence if he were actually nominated. This he could not afford to do.[50]

The ensuing campaign was unremarkable, almost quiet, since the outcome was now seemingly foreordained. Even the scandal surrounding the violent death in Washington, D.C., of W. P. Canaday provided little more than a temporary distraction for the Republicans. Canaday, the onetime editor and congressional aspirant from Wilmington, was found shot to death in his Washing-

48. "Eaves' State Convention." Rice had called a second county convention in New Hanover after quarreling with James H. Young at the first convention; Young said he had voted for Rice as a delegate as "he knew if he [Young] left him [Rice] at home, it would kill him."

49. "Against the colored leaders." James E. O'Hara and John S. Leary were touted as other possible nominees for attorney general.

50. While White may have been intrigued by the idea of running for attorney general, he was astute enough to realize how marginal were his chances of success.

ton office, shortly after notifying police that $130,000 in securities was missing from his office safe; it was an apparent suicide, though some suspected foul play. The champion of black political participation had left North Carolina almost a decade earlier, and few white Republicans had mourned his loss; even fewer did now. The Republican statewide ticket managed a respectable showing in November but still lost to the Democrats; the Populists won no statewide offices, either, although the combined votes of the Republican and Populist nominees for governor did outnumber those of winning Democrat Elias Carr. Had the Republicans not chosen to field separate statewide candidates, the story of 1892 might have ended differently; White's instincts, dismissed as too cautious at the time, now seemed eminently sensible in retrospect.[51]

Fusion with the Populists was still not acceptable to a majority of Republicans statewide; the process would require more time and thought. In just two years, however, fusion would emerge as a spectacularly successful gambit in General Assembly elections, and Republicans would regain the statewide success that had eluded them for nearly two decades.

Henry Cheatham fared slightly better than did most Republican statewide candidates in the Second District, but he was unable to withstand the political strains of the three-way split. Populist Thorne received nearly fifty-five hundred votes, taking votes from both parties, the most any third candidate would ever receive in the Second District. Cheatham was able to carry only three counties: Warren, Halifax, and Northampton, where the vote was neck-and-neck.[52]

Frederick Woodard carried the district's remaining six counties, amassing just under 45 percent of the total vote to Cheatham's disappointing 38 percent. Cheatham's showing had indeed been a dismal one; even in the counties that he carried, his vote totals had shrunk by an average of 15 percent since 1890. He had carried Edgecombe County overwhelmingly just two years ear-

51. *Raleigh Signal,* 29 September 1892; NCG, 1404–7. Canaday died September 27, 1892. Had the Populists and Republicans agreed on a joint nominee for governor, for instance, they might well have defeated Carr, whose plurality was just over 48 percent, and who drew about eight thousand votes less than the two other nominees combined. Republican Daniel Russell won a similar three-way race in 1896 with a plurality of less than 47 percent.

52. Anderson, *Race and Politics,* 348 (Table 18). Cheatham edged Woodard in Northampton by a mere 64 votes of 3,484 cast.

lier but now lost fully a third of his previous votes, losing badly to Woodard and receiving fewer votes than the opponent he had beaten there in 1890.[53]

Henry Cheatham's luck had run out; although most blacks continued to vote Republican, black voters were deserting him by the hundreds, according to gleeful Democratic observers.[54] If he had once again engaged in vote trading as a means to secure his reelection, the technique no longer worked. He had lost control of those blacks who had been persuaded to vote for local Democratic candidates and who did not return to the fold in the congressional race, choosing either the Democratic or Populist candidates instead.

But bleak as Cheatham's showing was, the statewide party fared even worse. Only one Republican legislator, black leader John H. Wright of Warren, won from the Black Second; apparent senate victor William B. Henderson of the Eleventh District (Warren and Vance) was later unseated. Outside the Black Second, a total of just four black Republicans managed to win house seats, a modest improvement over the 1890 showing. But none owed any gratitude to Cheatham, whose dimming political star had now been extinguished, perhaps for good.[55]

The only good news for Republicans from this election was for George White, who had warned his party against its rash actions. He had declined to seek higher office, standing on principle and declaring the Grand Old Party's future to be more important than his own. The party had neglected to heed his sensible advice this year, and had suffered a sharp defeat as a result. White's political star was now on the rise, his personal reputation stronger than ever. His major opponent was hobbled by a decisive loss and his own declining popularity. White's best year of opportunity, 1894, seemingly lay just around the corner.

53. Ibid. Compared to 1890, Cheatham's 1892 totals were dramatically smaller in all counties. Even where he won, he received an average of 15 percent fewer votes; he drew 47 percent fewer votes in Wilson, 24 percent fewer in Greene, and 10 percent fewer in Bertie, all of which he lost. In Edgecombe, he received only 1,514 votes; Mewboorne, his Democratic opponent, had received 1,651 votes in 1890.

54. Ibid., 202. Anderson cites separate comments from future district solicitor Walter E. Daniel of Halifax, in a November 1892 letter to Walter Clark, and the *Windsor Ledger*, 16 November 1892.

55. NCG, 471–3, 561. The five included house members William H. Crews and Tyrell L. Taylor of Granville County, James M. Watson of Vance, Robert W. Williamson of Caswell, and John H. Wright of Warren. Senator Henderson of Vance was unseated by a senate vote on January 24, 1893.

7

The Long Road to Congress

As 1894 opened, George White looked forward to victory in the Second District congressional race. His most worrisome opponent had been effectively eliminated in the unprecedented three-party contest of 1892, when Henry Cheatham had been unable to command the votes of all blacks. Recent history reinforced the negative forecast for Cheatham, since no man from either party had ever won a third term and no former congressman had ever come back from defeat to win another term in the Black Second. While defeated district candidates from both parties had been resurrected successfully, as in the case of James E. O'Hara after his 1878 defeat, none had ever won more than two general elections. The O'Hara precedent was also painfully relevant to Cheatham's situation, since Cheatham had capitalized on O'Hara's image as a loser in 1888 to deny him renomination; any strong challenger would surely return the favor to Cheatham in 1894.[1]

Personal estimates aside, George White was clearly the party's strongest possible challenger to Democratic incumbent Frederick Woodard. White's credentials were impeccable. He boasted two successful terms as district solicitor, with wide exposure throughout five of the congressional district's counties, along with a rare regional reputation for integrity. His legal ability had been widely applauded, even by Democrats, and he had the backing of strong

1. No defeated congressman in the district had ever come back to win either party's nomination; with the exceptions of John Hyman and James O'Hara in 1888, few Republicans even tried. The notoriously fickle district had spurned four sitting Republican congressmen for renomination, each time selecting a new nominee from the other race; two Democrats had also been defeated for reelection, along with O'Hara and Cheatham. Democrats W. H. Kitchin and Frederick Woodard had each lost the first time they were nominated.

leaders in his own party, both black and white. His solid reputation as an edu-cator, religious leader, and fraternal leader, along with his stable family life, underscored his image as a thoughtful and prudent candidate.[2]

Yet there were still drawbacks. Henry Cheatham might ignore logical ar-guments and run anyway, forcing White to expend valuable time and political capital gaining the nomination. In addition, White's home base of Craven was no longer among the Second District's counties, and he would not enjoy a hometown advantage in either the nominating convention or the fall elec-tion. Most importantly, however, he could not seek the Republican nomina-tion of the Black Second until he first established legal residency in the dis-trict. So he now chose to become a resident of Tarboro, in Edgecombe County, where his wife, Cora Lena, had been born and raised.

George White had apparently maintained two homes, one in New Bern and the other in Tarboro, as early as his 1887 marriage to Cora Lena. He may not have purchased a residence in Tarboro before 1897, when county records show he bought property at the corner of the town's Granville and Saint Patrick streets.[3] But Cora Lena and the children spent much time in Tarboro between 1887 and 1894, apparently to be near her mother and other relatives during her husband's extended absences. After 1890, when White began lay-ing firm plans for the 1894 race, he had begun visiting Tarboro more fre-quently, largely for purposes of his official travel, but also to be near his family.

The White household once again included three children after young George's birth in July 1893, helping compensate for the painful loss of daugh-ter Odessa seventeen months earlier. For a time, the household also included George White's father, who appears to have moved to New Bern earlier that year, perhaps because of declining health; Wiley White had retired from the Treasury Department in 1886 and from his subsequent job as a produce ven-

2. *Scotland Neck Democrat*, 22 November 1894; *Tarboro Southerner*, 27 September 1894; Anderson, *Race and Politics*, 211. White had always been "impartial in his work, showing neither favors to his own race, nor bitterness towards whites," wrote the *Democrat*. Incumbent Frederick Woodard stated in a letter written the day after the 1894 convention that he thought White the far stronger opponent. The *Southerner* called White "a courageous darky, especially in his official duties. . . . He was by far the strongest man in Edgecombe."

3. Reid, "A Biography," 48; Charles F. White, *Who's Who in Philadelphia* (Philadelphia: The A.M.E. Book Concern, 1912), 88. White purchased the Tarboro property on July 5, 1897, for the sum of $1,275, according to Edgecombe County records cited by Reid. He sold this property in 1900, but still owned a farm near Tarboro in 1912, according to *Who's Who*.

dor in 1892. Wiley White died in New Bern in early October 1893, and was buried in Greenwood Cemetery; a brief obituary in the *New Bern Journal* noted his age as seventy and the site of his funeral as St. Cyprian's Episcopal Church, with no mention of other survivors.[4]

Transferring his family and residence to Tarboro now became an eminently practical move for George White, since Edgecombe County was the true center of the judicial district. Living in Tarboro would reduce his travel time as solicitor; he was already on the road as many as half the weeks in any given year, including three to six weeks each year in Edgecombe Superior Court alone. By February, he made it official, although his duties as solicitor would require frequent visits to New Bern at least until the end of the year, when his term would officially end; he continued to own the New Bern house for another decade, and maintained law offices there as well. Newspaper editors who took note of White's formal move generally approved, envisioning him as an attractive potential nominee for the Republicans.[5]

At least one Second District resident, however, did not welcome White's appearance in Tarboro: Henry Cheatham, who took personal offense at his brother-in-law's attempt to gain the congressional nomination. In a revealing letter written during the summer of 1894, Cheatham told Congressman Thomas Settle that "White moved into this district to give me trouble on purely personal grounds." The two men had never competed directly before, but their public relationship now had lately begun to assume a "sharp, unpleasant character," indicating the possibility, at least, of personal dislike on one or both sides.[6]

4. Obituary for Wiley White, *New Bern Journal*, 4 October 1893. Wiley White was probably seventy-two at the time of his death; Treasury Department records listed his birth year as 1821.

5. "Superior Court, Spring terms 1887," *RN&O*, 6 January 1887; Anderson, *Race and Politics*, 206–7. Court schedules for the state, drawn up as much as a year in advance, were printed regularly by the Raleigh newspaper. The spring term schedule for the Second District in 1887, White's first year, allotted three weeks to Edgecombe—one in February, two in April—and a total of four weeks to Craven. Both the *Tarboro Southerner* of 15 February 1894 and the *Lasker Patron and Gleaner* of 21 June 1894, cited by Anderson, praised White as a candidate.

6. Henry P. Cheatham to Thomas R. Settle, 17 July 1894, Settle Papers, SHC; Anderson, *Race and Politics*, 208. Congressman Settle was a member of the arbitration committee, and received advice in the case from all sides; Cheatham neglected to mention that he himself had moved into the redrawn district in 1892 to be able to seek a third term. The characterization of the Cheatham-White relationship is Eric Anderson's.

Without a doubt, the two men's political visions differed widely. The older White saw himself as a reformer, ready to clean up the corruption and dishonesty that had lately seemed to plague the district's black leadership. Many blacks must have welcomed such a new, independent political force as their only hope of reclaiming white support and reasserting Republican dominance. White believed that merit was the best route to the top, not influence or personal connections; like many of his Craven colleagues, he believed that leadership must be rotated regularly to retain freshness and prevent concentration of power.

Henry Cheatham, on the other hand, seemed to believe the opposite. In his view, like that of James O'Hara before him, personal merit was useless without the right connections. Once established, leaders should remain in office for extended periods; this was the best way to make use of their experience. The two-term rule, as Cheatham saw it, was impractical at best, and detrimental to the party's long-term prospects. Having been officially unemployed and largely idle for two years, Cheatham longed for a rematch with Democrat Frederick Woodard; Cheatham had "always identified himself with the better class of white people," and in a head-to-head race, he believed his revitalized political machine could easily defeat the Wilson lawyer. George White's "reforms" were therefore a specific, personal threat to Cheatham; his brother-in-law's challenge could only be rooted in jealousy or personal hostility, not in principle, he told Thomas Settle.[7]

No letters document how or when White informed Cheatham of his decision to run, but it would have been uncharacteristic of White to surprise his brother-in-law with such plans, or not to explain them in some detail. It would also have been impractical to expect their wives, always such close friends, not to discuss such an important family matter as the Whites' impending move to Tarboro. So it seems certain that White told Cheatham of his intention to seek the nomination before he actually moved to Tarboro; the prosecutor, always so direct and frank in his political speeches, had nothing to gain by evading the issue, and may have even expected Cheatham's support. And while White may have felt some lingering resentment over Cheatham's

7. Cheatham's statements on the subject were self-serving at best. In his public speeches, he made much of his experience, though he had been only moderately effective as a Republican member of a Republican majority—and virtually the only black in Congress—between 1889 and 1893.

failure to support him fully at the state Republican convention in 1892—
when White had been defeated as a delegate to the national party convention, after Cheatham was chosen by acclamation—he rarely allowed personal
feelings to shape his political behavior, and he had never been given to public
criticism of an opponent's character.[8]

In all likelihood, White offered Cheatham a frank and pessimistic assessment of the other man's chances of winning the congressional seat, even in a
two-way race. Next he probably appealed to Cheatham's party loyalty; he
must have known the Populists would never endorse him as a "fusion" nominee, and the new party was certain to nominate its own candidate again if he
ran. Cheatham had proved he could not win a three-way race; insisting on
running would, under the circumstances, be detrimental to the party's overall
chances. Cheatham should therefore leave the choice to a new field. His day
in the center ring was past, and he should be the first to recognize it gracefully
and withdraw.

Unfortunately, any such appeal to Henry Cheatham's nobility was likely to
be a waste of breath. He had rarely shown concern over the dwindling number
of black legislators and officeholders in the Second District since he had first
run for Congress. Cheatham had reportedly been willing to trade off votes to
the Democrats in both his congressional elections; while the allegations were
never proven, they were both persistent and widely believed, and the results
of the elections only reinforced the belief. Cheatham, of course, was being
hopelessly unrealistic; he studiously ignored the obvious question of his own
potential effectiveness if the Democrats again won the house, or the related
question of why a congressman like Woodard, now of the majority party,
should be any less effective than an ex-congressman of the minority.[9]

So the principled reformer and his pragmatic opponent girded up for a

8. Anderson, *Race and Politics*, 204. Cheatham attempted to support himself by delivering
lectures across the North after leaving the House in 1893; Anderson cites a letter in which
Cheatham sought advice from Albion W. Tourgée, a noted former judge. The 1894 campaign
was an aberration for White, who sharply criticized both Cheatham and white Republicans during his postconvention tours; his previous campaigns had always been issue-oriented, and, while
partisan, never personal.

9. Anderson, *Race and Politics*, 184–5. In 1892, for instance, Cheatham ran about 100 votes
ahead of his party's local ticket, while the Democratic opponent ran behind his party's local
ticket by about the same margin. In his own defense, Cheatham could argue that his highest duty
to the party and its voters was to win the election, whatever means that required.

family battle of historic proportions, as the date for the nominating convention in Weldon drew near. Winning the nomination required gaining the
support of thirteen of the district's twenty-four delegates, all selected beforehand by county conventions. George White took an early lead in the delegate count, but based on both the district's recent history and Cheatham's
stubbornness, only one thing was certain: there would be no easy victory
ahead.

The week before the district Republican convention opened, White received an endorsement from an unexpected source, a reputable Democratic
newspaper in Northampton County. It was an odd omen for what would become the longest period of official deliberation for a nomination in the district's history: three months. George White was "undoubtedly the ablest man
in the [Republican] party who has been mentioned" as a candidate, wrote the
Lasker Patron and Gleaner, "and the Republicans of this county could do no
better than instruct their delegates to vote for him in the nominating convention." The newspaper's reason was simple and straightforward: "We want
to see good men nominated by all parties."[10]

Had the Northampton delegation done what its newspaper editor suggested, deliberations would have ended the first day, and White would have
won easily. But the peculiar dynamics of Black Second politics had already
spun away from an early decision. The convention, by all accounts, was distinctly in favor of White, who had claimed eighteen delegates in county balloting and expected to be nominated handily. Yet White received just eleven
votes on the first ballot, the balance having been redistributed among
Cheatham and others during the credentials process. Cheatham now held a
fighting total of nine delegates, and two or three white aspirants held the elu-
sive margin of victory.[11]

Ten additional ballots failed to break the deadlock between White and
Cheatham. On the twelfth, White apparently gained one of those votes but
was still one vote short of victory. The thirteenth ballot seemed to be shaping
up as decisive, with one of two probable outcomes: either the floodgates would

10. Editorial, *Lasker Patron and Gleaner,* 21 June 1894, cited by Anderson, *Race and Politics,* 209.

11. Joseph J. Martin and D. W. Patrick each received at least two votes on the first twelve
ballots; Hiram Grant received his single vote on the seventh ballot. The three were the first
white Republican candidates nominated since 1888.

open for White, or a continued deadlock would point the way to a compromise candidate. Up to this point, all accounts would later agree, at least on major details. The final ballot proved as unlucky for chroniclers as for numerologists, however; two separate, contradictory accounts were even published, side by side, in one district newspaper a week after the convention had closed.

As a reporter for Tarboro's *Southerner* observed in its first postconvention edition, "In many respects it was one of the most remarkable Republican gatherings on record. From the beginning the White and Cheatham factions had blood in their eyes, and they fought to the end, each side dying game. Both men claim this morning that they are nominated."[12] Henry Cheatham had been declared nominated, claiming that nomination only after winning over delegates committed to the two remaining white candidates on the final ballot, or so this account reported. But a second account was completely contrary, claiming the convention "went to pieces . . . at 3 o'clock . . . without making a nomination" and "broke up in confusion" after George White stormed the podium to denounce his foes "in unmeasured terms." White claimed that

> [t]wo or three hundred white Republicans of Lenoir, Wayne and other counties had determined to throttle the will of 16,000 negro voters . . . and that they were doing all they could to handicap the Republican party and thus elect a Democrat to Congress. He touched the Thirdites, and said if the Populists desired coalition, they must go to the Republican party. "For," he said "your little camp is too small to ask us into, and you are too young. You must come to us, we cannot go to you."[13]

For all its normal partisan zeal, the *Southerner* was unusually sympathetic to White, later calling him the "strongest man in Edgecombe" and praising him for his "courageous" performance as solicitor. The *Patron and Gleaner* echoed the same sentiments, calling White "the ablest man of his party in East Carolina now in public life." Both newspapers preferred him as the nominee, and had hoped for a peaceful settlement of the standoff in White's

---

12. "Another Report," *Tarboro Southerner*, 5 July 1894, reprinted from *RN&O*, 1 July 1894.
13. "In a Muddle: Contested Delegations and a Big Split," *Tarboro Southerner*, 5 July 1894; "Another Report," ibid.

favor.[14] But war now loomed on the political horizon, as White prepared to take his case directly to the voters.

White would not bolt the party, but instead announced a "vigorous and manly canvass of the entire district by townships, and as far as possible to instruct and re-unite the Republicans [by] honest means." His first volley was a one-page circular, dated the day after the convention and signed by both the candidate and convention secretary Henry Clay Holley. It claimed that George White's initial victory had been blocked by sheer fraud, in the shape of an "expressed plan several weeks before any county had held a convention." Unspecified anti-White forces had conspired to contest the delegates from any county declaring for White, and to substitute unfavorable delegates during the credentials process. George White had won a majority of votes on the last ballot, and had been "duly declared nominated, even though the convention's chairman refused to announce the results."[15]

The chairman, John Fields Jr. of Lenoir, quickly took umbrage at these "erroneous statements" and countered with a strongly worded circular of his own. After recounting his version of the credentials process, Fields blamed any delay in announcing the final vote—which was completely in Henry Cheatham's favor—squarely on "Bill Watson and Mr. White." Fields claimed that he had announced Cheatham's victory in unmistakable terms, and he was the legal nominee. But Fields was clearly determined to do more than correct George White's alleged factual errors here, as shown by his angry personal postscript: "P.S. Any other Republican pretending to be nominated by this convention, under these existing facts, could not be regarded *other than a fraud and an enemy to the party*" (emphasis added).[16] So much for any lingering hopes of party unity.

The unresolved contest dragged on through months of increasingly bitter public debate. At one point, White offered to drop out of the race if Cheat-

14. *Tarboro Southerner*, 27 September 1894; *Lasker Patron and Gleaner*, 27 September 1894. The *Patron and Gleaner* said White would have given Woodard a "close race," and was sharply critical of Cheatham's service to his constituents during his previous two terms.

15. "Hon. George H. White of Edgecombe, Republican Nominee for Congress, Second District, N.C.," circular dated June 27–8, 1894, in North Carolina Collection, University of North Carolina at Chapel Hill.

16. "Proceedings to the Republicans of the 2nd Congressional District of N.C.," undated [1894] circular signed by John J. Fields, in North Carolina Collection.

ham would do the same, both of them leaving the nomination to a third man of the party's choosing, such as Hiram L. Grant. This Cheatham refused to do. Finally, with the election upon them, both candidates agreed in September to seek neutral arbitration of the impasse; they signed a tersely worded agreement at the behest of frantic party leaders, including a member of the Republican national congressional committee, which regularly monitored such situations.[17]

Dated September 3, the agreement bound both men to abide by the decision of the arbiters: "Question having arisen as to the regularity of the Republican nomination in the Second district of North Carolina, and this question having been presented to the National Republican Congressional Committee, the undersigned hereby agree to submit their claims to the committee, and abide by their decision."[18]

Both contenders eventually appeared before the committee, which met almost three weeks later in Washington, D.C. Each man seemed hopeful; according to one newspaper account, Henry Cheatham expected to win the nomination outright, while George White expected the committee to select a third man. In anticipation of such a hearing, Cheatham and others had been writing letters since July to its members, including Congressman Thomas Settle of North Carolina's Fourth District. White was one of the few not attempting to influence Settle's decision; as one former solicitor to another, he may have felt such action unseemly.[19]

By the time he arrived in Washington to give his testimony, George White appeared to have given up all hope of receiving the nomination. His strongest evidence would have been solid proof of irregularities at the county conven-

17. "Political Notes," *RN&O*, 31 August 1894; Anderson, *Race and Politics*, 211. The newspaper predicted that both men might remain in the race until the end, despite the national committee's investigation. The committee included Republican congressmen and senators who "coordinated and assisted Republican campaigns."

18. "Cheatham is the Man, and the Democrats Will Have to Bestir Themselves if They Elect Woodward," *RN&O*, 27 September 1894. The newspaper printed the full text of the agreement in this story on the committee's decision.

19. "Cheatham Wins, and White will withdraw from the Congressional race in the 2nd District," ibid., 23 September 1894. Cheatham and "White left to-night for North Carolina and the decision will be sent to them. They are both hopeful, but Cheatham is more so than White," the newspaper wrote. Its editor combined several related stories from Saturday events into one long, disjointed front-page article in the Sunday edition.

tion level, magnified by evidence of the flawed credentials process at the district convention; either would have bolstered his case measurably, but in the face of pressure from the national committee, both he and Cheatham had voluntarily waived such investigations. White therefore aimed his brief testimony at convincing the committee to recommend Grant or another compromise nominee, one whom both candidates and the Populists could find acceptable. The Populists, he now knew, would not vote for a black nominee.[20]

Upon his arrival by train the night before he was to give his testimony, White told one reporter, perhaps only half in jest, that he "could not afford to bring a host of witnesses to testify for him," since he owned neither a railroad nor interest in one. The next day, White's testimony was cautiously optimistic. He told the committee he believed the "chances for Republican success are very good [and] much brighter than they were two years ago," particularly if the Populists chose not to nominate a candidate. "We will certainly give Woodard a close run."[21]

In his own testimony, Henry Cheatham agreed that the Republicans would win the election if the Populists did not put up a ticket, but insisted that if he were the candidate he would win either way. He expected a majority of seven or eight thousand votes. Cheatham had been in Washington a day earlier than White, and came out of his testimony "somewhat excited," telling the *News and Observer* he was hopeful, but "it was impossible to see what the end would be." Both men left Washington on Saturday, September 22, and each expected to receive news of a decision the following week. One member of the committee characterized the debate as "extremely hot," noting that Cheatham and White were "making a close contest."[22]

After two days of hearings, the seven-member committee was expected to deliberate for at least that long afterward. Surprisingly, however, the committee took only hours, issuing its decision the same night the hearing ended and awarding the nomination to Henry Cheatham, based on the results of the Weldon convention as reported by chairman Fields. "Barred from going behind the action of the District Convention," the committee implied that it had little choice but to endorse Cheatham. "We earnestly request and desire that every Republican in the district . . . will rally to the support of the Hon.

20. Ibid.

21. Ibid.

22. "The fight in the Second," ibid., 22 September 1894.

H. P. Cheatham, and see that a united and vigorous effort is made to secure for him such a sweeping majority" as the nominee deserved in a strongly Republican district.[23] Their decision ended the formal dispute, but the announcement would do little to unify the party in the Second District.

Sensing the irony of the situation, the *News and Observer* correspondent chose to inject a humorous anecdote of the day. A small goat, tethered outside the building where the hearing was held, had become the object of a conversation among those gathered to hear the final decision. One onlooker, supposedly "learned in the law," dubbed the creature "the scape-goat of the Republican party," whose fate was unmistakable:

> "As soon as the testimony has been given and the decision made, we are going to fasten all the sins on his back and let him take them over the mountains." After a laugh had been indulged in by all bystanders, the goat turned his head towards the speaker and bleated in a low tone, which indicated weakness. A colored brother who was enjoying the fun heard the goat, and, turning to the speaker, said: "Boss, hit's no use. Hit Kant be done. Dere's too many for him to carry, and he's too weak."[24]

If any scapegoat waited in the wings, it seems to have been George White. Upon arriving home, he was greeted with the news of his double loss: his own failure to secure the nomination, which he had expected, and Henry Cheatham's victory, which he had not believed possible. Both were due, he realized, to his agreement to waive investigation of the irregularities behind the convention.

What had really happened at the Weldon convention? Had the bizarre history of the Black Second simply continued its normal course, or was there a more sinister explanation? Had Henry Cheatham merely outwitted George White at the last possible moment, or had he stolen the nomination from his opponent? Was White just a poor loser, or was there a conspiracy to blame? Understanding the fifteen-hour sequence of events was difficult enough at the

---

23. "Cheatham Wins." Settle was the only southern congressman on the committee; Nebraska senator C. F. Manderson was acting chairman, and committee member Joseph W. Babcock, a Wisconsin congressman, was also chairman of the Republican executive committee. Committee secretary J. W. Graves had visited the district in August and early September.

24. "Cheatham is the Man."

time for politicians on the scene; reconstructing an accurate scenario from such widely varying accounts, a century later, is virtually impossible. There are no minutes to review, no living sources to ask. As one contemporary journalist observed, "[I]t is impossible to tell the result of a Republican convention in this district by being present and watching it. It produces the same result as does a cyclone." The only way to make sense of such bedlam, he said, was by "laying low, hugging the ground and revisiting the scene after the storm has past."[25]

The official transcript of Cheatham's contest, released in 1896, dealt only with fraud in the November election, and gave no answer to the mystery that still surrounds his come-from-behind victory at the convention. To better understand that situation, one must remember the context: a complex, volatile political backdrop involving players from three parties, none of which was unified. The Democrats, the Republicans, and the new Populists had all played a part in the Republican decision, all for their own reasons and often at cross purposes.

With some exceptions, the Populists were mostly disaffected Democrats, an outgrowth of the Farmers Alliance movement that had controlled the General Assembly briefly in 1891. They had fielded candidates in 1892, though with little success, and were only now gaining some key converts from both parties, such as James Mewboorne, Henry Cheatham's Democratic opponent in 1890. Blacks who could not yet bring themselves to vote for a Democrat were opting, in small numbers, for the Populist ticket. By 1894, the Populists' key to defeating the Democrats was "fusion" with the Republicans: dividing candidates between the two parties on a fusion ticket and uniting behind one candidate for each office. The Populists offered, unofficially, to fuse with the Republicans in the 1894 congressional race, but only if the Republican nominee was "not too objectionable"—almost certainly, a code for white.[26] Otherwise, the Populists would probably nominate their own candidate again, as in 1892.

25. "The 'Faithful' in Doubt: The Republicans of the Second District Have a Superabundance of Congressional Candidates," *RN&O*, 15 September 1894. "Such is the state of affairs as we glean it from the public press and other sources," the article closed. "There is but one fact that is conceded by White, Cheatham and everybody else—and that is Woodard will be re-elected."

26. *NCG*, 473; *Brief for Contestee*, 1–2; H. L. Grant to Thomas R. Settle, 2 July 1894, Settle Papers, SHC. Mewboorne was elected to the North Carolina senate in 1894 as a Populist from the Lenoir-Greene senatorial district. Populist leaders told Grant of their likely decision; Grant, of course, was a preferred nominee.

The other options for Populists were equally distasteful: either revert to voting for the Democrat, Woodard, or simply stay home. Their candidate in 1892, Edward Alston Thorne, had won more than five thousand votes in a three-way race, not enough to win but more than enough to ensure Cheatham's defeat.[27] In 1894, a Populist nominee had little chance of faring better. Their best hope was to persuade the Republicans to choose a new face, one acceptable to both former Democrats and committed Populists—in short, almost anyone except Henry Cheatham.

At the same time, the district's white Republicans saw their first opportunity in more than a decade to reclaim the house seat from both the Democrats and their party's own increasingly corrupt black members. To do so, however, they had to ward off an extremely popular black newcomer in George White; if White were allowed to win the election, the black claim to Republican power would only be strengthened.

Other factors remained to be considered as well. Although still representing a minority viewpoint within the GOP, the alleged race-baiting of Daniel Russell and others had clearly alarmed the party's white leadership. As recently as 1890, for instance, two of the party's nominees for Congress had been black, Cheatham in the Second District and George C. Scurlock of Fayetteville in the Third. While Scurlock had been decisively defeated by his Democratic opponent, the GOP still risked public identification as a party permanently controlled by blacks, rather than a biracial party with a significant number of black members, especially if Russell continued to circulate his rash charge that Henry Cheatham was the "real boss" in the party.[28]

Cheatham's defeat in 1892 had helped ease the party's difficulty, as had a continued decline in the success of black candidates across the Second District. While blacks continued to be overwhelmingly Republican, they were increasingly less visible from outside the party. A victory by George White, however, was sure to restore black ambitions to run more candidates and con-

27. Anderson, *Race and Politics*, 348 (Table 18).

28. *RN&O*, 22 August 1894; *Raleigh Signal*, 4 August 1892. Fayetteville businessman George C. Scurlock lost overwhelmingly to Democrat Benjamin F. Grady in the Third District race in 1890. The *News and Observer* mentioned the 1894 candidacy in the First District of "John P. Jones, colored, of Beaufort County . . . an aspirant for Congress"; Populist Harry Skinner of Pitt won that year's race. The *Signal* generally praised Cheatham in its own editorials, even though it differed strongly with Eaves; this August interview with Daniel Russell was a virulent attack on Cheatham and Eaves.

trol the party apparatus, both in the Second District and beyond. Former congressman Cheatham would be the perfect vehicle to derail George White; Cheatham's ambition had blinded him to the near certainty of his own second straight defeat in the redrawn Second District, and his presence was sure to distract White's supporters until it was too late.

If Cheatham's candidacy could keep George White from taking the nomination on the first ballot, and if a deadlock between White and Cheatham could be prolonged until both were exhausted, a compromise white candidate might become an option attractive enough to sway the convention. There was still a risk, of course, that Cheatham might actually win the nomination. But Populists would certainly then propose their own candidate, for whom white Republicans might be able to vote, and White might split the black vote by running independently; in either case, Cheatham would be finished, and White safely contained. The plan was a long shot, but a risk well worth taking for the long-term good of the party, so long as it was not too transparent.

John Fields long denied any involvement in the scheme but nevertheless seems the likeliest villain. Few others had the strategic position and knowledge required to manage such a complicated maneuver, which involved deftly sabotaging the credentials process, rigging the division of delegates to assure no clear leader going into the ballots, and managing enough votes on each ballot to ensure that White never won—all without leaving any fingerprints. The strategy seemed to work flawlessly, at first; however disappointed White and his supporters may have been by their loss of delegate votes, they voted to elect Fields as convention chairman by acclamation. Fields himself noted that the motion to do so was made by "one of Mr. White's friends," whom he did not name.[29]

George White suspected Fields's involvement from the outset, but could never prove it. A fuller explanation, which White offered nearly three months later to the *Raleigh News and Observer*, contains extra detail of the convention's denouement, but still leaves certain questions unanswered. When White gave this interview, he had not yet testified before the national committee, but he had had much time to reflect upon the events of that June night. "The plan which my opponents adopted was to raise contests in every county which I carried. By this means, seven illegal delegates were seated in

29. Fields circular.

place of the regular delegates who were for me," White told the newspaper. "I entered the convention under protest. On the 12th ballot one of these irregular delegates voted for me, and on the 13th ballot another. This gave me the necessary number of votes for a nomination."[30]

Chairman Fields had intervened at this point, by refusing to announce the results. "After the expiration of 3 hours and 20 minutes the Chairman announced that Cheatham had received the necessary 13 votes and that he was the nominee of the convention. Where the votes came from, which Cheatham claimed nominated him, I do not know," White said. "Cheatham claims that the two Northampton delegates voted for him to the last, but I have a written statement from one of those [irregular] delegates which states that he voted for me on the 12th and 13th ballots."[31]

If true, that statement was the only documented proof of Fields's treachery. Fields maintained that Northampton's delegates had both voted for Henry Cheatham on the final ballot, and further claimed that it was the change of four delegates from Lenoir and Greene—those previously committed to Patrick and Martin—that had given Cheatham the majority. Yet a switch of one Northampton vote on the twelfth and thirteenth ballots, of course, would have negated the Cheatham victory, producing a 12-to-12 tie. In George White's view, this realization was what had prompted Cheatham to ask Fields for a delay, and which very likely then drove a furious Watson up onto the podium to protest.

It is possible that in the confusion, anyone in physical control of the podium—anyone except John Fields, that is—may then have called on George White to speak, even though no formal announcement had yet been made of the Cheatham victory. A July newspaper account said White spoke in hostile anticipation of the nomination of a white candidate, although the sequence of events depicted is bewildering and slightly inaccurate, considering that it was George White who later agreed to a white compromise candidate.

Another witness claimed that W. W. Watson had run onto the stage as much as a half-hour earlier, creating a disturbance and throwing the convention into an uproar just as Fields was attempting to announce the ballot results. This was not unusual behavior for Watson, of course; he had done much

30. "White's Side of the Question: Says He Went into the Convention at Weldon with 18 out of the 24 Delegates, But was Cheated Out of 7 of Them," *RN&O*, 11 September 1894.
    31. Ibid.

the same in 1888, seeking then to defeat Henry Cheatham on behalf of George Mebane. In fact, the words attributed to White by the Raleigh newspaper—at least in reference to "white Republicans" and the Populists—sound far more like words the headstrong Watson would have said, not the far more astute (and usually less hot-headed) solicitor. Still, Cheatham specifically singled White out as the speaker, in his complaint to Congressman Settle.[32]

Assuming George White did make such an angry speech before the full convention, it seemingly would have come *after* Fields's announcement, not before. Why would any candidate have been allowed to address the convention unless balloting was ended? White never denied making the speech, and the sentiments in the newspaper's account are reflected in his circular, although he did not seem committed to a black nominee. His speech dealt specifically with losing the nomination, although here he probably referred to the credentials process; Holley's account may have been inaccurate on this point, at least.[33]

When "it became evident that these four votes were going to Cheatham . . . two more than he needed," White's angry supporters forced the convention to adjourn, in a virtual "coup d'etat, a row, a mob," the *News and Observer* wrote. After White's supporters rushed out "declaring he was nominated," the Cheatham faction quietly reassembled and nominated Cheatham, presumably making the announcement of the final ballot results only after White himself had departed, according to the newspaper. Secretary Holley's account represented only "how [White] would have been have been nominated *if the convention had lasted long enough*" (emphasis added). Holley, reportedly in the Bertie County jail for robbery in September, was unavailable to argue the point.[34]

The battle George White had apparently lost inside the convention hall soon spilled over into the district at large. His "manly canvass" of the district was sporadically reported in the press, leaving no doubt that White was determined to have another hearing, for he sincerely believed his own words: "If the will of the people had been regarded, 18 of the 24 votes in the convention

32. Anderson, *Race and Politics*, 211; H. P. Cheatham to Thomas Settle, 17 July 1894, Settle Papers, SHC. Anderson, citing *Contested Election Case of Cheatham v. Woodard*, 75, 79, describes the unnamed witness as "friendly to Cheatham."

33. White circular.

34. Ibid.; "The 'Faithful' in Doubt."

. . . would have been cast for me . . . [but] seven of the delegates who should have been seated were thrown out . . . *Might* here was *right,* and the voice of the people *was not in it. On the Sixth day of November next these voices will be heard*"[35] (original emphasis).

By the end of September, White had nothing left to gain by fighting his battle in the press; his statement to the *News and Observer* was the last he made before the election. It was just as well, since the newspaper viewed him somewhat dimly, as "vain and mouthy"; Cheatham, by flattering contrast, was "foxy and quiet." White was true to his word before the committee and did not oppose the Republican ticket headed by Cheatham. But he did not promise to campaign for the ticket or vote for Cheatham, and in fact did little to support the party in the fall. Even the partisan brief for Frederick Woodard, submitted later in response to Cheatham's contest before the U.S. House, acknowledged the importance of White's role after leaving the campaign: "It may well be presumed that Mr. White 'sulked in his tent,' and his large constituency, as represented by his delegates at the Convention, did not support one of whom their leader had spoken in no complimentary terms . . . White did not vote for contestant [Cheatham]."[36]

George White was a prisoner of his own inflexible conscience. He had agreed not to pursue the flawed credentials process, or the question of the convention's rigged final vote; he had promised in advance to abide by the decision of the national committee but had expected that committee to display Solomonic wisdom by discarding both candidacies. Perhaps his greatest fault here was naïveté, not vanity, but if he felt double-crossed by the committee—as he almost certainly was—he could not say so publicly. He could do nothing but wait.

As he pondered the events that had led to his loss, White must have considered, again and again, the fatal delay between the last two convention ballots. What had caused it? According to Fields, the delegations from Lenoir and Greene had changed their votes to Cheatham on the final ballot, and Fields had announced the results. Secretary Holley remembered the sequence differently: "On the 13th ballot, which the chairman refused to announce, stating as a reason that Mr. *Cheatham had requested him to wait a while,* Mr.

---

35. White circular.
36. "The 'Faithful' in Doubt"; *Brief for Contestee,* 7.

White received a majority of all the votes and was declared duly nominated" (emphasis added).[37] Both Fields and Holley were under strong pressure, Fields to sustain the decisions of his credentials committee in Cheatham's favor, Holley under some duress from his own delegation, if one is to believe an undated broadside recounting the results of a mass meeting in Holley's own Bertie County. The broadside denounced the actions of two pro-Cheatham delegates for "misrepresenting the wishes of the Republicans of Bertie," and affirmed White as the "Regular nominee." What actually happened seems almost surreal; even Fields's own tabulation of the Bertie vote had given those two votes to White, not to Cheatham.[38]

Yet if John Fields did announce Cheatham's victory and "legal nomination," as he claimed, why did he later feel constrained to attack George White's credibility so openly? Was it because he made no such announcement while White was present, perhaps waiting until White and his supporters had stormed out? Or was it an attempt to discredit Holley, the convention's own secretary? Indeed, Holley could hardly have left the proceedings before the gavel, since he noted the subsequent election of a new district executive committee; but he still insisted that the final ballot gave White the nomination.

Fields might have settled the issue by producing a report from the second secretary, but he chose not to do so, perhaps because his real purpose was to discredit White's larger claim of fraud in the credentials process. As chairman of the credentials committee, of course, Fields was bound to stand behind his group's report as "careful and impartial"; he could easily ignore White's claims as political sophistry. Had he been part of a well-orchestrated plan to deny White the nomination, as White so broadly hinted, Fields could ill afford to let such a challenge go unanswered. To ignore it would be tantamount to political suicide, and John Fields still had his own dreams to fulfill, dreams that did not include George White as an active threat.[39]

From all appearances, Fields had little to worry about, at least for the mo-

37. Fields circular. The county delegate votes on the first through twelfth ballots were recorded in White's circular, the vote on ballot thirteen only in Fields's circular.

38. White circular; *Brief for Contestee*, 7. At least one Bertie County resident, B. J. Askew, later told Congress that the two Bertie delegates seated at the convention had forged their credentials, while the regular delegates, committed to White, were denied admittance. Askew, chairman of the Bertie County Republican Committee, testified in Cheatham's behalf.

39. "To the Public," undated broadside, in Thomas R. Settle Papers, SHC.

ment. White had been effectively neutralized, if not actually neutered, by the national committee. His supporters were as disappointed as their fallen leader, and as helpless; some may well have followed his lead by staying at home on election day. It was Henry Cheatham's show now, but as White and others had warned, winning the Republican nomination was not the end of the story for Cheatham. The final six weeks of the campaign proved to be a virtual minefield, and Cheatham would later complain bitterly that election day fraud—always present in the Second District, no matter who won—had only added to his burden.

Disgusted at the presence of Henry Cheatham on the ticket, district Populists chose now to nominate their own candidate, former state senator Howard F. Freeman of Wilson. Dr. Freeman, an ex-Democrat, waged only a limited campaign, avoiding Halifax County completely. It seemed an odd decision, since Edward Thorne had drawn almost 10 percent of his 1892 vote from Halifax. Yet the results were ironic; even with a significantly smaller turnout, Freeman actually improved on Thorne's showing. Freeman drew higher vote totals in six counties than Thorne had, and almost matched Thorne's total vote from the larger 1892 election.[40]

The final tally of the three-way race was just as predicted in September by the *News and Observer*. Incumbent Frederick Woodard won in a virtual landslide, with just under 50 percent of the vote, handily defeating Henry Cheatham for the second time in a row. Cheatham finished a distant second, losing by 5,308 votes overall and carrying only Warren County, and that by a smaller total than before. His overall tally was a full 20 percent below 1892; this time he received just 9,413 votes, losing votes in all but one county, Lenoir.[41]

It was the worst defeat ever suffered by a Republican nominee in the Black Second, and spelled the practical end to Cheatham's elected career as a politician. The disastrous defeat, however, was barely noted by the exuberant state Republican Party, whose fusion with Populists brought a resounding joint vic-

40. Anderson, *Race and Politics*, 348–9 (Tables 18–19). Freeman received 5,314 votes, while Thorne had received 5,457 in 1892, including 450 in Halifax. Fields continued an active career in district politics and again chaired the district nominating convention in 1896.

41. Ibid. Cheatham had received 11,814 votes in 1892; this included 976 in Lenoir, where he received 1,114 in 1894. In Warren, the one county he carried in 1894, he received 1,511 votes compared to 1,683 in 1892.

tory at polls across North Carolina and an end to Democratic control of the General Assembly for the first time since the Reconstruction era. The Democrats were reduced to the role of opposition party, outnumbered by their combined rivals nearly two to one in the state house and, almost incredibly, more than five to one in the state senate.

If any consolation existed for the defeated—and there was very little to be found—the Democracy could at least boast that they had beaten Henry Cheatham at home, for the second time. And there was more irony buried in their statewide defeat: although the party had elected their smallest legislative contingent in recent history, just 54 out of 170 members, that total included nine from the counties of the Black Second. There were just five black legislators in the 1895 General Assembly, but for the first time since Reconstruction had begun, there were none at all from the Second District.[42]

Henry Cheatham, who had played a key role in helping defeat his fellow black candidates, would now play a curiously petulant role in sustaining their losses. In his contest of the election before the U.S. House itself, Cheatham argued that fraud after the fact had played the controlling part in his lopsided defeat; one of his active colleagues in the hearing was former solicitor John Collins, now out of politics himself, who cross-examined witnesses. Cheatham went to unprecedented lengths to bolster his case by assisting Democratic legislators in fending off postelectoral challenges from black Republican contestants in the Second District. It was a desperate and dangerous course, but Cheatham seemed to believe it would "materially strengthen his case before Congress," according to the *News and Observer*.[43]

Although he blamed his loss primarily on Democratic fraud and vote buying, Henry Cheatham was always quick to mention George White's "foolishness," as he had earlier called it: the months of persistent, hostile anti-Cheatham campaigning in a loser's revenge. Cheatham's repeated reminders

42. The black legislators elected in 1894 were William H. Crews Jr. and S. J. H. Mayes, both of Granville County; Moses M. Peace, Vance; Calvin L. Smith, Caswell; and James H. Young, Wake. Two black senate candidates, Elbert E. Bryan of Edgecombe and Scotland Harris of Halifax, unsuccessfully contested their losses.

43. *Brief for Contestee*; "Under the Dome," *RN&O*, 12 January 1895. Collins, who lost a legislative race in Halifax County, helped Cheatham cross-examine many of the witnesses. The column warned, "This legislature may turn out fairly elected men in order to help Cheatham in Washington, but it will avail him nothing."

were doubtless catalyzed by White's well-publicized opinion that his brother-in-law's latest tactic—the contest before the House—was "preposterous, and had no foundation in fact to sustain it . . . Woodard was fairly elected by an overwhelming majority. Even with Freeman out of the field, Mr. Woodard would have carried the district."[44]

It was certainly a coincidence, but an unnerving one nevertheless, that George White's law offices in New Bern burned less than a week after his comment appeared in a Raleigh newspaper, in one of three unexplained fires reported in New Bern in one day. The relationship between the two men was at its lowest point ever; much of the testimony compiled by Cheatham during his House contest, at least as printed by Cheatham's victorious opponent, seemed deliberately aimed at discrediting White, politely but surely.

If he did not blame actual fraud on White, he did hold his brother-in-law responsible for the poisonous anti-Cheatham atmosphere in many precincts. But Cheatham supporters could blame both men for the loss. One Cheatham voter testified that "Democrats were surprised at their vote being as large as it was. I heard some of them say so. The cause [was] this White-Cheatham mess."[45]

Ironically, Congress would eventually agree with Henry Cheatham that some fraud had undoubtedly occurred, but it would advise him of colder facts in its findings: even without fraud, he would still have lost the election. There were simply not enough votes available to him at that time. To win, he would have had to increase his vote total from 1892 by nearly one-third, and he had failed to give any compelling proof that he could have accomplished such a goal in a fraud-free election.[46]

George White had predicted the Republican defeat, even before he knew for certain that he would not be the nominee. He did not think fusion with the Populists was a panacea for his party's problems, at least not in the Second District. "There is no certainty of the colored vote being solid for it," he responded to a reporter's question. "It will take time and the development of the canvass to determine that question. The solidity of the colored vote is noth-

44. Ibid.
45. "City in Brief," ibid., 16 January 1895; *Brief for Contestee*, 60. The testimony came from Samuel Lawrence, an Edgecombe County merchant who had attended the county's delegate-selection convention and termed the events "very bitter."
46. *Henry P. Cheatham v. Frederick A. Woodard*, cited in Anderson, *Race and Politics*, 220.

ing like it has been."[47] His sensible observation would be borne out by subsequent events.

White would later assert, with just a trace of irony, that he had withdrawn from the 1894 race "in the interests of harmony in the party," the very phrase used by the national committee to describe its own decision. With greater irony, the U.S. House report and decision upholding Woodard's flawed but final victory was released on May 14, 1896, just one day after Cheatham officially lost the 1896 GOP nomination to White. Cheatham believed that White had engineered the delay in releasing the report, yet it is difficult to envision how or why White could have done so, even if he had wanted such a delay.

The 1896 loss was a doubly bitter defeat for the ambitious Cheatham, who never again ran for office, and a final vindication of George White's persistence in his long, painful struggle for leadership and dominance in the Black Second.[48]

47. "White's Side of the Question."

48. "Congressional Doings," *New York Times*, 15 May 1896. Had Cheatham been seated by the House, he would almost certainly have run for reelection in the fall. The coincidental timing of the report's release was noted by many, but the delay could only have been to Cheatham's benefit, since the report seated the incumbent, Woodard.

George Henry White. This photograph appears to have been taken at about the time that the congressman from Tarboro, North Carolina, was sworn in for his second term in March 1899.
Courtesy Library of Congress

The home of the Reverend Robert Owen Spaulding—a first cousin of Mary Anna Spaulding White, George White's stepmother—was built about 1870 in Sandy Plains, Columbus County, N.C. This 1890 photograph shows family relatives Jane Tuck Spaulding, Dollie Spaulding Evans, Mary Spaulding Gaines, and Cora Spaulding Pyles.
From Ann Courtney Ward Little, ed., Columbus County, North Carolina, Recollections and Records. *Reprinted by permission.*

View from the east of New Bern, N.C., ca. 1864. A busy port at the confluence of the Trent and Neuse Rivers near Pamlico Sound, New Bern was among the first southern towns seized by the Union, in March 1862. It quickly became a haven for escaped slaves and soon gained a majority of African American residents. Reproduced from an original print held by Tryon Palace, New Bern.
Courtesy North Carolina Division of Archives and History

William John Clarke, who became George White's mentor and law teacher in New Bern in 1877. The former Democratic state comptroller and onetime Confederate became an avid Republican after the Civil War, serving as a Superior Court judge.
Courtesy North Carolina Division of Archives and History

William Edwards Clarke (1850–1901), the son and law partner of William John Clarke. An active Republican and four-term state legislator, the younger Clarke defeated George White in a four-way race for the state senate in 1882.
Courtesy the Mary M. Barden Collection, New Bern, N.C.

John Campbell Dancy (1857–1901) was a prominent North Carolina journalist, religious leader, and Republican activist whose career paralleled George White's. Both attended Howard University in the 1870s, and they made their first joint political appearance at an Emancipation Day gathering at Beaufort, N.C., in 1879. Dancy served as U.S. collector of customs at Wilmington, N.C., before being appointed recorder of deeds for the District of Columbia in 1902.
Courtesy Library of Congress

Ebenezer Presbyterian Church, 800 Pasteur St., New Bern. George White was a founding member and elder of this church, begun in 1879 and completed in 1880. The edifice was destroyed by fire in 1922. Engraving reproduced from Lachlan C. Vass, *The History of the Presbyterian Church in New Bern, N.C.*
Courtesy North Carolina Division of Archives and History

George Henry White ca. 1886. This engraving appeared on the front page of the *New York Freeman*, the nation's most widely read African American newspaper, on February 5, 1887, along with a lengthy story on White's election as solicitor of North Carolina's Second Judicial District.
Reprinted from the New York Freeman, 5 February 1887

Craven County Courthouse, New Bern. As district solicitor from 1887 to 1894, George White often appeared in Craven Superior Court, held in this ornate structure built in 1883 and still in use today. This photograph appeared on a 1906 calendar. *Courtesy North Carolina Division of Archives and History*

Col. James Hunter Young. An African American newspaper editor and North Carolina legislator during the 1890s, Young helped George White win the Second District's Republican congressional nomination in 1896. He was also a key adviser to N.C. governor Daniel Russell, who appointed hm colonel of the Third North Carolina Infantry, a regiment of black volunteers during the Spanish-American War in 1898. *Courtesy North Carolina Division of Archives and History*

George White's residence at 519 Johnson St., New Bern. Beginning about 1890, White constructed this house around the small core of a one-story eighteenth-century building. He lived here until he moved to Tarboro in 1894, and his last two children, Beatrice Odessa and George Jr., were born here. White sold the house in 1903; it has since been restored, and its current owners, Duncan and Judy Harkin, have erected a private historical plaque to White at the site.

Photograph by the author

Henry Plummer Cheatham, George White's brother-in-law and political rival. This photograph of the young Cheatham may have been taken while he served as register of deeds in Vance County, N.C. (1885–1888). The Shaw University graduate was elected to Congress from the Second District in 1888 and 1890, later serving as recorder of deeds for the District of Columbia. Cheatham was married to Louisa Cherry, an older sister of George White's third wife, Cora Lena.

Courtesy North Carolina Division of Archives and History

Della White's graduating class, Scotia Seminary, Concord, N.C., 1897. White's only child from his brief first marriage, Della attended this teacher-training school before working as a music teacher in Tarboro. She later served on the Scotia faculty. She died of complications from scarlet fever in 1916 in Washington, D.C. None of the class members is identified here.

Reprinted by permission from Leland Stanford Cozart, A Venture of Faith: Barber-Scotia College, 1867–1967 (Charlotte, N.C.: Heritage Printers, 1976)

Josephus Daniels (1862–1948), one of the most influential journalists in the South, was also a power broker in the Democratic Party and an avowed proponent of white supremacy. He repeatedly attacked George White from the pages of his *Raleigh News and Observer*, the state's largest-circulation newspaper in 1900. Daniels later served as secretary of the treasury under President Wilson and ambassador to Mexico under President Franklin Roosevelt.

Courtesy North Carolina Division of Archives and History

HE DOESN'T LIKE TO LET GO,

TERM IN CONGRESS WORTH $5,000 A YEAR.

But most people think our only negro Congressman has had it about long enough.

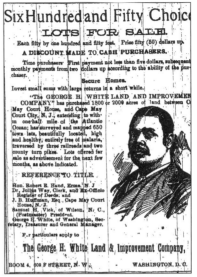

Six Hundred and Fifty Choice
LOTS FOR SALE.

Each fifty by one hundred and fifty feet. Price fifty (50) dollars up. A DISCOUNT MADE TO CASH PURCHASERS.

Time purchasers' First payment not less than five dollars, subsequent monthly payments from two dollars up according to the ability of the purchaser.

Secure Homes.

Invest small sums with large returns in a short while.

"The GEORGE H. WHITE LAND AND IMPROVEMENT COMPANY" has purchased 1800 or 2000 acres of land between Cape May Court House, and Cape May Court City, N. J., extending to within one-half mile of the Atlantic Ocean; has surveyed and mapped 650 town lots, beautifully located, high and healthy, entirely free of malaria, traversed by three railroads and two county turn pikes. Lots offered for sale as advertisement for the next few months, as above indicated.

REFERENCE TO TITLE.

Hon. Robert B. Hand, Erma, N. J.
Dr. Julius Way, Clerk, and Ex-Officio Register of Deeds; and
J. B. Huffman, Esq., Cape May Court House, N. J.
Samuel H. Vick, of Wilson, N. C., (Postmaster) President.
George H. White, of Washington, Secretary, Treasurer and General Manager.

For particulars apply to

The George. H. White Land & Improvement Company,

ROOM 4, 609 F STREET, N. W. — WASHINGTON, D. C.

This savage front-page cartoon from Josephus Daniels's *News and Observer* in mid-1900 satirized George White as a partisan elephant sucking at a congressional money-jug. White announced his retirement from office three months afterward.

Reproduced from microfilm, Raleigh News and Observer, 26 May 1900

This advertisement for the George H. White Land and Improvement Company appeared in the *Washington Colored American* for six months, beginning in December 1901. The drawing of White was also used for news purposes by the same paper, and continued to appear in the *Philadelphia Tribune* as late as 1913.

Reproduced from microfilm, Washington Colored American, 18 January 1902

Jeter Conley Pritchard. A leader in the North Carolina Republican Party and an early political ally of George White, Pritchard served in the U.S. Senate from 1895 to 1903 and afterward was a federal judge. His opposition in 1900 to continued officeholding by African Americans led to a bitter estrangement between him and White; the break may have prevented White from gaining an important federal appointment after he left Congress in 1901.

Reproduced from microfilm, Washington Colored American, 8 December 1900

This photograph of George White was taken sometime after he moved to Philadelphia in 1906. It was used for news purposes by the *Philadelphia Tribune* by 1915 and appeared with his obituary in the *Crisis*, house organ of the NAACP, in 1919.
Reprinted from Charles F. White, Who's Who in Philadelphia, *1912*

The People's Savings Bank of Philadelphia. George White opened his banking establishment at 1428 Lombard Street in January 1908 but by the end of that year had moved it to this building a block away at 1508 Lombard. White lived in an apartment on the third floor and died here in 1918.
Reprinted from Charles F. White, Who's Who in Philadelphia, *1912*

8

Into Congress: The First Term, 1897

Although he would face an experienced incumbent Democrat in the fall, with a likely third-party candidate also in the wings, George White enjoyed a rare advantage in the spring of 1896, as he accepted his party's nomination for Congress: Republican unity. At the Second District Republican convention in May, White had become the undisputed master of that group by a forceful display of personal strength. He had come from behind to squelch the chairman's second attempt to stack the credentials process in favor of his opponent, Henry Cheatham; by thus besting John Fields, White had denied his estranged brother-in-law's desperate bid for a fifth straight nomination. It was a personal triumph, but the effort had been difficult and draining, and White was not universally popular for his conquest. Still, he had made the best of a chaotic situation; one observer described the atmosphere at the Weldon convention's opening as "raising Merry Hades," with no consensus reached on any major issue during the first afternoon and evening sessions amid challenges to five pro-White county delegations.[1]

Fields had announced his tentative decision to appoint a credentials committee obviously sympathetic to Cheatham, just as he had done in 1894, but this time Fields was already chairing the convention and would not serve on

1. "The Row at Weldon," *RN&O*, 13 May 1896. "Cheatham wanted to be renominated [and] Grant of Wayne wanted the same plum; some of the convention wanted straight out action, and others wanted fusion. No definitive news had been received up to midnight," according to the account. Challenges had been raised against delegations from Bertie, Edgecombe, Halifax, Northampton, and Warren, all committed to support White.

the committee itself. During a late evening recess, "it was whispered around that Fields had been bulldozed by the White faction, and would 'take water,'" wrote the *Raleigh News and Observer* a day later. "The rumor proved true. . . . Chairman Fields, as pale as a ghost, arose and said for the sake of party harmony, he deemed it best to name a new committee on credentials. This he accordingly did, and the Cheathamites wilted." The new committee finally presented its report "near the midnight hour," and nominations were presented "without the least enthusiasm," including those for George White for Congress, Joseph J. Martin for elector-at-large, and two national convention delegates. White had "carried the day" in a showdown with those who had kept him from the nomination two years earlier.[2]

And what of Henry Cheatham, whose name was not presented for the first time in nearly a decade? He "took his defeat quietly, though he says he had been cheated out of the nomination. It certainly looked that way to a stranger," the correspondent closed. "Cheated" was an interesting term for the wily former congressman to use, considering his own reputation for covert deals. Still, White and his supporters had used almost every tool available to stop Fields and Cheatham. Hiram Grant, White's compromise choice in 1894 and later appointed secretary of the U.S. Senate, had sought just weeks earlier to strike a deal with Cheatham, for instance, but now found his deal instead with George White; Grant became a district delegate to the national convention.[3] White had also entered an informal alliance with radical free-silver advocate and fusionist James H. Young, a former Cheatham ally and a supporter of Daniel Russell, although White did not embrace the silver issue with the same fervor as Young.

The convention stretched on until about one o'clock in the morning, after delegates overwhelmingly nominated White and then glumly acceded to the statewide candidacies of Daniel Russell for governor and Jeter Pritchard for a full term in the U.S. Senate. Having won the Second District nomination at

2. "Second District Republicans: White nominated after nearly an all-night session," ibid., 14 May 1896. Now under the control of Josephus Daniels, the newspaper continued to favor Cheatham as the Republican nominee, although Daniels favored Woodard for reelection.

3. Ibid.; Anderson, *Race and Politics*, 229. Anderson quotes Cheatham lieutenant W. Lee Person on the Grant proposal; Grant still smarted from Cheatham's opposition to his Senate job, noted a year earlier by the *New York Times* (29 July 1895). Former Halifax register of deeds John H. Hannon, a black, was the other district delegate elected.

last, George White now assumed a powerful role in the statewide politics of his party. His district had been persuaded to support Russell at the upcoming state convention, despite the antipathy many blacks continued to feel for the man. White's new stature was recognized shortly by his selection as one of four at-large statewide delegates to the St. Louis convention in June, a fact duly noted by the *New York Times*.[4] But the political quiet in the Second District was to prove only temporary; Democrats were already weighing the prospect of renominating the increasingly unpopular Frederick Woodard, while at least some Populists sought to tap the ranks of Cheatham's disappointed followers for defectors; both groups would prove hostile to White, if for different reasons.

The Republican state convention two days later was another exhausting ordeal for White and his fellow delegates, lasting well into the morning hours as Russell battled the party's 1888 nominee, former congressman Oliver H. Dockery. The gubernatorial nomination gave rise to a marathon credentials process, fourteen hours and six indecisive ballots long. Conservative blacks like John Dancy and James E. Shepard supported Dockery with seconding speeches, while James Young pressed for fusion with Populists in a passionate speech for Russell. Young's new ally, George White, was reportedly indifferent toward the free-silver issue and had stubbornly opposed fusion in 1892, but as a practical politician, he now fulfilled the requirements of his necessary alliance.

Russell's creditable record on racial issues was marred by several intemperate speeches concerning the inability of most blacks to hold office, but with White's assistance, he was narrowly nominated over Dockery on the seventh ballot. Despite Russell's conciliatory acceptance speech, however, furious conservative blacks began laying plans to force him from the ticket or defeat him by luring black voters to support the separate Populist candidate; the estimates of black votes at risk ranged from thirty to fifty thousand.[5]

4. Jeffrey Crow, "'Fusion, Confusion and Negroism': Schisms among Negro Republicans in the North Carolina Election of 1896," *North Carolina Historical Review* 53 (October 1976): 378; Anderson, *Race and Politics*, 231; *New York Times*, 17 May 1896. Besides deriding Henry Cheatham as the "real boss" of the state Republican Party in 1892, Russell had also sharply ridiculed southern blacks as "mostly savages" in an unfortunate 1888 speech.

5. Crow, "'Fusion, Confusion, and Negroism,'" 377–8; Turner and Bridgers, *History of Edgecombe*, 311. The statewide gathering of black Republicans on July 2 sharply criticized

Meanwhile, Cheatham's supporters in the Second District were reportedly "determined to beat White if they have to go to the Democrats to do it." Eventual Second District Populist nominee D. Schuyler Moss of Littleton was already courting disaffected Cheatham disciples by mid-June with "a little money" and promises of further encouragement; he envisioned his own victory for Congress with the active assistance of Cheatham, in a letter to state Populist leader Marion Butler, North Carolina's other U.S. senator. "Cheatham is a personal friend of my father and he can turn this tide to me and says he will if I get the nomination," Moss wrote.[6]

Nothing concrete came of Moss's proposal, however; Butler and other Populist leaders were preoccupied with their own intricate plans for a carefully split fusion with the Republicans on the state level and with Democrats on the national level. Republicans at the statewide convention had agreed not to nominate candidates for several state offices, leaving those for Populist nominees to fill; mounting an aggressive campaign against White could be interpreted as a treacherous move.[7] Democrats were equally nervous about the fall election, the first since they had lost control of the General Assembly in 1894. Convinced they could carry the state for presidential hopeful William Jennings Bryan with the help of Populists, many believed they could choose a Democratic congressional nominee more acceptable than Woodard to Populist voters. Despite such reservations, however, Woodard was renominated in June. And Moss, whose own candidacy was floundering, was never allowed to campaign, for fear of provoking White into a more aggressive stance on the issue of gold versus silver.

Thus when "gold bug" George White appealed to Populists to support him in a September speech in Wilson—despite Populist support for free silver—many Democrats worried aloud that Populist indecisiveness might be fatal to Woodard's chances. White told his Populist audience that they held "the out-

Russell's nomination and endorsed Populist William Guthrie for governor. More than forty blacks from sixty-five counties attended, including Edgecombe County black leaders.

6. D. S. Moss to Marion Butler, 20 June 1896, Butler Papers, SHC.

7. Anderson, *Race and Politics,* 233–4. Besides Russell, Republicans had also nominated candidates for auditor, attorney general, and one of two supreme court justices. Populists nominated their own candidate for governor, along with candidates for secretary of state, treasurer, superintendent of public instruction, and the second associate justice.

come of the election in their hands"; this was true across the Second District.[8] The fusion campaign was a confusing one in many respects, with voters called upon to commit to memory an often complicated string of candidates from two parties. Democrats, meanwhile, tried to intimidate voters from the other two parties, charging that white Republican candidates were betraying the white race, and that neither Populists nor white Republican voters should be fooled by it.

Local GOP candidates whom Populists had agreed to support under fusion, like John I. Mozingo of Goldsboro, were specifically targeted by Democrats. The Wayne County sheriff's candidate had admitted he would vote for White for congressman, a move depicted by a local newspaper as racial heresy: "No more bitter and vindictive color line speeches have ever been made than by George White, the negro candidate for Congress." The *Goldsboro Daily Argus* offered no specific substantiation for its charge, apparently expecting white readers to accept it at face value, as many did just two weeks later.[9]

But there is no other evidence that George White made any inflammatory speeches, political or otherwise, during the 1896 campaign. He made at least one nonpolitical speech after his nomination, to graduates of Charlotte's private Biddle University, where he received an honorary doctorate of law, and of which he soon afterward became a trustee. His church newspaper, the *Afro-American Presbyterian*, certainly saw nothing untoward in his performance during the campaign, calling him "a gentleman of unblemished character and a representative of whom the race may well be proud."[10]

White was certainly not personally committed to the gold standard, the national Republican campaign's hottest issue. He had attended the St. Louis convention only as an unenthusiastic supporter of the party's final platform,

8. Ibid., 235. Anderson cites the *Wilson Advance* editorial of 17 September 1896 as symptomatic of Democratic concerns: "[White's] argument . . . was disgusting and should be condemned by every white man who believes in white supremacy." Fusion on the county ticket "has put the Populists under obligation to White and his crowd." Moss withdrew from the race a week before the election, too late to prevent ballots with his name from being cast; his largest vote came in Wilson County.

9. *Goldsboro Daily Argus*, 19 October 1896. Mozingo was later defeated as Democrats swept majority-white Wayne County.

10. Undated editorial, *Afro-American Presbyterian*, reprinted in *Raleigh Gazette*, 21 November 1896.

and his characterization by many as an ardent "gold bug" was hardly accurate. He and other Republicans were instead concentrating on civic issues of statewide interest, including the need for home rule and the protection of reforms carried out by the 1895 General Assembly; they were also preoccupied with appealing to black voters to avoid the dangerous risk of voting for any Democrat. White, of course, had voted to nominate William McKinley for president, and he professed admiration for the Ohio leader throughout the campaign; back home in "Bryan country," this seemed enough to feed the Democratic frenzy against the man who would soon become the nation's only black congressman.[11]

George White had actually been "discouraged" over the gold-standard provision before departing for St. Louis, according to the *News and Observer*, and once there, his mood had not improved: "All of us but five voted against the money plank," White said of his state's delegation, "but when it came to the adoption of the platform we had to take it as a whole." Described as the "leading colored man in the N.C. delegation" by the newspaper, White had "work[ed] actively among the negro delegates to hold as many in line as possible on the silver question." Silver organizers believed the key to defeating a gold plank at the convention was to "hold the negro delegates in line from the South," but according to White, that was "not an easy matter," since eastern organizers for gold had changed the minds of "many who came here talking for silver and the double standard." In the end, North Carolina's delegation voted overwhelmingly for silver, giving 14.5 of its 22 delegate votes to the silver plank, yet it was one of the few states to support that side of the issue. Few other delegations were swayed by the arguments of White or his colleagues; the gold standard plank was adopted by a vote of more than seven to one.[12]

George White was one of at least three black North Carolina delegates to

11. Crow, "'Fusion, Confusion, and Negroism,'" 378; "Straddler Pritchard," *RN&O*, 17 June 1896.

12. "Straddler Pritchard"; "McKinley and Hobart are the nominees, Silver Bolt led by Teller," *RN&O*, 19 June 1896. A fourth black delegate, Henry Denny of Catawba County, was selected but apparently did not attend the national convention. The race of state delegates and alternate delegates is not specified in convention listings; at least six alternates were known to be black, including W. S. Hagans, White's private secretary and companion on the train home, Hugh Cale, John H. Williamson, W. H. Crews Jr., J. E. Dellinger, and E. M. Green.

the national Republican gathering; others included John H. Hannon of Halifax County and J. P. Butler of Martin County. It was the first trip west of the Mississippi for White, now forty-three, and it must have been an enriching experience. But even as a traveler, White was cautious, almost provincially so; in a characteristic gesture, he chose to stay with friends in St. Louis rather than in a hotel, thus managing to avoid the embarrassing fate faced by other black colleagues, some of whom were refused accommodations by a number of St. Louis hotels. The North Carolina delegation stayed at the Laclede Hotel, one of only two local hotels that did not turn black delegates away, if only under pressure from the Republican executive committee, according to White. If the state's delegation escaped the racial slight suffered by others, many other black delegates were angered by their treatment in St. Louis, to the point of drafting a resolution protesting the discrimination displayed by area restaurants who refused to serve them.[13]

Discrimination against black Republican delegates had become a potent news story in the week before the convention opened. National committeeman and convention delegate James Hill of Mississippi was the first victim of the hotel lockout, having been forced to vacate his rooms at Hurst's Hotel; Hill returned from an evening meeting on his first day in St. Louis to find "the doors barred against him, as it were," wrote the *News and Observer* correspondent. Upon being informed that the clerk had "made a mistake in assigning him a room, every room in the hotel having been previously engaged," Hill withdrew to the home of William Dye, to remain there as long as the "Businessmen's League does not succeed in opening a hotel for him."[14]

Similar well-publicized instances were reported by other black delegates, although the St. Louis organizers claimed that it was due only to the lateness of their reservations. "When we got the convention we pledged ourselves to take care of the colored delegates and we are going to do it," said the League president, obviously stung by the adverse publicity; League members had subscribed fifty thousand dollars to build the massive convention auditorium, and felt they deserved praise for their efforts. "But those who waited until the last

13. "Negroes Hold a Mass Meeting, They Want a Plank Adopted Denouncing Lynching in the South," *RN&O*, 16 June 1896.

14. "Is Still a Problem, What to Do with Negro Delegates to National Conventions, All the Rooms 'Engaged,'" ibid., 10 June 1896.

minute will have to take what they can get, so long as it is clean and good. White men cannot get accommodations at the hotels now."[15]

Unconvinced, more than a hundred black delegates and alternates met on June 15 to organize a complaint to the full convention over their mistreatment, as part of a larger caucus on political issues; the group also voted overwhelmingly to endorse the gold standard and called for a platform plank denouncing lynching in the South. Only six delegates at the mass meeting voted for silver, presumably led by George White, who had arrived in St. Louis the night before; it was his first opportunity to meet many of the nation's leading black Republicans as an equal, including fellow delegates James Hill, Judson W. Lyons of Georgia, and former congressman Robert Smalls of South Carolina, along with alternate delegates Dr. S. E. Courtney of Boston, John P. Green of Ohio, and George Knox of Indiana. White's old friend T. Thomas Fortune was also present as an observer-journalist, as was editor W. Calvin Chase of Washington, D.C.[16]

White went on to serve on the convention's Committee on Rules and Order of Business and earned respect for his performance at the St. Louis gathering despite his disappointment over the silver plank's defeat. Upon his return home, White was called upon to participate in the McKinley campaign as a traveling speaker, mostly speaking to blacks across North Carolina and reportedly in a few northern states; it is not clear in which other states he traveled, but it seems he was accompanied by other black leaders, including former state senator John P. Green of Ohio and former congressman John R. Lynch of Mississippi. His companions may even have included two nationally renowned leaders of the race, John Mercer Langston and Blanche K. Bruce, both facing the last political campaign of their lives.[17]

15. Ibid. The Businessmen's League president, S. M. Kennard, promised that "dozens of restaurants will feed colored delegates during convention week."

16. "Negroes Hold a Mass Meeting." Fortune and Chase were not delegates but were active in the convention's black protest movement. Former congressman John Mercer Langston sent a letter endorsing the movement, as well.

17. George H. White, letter to the *Washington Post*, printed 23 April 1901; "John Patterson Green," in Thomas Yenser, ed., *Who's Who in Colored America* (New York: Who's Who in Colored America Corp., 1941), 214–7. White cited his 1896 campaign travels in his 1901 letter to the *Post*, but probably spent most of that time in North Carolina; by 1900 he expanded his campaign travels to seven states. *Who's Who in Colored America* notes that Green traveled "during several Republican campaigns" with White, former congressman John M. Langston, and for-

Whatever contribution George White made to the 1896 McKinley effort, he was fast becoming as popular in his party outside North Carolina as at home, perhaps even more so. While the Cheatham-backed movement to defeat White had all but evaporated by September, after Populists and Republicans finalized their half of the fall fusion plan, White's alliance with James Young had left a bitter taste in the mouths of conservative black leaders who distrusted Young as an opportunistic holdover from the old revenue-ring days of the early 1890s. Young still had influential enemies in the party, a fact of which White was now acutely aware; among them were Cheatham's supporters. Young, now arguably the most popular black politician in the state, had previously been a close ally of Cheatham's, and his defection to White in 1896 aggravated Cheatham's personal dispute with his brother-in-law.[18]

Whatever their differences, George White and James Young did share a strong belief in education as the key to advancement by North Carolina blacks as well as a deep interest in black social organizations as another mechanism for advancement. They saw politics as more than simply a "means of protecting the Negro's status from prejudice and violence," as the conservatives argued. Young was a pragmatic realist; while conceding that blacks still had legitimate "grievances against certain Republicans" who were no more sympathetic than most Democrats to black aims, he emphasized that the Grand Old Party at least permitted blacks "to vote and scuffle" for offices, while the Democrats wanted to take away their right to vote.[19] Young's personal commitment to the candidacy of Daniel Russell was a sincere one, and White respected that belief; although White and Russell would never be close, White's support for Russell in the fall election was thoughtful and solid.

The 1896 election was the first to be conducted under the state's reformed election law, which had reversed decades of Democratic erosion of basic protection for minority voters of both races. Victors in the fusion election of 1894

---

mer U.S. senator Blanche K. Bruce; both Bruce and Langston were in failing health in 1896, however, and dead by 1898.

18. James Hunter Young (1859–1921) was a former Raleigh city council member, internal revenue clerk in Wilmington, and member of the 1894 General Assembly.

19. Crow, "'Fusion, Confusion, and Negroism,'" 368–9. Young was reelected to the General Assembly in 1896, his last elected post. But he was appointed chief fertilizer inspector for the state by Governor Daniel Russell before Russell made him a full colonel in the North Carolina Negro Battalion during the Spanish-American War.

had swiftly enacted the sweeping changes, which guaranteed each of the three parties a judge and a registrar at every poll to ensure honest elections. Among other important new provisions, the elected superior court clerk in each county was given authority to count votes, and the old county board of canvassers was abolished; obstacles to black registrants and voters were also removed under the new law, including the dropping of the troublesome prohibition against "devices" on the ballot. A flood of new black registrants had been predicted as a result, and Populists in the eastern counties were reportedly poised to appoint black judges and/or registrars, in order to reinforce the appeal of fusion to black voters.[20]

But both Populists and Democrats were troubled by the aggressive recruiting behavior of Republican managers in the eastern black-belt counties. Some distrustful Populist leaders suspected that the Republican registration efforts were a Trojan horse of sorts, paving the way for the black takeover of counties after the election, when the Populists were no longer useful. Future congressional candidate James B. Lloyd of Tarboro said he understood "their little game. . . . They are dependent on us to get their voters out, and if they then see they can 'stand alone,'" Republicans would undoubtedly display "more independence" in the future.[21]

Former Democratic congressman W. H. "Buck" Kitchin, having emerged from a brief flirtation with Populism, charged that as many as eight thousand unqualified black Republicans had been registered, including minors, criminals, and residents of other states. The Republican Party's Winston newspaper did not confirm Kitchin's allegations, but did gloat that the "negro vote registered so far . . . has swollen the Republican strength enormously," which could only help Republican candidates in November.[22]

The 1896 campaign proved the strangest in North Carolina history. Populists had agreed, for instance, to divide the electoral vote with Democrats for William Jennings Bryan, the joint nominee of both national parties, while seeking to help elect black McKinley supporters to the General Assembly and

20. Ibid., 379–80.

21. Anderson, *Race and Politics*, 236. He cites an October 9, 1896, letter from Lloyd to Marion Butler.

22. Crow, "'Fusion, Confusion, and Negroism,'" 380; Kitchin to Marion Butler, undated, Butler Papers, SHC. The *Winston Union-Republican* made the statement in its edition of 15 October 1896.

ensure the reelection of conservative Republican Jeter Pritchard to the U.S. Senate. If successful, their fusion plans with Republicans would guarantee that blacks would be elected as magistrates and county commissioners in the east—in the first such election allowed in twenty years—even though many Populists were openly antagonistic to the prospect of black officeholders. "The time has not come for the negro to rule and govern the white people of the state," the Populist convention chairman had declared in mid-August, warning that "whatever we do we must recognize that the white man must rule in North Carolina."[23]

Populists, meanwhile, shrewdly divided up the future congressional delegation with Republicans, expecting the GOP to carry only the Second and Fifth Districts, where George White and incumbent Thomas Settle were running, respectively. As election day approached, confusion mounted; Democrats were furious with the Populists, Populists were increasingly nervous about their "deals" with both parties, and Republicans were more confident than either of their opponents, especially in the Second District. By the end of October, black opposition to White had all but collapsed, while the Populist nominee had formally withdrawn in a last-ditch effort to bolster the chances of reelecting Frederick Woodard. Daniel Russell was set to become the state's first GOP governor in two decades, after having convinced blacks to unite behind him largely by stirring up fear over what would happen if the Democrats won. His black lieutenants carefully pointed to Mississippi and South Carolina, both of which had recently disfranchised their own black voters, as examples of what lay ahead should Russell be defeated and Democrats allowed to undo the election-law reforms.[24]

Strange or not, the election of 1896 was the state's fairest election since Reconstruction in terms of the honest counting of votes, as well as the most heavily subscribed; it produced a remarkable turnout of more than 85 percent of all eligible voters, including an estimated 87 percent of black voters.[25] In all, more than 330,000 votes were cast, nearly 20 percent more than in 1892,

23. Anderson, *Race and Politics*, 233–4. The speaker was Congressman Harry Skinner, who characterized the Populists as having become "a harlot between the old parties," quoted by the *Raleigh Caucasian*, 20 August 1896.

24. Crow, "'Fusion, Confusion, and Negroism,'" 383.

25. Ibid. Crow notes that all sixteen black-belt counties voted Republican, delivering almost twice as many Republican votes in 1896 as in 1892.

and the results were an equally stunning victory for the fusionists, as Republicans and Populists swept the state and all but one congressional district. Presidential contender Bryan won North Carolina in a nationwide losing effort, and William W. Kitchin became the state's only Democratic congressman, defeating Thomas Settle in the election's one true upset. George White won an absolute majority in the Second District, drawing nearly 52 percent of the vote and carrying five of the nine counties; two other Republicans won seats in the far western districts, although Populists won the state's five remaining seats.

The most illustrious winner, of course, was Daniel Russell, who received a narrow plurality over his two opponents in his quest for a four-year term as the state's highest official. Russell's Populist rival, William A. Guthrie, had withdrawn on the eve of the election in favor of Democrat Cyrus Watson but still garnered about 9 percent of the vote. Russell won by a margin of just eighty-five hundred votes, drawing 46.5 percent of the total to 44 percent for Watson.[26]

Populists dominated the General Assembly, taking almost half of the senate and more than a third of the house. To control both bodies, of course, they needed to share power with Republicans, and that uneasy alliance would continue until 1898; together, they outnumbered the Democrats by a margin of three to one. At least 12 blacks were elected to the 1897 legislature, including Senators W. Lee Person of Edgecombe and William B. Henderson of Vance; Representative Young of Wake, reelected convincingly, was among 10 black members of the new House. In all, 21 of the 22 new legislators from the Second District were either Populists or Republicans, including seven black Republicans who had benefitted from George White's presence on the ticket. And in a rare instance of racial solidarity, Edgecombe County elected both an all-black legislative delegation and an all-black list of justices of the peace; neighboring Bertie County voters elected 16 black magistrates. It was the last time either county would place so many blacks in office.[27]

It was a deeply satisfying triumph for George White, soon to be sworn in as the nation's only black congressman. His persistence had been rewarded, and his diligence had earned him the highest office voters could yet hope to be-

26. NCG, 1406. The 330,000-plus votes cast in the 1896 governor's race was quite a jump from 1892's just over 280,000.

27. Anderson, *Race and Politics*, 238.

stow upon a member of his race. He had drawn more than nineteen thousand votes, over twice as many as Henry Cheatham had received in the same district two years earlier. White's total vote in eight common counties even rivaled James O'Hara's drawing power of 1884, in O'Hara's two-man race with the same major opponent, Frederick Woodard.[28]

Returning to his former home of New Bern, White was greeted by about three thousand cheering citizens and was carried through the streets in a buggy drawn not by horses but by his old friends and supporters. He received a comparably hearty welcome the following week in Wilmington, the state's largest city, according to a series of highly flattering articles printed in the *Raleigh Gazette* by editor James H. Young, White's newest ally.[29] Since White had campaigned tirelessly for William McKinley, now it was White's turn to bask in the reflected glory of a popular new Republican president.

George Henry White took his seat in Congress on March 15, 1897, becoming the fourth black man to represent North Carolina's Second District in the U.S. House of Representatives. It was a solemn occasion for the Tarboro lawyer, and the culmination of seventeen years of steady political campaigns; the event marked his official return to the nation's capital, two decades after his graduation from Howard University. He was the only African American in the 55th Congress, but, ironically, was not the only George White to be sworn in that day; George Elon White, an Illinois Republican, was entering his second and final term in the House.[30]

The two George Whites were members of an overwhelming Republican majority in their chamber, and voted with 198 party colleagues to reelect Maine's Thomas B. Reed House Speaker over Democratic challenger Joseph W. Bailey of Texas by a vote of 200 to 114. Two other Republicans also hailed from North Carolina, Romulus Z. Linney and Richmond Pearson; the rest of

28. Ibid., 346–9 (Tables 14, 19, 20). Henry Cheatham tallied 9,413 votes in his fourth and final race in 1894, compared to nearly 17,000 in 1888. Had they run in the same eleven counties, White might well have outpolled O'Hara, but Craven, Jones, and Vance Counties were no longer in the Second District. White received more votes in Wayne in 1896 than O'Hara had in 1882, when he carried Wayne by default. In eight counties where they both ran, White drew 17,173 votes, O'Hara 17,448; White outpolled O'Hara in Halifax, Warren, Bertie, and Lenoir.

29. *Raleigh Gazette*, 21 November 1896, 28 November 1896, and 5 December 1896.

30. George Elon White (1848–1935) of Chicago was defeated for reelection in 1898. Yet a third George White (1872–1953), this one an Ohio Democrat, also served three terms in Congress during George Henry White's lifetime (1911–1915, 1917–1919).

the state's House delegation were Populists, with the lone exception of Democrat W. W. Kitchin of Roxboro, who voted for Bailey. Populist members gave their 21 votes to John C. Bell of Colorado. George Henry White, of course, owed his election, in part, to the Populist-Republican fusion, but as a member of Congress, he voted almost exclusively with his own party and for his president.[31]

Ordinarily, the new Congress would not have met until December, but this was a special session called by McKinley, beginning a mere fortnight after his inauguration. New congressmen were still recovering from the festivities when they were suddenly faced with a host of appropriations bills and the controversial Dingley tariff. Perhaps because of the rush to deal with these issues, George White's appearance on the Washington scene was scarcely noted by the press. Yet he must have attended many of the inaugural events, and was probably accompanied to some of them by Cora Lena; she spent little time in Washington, however, until the family moved there two years later.[32]

White's first address in Washington was at 1203 16th Street, NW, less than a block from his father's former home where he had lived as a student, but he soon moved to an address nearer the Capitol, on "A" Street, NE, according to congressional records; this was apparently a boardinghouse. He traveled often to North Carolina during 1897, both because of the illness of unnamed family members and for legal reasons, particularly a client's ongoing court case in Wilmington. The congressman did not purchase a home in the District of Columbia until following his 1898 reelection, after Cora Lena's health failed; she and one daughter moved to Washington for good only in January 1899, soon followed by other family members.[33]

31. The Populists and Republicans had little in common on national issues; the Populists had fused with Democrats by endorsing William Jennings Bryan, even though they named a separate vice-presidential candidate.

32. "One Colored Man named White," *Washington Evening Star,* 15 March 1897; "Gossip Heard at the Capitol," column, *Washington Post,* 18 March 1897; "Tarboro and Eastern Snap Shots," *Raleigh Gazette,* 11 September 1897; also, "Eastern Snap Shots," *Raleigh Gazette,* 5 June 1897. The brief *Star* subheading came in a longer story on the special session; the *Post* noted plans by Howard alumni for a reception in White's honor. The *Gazette* hinted in September that Mrs. White and the younger children had remained in Tarboro during much of the first session; George Jr. had been ill early in the summer, and Della was in Macon, Georgia.

33. *Congressional Directory,* 55th Cong., editions corrected through March 12, 1897; June 24, 1897; and January 12, 1899. By June 1897, White had moved to 316 "A" Street, NE, near the

The first session of the 55th Congress was scheduled by McKinley to capitalize on his popular mandate, giving the opposition little time to devise a strategy to block the new tariff. Thus the spring of 1897 became a busy one for George White, who shuttled between Washington and North Carolina on several occasions beginning as early as March 19, when he received his first leave of absence, "on account of sickness in his family," for four days. On April 10, he would receive a second leave, this one for ten days, "on account of important business," apparently to attend the court case in Wilmington; this was followed by another ten-day request for a combination of business and family illness, granted on April 23. In between these trips, he found time to introduce his first bill—one seeking relief for former congressman Robert Smalls of South Carolina—and to make his first recorded speech on the floor of the House, delivered on March 31.[34]

George White's maiden speech was brief but pointed, combining humor with a concise analysis of the beneficial effects of the proposed protective tariffs on his constituents, especially on those involved in the lumber industry. The Dingley tariffs were to be the highest ever imposed on foreign goods, amounting to what some called the blatant protection of monopolies in major industries; the concept was ardently opposed in much of the Democratic South, but Republicans held the upper hand in this Congress. In his allotted five minutes, White argued that the bill's lumber schedule "commends itself especially to the Southern people who have to labor to get bread and meat for their families." Mill workers had been among the hardest hit by the inadequate protections of the Wilson-Gorman tariff, which had allegedly caused widespread forfeiture of contracts by busy lumber mills and forced them to shut down in the face of unfair competition from cheaper imports.[35]

"There is a growing sentiment . . . that the industries and the labor of

Capitol. By early 1899, he had moved to a house at 1412 17th Street, NW, and was now listed as "accompanied" by his wife, a daughter, and two "other ladies," perhaps other relatives.

34. *Congressional Record*, 55th Cong., 1st Sess., 30, 1:90, 1:550–1, 1:677; "Eastern Snap Shots," *Raleigh Gazette*, 24 April 1897. According to the *Gazette*, "Congressman White spent the week in Wilmington, attending court." H.R. 1824 was referred to the Committee on War Claims, but never passed. Smalls, a five-term congressman from South Carolina, had sailed a Confederate steamer-gunboat out of Charleston and turned it over to Union forces in 1862.

35. *Congressional Record*, 55th Cong., 1st sess., 30, 1:550; Samuel Eliot Morison, *The Oxford History of the American People* (New York: Oxford University Press, 1965), 795–800. Morison summarizes the Wilson-Gorman tariff of 1894 and the Dingley tariff of 1897.

America shall be protected against the pauperism and the cheap labor of foreign countries," White said, declaring that the South's black laborers wanted "bread and butter [and] pay for an honest day's work." Democratic protests were dismissed as irrelevant: "finespun campaign theory" from the advocates of "'free trade' . . . 'free whisky' . . . and 'free silver' . . . the Southern element of the Democratic party has advocated 'free' everything except free ballots and free negroes."[36]

White then departed from the tariff's defense to pursue an open challenge to southern Democrats on two issues dear to his own heart: employment and voting rights for black Americans. It was the opening salvo in what would become a familiar litany of the obstacles being placed in the paths of blacks struggling to emulate white Americans; over the course of the next four years, his speeches would echo and expound upon these themes at length. In March 1897 he was "here to speak . . . as the sole representative on this floor of 9,000,000 [Americans], 90 percent of whom are laborers . . . who want something now upon which body and soul can be kept together."

Since the vast majority of blacks still lived in the South, where disfranchisement and discrimination were most prevalent, it was inevitable that White would reserve his sharpest words for the region's ruling Democrats, particularly those who claimed they alone understood the needs of southerners. Democrats had bristled at recent Republican charges of "incompetency" in their management of southern states, and White now mocked them for sheer hypocrisy: "Well, I am a Southerner to the manner born and reared, and am usually in sympathy with the South, but when Democratic members on the other side of this House drag into this great Congress of the United States the expressions of the Southern plantations in regard to 'the darky and the heels of a mule,' then I think the imputation [of incompetency] is a correct one."[37]

One South Carolina congressman had accused southern Republicans like Romulus Linney, White's fellow North Carolinian, of not properly representing the "popular sentiment of the South" on the tariff. White turned on that critic with a withering phrase: "I think, Mr. Chairman, that it comes with bad grace from the gentleman to talk of misrepresentation of the Southern people when he considers the fact that 130,000 voters in his State are not allowed to

36. *Congressional Record*, 55th Cong., 1st sess., 30, 1:550. This remark drew applause from the Republican side and the galleries, which probably held a number of black observers.
37. Ibid.

vote at all." In a sly jab, he admitted he knew little of South Carolina "as it now is," but that he had been more familiar with it "when it was a State in the Union, with the privileges of sister States."[38]

It was George White's last recorded word during this four-month session, but he had made his debut, and the Dingley tariff soon passed the House, by a party-line vote of 205 to 122. White next turned his attention to more routine matters, including the recommendation of postmasters and others for appointment by the president; by the end of the first session in July, he had successfully recommended 39 persons, including 23 blacks as postmasters in the counties of the Second District, according to the *Raleigh Gazette*. Much of White's future notoriety resulted from this specific action, since it produced the first blacks in influential public positions in many small towns across the Black Second. Henry Cheatham had obtained fewer than a dozen black postmasters in his first year as congressman under President Harrison, but even this number had been startling, since before 1889 there had never been more than one or two black postmasters at any one time in the entire district.[39]

White's pace—twice as many appointments as Cheatham in the first four months—was remarkable. While few of his initial group of black appointees served large post offices, one large town, Rocky Mount, and two county seats, Halifax and Windsor, were among the first group to receive black postmasters. The rest were scattered across the district, mostly in "obscure and unprofitable places like Lawrence or Ridgeway," but were still highly visible to each area's white population. And like Cheatham before him, White faced an uphill battle at times; at least two of White's appointees eventually went to jail for misuse of funds, along with a third appointee he had recommended in neighboring Nash County. At least one of his nominees was even rejected by the Senate. Yet the pace would continue into 1898, with at least two major dis-

38. Ibid.

39. "About People You Know," *Raleigh Gazette*, 31 July 1897; Anderson, *Race and Politics*, 243–50. Anderson gives a partial list of black postmasters in the Second District between 1897 and 1901 in Table 6 (246). The *Gazette* noted the appointment of the black Israel D. Hargett as postmaster at Rocky Mount, one of the few "paying" offices in the district; White nominated white Republicans for post offices at Goldsboro, Kinston, and Tarboro. Because of its geographical split between Edgecombe and Nash Counties, Rocky Mount's federal appointments were often divided between congressional districts. Most of the town lay inside Nash County, assigned to the Fourth District in the 1890s, but the postmaster's appointment—a lucrative one despite the town's small size—apparently went to the Second District's congressman.

trict towns, Wilson and Weldon, benefitting from the next year's crop of black appointees.[40]

Democrats and white patrons in the district were angered by the sudden upsurge in such appointments, coming on the heels of the elections of black magistrates and the hiring of black constables, policemen, and jailers in many counties. Postmasters were not policy makers, but few public officials had such close dealings with so many citizens on a regular basis; to many observers, it was a replay of the excesses of the Reconstruction era, with no end in sight to "Negro domination." Because some postmasters—especially in rural areas and small towns—actually had their offices in their homes, white patrons were often forced to visit black neighborhoods to transact their postal business, which they often resented. George White's rumored plans in mid-April to appoint a black cadet to West Point had confirmed the worst fears of many Democrats about the new congressman, who had earlier proposed the appointment of a black U.S. consul at Victoria, British Columbia; this had occasioned White's first known visit to the White House, when he filed nomination papers for Capt. John P. Leach.[41]

White's hometown newspaper, the *Tarboro Southerner*, was among those watching the appointments and commenting regularly, often with more than a little sarcasm. "Any office held by a negro under former Administrations is considered by that race to belong to it, and they will raise a howl if they do not get it," the *Southerner* wrote on April 22, in a comment on the Rocky Mount postmastership. By June 10, the newspaper warned that "there will soon be no one left to manage the campaign and pull the legs of office seekers" if President McKinley continued his current pace of black appointments in the district, and tweaked White for his energetic pursuit of jobs "for those who worked so hard to bring about his election."[42] If the congressman was aware of

40. Anderson, *Race and Politics*, 246. According to Anderson, Bertie County was reported to have nine black postmasters by 1898. White's appointees at Rocky Mount and Tillery were removed from office and imprisoned, along with Battleboro postmaster Clinton W. Battle, whom White had recommended to Populist colleague William F. Strowd.

41. "Washington Report, Seymour's Mantle," *RN&O*, 1 April 1897; "No. Carolina's Colored Congressman May Appoint a Negro," *New York Sun*, reprinted in *RN&O*, 23 April 1897. State senator W. Lee Person accompanied White on this visit, when the duo reportedly encountered Cheatham, who was seeking a separate appointment.

42. "Frank Powell's National Capital Notes," *Tarboro Southerner*, 22 April 1897; untitled editorial asides, *Tarboro Southerner*, 10 June 1897.

the developing unease at home over his record of appointments, however, he gave no sign that it bothered him.

White continued his hectic travel schedule throughout the summer, attending daughter Della's graduation from Scotia Seminary in Concord, North Carolina, in late May, then returning to Washington to deliver the annual commencement address at his alma mater, Howard University. In late June, he and Cora Lena visited Baltimore, Maryland, and Wilmington, Delaware, apparently for a brief vacation after young George's recovery from a serious illness. White returned to Tarboro after the recess of the first session of Congress on July 24, then immediately left for Wilmington on legal business, returning by mid-August for "a few days of much needed rest at his home" before a quick family trip to New Bern.[43]

His "graceful and accomplished" daughter Della spent much of the summer in Macon, Georgia, with her stepmother's sister, Mrs. Eustace E. Green, celebrating "a brilliant season" after her graduation from Scotia; she returned to Tarboro in mid-August to begin her teaching job in the town's public school. In her absence, tragedy nearly struck the White family, when Della's sister and brother were trapped in a buggy drawn by a runaway horse. Only the intervention of a heroic stranger stopped the horse and prevented "a serious accident," according to the *Tarboro Southerner*; nine-year-old Mamie and four-year-old George Jr. were frightened but not injured, while Tom Brown, the hero, drew the *Southerner's* special praise for his courage.[44]

After the family's vacation in New Bern, Congressman White returned to Washington in early September. Although the Congress would not reconvene for three months, he was undoubtedly eager to begin planning for the second session; he had been appointed a member of the House Agriculture Committee on the final day of the first session, and may have attended committee working sessions during the recess. He did return to North Carolina in October, still tending to legal affairs in Wilmington and New Bern, but by December 6 had settled in Washington once again, when the 55th Congress convened its second session.

43. White's travels were regularly noted by the *Raleigh Gazette*.

44. "Tarboro and Eastern Snap Shots," *Raleigh Gazette*, 14 August 1897; *Tarboro Southerner*, 29 July 1897. Black passerby Tom Brown saved the children; "the writer does not know Tom, but having witnessed his conduct on this occasion, he is prepared to believe good things of him," wrote the journalist.

This session was a far busier one for White, who introduced seven bills and joint resolutions in the seven months, as well as a dozen petitions and papers from a variety of constituents and other organizations. All but one of his bills involved requests for various kinds of relief for individuals, including the family of a black South Carolina postmaster murdered in early 1898 by an armed mob of whites in Lake City; all were referred to various committees on claims, military affairs, or the post office, and none were passed. The seventh bill, H.R. 9421, was a proposal for incorporation of the National Colored American Industrial Association No. 1; it was referred to the Committee on Manufactures, but was not passed by the House.[45]

The Lake City postmaster's murder had been front-page news throughout much of the South. On February 21, 1898, a group of armed white men had attacked the postmaster, Frazier J. Baker, and his family, killing Baker and one son before burning down their house. White's joint resolution, read to the House ten days later, sought $1,000 in financial relief for Baker's widow and their five surviving children, "now suffering even for medical treatment and other necessities of life." Consent to the resolution was blocked, however, when Congressman Charles L. Bartlett of Georgia objected to its formal introduction, thereby preventing White from speaking further. A testy exchange moments later between White and Speaker Thomas Reed failed to resolve the issue, after Reed announced that White's request was "not in order."[46]

House Resolution 171 was read aloud but not discussed; its referral to the Committee on Post-Office and Post Roads was an unhappy omen despite widespread sympathy for the Baker family. White had intended to ask for a much larger sum—$50,000 in assistance—but later told antilynching activist Ida Wells-Barnett he had reduced it to $1,000 "because he thought the southern congressmen would not object to that sum." She retorted that White "did not know the South as well as I had hoped for; if he did, he would know that they would object to the compensation of five dollars" purely on principle.

45. *Congressional Record*, 55th Cong., 2d Sess., 31, Index, 1:538. The list of bills, joint resolutions, and petitions and papers introduced by White during the second session is contained in the index. The following were subjects of relief attempts: Rebecca Bly (H.R. 10629), C. G. Holt (H.R. 8653), the Baker family (H. Res. 171), Mary Moten (H.R. 5319), Willis Pinner (H.R. 5320), and Hardy Spencer (H.R. 8332, to remove a charge of desertion).

46. Ibid., 1:2427.

Despite having a newborn son to nurse, Mrs. Wells-Barnett spent five weeks in Washington lobbying White to withdraw his bill, as well as pleading with the committee chairman to report it out so it could be voted on.[47]

Neither White's admirable intentions nor Wells-Barnett's stubborn quest were successful, however; even her personal intervention with President McKinley proved futile. Illinois representative William Lorimer had promised Wells-Barnett to offer a "more adequate" measure, which might well have passed the House, but declined on parliamentary grounds to take action until White's bill was disposed of. After war was declared on Spain in April, Lorimer warned Wells-Barnett that action would have to be delayed until after the war ended; she returned to Chicago only to learn that her well-publicized campaign had created a strong backlash against both her and the issue. As expected, White's resolution died in committee, and no similar bill was ever again offered. The matter remained a sore point between Wells-Barnett and White for years, and may have been one reason Wells-Barnett objected to the language of White's proposed antilynching bill in 1900.[48]

White's attempts at speaking were more successful on four other occasions during the session, particularly his first long speech, on January 11, 1898. The subject was civil-service reform, and Congressman White was addressing the "Committee of the House as a Whole." He presented his case with zest and humor, even managing artfully to digress into foreign affairs on two occasions and disfranchisement of black voters on a third, all without losing his audience's attention. He said he despised the Civil Service Commission, which he labeled as unconstitutional, and called for its replacement by a decentralized system of "fitness bureaus" within each federal department, "because the head of a Department knows better than the commission can know the character of the work done" there. Citing examples of abuse of the current law, he warned defenders that the concept of a merit system, as originally intended under the

47. Alfreda M. Duster, ed., *Crusade for Justice: The Autobiography of Ida B. Wells* (Chicago: University of Chicago Press, 1970), 252-4. Wells-Barnett died in 1931; her memoirs, edited by her daughter, were published four decades later.

48. Ibid. Wells-Barnett was accompanied to the White House by Illinois senator William E. Mason and seven Chicago-area congressmen, probably including Lorimer. She does not mention White's 1900 antilynching bill in her own book, but her dissatisfaction with its language is noted by her biographers, including Linda O. McMurry in *To Keep the Waters Troubled: The Life of Ida B. Wells* (New York: Oxford University Press, 1998).

law, had degenerated into a wasteful bureaucracy that now threatened instead to "revolutionize the internal workings of our entire system."

White went on to characterize Republicans as the "true reformers" on the issue, before revealing his own personal views on the matter. Democrats claiming to represent the "merit system" had derided Republicans as "spoilsmen," but White claimed that the opposite was true. "We are the ones who would perpetuate some form of civil service," he said. "We are the ones who believe in merit, but we also believe, or I do at least, and I proclaim it as my doctrine, that to the victors belong the spoils; or, in language a little more primitive, if you please, the ox that pulls the plow ought to have a chance to eat the fodder."[49]

The Civil Service Commission, he said, "without regard to merit, without regard to fitness, pulls its ample india-rubber folds over 48,000 men and women," allowing such abuses as the two White now described: an infamous ballot-box stuffer from his own Second District, who had obtained a lifetime appointment as a common laborer at the Interior Department under the Cleveland administration, purely on the basis of his Democratic affiliation; and a second man, who had failed the "merit system" examination, but then obtained a civil service appointment, advancing through the ranks until he had become a bureau chief responsible for examining applicants under the very system whose entrance examination he had once failed. Neither man could be replaced, for both now held "life tenure."[50]

George White's fifteen-minute speech brought strong applause and cheers from the floor and the galleries, leading the chairman at one point to gavel all listeners into order. His references to long-promised "aid to Cuban sufferers" and the recent overthrow of Hawaiian Queen Liliuokalani by U.S. citizens were unrelated to civil service reform, but nonetheless pointed. The Republican Party platform of 1896 had promised to aid Cubans, but U.S. Government boats still intercepted relief shipments; Hawaii's legal government had been overthrown while the (Democratic) administration gave tacit approval.

49. Ibid., Index, 1:541–2. White's original allotment of time had expired, but he was now granted an additional ten minutes by unanimous agreement. He was interrupted seven times by applause or laughter, with "loud and prolonged applause" at the end of his speech.

50. Ibid., 542. White claimed he had tried to recommend a new laborer for the job but was informed it was covered by civil service; the Interior Department appointment clerk was a Democrat.

Disfranchisement of blacks was patently unconstitutional, asserted White, and still the Congress did nothing to halt it. All were at variance with his concept of just and proper governmental actions, and the civil service system was no different. "I make no profession to be a great constitutional lawyer," White said, but the "evasive arguments" advanced in defense of the law would have driven Charles Dickens's "Artful Dodger . . . away in shame because of his inability to cope with these gentlemen."[51]

White's next major speech, delivered on March 7, dealt with his attempt to create an artillery regiment specifically for blacks in the U.S. Army, mirroring the Army's provisions for two black regiments each of cavalrymen and infantrymen. Black soldiers had certainly proved their worth during the "recent rebellion," yet nearly four decades later, they were still barred from serving as artillerymen. The army had simply refused to create such a regiment on its own, and since no regiments were integrated, there were no black artillerymen.

This was no plea for special privilege, White said, but for "a man's chance, a man's protection; in fact, all the privileges of an American citizen." With war against Spain clearly on the horizon, "I pledge you that the black phalanx is ready to be mustered in, one-half million strong."[52] Blacks deserved this opportunity based on their record of faithful service during and after the war, without indulging in "strikes, tumult, riots, or labor organizations." But their loyalty to the Union had not always been justly repaid, as was "painfully evidenced by the almost daily outrages [of] lynchings, murders, assassinations, and even cremations of our people all over the Southland." Protesting such inhuman treatment, blacks had been callously referred back to the "several States and their governments [because] the nation has no power to interfere in the premises."

Yet regardless of its faults, this "grand old Union" still held the loyalty of its black citizens. Black citizens would be content with nothing less than equal treatment under the law, White continued, calling on the Congress to "remove all statutory barriers prescribed against us." He now uttered his most famous phrase, in the first of many iterations:

51. Ibid. White scored the unwillingness of Congress to punish offending states in the South, which had limited the franchise so severely that as few as 5,000 (white) voters might decide an election in some districts, compared to a national average of 30,000–50,000 voters.

52. Ibid., 1:2556.

You have two hundred and fifty years the start of us; and if you are honest, if you are fair, if you are not cowards, and of course you are not, you
certainly will be willing to accord to us at this late day all the rights of
American citizens enjoyed by you. *An even chance in the race of life is all*
that we ask; and then if we cannot reach the goal, let the devil take the
hindmost one![53] (emphasis added)

For technical parliamentary reasons, White was unable to propose the specific amendment that occasioned this speech; his proposal was therefore symbolic only, if compellingly so. Still, he called it a "sad commentary" that such
an amendment was even necessary to allow black soldiers to serve as artillerymen. For the first time since entering Congress, White had now publicly expressed his unequivocal belief in the equal rights of all black citizens under
law in America. Again his speech drew loud and prolonged applause, but not
all hands were clapping; as the war with Spain neared, the first shots were also
being fired in a smaller domestic skirmish in North Carolina. "White supremacy" would soon be the watchword in this campaign to defeat the nation's only black congressman, as the forces of reaction gathered steam for the
coming fall election.

Like many politicians before and since, White was not always sensitive to
his image in the press or to the need to court journalists. A careful, private
man, he had done little to seek favorable publicity before his 1896 election,
preferring to deliver his message in personal speeches, few of which were
reprinted; his notices were therefore laudatory but limited. After his election,
however, that situation had undergone a rapid change, as he now became
"good copy" in the journalistic parlance. Black newspapers such as the *Raleigh*
Gazette and Washington's *Colored American* began to carry longer stories
about him, emphasizing his personal charisma and exaggerating his impact on
the national scene; he was the first black superstar, the political savior of his
race, and nearly every word that he uttered quickly appeared on the printed
pages before hundreds of eager readers, often picked up and reprinted in other
black publications. While the mainstream white media had not completely ignored George White, editors of most white newspapers—especially in Democratic North Carolina—seemed less awestruck than their black colleagues,
printing few accounts of his early speeches and often mentioning him only in

53. Ibid.

passing, outside the editorial page. For the white community, White was generally less of a lasting phenomenon than an irritant; the less said, the sooner he might fade away.

That, too, would soon change, if only for the worse, in the wake of a strategic error White committed in the early spring of 1898. It seems he made some incidental use of "franked" envelopes to mail copies of a commendatory article from the *Colored American* to his friends in North Carolina. The articles in question, which dealt with White's March 7 speech, ended up, to his chagrin, in the hands of a white Raleigh newspaper. The *Morning Post* roundly criticized him for abusing the congressional franking privilege, and then thwarted his attempt to explain the situation by letter as "purely an oversight." In White's words, the *Post* printed only "garbaged extracts" of his letter; stung by the editor's apparent animosity, he then furnished a copy of the letter to his hometown newspaper, which reprinted it without comment, to his advantage.[54]

This first of many such barbs from the white press was a new and unsettling experience for the proud and proper congressman. White had rarely encountered open hostility from powerful journalists, although as early as 1888 mistreatment by Josephus Daniels of the *Wilson Advance* had constituted a warning signal. Since White's election to Congress in 1896, even Daniels—now the publisher of the state's largest newspaper—had been largely neutral, even charitable, to the Tarboro lawyer. But as his record of appointments and the tenor of his speeches received increasing publicity, the new celebrity accorded him in Washington and elsewhere soon proved to carry a hidden cost at home. Only the outbreak of war would interrupt the criticism, but only temporarily.

White continued to shuttle between Washington and North Carolina during the second session of the 1898 Congress, requesting a total of at least twenty-nine days of official leave from the House on seven occasions between December 6, 1897, and April 13, 1898, almost all for "important business," presumably legal cases. He was in North Carolina on April 18 when word

54. "Letter from Congressman White," 11 April 1898, *Tarboro Southerner*, 14 April 1898, containing a letter to the editor of the *Raleigh Morning Post*. The article mailed earlier was probably from the *Washington Colored American* of 19 March 1898; "Only an Equal Chance" contained the entire text of White's March 7 speech and described him as "the race's brilliant representative in Congress."

came that war would soon be declared on Spain, and despite his best efforts, he arrived back in Washington too late to vote at the all-night session, as he told the House on April 19, just before its noon recess: "I was unavoidably absent last evening, having traveled 450 miles yesterday and last night in the attempt to get here for the purpose of voting on the Cuban resolution," he told his House colleagues. "I got here at 8 o'clock this morning, after the vote had been taken last night; and now desire to say that if I had been present, I should have voted in the affirmative on the final passage of the resolution."[55]

Such a personal explanation as White's was not unique; at least one other congressman sent a similar message from his sickbed. But the urgency with which White had returned was sadly comical. At the beginning of his trip, he had missed an April 13 vote on a related joint resolution that recognized the independence of Cuba, and now he had missed the declaration of war by a few hours. One purpose of the trip had apparently been to deliver his letter on the franking incident to the *Southerner* in Tarboro, in time for its Thursday publication deadlines; had he been less concerned with protesting his innocence, perhaps, his apology to the House might have been unnecessary.[56]

Just three days after his return to Washington, White made his final House speech of the session, offering his observations on the contest between Congressman Edward Carmack of Tennessee and challenger Josiah Patterson. Both were Democrats, and according to White their contest had been clouded by conflicting claims over "how the negro vote was cast in that district"; but he cared less for the outcome in this instance than for the opportunity to speak once again about the evils of disfranchisement, using the neighboring state of Mississippi as his example. White estimated that as many as 150,000 Mississippi blacks had been denied the right to vote in the 1896 election, leading him to question "whether or not there is a republican form of government in the State of Mississippi" and other southern states with similar records of disfranchisement. That congressmen from these states "can come here and occupy seats by the suppression of the vote of their district, simply because they are of a different complexion, of a different race or different politics" was anathema to him. But he did not expect his white listeners to "feel

55. *Congressional Record*, 55th Cong., 2d Sess., 31, 1:4086; also, Index, 1:538.

56. He presumably had other business to transact in Tarboro but was determined to have his letter printed in unexpurgated fashion by a friendly source as soon as possible. Hand delivery by April 14 was the only way to ensure its timely publication that week.

this as I do," for he was unique in one respect: "I am easily the leader of one thing, and that is the black phalanx on this floor. I have no rival, and I will not be disturbed in that leadership."[57]

The eight-minute speech was vintage White, rolling easily between humorous jabs at his Democratic opponents (and even at his own status) and more serious analyses of the South's wrongful treatment of its black citizens, with both dry statistics and lyrical turns of phrase, as in "The lifeblood of the Union is being sapped; little by little it may be, but surely sapped." Yet it was White's gradually increasing obsession with disfranchisement—second only to lynching as a subject in his future speeches—which had begun to distinguish him from his black predecessors in the Congress. Few had dared to make so many speeches in their first year, and almost none had raised so potent an issue in such an elegant fashion, never shrill yet difficult to ignore.

The second session ended in early July, with the Spanish-American War still technically underway; the Spanish, overpowered on all fronts, sued for peace after July 15, and signed a preliminary armistice in mid-August. Despite George White's earlier hopes, no black artillerymen were sent to fight in Cuba, which surrendered less than four weeks after American forces landed; his cohort James Young was now a colonel in the North Carolina regiment but saw no overseas action during the three-month war. But even as the "splendid little war" ended and White returned to North Carolina for the summer and his expected renomination, a nasty little political war was ready to resume in his home state with surprising ferocity.

Young's appointment by Russell "unleashed a barrage of racist rhetoric against him," helping set the tone for the fall election; the all-black regiment was mustered out in early 1899.[58] By the middle of the fall, the first casualties of the white-supremacy campaign were recorded and the fragile stability of Republican-Populist fusion demolished for all time. Young and White, allies since just 1896, now faced the political whirlwind together.

57. *Congressional Record,* 55th Cong., 2d Sess., 31, 1:4194.
58. "James Hunter Young," *DNCB,* 6:297.

9

Facing the Lions: Reelection to a Second Term

Neither the subject nor the text of his speech at Alabama's Tuskegee Institute has been found, but George White must have long pondered his choice of words for the May 1898 commencement address there. The school, run by the emerging black leader Booker T. Washington, had become the symbol of black accommodation to segregation during the 1890s since Washington's famous "Atlanta Compromise" speech in 1895, and Washington had himself become a symbol of "acceptable" black leaders, a man publicly admired by white conservatives, both for the economic self-reliance he preached and his disavowal of an activist approach to civil rights for blacks.[1] White certainly agreed with Washington on the need for self-reliance and certainly disagreed with him on civil rights, but on Washington's theory of industrial education for blacks, there was a more nebulous balance of ideas between the two men. The theory ran counter to White's fundamental beliefs, and his own hard-won education—even in a normal school for teachers twenty years earlier—had been more academic than vocational. Yet White had never advocated liberal-arts education for black children as a panacea, and in any event, the congressman would hardly dare to argue with the theory of industrial education on his host's home ground, in front of the man's disciples. It was far wiser to praise the educator diplomatically and encourage his followers to continue in the pursuit of their goals rather than urge them to question the mindset of their leader.

1. Gatewood, *Aristocrats of Color*, 302–3.

White spoke on the Tuskegee campus on Thursday, May 26, 1898, where he was "received with great enthusiasm," according to one brief account. It was part of a week-long swing through the southeast for White, who had requested a leave from Congress, also making stops in Atlanta and Macon, Georgia, on his return trip. In Atlanta, he addressed the Douglass Lyceum at Big Bethel Church, and in Macon he visited the family of his wife's sister.[2] But the major purpose of his trip was clearly to make the pilgrimage to Tuskegee and to establish a working relationship with the enigmatic Washington. It is not clear when the two men first met, but this may have been the first time. Their backgrounds were too different to expect a close friendship to develop; Washington probably felt more affinity on both personal and philosophical levels for Henry Cheatham than he did for Cheatham's brother-in-law. But as two practical men, White and Washington must have foreseen their eventual need to work together, despite the barriers that prevented an outright alliance. If there was no immediate mutual trust in 1898, neither would there ever be any sign of animosity between the two. What seems to have developed is a highly proper and cordial relationship, grounded in respectful disagreement for the other's positions but flexible enough to grow and mature as the two men came to understand each other more deeply.

Theirs was to be a cautious, unspoken compact of divergent strategies. Booker T. Washington had chosen a nonpolitical course of action in leading his race during a difficult period, but his political instincts remained active and shrewd; he understood and appreciated George White's dedication to protecting the rights of American blacks, but saw no effective way to reverse the dominant viewpoint among the white majority, now determined to reduce blacks to second-class status. Although he would quietly battle the effects of Jim Crow laws and segregation on his people, Washington would not openly challenge or malign the system that imposed them.[3] By contrast, George White had become the last political lightning rod of black America, if almost unwittingly so—defying the injustice he witnessed by speaking out against it at every available opportunity, in effect daring the system to punish him for his increasingly blunt candor while stirring his followers to protest the same mistreatment. George White hoped to shame the nation into changing its

2. "City Paragraphs," WCA, 28 May and 11 June 1898. Della White had spent the previous summer with Eustace and Georgianna Green, who had lived in Macon since about 1890.
3. Ibid.

collective mind; he would not question Professor Washington's sincerity or his actions, but could not follow the same quiet course. His words might be interpreted as heresy by the white establishment of the South, but that was a chance he felt compelled to take; if he could rouse the Congress and the rest of the nation to action, it was a risk well worth taking.

The philosophical divide between White and Washington mirrored the larger, growing divisions among the race as a whole, as conservative blacks battled to preserve their material gains while outspoken black intellectuals criticized the political system that seemed intent on abandoning their race. Washington was a former slave, White raised as a free child during the last days of slavery; their common memories of the institution would link them, but as new generations that had never known slavery grew to adulthood, the influence of older blacks born during the slave era would begin to decline sharply. As common memories faded, the fragile solidarity among post-Reconstruction black leaders would also begin to unravel, yet it is clear that Washington and White maintained a friendly, helpful professional rivalry for the better part of a decade after the Tuskegee speech.

George White did bring away a new awareness of the worth of industrial training for black citizens from his Alabama visit. He continued to believe that talented blacks should receive university-level liberal-arts educations, but he discarded his old prejudice against industrial education after seeing it in action at Tuskegee. "I confess I went there with some misgivings," he told an audience a year later at Hampton Institute, Tuskegee's mother school,

> but when I found one-third of the property of that little town owned by the school, when I saw there 1100 boys and girls, 88 teachers, and $350,000 worth of real estate, and learned that the many buildings had been erected by boys from the crude masses; when I saw students from all conditions of life . . . all learning how to support themselves and live as they should—when I saw all these things, my prejudice vanished, and now I am a firm supporter of the industrial idea.[4]

Few letters from this early period illuminate the White-Washington relationship, and most that do survive are one-sided, from George White or his

4. "Congressman White's Address," *Southern Workman and Hampton School Record*, July 1899, 244–5. White spoke at Hampton Institute's 31st commencement on June 15, 1899, along with Howard professor Kelly Miller and former U.S. minister to Liberia John H. Smyth. The text of his address was printed here.

wife to Booker T. Washington. But a clearer sign lies in the pages of the *Colored American,* which unflaggingly praised and supported White's efforts until its 1904 demise. Washington quietly subsidized that newspaper and advised its editor, Edward Elder Cooper, and the newspaper took no editorial stands that might have displeased its powerful patron.[5]

After his speeches in Tuskegee and Atlanta, George White returned to Washington in early June to begin a busy summer. In addition to congressional duties, over the next eight weeks he also traveled on a nearly continuous basis, including several trips to North Carolina, a side trip to Baltimore with his wife, and a lengthier trip to the Midwest in late July after attending the Republican state convention in Raleigh. He also received an honor from his alma mater, Howard University, during that school's summer commencement: an honorary master's degree, one of three it awarded that year. This was neither the first nor the last honorary degree White received, but must surely have been the most personally meaningful for the farmer's son from Bladen County, who had recently become an honorary trustee of Howard.[6]

In May White also received an audience with the nation's chief executive to discuss the issue of black service in the U.S. Army as it prepared to invade Cuba. Only a brief newspaper account documents the largely symbolic meeting; few blacks were sent to fight in Cuba, although those who did see combat distinguished themselves by their valor. The black artillery regiment that White sought was never created; the four black army regiments sent to Cuba were existing units, the Ninth and Tenth Cavalry and Twenty-fourth and

5. Gatewood, *Aristocrats of Color,* 62; BTW to Edward Elder Cooper, 28 April 1904, and Richard W. Thompson to BTW, 3 September 1900, BTWP. Despite disclaimers, Booker T. Washington provided both moral encouragement and indirect payments to Edward Cooper and the *Colored American;* he may have paid the salary of the paper's managing editor, Richard W. Thompson, who remained there largely at BTW's encouragement while employed full time as a federal clerk. Both men also maintained a lengthy correspondence with BTW.

6. "City Paragraphs," WCA, 18 June 1898; *Howard University Directory of Graduates, 1870–1985* (White Plains, N.Y.: Bernard Charles, 1986), xii; Dyson, *Howard University: The Capstone,* 421. Other recipients of honorary master's degrees in 1898 included I. Oyabe and Mark Thompson; U.S. consul Richard T. Greener and Howard Law Dean William F. Bascom each received an honorary doctorate of law. In 1896, White had received honorary LL.D. degrees from Livingstone College and Biddle University, and in 1900 received an honorary Ph.D. from the Agricultural and Mechanical College of Alabama in 1900. According to Dyson, White became an honorary trustee of Howard in 1897 and remained one until his death; the primary function of this board was to advertise the university across the country.

Twenty-fifth Infantry.[7] Nevertheless, being heard in the White House was an encouraging sign for a freshman congressman.

Two weeks before he left for Tuskegee, White had requested the audience with President McKinley to press his case for equal treatment of black soldiers by the army following a "savage attack" by the *Washington Post* "upon Negro leaders and organs, and its contemptuous reference to the colored soldier." While the *Post's* critical recent editorials could hardly be characterized as "savage," they had struck a racial nerve.[8] In describing the May 11 meeting, the *Colored American* called White's efforts "a long step in the right direction," since McKinley had "assured Mr. White of his sympathy with the movement for a larger recognition of the Negro soldiers, and expressed high regard for the valor and capacity of the colored comrades, knowing their worth from actual contact in the field. He stated that at least five regiments would be made up of colored men, and they would be commanded by their own efforts."[9]

The meeting is the only recorded private encounter between the two during McKinley's term of office. It was also the second dramatic event within a week for George White; days earlier, he had been renominated without opposition by Second District Republicans at a convention in Weldon. "Few men in either party have in so short a time attracted the attention of this gentlemen for taking hand in the heat of debate," wrote the *Colored American*, which had earlier called his renomination (and reelection) "a foregone conclusion. He is making his presence felt, and the race feels justly proud of him."[10]

7. "Black Troops Fight in Spanish American War," in Christian, *Black Saga*, 284. Four new volunteer regiments of black soldiers were formed but none saw action in the brief war although nearly two dozen black sailors had died aboard the U.S. battleship *Maine* in Havana harbor in February.

8. The *Washington Post* editorials, entitled "Civilians' Rights in War Times" (22 April 1898) and "Washington and the War" (25 April 1898), both "criticize[d] the tone and temper of some of the colored troops—men of the Twenty-Fifth Infantry"—for rowdy behavior in protesting their transport in segregated "Jim Crow" train cars. Black leaders were outraged at the criticism.

9. Untitled editorial, WCA, 14 May 1898. It called White's visit "his latest signal service [to his] constituents . . . the colored people of the entire country."

10. *Colored American*, 14 May 1898; "Sharps and Flats," ibid., 7 May 1898. The latter column referred to White's remarks in the Patterson-Carmack contest, remarks the newspaper called "forcible, convincing and at times humorous."

More than a few white Republican leaders were equally satisfied with White's performance thus far, including New York congressman George N. Southwick, who paid special praise to the North Carolinian in a letter to journalist J. E. "Grit" Bruce, which was reprinted in the *Colored American* on June 11. "I can vouch for the fact that his fellow Republicans in the House regard him as a most capable and worthy man," Southwick said, while admitting that their Democratic colleagues—particularly southerners, "on whose minds the instrument of human slavery has made a deep impression"—did not necessarily agree.[11]

Southwick's letter, one of the few favorable contemporary descriptions of George White that did not come from an African American source, paints a detailed and revealing portrait of the young congressman at the end of his first year in office: "Mr. White is sturdy of frame and limb, sturdy of voice, sturdy of Republicanism. He is an orator of no inferior degree of excellence. With depth of mind, breadth of experience and charm of manner he combines an instinct of humor well developed which attracts the sympathy and support of all his colleagues, except those to whom color is an insuperable barrier."[12]

White's "witty sallies" had frequently elicited rounds of applause from his Republican colleagues in the House, if not from the opposition, Southwick wrote, and he overlooked the "petty prejudices manifested against him by his Democratic colleagues from the cotton belt" in a "calm, courteous and conservative" fashion, "while winning the esteem, even the affection of his Republican associates." Moreover, Southwick added, "Mr. White reveres the principles of the party of Lincoln and Grant. The crack of the party whip is never necessary to get him into line for Republican measures of legislation. He is a stalwart among Stalwart Republicans."[13]

George White was "a credit to the colored race and to the American people," in Southwick's estimation, and had already become "one of the most

11. "Southwick Praises White, Letter to J. E. Bruce," letter reprinted in the *Colored American*, 11 June 1898. John Edward Bruce (1856–1924) was a well-known black journalist who established the publication *Grit* in 1884 and often wrote under the name of "Bruce Grit." George Newell Southwick (1863–1912) was in his second term in Congress from Albany; the former journalist and New York state committee chairman was defeated for reelection in 1898 but reelected in 1900, and served until retiring in 1910.

12. Ibid.

13. Ibid.

prominent Republicans in the House . . . by reason of the many excellent qualities . . . attributed to him, as well as by reason of the ebony color of his skin."[14]

The two congressmen would soon demonstrate their party solidarity on the question of annexing the Hawaiian Islands, voting with the majority to annex the tiny Pacific republic. With the Spanish-American War in full swing and the U.S. invasion of Cuba less than a week away, the security of Hawaii had become a timely and worrisome issue; the expected conquest of the Philippine Islands made it necessary to resolve Hawaii's request for annexation before territories taken by military conquest were to be considered. Democrats had sought instead to guarantee the independence of the Hawaiian Republic by declaring any hostile action against Hawaii to be an act of war against the United States. But the minority report of the House Foreign Affairs Committee, recommending continued independence for Hawaii, was rejected overwhelmingly by the House on June 15, just before the body voted by an even larger margin to approve the joint resolution annexing Hawaii.[15]

George Southwick and George White were among the majority of 204 congressmen who voted against the independence resolution, and moments later they joined a total of 209 voting for the annexation, including five Democrats who had previously supported independence. Both majorities included 17 southerners: 11 Republicans, 5 Democrats, and 1 Populist.[16] The South as a region generally opposed annexation and favored independence for Hawaii, with 63 of the region's congressmen voting against the majority in each case.

Whether the regional vote was on the basis of party loyalty or of geo-

14. Ibid. The term "ebony," used here by Southwick to describe White's skin color, was already a generic term for persons of African descent; White's complexion was not black but reddish-brown.

15. *Congressional Record*, 55th Cong., 2d Sess., 31, 1:6018–9. The votes were 204 to 96 against the independence resolution and 209 to 91 for annexation; another 55 congressmen either abstained or were absent from each vote. Hawaii's precise status would remain unclear until it was declared a U.S. territory in 1900.

16. Ibid. Democratic congressmen outnumbered Republicans from the South in 1898 by more than six to one; there were only 11 Republican House members from former Confederate states, compared to 74 Democrats and 5 Populists. Of 17 southern congressmen opposing Hawaiian independence and supporting annexation, 5 were Democrats: Reps. Lewis and Livingston of Georgia, Norton of South Carolina, Taylor of Alabama, and Young of Virginia.

graphic sensitivity to the specific issue, or both, is not clear; at any rate, the only five Democrats to break ranks on the independence vote were southerners. But both votes may have been symbolic as well, expressing opposition to any separate future attempt to make Cuba a state. That largely black island had been briefly considered for annexation by the Confederacy during the war, purely as a strategic move against the Union, although nothing had come of the proposal. Annexing territory with a nonwhite majority was a problematic question for many southerners, who did not want to facilitate the eventual entry into the Union of nonwhite states, but who remained understandably nervous about appearing to oppose the administration's very popular war against Spain.[17]

Owing to his frequent absences from the floor in 1898, George White had missed many of the important votes on Cuban independence and the declaration of war. It seems likely that some of these absences were intentional. White may also have preferred to miss the Hawaiian vote, since he had strong feelings on the subject and the related issue of the treatment of nonwhite foreign peoples by the United States. He had referred caustically to previous U.S. acquiescence in the Hawaiian coup of 1893 and the subsequent mistreatment of Queen Liliuokalani, and probably believed that Hawaii should return to being an independent kingdom. Party loyalty and the urgent circumstances of war, however, overruled his independent streak on the issue; whatever misgivings he may have harbored, White made no comment in the record about the equity of the annexation.

Soon after the vote, White received three days leave of absence "on account of important business," and he was absent from the House during much of the remainder of the session. He requested and received another six days of leave on June 30, also for "important business," and the House adjourned in his absence on July 8. The third and final session of the Fifty-fifth Congress was scheduled to begin five months later on December 5, after the fall election.[18]

Before Congress opened again, George White would become a far more controversial figure at home, as a result of a speech he delivered during the

17. Ibid., 1:3819, 4042, 4056, 4060, 4068, 6100, 6566, 6601. White was granted leave on June 17 and June 30.

18. Ibid., 1963, 4347, 4691, 6180 (leave granted); 3814 (Hawaiian government bill); Anderson, *Race and Politics*, 291. Anderson cites the conference committee action, which Democrats claimed was due to criticism from White and others.

third week of July. North Carolina Republicans were gathered for their annual convention in Raleigh amid reports of the surrender of Santiago, Cuba, to the American invasion force and preparations for the impending clash of American and Spanish forces halfway around the world in Manila. What might have passed as an essentially unremarkable political event became a high political circus in the hands of the *News and Observer*, which seemed intent on setting the stage for a domestic battle to rival the foreign conflict so dominating the nation's front pages.

The Raleigh newspaper's page-one headline on July 21, 1898, included a tantalizing reference to the speech made there the day before by the state's most famous black Republican: "'More Negroes Made to Order to Fill Offices,' Cried Congressman White." But George White's speech, notable as it must have seemed, was confined to excerpts on the jump page inside; before readers could get there, they were forced to wade through a lengthy account of other convention business and the "variegated crazy-quilt" of complexions and physical appearance. From the "red beard" and "red face" of two white party leaders, readers were led to the "black face of Abe Middleton, the ginger-cake color of John C. Dancy and the whiter face of Col. James H. Young, dressed out 'spic and span' in his full regimentals."[19]

James Young had only recently been appointed by Governor Russell as colonel of the Third North Carolina Infantry, an all-black volunteer regiment in training for reserve use by U.S. forces abroad. As the state's highest-ranking black appointee, Young quickly came under the *News and Observer*'s increasing fire, along with Governor Russell and other Republican leaders. It was obvious from the outset of the July article, however, that the paper's main object of ridicule would be the despised "social equality" displayed at the biracial convention: "African and Caucasian kissed each other; octoroon and mulatto joined hands," and all were joined by Governor Daniel Russell and white colleague Dr. R. M. Norment, "who voted to honor Fred Douglass because he was half white and half black."[20]

19. "Negroism Exalted, The Republican Convention Heartily Endorsed Everything in Sight, Russell's Policy is Unanimously Endorsed," *RN&O*, 21 July 1898. Former state senator Charles A. Cook of Warren County owned the red beard, Eighth District congressman Romulus Linney the red face. Middleton was the appointed doorkeeper of the North Carolina house, Dancy the appointed U.S. collector of customs in Wilmington.

20. Ibid. Although the regiment never saw action in Cuba, even Democrats grudgingly admitted later that Colonel Young and his men had prepared and performed well. As a Robeson

White, John Dancy, and Abe Middleton were among fifteen members elected to the party's state executive committee; Dancy had earlier been elected convention secretary and a member of the committee on resolutions. It was hardly surprising, then, that both Dancy and White addressed the convention in turn, but to the *News and Observer*, their remarks were hardly coincidental: "the big guns were fired by Dancy, the negro collector of the Wilmington custom house, and Geo. H. White, the negro Congressman from the Second District." Dancy's brief remarks prior to the platform's adoption were characterized as a "war speech . . . attributing everything done in war as a Republican victory. He was cheered most when he praised the black soldiers," leading neatly into the platform's call for "a vigorous prosecution of this war to a triumphant conclusion."[21]

Mild ridicule of Dancy, however, soon gave way to an openly sarcastic attack on White, who had "denounced with bitterness the Democratic position and defended the placing of power in the hands of negroes, and heaped his abuse upon those who wanted to keep the government in the hands of the intelligence of the country." There is no written copy of the speech to verify the next words, which went on to haunt George White through the end of his career in North Carolina, but the *News and Observer's* abbreviated version of what must have been a much longer speech soon became sacred text to white supremacists across the Tar Heel State.

White began in a partisan but relatively restrained fashion. "I have noticed men who did not like the name Republican, who stopped at the halfway house, calling themselves Liberals or something like, but they all wind up finally as straight-out Republicans," he said. "Two years ago I hardly knew whether to say I was in favor of free silver or not. My experience now has taught me that 10 to 1 [one] will not do. I am like the man who would not travel on a certain train, because it left his town at 10 to 1." This joking reference to the "gold standard" issue and his own mixed feelings on the issue gave little hint of the next quote, obviously lifted from whatever context he might have intended to give it: "You dare not enter my door to enjoy social equality unless I invite you there. We are not afraid of social equality."[22]

County legislator, Norment had led the tribute to Frederick Douglass after his death in February 1895, for which the General Assembly adjourned for a day.

21. Ibid.

22. "The Negro White Speaks," subheading, ibid.

Such a direct challenge to segregation was bad enough in the jaundiced eyes of the state's largest newspaper, and it was merely a lead-in to "the lowest plane upon which any man, white or black, ever talked to the people about. It showed the low tone of the convention and the unworthy mind of the Congressman," wrote the unnamed observer. "The hurrahing and cheering was such as was heard twenty years ago in the days before the taxes of white men gave them schools," as White allegedly delivered the fateful phrases:

> I am not the only negro who holds office. There are others. *There are plenty more being made to order to hold office. We are the modestest people in the world, and don't hold as many offices as we will. I invite the issue.* If you will come into my district we will have a joint debate. I am going to hold up the hands of Jeter C. Pritchard, Daniel L. Russell and William McKinley. We imitate white men. You steal and so do we. You commit crimes and so do we.[23] (emphasis added)

The juxtaposition of White's excerpts bordered on libel, although political speeches of the day often contained far worse inferences. White soon sat down "amid thunders of applause," according to the main story, after praising Governor Russell "for putting negroes in command of regiments, and putting negroes in high positions." In a sidebar on the same page, however, the newspaper gave a somewhat different version of White's words, under the headline "Convention Kinks."[24] That the two versions varied significantly—particularly in one key expanded sentence involving the central "issue"—did not seem to trouble the editor who placed them side by side, with no word of explanation or apology to the reader.

In this excerpt, White seemed even more explicit and provocative than before: "There are many other negroes that are going to hold office. They are being built to order. I want to invite *the issue of the white man against the negro.* I want to meet it in the black belt, *and whether they meet me or not, I am going to have them to hear me*"[25] (emphasis added). That any black politician might have made such an angry challenge to the state's white leaders is certainly

23. Ibid. Paragraph breaks have been eliminated from this quotation and certain phrases highlighted for emphasis, but otherwise this section of the story appears just as it did in 1898.

24. "Convention Kinks, That Fell from Negro Nooddles [sic] and Other Tangles," *RN&O*, 21 July 1898.

25. *Raleigh Morning Post*, 21 July 1898, cited in Anderson, *Race and Politics*, 258–9.

possible, particularly in a heated setting before a friendly partisan audience. That it was George White, usually so eloquent and thoughtful, who desired to set the races against each other is possible, if extremely unlikely; alienating nervous white Populist allies at the beginning of a crucial election campaign was neither a wise nor prudent act, and the eminently sensible White had never taken such a political risk so publicly before. If he did utter the phrase as recorded, it would indeed have been startling to his white listeners; the convention adjourned almost immediately after his speech, perhaps even in a state of shock.

Assuming the accuracy of either account, an obvious question is why the newspaper felt it necessary to print two versions of the speech on one page; why it placed the stronger version in a secondary story is even more difficult to explain. Perhaps White had simply paraphrased himself later for emphasis; perhaps it was a simple error, committed under deadline pressure; or perhaps separate reporters had written the two accounts, one taking more complete notes. Most likely, however, it was a sign of Josephus Daniels's creative journalism at work, in the sensational "yellow" style so popular in the era.

An account in the *Morning Post,* Daniels's smaller Raleigh competitor, seems to bear out the last alternative. No particular friend of George White's, the Democratic newspaper had nevertheless covered the same speech, and had produced an account of the congressman's speech that sounds considerably more like his normal style and content. Its smaller readership, however, meant that fewer citizens saw the calmer, more reflective version, printed on July 21: "No white man dares enter my home unless invited there, and I dare not enter any white man's home unless invited there. The laws of the land do not regulate social equality. Man regulates the social problem for himself. There's nothing in this social equality plea. It's a [campaign] scheme to get in on."[26]

Even the truculent promise of more black officeholders, recounted twice by the *News and Observer,* seemed mellower to the *Morning Post* reporter, who heard White say this: "The Democrats are going to say that I am a negro office holder. Yes, and there are going to be more just like me. The Constitution gives me the right to vote and this gives me the right to hold office." Weeks later, White himself told the *Morning Post* that his speech had been badly mis-

26. Ibid.

quoted (by others) and that he did not favor raising the question of race at all.[27] By then, however, the pendulum of white public opinion had swung against him with the force of a hurricane, led by the drumbeat of Josephus Daniels and the gathering forces of white supremacy.

The *News and Observer* was certainly appalled at the reports it printed; it had quickly condemned White's fiery words through a surrogate, quoting one unidentified black observer as saying, "I was ashamed of my race, that when it has a chance to put a man in high position, selects a man who will make so mean a speech." But its editorial policy, never far from the surface of its political coverage, then leapt onto the news page outright, characterizing "[e]very North Carolinian who loves his State [as] ashamed of the cheers that greeted the coarse and low utterances. It shows that negroes always put their worst representatives forward."[28]

Within days, other North Carolina newspapers, notably the *Wilmington Morning Star*, had picked up Daniels's lead, lashing out at the "malicious windbag" George White for his "vulgar, shameful" speech, which "pandered to the negro feeling and toyed with negro ignorance and negro aspiration." Blacks had charged the Democrats with "drawing the color line," then proceeded to do the same thing in their own party, claimed the *Morning Star*. By early fall, the chorus had grown to include White's hometown newspaper, the *Tarboro Southerner*, previously favorable toward the congressman but now determined to defeat him, if possible: "From now until election day, North Carolina's political war will be waged squarely upon the color line. . . . There will be no middle ground."[29]

The color line had indeed been drawn in no uncertain terms, whether by George White or his detractors, and the fall campaign soon developed into the bitterest and most potentially violent one in the state's history. But whatever the short-term effects of his speech, White did not linger in the state

27. *Raleigh Morning Post*, 2 September 1898, cited in Anderson, *Race and Politics*, 259. According to Anderson, "the Democratic press was furiously promoting the notion that blacks were the aggressors in North Carolina racial conflict . . . and the remarks attributed to White served to illustrate this contention."

28. "The Negro White Speaks."

29. "There Will Be More," editorial, *Wilmington Morning Star*, 23 July 1898; untitled editorial, *Tarboro Southerner*, 8 September 1898. Both newspapers began to refer to the White speech regularly as the election neared.

long enough to hear much of the immediate criticism. By July 22, he was in Chicago, accompanied by an acquaintance from that city's art institute and en route to Omaha, Nebraska, for the Republican League's national convention. It was there that a curious incident occurred which may have deepened George White's resolve to battle the nationwide encroachment of racial segregation.

According to a report from the *Illinois Record*, White and his companion, Robert Thomas, "were refused service at the Allen Restaurant, 246 State Street, Chicago," and had reacted by threatening the restaurant's "prejudiced proprietor" with civil suits as a result. In reprinting the story, the *Colored American* called it a "strange showing for big-hearted, free and magnanimous Chicago . . . the gentlemen must have stumbled unwittingly into a cheap hash-house . . . about the only kind that are afflicted with color-phobia in the Windy City."[30]

Upon his return from Omaha in early August, White attempted to redress the inaccurate reporting of his speech by the *News and Observer* and other papers, but his efforts were already too late; the momentum against him was building rapidly. Fusion campaign literature was distributed denying the language attributed to White at the convention, but even affidavits from those who had been in the audience seemed useless against the rising tide of negative media coverage.[31]

Two relevant events had occurred in White's absence. First, the Populists of the Second District had chosen their nominee for Congress. White's opponent would be another Tarboro resident, James B. Lloyd, a close associate of U.S. senator Marion Butler; Lloyd was to be given stronger backing than the luckless D. S. Moss in 1896, it seemed. Second, and more insidious, the White Government Union was unveiled. A new organization open to membership by any white man willing to join the Democrats in the fight for white supremacy, the WGU was the brainchild of former Republican Francis D. Winston, now a proud defector to the Democrats, and was openly endorsed by the Democratic Party's statewide chairman, former congressman Furnifold M.

---

30. *Illinois Record*, 23 July 1898, reprinted in "Political Pointers," WCA, 30 July 1898. "These men are both able representatives of our race, men whose intelligence and position in life deserve proper consideration from all classes," said the indignant *Record*, claiming both men would "look after the case upon their return from Omaha."

31. Anderson, *Race and Politics*, 259.

Simmons. Simmons promised that only "honorable, legitimate and proper methods" would be used by the WGU, whose goal was to organize a chapter in every county by the end of August. But the organization was plainly intended to restore white unity by intimidating any white voter who did not willingly follow the Democratic banner, as Simmons delicately hinted to the *Kinston Free Press:* "Our state is the only community in the world, with a majority of white voters, where the officers to administer the government are the choice of negroes. . . . This condition has been brought about by an unfortunate division among the white people, and it is likely to continue until that division is removed."[32]

The tone of the campaign was dictated by Democratic journalists, whose repeated attacks on George White became shriller as the election drew near. Democrats in the Second District declined even to nominate a candidate against White, hoping to coerce Captain Lloyd from the sidelines into a vigorous tirade against "negro domination." The *News and Observer* pressured Lloyd to "place himself at the head of the white column," while the *Wilson News* echoed an oddly ironic Darwinian theme, calling the two-man race "a case of the survival of the fittest."[33] Three other newspapers—the *Kinston Free Press, New Bern Journal,* and *Wilmington Morning Star*—engaged in a contest of sorts, attempting to name all the various offices held by blacks in the eastern counties after White accurately pointed out in a speech at Jackson that blacks were already a majority in many counties "and could elect a negro to every office" but had never done so. The *Free Press* won the contest, running its list under a simple but eye-catching three-word headline: "Nigger! Nigger! Nigger!"[34]

Although both were under pressure to play more extremist roles, candidates Lloyd and White struggled to practice politics as usual, despite the maelstrom of racial invective around them. In every appearance, White scoffed at the charge of "Negro domination" and counseled his followers to remain calm

32. *Kinston Free Press,* 10 August 1898, cited in Anderson, *Race and Politics,* 261–2.

33. *RN&O,* 2 September 1898, and *Wilson News,* 3 September 1898, both cited in Anderson, *Race and Politics,* 261–2.

34. *Kinston Free Press,* 3 September 1898, and *New Bern Journal,* 2 September 1898, both cited in Anderson, *Race and Politics,* 264; *Wilmington Morning Star,* 3 September 1898. Each reacted to coverage of White's comments after the Northampton County Republican convention, as quoted by the *Rich Square Patron and Gleaner* and *Raleigh Morning Post* of 1 September 1898.

and obey the law. He had repeated the same admonitions against disorder to his listeners in Kinston, Windsor, Goldsboro, Wilson, Tarboro, and other points, he told the *Raleigh Morning Post* in a letter published in early October, but not all newspapers agreed. Even in describing his moderate speech to Republicans at Windsor, the local *Ledger* called it "the reverse nature as the one he made at the Republican State convention. Undoubtedly he has been advised along that line." The *Tarboro Southerner*, intent on criticizing white Republicans for having hearts "as black as midnight," damned him with faint praise after his address at the Edgecombe County convention: "In White we recognize a man far above the average of his race and by long odds superior to the whites who took part in the convention."[35]

To his credit, James Lloyd refused to play the public stooge as the Populist nominee, though his private tactics indicated his strong sympathies for a return to a political system dominated by white voters. He campaigned doggedly on purely national issues, advertising himself as a "white man, a W. J. Bryan and a silver man, and said the people . . . ought to vote for him because he represented their interests," but his rhetoric failed to galvanize interest among voters. On a strategic level, Lloyd endured the intricate local aspects of fusion in his own Edgecombe County, where Populists had accepted two black Republican legislative candidates in hopes of electing a Populist to the third seat, but then attempted unsuccessfully to persuade the black Republican candidate for solicitor, Robert W. Williamson, to withdraw in exchange for "the solid [Democratic] vote of this Dist[rict]." Fearful of violence, Lloyd advised Marion Butler not to attempt to speak in the Black Second, where even the eight-term mayor of Tarboro, W. E. Fountain, an active Populist, was believed to be in grave danger for his fusion activities.[36]

The campaign tottered on the brink of absurdity as octogenarian Curtis H. Brogden, a former Reconstruction-era governor and Republican congressman, publicly denounced White as "an unprincipled, swaggering demagogue [and] the most objectionable negro in the State as a politician." At a subsequent speech in Rich Square, White allegedly told his black audience "to get their guns and ammunition ready" in order to "demand their rights at the polls"; White's denial of such words fell on deaf ears, except those of the *Raleigh*

35. *Windsor Ledger*, 22 September 1898, cited in Anderson, *Race and Politics*, 266; *Tarboro Southerner*, 22 September 1898.

36. J. B. Lloyd to Marion Butler, 14 October 1898, Butler Papers, SHC.

Morning Post, which at least printed his letter.[37] James Lloyd had all but with-drawn from the race in frustration by the second week of October, when the *News and Observer* eagerly trumpeted a sensational new incident as clear evidence of White's not-so-hidden agenda of "social equality."

Newspaper accounts of the infamous "circus incident" vary, but there seems little doubt that George White, either alone or in the company of a group of women and children, did attend John H. Sparks's circus in his hometown of Tarboro on October 8. Perhaps he was seeking relief from the heat of the campaign, but if so, he found little solace inside the tent. The *Greenville Reflector* reported that White "took a seat among the white people," refusing to move when requested and "saying he was as good as the white people and that he would not sit with the negroes." Four policemen and twenty circus employees later, White and his entourage left the tent voluntarily but still protesting, according to the *Reflector.*[38] Not content with simply reprinting this account, the *News and Observer* quickly sought out at least five Tarboro whites to sign affidavits affirming and embellishing the tale of the "great big black, burly leader of the fusion forces in North Carolina" and his demand for social equality; their affidavits were the basis for a longer follow-up story two days later.[39]

Yet the entire story was outlandish at best. George White may have attended the circus, but the *Tarboro Southerner* made no reference to any such incident in its next edition, even after the intervening reports had been published. With his deep devotion to his family, he would never have countenanced their public humiliation or possible exposure to rough treatment by a hostile crowd. Still, White ignored the publicity; his only recorded reference to the matter was a flat denial in a letter to the *Kinston Free Press* nearly two years later, after a similar seating incident, this time on a train from Goldsboro

37. *Raleigh Morning Post,* 6–7 October 1898, cited in Anderson, *Race and Politics,* 266–7. The *Post* accepted White's explanation, expressing surprise at the original report of "incendiary language" and doubting that such an intelligent man would have ignored the consequences of such incitement.

38. "Here's Result of Russellism, The Negro Congressman Demands to Sit with White People at Circus," *Greenville Reflector,* reprinted on page one, *RN&O,* 12 October 1898.

39. "Good As White Folks, That's What Congressman White Said. He Leaves the Circus Rather than Sit on Seats with His Own Race, He Demands Social Equality," *RN&O,* 14 October 1898. A local lawyer, a merchant, and two soldiers signed one affidavit, and a circus employee signed a second.

to New Bern, had been reported. "I have never had, have not now, nor do I ever expect to have any hankering to push myself among any class of people where I am not wanted," White wrote in July 1900. "The circus incident to which you allude . . . had no foundation in fact."[40]

The origin of the circus story is as difficult to fathom as one that appeared two weeks later in the *Wilmington Messenger*, supposedly involving 150 Lenoir County "Rough Riders" who had physically prevented George White from disembarking his train in Kinston for a campaign speech. Even the *Kinston Free Press* called the story "a fake," and White publicly denied that anyone in Kinston had intimidated him. Yet a week later, a new type of intimidation appeared in the *News and Observer* in the form of an article accusing members of White's family of fomenting racial strife and planning to commit armed violence; Josephus Daniels's newspaper had in effect declared war on George White six days before the midterm election.

The boxed front-page article used enlarged boldfaced type—the size of ordinary headlines, and two columns wide—to make its sensational charge, under a headline almost as long as the story itself: "Negro Women Active, Congressman White's Wife Gets Rifles and his Daughter Asks Negro Women Not to Work for White People." Datelined Tarboro, the first paragraph claimed that Mrs. White had "received an express package containing rifles, name of shipper withheld," the preceding Friday, but the story offered no other details or any evidence to support the charge. A second paragraph claimed, "on good authority," that White's daughter—obviously Della, now eighteen and teaching in Tarboro—"is circulating a petition asking all colored women to refuse to work for white people."[41]

For all the inflammatory implications of these two sentences, it was the article's unrelated final sentence that revealed the true purpose of the story as an unmistakable call to arms, if only among its white Democratic readers: "The white people are ready and prepared for any emergency." And in case any *News and Observer* reader might doubt the severity of the situation, a story from the *Richmond (Va.) Dispatch* appeared just below, in normal-sized type but also boxed for effect. It recounted reports of an unnamed black officeholder from Wilmington who had attempted to purchase "a supply of arms

40. Letter to the editor from George H. White, *Kinston Free Press*, 30 July 1900, commenting on an editorial in the same newspaper on 23 July 1900.
41. "Negro Women Active," *RN&O*, 1 November 1898.

and ammunition" in Norfolk and Baltimore one day before Mrs. White's package had arrived. The buyer reportedly said he "regretted the necessity for an armed conflict," but "his people were thoroughly prepared for it." A special correspondent in Washington had somehow obtained the information, which was "of a most authentic character."[42]

By then, the campaign for Congress in the Second District had degenerated into virtual chaos. Lloyd, the Populist candidate, apparently offered to withdraw from the race in favor of an unnamed new candidate who could unite white voters; while even Lloyd still refused to endorse the Democrats' call for white supremacy, the "circus outrage" had convinced him that fusion between the Populists and Republicans should be halted immediately. Democrats quickly held what was later described as "an immense mass meeting" in Goldsboro on October 28, determined to crush the possible success of fusion by stirring up the urgency of their appeal to white voters. Feelings ran high in both the Democratic and Populist camps; when the respected former governor and ex-U.S. senator Thomas J. Jarvis stepped forward to call for an end to "Negro domination" in the state, it was painfully obvious that the bandwagon was now rolling.

Populist leader W. E. Fountain, the recent object of abuse and threats of violence, threw in his party's towel and demanded the defeat of George White. "I will leave nothing undone to accomplish this," he told the suddenly enthusiastic audience. Within days, he had announced his own independent Populist candidacy for Congress; a man reborn, he had emerged as a supporter of white supremacy.[43] Fountain was the Democratic candidate in all but name, as Lloyd pointed out dismally; their personal feud was exacerbated by a stubborn district committee, which had refused to let Lloyd resign and allow Fountain to run as the regular Populist nominee.

It did not seem to matter in the end; Fountain's last-minute effort did not

42. "Negroes Buying Guns, A Negro Office-Holder Visits Norfolk and Baltimore to Make Purchases," datelined Washington, D.C., from *Richmond Dispatch*, 29 October 1898, and reprinted in *RN&O*, 1 November 1898.

43. Anderson, *Race and Politics*, 273–6. Populist leaders had formally considered a Democratic proposal to drop Lloyd and substitute a more acceptable candidate a week before the mass meeting, but had declined to endorse it. Also speaking in Goldsboro were William A. Guthrie, 1896 Populist candidate for governor, and Furnifold Simmons, now state Democratic chairman. Fountain, former mayor of Tarboro, was a previous state Populist chairman.

deny George White reelection, but it did settle the political turmoil by effectively killing off the Populist Party. Mayor Fountain drew almost as many votes—just under fifteen thousand, or 42 percent of the final vote—as had Woodard, the Democratic incumbent, in 1896, and might have drawn more had his ballots actually been distributed into every precinct. Captain Lloyd drew the votes of hard-core Populists, although his total was slightly lower than that of D. S. Moss in 1896; each candidate ended up with about 7 percent.

Overall voter turnout declined by nearly 2,500 votes (6 percent) from 1896; most of this came in predominantly black counties, such as Halifax, the district's largest. Pressure against black registration reduced the entire turnout to 3,951, or four votes fewer than George White alone had received two years earlier, when more than 6,000 votes had been counted in Halifax.[44]

White's 1898 total was 49.5 percent of the Second District vote; only the presence of two minor candidates and a scattering of other votes kept him from an outright majority. This time, he carried just four of the district's nine counties—Bertie, Halifax, Northampton, and Warren—yet his margins in those four predominantly black counties were insurmountable. But for the first time, he lost his home county of Edgecombe, with Fountain taking that race by thirteen votes; that it was the home of all three final candidates certainly made it a fierce battleground on election day, even though Populist Lloyd managed only eighty-seven votes there.

For the second straight time, Democrats had been unable to defeat the nation's only black congressman but had decimated the ranks of both Republicans and Populists in almost every other race. This had been the primary objective for the Democratic Party, after all: not simply to defeat the fusionists, but to obliterate all the reforms enacted by the past two legislatures, in which Democrats had been embarrassingly outnumbered by their combined opponents. And it was an amazing reversal by any measure. The 1899 General Assembly contained an enormous Democratic majority of four to

44. Anderson, *Race and Politics*, 275–6, 349–50 (Tables 20, 21). Anderson's tables show 37,808 votes tallied in the Second District in 1896, including 6,216 in Halifax; 35,472 votes were tallied in 1898, or about 6 percent fewer. Vote totals declined significantly in Bertie, Halifax, and Northampton, all with black majorities; increases were recorded in Wilson, Greene, and Lenoir—with white majorities—while two black counties (Edgecombe and Warren) had smaller increases.

one, although the exact number would not be known until several contests were decided during the session; all were ultimately won by Democrats. Only 30 fusionists were seated in the 170-member General Assembly: 28 Republicans and 2 Populists. But nowhere was the turnaround more noticeable than in the counties of George White's district, where 18 of the 23 legislators were now Democrats and from which only 4 Republicans, all black, and 1 Populist would now go forward to represent the Black Second in 1899.[45]

North Carolina was barely recovering from the shock of the November 7 election when the first aftereffects of the white-supremacy campaign hit home. Wilmington, the state's largest city, was struck by the worst racial violence in state history; at least seven and perhaps as many as thirty black citizens were killed after a mob of six hundred armed whites literally overthrew the city government and began expelling white Republicans from the city itself. Hundreds more black residents fled the city, hiding in nearby swamps and woods for days to escape the mob, while both the Republican mayor and the city attorney were among those banished to the North for sanctuary. Alex Manly, editor of a black newspaper, was forced to flee for his life. Two months earlier, he had dared to print a sarcastic editorial on lynching; now his newspaper's building had been burned to the ground.[46]

Wilmington was not known for such violence, although the white minority in the city had grown increasingly restive under the renewed Republican rule, both black and white, during the past decade; three blacks had served on the city's board of aldermen in 1897, and a number of blacks held public positions, including fourteen policemen, a handful of deputy sheriffs and as many as forty magistrates.[47] The *Morning Star*, in much the same fashion as the *News and Observer*, had sharply stepped up its verbal attacks on Republicans and "Negro domination" during the final weeks of the 1898 campaign, and

45. NCG, 476–8. The four black Republicans were state senator Thomas O. Fuller of Warren and house members W. C. Coates of Northampton, John Y. Eaton of Vance, and John H. Wright of Warren. Populist senator W. E. Harris, a white, was elected in Northampton. Isaac H. Smith of Craven was the only other black elected to the house in 1898.

46. Various accounts of the Wilmington race riots exist; one thorough treatment is Henry L. Prather, *We Have Taken a City: Wilmington Racial Massacre and Coup of 1898* (Rutherford, N.J.: Associated Universities Press, 1984). Most reports list seven blacks as killed, although Lefler and Newsome cite ten deaths in *North Carolina*, 559, and Jeffrey Crow between seven and thirty in *A History of African Americans in North Carolina*, 115.

47. "Forty Negro Magistrates," *Wilmington Morning Star*, 20 August 1897.

had undoubtedly inflamed local sentiment. The situation turned deadly on November 8, after editor Manly of the *Daily Record* and other black leaders refused orders to appear before an all-white citizens' committee.

Newspaper coverage of the race riot was hardly objective, but when a new Wilmington city government composed entirely of white Democrats replaced the elected Republican administration, the *News and Observer* gleefully announced that "Negro rule is at an end in North Carolina forever. The events . . . at Wilmington and elsewhere place that fact beyond question."[48]

The postfusion era of black voters and black elected officials was not yet over in North Carolina. Certain local officials in Black-Second counties were still black, including the recently elected registers of deeds in Northampton and Warren Counties. Voters in Bertie County had elected seven black magistrates and two constables. The Second Judicial District had even come within an eyelash of electing another black solicitor, until Robert W. Williamson's apparent victory was quashed by county clerks in Northampton and Halifax Counties, who rejected 427 Williamson votes. George White would be in office for another two years as well, along with four other fusionist members of the state's congressional delegation: both U.S. senators, Populist congressman John W. Atwater of the Fourth District, and Republican congressman Romulus Z. Linney in the Eighth.[49] Stopping such elections would require more than intimidation of stubborn white voters, the Democrats knew. It would require a step of dubious constitutionality: disfranchisement of black voters. But having assumed the garb of white supremacy, the state Democratic Party was not about to turn back now.

White had many ties to Wilmington, and an affectionate regard for its people. He had practiced law in the New Hanover County courts and received a hero's welcome from the citizenry after his first election to Congress in 1896. It was hardly surprising that he would later describe the Wilmington riot as "the miserable butchery of men, women and children" who were innocent of any crime. In a highly publicized speech on lynching delivered to the U.S. House in early 1900, he interjected a fearful picture of the aftermath of the 1898 violence: "the horrible scene of the aged and infirm, male and fe-

48. Editorial, *RN&O*, 13 November 1898.

49. Marion Butler's Senate term would not end until 1901, Jeter Pritchard's only in 1903. In addition, Ninth District Republican Richmond Pearson was restored to his old House seat after his successful contest in 1900.

male, women in bed from childbirth, driven from their homes to the woods, with no shelter save the protecting branches of the trees of the forest, where many died from exposure, privation and disease contracted while exposed to the merciless weather."[50]

White made no claim for the accuracy of this depiction, and he was obviously not present in Wilmington when it happened, yet his description has long been taken to be valid. His intention that day was more to counteract the equally vivid comments—all too one-sided, in his opinion—previously made by a Georgia congressman as a justification for lynching, about the "fiendishness" of a specific case of rape, of which two distinctly opposing accounts had been given. Such images as White later presented, however, must have danced in his head on New Year's Eve 1898, after the congressman led members of the executive committee of the new National Afro-American Council to call on President McKinley at the White House to plead for McKinley's attention to the issue of lynching.[51]

The delegation consisted of nearly two dozen of the nation's most prominent black leaders, including former congressmen Henry Cheatham and George W. Murray, one former governor—Pinckney B. S. Pinchback of Louisiana—council president and AME Zion bishop Alexander Walters, and journalist Cyrus Field Adams. They requested that President McKinley "use his good offices in presenting to Congress the subject of the recent lynchings of colored men in the Carolinas," a subject in which he had little active interest. In a general way, they also asked him to "exert his influence in all proper ways to improve the conditions of the colored race," a course of action more likely to be realized.[52]

The National Afro-American Council had been created three months earlier in Rochester, New York, to succeed the defunct Afro-American League set up by Fortune but disbanded in 1893. The group had concluded a two-day special session in December at Washington's Metropolitan Baptist Church when the decision was apparently made to call on the White House, after John P. Green's unfortunate remark that "President McKinley was advised by black men not to mention the North Carolina and South Carolina riots in his annual messages to Congress" angered Fortune and other members,

50. *Congressional Record*, 56th Cong., 1st Sess., 2151.
51. "The Negroes Appeal," *RN&O*, 2 January 1899.
52. Ibid.

nearly disrupting the meeting. It is doubtful that White attended this special session, since he was not yet a member of the executive committee, but he may have agreed to shepherd the delegation through the White House visit as a personal favor to Walters. When Fortune demanded to know the identities of the "black Judases," Green was forced to admit that his information was secondhand, and he had not asked his informant—a "close personal friend of the President"—for their names. It was a humiliating blunder for Green, who had agreed at the last moment to replace George White in giving the scheduled address on "Protection of American Citizens," despite his apparent lack of knowledge about the subject's finer points.[53]

Had the far shrewder White been present, he should have been able to defuse the situation with minimal effort; his sensible solution after the fact was to shepherd the council's delegation through the White House for a brief meeting with the president, probably as a personal favor to Bishop Walters, perhaps even out of sympathy for the hapless Green. White was not yet a member of the council, but became active in the organization soon afterward and was later elevated both to the executive committee and its special operational subcommittee.

President McKinley had only recently returned from a triumphal tour of the South, having attended the Atlanta Peace Jubilee and addressed the Georgia legislature before visiting students at the Tuskegee Institute at Booker T. Washington's invitation, among other stops on an eight-day December swing. But McKinley's continuing silence on the question of sensitive racial matters was well noticed and favorably interpreted by southern whites; despite the pleas of northern whites to intervene in the South's "crusade against the

53. Cyrus Field Adams, "Special Session of the National Afro-American Council," in *The National Afro-American Council* (Washington, D.C.: National Afro-American Council, 1901), 6; "The Council at Work," WCA, 6 January 1900. Adams's account of this session says it was held in Washington on December 29–30, 1899—obviously a typographical error, falling as it does between separate accounts of the 1898 organizational meeting and the Second Annual Convention held in Chicago seven months later (August 17–19, 1899). White joined the subcommittee at a semiannual executive committee meeting in Washington in late 1899. "Official Programme, First Annual Meeting of the Afro-American Council, etc." John Green and seven other council members were slated to discuss White's speech during the December 29 evening session, according to the printed program. Minutes indicate Green was whisked off the stage into a hastily called session of the Committee on Address, where he explained the circumstances in private, after which the committee's chairman relayed the details to the audience.

Negro," as voiced by wealthy industrialist John E. Milholland of New York, McKinley never referred to the recent Wilmington riot or related matters such as disfranchisement. George White had personally begged the president in a December 12 letter to consider stopping at Greensboro's A & M College, "for an hour or so between trains," while en route through North Carolina to Georgia on December 13, or on his return. "The citizens throughout the State would greatly appreciate a visit from you to this Institution," which White described as the "only institution for Colored that receives any national support."[54] White's letter doubtless arrived too late to change the president's itinerary; accepting the delegation's visit may have been McKinley's belated attempt at a reply, since there is no record of any other response from the White House.

Despite his disappointment at McKinley's silence, White remained hopeful; even so, he was preoccupied with the situation back home in North Carolina, more so than most of the Afro-American Council delegation. He was preparing to convene a meeting of at least fifty black leaders in the state just three weeks later to draft a memorial to the General Assembly expressing the race's concerns over issues of security and citizenship rights. The Council of Colored Men of the State met as planned in Raleigh January 18–19, 1899, and elected White as its first president. The *News and Observer*, apparently in a mellower mood since the Democratic legislature had convened, described White as "the author of the meeting and its moving spirit," and the group itself as "a representative body of colored men, being composed of many of the most intelligent members of the colored race of the State."[55]

Both this council's ultimate memorial and a separate address to North Carolina's black citizens were "conservative," according to the newspaper;

54. Richard B. Sherman, *The Republican Party and Black America: From McKinley to Hoover, 1896–1933* (Charlottesville: University Press of Virginia, 1973), 11–3; George H. White to William McKinley, 12 December 1898, McKinley Papers (microfilm), Library of Congress. Sherman cites a letter from Milholland to McKinley, 14 November 1898, in McKinley Papers, Library of Congress. Some blacks were already openly critical of the president in 1898; the National Race Protective Association condemned McKinley's inaction on December 19 as he returned from Georgia. North Carolina's Agricultural and Mechanical College for the Colored Race had been established in 1891 at Greensboro; Professor James B. Dudley, president of the college, asked White to extend the invitation to McKinley.

55. "Negroes Meet Today, Convention Called to Memorialize the Legislature," *RN&O*, 18 January 1899; "The Negroes Appeal," ibid., 19 January 1899.

"cooler heads, who were largely in the majority," voted down a more "sensational and radical address." As presiding officer, White may have felt compelled to accept the majority report even though it was less direct than he would have chosen to be, but it is not clear that he openly favored anything more provocative; a Charlotte newspaper depicted him as among those favoring explicit language on emigration "in case the Democrats made their stay in North Carolina intolerable," although no other newspapers noted this. More than a year later, after the disfranchisement amendment was passed, White publicly began to urge blacks to emigrate from North Carolina.[56]

One visible moderating influence seems to have been that of Thomas O. Fuller of Warren County, the only black member of the state senate. Fuller presented the council's memorial to that body on January 19, noting that there was "considerable interest among the colored people of the State, that some of them—in view of possible legislation—were reluctant to fulfill contracts previously made." But Fuller, a minister, said the council had decided against calling for widespread emigration, choosing instead to "recommend [blacks] to continue to live at peace with their neighbors, and to go quietly about providing for their homes and attending their schools." Fuller soon left for Tennessee, but said he had attended the council meeting and "used his best endeavors to see that nothing rash was done." Years later he expressed guarded admiration for George White in his own autobiography, but made no mention of the Council of Colored Men or his opinion of its effectiveness.[57]

The council hoped to head off any sudden movement on the issue of disfranchisement, which the General Assembly was now considering. By the end of the session, however, a proposed constitutional amendment was passed for submission to voters in August 1900; if approved, the amendment would disfranchise all illiterate voters, black and white, although a "grandfather clause"

56. William A. Mabry, "White Supremacy and the N.C. Suffrage Amendment," *North Carolina Historical Review* 13 (January 1936): 1–24. The other newspaper was the *Charlotte Observer*, 19 January 1899. White cautiously broached the subject of emigration when testifying before the Industrial Commission in February 1900; he began calling for moderate emigration in his farewell interview with the *New York Times* in August 1900.

57. "Adjourned After the Morning Hour," *RN&O*, 20 January 1899; Thomas O. Fuller, *Twenty Years in Public Life* (Nashville, Tenn.: National Baptist Publishing Board, 1910). In his autobiography, Fuller recounted his pastoral call to Nashville in the early 1900s. He remained in Tennessee for the rest of his career; the 1899 term in the North Carolina senate was his only foray into politics.

would exempt any illiterate man with a male ancestor eligible to vote in 1867. Since blacks had not been given the vote again until 1868, the exemption was clearly intended only for whites; almost all blacks would be prevented from voting, since even educated blacks could expect to fail the rigorous tests given by white registrars.[58]

Such a prospect was highly distressing to George White and other prominent blacks, but few yet believed that a majority of the state's voters would favor such an obviously unfair tactic. White, not easily daunted, believed in the essential good character of the people of North Carolina. He had praised his native state, despite its faults, to audiences in both Boston and Halifax, Nova Scotia, during his December lecture tour. In Halifax, he had addressed the Cornwallis Street Baptist Church on December 4 at the invitation of its pastor, Rev. J. Francis Robinson, speaking on "the Negro and The South." White had also become the first black man ever "known to dine in Cook House as a guest."[59]

White's December 1 speech at Boston's Charles Street AME Zion Church received considerable coverage from the *Boston Globe*, which reprinted quoted sections of his text at length. The speech revealed a curious ambivalence toward the prospects for continued political participation by southern blacks, who faced a painful dilemma if they remained in their homeland: either to fight for their rights and face "being annihilated" by "cowardly assassins," or to "surrender to the dominant race in this country those civil and political rights . . . thus virtually becoming slaves." Only by leaving the South could blacks hope to maintain both their safety and self-respect, he warned; emigration to other parts of the country was the only sensible way to diminish both the potential for violence and the "false howl of 'negro domination.'"[60]

That his native state had fallen victim to the spread of antiblack senti-

58. NCG, 476. The 1899 General Assembly met in three separate sessions: the regular session, from January to March 1899; the first adjourned session, June 12–14, 1900; and a second adjourned session, July 24–31, 1900. It was the first North Carolina legislature to hold an extra session in twenty years; the proposed constitutional amendment consumed much of its discussions.

59. "Political Chitchat," WCA, 10 December 1898; "Here and There: Congressman White Lectures," ibid., 17 December 1898.

60. "Simple Justice, That Is All the Southern Negro Wants," *Boston Globe*, 2 December 1898. This 1,300-word article, which the *Globe* placed on its second page, contains the longest printed version of a speech by George White ever found outside the *Congressional Record*. In all, more than 1,000 words were quoted from what must have been a much longer speech.

ment and murderous violence puzzled and saddened George White. Despite a local history of "friendly relations" between the races, North Carolina officials now seemed either unwilling or unable to stem the tide; the recent riot at Wilmington had "beclouded and dishonored," perhaps irrevocably, the "hitherto proud name of the 'Old North State.'" Even the federal government seemed powerless to prevent recurrences of the violence, White said: "It throws up its hands in holy horror and reminds us that its own brave, patriotic and long-suffering black citizens are without remedy under the stars and stripes under which they have so often fought, and that our redress is relegated to the states."[61]

Yet White's message was not without hope. He urged New England's leaders to visit the South and "help us to arouse this nation from its state of lethargy . . . before the putrefying cancer destroys the body politic." His audience in Boston, at least, was receptive, and White returned to Washington hopeful and more determined than ever to continue the struggle for the rights of his race. He had weathered a difficult and sometimes brutal campaign to win his own reelection against the odds. White was now recognized as a national spokesman for his race—indeed, the highest black elected official in the nation. He planned to use his new prominence to advance the cause of black civil rights, and with a Republican majority in Congress, he had strong hopes for success. But the struggle was now entering a delicate and uncertain new phase, and he soon found that he needed more than mere resolve to keep those hopes alive.

61. Ibid.

10

The Second Term in Congress

His narrow reelection in November 1898 after a depressing and painful campaign must have made George White pause and reflect upon the events of the preceding six months. Horrified by the deadly spectacle of the Wilmington race riot, wounded by the gratuitous verbal attacks on his family, saddened by the defeat of so many of his fellow Republicans at home, he may well have welcomed the chance to retreat to Washington and points north, where the atmosphere was less poisoned by racist name-calling.

He returned to Washington briefly, preparing to resume his official duties as a member of the final session of the 55th Congress. But having already scheduled trips to Nova Scotia and Boston as part of a speaking tour, he was unable to attend the first days of the session, which opened on December 5, 1898. He arrived back in the capital within the next week; his letter to President McKinley requesting a stop in Greensboro was dated December 12. His first recorded vote was on a Senate bill appropriating funds for the holding of a new Philadelphia industrial exposition, scheduled for 1900; he voted in favor of the bill, which passed by a strong majority. He then appears to have spent most of the next month in Washington, filing his next official request for leave on January 12, after which he spent a total of eight days in North Carolina, including several days in Raleigh presiding over the new statewide Council of Colored Men.[1]

George White's family moved to Washington with him following the 1898

---

1. *Congressional Record*, 55th Cong., 3d Sess., 32, 1:315. The vote took place on December 19, 1898.

election, probably because of the adverse effects of recent publicity; White later blamed Cora Lena's broken health on the grievous effects of the campaign, which had, of course, included unfounded rumors of her involvement in the arms trade. The family lived temporarily at a house on Washington's 17th Street, NW, from which they soon moved to a nearby house, apparently newly built, on 18th Street. This house was located in a section of the city known as the "Strivers' Section," between Dupont Circle and Shaw neighborhoods. Many affluent African Americans chose to move here in the early twentieth century, including noted architect Calvin T. S. Brent, among others.[2]

At least one of his daughters accompanied them, probably Mamie, now eleven years old; the *Congressional Directory* listing for White in early 1899 lists him as accompanied by his wife, one daughter, and two "other ladies," possibly a relative and Cora Lena's private nurse. Della, nineteen, and young George, five, initially remained in North Carolina, although both moved to Washington by mid-1900.[3]

Cora Lena's health now became a major issue for the White family. In a January 1902 letter, she told Booker T. Washington that she had already been an invalid for three years, indicating the onset of her health problems as early as the campaign of 1898. She did not indicate the nature of her illness, which was revealed publicly only after her death in 1905 as chronic neurasthenia, a debilitating and somewhat mysterious ailment requiring more or less constant care, including a private nurse.[4] This may have been the primary reason she

2. Sandra Fitzpatrick and Maria R. Goodwin, *Guide to Black Washington: Places and Events of Historical and Cultural Significance in the Nation's Capital*, 2d ed. (New York: Hippocrene Books, 1990), 225. Bounded by 15th and 18th Streets, R Street, and Florida Avenue, NW, the "Strivers' Section" was called "a community of Negro aristocracy." Architect Brent, who lived three blocks away from White, designed many of the houses along U and V Streets. In 1980, a portion of the surviving section was declared a historic district; White's rowhouse had already been demolished by then, although houses similar in age and style still line nearby blocks.

3. *Congressional Directory*, 55th Cong., 3d Sess., edition corrected through January 12, 1899. The temporary house was located at 1412 17th Street, NW. The house White purchased was five blocks away at 1814 18th Street, NW; the family had moved to 18th Street by late November 1899, when White hosted a large dinner, according to the *Colored American* (9 December 1899). All three children lived there in mid-1900.

4. Cora Lena White's death certificate was signed in January 1905 by her attending physician, Dr. Sterling Ruffin; it listed the immediate cause of death as asthenia (duration two weeks) and the primary cause of death as chronic neurasthenia (duration seven years).

moved to Washington when she did, since specialized medical care was not available to her in Tarboro.

Having her older sister nearby must have been a comfort to Cora Lena; she and Louisa had spent little time together in recent years, especially after Henry Cheatham's appointment as recorder of deeds for the District of Columbia in 1897. Their children were close in age, allowing the families to mix easily; Mamie Cheatham and Mamie White had both been born in 1887, while Plummer Cheatham was the same age as Odessa White, who had died as an infant in early 1892. Charles Ernest Cheatham was the oldest, born in 1886. All doted fondly on George Jr., the youngest cousin, born mid-1893. The children spent much time together, the political feud between their fathers having ended.

Despite the precarious nature of Cora Lena's health, the White family seems to have entertained fairly often, holding at least one large dinner for friends and political acquaintances each year. Edward Cooper, editor of the *Colored American,* was a frequent guest, as were Henry Cheatham, Judson W. Lyons, and John P. Green, as well as journalists and others; the annual holiday dinners at White's "handsome" home invariably received coverage in Cooper's columns. White was the "ideal host," mixing political chat with good food and musical entertainment, such as that provided by his younger daughter, son, and niece at the first such dinner, held at the house on 18th Street in November 1899.[5]

Having his family in the same city removed much of George White's need to travel to North Carolina as often as before. He seems to have ceased the bulk of his legal work in the state after the 1898 election, for there are no mentions of any "important business" trips there in 1899. He had apparently concluded the cases that had occupied so much of his time in 1897 and 1898; the collapse of Wilmington's Republican administration and the expulsion of high-ranking white Republicans had almost certainly removed any chance for further legal work there. After returning from Raleigh in January 1899, White began to concentrate on his congressional duties and his growing involvement in civil rights activism, including the National Afro-American Council, on whose executive committee he would soon serve.

5. "City Paragraphs, Mr. White as a Host," WCA, 9 December 1899. One guest at this dinner was Alex L. Manly, now editor of the *Washington Daily Record*. Edward Cooper began to comment regularly on the state of Cora Lena's health after this dinner.

White delivered his first major speech of the third session of the outgoing Congress on January 26, 1899, just a week after the Raleigh convention ended. The talk was expected to deal with a bill to extend the standing army of the United States, the war with Spain having been concluded some months earlier; while White did address that issue in his opening, he quickly steered the subject to "another great problem that confronts us . . . the race problem." He apologized in advance to the House for changing the subject, but the ten million American blacks he now represented "have no else to speak for them, from a race point of view, except myself." The momentous twenty-minute speech drew prolonged applause from his Republican colleagues, although it probably sat less well with those groups from the South and other regions that White labeled "sectional cowards."[6]

"I have heard my race referred to in terms anything else than dignified and complimentary," he said with rising emotion. "I have heard them referred to as savages, as aliens, as brutes, as vile and vicious and worthless, and I have heard but little or nothing said with reference to their better qualities, their better manhood, their developed American citizenship." To Congressman John S. Williams of Mississippi, who had recently waxed eloquent about "white supremacy" in his own state, White tossed the words back, with bitter sarcasm: "Just here permit me to say that I have no respect for a 'supremacy,' white or black, which has been obtained through fraud, intimidation, carnage and death."[7]

White's anger had been building throughout the entire 55th Congress. For such men as Williams to argue that blacks posed any threat to "the Anglo-Saxon ruling this country" was sheer nonsense; by numbers, they were no threat at all. "We constitute as a race less than one-seventh, possibly, of the population. We have been enslaved; we have done your bidding for 240 years without any compensation; and we did it faithfully," he said with great emphasis, and it was "ungracious now . . . to be unwilling, at this late day, to give us a man's share in the race of life." Only the "force of circumstances"—not any inherent defect—had created the condition of blacks' inferiority to whites that now existed in the United States.

6. *Congressional Record*, 55th Cong., 3d Sess., 32, 1:1124–6. "I trust ere long we shall have the manhood to stand up in our places and meet [the race problem] like American citizens, not like sectional cowards," White said at the outset.
7. Ibid., 1124.

"Yes, by force of circumstance, we are your inferiors. Give us 240 years the start of you, give us your labor for 240 years without compensation, give us the wealth that the brawny arm of the black man made for you, give us the education that his unpaid labor gave your boys and girls, and we will not be begging, we will not be in a position to be sneered at as aliens or members of an inferior race," White continued, now rolling along at his polished best. "We are inferior. We regret it. But if you will only allow us an opportunity we will amend our ways, we will increase our usefulness, we will become more and more intelligent, more and more useful to the nation."

It was the first time George White had given such an extended public display of his views on the place of black citizens in the American social system. His years of observation as a teacher, principal, lawyer, and prosecutor had been distilled into one simple statement, which he now presented for the consideration of his listeners, after a moment's pause, no doubt, for emphasis: "It is a chance in the race of life that we crave."

This was a slightly refined, softer version of the pointed phrasing he had used ten months earlier: "an even chance in the race of life is all that we ask." He had now dropped the qualifying word "even," and made the desire a more wistful one, by substituting "crave" for "ask"; perhaps the bitterness of the recent campaign had forced him to rethink any new appeal for civil or social equality, or perhaps the beginnings of despair were creeping into his mind. He was now demanding the simple recognition of black humanity.

If despair did threaten to overtake him, he recovered with a facetious touch. Special legislation was not the answer, nor was "40 acres and a mule . . . The mule died long ago of old age, and the land grabbers have obtained the 40 acres. We do not expect any of those things," he said. "But we have a right to expect a man's chance and opportunity to carve out our own destiny. That is all we ask, and all we demand."[8]

His race was facing "a crucible, a crisis—a peculiar crisis," he warned. The problem was no longer confined to the South, but had now become a national problem, spurred by the stubborn reaction of many blacks to recently increased levels of oppression—specifically disfranchisement, though he did not yet name it. "This tendency on the part of some of us to rise and assert our manhood along lines is, I fear, what has brought about this changed condi-

8. Ibid. White had used the similar phrase in his speech of March 7, 1898, on the proposed creation of two black artillery regiments in the U.S. Army.

tion," he said, with no hint of apology in his manner. The time for apologizing had long since passed.

Endless discussions of the constitutionality of such "oppression" only evaded the real issue of justice, in his view. He recounted an anecdote of a judge, preparing his students to be examined for licensing, who warned them that when the law was in their favor and the facts against them, they must "lean hard on the law"; when the facts were in their favor but the law against, "lean hard on the facts." But when both the facts and the law were against them, "you must beat around the bush." White charged that whenever American law or the Constitution was forced to deal with the rights of blacks, the system reacted this way, especially when blacks had both law and facts on their side.[9]

After Congressmen Williams and John M. Allen of Mississippi had repeatedly "slurred" his race, White used that state's entries in the *Congressional Directory* to calculate total black votes cast there in 1896 in five of seven congressional districts, arriving at a figure of 45,867, "out of a total vote of between 250,000 and 300,000." In South Carolina, the situation was marginally better, by his numbers: 56,953 votes cast in five districts, out of about 250,000 estimated. Both states had recently taken the vote away from black citizens.[10]

Proponents of disfranchisement should not be allowed to have it both ways, White argued. He said he would not "grumble about the number of votes that you cast down there in South Carolina," but called on Congress to ensure that all states "ought to have the benefit of the votes that are allowed to be cast in their representation on this floor, and no more." If blacks were "unworthy of suffrage," if disfranchisement was deemed "necessary to sustain white supremacy," then states practicing it should not be allowed to count "the poor men, black or white, who are disfranchised." No one had raised such an issue before "because the boot does not pinch anybody else as it does me and my race. But it will come home to you. You will have to meet it."[11]

Despite his somber tone, White claimed not to be a pessimist; instead, he

9. Ibid. While White did not name the "learned old judge," it sounded much like something William J. Clarke would have said to his own pupil in 1878.

10. Ibid.

11. Ibid., 1125. Directory entries generally listed the votes cast for the winning congressman in each district, total votes for presidential candidates when appropriate, and the estimated voting population for each district. In both Mississippi and South Carolina, only five districts listed numbers of votes cast for Congress in 1896.

believed that the "negro problem in less than fifty years will be a thing of the past," that "the color of a man's skin . . . will cut no figure at all." But this would not occur through assimilation, because blacks were not asking to be "amalgamated; we do not ask for anything but to remain a distinct and separate race as we are, and to be permitted to work out our own manhood and womanhood. We do not expect anything else." It would occur only if the Congress was fair and patient with blacks, who would develop into worthy citizens with proper guidance and incentive, if they were treated justly in the meantime. When their development was complete, of course, blacks would be entitled to far greater representation than they now received; so far they had remained passive about this, being warned not to be "uppish," to "be still; to keep quiet," even in the face of "hundreds and thousands" of lynchings.

Numerically, blacks were already entitled to fifty-one representatives in Congress, thirteen U.S. senators, at least one Cabinet position, and one Supreme Court justice, yet White was still the only federal representative of ten million blacks. "How long," he asked, "must we keep quiet?"

In closing, White reached for humor once again, recalling a Saratoga man's remark, made during the off-season, that his resort area depended on "skinning the visitors" in the summer. "I can very well understand that," White had replied, "but how do you get along in the winter?" The old man's answer came slowly: "'Then . . . we skin each other.'"

"Gentlemen, the process of skinning the negro is nearly over," White said to gales of appreciative laughter. "You have about completed the job. Gentlemen of the North, of the East, and of the West, yes, and you of the South, when that is done you have got to have somebody to skin, and you will turn on each other, and then possibly the negro will get his just deserts."[12]

Returning to the military theme, White renewed his support of "acquisition of all of the territory that is within our grasp" after the recent war with Spain. But first Congress must "recognize your citizens at home . . . give them the rights that they are justly entitled to," before going out to extend American civilization and Christian culture to the Cubans, the Puerto Ricans, the Philippine Islanders, and the Hawaiians. If Congress did this, all Americans would "rejoice with you in that we have done God's service and done that which will elevate us in the eyes of the world."[13]

12. Ibid., 1126.
13. Ibid.

The speech was well received by Republicans, although no proposal for re-duction of representation in southern states was considered until late in the next Congress, at the end of White's term, and then without success. White made briefer remarks on three later occasions before the House adjourned on March 4: twice on the need for appropriations for capital projects in North Carolina—continued improvements to Fishing Creek by the U.S. Army Corps of Engineers and the construction of a federal building at Durham—and once on a Colorado colleague's bill to restore a homestead claim to a dis-abled black Army veteran. All these actions showed White's concerns for the needs of the people, as he put it: the farmers along Fishing Creek, the citizens in a fast-growing urban center, the veteran unable to meet the requirements of the law due to injuries received in combat.[14]

But the January 26 speech would remain the longest and most controver-sial of White's first congressional term. Its intellectual division between ap-peals for justice and fair treatment for blacks on the one hand and for punitive treatment of certain states in his native South on the other, made it dis-jointed, and because it dealt with no specific bill or appropriation, but with an issue few could readily identify with, it may have been less than effective, purely as a tool. But its range of emotion, its moments of grand eloquence, and its magnificent delivery made it a memorable speech for his listeners. Its com-plexity symbolized the "peculiar crisis" George White was now going through on a personal level. Having been exposed to the rawest edges of social and po-litical injustice, and beginning to despair for the future of the race he had come to represent, he could choose to lash out angrily at his tormentors—an ultimately futile, if cathartic, course—or he could seek to persuade them of the error of their ways, both by force and by gentle reason. As his speech dis-played, he had not yet decided which course to follow, but gave notice of both; over the next two years, his choice emerged.

After the adjournment of the 55th Congress in March 1899, White en-joyed the longest period of unrestricted activity during his tenure in Congress, a period of nearly nine months. Although his duties to his constituents con-

14. Ibid., 1369–70, 1994, 2894. The Fishing Creek amendment to an appropriations bill was denied; the Durham, N.C., appropriation requested by his Democratic colleague, W. W. Kitchin, repeated an unsuccessful request in the previous Congress and also failed here; the bill to extend Isaiah Mitchell's expired time limit (H.R. 7915) was passed, although with amendments to which White objected.

tinued, he had to attend no formal daily sessions until the 56th Congress convened in early December. There is no precise record of his trips to North Carolina during the rest of 1899, since he was not required to submit requests for leave of absence, yet he certainly spent as much time as he felt necessary in the Second District. The Council of Colored Men may also have met periodically during the recess, although there is no public record of another 1899 meeting after the January convention; if there was one, White would certainly have made every effort to attend.

He took at least two long trips out of Washington during the summer, one to Halifax, Nova Scotia, for a return lecture in late July and a second to Chicago for the annual convention of the National Afro-American Council in mid-August. His family may have accompanied him on one or both of these trips, although Cora Lena was regularly confined to her bed by the end of the year and seems to have traveled little, if at all, after moving to Washington. The two younger children, Mamie and George Jr., were both living in Washington by November; Della was in Concord, North Carolina, teaching music at her alma mater, Scotia Seminary, but moved to Washington before the end of 1900.[15]

Cora Lena's father, Henry Cherry, probably died in Tarboro during this year, and the family would undoubtedly have returned to spend time with Mary Ann Cherry as soon as possible. Cherry had continued to work as a merchant in his grocery and liquor businesses in the 1890s and would have been in his mid-sixties in 1899. But a far sadder event occurred toward the end of the year, when Cora Lena's older sister, Louisa Cherry Cheatham, died at the age of thirty-six of unspecified natural causes. Little is known about Louisa Cheatham's death; there is only a brief reference a year later in the *Tarboro Southerner* to "her fatal illness."[16] After her death, her three children re-

15. George B. Cortelyou to George H. White, c/o Halifax Hotel, Halifax, Nova Scotia, 27 July 1899, McKinley Papers (microfilm), Library of Congress; "Second Annual Convention of the National Afro-American Council, August 17–18–9, 1899, Chicago, Ill.," in *The National Afro-American Council*, 6; "Testimony of Hon. George Henry White," *Report of the Industrial Commission on Agriculture and Agricultural Labor, Vol. 10* (Washington, D.C.: GPO, 1901), 425. White testified before the Industrial Commission on February 8, 1900.

16. Kenzer, *Enterprising Southerners*, 60; *Tarboro Southerner*, 30 August 1900. Henry Cherry was dead by mid-1900, when his wife was listed as a widow in the 1900 census of Tarboro; he was last noted as alive in late 1898 by Kenzer. In an editorial criticizing White's *New York Times* "exile" interview, the *Southerner* said that "H. P. Cheatham's wife was her [Cora Lena White's] sister; her fatal illness was not due to politics any more than Mrs. White's."

mained in Washington with their father, who still served as D.C. recorder of deeds.

Louisa's death must have been a great shock to Cora Lena White; while she still had one older half-sister and several brothers alive, she had always been closest to Louisa, even during the political estrangement of their husbands. The death thus deprived Cora Lena of her closest friend, at a particularly lonely time in a new city; her depression over the loss of her father and sister may have contributed to the worsening of her own illness.

Yet Cora Lena's condition did not prevent her husband from holding an active membership in various organizations. George White's growing involvement in the National Afro-American Council had been catalyzed in part by a banquet given in his honor in early January, days after he had facilitated its executive committee's call on President McKinley. Held at a well-known black restaurant, the Delmo-Koonce, the January 3 dinner attracted a glittering array of the nation's black leaders to pay tribute to White for his continued leadership of the race, particularly after his reelection two months earlier. Such leaders as Bishop Walters, Judson W. Lyons, Henry P. Cheatham, George W. Murray, and Pinckney B. S. Pinchback toasted White's accomplishments. Fellow Howard graduate Jesse A. Lawson, now a professor in New Jersey, summed up the group's reasons for its tribute in one lengthy sentence: "It required a man of the heroic mold to pass through the ordeal to which you have been recently subjected and come through without a scratch, and because of your manly bearing under the most trying circumstances, and the fact that you have never betrayed any trust committed to your keeping."[17]

White's own speech at the dinner reflected his growing exasperation with the press, which he believed was responsible for a recent shift in "public sentiment" toward American blacks. "We are without one of the great lovers we formerly had—the press," he said. "The crimes of the Negro are exaggerated, his virtues minimized, and there is no one to contradict the lies that are told." His own recent experiences with the *News and Observer* and other newspapers in his home state were not mentioned, but everyone in his audience surely understood the reference.

Public sentiment had once had a powerful role in keeping blacks in slavery, until abolitionists had worked to change its image into that of an "accursed institution [that] threatened to crush the life out of the republic," he

17. "Homage to a Race Leader," WCA, 7 January 1899.

said. Now public sentiment was operating in the opposite direction, despite all the efforts of blacks to prove themselves worthy of citizenship. In thirty-five years, America's black population had grown "from a penniless slave of four and a half millions to a prosperous race of over ten millions," yet few outside the race seemed to notice.

Neither emigration nor amalgamation (race mixing) would solve the problem, he declared; blacks would simply not emigrate, except as individuals in search of economic betterment, while amalgamation "weakens both races." Only by providing positive incentives for blacks would the American society produce a worthwhile long-term outcome. "All the sensible Negro clamors for is a man's chance in the race of life, and then if he fails, the fault lies with no one but himself," he intoned.[18]

White was foreshadowing his lengthier speech three weeks later on the floor of the U.S. House, but on this night, his appeal was strictly to members of his own race. Within seven months, he was elevated to the council's executive committee, a further sign of his new standing among his peers. Council president Walters spoke next, calling for the "perfection of a strong national organization, covering every state," and the establishment of a daily newspaper, "in which the issues could be kept before the public." Both would be expensive projects, but Walters said he saw no reason why as much as fifty thousand dollars could not easily be raised as seed money.[19]

George White was now regularly hailed as a hero by his race, and his increasing prominence would have an interesting effect on his performance in the next Congress. By year's end, he unveiled formal plans to introduce a bill to make lynching a federal crime, gambling that public pressure from a united black leadership, sympathetic northern newspapers, and white civil-rights leaders would succeed in convincing Congress to pass the law and the president to sign it. The proposal had strong support from almost all black leaders, but placed White almost alone in the public spotlight as he prepared for what one black newspaper called "the fight of his life."[20]

The pressure was indeed strong from all directions; expectations from White's own race were perhaps unrealistically high, and failure was sure to undermine his credibility. In addition, 1900 was a presidential election year, and

18. Ibid.
19. Ibid.
20. "The Political Horoscope," ibid., 13 January 1900.

neither Congress nor William McKinley would be easily won over, even by White's persuasive rhetoric. But it was a risk he seems to have been determined to take. Because of his elected office, White had now accepted his role as the de facto national political leader of American blacks. With regard to his personal qualities he was certainly a strong leader, but there were two major drawbacks: first, the narrowness of his base, and second, the precariousness of his position, since he had a diminishing chance of reelection. Moreover, White was neither the only black political leader nor the single strongest, as he would gradually discover; his inability to build a lasting consensus among all factions would be a nagging disadvantage in his legislative quest. He had taken on a heavy responsibility, far heavier than he could have known, and few shoulders were offered in support.

For the moment, however, White enjoyed much favorable public attention from all quarters of the black community, including Howard University, whose law school invited him to address its faculty and students in March 1899. Excerpts from his lengthy speech were reprinted in the *Colored American*, revealing White's conservative, practical approach to law and a dedication to small-town values such as civic pride. White himself had not finished his legal training at Howard, of course, and his old-fashioned experience of having read the law under the guidance of a small-town attorney caused his provincial roots to be conspicuously visible.[21]

The advice he gave was thus well-intentioned and sound, but not particularly practical in the eyes of youthful students. He warned them to resist the tempting but illusory offer of security in a government job, particularly in Washington; friends from his own days at Howard two decades earlier had succumbed, and were still in Washington, he said, "still paying rent, and they cannot get away if they want to." A dedicated lawyer should be prepared and willing to go where he could do the most good; for black lawyers, that was the South, where most blacks in America still lived. "The people of that section need your talents, your services and your ability . . . I firmly believe you can . . . be a credit to the community in which you locate, and an honor to the race to which you belong," he said.[22]

White explained that he did not yet agree with Booker T. Washington's

21. "Cong. Geo. H. White Speaks, The Students and Faculty of Howard Law School Entertained by the Eloquent North Carolinian," ibid., 18 March 1899.
22. Ibid.

theory of industrial education as the "panacea of all our ills, and the acme of all our accomplishments." Such a view was useful, as he would repeat at Hampton Institute three months later, but it was incomplete. What was also needed was "professional men and women along different lines." The average lawyer faced a hostile public perception of lawyers as "liars, unscrupulous and untrustworthy," and it was up to younger lawyers to disprove this incorrect stereotype. In order to succeed permanently, White thought, "a lawyer . . . must be an honest and honorable man; must deal fairly and squarely with his clients."[23]

White went on to claim that he had never found anything that "prevented a successful lawyer from being an honest, dignified, truthful, Christian gentleman," although lawyers were forced to be more thoroughly prepared than other professionals. He contrasted this situation to that of the medical and theological professions: "The doctor has no one to dispute the *ipse dixit* that he advances in the diagnosis of the nature of his patient's illness, and if an error is committed in medicine it is buried under six feet of earth"; likewise, the theologian was also free to "advance his own orthodoxy about which there is no dispute, as it is accepted by his hearers as the fact." Lawyers, however, were compelled to fight almost daily for "every inch of [legal] ground," and as professional warriors were rarely afforded the luxury of resting on their laurels, either publicly or privately.[24]

The congressman cautioned his listeners to strive to become "moulders of public sentiment," inasmuch as many lawyers tended to become legislators and political leaders. "Have a mind of your own; be original thinkers with opinions of your own." Their education would not end when they left the classroom but would require long years of continuous study in practice; formal schooling was "only a starting point" to the eventual goal: becoming a "useful, intelligent and industrious citizen."[25]

Three months later White made another important speech before black students, this one at Virginia's Hampton Institute, the ideological parent of Booker T. Washington's Tuskegee. Speaking at the school's thirty-first commencement in June, White recounted his visit to Tuskegee a year earlier in glowing terms, praising the offspring to the proud parent. Both schools were

23. Ibid.; "Congressman White's Address."
24. "Cong. Geo. H. White Speaks."
25. Ibid.

filling a deep-seated need for the race, that of "Negroes engaged in industrial pursuits throughout the South." White believed that the complementary demand for higher education among blacks—while "indispensable to a limited number" of black students—"we have now met in all measure." Industrial education was now of paramount importance; there was clearly "an abundant supply of ministers, doctors and lawyers" for the race, and what was needed now was "the skilled hand of the mechanic."[26]

Acknowledging the growing ideological chasm between Washington's accommodationism and the more militant advocacy of total equality in education, White sought to bridge the two viewpoints. "There are two distinct classes of schools now contending for the mastery, those for higher and those for industrial education." Both were necessary, and "I think there ought not to be any unfriendly feeling between them." He himself was part of the problem, he hinted; while ashamed to admit that he had passed by the campus for two decades without "interest enough to visit this school," he had learned the error of his ways. "Now that I have come once, I assure you I shall come again."[27]

Offering a parting word of caution, White sounded a curiously disquieting note as he completed his address. "Your success does not depend on your diploma," he reminded them. His own "piece of parchment from Howard" lay tucked away in his own desk, "where I never see it. Why? Because I realize that I must make my own way . . . your success will depend . . . on yourself, on your own manhood and womanhood." His words perfectly complemented those of Hampton's president, Dr. David H. Greer, who had warned the same listeners not to try shifting the blame for the race's problems onto anyone else. "I cannot agree with the author of the 'White Man's Burden,'" Greer had stated. "The black man's burden is the black man's burden, and though the white man must help him find out how to bear it, he must himself work out his own salvation."[28]

By year's end, White had taken up the "black man's burden" in every sense of the word and put his own advice to the sternest test yet. As the 56th Congress prepared to open in December 1899, White's intention to introduce his bill to make lynching a federal crime was widely known. The *Washington*

26. "Congressman White's Address."
27. Ibid.
28. Ibid.; also "Dr. Greer's Address," *Southern Workman*, July 1899, 243–4.

Post had already responded negatively to the report and a draft of the forth-coming bill, claiming that its provision, as recounted by the *Colored American*, to "confer upon the federal officers co-ordinate powers with state author-ities for the protection of mobs of persons accused of crime" was both unconstitutional and a "dangerous" measure. For his part, Edward Cooper of the *Colored American* expected "one of the most bitter and significant fights that have graced or disgraced the House since the passage of the 'war amend-ments'—but let it come." He did not claim to know whether White's bill was in fact constitutional, but declared that the issue itself was too important to be dismissed over a technicality. "The method of getting at it [controlling lynch mobs] is merely a question of detail," he wrote.[29]

In early January 1900, the black paper again called attention to the bill, depicting White as "preparing to make the fight of his life in behalf of the peo-ple he represents—the 10,000,000 Negroes of the United States." The news-paper strongly encouraged him in the effort, but cautioned him to "be careful of his health, for much depends upon his vigor and ability to bring to bear his best thought and action. He is burdened with a multitude of obligations, and the strain is enough break down three ordinary men."[30]

Within a few weeks George White introduced H.R. 6963. Its wording was not unexpected, but its context was delicately balanced; with the North Carolina constitutional amendment on disfranchisement barely six months away from a vote, each word White uttered involving race was being carefully examined by observers at home, including the ever-vigilant Josephus Daniels. Their uneasy truce had lasted for nearly a year now, since the meeting of the Council of Colored Men, but it apparently would not last out the century; even white Republican leaders at home feared unleashing the journalistic guns of the *News and Observer* and counseled a low profile for black leaders on the issue.

But as recently as December 1899, the issue of North Carolina's proposed suffrage restrictions received a low priority for the congressman from Tarboro, who was preoccupied by matters other than potential political firestorms in his home state; instead, personal and professional matters of unusual signifi-cance consumed his time. Along with preparing the antilynching bill, he was facing equally weighty concerns at home. Cora Lena's health was continuing

29. "Now for Mr. White's Bill," editorial, WCA, 6 January 1900.
30. "The Political Horoscope."

to degenerate; she had now been an invalid for more than a year, and would shortly fall into a near-fatal coma.

The year ahead in Congress promised to be unusually busy on all fronts. White's two new committee assignments, announced by the speaker in mid-December, included seats on both the Committee on Agriculture and the Committee on the District of Columbia. It was his second term on the agriculture committee, and it led in part to his testimony before the Industrial Commission. But it was the second appointment that more fully displayed the growing confidence of House Republican leaders, when they chose White to replace a retired colleague—George E. White of Illinois—in the seat. According to one newspaper account, Speaker David B. Henderson had earlier "characterized the North Carolinian as one of the brainiest representatives of the Negro race that he has ever met, and it is a very few he has not known personally."[31]

White was one of the only black congressmen ever to serve on the District of Columbia committee. On the committee there were a handful of Deep South Democrats with whom he had little in common, including Asbury Latimer of South Carolina, Adolph Meyer of Louisiana, Peter Otey of Virginia, and Thetus Sims of Tennessee. Two Maryland Republicans, Sydney Mudd and George Pearre, also served on the Committee, but White's strongest personal relationships were with two of its northern members: Charles F. Sprague of Massachusetts and Alfred C. Harmer of Pennsylvania, now serving their last terms in Congress.[32]

For all the competing issues, however, the question of disfranchisement was never far from White's thoughts. Although he remained largely unknown outside North Carolina and the halls of Congress, he did gain limited national exposure from the publication of his article on the subject of disfranchisement in the January 18 edition of New York's *Independent* magazine. "The Injustice

---

31. *Congressional Record*, 56th Cong., 1st Sess., 33, 1:573–4; "Speaker Henderson: The Afro-American Has a Friend in the Chair of the National House of Representatives," *WCA*, 2 January 1900. Henderson was expected to give White a "handsome committee assignment." In a separate column, the newspaper proclaimed, "We Would Like to See . . . Congressman White on the District Committee."

32. Sprague, a wealthy two-term representative from Boston, developed a personal friendship with White, but retired from Congress in 1901 and died in 1902. Harmer, a veteran Philadelphia representative, died in March 1900.

to the Colored Voter," White's first article of any length in the mainstream press, was one of two opposing articles on the subject of the disfranchisement of southern blacks. White's article favored a proposal by Indiana congressman Edgar Crumpacker to reduce representation of certain states in Congress to the levels of their registered voting populations rather than their total populations.[33]

A second article, by Mississippi's Hernando D. Money, entitled "Shall Illiteracy Rule?" took strong exception to the Crumpacker bill. Senator Money's article defended Mississippi's approach to the franchise; many states that restricted suffrage on literacy grounds, such as Massachusetts, would be similarly affected by Crumpacker's language.[34] But White argued that disparities across the South, due to disfranchisement in many states, were egregious enough to deserve specific punishment; fewer voters participated in congressional elections in some entire states—Mississippi, for instance—than in his own district alone. North Carolina's new and unfair election law effectively penalized all black voters; if the state amended its constitution as proposed, the effects on literate blacks would only be magnified by those provisions.

While the *Independent* did not circulate widely in the South, and while its articles drew little immediate public comment, White's arguments undoubtedly nettled Josephus Daniels, who remained convinced of White's "militance" and hostility toward the white race. White, whose upcoming testimony before the Industrial Commission on Agriculture and Agricultural Labor would demonstrate precisely the opposite viewpoint, probably did not care what any disfranchisement advocate thought. In any event, he was still distracted by personal matters; Cora Lena had been "dangerously ill" in January, so near death at one point that Mary Ann Cherry had come up from Tarboro to nurse her daughter. The absence of White's private secretary, W. S. Hagans, who had spent much of the recent holiday season at home in Goldsboro, had complicated matters at his office; fortunately for his boss, Hagans returned to Washington at about the same time as Cora Lena's latest setback.[35]

33. George H. White, "The Injustice to the Colored Voter," *Independent* 52, 18 January 1900, 176–7.
34. H. D. Money, "Shall Illiteracy Rule?" *Independent* 52, 18 January 1900, 174–5.
35. "City Paragraphs," WCA, 13 January 1900. White had also been preoccupied by frequent meetings of the National Afro-American Council's executive committee, recounted by

Hagans's assistance in preparing White for his appearance was vital. The congressman's lengthy testimony before the Industrial Commission in early February was to be his most comprehensive statement ever on day-to-day life for blacks, past and present, in North Carolina, and its depth of detail reflected rigorous studying beforehand. Freed of partisan implications by an express prohibition on discussion of political matters, the statement was instead devoted to an analysis of North Carolina law regarding landlords and tenants, specifically of farms. White acknowledged that he had not "been on a farm since I was a man," but as the only black in Congress, he believed it useful to speak for his race, many of whom were small farmers and sharecroppers. He also noted that his experience as solicitor had given him a special insight into the workings of the law in North Carolina.[36]

White's comments were wide-ranging and illuminating, combining personal observation and careful compilation of useful statistics and giving a unique picture of the economic environment in which North Carolina's poorest agricultural workers lived. He noted that not all black farmers were poor; his private secretary's father had recently died, he said, leaving his two sons an estate exceeding $40,000, all accumulated in agriculture since the war. The Hagans heirs now owned "as good farming land as any in the county, in several plantations." But most of the state's black farmers were tenants, not landowners, and their livelihoods depended on fair treatment by the owners of the land they worked.

Economic issues aside, White's remarks on his personal experiences in North Carolina were frequently just as intriguing. Asked about the condition of his state's public schools, he noted that he had "never sent one of my children to a public school in North Carolina in my life," preferring to use private schools for their education; most were church-run schools, he added, although almost all were located in urban settings. He discussed the teacher-training programs for North Carolina blacks at some length, citing almost all of the

---

the *Colored American* in January as dealing with his proposed bill. Mrs. Cherry had returned to Tarboro by June. Hagans was the brother of Henry E. Hagans, a delegate to the Republican National Convention with White later in the year.

36. "Testimony of Hon. George Henry White," *Industrial Commission*, 416–33. George White's nonpolitical testimony before the Industrial Commission was one of the longest statements he made during his political career. He began testifying at 2:55 P.M. on Thursday, February 8, and his remarks covered eighteen single-spaced pages of the commission's final report.

public and private black colleges open in 1900, including the normal schools, which he had been instrumental in establishing. Among private colleges, White commented specifically on Scotia Seminary, where "my daughter [Della] was educated . . . and is a teacher of music there now"; an unnamed nephew, probably Charles F. Green, had also recently graduated from a private black college, probably Biddle University, which White now served as a trustee.[37]

Perhaps the most revealing portion of the testimony came in response to a question on the "general condition of the colored people in your state." White termed it "a bad state of affairs," one exacerbated during the last two years by politics. Until then, he said, "the best feeling that I have known anywhere in the Southland existed between the whites and colored in our State. . . . It is difficult for an illiterate white or colored man to differ in politics without differing in church, business or anything else." Rigid black dependence on the Republican Party, "whether wisely or not, I will not say," had helped cause the most recent deterioration, since "that party has recently been overthrown, and in my opinion the most vicious element of the white race is now in possession of the State." White said he was pessimistic about the situation, noting that "the way looks dark for the future"; the "bad feeling" created by "dragg[ing] the race into politics" had died down somewhat, but still not completely, after the Wilmington riots of 1898.[38]

Another obstacle was intemperance, which White called "the curse of our race, one of the greatest curses of the colored man"; for a black man, drinking whisky was a "cultivated appetite . . . he never had it until his emancipation." The black man was a "great imitator, and unfortunately for him, he has imitated his white brother in these vices as well as his good qualities. Hence his propensity for drinking whisky," White said. "It is his misfortune. I am not trying to shift the responsibility, but it is his misfortune."[39]

Asked about separatism and emigration as possible solutions to racial un-

37. Ibid., 422, 425. "He was a farmer; started with nothing. He was a colored man, and he was worth easily $40,000," White said of the elder Mr. Hagans. The nephew was probably Charles F. Green, nineteen-year-old son of Eustace and Georgianna Green. Biddle (now known as Johnson C. Smith University) and Howard were the only two schools White claimed to have served as a trustee.

38. Ibid., 426.

39. Ibid., 427.

rest, White suggested that "a gradual thinning out" of blacks from the South would be one answer to the "overcrowding," but that neither large-scale emigration or "aggregation" in certain southern areas would work, for practical reasons. The two races were locked by circumstance into southern coexistence, and thus were naturally interdependent, he argued. But proximity compelled an unequal status for the two races: "perfect equality of the two races, either in education, industry, or politics, is next to the impossible." In a perfectly fair situation, of course, blacks should be admitted to equality with whites, but the far superior position of the "white man's superior civilization from long years in advance of him, and his supremacy, wealth and superior education, would tend to keep the colored man his inferior."[40]

It was a logical viewpoint, yet a highly personal one, and its sentiments were advanced by one of the few black men in a position to challenge white misconceptions about the potential of his race for advancement. George White's practical nature could not disguise his essential optimism here, but as he and other North Carolinians would learn, the white man with his "superior civilization" had no intention of allowing blacks to compete on an equal basis. In the political arena at least, black equality was an increasingly endangered concept, and those who defended it were in danger of losing their positions and their credibility.

40. Ibid., 428.

11

The Showdown over Disfranchisement

As 1900 opened, the deceptively quiet standoff between George White and Josephus Daniels had held for nearly a year. After its vitriolic campaign attacks of 1898, the *News and Observer* had begun referring to Congressman White in a curiously quieter, almost respectful fashion since early 1899. White's public restraint after the Wilmington violence may have been a major factor, since he said nothing to provoke Daniels further and seems to have emerged as a less threatening figure in Daniels's eyes after helping organize the state's new Council of Colored Men and serving as its first president. The group's prudent opposition to unspecified "sensational and radical measures"—presumably work stoppages and large-scale emigration to the North and West—undoubtedly pleased Daniels, who had no wish to see the economic unrest such measures would bring.[1]

If Josephus Daniels eased his criticism of George White because he believed White had "come around," however, he was mistaken. A year had passed since the council was formed, and White would soon begin to preach the virtues of limited emigration for blacks, especially in his testimony before the Industrial Commission in February 1900. And even while White had remained publicly silent on the subject of emigration, he had continued to work behind the scenes to keep the story of the Wilmington riots from being forgotten and had tried quiet, if unsuccessful, intervention with President McKinley.[2] White had

---

1. "Adjourned After the Morning Hour," *RN&O*, 20 January 1899.
2. George H. White to William McKinley, 12 December 1898, McKinley Papers (microfilm), Library of Congress.

also undertaken his fateful attempt to protect black Americans by drafting the antilynching law making death by mob violence a federal crime punishable by execution.

Josephus Daniels's restrained tone in public references to George White during 1899 was no sign of any major philosophical shift, nor of a new mellowness in his personal feelings toward White, whom he admittedly detested; if anything, it may have signaled Daniels's grudging repentance for having helped inflame racial animosities and set the stage for Wilmington's recent violence. The journalist remained adamantly opposed to political or social equality for blacks, and his *News and Observer* continued to press for such measures as the proposed North Carolina constitutional amendment aimed at removing black voters from the political equation as soon as possible. There is no indication that the two men ever corresponded or carried on extended conversations; even though they must have met on several occasions, forty years later Josephus Daniels mistakenly described the congressman's skin color as "very black" in his memoirs, perhaps superimposing personal distaste for White on his recollections.[3]

In retrospect, it would be easy to characterize Josephus Daniels's views as simple racism, but the truth is somewhat more complicated. As one of the "New White Men" of the postwar South, he was emphatically determined to rid North Carolina of black political power, including "Black Best Men" like George White. But even in his haste to depose White, Daniels showed a particular independence in other ways, taking pains to underscore his own personal opposition to the crime of lynching: "What is wanted is a public sentiment . . . so stern in its condemnation that it will beget a few clean-cut jury convictions," Daniels wrote in early 1899. "Then, and not before, lynchings will cease. . . . The lyncher is no legitimate product of our civilization." That Henry Cheatham soon quoted his words in an interview with a widely read Washington newspaper, which was printed along with a stirring tribute to Daniels, was an unexpected but welcome reward; it also helped explain Daniels's sincere respect for Cheatham, although it threw no light on his aversion to George White.[4]

3. Daniels, *Editor in Politics*, 285. "He was thick-set and very black," Daniels wrote of White in 1941.

4. Gilmore, *Gender and Jim Crow*, 62–3, 66–7; "Cheatham Talks against Mob Law, Public Sentiment Averse to Lynching of Criminals," *Washington Evening Star*, reprinted in *RN&O*, 14 May 1899. The terms "New White Men" and "Black Best Men" are borrowed from Professor

The Daniels-White feud had simply become dormant, as observers would soon discover. Even an issue on which they seemed to agree—the evil of lynching—was a potential spark to the dry tinder of their détente. The truce would soon escalate into a shrill verbal war, as the nation's only black congressman took an increasingly public and unpopular stand against the crime of lynching, and with it found himself up against his old nemesis, North Carolina's most powerful journalist.

White's political future was linked inextricably to that of the disfranchisement amendment, which he bitterly opposed on behalf of the black voters who would be most affected by its passage. Yet his political position was a delicate one; white Republican leaders at home strongly discouraged any public statements on the amendment by black leaders, fearing that public opposition by blacks would openly antagonize the Democrats during a close election.

Although the *Independent* magazine did not circulate widely in the South, and its articles drew little immediate public comment, White's arguments undoubtedly nettled Daniels, who remained convinced of White's "militance" and hostility toward the white race. Daniels's imminent explosion was not based on the *Independent* article, but was rooted in White's antilynching bill and the congressman's related brief remarks on the floor of the U.S. House just two weeks later.

On January 20, two days after the article appeared, White introduced his bill to make lynching a treasonable federal offense. For technical reasons, he was unable at the time to read either the text of H.R. 6963 or an accompanying petition, purportedly signed by more than two thousand citizens of Massachusetts and "urging legislation making lynching and mob violence a crime against the United States, providing penalties therefor, and for the creation of a central detective bureau at Washington, with branch offices in various sections of the county, to collect and transmit information of the movements of such lawless bodies." Both the bill and petition were promptly referred to the House Judiciary Committee, from which the bill never again emerged. Nonetheless, White later addressed the issue at length and offered at

---

Gilmore, whose comments on an earlier version of this chapter were invaluable. Cheatham called Daniels's statement "the clearest, bravest and most convincing defense of Southern honor, dignity and patriotic character that I have read," and called Daniels "one of the strongest political factors in American journalism."

least four similar petitions from various areas, including his future home of Philadelphia and the states of New York, Texas, Massachusetts, Virginia, and Florida. All four, bearing a combined total of over a thousand signatures, were referred to the Judiciary Committee.[5]

White had drafted the bill with the assistance of two black colleagues, assistant librarian of Congress Daniel Murray and Boston lawyer Edward E. Brown, both also members of the new National Afro-American Council. The three had worked closely with Justice Department lawyers, including U.S. Attorney General John W. Griggs, to achieve at least a semblance of constitutionality in the proposal; White reportedly expected President McKinley to endorse the bill as well.[6]

Yet even a sympathetic observer later described the bill as "crudely drafted and not likely to win over those numerous Congressmen who had honest doubts about the constitutionality of federal intervention." One major obstacle was its provision making the murder of an American citizen by mob action into a treasonable offense; U.S. citizens convicted under the law would be subject to the regular penalties for treason, including execution. It was not the first antilynching law ever proposed, since former president Benjamin Harrison had suggested a federal law eight years earlier. But Harrison's proposal, never enacted, applied only to the lynching deaths of foreign nationals living in the United States; White's bill was the first to prescribe severe penalties for mob-related deaths of American citizens.[7]

White's proposal had long been an open secret among legislators and observers alike. Both supporters and opponents were preparing for a public battle, yet not everyone fit neatly into either category; there were those like Josephus Daniels, who fell somewhere between. Daniels was an outspoken op-

5. *Congressional Record,* 56th Cong., 1st Sess., 33, 1:1017, 1022, 1598, 3112, 3550, 5931.

6. "Mr. White's Bill," editorial, *WCA,* 2 December 1899. White and Daniel Murray, the assistant librarian of Congress and an active member of the National Afro-American Council, had met with "Attorney General [John W.] Griggs and other gentlemen high in authority." Brown, a highly respected black lawyer in Boston, had spent much of December in Washington, working on the draft with White; Brown apparently also collected signatures on the antilynching petition. "The President has promised his aid to Mr. White's measure," the editorial noted.

7. Sherman, *The Republican Party and Black America,* 15 (footnote). President Harrison's proposal was presented in his December 1891 message to Congress. Sherman also described White's bill as "crudely drafted."

ponent of lynching, but no friend of federal intervention to stop it or anything else properly handled by the states; his distaste for White's previous statements on related subjects must have returned with a vengeance as he read the provisions of the new proposal on lynching. To oppose the bill, however, would be equated by many as endorsing criminal behavior by mobs; seething at his predicament, Daniels must have been overjoyed on January 31, when he saw an opportunity to crucify the militant messenger and weaken his bill, perhaps irrevocably, without appearing to favor lynching.

Others hardly noticed the red flag Daniels found: an interjected remark by George White on the House floor during another North Carolina congressman's speech. But the *News and Observer* was suddenly energized by fury, and began pursuing White relentlessly; its biting editorial on February 2 characterized the congressman as "venomous, forward, slanderous of the whites, appealing to the worst panderers of his own race."[8]

On its face, White's January 31 statement was almost innocuous, scarcely provocative, at least not as its text later appeared in the *Congressional Record*. Irritated by Texas congressman Robert Burke's rude questioning of Romulus Linney during Linney's speech, White had requested permission to answer a Burke question, "since my race is assailed." Burke had asked Linney "to state what proportion [of lynchings] is due to assaults by colored men upon white females"; Linney vigorously retorted that all races had been victims of lynchings, if "more Negroes than otherwise, it is true." But Linney had also fumed that Burke was typical of bigoted southern Democrats: "There you have it, Mr. Chairman; you can not discuss any question with a Southern Democrat . . . that he does not holler 'Nigger.'"[9]

White's recorded response, somewhat more measured than that of the famously belligerent Linney, was part fact, part opinion: "I have examined that question, and I am prepared to state that not more than 15 per cent of the lynchings are traceable to that crime, and there are more outrages against col-

8. "The Colored Member," editorial, *RN&O*, 2 February 1900.

9. *Congressional Record*, 56th Cong., 1st Sess., 33, 1:1365. Linney's original topic had been the election of U.S. senators; he had digressed to the topic of lynching via the related topic of disfranchisement, perhaps to give White an opportunity to speak. Burke, of Dallas, said he was "as much opposed to [lynching] as any man in the U.S. . . . But in justice to the House, should not the gentleman state the fact that in almost every instance, the lynching occurs in consequence of [rape]?"

ored women by white men than there are by colored men against white women."[10]

The *News and Observer* openly detested Romulus Linney and quickly sought to link both Linney and White to the infamous "Manleyism," which had allegedly helped set off the 1898 Wilmington racial riots. Alex L. Manly's editorials in Wilmington's *Daily Record*, a black weekly newspaper, had infuriated white supremacists across the state in the three months preceding the 1898 general election; one of them had been reprinted widely and had particularly incensed Daniels and other "New White Men." Manly himself was in permanent exile in the North, having fled Wilmington after a white citizens' council had demanded he shut down his newspaper the day after the election.[11]

In retrospect, the *News and Observer* blamed the lingering effects of "Manleyism" for the alleged excesses of Daniel Russell and the state's black-majority Republican Party. "It is bad enough that North Carolina should have the only nigger Congressman," sneered the newspaper's editorial writer, almost certainly Josephus Daniels or a closely watched associate. "What shall be said when that nigger Congressman gives utterance to the following on the floor of the House," then printing a noticeably different version of White's previous statement: "'I have investigated the lynchings in the South and find that *less than 15 percent* of them are due to the crime of rape. And I desire to announce here that *if it were not for the assaults of white men upon black women, there would be less of the other class*'"[12] (emphasis added).

"Thus does the Manleyism of 1898 show its head in 1900. Manley [sic] slandered white women in a scurrilous negro newspaper having a local circulation; White justifies assaults by negroes on white women by slandering white men in a speech in the Congress of the United States," complete with an audience of loudly applauding blacks, the editorial continued. "As far as this particular negro is personally concerned, he may be dismissed as beneath

10. Ibid. This was probably a small part of a longer speech White still expected to make; he had not been allowed to read his petitions aloud when introducing his antilynching bill eleven days earlier, due to a procedural objection by Tennessee congressman James D. Richardson.

11. "The Colored Member." Alex Manly's editorials had appeared in the *Wilmington Record*, whose offices were burned down by the white mob during the riot. Manly himself had escaped, and now lived and worked in Washington, D.C.

12. Ibid.

contempt. [But he] is regarded by his race as a leader . . . as a fresh manifestation of negroism of what the negro's attitude is toward the white man, now and always, its significance should not be allowed to escape us."

Intensifying its tone, the *News and Observer* went on to label White ("the negro in office") as "the enemy of the white man . . . a menace to the peace of the commonwealth and a danger to the safety of both races." The white people of the state "have had enough of Manleyism. They have had more than enough of negro Congressman White. He must be made an impossibility for the future, and will be."[13]

There were now two competing versions of what George White had said. Both were roughly the same length; the *News and Observer*'s version, which it attributed to the Associated Press, contained fifty-two words, six more than the passage printed in the *Congressional Record*. Yet the two versions were textually distinct, containing just fifteen identical words. Indeed, White's spoken remarks had been so brief—requiring no more than thirty seconds—that the AP reporter may not even have heard all of them and may have reconstructed the speech from other accounts; the reporter clearly did not use the *Congressional Record* as a source.[14]

Days after the *News and Observer*'s editorial appeared in print, White rose to address the full House on a question of personal privilege. On February 5, 1900, he asked that the newspaper's February 2 editorial be read aloud and printed in the public record in order to "give that vile, slanderous publication the widest possible circulation . . . that the world may see what the poor colored man in the Southland has to undergo from a certain class."[15]

White then amplified his January 31 remarks, after pausing to "exonerate a very large percentage of the white people of North Carolina, my native State. No better people live anywhere on God's green earth than some of them." White specifically exempted "this fellow who edits the News and Observer," however, from membership in that group of "no better people." Josephus

---

13. Ibid.

14. The identical words are: "I have . . . that . . . than 15 percent of . . . are . . . to . . . crime . . ., and . . . white men . . . women . . . there." The AP report differs in certain key phrases, using "black women" rather than "colored women"; using "due to the crime of rape," rather than "traceable to that crime"; and "less than 15 percent" rather than "not more than 15 percent."

15. *Congressional Record*, 56th Cong., 1st Sess., 33, 1:1507. The House clerk then read the *News and Observer* editorial in its entirety.

Daniels's editorial was both slanderous and a form of literary pollution, in White's opinion, and "[u]nfortunately, men of the type of him who wrote that article are now in the ascendency" in North Carolina.[16]

"I desire to repudiate as slanderous and wholly untrue the utterances there attributed to me," White said of the editorial. While he had indeed made a statement during Romulus Linney's speech, his words had been taken from a "paper I read before a local organization of this city," based on a personal investigation he had undertaken in the summer of 1899. "I found that less than 15 percent of the lynchings in this country were for assaults committed upon women, not in the South, but in the entire United States. I repeat that utterance."[17]

But the former prosecutor had never condoned rape of any variety, and he certainly had never attempted to justify assaults by black men upon white women on the ground that white men did the same to black women. "I said that there were assaults occasionally committed upon women . . . and [some] were also committed by white men upon black women, as evidenced by the great numbers of mulattoes in the Southland"; anyone visiting the South could readily see the truth of White's statement for himself. "I repudiate as much as any man can anyone, whether he be a white brute or a black brute, who commits an assault upon any woman. . . . I think such a man ought to be hung—hung by the neck until dead. But it ought to be done by the courts, not by an infuriated mob such as the writer of that article would incite."[18]

White had now accused Daniels of favoring lynch mobs—certainly an unfair, if understandably provoked exaggeration of the publisher's position—but there was more. In White's opinion, the article was an obvious prelude to the August election in North Carolina, set to decide the fate of the disfranchisement amendment. It was but one example of "what we have got to contend with—an absolute perversion of and slanderous misrepresentation of the truth." White now offered himself for personal judgment by his House colleagues, "both Democrats and Republicans, with Populists thrown in," to determine whether "my character and conduct for the last three years on this floor . . . has conformed to the description given by this fellow."[19]

16. Ibid.
17. Ibid.
18. Ibid.
19. Ibid.

Listeners applauded the angry speech, though for once the applause was not "loud and prolonged." Few among them would have congratulated White for making such fiery remarks about Josephus Daniels, sensing the advent of even harsher words from the powerful publisher in retaliation. Daniels's response would be quick indeed, and at least two of those House members present were already planning to aid him in the attack.

In an explosive front-page item on February 10, the *News and Observer* now produced still another version of what White had said on January 31, this one longer and more inflammatory than either version previously printed. Two unnamed North Carolina congressmen had "procured from the official stenographer an exact copy of what White really said in his notorious interruption of Congressman Linney"; in addition, the newspaper charged Romulus Linney with "taming down" White's remarks by requesting the record be "doctored." Linney's consent to such changes prior to publication was arguably necessary, since White had interrupted him but had not made an independent speech.[20]

The stenographer's newly discovered notes now showed White uttering a total of seventy-four words: "I have investigated the facts in regard to these lynchings for the past two and a half years, and I say that less than seventy-five per cent of the lynchings which have occurred in the United States were chargeable to the cause stated; and that if there were not outrages and assaults committed—not upon white women by black men, but by white men upon black women, there would be less of the other class."[21]

The *News and Observer* article went on to point out apparent discrepancies between what White claimed to have stated, as printed in the original *Record*, and what the notes of the stenographer allegedly showed. But the newspaper failed to explain any of the discrepancies between its own original editorial and this new version. Perhaps the newspaper's errors were inconsequential in its own view, since George White and Romulus Linney were the true culprits here; in his February 5 "diatribe," White had "modified his state-

20. "What the Negro Really Said, and How He Afterward Tried to Get Out of It. Stenographer's Notes Show the Speech was 'Doctored' Before It Went on Record. Was It Revised with Linney's Consent?" *RN&O*, 10 February 1900.

21. Ibid. Since this version was quite different from what the Associated Press had originally reported, it seemed increasingly likely that the AP reporter had not even been present on January 31.

ments still further and tried to make it appear that he had not said what he did say," and Linney, in turn, "seems to be bent not only on slandering the good name of his State but resolved to put a new Federal election law" on the nation's books.[22]

What seems more probable than the newspaper's conclusion—that Congressmen White and Linney had somehow conspired to alter a public statement, for whatever reason—is that Josephus Daniels was determined to punish both White for speaking on the subject at all and Linney for allowing him the opportunity. In its Sunday edition of February 11, the *News and Observer* reprinted its February 10 article, along with an accompanying article on Linney's original speech, which had barely been mentioned in previous stories. New additions included sidebar articles on White's infamous July 1898 speech before the state Republican convention, White's plans to sue a Pittsburgh restaurant for refusing to serve dinner to him and black attorney Walter E. Billows, and the opening of the Republican "Anti-Amendment Campaign" in U.S. senator Jeter Pritchard's hometown of Marshall. Topping the page were drawings of both Linney and White, pointing their fingers in reproach.[23]

The battle of wills was once again under way in full force, as the critical decision by North Carolina's citizenry on disfranchisement drew nearer. If Josephus Daniels had his way, the last word would belong to the *News and Observer*, which now trumpeted the cause of white supremacy on a regular basis. Those "white and black Radicals . . . fond of denouncing the News and Observer because it exposes their desire for social equality" would be vanquished in the end; "if such folks didn't denounce the News and Observer, it would be unworthy of the confidence of all believers in White Supremacy," the newspaper wrote on its front page.[24]

If social equality was on George White's agenda, there was no evidence of it in his next speech before the House, the longest speech he had ever given in Congress. The speech came on February 23, 1900, during debate on a bill to impose a tariff upon the newly acquired possession of Puerto Rico, but White dealt only in passing with that issue. His primary subject was the anti-

22. Ibid.
23. "The Negro White Demands Social Equality, 'Doctored the Record,'" ibid., 11 February 1900.
24. Ibid.

lynching bill—"A Bill for the Protection of All Citizens of the United States Against Mob Violence, and the Penalty for Breaking Such Laws"—whose text he was now able to enter into the *Congressional Record* for the first time.

Much of White's speech was devoted to repeating the words of other congressmen, notably Mississippi's John S. Williams and Georgia's James M. Griggs, along with Alabama's senator John T. Morgan. Williams, Griggs, and Morgan had spoken on related subjects, including both the purported unfitness of blacks for American citizenship and the subliminal characterization of all black males as potential rapists, and Griggs had given a graphic account of Sam Hose's alleged-rape case. White spent a significant portion of his time offering the "other side" of that case, which had been established under oath by a disinterested white witness, and suggested that Griggs might well have chosen to depict the pathetic aftermath of the 1898 Wilmington riots, which White now described. White observed drily that Griggs seemed especially intent on "riveting public sentiment" upon the imagined potential for criminal behavior of "every colored man of the South."[25]

Since the end of the Civil War, "fully 50,000 of my race have been ignominiously murdered by mobs, not one percent of whom have been made to answer for their crimes," George White proclaimed. It is worth noting that White did not claim that 50,000 blacks had been lynched, which would have been a clear exaggeration of the actual number; yet many listeners heard just that, and he was later criticized for using this figure. The difference between lynching and "ignominious murder by mobs" was more semantic than real in a political debate, at least, and the language of White's bill equated murderous mobs with "lynching bees." Even White seemed somewhat aware at the time of the impact of the very large figure of 50,000, by his careful tabulation minutes later of the total of recent lynchings of persons of all races—229, by his count, in the years of 1898 and 1899. Still, the proportion of blacks of those recently lynched was startlingly large: 213 of the 229, many for serious crimes but just as many for alleged offenses as lowly as "wanting to work (7)," "talking too much (2)," and even "nothing (2)" or "no cause stated (3)." Fewer than one-fifth (33) of the lynchings in those two years had been for "assault,

25. *Congressional Record*, 56th Cong., 1st Sess., 33, 1:2151. No provision was included here for creating a central detective bureau in the federal government, an unpopular idea previously considered; the idea of coordinate powers between state and federal governments was also dropped. White's description of the Wilmington scene is given in chapter 9.

criminal or otherwise," which doubtless included rape; more, in fact, had been
lynched for the offense of murder. At least one-third had been killed without
any charges ever being brought against them, he said.[26]

White also read into the record three newspaper articles, including a
lengthy editorial from a New York newspaper praising Linney's and his remarks to the House on January 31. A second article, from the *Roanoke (Va.)
Times*, described the "horrible mistake" committed by a Newport News,
Virginia, lynch mob when an alleged rapist was killed but later cleared by the
admission of the woman involved. A third article, taken from the pages of the
News and Observer itself, detailed the arrest of a white Robeson County magistrate for the rape of a disabled black woman; only days earlier, the same magistrate had presided over the arraignment of a black man, charged in a separate rape and eventually executed for that crime.[27]

The longest portion of White's speech was given to the reading of a
lengthy letter from former Massachusetts attorney general Albert E. Pillsbury,
a legal professor who offered convincing arguments for the constitutionality of
a carefully worded federal law against lynching. Pillsbury argued that the political obstacles were far greater than the constitutional issue: "If the Republican party leaders consider that any attempt at legislation of this character is inadmissible for political reasons, I can understand it, though I do not

26. Ibid., 1:2152; Sherman, *The Republican Party and Black America,* 174; Robert L.
Zangrande, *The NAACP Crusade against Lynching, 1909–1950* (Philadelphia: Temple University
Press, 1980). An exhaustive NAACP study, cited by Zangrande, estimated that 3,224 victims
were lynched in the U.S. (78 percent of them black) between 1889 and 1918, an average annual
rate of just over 100 lynchings. Even if the rate had decreased dramatically in the 1890s, as the
NAACP believed, the average rate from 1865 to 1889 would have had to exceed 1,000 per year
to meet a 50,000 total by 1900. Most historians agree that White's figure was excessive, perhaps
by a factor of ten; White gave no official source for his figures, which he attributed to his own
"little investigation" of lynchings between January 1, 1898, and October 20, 1899. Of 166 lynchings in the period ending April 25, 1899, 156 victims were black, and 155 had been lynched in
the South. Of 63 lynchings in the second period, "there were 1 Italian, 1 Cuban, 4 white men
and 57 negroes."

27. *Congressional Record,* 56th Cong., 1st Sess., 33, 1:2152–3. The articles were as follows:
"How 'usual' is the 'Crime,'" *New York Press,* 2 February 1900; "The Terrors of Mob Law,"
Roanoke Times, undated; "Sensation at Lumber Bridge—Magistrate Who Tried Reuben Ross
Charged with Rape," *Fayetteville (N.C.) Observer,* undated, reprinted in *RN&O,* undated
[February 1900].

agree to it. The legal proposition that the United States . . . has no power to protect [its citizens] in their lives within sight of its own capital . . . is so monstrous that it is not to be conceded until affirmed by final authority."[28]

White then disavowed "any intention of harshness" or any wish to create "friction between the races or the sections of this country"; his only purpose, he said, was to raise his voice "against a growing and, as I regard it, one of the most dangerous evils in our country." His race had "no one else to speak for them here from a racial point of view."[29] It was a curiously revealing statement. White was certainly committed to the concept, or he would never have undertaken this lonely crusade, but as a shrewd politician, he had to be aware of his vulnerable position in launching this bill, particularly with "soft" support from the predominant white wing of his party. Even a popular Republican president had been unable to spark consensus interest in an antilynching bill less than a decade before. If White was counting on a concerted effort from McKinley, few others expected the president to take such a controversial stand in an election year, particularly as the "lily-white" wing of his own party was assuming more and more prominence.

The speech was White's last major effort of the session; during the remainder of the winter and spring of 1900, he spent much of his time introducing private bills and petitions, mostly involving constituents' claims for pensions or other financial relief. His family life was becoming more settled, with Cora Lena's health now apparently stabilized and his three children now living with them in Washington. On March 13, he was admitted to the Bar of the U.S. Supreme Court, having been licensed to practice law in the District of Columbia since 1899. Soon afterward, rumors began to circulate that the Whites had left North Carolina for good; the Colored American took special pains to quash a mid-April report that White was planning to move to Ohio to begin practicing law there.[30]

28. Congressional Record, 56th Cong., 1st Sess., 33, 1:2153–4. White said he offered Pillsbury's statements, which were contained in a letter "to a friend of his in this city," by permission.

29. Ibid., 1:2154.

30. Ibid., 1:151, 166, 372, 594, 791, 793, 1021; "City Paragraphs," WCA, 3 February, 3 March, 17 March, and 7 April 1900; Reid, "A Biography," 52; "The Political Horoscope," WCA, 14 April 1900. Henry Cheatham had last introduced the Freedman's Savings bill in 1892; James O'Hara had twice introduced similar bills. Both Cheatham and O'Hara had also sponsored bills

White was occupied briefly during late March and April with helping to quash proposed changes in the office of the D.C. register of wills. This intervention was successful, as White wrote Louis A. Dent on April 18; "I thought then, and believe now that I was right, and usually have the courage of my convictions." But he was increasingly preoccupied with domestic political matters from his home state, including his own renomination and the approaching vote on the disfranchisement amendment. The day after writing Dent he was back in Tarboro to attend the Edgecombe County Republican convention, aimed at selecting delegates to the upcoming district convention as well as four delegates to the May statewide convention. White was chosen for both delegations, but the Edgecombe meeting was unenthusiastic and sparsely attended, according to the hometown *Southerner*, which recorded only about two dozen blacks (and no whites) present. A week later, the Second District convention took the unusual step of agreeing to postpone indefinitely the nomination of a party candidate for Congress, apparently with White's blessing; White and Henry E. Hagans were chosen as district delegates to the Republican national convention. With the statewide GOP under extreme pressure from "lily-whites" to deemphasize black membership in the party, this may have been the only way White could expect to attend the national convention.[31]

White's visibility at the state Republican convention in early May was limited; even though the North Carolina party's rank-and-file remained over-

---

to reward Robert Smalls for his wartime heroism. The *Colored American* stated that "Mrs. George H. White shows many gratifying signs of improvement." The date of White's admission to the bar of the high court is from Reid. The *Colored American*, 14 April 1900, quashed the rumor of White's plans to move to Ohio.

31. George H. White to Louis A. Dent, 30 March 1900 and 18 April 1900, Louis A. Dent Papers, SHC; *Tarboro Southerner*, 26 April 1900, quoted in Anderson, *Race and Politics*, 301. The newspaper called the delegates "forlorn," noting that the "old scenes of noise and disorder were all lacking." For the first time since 1880, the district did not send one delegate of each race; the statewide convention had traditionally selected the Second District's congressional nominee as an at-large delegate in presidential years, such as O'Hara (1884), Cheatham (1892), and White (1896). Due to Pritchard's active opposition, however, going as a district delegate may have been White's only hope of attending the national convention.

According to the *Tarboro Southerner* of 17 May 1900, there were only eighteen black delegates in Raleigh, compared to 180 in 1896. Cheatham, nominated as a delegate to the national convention, withdrew before the vote; four whites were named at-large representatives.

whelmingly black, fewer than forty black delegates were even there, less than a sixth of the total number of attendees and many fewer than in recent years. For the first time since 1892, White was not asked to address the convention, a sure sign of his declining popularity. He was also being deserted by certain white leaders in his own district, including Hiram Grant, whose endorsement had been key to White's 1896 nomination; Grant told blacks in Goldsboro in April that "you have not a worse enemy to your race . . . [than] George H. White," who had "drawn the color line in this district." Grant now claimed he had always opposed black officeholders, although at least one black political leader took him to task, in a letter to a Democratic newspaper, for having a selective memory.[32]

Like Hiram Grant, other white North Carolina Republicans were living under a desperate air of self-delusion, hoping that by minimizing the image of black members, the GOP might somehow maintain the fiction of Populist-Republican "fusion" unity through the end of the campaign. Unnerved by the rapid growth of local white-supremacy clubs, Republicans stopped assisting routine registration efforts in eastern counties, leaving that effort to Populists whose past devotion to black voter registration had hardly been enthusiastic. With strict new registration rules imposed by the 1899 legislature, many blacks felt deserted by their party and simply refused to come forward to register at all.[33]

If anyone maintained a sense of public optimism under the circumstances, however, it was George White, who blithely insisted in May that North Carolina voters would reject the constitutional amendment, albeit only in a Washington, D.C., newspaper; he told the *Colored American* in mid-May that he expected rejection by a "more than 40,000 majority." He had just returned from North Carolina, where he saw "no suggestion of the bitterness and strife presented through the Democratic newspapers"; even in Tarboro, he said, white citizens had "com[e] across the street to shake hands with him and discuss current events." He also expected early consideration of his antilynching bill, "which has been sleeping in the judiciary committee."[34]

32. Anderson, *Race and Politics*, 299–300. The Reverend C. Dillard, a black clergyman, wrote to the *Goldsboro Daily Argus* the day after Grant's speech, claiming that Grant now opposed "educated negroes" who refused "to be pliant tools in the hands of designing politicians."
33. Ibid., 305.
34. "Congressman White Thinks the Proposed Amendment Will be Defeated by North Carolina's Right-Minded Citizens," WCA, 19 May 1990.

White may have viewed the recent House decision to seat former North Carolina congressman Richmond Pearson, after Pearson's lengthy contest against Democrat William T. Crawford, as a good political omen.[35] White may have also been encouraged by the announcement that Bishop Walters planned to step down as president of the National Afro-American Council in August, reportedly in the North Carolinian's favor. But as the August referendum neared, his outward good spirits were shaken by the *News and Observer's* resumption of political attacks on him.

Front-page political cartoons became a regular feature of the Raleigh newspaper in 1900, and almost all were racially tinged, featuring comically dressed blacks and befuddled white Republicans, sometimes violently attacking white Democrats, who were more often than not protecting white women from certain ravishment. The humor was often laced with acid, which fairly dripped from a particularly pointed May 26 caricature depicting George White as a bizarre elephant-like creature sipping from a jug labeled "Term in Congress Worth $5,000 a Year."[36] The caption read "He Doesn't Like to Let Go," and the cartoon apparently celebrated the selection by Second District Democrats, just a day earlier, of the only congressional nominee so far in 1900: Claude Kitchin, son of the infamous W. H. "Buck" Kitchin, the district's congressman from 1879 to 1881.

White had not yet made a final decision to forgo renomination, although he had to appreciate the increasing odds against his reelection. Without his usual strong support from the state Republican Party, and absent the support of formerly dedicated white district leaders like Hiram Grant, he faced an uphill battle against Claude Kitchin. In defeating ex-congressman Frederick Woodard and others, the younger Kitchin had survived a marathon selection process in Goldsboro, emerging only on the convention's 120th ballot, but the Democrats were already predicting his certain victory in November.[37]

35. Pearson was seated by the House on May 10, 1900; he had previously served the Ninth District from 1895 to 1899, while Crawford had served it from 1891 to 1895 and from March 1899 until Pearson's seating.

36. "He Doesn't Like to Let Go," cartoon, page one, *RN&O*, 26 May 1900. The creature, with a black face atop an elephant's body (labeled "G.O.P."), was "our only negro Congressman," whom voters were convinced had been in office "long enough."

37. Anderson, *Race and Politics*, 302. The *Goldsboro Daily Argus* (cited in Anderson) said on May 25 that Kitchin's election "is already a fact beyond the possibility of contravention."

Since January, George White had encountered strong verbal criticism from unnamed white Republican leaders who feared he was "desirous of making any kind of a deal to get reelected." A "prominent white Republican" complained to a Goldsboro newspaper in May that Second District blacks were "so 'uppish' that we can't make them stay in the background" until after the amendment vote, "and that fellow White, d—— him, is the cause of it."[38]

White had made no such deals by the time of the state GOP convention in May, but he harbored no illusions about the likelihood of a clean, civilized campaign; having served alongside Claude Kitchin's older brother William in the current Congress, he was well aware of the antipathy the Kitchin family felt toward black officeholders. In this expectation, White would not be disappointed; one of Claude Kitchin's earliest speeches was a two-hour exhortation in Goldsboro to white supremacists to halt alleged Negro hopes of "domination over us and our loved ones."[39]

The strain of the political infighting was beginning to show in White's public speeches, and by the end of June, he was apparently resigned to his lot; his speech to the Edgecombe County party regulars on June 30 was "quite conservative," according to the *Tarboro Southerner*, and included his own declaration that he was "out of politics so far as wanting office." He advised blacks to "register and vote, but create no disturbance and to strive to cultivate harmony and good feeling between the races."[40]

White's sober new approach was perhaps due in part to his experiences at the national Republican convention a fortnight earlier. White and Henry Hagans had journeyed to Philadelphia as the state's only black delegates;

38. J. T. B. Hoover to Marion Butler, 14 March 1900, Butler Papers, SHC; Anderson, *Race and Politics*, 301; John Addison Porter to George H. White, 20 January 1900, McKinley Papers (microfilm), Library of Congress. Anderson cites the *Charlotte Daily Observer* (January 1900) and the *Goldsboro Daily Argus*, 3 May 1900. Populist district supervisor Hoover complained to Marion Butler that White had intentionally included black men among potential census enumerators for the 1900 census in Warren County; Porter's letter acknowledged White's recent request to appoint Thomas J. Calloway to an unspecified federal post.

39. Anderson, *Race and Politics*, 303. William Walton Kitchin (1866–1924) of Roxboro served North Carolina's Fifth District from 1897–1909 and later served as governor. Both he and Claude (1869–1923) were sons of former congressman William H. "Buck" Kitchin. Claude's speech was recounted in the *Raleigh Morning Post*, 16 June 1900, which Anderson cites.

40. "The Republican Convention," *Tarboro Southerner*, 5 July 1900. The *Southerner* had written on 3 May 1900 that "It is believed that the present representative, George H. White, can [still] have a renomination if he wants it."

there were noticeably fewer black delegates in Philadelphia than at the 1896 gathering in St. Louis, and their participation was far less publicized. Former congressman John Roy Lynch of Mississippi offered an unsuccessful amendment to the national platform that echoed the forthcoming Crumpacker amendment, favoring the reduction of representation in Congress under terms of the Fourteenth Amendment for states that disfranchised black voters. White offered support by insisting that two of the convention's own rules be read twice, visibly annoying the convention chair. The platform eventually condemned "devices of State governments, whether by statutory or constitutional enactment, to avoid the purpose of this amendment" as "revolutionary," but declined to endorse John Lynch's solution.[41]

In like manner, the full convention declined to endorse a strong platform plank on lynching as offered by the National Afro-American Council to the convention's subcommittee on resolutions in Philadelphia, when White had chaired the council's delegation before the subcommittee. It was certainly a disappointment for White, whose antilynching bill was trapped in the House Judiciary Committee and unlikely to emerge before the November election. He had undoubtedly hoped the party would endorse some form of antilynching language, which would bolster his bill's chances of passage and possibly strengthen his own chance of gaining the presidency of the Afro-American Council in August in Indianapolis. He continued to look for promised help on the antilynching bill from President McKinley, but T. Thomas Fortune's earlier characterization of the president as "a man of jelly" must have echoed ominously in his ears.[42]

White voted to renominate President McKinley, with New York governor

41. *Official Proceedings of the Twelfth Republican National Convention, Held in the City of Philadelphia, June 19, 20 and 21, 1900* (Philadelphia: Dunlap Printing, 1900), 100–1; Donald Johnson, *National Party Platforms, Volume 1, 1840–1956* (Urbana: University of Illinois Press, 1978), 124; "Is Lynch to Blame?" editorial, *Cleveland Gazette*, 30 June 1900. Well-known black delegates included Judson W. Lyons, W. A. Pledger, and H. A. Rucker of Georgia; Walter L. Cohen of Louisiana; and James Hill of Mississippi, plus a number of black alternate delegates. John Lynch was "wholly responsible for the mutilation and practically the ruination" of the council committee's resolution, said *Gazette* editor Harry C. Smith; substitute wording adopted by unanimous vote of the subcommittee was unsatisfactory.

42. Sherman, *The Republican Party and Black America*, 13; "Attack on the President," *New York Times*, 11 May 1899. Fortune called McKinley "a man of jelly who would turn us loose on the mob and not say a word," according to Sherman. The remark came before Afro-American Conference (religious) delegates, according to the *Times*.

Theodore Roosevelt as his new running mate, but left the convention with empty hands and a heavy heart. His hopes for the antilynching bill and the council office now depended on the outcome of the vote on disfranchisement in his home state, as did his slowly fading chances for reelection to Congress in the fall. Despite White's own disclaimer of interest in the congressional nomination, his Second District party had as yet made no move to nominate anyone else, and he would certainly not have refused an earnest draft. No other candidates were yet willing to challenge him, although some white Republicans had already begun considering possible white nominees for the first time since 1894. As a practical matter, White knew that he was of more use to the antiamendment campaign as a seemingly disinterested statesman than as an active candidate, and that campaign of principle was more important to him than his own run for office.

However pessimistic he may have been regarding his own situation, White stubbornly refused to believe that a majority of North Carolina voters would endorse white supremacy by voting to restrict suffrage. As late as election week he was still predicting rejection by a large majority unless the Democrats stole the election by fraud; even then, White seemed to believe the courts would intervene to overturn the election, the amendment, or both.[43]

Democrats had previously decided to hold the state's 1900 gubernatorial election in August, returning to the pre-1880 schedule that had divided state and national elections between August and November. Such a schedule would now allow the constitutional amendment to be voted on separately from national contests. In the governor's race, Democratic candidate Charles Brantley Aycock was a heavy favorite to replace the increasingly unpopular Daniel Russell, who was not allowed to succeed himself. With the astute guidance of state Democratic chairman Furnifold Simmons, Aycock had eagerly assumed the white-supremacy mantle while shrewdly defusing the potential issue of the disfranchisement of illiterate whites by pledging to expand and improve the state's educational system.

The pledge was a blatant effort to sway sentiment among normally pro-Republican whites in the western end of the state. Under the amendment's "grandfather clause," most illiterate whites would be permanently exempted from disfranchisement by simply registering before 1908, if their ancestors had

43. WCA, 4 August 1900.

been entitled to vote in 1867. Conversely, few blacks could expect to meet that standard, since free blacks had been barred from voting in North Carolina after 1835, and black men had been given suffrage rights again only in 1868. Any white man who could read and write by 1908 would afterward be able to register to vote, and illiterate whites registered before 1908 would continue to be able to vote thereafter. Yet even literate blacks would face the official obstacles of the new, stricter registration procedure.[44]

The reappearance of "Red Shirt" campaigners in the summer of 1900 also minimized the chance that North Carolina voters in some areas might even hear the opposite view, as argued by nervous Republicans: that the amendment was undemocratic at best and would still deprive thousands of illiterate whites of the right to vote. The Red Shirts were Democratic men attired in distinctive red apparel, first prominent during the 1898 campaign. Their return in 1900 was certainly intimidating, if not actually violent, causing one Republican candidate to cancel his speaking tour from Weldon to Wilmington because he encountered hecklers at every railroad stop. Other Republican speakers were sometimes discouraged from speaking by the "strong measures" of the Red Shirts, particularly in the heavily black counties of eastern North Carolina, according to Trinity College history professor John Spencer Bassett. Their combination of physical terror against prospective black voters and social terror against whites was inexcusable, Bassett wrote at the time.[45]

Both the Populist and Republican ranks were gradually being depleted by the war of nerves being waged by the Democrats, yet opponents of the amendment continued their fight in the face of overwhelming odds. Cyrus Thompson, the Populist candidate for governor, urged opposition to the amendment as late as mid-July, when he spoke to party faithful at a Warrenton convention; meanwhile, George White assumed personal control of the Edgecombe County Republican campaign, becoming chairman of

44. Lefler and Newsome, *North Carolina*, 560–1.

45. Helen G. Edmonds, *The Negro and Fusion Politics in North Carolina, 1894–1901* (Chapel Hill: University of North Carolina Press, 1951), 212; Lefler and Newsome, *North Carolina*, 595. A week later, John Spencer Bassett wrote about the election in the *Outlook* 45 (11 August 1900). Bassett later edited the *South Atlantic Quarterly*, a scholarly journal whose "advanced views" on race and Booker T. Washington alienated Josephus Daniels and others, leading to a public campaign for Bassett's dismissal in 1903; he was retained by trustees.

the county party's executive committee. No polling techniques existed at the time to measure public opinion, but vocal opposition to the amendment was apparently strongest in the heavily Republican western counties, where few blacks lived; voters there feared that illiterate mountain whites would be victimized by Democrats, despite assurances to the contrary. Republican leaders in the east continued to suggest that black voters leave the issue up the courts rather than risk a white backlash by making a public issue of their opposition.[46]

Even without fraud, the Democrats would likely have won the election, but they nevertheless decided to take no chances in the August balloting. Charles Aycock was credited with a resounding victory over Republican Spencer Adams, 186,650 to 126,296. Aycock claimed just under 60 percent of the total vote, carrying 73 of the state's 97 counties. In many instances, however, the returns were little short of preposterous: Edgecombe County went 91 percent and Halifax 88 percent for Aycock, with thousands of black votes either ignored or "converted" to Democratic ballot boxes. In Halifax, the total vote counted exceeded the county's entire population of adult males by more than 200 votes, an absurdity that only shell-shocked Republicans seemed to notice. A remarkable 67 percent of the state's black voters made the courageous trek to the polls, although their votes were too few to defeat Aycock or the constitutional amendment, even had they been fairly counted; many Populists, on the other hand, and even some Republicans, appear to have voted Democratic or stayed home.[47]

The victory of the constitutional amendment was somewhat less impressive than Aycock's, but still monumental in its own right. Sixty-six counties gave a majority to the amendment and thirty-one opposed it; the total was

46. Lefler and Newsome, *North Carolina*, 561; "Wednesday at Warrenton," *Littleton True Reformer*, 25 July 1900; "Congressman White County Chairman," *Washington Daily Record*, reprinted in *Littleton True Reformer*, same date. Thompson was replaced by Republican nominee Spencer Adams as the Populist candidate for governor shortly before the election, under a fusion agreement with Republicans; Thompson became the fusion candidate for secretary of state.

47. Anderson, *Race and Politics*, 306–7; Crow, *A History of African Americans in North Carolina*, 117. Halifax officials reported 7,495 votes, although the U.S. census showed just 7,249 adult males residing in the county, more than 60 percent of them black. Aycock's total in Edgecombe was more than twice that of any previous Democratic candidate for governor, in a county that Daniel Russell had carried by 60 percent four years earlier. Crow estimates the black turnout in August 1900 at 67 percent.

182,217 votes for the amendment to 128,285 against. Only three eastern counties, none of which had black majorities, voted the amendment down: Brunswick, Camden, and Sampson. Only 2 opposing votes were counted in New Hanover, scene of the deadly racial riot two years earlier, out of nearly 3,000 cast; the figures were barely less lopsided in the Black Second counties, where Warren voters came closest to defeating the amendment, giving only 43 percent of the vote for disfranchisement. In the eighteen counties with black majorities, the average vote was three to one in favor; in George White's home county of Edgecombe, the vote was nine to one in favor, even though registered black voters outnumbered white voters by as many as 400.[48]

That the Democrats had stolen the election was obvious, even to some Democratic observers, who nevertheless defended the tactics as being for the greater good of the state. For thousands of black voters who had braved Red Shirt threats to go to the polls, the loss was disheartening enough; the fact that most of their votes were not even counted properly was a depressing reminder of just how far down the political ladder they had fallen. While they might yet attempt to vote until 1902, it seemed a useless gesture; with the lily-white wing of the Republican Party now firmly in control, they had effectively been jettisoned by their own party. Blacks no longer held any political power in counties they had until recently helped to rule, in the last state where their votes had elected legislators from their race. Four years earlier, black voters had played a key role in electing North Carolina's governor; four years hence, most would not even be allowed into the polling booths.

As their leader and moral guide, Congressman White was devastated. A close election might still have been challenged successfully in the courts; a runaway landslide, however suspicious, was beyond legal reproach, practically speaking. For weeks White pondered his options, after returning to Washington for rest and preparation for travel, this time to Indianapolis for the National Afro-American Council's annual convention.

Shortly before he left Washington for Indiana in late August, White gave a lengthy interview to the *New York Times*. The resulting article, a revealing and unusually bitter portrait of a man whose political future had just col-

48. Edmonds, *Fusion Politics*, 209. Edmonds cites figures from the *North Carolina Manual* (1913). Most of the counties opposing the amendment were in the central and western sections of the state; the suffrage question actually cut across party lines, since seven counties supporting Democrat Aycock also voted against the amendment for which he campaigned.

lapsed, appeared in the Sunday edition of the newspaper on August 26, two days before the council convention was slated to open. "I cannot live in North Carolina and be treated as a man," he told the *Times* correspondent, noting he planned to leave the state permanently and had "made up my mind not to be a candidate for renomination to Congress."[49]

While he himself had once felt perfectly comfortable practicing law in the state, White said, "I cannot feel so any longer. I expect to practice law in New York, or if not there, I shall settle in some State up this way." He described the disfranchisement of his race in North Carolina as "merely a symptom of what is going on there," and called "the political part of it . . . a mere subterfuge . . . a means for the general degradation of the Negro."[50]

White gave three specific reasons for his decision to leave Congress, including the poor health of his wife, "a refined and educated woman . . . [who] has suffered terribly because of the attacks on me." Cora Lena was currently ill in New Jersey, he said, and he feared she would be "an invalid for a long time." This was his primary concern, he explained, adding that

> My wife's health has been wrecked on account of the maliciousness of the political attacks made upon me, and I am sure the excitement of another campaign would kill her; secondly, I am satisfied I could not secure a certificate if I were elected; and thirdly, I must devote myself to some employment that pays me. I have not sufficient means to carry on a political fight that can only prove expensive.[51]

George White believed he had been singled out as the "target for those who have been fighting against the Negro race in North Carolina, and nothing has been too hard to say of me." But the real loss to the state would not be his departure, he predicted; it would be the forced immigration of as many as fifty thousand blacks from North Carolina to other states during the next decade. He personally opposed colonization in any one location, "for that would result in a repetition of what has taken place . . . in the South generally"; he proposed instead that blacks should "go to the West and to the

49. "Southern Negro's Plaint, Congressman G. H. White Forced to Leave North Carolina; Will Not Re-Enter Congress; Wife a Physical Wreck Owing to Attacks; Advises Negroes to Migrate West," *New York Times* (Sunday), 26 August 1900.
    50. Ibid.
    51. Ibid.

North, but especially to the North . . . [and] should lose themselves among the people of the country. A few families could settle here and there. Then their children will be better educated." This would also benefit the majority of his race, who "must of necessity remain in the South"—apparently by reducing white resentment against them—although he expected fully a "third or a half of the colored population of North Carolina will leave the South eventually," including immigration to the new territories of "Cuba, Porto Rico, Hawaii or the Philippines."[52]

White spared no one his anger, reserving some of his sharpest words for his state's Republican Party: "The fact is, the white Republicans of North Carolina are Republicans in order to get the Negro vote to maintain them in office, but they do not want the Negroes to hold office." He mocked Republican senator Jeter Pritchard, who had recently promised to join the state's Democrats in passing new legislation to place the "black counties" under white control (as in the period from 1876 to 1894), rather than disfranchise blacks; Pritchard now opposed blacks in office, although he owed his two elections to the Senate to strong black support. White called for an end to black dependence on the GOP, stating it was now time for the black man "to think for himself and act for himself. He must paddle his own canoe."[53]

The *Times* called White "one of the best-known figures in the Fifty-Fifth and Fifty-Sixth Congresses . . . a stalwart, good-looking man and a good speaker," as well as "the only colored man in Congress." His departure from the House was "one of the most significant results of the race trouble in North Carolina," in the opinion of the writer, who specifically mentioned White's recent speech "on the lynching question." Almost all of White's major career accomplishments were in fact dutifully listed, although his work on behalf of the National Afro-American Council was not among them.[54]

The interview was undoubtedly cathartic for White, who had now publicly expressed his feelings to the nation. But not all *Times* readers in North Carolina were impressed with his reasoning or sympathetic to his plight, of course. In his hometown, the *Southerner* dropped its previous cordiality to ridicule him openly: "George H. White says he will keep his voting residence here until the Supreme Court has determined the constitutionality of the

52. Ibid.
53. Ibid.
54. Ibid.

Amendment. George will stay here if he can get a job." As for the interview itself, the *Southerner* chided White for "making about as many misrepresentations of the South and this section as one can well do in the same space."[55]

The *News and Observer* attributed a subtler motive to White, in reprinting the Tarboro comment within an editorial entitled "May Be Playing False." The congressman "knows if he shows his hands, the negroes cannot be organized for McKinley. . . . These negro leaders may be playing possum, and it will do to watch them," wrote the Raleigh newspaper. White hoped to lull the Democrats into complacency in the fall election, but "no sort of sedative will put the N.C. Democracy to sleep while the votes of 120,000 are cast for McKinley."[56]

What prompted White to grant the interview at this particular moment is not known; perhaps he felt that such publicity might help his campaign for president of the Afro-American Council, by announcing his retirement from the political arena just before the convention opened. If this were true, even mentioning the council in the article might have been seen as self-promotion and might change the tenor of the interview entirely. At any rate, there was no consensus in the black community about White's suitability for the office; at least one major black newspaper had recently questioned the wisdom of electing a partisan political figure like White to the council's helm, since the council itself was vigorously nonpartisan.[57] Alexander Walters might yet be prevailed upon to continue as council head, and it was not at all clear that George White even remained interested in challenging Walters under the current circumstances.

Perhaps, for once, George White's temper simply prevailed over his usual practical and calm demeanor; in any event, the publicity failed to enhance his strength at the convention, where he drew no office at all, perhaps by choice. The convention met for four days (August 28–31) in the senate chamber of the Indiana State House, where Walters was indeed reelected to a third term

55. Untitled editorial and "George White on the Amendment," both in *Tarboro Southerner*, 30 August 1900.

56. Untitled editorial, *RN&O*, 27 August 1900.

57. Untitled editorial, *Cleveland Gazette*, 26 May 1900. According to this piece, "Congressman White may be just the man for the place in the estimation of Bishop Walters and others, but there are those who feel that he is too deeply imbedded in politics for a such a position. The president of the Council should be a man who is above political influence."

as president. White did suggest that the council consider electing a national organizer, a post then given to crusading journalist Ida Wells-Barnett of Illinois, who had been active in the council's antilynching bureau but reportedly opposed White's bill as ineffective. The congressman undoubtedly welcomed her active participation in his own cause, but he took strong exception to the appearance at the council of a man for whom he now had little use—U.S. senator Jeter Pritchard, North Carolina's Republican member of that body since 1895—and from whom he expected to hear nothing of interest.

Pritchard had been personally invited to address the council by Bishop Walters, as approved by the council's invitation committee, and his subject was a timely one: "Why the 13th, 14th and 15th Amendments to the Constitution of the United States Should Not Be Repealed." Just before the speech began, however, George White "offered vigorous objections, saying he would not consent to the organization's being addressed by any man who said that he would favor withholding political office from Afro-Americans when they were in the majority"; others at the convention agreed, although the speech went ahead as scheduled. Senator Pritchard's speech turned out to be "a very able one, with the exception of one or two distasteful remarks," according to journalist and council vice president Harry C. Smith's account; J. Milton Turner of St. Louis, a former U.S. minister to Liberia, responded cordially to Pritchard's remarks as well.[58]

The council declined to take an active part in the 1900 political campaign, though many of its members were personally active afterwards, including both George White and John P. Green of Ohio, and even one of its officers, Cyrus Field Adams. White campaigned in Ohio for William McKinley in mid-September, probably accompanied by John Green. The Ohio trip was apparently one of many for White that fall; he later recalled that he had canvassed "seven different states" during the 1900 McKinley campaign, although the list did not appear to include North Carolina.[59]

There, Republicans of the Second District had finally met in September to nominate a "caretaker" candidate for the fall's congressional race, in the wake

58. "Fired Out!" *Cleveland Gazette*, 8 September 1900; "Third Annual Convention of the National Afro-American Council," minutes, in Adams, *The National Afro-American Council*, 9.

59. *Washington Bee*, 15 September 1900; WCA, 28 October 1899; "Ex-Representative White: Why He Is Entitled to Consideration at the Hands of the President," letter to the editor, *Washington Post*, 23 April 1901.

of George White's final withdrawal and his conspicuous absence from the scene. Eight members of the district executive committee—five blacks and three whites—met on September 14 to select a white nominee, former First District congressman Joseph John "J.J." Martin. Having more recently served as Tarboro's postmaster, the sixty-six-year-old Martin had sought the Second District nomination in years past without success. Still, as the *Tarboro Southerner* admitted, the committee had "probably selected the best man in [the] party," even if he had little chance of beating Claude Kitchin.[60]

George White had much respect for Martin, a former prosecutor who had preceded John Henry Collins and himself as Second District solicitor (1868–1878), but the congressman took no interest in the fall campaign or the election itself in North Carolina. In an open circular distributed to the district's executive committee and other party members in early October, White said he could no longer support the state's GOP leaders, who had betrayed black party members. "I wish to state here and now that I will never follow such leadership again. . . . I have lost faith in . . . so-called Republicans that we have at the head of affairs in our State at this time." He explained that one reason he had declined to run again for Congress was that he would not enjoy the "hearty cooperation of many of the white Republicans in the State," and he sharply criticized Pritchard, Hiram Grant, and party chairman A. E. Holton for suggesting legislation to prevent blacks from holding office.[61]

White's withdrawal from politics had certainly removed any vitality from the local campaign trail; the fall election was one of the quietest on record. For the first time in three decades, no black candidate's name appeared on the Second District ballot, either as a Republican nominee or as an independent. While more than 35,000 votes were tallied across the district in November, the conclusion was never in doubt; Claude Kitchin defeated J. J. Martin by a margin of nearly two to one. Carrying all nine counties, Kitchin claimed 22,901 votes, Martin just 12,521. Again, as in August, the official results ranged from highly suspect to all but impossible; no Democratic candidate had ever won more than 16,051 votes in the Black Second, Furnifold Simmons having set that record in his 1888 defeat.[62]

60. *Tarboro Southerner*, 20 September 1900.

61. Anderson, *Race and Politics*, 310–1. He cites reports from the *Scotland Neck Commonwealth*, 11 October 1900, and *Windsor Ledger*, 25 October 1900.

62. Anderson, *Race and Politics*, 350 (Table 22).

Now, in contrast, Martin's closest margin was in Warren County, where he won 43 percent of the vote; in his own Edgecombe County, he received barely a third of the total. Martin may well have planned to challenge the results, but his unexpected death on December 18, 1900, closed the books permanently on the election; it was, coincidentally, the day of George White's forty-eighth birthday.[63]

The vote for president in North Carolina was considerably closer than had been the summer election for governor, although this was due as much to a drop in Democratic turnout as to anything else. William Jennings Bryan defeated William McKinley in North Carolina by a margin of just under 25,000 votes; Governor Aycock had received 29,000 more votes in August than Bryan did now, and McKinley received 6,000 more than had Aycock's challenger, Adams, in August. In all, the state's presidential voting tally had declined by 40,000 from 1896; even with the same two candidates, 18,000 fewer Democrats bothered to turn out this time.[64]

For the first time since 1866, not a single black was elected to either house of the General Assembly. No blacks were elected to any offices in any of the counties of the Black Second, which had finally been "redeemed" for the Democracy by Charles Aycock, Furnifold Simmons, and Francis D. Winston. For practical purposes, the Black Second had ceased to exist as a political entity; while black voters were still a registered majority in Edgecombe and Warren Counties, for instance, their votes were essentially worthless, even locally.

Two months earlier, just after the passage of the disfranchisement amendment, the *Tarboro Southerner* had quipped, "The George H. White supremacy no longer reigneth in Edgecombe. Selah."[65] Its comment was premature, since White remained in office until March 1901, but from this point on, the Republican Party's supremacy in the state was over. Indeed, the era of truly competitive two-party politics in North Carolina was over, for the next half-century and more.

For Josephus Daniels, the victory was a sweet one. His beloved Democratic Party had routed the forces of radical Republicanism and "Negro domination"

63. Ibid., 311. Martin's obituary, carried in the *Tarboro Southerner* of 20 December 1900, described him as "kind-hearted" and a "model postmaster."

64. NCG, 1335.

65. Untitled editorial, *Tarboro Southerner*, 5 August 1900.

in North Carolina, and ended the reign of the man he later characterized in his memoirs as the "most militant of the Negroes elected to Congress," describing White's 1900 speeches as "bitter and vicious."[66]

For George White, there was little to do but ponder the future and look for another job. His political career in North Carolina was officially ended, and his eyes were now trained on a self-imposed exile in the North. His mood must have been dark and his thoughts angry as he considered his reward for twenty years of faithful public service. He was not given to swearing in public, but one chronicler records him as cursing his birthplace: "May God damn North Carolina, the state of my birth."[67]

White would make the somber trip back to Washington sometime in November. The second and final session of the 56th Congress convened on December 3, 1900 and lasted three months, but it occupied little of White's time as he spoke on only four occasions during the session. Two of these speeches were very brief remarks and one was a lengthier discussion of a bill White still hoped to pass. His "farewell" speech on January 29, 1901, the last time he addressed the U.S. House, was by far the longest.

On each of these carefully selected occasions, White sought to make a specific point, both political and personal—in effect, they compose a four-part commentary on his career and philosophy. His talk on December 8 was one of many eulogies offered by House members to their fallen colleague, Alfred C. Harmer of Pennsylvania, who had died earlier in the year. A fourteen-term veteran of Congress, Harmer would probably have been embarrassed by the attention showered on him that day; he had rarely spoken on the floor of the House, but was famous for the quality and thoroughness of his committee work, particularly on the District of Columbia committee, where he had recently served with White. It is quite possible that the two had met much earlier, perhaps in 1876, when White worked at the Centennial Exposition in Philadelphia and Harmer was a young congressman from that city, then in his

66. Daniels, *Editor in Politics*, 336.

67. H. Larry Ingle, "George Henry White," in David Roller and Robert Twyman, *Encyclopedia of Southern History* (Baton Rouge: Louisiana State University Press, 1979), 1337. Ingle cites his own unpublished paper, "White," and Elmore, "North Carolina Negro Congressmen," as sources of this quote. In turn, Elmore cites Turner and Bridgers, *History of Edgecombe County*, 323, as the source of the quote; Turner and Bridgers locate its origin as an unspecified speech of July 1900.

second term. As the longest-serving congressman, Harmer had been selected to administer the oath of office to the new speaker, David Henderson; the so-called Father of the House had then lapsed into serious illness.[68]

"Mr. Chairman, there are two periods in the life of every public man which provoke attention," White's eulogy began. "If he has enemies or opponents, when he starts out . . . the worst possible phase of his character is ventilated to the world. The tongues of his maligners will run at rapid pace." The second period began after his death, causing a reverse effect of excessive praise, when "the virtues of this man's life are portrayed and his morals are held up in a glittering galaxy of beauty." Alfred Harmer, said White, was an exception to both general rules: he had lived such an exemplary life that no maligners could be found at its opening, nor was any exaggeration needed at its close.[69]

"He was not noisy, but he was grand, useful, noble, in every instance, and in every purpose strictly honest," White went on. "With him wrong was a foe; with him, right was a duty. He sought to know the right, and always had the courage to do the right, and at the close of a long, eventful and useful life he was doubtless prepared to receive the divine blessing, 'Well done, good and faithful servant.'" And unlike the proverbial prophet, honored everywhere except at home, Harmer had commanded the respect and affection on his fellow congressmen, "whom he knew longest and knew best."[70]

White's tribute to Harmer was genuine and heartfelt, but it contained an even deeper message of the seeming futility of politics as a profession, at least for ordinary men. One's self-worth was pilloried at the outset and praised only when he could not hear it, one's accomplishments never assessed fairly or adequately rewarded during one's lifetime. How rare the exceptional man, like Alfred Harmer, who could transcend the normal rules and set an example "worthy of the emulation of the young," how seldom the true worth of a statesman acknowledged or appreciated by his peers at the time of his accomplishments.[71]

By January 8, White felt compelled to criticize the systemic unfairness of a political structure that tended to stifle dissent on matters of critical impor-

---

68. *Congressional Record*, 56th Cong., 2d Sess., 33, 2:5.

69. Ibid., 2:192.

70. Ibid.

71. Ibid.

tance. The occasion was the pending vote on the Crumpacker amendment to the Burleigh reapportionment bill, based on the results of the 1900 census. Congressman Edgar D. Crumpacker of Indiana, a former judge, had protested the majority report of the Committee on the Census, which ignored the actions of southern states in disfranchising black voters and proposed to allot representation to those states sheerly on the basis of population. Under the Fourteenth Amendment, Crumpacker said, Congress had no discretion to ignore the punitive and unfair actions of states such as Louisiana, Mississippi, South Carolina, and now North Carolina, but must act as a "countervailing force" to injustices there. "If the negro is not entitled to the protection of political laws," he asked, "under what laws is he entitled to protection?" Legislation such as Crumpacker favored in his minority report—ultimately reducing the number of representatives given to offending states—"cannot put brains into the heads nor character into the lives of the people, but it can set in motion forces that will tend to encourage a healthy and honest growth of civil life."[72]

White had attempted mightily to be heard on the question, claiming that as the "sole representative of one-eighth of the entire population," he should have a voice on matters directly affecting his race, but he was never allowed to address the issue directly. As the reapportionment bill approached its vote on January 8, 1901, much of the discussion had centered on Crumpacker's minority proposal—which had sparked furious denunciation from southern Democrats but little comment from those who favored it—under strict rules established by the House leadership and carried out by the floor managers of both the majority and the minority reports on the bill. Only two other congressmen, Democrat John Fitzgerald of Massachusetts and Republican Charles Grosvenor of Ohio, had spoken in favor of the Crumpacker amendment when White was finally recognized for a brief comment, after general debate had been closed.[73]

In sheer frustration, White had agreed that he would "not refer to the matter under consideration now," although he hinted unmistakably at his anger at

72. Ibid., 2:486; Sherman, *Republican Party and Black America*, 18. Crumpacker's proposal suggested that as a result, Louisiana should expect to lose three of its seven representatives, Mississippi three of its seven, South Carolina two of its six, and North Carolina three of its nine.

73. Sherman, *Republican Party and Black America*, 18; *Congressional Record*, 56th Cong., 2d Sess., 33, 2:737.

House leaders for allowing his race to be "so grossly misrepresented and maligned" by speakers from three separate states without the courtesy of a reply. "They have spoken of my people as a thing to be managed. . . . Can they manage us like oxen? I want them to understand that, removed as we are thirty-five years from slavery, we are to-day as you are, men, and claim the right of the American citizen and the right to vote."[74]

"I did think, and I thought it rather strange, that the gentlemen managing the two sides of this question . . . after my people had been so slandered, might have accorded me an opportunity to defend them, as only two or three gentlemen [Fitzgerald and Grosvenor] have taken the opportunity to do. God bless them," White said, and "God bless Judge Crumpacker, who has taken occasion to stand up in his place as a man and has said a word in defense of these people . . . who since their emancipation have served their country faithfully" as Republicans.[75]

The Crumpacker amendment was defeated shortly afterward, 136-94, and the unpopular proposal to punish southern states was laid aside permanently. The passive attitude of the Republican leadership, caught up so tightly in its own battle between its lily-white and traditional wings, had been unwilling to risk a political war with the South, even as it relinquished the potential votes of nearly one million blacks now left without a citizen's right of suffrage, and soon to be left without a single representative in Congress. White was indignant, but resigned to his lot; as a lame-duck congressman, he had almost no leverage with the leaders of his party in the House, and there was still one bill he hoped to have passed, that to establish "a home for aged and infirm colored people." He had introduced House Joint Resolution 67 appropriating money for this purpose in December 1899.

Two weeks later, the actual bill, H.R. 10305, reached a vote. It appropriated the sum of $100,000—all left-over "moneys, arrears of pay and bounty which are due to the estates of deceased colored soldiers" from the war—to

74. *Congressional Record*, 56th Cong., 2d Sess., 33, 2:737. White mocked the youth of the three southerners—from Alabama, South Carolina, and North Carolina—"as an extenuating circumstance for their vile words against my people."

75. Ibid., 2:737 and Appendix, 2:88–90. Congressman Grosvenor entered into the *Record*, as an appendix a sympathetic article he had written months earlier on "The Negro Problem in the South," as well as an editorial from the *Raleigh Morning Post* on economic problems likely to face North Carolina after black voters were disfranchised.

construct a "national memorial home for aged and infirm colored people" in the District of Columbia. Such funds would remain indefinitely in the U.S. Treasury, and no claims against the funds were likely to be pursued by any legal heirs, due both to the length of time and the lack of legal documentation, White explained on January 21. Since most of the soldiers affected had been slaves, their marriages had not been recorded and their children would have great difficulty in proving their entitlement. The actual sum available amounted to nearly a quarter of a million dollars, and the remainder of the fund would be used to create an endowment fund for long-term maintenance.[76]

The Committee on Military Affairs had reported the bill out favorably, allowing White to call for a suspension of the rules and an immediate vote. White argued forcefully that the money in question "does not properly belong to the United States," but was "simply a kind of trust fund in the custody of the United States and under its control"; using it to assist the elderly and the sick of the race was certainly more beneficial then leaving it in the Treasury indefinitely. During a brief debate centering mostly on whether the home should be restricted to residents of the District or open to any black resident of the country, White was assisted by Congressman Charles Grosvenor of Ohio and other supportive members in responding to questions and objections; the bill was then passed without additional amendments on a vote of 135 to 59, and sent to the Senate for its consideration.

Although a similar bill had been passed by the Senate nearly three years earlier, but not enacted by the House, this time the bill was debated but not approved by the Senate.[77] White's handling of the challenge showed that even under trying circumstances, he still knew how to work with helpful colleagues in a constructive fashion for an agreed-upon purpose; this time, he did not insist that the issue be cast in racially charged terms, and he was successful, at least in the short range.

When White next rose to address the House eight days later, it was to deliver his final remarks to that body. The address, which came to be called his

76. Ibid., 2:1268.

77. Ibid., 2:1268–71. The bill was "passed over" by the Senate after being reported out favorably by the Committee on Education and Labor; see also 1288, 1821, 2504, 3499, and 3503. Previous Senate action in June 1898, on the similar bill, is described in the House Committee report at 1268.

farewell speech, was the lengthiest speech of his career, and portions of it were reprinted for decades in anthologies of black literature. It was divided into a brief introduction and three distinct parts, each covering a different aspect of the central theme of racial justice and fair treatment of black citizens. White had been granted time to speak during debate on an agricultural bill concerning, among other things, the continued distribution of free seeds by the Department of Agriculture; White's other major committee had recently debated the bill. His introduction dealt briefly with the bill and his own observations on the rapid growth of the federal bureaucracy dealing with such programs.[78]

That being said, he launched into the meat of his speech: "a plea for the colored man, the colored woman, the colored boy and the colored girl of this country." What he had been prevented by circumstance from saying three weeks earlier during the general debate on reapportionment and the Crumpacker bill was now offered at some length, covering more than two pages of the *Congressional Record*. "I therefore must embrace this opportunity to say, out of season, perhaps, that which I was not permitted to say in season," he began. In response to specific remarks by North Carolina's W. W. Kitchin on the fitness of black citizens to vote, White pointed out the results of the recent election on the state's constitutional amendment. In Kitchin's hometown of Scotland Neck, for example, the total registered vote at the time of the election had been 539; total votes counted, however, had been nearly double—831—and Democratic by an eleven-to-one margin, although registered Republicans outnumbered Democrats nearly two to one. There, Democratic fraud had been based on senseless charges of "negro domination in that State," and White blamed Kitchin's "wild and spasmodic notions" regarding the subject on his youth. White was less charitable in referring to Alabama's Oscar Underwood, whose threatening remarks he compared to those of a murdering highway bandit; Underwood had recently claimed that any attempt to enforce the Fourteenth Amendment in the South would bring deadly retaliation.

A highwayman commits murder, and when the officers of the law undertake to arrest, try and punish him commensurate with the enormity of his crime, he straightens himself up to his full height and defiantly

78. Ibid., 2:1634–8.

says to them: "Let me alone, I will not be arrested, I will not be tried, I'll have none of the execution of your laws, and in the event you attempt to execute your laws upon me, I will see to it that many more men, women or children are murdered."[79]

Alabama's opposition to the Constitution was startling, yet no more so than Underwood's revisionist assertion that blacks "have been thrust upon the whites of the South," as if slavery had never existed. It was similar to the assertions by "some members of the Republican party to-day—'lily-whites,' if you please—who, after receiving the unalloyed support of the negro vote for over thirty years, now feel that they have grown a little too good for association with him politically, and are disposed to dump him overboard." As for the poetic observations of White's witty colleague on the agriculture committee, Peter Otey, that "justice is merely relative," and could exist "among homogeneous people" as equals, but never among "heterogeneous people," White scoffed. He reminded Stanyarne Wilson of South Carolina that while Reconstruction had indeed elevated a "few ignorant, gullible and perhaps purchasable negroes" to high posts in that state thirty years earlier, the corruption had been mainly the fault of northern carpetbaggers and their "diabolical purpose."[80]

In the second section of his address, White attempted to demonstrate the advances blacks had made: increased literacy, economic leverage, professional advancement, more than $50 million in church and school property, another $750 million in farms and homes. "All this we have done under the most adverse of circumstances. . . . The new man, the slave who has grown out of the ashes of thirty-five years ago . . . asks a fair and just judgment." This included White's antilynching bill, "which still sleeps sweetly in . . . committee," and the separate bill to reimburse Freedman's depositors, for which White once again pushed at length.[81]

White's final remarks, offering a "brief recipe for the solution of the so-called American negro problem," were touchingly sad: "Help him to overcome his weakness, punish the crime-committing class by the courts of the land, measure the standard of the race by its best material, cease to mold prej-

79. Ibid., 2:1635–6.
80. Ibid., 2:1636–7.
81. Ibid., 2:1637–8.

udicial and unjust public sentiment against him . . . obliterate race hatred, party prejudice and help us to achieve nobler ends, greater results and become more satisfactory citizens to our brother in white."[82]

White's closing lines were among the most widely remembered and widely quoted lines from any speech by a black American for the next half century: "This, Mr. Chairman, is perhaps the negroes' temporary farewell to the American Congress; but let me say, Phoenix-like he will rise up some day and come again. These parting words are in behalf of an outraged, heart-broken, bruised, and bleeding, but God-fearing people, faithful, industrious, loyal people—rising people, full of potential force."[83]

A poignant paraphrase of Sir Walter Raleigh's centuries-old defense of Lord Bacon drew thunderous applause as White left the floor for the last time: "The only apology I have to make for the earnestness with which I have spoken is that I am pleading for the life, the liberty, the future happiness, and manhood suffrage for one-eighth of the entire population of the United States."[84]

George White's term in Congress concluded five weeks later, to the less admiring words of a North Carolina legislator. Rising to address an all-white audience in Raleigh at noon on March 4, Representative Watts of Iredell led a collective jeer at the departing figure. "Geo. H. White, the insolent negro, who has so long represented the proud people of North Carolina in the Congress of the United States, has retired from office forever," Watts declared. "We have a white man's government in every part of the old State, and from this hour no negro will again disgrace the old State in the council chambers of the nation. For these mercies, thank God."[85]

82. Ibid.

83. Ibid.

84. Ibid.

85. "Under the Dome," *RN&O*, 5 March 1901. Watts noted that U.S. senator Marion Butler, the other "renegade," had also retired.

12

Life after Congress: Testing the Currents, 1901

Like many retiring congressmen, George White faced a quandary in early 1901: he no longer had a job, but was not ready to leave Washington. His national party was securely in power, and President McKinley, for whom he had campaigned tirelessly, had just been reelected comfortably to a second term. If White were to seek a federal appointment, he fully expected the president's blessing and the support of party leaders. Still vigorous at forty-eight, he had been a highly visible celebrity—as the only black member of Congress—for four years. He was warmly endorsed by his fellow party leaders, personally liked by many; he had also been sure to write McKinley a personal note of congratulations after the election.[1]

There were, as well, recent precedents for midlevel black appointments by this president. McKinley had appointed White's brother-in-law, Henry Cheatham, recorder of deeds for the District of Columbia in 1897. The late Blanche K. Bruce of Louisiana had served as register of the Treasury from 1897 until his death a year later and Judson W. Lyons of Georgia had succeeded him in 1898. Both jobs had been designated almost exclusively for black appointees since Reconstruction. They were half of the so-called top four, along with the posts of minister to Haiti and minister to Liberia, then held by William F. Powell of New Jersey and Owen Lun West Smith of North Carolina, respectively.[2]

1. Congressman George N. Southwick (R-N.Y.) to John E. Bruce, reprinted in *WCA*, 11 June 1898.

2. Bruce (1841–1898) of Louisiana, the first black to serve a full term in the U.S. Senate

Still, a major appointment was no certainty for George White. There were obstacles. For all his personal dedication and visibility, White had not been particularly successful as a legislator. Two terms had hardly been long enough to build the substantive reputation he needed to gain a significant federal position; only one of his bills had been passed, while none of his committee assignments had been noticeably productive. Worse, he had infuriated many southern congressmen with his obstinate refusal to play the quiet foil to smug pronouncements about his race. His southern base of support had been decimated by the imminent disfranchisement of most black voters in North Carolina. And while he was generally respected by black leaders, he was not universally revered by his race, as he would learn shortly.

Just how high could White set his sights? He and several other black Republicans had campaigned for McKinley with vigor, even in the face of increasing criticism from fellow blacks who were disenchanted with the president's inattentiveness to their needs. But now an unsettling undercurrent was on the political front. Flagrant disfranchisement of black voters by the southern states had gone unpunished by Congress, and the rate of lynchings was still unacceptably large.

Worse, "Jim Crow" laws were also appearing across the South, promising "separate but equal" status for blacks. It was the beginning of the new American apartheid, sanctioned by the courts and nervously ignored by racial moderates. Deeply troubled by these developments, George White had not wished to leave Congress in 1900, where he felt secure, useful, and important; the four-year drumbeat from much of the black press ("the only representative of 10,000,000 Americans") had personal resonance for him as the premier spokesman for his race.[3] He had privately hoped for at least one more term; there were bills he wanted to introduce, principles he wished to uphold, statements he needed to make. Few jobs outside Congress would offer him so powerful a platform; consequently, he had not withdrawn formally from the race until the last possible moment in 1900.

His last active campaign, in 1898, had been fought under vicious circum-

---

(1875–1881), also served as register of the U.S. Treasury (1881–1885) under Presidents Garfield and Arthur and as recorder of deeds, District of Columbia, under President Harrison. Smith (1851–1921?) of North Carolina was minister to Liberia from 1898 to 1902; Powell (1848–1920) of New Jersey, minister to Haiti from 1897 to 1905. Both were appointed by McKinley.

3. Variations of this phrase were often used by the *Colored American* and other black newspapers, such as the *Cleveland Gazette* and *Indianapolis Freeman*, to refer to White.

stances, amid the opening of the legendary white-supremacy campaign in North Carolina. The 1900 election had promised more of the same mudslinging; the August passage of the disfranchisement amendment to the state's constitution had been a stinging personal affront to White, who had publicly predicted the amendment's rejection at the polls as late as May. Even after the amendment passed, black citizens would remain technically eligible to vote until 1902, but White knew that most blacks would too frightened to go to the polls in November.

His practical nature—and his pride—had finally convinced White not to run again in 1900. He had never lost a general election in the Black Second, and he did not want to bow out of politics a loser. By the time his vocal and well-publicized withdrawal announcement in the *New York Times* underscored his disappointment at being forced into political exile, White had already quietly sold his home in Tarboro in anticipation of his family's permanent relocation to the North, even if he stayed behind.[4]

George White simply could not go home again. He had been accustomed to equal treatment, at least in the counties of the largely black congressional district where he had lived since 1877; to go back as a second-class citizen was anathema to him. Henry Cheatham would do just that by early 1902, eventually to run an orphanage near Oxford, but Cheatham seems to have cared less than White for the trappings of power; financially well off from Washington real-estate investments, he was also tired of politics. He had spent an increasing amount of time in North Carolina during his last two years as recorder of deeds, and had been forced to retire from that position in late 1901, under the shadowy circumstances of an alleged scandal. He had then moved back to North Carolina, taking his new wife, Laura, with him; they soon began another family, to add to the three children from his first marriage.[5]

Henry Cheatham's second marriage in 1901 had loosened his family ties to

4. "Southern Negro's Plaint," *New York Times*, 26 August 1900; Reid, "A Biography," 48.

5. DNCB, 1:360; *Washington Bee*, 1 April 1905; *Dictionary of American Negro Biography*, 103. Cheatham's fourth child, daughter Susie Clayton Cheatham, was born when he was forty-seven. His new wife was Laura Joyner of Brancheville, Va., whom he married October 30, 1901; Logan and Winston name two more sons, Richard and James Cheatham. The new Mrs. Cheatham was reportedly well-to-do, refined, and educated; both the *Colored American* and the *Bee* had linked the widower romantically with a number of unnamed women, including a Tennessee "aristocrat" just weeks before his marriage.

George White. Their political differences in the past had always been a source of strain, and the bitterness of the 1894 and 1896 battles for the congressional nomination had nearly sundered the Second District Republican Party and rendered them polite rivals who were never again really friends. One suspects that only the affection between their wives kept them civil after that experience. Louisa Cheatham's sudden death in 1899 had deeply depressed Cora Lena White, whose own health had already given way.[6]

When George White had blamed Cora Lena's poor health largely on the maliciousness of the political attacks on him and had listed it as one of three reasons for his retirement from Congress, the *Tarboro Southerner* had jeered at his reasoning, claiming neither Cora Lena's illness nor Louisa Cheatham's death was related to politics. By 1901, some believed White wanted to succeed his brother-in-law as D.C. recorder of deeds, thus keeping the black tradition in that job alive.[7] But it went instead to another black North Carolinian, John C. Dancy, in early 1902, after a flurry of rumors of Cheatham's impending reappointment.

Newspaper reports in the last weeks of 1901 attributed Cheatham's failure to the willful intercession of other black leaders, such as the Arnett family, even in the face of his endorsements by white North Carolina leaders, but speculation that the Dancy appointment may have been helped along by Cheatham as a parting shot at his brother-in-law was probably unfounded. Whatever their differences, both men seem to have been too gentlemanly for such intrigue; Cheatham was still welcome in George White's home at family events, and White had referred to him respectfully in a speech at Howard University in February 1901.[8]

6. The nature of Louisa Cheatham's illness was never specified. Cora Lena White's illness, never publicly described before her death, was chronic neurasthenia; it required serious surgery on at least one occasion.

7. Untitled editorial, *Tarboro Southerner*, 30 August 1900; August Meier, *American Negro Thought, 1880–1915* (Urbana: University of Illinois Press, 1973), 112; George H. White to BTW, 7 October 1901, BTWP. White's appeal to Washington was for a Treasury auditor's job.

8. *Cleveland Gazette*, 21 December 1901; "Howard University in Public Life," *WCA*, 2 March 1901. AME Zion bishop Benjamin W. Arnett and his son, Henry Y. Arnett, made such serious personal accusations against Cheatham that "President Roosevelt refused to countenance [them] until they were placed on file in the form of affidavits." The younger Arnett was a clerk in Cheatham's office; the Arnetts' candidate, Dr. John R. A. Crossland, was passed over by the president for recorder, but later served as minister to Liberia (1902–1903).

What White could *not* do was emulate Cheatham by surrendering his "manhood"—the turn-of-the-century code for pride of race—to beg for a job in the same towns where he had so recently been a political aristocrat. Above all, White believed in setting an example for his fellow blacks; he felt he had earned the right to expect a reward for his efforts on behalf of the Republican Party and believed his supporters expected him to insist on that reward. He had been a faithful party workhorse on the House floor and the campaign trail, and had defended the spoils system in Congress, whatever private resentment he may have felt at the scarcity of black recipients of the spoils.

The family's needs were a significant and expensive factor in any decision. The invalid Cora Lena's health would not permit a difficult move. The Whites' hopes to educate the teenaged Mamie and the young George Jr. in private schools required an income at least roughly comparable to that of a congressman (an annual salary of $5,000 during his terms). The family was settled into the house on 18th Street; Della, still a music teacher, had recently begun working in Washington.[9] To move them back to the racial uncertainty and social hinterlands of Tarboro was unthinkable.

So George White chose, however reluctantly, to stay on in Washington and play the game a while longer. With luck, and the support of the right friends, he could expect to be taken care of, but what were his political options? Could he handle himself adroitly enough to accommodate the condescension of white political masters in order to achieve the goals he seemed to aspire to? Neither answer was clear.

But the proper choice of a transitional job for White was clearer to some than to others in 1901. To Edward Elder Cooper, local editor and veteran booster of White, there was no question: an auditorship at the Department of the Treasury seemed suitable, with an annual salary of $4,000, comparable to that of congressmen. Nothing less would be acceptable to Cooper, and by implication, neither would it be to White. None of the six auditor's slots at the Treasury were yet vacant, but this was of little consequence to Cooper. In fact, only one of the six auditors, the luckless William Youngblood, would be gone

9. U.S. Census, Washington, D.C., 1900; "Testimony of Hon. George H. White," *Industrial Commission*, 425. The White residence listed Della, twenty; Mary (Mamie), twelve; and George Jr., seven, in addition to their parents. George White told the Industrial Commission that he had never sent any of his children to public school in North Carolina, and claimed that many black families preferred to educate their children in private schools.

by the end of 1901; his position seems to have been the goal eyed by Cooper, though this was never specified. Cooper's persistent editorial comments in the *Colored American*, Washington's lively black weekly, pushed the auditor's position for his friend White throughout 1901. Cooper may have acted independently, but his comments bore the authentic ring of an insider's confidences; whether White encouraged him or simply acquiesced is another question.

Other prominent blacks had recently held similar appointive positions, including the "top four." One of the Treasury auditor's jobs had previously been held by John R. Lynch, a black former congressman from Mississippi, under President Harrison (1889–1893). It was not of the top rank, but carried a comparable salary, which seemed to be the cutoff criterion; George White was too well-known to risk accepting a minor post, or a "crumb," as Cooper would soon describe it. There were also practical reasons for this type of appointment; it would not necessarily require confirmation by the Senate, where southern leaders would probably set off a public firestorm or even a filibuster. North Carolina's senior senator, Jeter Pritchard, had publicly opposed black officeholders, though he apparently did attempt to help Cheatham in late 1901. Ever proud, White wanted to be offered a position with no strings attached: a palpable tribute to his fitness, not a grudging favor.[10]

Cooper's efforts on White's behalf soon came to resemble a modern-day public relations campaign. Since 1898, the weekly columns had regularly carried a variety of laudatory comments about the congressman: coverage of his local speeches, descriptions of his rhetorical prowess, references to his speaking engagements elsewhere, even vague progress reports about Cora Lena's improving health. As a booster, Cooper was no neophyte; his methods were certainly effective enough for a limited audience, but he could be naïve at times, and seemed almost manipulative at others. Cooper's particular specialty was effusive editorials, praising White's "manhood" and unique political stature.

10. *Congressional Directory*, 53rd Cong., edition corrected through December 1, 1894; Emmett J. Scott to BTW, 14 December 1901, BTWP. As third auditor of the Treasury Department, John Roy Lynch handled affairs for the Navy Department. The rankings were removed and the titles and duties changed in the 1894 reorganization of the Treasury Department. Pritchard was on better terms with Cheatham, whom he had helped obtain the initial appointment as recorder in 1897; he also supported Cheatham for reappointment but regretted it after hearing the Arnetts' charges, according to Scott.

To be sure, there was no one quite like George White on the national scene, nor would there be for another generation; even he himself knew he would probably be the last of the post- Reconstruction era's black congressmen.[11] Cooper was no mere sycophant, however, and the purpose of his overly fulsome praise was not merely to flatter White. At least in part, he seems to have intended to shore up White's support among moderate and conservative blacks by defending his patron against unfair comparisons, for instance, with the powerful emerging leader Booker T. Washington. Cooper was always careful to mention other black leaders in his editorials, alienating no one, while subtly reminding readers that no one else had George White's recent political record or recognition level.

Yet Cooper's astuteness was flawed and incomplete. He was receiving quiet financial support from Booker T. Washington, and may have been following Washington's instructions, or at least doing what he assumed the Tuskegee leader wanted.[12] But he lacked both the subtlety for the task at hand and the finesse for political negotiations in general; what might sound elegant in a speech often was reduced to near-banality on the printed page, particularly to those not accustomed to the verbal swaggers and flourishes common in the black press of the period. And it was at precisely those listeners, in the white community, that Cooper was now aiming his messages.

Witness Cooper's response to a critical January 1901 editorial in the Cleveland *Gazette* ("a blow from a friendly quarter"), in more or less typical language:

> Hon. George H. White is the peer of any member on the floor at the Lower House of Congress. As an orator he is equal to any and superior to many of them. He does not lack in moral courage, stamina and in manhood. He has been in public life now nearly twenty years, and not

11. In his farewell speech to Congress in January 1901, White called his impending departure "the Negroes' temporary farewell" to that body. Other black candidates sought seats in Congress after 1901 and some won party nominations, but the next black congressman, Oscar DePriest, Republican of Chicago, was not elected until 1928.

12. See, for example, BTW to Edward Elder Cooper, 28 April 1904, in Louis R. Harlan and Raymond W. Smock, eds., *The Booker T. Washington Papers* (Urbana: University of Illinois Press, 1972–89), 7:488–9. It is not clear how often or how much Washington contributed to Cooper's newspaper, which was rarely profitable, nor is it clear when BTW began the subsidy, but the 1904 letter to Cooper hints that it had been going on for some time.

one spot is there in his public career to mar his good name or his willingness at all times to stand up for the race. *The Negroes of this country need more men of the Geo. H. White ilk,* and it is the duty of every loyal, intelligent Negro to stand by such men when they are in the right. Mr. White is alright. Don't forget that.[13] (emphasis added)

The *Gazette* had dared to mock the "great" White for his silence during the floor debates on the ill-fated Crumpacker amendment, which had sought to penalize southern states for disfranchisement of black voters by reducing their representation in Congress. The *Colored American* had lectured *Gazette* editor Harry C. Smith on the rules of the Congress, which Cooper claimed had hampered White's active efforts to be heard.

A few days before White retired from Congress, Cooper began to adjust both the tenor and the velocity of his comments. On March 2, the *Colored American* heralded White's upcoming testimonial dinner, still three weeks away. White had been licensed to practice law in Washington since early 1899, and was admitted to the bar of the U.S. Supreme Court in 1900; Cooper soon mentioned White's new law practice in glowing terms: "George H. White has entered upon the active practice of law in this city, and is making an excellent impression upon all the courts in which he appears. He invariably wins his cases by his tactful and finished methods, and is equal to the best counsellors now before the District bar."[14]

The next step was to portray White as the irresistible choice of a united black community for a high-ranking federal job, in order to bring more pressure to bear on McKinley. Cooper would need outside help for this phase of his campaign, and received it, for once, with exquisitely good luck.

Luck had not always come Cooper's way, although he had survived even the most difficult obstacles with a certain gritty style. Born a slave in Tennessee just before the war, he had migrated to Indianapolis, where he was the only black member of his graduating class at Indianapolis High School; he had also spent a summer waiting tables in Philadelphia during the Centennial

13. Untitled editorial, *WCA*, 19 January 1901. Smith soon admitted that his own sources had been faulty and publicly apologized in his own newspaper, but Cooper never acknowledged the apology.

14. "City Paragraphs," ibid., 9 March 1901. The nearly shameless commercial plug for White's law practice even listed his business address, in the Capital Savings Bank building, 609 "F" Street, NW.

Exposition. After high school, he had quickly launched a journalistic career, helping to found the weekly *World* in 1884 while working for the Indianapolis post office. Cooper later started the Indianapolis *Freeman* in 1887, then sold it to George L. Knox in 1891, after encountering severe financial and legal difficulties; it is not clear whether he had to stay away from Indianapolis to avoid facing charges. He relocated in Washington in 1893 to found the *Colored American,* but he always retained an affectionate respect for his Indiana ties and the *Freeman,* which he quoted regularly and admiringly on the pages of his own newspaper. Both newspapers were strongly Republican in their political leanings.

As luck would now have it, the *Freeman* obligingly singled out George White as its prime candidate for "race pilot" in a lengthy editorial of March 9, 1901. A singularly bookish and almost impenetrably obscure analogy between oppressed blacks in the United States and Irish patriots, the editorial referred at length to Washington Irving's poem, "Conquest of Granada," and the ill-fated Boabdil El Chico, who had nobly led the Moors during their final years in Spain. Cooper may have misunderstood the message, or simply ignored the major thrust of the editorial, which likened White to Boabdil and depicted a "spiritual death" for blacks in America under his valiant leadership. But perceptively or not, Cooper now refined this message to meet his own needs, portraying White on March 23 as one of several "race pilots," while being careful to include no potential rivals for a federal job:

> The Indianapolis Freeman calls for a race pilot and thinks, all things considered, that Geo. H. White is the man for the emergency—the Parnell of the situation. *Mr. White is indeed a most capable and courageous man and practically speaking, is the most available figure we have.* It is not likely that the Negro will come to the wisdom of following a single leader during this century. In the meantime, it would be well to stand by the several forces who lead in the various departments of activity—such as Washington in education, Walters in the church, White in politics, the True Reformers in business, Dunbar, Chesnutt and others in literature, DuBois, Miller, and the like in sociological inquiry. After all, this may point a way out for the present.[15] (emphasis added)

15. "As to a Race Pilot," editorial, ibid., 23 March 1901. Entitled "A Pilot the Demand," the *Freeman*'s original editorial had also mentioned Booker T. Washington prominently; although

For good measure, elsewhere in the same issue Cooper noted a "rumor": "It is reported that Hon. George H. White will practice law in New York." (This was not new, as White himself had indicated as early as 1900 that he might practice there.) The March 30 and April 6 issues next carried lengthy reports of the March 22 testimonial dinner. A festive event held at the city's Metropolitan A.M.E. Zion Church, it was attended by an estimated three thousand persons, among them a glittering array of black notables from all walks of life. It was the "proudest moment of (White's) life," according to Cooper, who said the testimonial provided "the greatest Negro Congressman . . . [with] the heartiest demonstration of confidence and respect that has ever been given to any member of the race anywhere."[16]

A smaller tribute three days later by members of the Pen and Pencil Club provided Cooper with yet another opportunity to trumpet White's praises. "The unanimous verdict, gathered from the tone of the talks, was that George H. White represented in his eminent personality, wisdom, courage, fortitude, honesty, manhood and spirit of self-sacrifice the potentialities that made him, willy-nilly, the natural leader of the Negro of this country," Cooper wrote. "It was demanded that he be placed by the powers in a position where he could continue the battle for the race without fear that the wolf of necessity would be apt to visit his door."[17]

The *Colored American* then printed another timely letter, this time from a reader named D. C. Covington, of Wilkesboro, North Carolina—a coincidence, perhaps, but in Cooper's eyes a helpful one. "We have a large number of the very best Negro lawyers from which to select an able representative for the Federal judgeship in the Philippine Islands," Covington wrote. A federal judgeship for a black was not yet a practical goal, even for as skilled a lawyer

---

describing him cryptically as "not a political leader"—technically true, since he never ran for office—the *Freeman* had actually endorsed BTW as the better choice, saying "he could not make things much worse" than the politicians who had preceded him.

16. "Rallying to a Noble Standard," ibid., 6 April 1901.

17. "Pen and Pencil Club Tribute," ibid., 30 March 1901. The *Indianapolis Freeman* devoted two columns of its front page on April 27 to accounts of the testimonial dinner and Pen and Pencil Club tribute, under a lengthy series of headlines: "An Honored Guest, One of the Race's Leaders the Recipient of Highest Praise from the Nation's Best," etc. "Mr. White displays a wisdom that was not understood by many of the leaders of the older time, and which might be emulated by some of those who essay to reach the front," the article closed.

as White, but perhaps the suggestion might hasten the announcement of an auditorship. Covington included White in a long list of worthy black candidates from all areas of the country: "See the list of able lawyers I present: Congressman George H. White of North Carolina, Edward Everett Brown of Boston, Mass., E. M. Hewlett of Washington, D.C., Harry S. Cummings of Baltimore, Md., J. Madison Vance of Louisiana, W. A. Pledger of Atlanta, Ga., J. C. Napier of Tennessee, D. A. Straker of Michigan, Judge J. B. Raymond of Pennsylvania, John S. Leary of North Carolina. If either of the men mentioned were appointed, I have no doubt in the world but that he would make a most excellent judge for the Island."[18]

Cooper now launched a frontal assault on the coveted White House appointment with two fateful sentences in his April 13 issue of the *Colored American*. "Information comes from a very good source that Ex-Congressman George H. White is slated for appointment as one of the auditors of the Treasury, at a salary of $4,000 per annum, " Cooper wrote. "That would be about the kind of place to give this courageous leader—if President McKinley has nothing better he can drop over in his direction."[19]

And on April 20, Cooper resumed his now-breathless praise: "George H. White has reason to be the proudest Afro-American in the country. His stewardship has recently been eloquently and substantially indorsed, and his leadership of the race in politics and legislation has been unanimously confirmed. He is worthy of every encomium bestowed."[20] But neither Cooper nor White was prepared for the inevitable counterattack, and their overreactions belied their reputations for political acumen. A more restrained, calculated response would have been much wiser, but no cautious elders were offering counsel, if indeed outsiders were even being asked for advice.

The first roadblock appeared on April 18, between the dates of the two

18. Letter to the editor from D. C. Covington, *WCA*, 6 April 1901. On May 6, Covington narrowed his endorsement to John S. Leary of North Carolina. The first appointment of a black federal judge came three decades later, when Franklin D. Roosevelt appointed William H. Hastie in the U.S. Virgin Islands (1937–1939).

19. Untitled editorial, ibid., 13 April 1901. Cooper never identified his source; White was in North Carolina on his first trip home since retiring from Congress, as noted in the April 6 issue. White returned in time to read the *Post* editorial of April 18 and its story of April 20, and to respond by April 22; his letter was printed on April 23, 1901.

20. Untitled editorial, *WCA*, 20 April 1901.

Cooper editorials previously cited; it may even have been in specific reaction to Cooper's April 13 mention of the auditorship. It came on the editorial page of the *Washington Post*, one of the city's major mainstream dailies; neither a fan nor foe of White during his four years in the House, the *Post* had rarely mentioned his name at all in news stories, and apparently only once (March 1897) on the editorial page.[21] The newspaper now suggested that White's first duty was to his people of North Carolina; the unusually personal lecture signaled the less-than-friendly reaction White's appointment could be expected to generate farther south.

The day's lead editorial, it was entitled simply "Mr. White's Dilemma." Its tone was not hostile, at least not initially, but was rather that of a wise, somewhat dyspeptic schoolmarm, firmly lecturing her headstrong scholar. "Hon. George H. White, who was the only colored member of the last Congress, says that he has not yet decided whether he will return to North Carolina," the *Post* began. "He is, we understand, an applicant for an appointment by the President—auditor or something equally desirable—and, of course, should the President favorably consider his aspirations he will remain in Washington. But, in the other event, the quandary would still confront him." White's choice was a cruel one, of course,

> between North Carolina, the State of his birth, the State in which he was educated, licensed to practice law, and honored with a number of political appointments and promotions—the State in which he rose to eminence—and some Northern community where he can benefit neither himself nor the people of his race. He is reported as having said that, if the North Carolina election law shall receive the ratification of the courts, he will abandon North Carolina and make his home in Washington or New York. Let us hope that this resolve is not irrevocable, and that Mr. White will at least hold the alternative open.[22]

The *Post* reminded White of "his obligations to the colored people of North Carolina," who now depended on him for "his counsel and protection

21. The *Post* had printed a courteous account (18 March 1897) of plans by Howard University alumni to give White "an elaborate reception" after he was sworn in as a member of Congress, under the heading "Gossip Heard at the Capitol"; it was quickly reprinted by the *Raleigh News and Observer*.

22. "Mr. White's Dilemma," editorial, *Washington Post*, 18 April 1901.

more than ever." For White to claim personal ill treatment or oppression in North Carolina was absurd; his very presence in Washington was proof of his good fortune there. Whatever good White might have accomplished as a politician, he could not easily shed the burden of his racial background: "in fact, he stands a living, breathing illustration of the truth we have so often asserted—*that a self-respecting colored man of brains, ability, and virtue has larger opportunities and wider vistas at the South than at the North.* From what Northern States . . . have come such men as Bruce, Pinchback, Lyons, White, Lynch—a dozen others we might name?"[23] (emphasis added)

What the *Post* neglected to point out, of course, was that many of the South's native blacks who had emerged as postwar leaders had done so only after being educated in the North, often escaping from slavery to do so. Nor did it stop to reflect that of the leaders it named, only George White had spent as much as half his adult career in his own home state. Bruce, Pinchback, Lyons, and even Lynch had come to Washington to stay; White had been there only four years.

The *Post* next engaged in highly specious generalizations about regional differences in treatment of the races: "At the North they are vastly fond of bewailing the negro's wrongs, and denouncing the Southern whites for treating them with cruelty; but what have the Northern people ever done for the advancement, the exaltation of the colored people who live among them? What New England town would put up with a negro mayor? What first-class New England hotel would throw wide its doors to negro custom, no matter how decent and well-behaved?"[24]

This was sheer sophistry, at best. Washington remained one of the nation's

23. Ibid. The unstated issue, racial demographics, was never openly addressed by the *Post*; its editorial policy, however, subtly discouraged more blacks from moving to the capital city, where ninety thousand already lived. Its considerably less moderate news policy allowed sensational treatment of stories involving black criminals and unfortunates. Among those black leaders the *Post* did not name were John Green, Cyrus Adams, and William Powell—all from nonsouthern states—and Owen Smith, John Dancy, and Henry Cheatham, all of North Carolina. The curious oversight indicated at least a nominal "ranking" by the *Post*, since Bruce was dead, Lyons and Lynch already held federal positions, and only Pinchback was being considered for appointment.

24. Ibid. Blacks were only beginning their exodus to the North and Midwest, and their chances of winning elective office outside the South were unlikely, at best. In the North, blacks might not be accepted at hotels, but at least they could still vote; up to 90 percent of the nation's blacks lived in states of the former Confederacy, where they were almost completely disenfranchised.

most rigidly segregated cities, and was certainly no better than its northern counterparts; the *Post* ignored the more tolerant atmospheres of Massachusetts and other northeastern states with small black populations, or such cities as Philadelphia, where blacks had long played a significant role in local politics. Washington's population was gradually approaching a black majority, and the purpose seems to have been to avoid encouraging more blacks to move there.

White's mission, the *Post* declared, "is at the South, in the land of his birth, among his own people. He can do much there. *He can do nothing here or farther North*" (emphasis added). The *Post* briefly reflected on the new laws of North Carolina before congratulating itself for its own wisdom; it had examined the changes in that state's election law and found them imperfect, even troubling, with "much . . . to deplore and criticize." Yet it found positive characteristics, as well: "at least they mark a progress in the right direction; at least they set a new and higher value on the franchise and partially lift it from the foul gutter in which it had lost its significance, its honor and its dignity. The march toward betterment has been set in motion. *Mr. White's place—the place of every colored man of his class—is in the van*"[25] (emphasis added).

The self-righteousness of the newspaper's position was not lost on George White. For all his likely indignation at the editorial, however, it was only a front-page barb two days later, buried in an otherwise unremarkable news story, that drew first blood. The story concerned William Youngblood, Treasury auditor for the Interior Department, and his expected transfer due to unspecified "friction" in the office. The story bore the headline "May Transfer Mr. Youngblood," and announced that among the candidates to succeed him were two former Republican congressmen, William F. Aldrich of Alabama and George H. White.

Had the story ended there, there would have been little to complain about. Unfortunately, it did not: "But it is not at all probable that Mr. White will be given as good a place as an auditorship, which pays $4,000 a year. *Mr. White will be entirely satisfied with a place as deputy auditor which pays $2,500 a year*, and it is not improbable that such an office will be bestowed upon him"[26] (emphasis added).

25. Ibid. The *Post* conveniently glossed over the inherent unfairness of the "grandfather clause" and similar devices that enabled illiterate white men to vote but effectively denied educated black men the same right.

26. "May Transfer Mr. Youngblood: Ex-Representative Aldrich Talked of for Position as

This was an unexpected slap at George White, and a bitter disappointment besides. His previous encounters with the mainstream white press, if infrequent, had usually resulted in deferential, encouraging accounts of his interviews on newsworthy topics, at least outside North Carolina. This was different; the *Post* editorial may have lacked balance, but the separate story had crossed the line into untruth. Similarities between editorials and news stories in those days were significant; only the placement in a newspaper, for instance, could distinguish them in many cases. In this case, it was the combination of the two that White found personally offensive.

White rarely spoke in haste or rancor, but this time his temper got the best of him. His long and indignant response, printed five days later by the *Post*, did little to repair the damage to his hopes, and did nothing to improve the indigestion of his now-nervous supporters. White was a stirring and popular speaker, but was unaccustomed to the irrevocable nature of his own words in print and their effect on readers unfamiliar with his style of speech. He had written only rarely for mainstream publications. In preparing speeches, he obviously pondered the biblical and mythological references he loved to use as metaphorical flourishes, and audiences regularly applauded his clever quips.[27]

Had he but considered the impetuous example of Pandora, he might have reconsidered sending this letter. For like her, he was opening up a box he could never reclose, but a box with one important difference: at the end of the story, Pandora's box still contained hope, but George White's box would not. His anguished response, sounding more like a speech than a public letter, appeared without comment on an inside page in the April 23 edition of the *Post*, under the headline, "Ex-Representative White: Why He is Entitled to Consideration at the Hands of the President." It was heartfelt but naïve, and its impact on his remaining chances for an appointment was immeasurably negative. Yet he must have felt he had no choice except to defend his honor.

Auditor," *Washington Post*, 20 April 1901. The reasons for Youngblood's transfer were not specified, but were "not altogether discreditable for him," and involved "controversies concerning some of his constructions of the laws," as well as "some friction in the office between him and his employees."

27. He had published just one magazine article, "The Injustice to the Colored Voter," in January 1900. His rather wooden writing style was far less moving than his speaking style; his speeches in the *Congressional Record* were invariably followed by notations of "loud and prolonged applause."

The letter opened sensibly and cautiously, with White recounting his surprise at seeing his name in the *Post*'s editorial column. "The reference made concerning me in the columns of The Post during my four years' stay in Washington wholly unprepared me for the recent advice and seeming interest contained in one of your leading editorials of a few days since, giving reasons why I should return to North Carolina and there remain," he wrote. What the *Post* wrote "would have been all true in the main three and a half years ago, as I at that time had not the remotest idea of changing my domicile from the State of my nativity," but much had changed since then "as far as the colored man is concerned. Your [April 18] editorial gives only one side of the question."[28]

White then utilized his knowledge of "moral philosophy," listing two cardinal principles "for which our forefathers fought—I say 'our,' for the Negro was there: that taxation and representation go hand in hand; and . . . that of one flesh and blood God created all men, and endowed them with certain inalienable rights, among which are life, liberty, and the pursuit of happiness." Not even the *Post* could pretend for a moment, he said, "that these basic principles are meted out to the Negro race in North Carolina . . . under existing conditions. I feel that my place is where I can best care for my own household and do the most good for the race with which I am identified, whether that be in North Carolina, the District of Columbia, East, West, or North."[29]

White's primary complaint, however, was the April 20 news article and its glaring inaccuracy: "Just where your reporter got the information that I would be so easily contented with so small a position [as deputy auditor] I am not advised." Such a statement had certainly not come from him, he might have added. But his tone was gradually becoming defensive, and his reasoning labored. "Why should I be 'satisfied' with a position of less dignity and salary than any other man situated as I am?" he asked. "On the score of merit permit me to say that I have served faithfully the Republican national party in every

28. "Ex-Representative White: Why He Is Entitled to Consideration at the Hands of the President," letter to the editor, *Washington Post*, 23 April 1901. Note that he pushes the issue back to late 1897—"three and a half years earlier." He had hinted broadly in his 1900 *New York Times* interview that the 1898 campaign had been a major factor in his change of heart; this is a subtler indication of his state of mind before that campaign had even begun.

29. Ibid. White had taken a course in moral philosophy during his last year as a student at Howard, and may have taught it while a principal.

campaign during the past twenty-seven years, wholly without reward or one dollar's compensation, or even applying for a government position up to this year."

Technically, the statement about never applying for a government position is suspect, since White had served for several years as principal of the state normal school at New Bern—an appointive position for which he had certainly applied—and he had worked for the U.S. Coast Survey for nearly six months in 1876. But here he was undoubtedly referring to high-level patronage jobs. He was careful to describe his political positions as "direct from the people at the ballot-box. I was delegate-at-large to the St. Louis convention, and again a delegate to the Philadelphia convention. . . . I gave my time and efforts unstintingly in each of the campaigns in which [McKinley] was elected, even at the cost of my own health in the canvass of seven different States last fall." Why, indeed, should he then expect "of Mr. McKinley a position of less moment than Mr. Aldrich, or any other of my colleagues of the Fifty-fifth and Fifty-sixth Congresses?"[30]

If the *Post* doubted the depth of his support, White claimed to hold "endorsements and recommendations from 189 Republican Members and Senators of the Fifty-sixth Congress" requesting his appointment. He also cited "strong letters from several chairmen of state Republican committees, including North Carolina, together with the national committeeman from that State," among others. Somewhat less modestly, he went on to quote from a letter written by Senator Nathan B. Scott of West Virginia, chairman of the national speaker's committee in the 1900 campaign, who had reportedly written the president to say that "no speaker in that campaign did more to secure the election of Mr. McKinley than myself."[31]

Naming his endorsers was at best a risky move, but White obviously felt justified in claiming support from many of his party's white leaders, even if none of them stepped forward to support him publicly. He was, however, overstating that support slightly, since his undated endorsement list contained just 177 members of Congress—including four senators and one nonvoting delegate from Oklahoma—and only 185 names in all; the other eight were North Carolina political leaders and a handful of prominent black leaders from

30. Ibid. Interestingly, White does not deny speaking to the *Post* reporter, indicating that he may in fact have done so; here he shrewdly disputes only the reporter's exact wording.

31. Ibid. No copy of Scott's letter could be located among the McKinley papers.

Washington, D.C. All the members of Congress, not surprisingly, were Republicans, although at least two of them might have changed their minds since signing it, for different reasons: Senator Jeter Pritchard of North Carolina, whom White had criticized publicly on several occasions, and Representative Charles F. Sprague of Massachusetts, whose failed dinner party for White and other District of Columbia committee members had been a public spectacle in February. One notable absentee from the list was William F. Aldrich, the Alabama congressman who was White's apparent competitor for the job; the names of another dozen or so other GOP congressmen were also missing, although they may simply have been absent from Washington when the list was circulated.

Why Pritchard had chosen to sign the endorsement at all is a mystery, considering the poor relationship between the two men. There seemed to be little need for it, and few senators seem to have been asked to sign; even Nathan Scott, whose letter to McKinley had been quoted by White to the *Post,* was not among the signers of the list. The only other senators were Matthew Quay of Pennsylvania and William Mason of Illinois—two outspoken supporters of White—and Iowa's Jonathan Dolliver, a House member himself until his elevation to the Senate in December. The list itself appears to have been drawn up sometime after the final session had opened in December, perhaps as late as its adjournment in March.[32]

If the list of endorsers was less than rock solid, so were George White's estimates of support from his race and of the Republican loyalty among his race. Like many black Republicans, he believed that the Democrats had little to offer black voters, and ignored their slowly increasing numbers. The Republican Party at least had the earned advantage of historical ties, despite the growing strength of its lily-white movement. So White confidently claimed support from an overwhelming majority of the members of his own race: "I will be pardoned for saying that I believe I have the accord and good wishes of at least 90 per cent of the 10,000,000 of Negroes of the United States, 90 per cent of whom are Republicans, in the recognition I seek. Again, I ask, why

32. "Geo. H. White Makes Application for Auditor: Brief," folder among records of the U.S. Treasury, National Archives. The list of his endorsers contains 185 names, of whom 177 had been members of the 56th Congress; 7 of those signing had been seated only on December 3, 1900. One likely signer, New Hampshire's Frank Clarke, died on January 9; another, Maine's Charles Boutelle, resigned on the last day of the session, March 3.

should I be 'perfectly satisfied' with the position indicated in your article of Saturday?"[33]

George White had now vented his spleen, even at the risk of sounding more like a grasping job seeker than an innocent victim. Yet if White believed that his letter would end the matter—that the *Post* would, perhaps, apologize, or simply say nothing else—he was mistaken. Two days later, the *Post* sneered at White's explanation, smugly noting that "Ex-Representative White resents the notion that he should go back to North Carolina and resume his private citizenship. That is not an uncommon feeling on the part of a winged states-man."[34]

As White would soon learn, his name was already fading from the list of those politically welcome at the White House. His May 31 attempt to gain an audience with President McKinley was gently rebuffed by the president's gate-keeper, George Cortelyou, who suggested White "submit a written statement of the matter which you desire to bring to his notice." Chastened, White re-sponded with a note of sympathy, apparently for the recent poor health of Mrs. McKinley, which Cortelyou acknowledged on June 4.[35]

Sadly, not even all the members of his own race were willing to support him in this quest. His claims of near-total support within his own race seemed significantly less credible as the months wore on, and his distance from power increased. As the blacks' former representative, he was now expendable to some, including a small but growing number to whom the Democratic Party had now become the preferred vehicle of their hopes and dreams—a harbin-ger of the political sea change yet to come.

33. "Ex-Representative White: Why He is Entitled."

34. Untitled editorial, *Washington Post,* 25 April 1901.

35. George B. Cortelyou to George H. White, 1 June 1901 and 4 June 1901, McKinley Papers (microfilm), Library of Congress. White's incoming letters, dated 31 May 1901 and 3 June 1901, are mentioned in Cortelyou's responses, but neither could be found in the McKinley Papers.

13

Dueling Editors and a "Winged Statesman"

At this point in mid-1901, cooler hands than those of Edward Cooper would probably have shelved George White's quest, at least while the air cleared. But Cooper apparently could not suppress his fervor; his Saturday columns stubbornly continued the series of pronouncements, which did little to improve the situation.

The April 27 editorial in the *Colored American*, entitled "Mr. White Is Not a Cheap Man," repeated themes from the former congressman's letter to the *Post*, expressing pleasure that White "has so promptly sat upon the rumor . . . that one of the Treasury auditorships would probably be conferred upon a prominent white Southern Republican." White had clearly refuted the *Post*'s "intimation . . . that a $4,000 place was too good for a Negro, even of Mr. White's eminence and strong party service." After all, "Mr. White is a representative of the most loyal contingent the republican party has within its ranks today, and he cannot afford to accept any position that is not commensurate with his own dignity and that of the people for whom he stands. He is not in politics for a living, but with a good place as a leverage, he can be of more value to the race than in a purely private capacity."[1]

Because of White's faithful service, the *Colored American* expected that he would "soon be called to a position befitting his character and attainments." Cooper's editorial was aimed primarily at the White House, but his closing argument was clearly crafted with the *Colored American*'s typical audience in

1. "Mr. White Is Not a Cheap Man," editorial, WCA, 27 April 1901.

mind: "The race is reaching an enviable position when it can grow a *leader who is strong enough to decline the crumbs, and who insists on sitting at the first table or none*" (emphasis added). This was nothing less than an ultimatum. At best it was a calculated gamble with attendant risks: the administration might ignore it as a bluff, or, worse, write off George White as not worth the effort. But at least in Cooper's mind, McKinley must have wanted the former congressman to serve, and in a senior position; the president needed only to be convinced of White's determination. And whatever else George White desired, he could not afford to disappoint his own race.

Cooper's tactic of verbal overkill lacked the subtleties of delicate backstage maneuvering, leaving little room for compromise on either side. Still, what might have passed unnoticed among all but the limited readership of the *Colored American* seemed to be evolving and acquiring a life of its own, as it moved into a stronger phase: a fading squall blowing itself up into a hurricane, away from land but turning back with ominous fury. Cooper's journalistic instincts, usually good, seemed to fail him at this point. Ever the gossip, he could not resist resurrecting a curious episode involving another retired congressman, Republican Charles F. Sprague of Massachusetts, with whom White had served on the District of Columbia Committee during their last term together in the House. The story was no longer news; the event had occurred two months earlier, and the *Colored American* itself had already reported it twice, first in February and again in late March. It was hardly relevant to the current situation—both men now being out of Congress—and in a later day, might even have provoked a libel suit. But Cooper must have believed it would buttress his current cause, or he would hardly have included it on the same editorial page, adjacent to his commentary on White's letter: "Congressman Draper [sic] withdrew invitations for a committee dinner because of complications growing out of an invitation to Congressman White, which the latter accepted. Mr. Draper then went crazy. It is not our purpose to say that the two facts were related in any way. We merely give two contemporaneous facts that occurred."[2]

Was this intended as a parable? Did Cooper mean to equate Sprague's snub

2. Untitled editorial, ibid., 27 April 1901. The newspaper misspelled Sprague's name in this brief account, but there was no mistaking the hapless protagonist, whose story was well known throughout official Washington. Sprague died early the next year in a Providence, Rhode Island, hospital.

of White with the offer of a second-rank job by the McKinley administration? Was he suggesting that a better job (the auditorship) had been considered but withdrawn? And did Cooper understand the essentially poor taste of raising the Sprague affair again, so late in the game? His first mention, weeks earlier, had been relatively innocuous, as had most other journalistic references; the *Cleveland Gazette* had reported the dinner story at some length in February, in slightly less lurid fashion. The March follow-up, however, contained the news that Sprague, "just retired from Congress, has been confined to an insane asylum in Boston. His health has been failing for years."[3] The *Colored American's* less charitable linking of the two events could only have raised eyebrows in official Washington, as a fresh reminder of White's alleged penchant for demanding equal treatment on a social level, perhaps even of his growing desperation.

The newspaper's tactic may not have had an effect on the White House decision makers, but was hardly a prudent move in any case. Cooper's words were also insulting on a personal level; weeks earlier, he had characterized Sprague as "evidently lacking in vertebrae. Daniel Webster would have given the dinner if only the Commissioners, Mr. White and himself had been present."[4] Sprague, now indisposed, was no Webster, but then Cooper was hardly the best judge of polite behavior—or political wisdom, apparently.

Cooper continued his pursuit of the White appointment on May 4, this time with three separate defensive jabs. Two were short pieces on separate pages, under the breezy regular heading "We Would Like To Know." The first asked, "Why the Washington Post is so concerned about the future of George H. White, who has so amply demonstrated his ability to take care of himself?" The other almost surreally wondered aloud, "If Gov. Pinchback and George H. White are not about due to 'land'?" Pinckney B. S. Pinchback, a successful

---

3. "Color-Liners Not Invited, Mr. Sprague to Give a Dinner in Place of the One that Was Called Off," *Cleveland Gazette*, 23 February 1901; "Shreds and Patches," *WCA*, 23 March 1901. The *Gazette* said the dinner was "originally arranged in honor of the commissioners of the District of Columbia," in order to introduce commissioners to members of Sprague's committee, which included White; a second dinner for the same commissioners was given for various House members, but no one who had refused Sprague's earlier invitation was now invited. The *Colored American* spelled Sprague's name correctly in its first mention on February 16, when it said only that the dinner "did not come off."

4. "Shreds and Patches," *WCA*, 23 March 1901.

Washington lawyer and member of the city's black social elite; had last served on the federal level as a marshal in the 1890s. A popular speaker on the black circuit, Pinchback liked to recount his undeniably fascinating political career, including his brief (one month) tenure as governor of Louisiana thirty years earlier and the fabled "railroad race" that had preceded that tour.[5]

Cooper had previously lumped White with both the opportunistic Pinchback and New York Age editor T. Thomas Fortune as prime candidates for McKinley appointments. Only weeks earlier, Cooper had added the three to the list of "[Caucasian] tall figures" who had been defeated in 1900 and were now receiving rewards from the president.[6] Continuing to link White to either man now was of questionable practicality. Pinchback's lavish lifestyle and unorthodox business dealings contrasted sharply with the more strait-laced White; the fiery Fortune was brilliant but erratic, and militant journalists were not always considered acceptable social company in that day. But Cooper forged ahead, as usual, with whatever weapon happened to be at hand.

The Colored American's lead editorial on May 4, couched in vintage Cooper language and almost sputtering with anger in defense of his wronged patron, revealed the editor's obsession with winning. "George H. White's [April 23] letter to the Washington Post was the statement of a man, and went straight to the marrow of the situation. He claims the right to go where he can do best for himself, for his race, and for his household," Cooper wrote. "It is the case where a white man is concerned, but it is far from the case when the Negro enters the equation. Mr. White should be given a position under the government commensurate with his standing and party service, and he should accept no other."[7]

According to Cooper, White's letter was "the frank declaration of a man who knew his place, and who wished to show that there were plenty of friends who were in sympathy with his contention." The former congressman had not erred in referring to his endorsers, as others seemed to think, for "he knew that indorsements locked up in an official safe would grow cobwebs, but that an

5. Foner, Freedom's Lawmakers, 171. On April 13, in a brief editorial aside, the Colored American had listed the trio as "Booked to 'Land.'"

6. "Do Not Forget the Negro," editorial, WCA, 6 April 1901. Listed were former U.S. senators Carter, Thurston, Chandler, and "others of the Caucasian hue."

7. Untitled editorial, ibid., 4 May 1901.

open card in a live newspaper would solve the combination and 'call them up for examination.' Mr. White is too valuable a man to be ignored when the honors are passed around."[8]

Cooper risked alienating some of these endorsers by dragging them into a public argument over how high White's appointment should be. No names were listed; White's letter had simply cited all the Republican members of the previous House, although as recounted earlier, the actual list contained only 173 House members, plus four U.S. senators. The editorial chess match in Washington between the small weekly and its much larger daily opponent now approached checkmate, with White in danger of becoming a pawn in the struggle. Limited to its one Saturday edition, the *Colored American* could not match the tactical shrewdness of the *Post,* whose next move was sure to leave Edward Cooper fuming for five long days until his own next edition could appear.

A letter from J. C. Cunningham ran in the May 6 (Monday) edition of the *Post,* under the provocative headline, "Question of Common Sense: Ex-Representative White's Attitude, as Voiced by One of His Race." No accompanying editorial was needed, for none could have performed the task with such deadly effectiveness; even Cunningham's reputation within the black community as a prolific and pompous know-it-all did not matter. Up to now, the *Post* had slighted George White's loyalty to his race, but had refrained from attacking him too openly. Now, without uttering a word of its own, the newspaper could both ridicule the former congressman's personal judgment and cast doubt on his integrity. Cunningham's words were also the first sign of a break, however small, in White's supposedly solid racial ranks. "A great deal is being said of Ex-Congressman George H. White in regard to his 'manhood' in refusing a deputy auditorship if offered him by the President," Cunningham wrote.

"We are informed that this position pays a salary of $2,500 per annum." If this were accurate, he said, "it seems to us that Mr. White would show more 'manhood' and common sense in accepting such a position than by refusing it. Such positions don't come to a man of Mr. White's color every day; it matters not what he did during the preceding national campaign." According to Cunningham, White was "an able man, and the colored people would be glad

8. Ibid.

to see him get all he wants." Yet his personal selectiveness bordered on greed, "since Mr. White don't care to accept of anything much short of a 'Cabinet' position—a place for which only white men need apply—it seems to us that he would show his great love for his race by giving his influence to secure the deputy auditorship for one of his worthy constituents."[9]

No loyal black North Carolinian would feel himself "insulted" at such an offer from the president, even if it were beneath White himself; in fact, White would be better off refusing any "fat Federal job," which generally gave black leaders "the lockjaw," Cunningham now said, assuming a more venomous tone. "They invariably become deaf, dumb, and blind to the good and welfare of our people just as soon as the President signs their commissions." Of course, White could prove to be an exception to that rule, but Cunningham wondered aloud if White, after serving in Congress, might have forgotten to which race he belonged:

> Mr. White should not overlook the fact that although he occupied a seat with Mr. Aldrich and others in the Fifty-fifth and Fifty-sixth Congresses, he is still looked upon as a colored man along with the rest of his colored brethren. If he desires to lead and to help his people he would do well to follow the example of Prof. Booker T. Washington— go out among his people and get them interested in business enterprises, so that the young men and women graduating from the schools and colleges may have something to do for an honest living.[10]

Such a vivid contrast to Washington, whose accommodationist star was currently rising over the more aggressive stance of White and others, was not at all what Cooper wanted Republican leaders to see in print at this point. But Cunningham, almost as if on cue, had one final sting to impart: "Since Mr. White cannot afford to accept a $2,500 position if offered by the President, and since it is said that some loyal white Republican will get the place that he (Mr. White) thinks he is heir to, the colored people of this country may rejoice over the fact that he will still remain with us and help battle for our rights as American citizens."[11]

9. "Question of Common Sense, Ex-Representative White's Attitude, as Voiced by One of His Race," letter to the editor from J. C. Cunningham, *Washington Post,* 6 May 1901. The writer was not further identified, but was still writing letters to the *Washington Bee* in 1919.

10. Ibid.

11. Ibid.

Cunningham's heavy sarcasm did not disguise the plainer truth from *Post* readers: the common knowledge that George White had been unable to deliver federal protection from lynching for blacks, or to stop his own state from following the rest of the South into disfranchising its black voters. He had made speeches, but had accomplished little else. J. C. Cunningham's opinions clearly represented only a minority within the black community, yet his implication—that blacks would be no better off for all White's well- publicized stubbornness, with or without an appointment—was not a good omen. His example of Booker T. Washington out working for his people, while White was simply grasping for himself, was particularly unflattering.

If either White or Cooper had a response to this latest strike by the *Post*, there is no record of it during the rest of May 1901. The few references to White in the *Colored American* during the next two weeks were mostly routine, such as the account of a May 2 "planked shad dinner" in White's honor. It was a particularly pleasant diversion for White, who was helping raise funds for the legal expenses of the National Afro-American Council and seemed in his element among friends. "Th[e] distinguished gentleman was never more witty and eloquent. The rafters shook with applause after his speech." If White was nervous about the appointment, Cooper at least saw no sign of it.[12]

On May 11, White's picture, along with those of Ashley M. Gould, Hiram Watty, and Rev. Owen W. Waller, appeared on the *Colored American*'s editorial page under the heading "Men of the Hour." On May 18, the paper mentioned White twice. The first was its brief coverage of a meeting of the District Afro-American Council, which White served as president, and the speeches made there by Pinckney B. S. Pinchback, John P. Green, and White. The second was Cooper's listing of his perennial trio of appointees-in-waiting, under a column of events "We Would Like to See: T. Thomas Fortune 'land.' George H. White tendered an auditorship of the Treasury. Some substantial recognition accorded the stalwart P. B. S. Pinchback."[13]

12. "Up the Palisades," and "Men of the Hour" (picture series), both in WCA, 11 May 1901. The dinner drew a number of White's friends: Dr. W. S. Lofton, Dr. F. P. Laney, C. C. Curtis, Felix Bryan, Robert Drew Sales, and A. O. Stafford. Other "Men of the Hour" on May 11 were well known regionally; Gould was U.S. attorney for the District of Columbia, Watty a member of the Baltimore city council, and Waller the rector of St. Luke's Episcopal Church, Washington. (Cooper later felt compelled to explain that Gould, the only white chosen, was not a Negro.)

13. "We Would Like to See," WCA, 18 May 1901.

338 | George Henry White

The *Colored American* did not mention White at all in its edition of May 25, although the "City Paragraphs" column did refer to Cora Lena's slow improvement "from a long illness." Across the nation, however, other black editors were beginning to show a growing interest in White's situation; at least six black weeklies across the country had now taken up the issue, with somewhat varying angles. In Indianapolis, the *Freeman* and its Democratic crosstown rival, the *World*, engaged in a gentlemanly tennis match over White's status. On May 4, the *Freeman* printed excerpts from White's earlier letter to the *Washington Post* before offering its qualified endorsement of the ex-congressman:

> . . . it should be borne in mind that there ought not to be too much letting down in securing a political office after serving in such a high capacity . . . many of us would prefer to remain humble rather than be exalted at a certain kind of expense. We hope to see quality in kind in those who have something to stand for. Our last Congressman should not put forward too much effort to secure an appointment. His services are known; he is known.[14]

This seemed to confuse the *World*, which reprinted the *Freeman's* piece and asked, innocently, for elucidation: "What does the Freeman mean? In the first place it declares that it is naturally in favor of Mr. White, and then advises him not to put forward too much effort to secure an appointment. And what are we to understand by 'quality in kind?'"[15]

Surely the *Freeman* did not intend to disparage "the quality of Hon. George H. White's ability or statesmanship," the *World* countered. White was certainly not alone in seeking presidential reward after leaving Congress, and he was at least as qualified as ex-senator Thomas Carter of Montana, whom McKinley had appointed as a member of the U.S. Commission to the Louisiana Purchase Exposition in St. Louis. "Mr. White knows what he wants, and has probably placed a correct estimate on his merits and ability," while all Tom Carter had done was filibuster. Carter was an easy target, but the *World* could not resist parting without a final cross-the-net lob at the *Freeman*, which "talks learnedly about remaining humble at a certain kind of expense.

14. "Hon. George H. White," editorial, *Indianapolis Freeman*, 4 May 1901.
15. Untitled editorial, *Indianapolis World*, 18 May 1901.

Would it be exalting the race to refuse Mr. White the $4,000 auditorship he asks for and insist upon him accepting the $2,500 deputy auditorship he does not want? We think not, and if we were 'naturally' for White we would try to help him reach his aim."[16]

The *Freeman* returned the volley on May 25, sticking by its first editorial, if in somewhat less labored style. It insisted that the *World* knew exactly what this argument entailed: "It is a question of propriety only." The *Freeman* wished White success, but also wished he would keep in mind that "the people will expect that he conduct his campaign along those lines usually employed by Congressmen, and not like an unknown man who depends upon superabundant political activities." After all, the office deserved its own dignity in the minds of the voters:

> Mr. White is fully competent and worthy and should succeed. . . . [But] the question does not reduce itself to what he wants, nor whether it would be exalting to do this or the other. Let it be for $4,000 or for $2,000, the more the merrier. But it is whether Mr. White, standing for so much more than other Congressmen, with his double-dutied representation, can afford to be active in [such] a campaign.[17]

Meanwhile, the *Colored American*'s own crosstown rival, the *Washington Bee*, was busy questioning White's decision not to return to North Carolina, but to practice law in the North—this time for practical reasons. *Bee* owner and editor W. Calvin Chase was himself an attorney; he was also no friend of Edward Elder Cooper's. Chase argued grumpily that black jurors "to a great extent are failures. . . . The negro jurors [tended to] dislike to see a colored attorney succeed." Influenced more by white jurors and attorneys, they often forced black attorneys to "excuse negro jurors when they are called to sit upon a case of a negro."[18]

Chase based his claim on years of "experience and observation," having written about the city since the early 1880s and practiced law there since 1889. Cautioning White not to expect to transcend the facts, he urged the re-

16. Ibid.

17. Untitled editorial, *Indianapolis Freeman*, 25 May 1901.

18. Untitled, undated editorial, *Washington Bee*, reprinted in the *Bee*, 11 May 1901. Washington native Chase (1854–1921) had founded the *Bee* in 1882, and was admitted to the bar of the District of Columbia in 1889 after attending courses at Howard Law School.

tiring congressman to reconsider his decision. At least one southern newspaper, the *Charleston (S.C.) Messenger*, then picked up the *Bee's* theme and embellished upon it: "Washington, D.C., is not the only city that is bull-headed on such important questions, but in other cities like Charleston and Columbia the situation is even worse, for negro lawyers, they would perish and die if their support depended upon the patronage of the colored people in the criminal courts."[19]

Remedying this situation required a "closer union between the colored people," including those in self-imposed exile, like George White, who owed their success to "the poor struggling negro who is left to face the music and do the best he can" back home in the South, "after the exit of one whom the people thought would stand by them in all the obstacles that confront them daily and be a sharer in their joys as well as their sorrows. *A man who the colored people have stood by, like Congressman White of North Carolina, should die with the people who made him and esteem him still*"[20] (emphasis added).

An Illinois reader of the *Bee* was the *Springfield State Capital*, which also agreed with Chase's comments about White's decision to leave North Carolina, a state it said desperately needed its "strong men" now. "Mr. White no doubt has a reason for taking up his residence outside the scenes of his people's woes, but strong as may be his emotions when in the midst of these things, he should help win back all they and he have lost." Furthermore, "As he has been their leader in the past he should be their counselor at the present, and refuse to be driven from his home by disfranchisement. The braver Negroes of North Carolina (and of all states where vicious legislation takes place, for that matter) will yet conquer all their trials. Will Mr. White help them?"[21]

Meanwhile, the *Cleveland Gazette* was also getting involved in the midwestern debate over propriety. Its primary object, however, was not George White, but someone close to him: a friend and fellow "exile," John Paterson Green. Green, a native of White's New Bern who was seven years older than the congressman, had grown up in Ohio. Before moving to Washington in

19. "Congressman White's Return," editorial, *Charleston (S.C.) Messenger*, 4 May 1901, reprinted in *Washington Bee*, 11 May 1901.

20. Ibid.

21. "Why Leave?" editorial, *Springfield (Ill.) State Capital*, 4 May 1901, reprinted in *Washington Bee*, 11 May 1901.

1897, Green had established his political credentials in his adopted state as one of a handful of black state legislators in the 1880s and 1890s, and on the campaign stump for the Republicans in 1896. He had traveled on the Mc-Kinley campaign trail with White and their colleague, former congressman John Roy Lynch, now a U.S. Army paymaster.[22]

During his career, John Green had run afoul of at least one prominent black politician and journalist, *Gazette* editor Harry C. Smith. Green's acceptance in 1897 of a low-level political appointment—as postage-stamp agent in Washington—had been proof enough to Smith of Green's unworthiness, and Smith thereafter never missed an opportunity to voice his disapproval of Green. When Green's belligerent behavior at the Afro-American Council convention in Indianapolis in 1900 led to a shoving match and his ejection from the meeting, Smith gleefully turned the incident into front-page news, complete with a belittling cartoon showing Green shouting and weeping.[23]

So it was with barely concealed delight that the *Gazette* picked up Cooper's catchy "cheap man" theme from the *Colored American* editorial, using it to make cheap fun of Green. If George White was not "cheap" by virtue of his refusal of such a low-paying job, then John P. Green could only be "cheap" for accepting one: "According to our contemporary, John Green (an ex-state senator), formerly of this city, now a $2,500 a year chief clerk in the government stamp department at Washington, is 'a cheap man.' Those of us who have known John for years are not inclined to question the American's estimate."[24]

Smith had equally disparaging words for Green's colleagues, including

22. *Who's Who in Colored America, 1929,* 334; *Dictionary of American Negro Biography,* 265–7; Foner, *Freedom's Lawmakers,* 139. Green (1845–1941) had moved with his mother to Ohio after his father's death. He graduated from Ohio Union Law School in 1870, then served three terms in the Ohio legislature between 1882 and 1893, as well as a decade as an elected justice of the peace in Cleveland. Lynch (1847–1939) served as major paymaster of the U.S. Volunteers from 1898 until 1906, when he was appointed captain and paymaster in the regular army; he had served in the U.S. House for two full terms and part of a third before retiring from elective politics in 1883, and was a delegate to at least five national Republican conventions between 1872 and 1900. As temporary chairman of the 1884 convention, Lynch was the first black to deliver a keynote address.

23. "Fired Out! John P. Green's Fate at the Afro-American Council Meet of Last Week," *Cleveland Gazette,* 8 September 1900.

24. Untitled editorial, *Cleveland Gazette,* 4 May 1901.

White and T. Thomas Fortune, "who were more loyal to McKinley last fall than they were to the race, and who are said to be waiting patiently for the President to knock a political 'plumb' (office) into their hands." All three would be "sadly disappointed" for a simple reason, predicted Smith: "McKinley is too busy dodging the question of disfranchisement and turning down the faithful 'old-guard' Afro-American republicans in the south and appointing to office, in their stead, 'gold democrats' (white) to do anything for northern Afro-Americans."[25]

The *Gazette* had already crossed swords with its Washington counterpart once that year, in January, over White's faultily reported "silence" on the floor of Congress regarding the Crumpacker amendment to the Burleigh reapportionment bill. Cooper had scored his fellow editor for that misstep, and now struck back with a May 18 editorial, defending Green as an "honorable man" who "naturally resents the idea . . . that a man cannot hold public office without becoming a trimmer and an apologist for the mistakes of an administration." Moreover, Cooper thought, "Mr. Green holds his first political office, and he is doing his duty nobly . . . we suggest that small fry talkers and penny-a-liner writers let him alone, and cease the petty nagging that sets them down as a distinguished relative of the animal which Balaam rode upon a historic occasion."[26]

The longstanding rivalry between Cooper and Smith, dating back to at least 1899, now erupted into open hostility. On May 25, the *Gazette* said Cooper "would take the first prize as a venter of hot air, even on the midway at the Pan-American exposition," for his "ridiculous" defense of Green. Smith also twisted his editorial knife with a less-than-flattering portrait of George White, who had refused "a deputy auditorship because he does not regard it as a good enough place and which, by the way, has not as yet been offered him." So far, this was all the reward the ex-congressman seemed likely to receive "for his McKinley shouting of last fall and for subserviency . . . while in Congress. He is not the only one. There are others—Afro-Americans, too."[27]

Such baiting soon worked, and Cooper minced no words in chastising Smith anew. The *Colored American*'s response bore the title "As to Cheap

25. Ibid. Although no fan of Cooper's journalistic ability, Fortune tactfully decided to stay out of this argument and printed no comments.
26. "Fair Play for Hon. John P. Green," editorial, WCA, 18 May 1901.
27. Untitled editorial, *Cleveland Gazette*, 25 May 1901.

Men," and clearly had a double meaning, for Smith's tactics were judged gratuitous indeed. "The Cleveland Gazette goes out of its way to insinuate that Senator John P. Green is a 'cheap man,' because he accepted a $2,500 position—a grade which Hon. George H. White declines in advance," wrote Cooper. "Why doesn't the Gazette do a little thinking sometimes and get away from its petty prejudices?"[28]

Green was holding his "first political office," and was lucky to be making $2,500 a year, Cooper snapped. In contrast, White's federal salary history ("four years at $5,000") placed him "among the law makers who have been placed on commissions at salaries equal to the ones they have been enjoying" (obviously referring to Montana's Carter, among others). "To treat Mr. White less generously would be a demotion for him, and a discrimination under which he could not comfortably rest," the Colored American fumed. "Mr. Green is on the upward trend, and is complacent. For Mr. White to take a backward step would be a march for the bargain counter—the cheap side. Sit down, Smith!"[29]

The flurry over Green came as a momentary distraction from the gloomy silence out of the White House. The auditor's position previously filled by Youngblood was now vacant, but Harry Smith had been right that it would not be used to reward an outsider. Instead, by year's end it went to Youngblood's previous deputy, Robert S. Person, who then held the job for several years.

The cult of personality and power within the small world of black journalism was fascinating to watch; its players were often beguiled by an elevated sense of their own importance. Cooper, for instance, was continually competing for top billing in the nation's black press with Smith and a select few others: Fortune of the New York Age, Christopher J. Perry of the Philadelphia Tribune, and George L. Knox of the Indianapolis Freeman, among others who held sway outside the nation's capital, and at home, Chase of the venerable Washington Bee. A Cooper spat two years earlier with Ralph Waldo Tyler of the Columbus (Ohio) Daily Dispatch had drawn a bemused comment from Fortune's Age, ending up as a reprint on the editorial page of Smith's Gazette: "[Cooper and Tyler] are having a tiff on relative veracity and probity which

28. "As to Cheap Men," editorial, WCA, 1 June 1901.

29. Ibid. The obsession with salary illustrates the fact that it was the single most significant measure of success, and, moreover, that equal salary with whites was a sacred concept.

makes the Hon. Harry C. Smith, of The Cleveland Gazette, very happy, and which the rest of us are watching with subdued interest."[30]

Chase himself occasionally fanned the flames, calling Smith "the Ohio bombast" and admitting that he (Chase) and Cooper did not care for each other. Such personal comments about other editors, if not frequent, were a recognizable characteristic of the lively and somewhat unpredictable nature of the black print medium, still in its adolescence at the turn of the century. Outspoken black editors often dabbled in politics as well: Harry Smith was elected three times to the Ohio legislature before being defeated for reelection in 1900, while Chicago Appeal editor Cyrus Field Adams had been appointed assistant register of the U.S. Treasury in 1901 after serving as a Chicago-area town clerk. Even Edward Elder Cooper, not too surprisingly, would seek employment with the District of Columbia Commission in 1905, after closing down the Colored American in late 1904 and failing to succeed with a second newspaper.[31]

What may have been an amusing sideshow to some was doubtless exasperating to others. The George White affair was now beginning to divert attention from the truly serious racial questions of the times: lynchings, southern disfranchisement, and separate educational facilities. It was also exacerbating a new tactical split between Booker T. Washington and the older leadership in the nation's black community. But Edward Cooper rarely paid heed to the opinions of others when it came to the subject of George White; by June 15, he had resumed the quest in a brief editorial aside: "Congressman George H. White is possessing his soul in patience, 'waiting until his change comes.'"[32]

White had, in fact, wisely absented himself from the public discussions of his hopes for an appointment. His only recorded comment of any type during the summer was in response to an informal "poll" of local leaders on the impact of the new North, East and West Association, which had honored John

30. "Doings of the Race," Cleveland Gazette, 16 December 1899.

31. As listed under "Executive Branch, Department of the Treasury," in the Congressional Directory, 56th Cong., edition corrected through January 8, 1901, and 57th Cong., edition corrected though November 29, 1901; "What I Saw and Heard," Washington Bee, 25 November 1905. Editor Harry Smith later called Adams's appointment "a reward of his questionable conduct" in 1900—that is, for circulating a petition condemning the Afro-American Council for not endorsing McKinley for reelection.

32. Untitled editorial, WCA, 15 June 1901.

P. Green with a recent banquet. "Just say for me that I have nothing to say upon the subject," White had told Cooper, reportedly with a smile. No one else had a comment on the question, either, but on a slow day, even the lack of a comment was newsworthy enough for Cooper to report.[33]

White would also have no comment on the sad news from his former hometown of New Bern later that month: the death by drowning of his old friend and political rival, William Edwards Clarke. In a bizarre accident on the Trent River, Clarke and his two young daughters died when their aging rowboat disintegrated during a Friday evening family outing with a neighbor's young son. Clarke, by all accounts an exceptionally strong swimmer, was apparently pulled under while trying to save his frantic daughters; their intertwined bodies were found shortly afterward. The former legislator and postmaster was fifty years old, just two years older than White.[34]

Soon the *Colored American,* in its June 22 edition, "Wanted to Know [w]hen the Administration will find those comfortable berths for George H. White and P. B. S. Pinchback." If Clarke's untimely death was an omen of things to come, Edward Cooper blithely ignored any mention of it, choosing instead to describe White's scheduled appearance at the upcoming National Afro-American Council convention in Philadelphia, representing Washington's Second Baptist Church Lyceum, one of White's regular speaking forums. White, no longer a council officer, may have needed a formal designation to gain entry, since he planned to run for council president.[35]

Shortly afterward, Cooper predicted that "Hot Weather Will Subside" when two events, among others, occurred: "When the Administration takes care of the Hon. George White to the tune of a $5,000 berth [and] Gov. Pinchback is properly rewarded for his lifelong services to the grand old party."[36]

In a separate editorial in the same issue, Cooper took pains to help John P. Green put an end to distasteful rumors of his "designs upon the office of the Register of the Treasury or Recorder of Deeds, now so capably filled by Messrs.

---

33. Untitled editorial, ibid., 8 June 1901. Cooper described White as "up to his ears disposing of his correspondence" in his office at the time.

34. *New Bern Daily Journal,* 29 June 1901.

35. "Wanted to Know," WCA, 22 June 1901; "Washington, D.C.," *Indianapolis Freeman,* 27 July 1901.

36. "Hot Weather Will Subside," WCA, 13 July 1901.

Lyons and Cheatham. There is nothing in the rumor."[37] Green had publicly removed himself from consideration for either job, according to the *Colored American;* no source for the widespread rumor was cited, and there was nothing but silence, for once, from Green's nemesis, the *Gazette*.

Cooper also politely reminded President McKinley that George White was still waiting for the offer, as if there could be any doubt. "The administration should hasten to recognize the political services of the Hon. George H. White. The recognition, of course, should be commensurate with his standing as a public man, and the elected representative of 10,000,000 citizens of the republic," Cooper wrote. "A treasury auditorship would just about fit Mr. White."[38]

But by now, the last phrase was beginning to sound almost perfunctory. There would be no offer at that level from McKinley, not for the moment. Perhaps once the public storm had blown over, the president would reconsider and find a new vacancy for the exiled North Carolinian; this was Cooper's unstated hope. In the meantime, there were other possibilities to be advanced, in case the auditorship had slipped away. Cooper provided a novel suggestion for an alternate position for White and several others in a midsummer editorial that reprised the previous calls for special posts for black leaders, like those offered to Carter and other defeated white politicians: "A commission of 5 to go to Porto Rico, the Philippines and Hawaii, to report on industrial conditions and suitability for colonization by laboring classes, would be a splendid opening for the right men, and would do the country a lot of good. Mr. White, Gov. Pinchback, Mr. Fortune, Col. Pledger, Messrs. Lawson, Durham, Jones, Knox and Napier would afford a fine field for the selection of appropriate timber."[39]

By August 10, the *Colored American* had grown almost desperate, describing White in a brief editorial note as "ready to receive any official communication which the distinguished gentleman at the White House may wish to bring to his attention." As White's distance from Congress grew, Cooper feared his stock might be losing its value. Cooper's campaign was grasping at straws a week later, when the *Colored American* claimed that "White is to be an auditor of the Treasury, when the President returns" to the capital.[40]

37. Untitled editorial, ibid., 13 July 1901.
38. Untitled editorial, ibid., 20 July 1901.
39. "A Hint to the President," editorial, ibid., 20 July 1901.
40. Untitled editorial, ibid., 10 August 1901; "Dame Rumor Has It," ibid., 17 August 1901.

Only the autumn resumption of political activity would bear this out. But during the president's late-summer absence from Washington, George White's prestige would suffer another blow, this one from within the highest ranks of the nation's black community. Bishop Alexander Walters had considered stepping down as president of the National Afro-American Council as early as the middle of 1900, when the fledgling organization held its third annual convention in Indianapolis; some observers had then suggested White as a replacement. But opinion in the black community had been divided at the time. The council was a determinedly nonpartisan organization, and its constitution forbade its involvement in politics; selecting an active politician to lead the organization could be a dangerous precedent, as the *Gazette* had eagerly pointed out: "Congressman White may be just the man for the place in the estimation of Bishop Walters and others, but there are those who feel that he is too deeply imbedded in politics for such a position. The president of the Council should be a man who is above political influence."[41]

White was already one of nine members of a special council subcommittee responsible for operations of the body between its annual conventions; of those nine, he was the only member holding elective office in 1900, but hardly the only political player. Others included Professor Jesse Lawson, chairman, and such notables as Pinchback, U.S. Treasury Register Judson W. Lyons, and Boston's Edward Everett Brown.[42]

The council's determination to stay out of partisan politics led to an embarrassing drama at the 1900 convention, growing out of efforts by some members—most notably, John P. Green and Cyrus Field Adams—to force the body to endorse the candidacy of President McKinley. In the end, Bishop Walters had been reelected in Indianapolis, the council had declined to endorse McKinley, Green had been forcibly ejected from the floor, and White had taken no elected office at all.[43]

A year had passed since then, and White was no longer an active politician, at least in terms of seeking elective office; his availability for the council presidency was clear, as was his own desire to hold the office. But by August

41. Untitled editorial, *Cleveland Gazette*, 26 May 1900.

42. "The Council at Work," WCA, 6 January 1900. Other subcommittee members appointed at the annual session were H. T. Johnson of Pennsylvania, Richard W. Thompson of Indiana, and Daniel Murray of South Carolina; all three lived and worked in the Washington area but represented their home states.

43. "Fired Out!" *Cleveland Gazette*, 8 September 1900.

1901, Bishop Walters had decided to stay on, and apparently explained this to White only in Philadelphia as the convention opened. The most White could hope for was one of nine vice-presidencies, distinctly disappointing in terms of national stature. Of the nine men previously elected, at least two were mere journalists (Fortune and Smith), and none had held any important national position outside the council.[44]

Newspaper reports of the results of the 1901 convention are contradictory, but paint a revealing picture of the council's Byzantine internal politics. The *Gazette* chose to believe unconfirmed reports that White would resign from his new vice-presidency in protest against Walters's consecutive decisions to stay on (a "sore spot" left over from Indianapolis), and chided White in advance for his bitterness: "We thought Cong. White too big a man to be so small over anything."[45] The *Bee*, however, labeled the convention "A Farce" in its front-page headline, all but accusing Bishop Walters of double-crossing White at the last possible moment.

Bishop Walters had been reinstated to the nominating committee's list just before the vote and had easily defeated White, who nearly stormed out of the meeting before "dozens of delegates got upon their knees and begged him not to go." Emmett Scott called it "the only unpleasant feature of the Convention . . . George H. White was slaughtered." (Scott thought this "for the best, as he only wanted to use it as a weapon to help him politically.") White agreed to accept the lesser position, but returned to Washington "much disgusted." The incident created bad blood among the factions, declared the *Bee*, and was "the worst meeting ever held" by the council.[46]

Predictably enough, the *Colored American* struggled to find something positive about the situation. White's "manly course" in accepting the lesser job "had made for him many friends," and he "went out of the session a stronger man in the organization than at its opening, and it is believed that some day he may yet, if he so desires, achieve his honorable ambition to be president of

44. Ibid. Other new vice-presidents were W. A. Pledger, Ernest Lyon, O. M. Woods, Col. M. Marshall, Bishop George W. Clinton, William H. Steward, and Mrs. Lillian Fox. Cyrus Field Adams was elected secretary.

45. Untitled editorial, *Cleveland Gazette*, 24 August 1901.

46. "The Afro-American Council: The Meeting a Farce, Bishop Walters Defeats Ex-Congressman White," and "Ex-Congressman White Indignant," *Washington Bee*, 17 August 1901; Emmett J. Scott to BTW, 13 August 1901, in Harlan and Smock, *The BTW Papers*, 6:195. Scott (1873–1957), a former journalist, was Washington's private secretary and confidant.

the Black Congress, and should that day come, he will find in the membership as loyal supporters of his administration as they are now the supporters of the present one."[47]

White would duly report his defeat to the Second Baptist Lyceum in October, and the *Bee* began predicting regularly that the council would disband any day. The body would still be struggling in late 1905, however, when another disruptive convention (this one in Detroit) forced a "purge" of its membership. Walters served as head until 1902, when T. Thomas Fortune was elected to succeed him; by then, White would presumably have lost interest in holding the post.[48]

With Walters's reelection in Philadelphia, the former congressman's prospects for any type of important national position outside the federal government had been dashed. He could now only wait for the return of the president to Washington, and for any consoling news that McKinley might bring back with him. But fate would soon intervene in a dramatic way, as the president's trip to Buffalo in early September to visit the Pan-American Exposition produced the stunningly unthinkable event—attempted assassination by a crazed gunman, and McKinley's valiant battle to recover—which took first priority in almost all newspapers during the second week of the month. Most newspaper editorials refrained from any overtly political statements during the week after the shooting, as the nation waited and prayed for the wounded president to recover; for a time, it appeared that he would rally and survive.

Impatient to the end, the headstrong Edward Cooper chose the *Colored American*'s edition of Saturday, September 14, to repeat his plea on White's behalf. Under a column entitled "Isn't It Time For," he called on the president, supposedly well on his way to recovery, "to remember Congressman White." Cooper's sense of timing, for once, was dreadful; on that same day, William McKinley succumbed to gangrene caused by gunshot wound.[49] The

47. "Echoes of the Afro-American Council," WCA, 31 August 1901.

48. "Negroes Hostile to B. T. Washington, Demonstration at Afro-American Council in Louisville," *New York Times*, 3 July 1903. Walters (1858–1917) served as head until 1903 and from 1905 to 1908. Fortune (1856–1928), reelected first vice-president at Philadelphia in 1901, was elected to succeed him in 1902; he was also the founder of the short-lived Afro-American League. He suffered a mental breakdown in 1907, but regained his health to work for the *Philadelphia Tribune* and Marcus Garvey's *Negro World*, among others.

49. "Isn't It Time For," WCA, 14 September 1901; Margaret Leech, *In the Days of McKinley* (Westport, Conn.: Greenwood Press, 1975), 600–1. Cooper could hardly have foreseen the enor-

nation was horror stricken, Cooper was certainly mortified at his faux pas, and George White was no less moved than many of his fellow Americans; from all indications he genuinely admired McKinley and had campaigned for him with unmistakable fervor in 1900.

But the death of the president meant more than merely personal sadness for White. It effectively extinguished any hopes he might have for a significant appointment, for now there would be a new chief executive, one whose loyalty to black leaders was based less on political reward than on philosophical acceptability. The new president was Theodore Roosevelt, with whom White had virtually no connection; Roosevelt's public regard for Booker T. Washington—whom he even invited to dine at the White House within weeks of his own inauguration, much to the public's shock—signaled the end of an era for George White. While Roosevelt might still consider White for a minor post, nothing as visible as the hoped-for auditorship, or an equivalent job with similar salary, would be forthcoming.

Edward Cooper continued to mention White fondly in the columns of the *Colored American*, but with gradually decreasing frequency. White's picture ran as a "Man of the Hour" on October 5, and Cooper reminded President Roosevelt twice in October of White's availability for an important post. There were other mentions of the former congressman by the *Colored American* on into 1902, but they seemed almost halfhearted. Much of this publicity dealt with White's new blacks-only industrial colony in southern New Jersey, as yet unnamed. White began advertising his land development company in the *Colored American* in late 1901, and continued for about six months.[50]

Whenever possible, Cooper mentioned members of White's family and noted the former congressman's speaking engagements, but, practically speaking, the campaign for high office for George White was now over. It had ended in October when Booker T. Washington failed to respond favorably to

mity of this faux pas, since the *Colored American* went to press on Friday evenings for early Saturday distribution. McKinley had been reported as recovering steadily until Friday night, September 13, when news flashed of his worsening condition; he died in his sleep about 2 A.M. Saturday, September 14.

50. "Men of the Hour," picture series, WCA, 5 October 1901; "We Would Like to See," ibid., 12 October 1901; untitled editorial, ibid., 19 October 1901. Other "Men of the Hour" were Charles W. Anderson, Bishop W. B. Derrick, and Maj. Charles R. Douglass. Advertisements for the George H. White Land and Improvement Company appeared each week in the *Colored American* for six months after 7 December 1901.

a private letter from White, requesting Washington's intercession with the new president.[51]

The letter, dated October 7, 1901, was a sad commentary on White's reduced importance in Washington and the speed with which it had occurred. Until his departure from Congress, White had needed no assistance in gaining an audience in the McKinley White House, and before the 1900 election, White's success in obtaining appointments for other black leaders had been remarkably high. Now he was forced to ask someone else for help in gaining access to the Roosevelt administration; he had been unable even to obtain an appointment with the new president, according to Emmett Scott's account.[52] No matter how cordial this gatekeeper might be, it was a letdown for the very proud George White. Despite the difficulty of accepting the snub, White was realistic, as his letter proved.

"I have just returned from a visit to the White House, where it was intimated to me that in my fight for an Auditorship under the Treas. Dept. here, a letter from you would greatly strengthen my chances," White wrote by hand from his office; he had sent his secretary home. "I am aware that your work is entirely divorced from politics and office seeking. But I want you to please help me in this instance by writing a personal letter addressed to Pres. Roosevelt, giving him the estimate you have of me from my public life and your personal knowledge of me."[53]

The polite language barely concealed White's growing desperation. Without such a letter, the lucrative appointment would slip away forever; the only obstacle was his famous pride, which he was now forced to set aside. "I would always greatly appreciate the favor," he wrote, "and endeavor to so conduct myself in the future as never to cause you to regret your act." The letter should be returned directly to him, White asked, "that I may hand it to the Pres. in person."[54]

The deed was done; the "winged statesman" had gone begging. But the hu-

51. George H. White to BTW, 7 October 1901, BTWP. A handwritten notation on the top of the letter, apparently made by BTW or his secretary, read "Not Answd, 10/9."

52. Emmett J. Scott to BTW, 4 October 1901, in Harlan and Smock, *The BTW Papers*, 6:212. Scott had been at the White House that day to meet with Roosevelt, while others—such as White, [Henry?] Arnett, and Paul Laurence Dunbar—"were waiting to see the President but failed."

53. George H. White to BTW, 7 October 1901, BTWP.

54. Ibid.

miliation was not finished. The appointment went to another less controversial man, the former auditor's white deputy. There would be no formal written answer from Tuskegee to the request, not for months to come, at least—and even then, coaxed forth only by the pitiful, covert plea of George White's ailing wife. But it is almost certain that White learned the answer earlier than that. Washington's notorious dinner with the new president had taken place within a fortnight of White's letter, and the Tuskegeean must have used the occasion of his visit to alert White to the negative reality he now faced. How assiduously Washington may have pushed while at the White House on October 16 is not known, but the explanation he offered later—of Senator Jeter Pritchard's fatal opposition—was certainly not unexpected, however convenient it may have seemed.

White understood, of course, that Washington held no personal grudge, and that his lack of assistance here was both strategic and prudent. Washington's stated preference was for a small number of conciliatory members of the race in public office—John Dancy, for instance—and his shrewdness prevented him from wasting recommendations. He apparently took no part in the rancorous debate in December over the doomed reappointment of Henry Cheatham as recorder of deeds for the District of Columbia; he would easily have sized up the situation as a no-win battle.

Roosevelt's appointment in early 1902 of Dancy to succeed Cheatham was an anticlimax to a distressing affair. Dancy was named to the post after a covert battle by Cheatham's enemies, notably Bishop Benjamin Arnett and his son Henry, succeeded in convincing Roosevelt not to reappoint him; Cheatham's involvement in an obscure sexual scandal seems to have been the final obstacle. Despite Cheatham's recent remarriage, letters involving an unnamed woman had recently surfaced, besmirching his reputation; the opportunistic Arnetts had also made serious managerial and legal charges against Cheatham, which led to an investigation by the U.S. attorney general. Senator Jeter Pritchard, who had backed Cheatham in 1897 and continued to support him to Roosevelt, was "mortified" at the facts, according to one well-placed observer, Whitefield McKinlay; the Washington press gave coverage to the charges, which appeared technical in nature, not criminal.[55]

55. Whitefield McKinlay to BTW, 14 December 1901, in Harlan and Smock, The BTW Papers, 6:347; "Cheatham Must Vacate, President Decides Not to Reappoint Him as Recorder of Deeds," Washington Post, 18 December 1901. McKinlay, a prosperous black businessman, quickly

It is entirely possible that Booker T. Washington, who generally recommended just one candidate for a position, then turned to Dancy as a reliable bureaucrat with an acknowledged record of service. If White was ever seriously considered for this position, there is no evidence of it; neither he nor the ever-present John P. Green were even discussed in the press as possible appointees, for instance, although Green may have harbored loud private hopes.[56]

The situation was demoralizing on other fronts, for both Booker T. Washington and the race as a whole. Washington's longtime ally, T. Thomas Fortune, had recently embarrassed himself with a conspicuously drunken speaking engagement in front of the local Bethel Literary and Historical Association, according to Whitefield McKinlay, who warned Washington to "diplomatically cut loose" from Fortune and Bee editor W. Calvin Chase, a strong critic. In an uncharacteristically frank reply, Washington bemoaned the "difficult and embarrassing" situation he now faced and the impossibility of "shak[ing] off at once the old time men and old time influences." Apparently well aware of Fortune's weakness for alcohol, he had warned Fortune, to no avail, against "being led astray" at the Washington appearance. Yet however repugnant their behavior might be, Washington depended on influential journalists such as Fortune and Chase to present his views to the race. "Public sentiment among our people . . . is very largely moulded and educated by the [black] press," he believed, arguing that he could not counter recent accusations "by certain parties in Washington . . . of giving more attention to what is called the 'old crowd' who . . . stood manfully in the earlier and darker days" if he ignored Chase and Fortune.[57]

Booker T. Washington continued to nurse a relationship with the increas-

---

became a liaison between BTW and the White House; he had "just learned" that neither Cheatham nor Crossland would be appointed, and quoted John Dancy's account of Pritchard's reaction. The *Post* article gave few specifics, but the subheadline read as follows: "Attorney General Reports Foundation for a Charge of Technically Violating a Federal Law."

56. See, for instance, an untitled editorial, *Cleveland Gazette*, 21 December 1901. Ever unkind to his old foe, Harry Smith said it was "strange that the Arnetts could find no one in Ohio to back for the [Recorder's] post, especially since it has been a nightly dream for nearly four years for John P. Green."

57. Ibid.; also BTW to Whitefield McKinlay, 16 December 1901, in Harlan and Smock, *The BTW Papers*, 6:348–9.

ingly unstable Fortune, but enjoyed little success in his attempts to cultivate the independent and notoriously prickly Chase. He had somewhat better luck in his dealings with Edward Cooper of the *Colored American*, but that publication would soon fail. Washington continued to endorse qualified candidates of the race to Roosevelt, who invariably honored the recommendations, but at a considerably slower pace than in the McKinley years. After 1906, the appointments of blacks to major offices would almost cease, following the maturation of the lily-white movement within the Republican Party, and due partly to Washington's decision to recommend relatively few blacks for major appointments. Henry Cheatham, quietly disgraced, seems to have sought only one more appointment, in 1906, but did not receive it; in 1907, he began running an orphanage in Oxford, N.C., where he remained active until his death three decades later.[58]

Cheatham's successor Dancy and longtime treasury register Judson W. Lyons continued as federal servants for several more years during the waning Republican era, which ended with Woodrow Wilson's election in 1912. Edward Cooper's other favorite, John P. Green, ended his federal service in 1906 and lived on as a respected elder statesman, along with John R. Lynch and a handful of others from the glory days of the 1880s and 1890s. Lynch served as a paymaster of the U.S. Army for nearly a decade, and both he and Green lived on in retirement into their nineties.[59]

George White, however, would never reach the pinnacle of a federal appointment again. Less surprisingly, perhaps, neither would the wealthy Pinchback nor the deteriorating Fortune, both of whom owed their allegiance to the McKinley-Hanna wing of the Republican Party, not to the "progressive" wing now controlled by Roosevelt. At any rate, neither man cared for the actual responsibility of office as much as did White, who had always been a dedicated public servant. An inner fire seems to have been extinguished in him

58. Cheatham's goal may have been to succeed John P. Green as U.S. postage stamp agent after Green retired in 1906. In any event, both President Roosevelt and Postmaster General George B. Cortelyou—McKinley's private secretary in 1901—remained well aware of the 1901 scandal, which forced Cheatham to retire from public life.

59. Green (1845–1940) and Lynch (1847–1939) continued to be active until their deaths, Green in Cleveland as a lawyer and Lynch in Chicago as a prolific writer. Judson Lyons (1860–1924) served as Treasury register until 1906; John Dancy (1857–1920) served as recorder of deeds until 1910.

by this futile quest, yet if he was depressed by this failure to maintain a seat near the center of power, he gave little public sign of it. There may have been few thundering speeches after 1901, but there were simply fewer opportunities for him to press his case for fair treatment for blacks, and fewer interested audiences among the apathetic white majority.

Much more than a simple political tide for one man had turned. American society itself seemed to be turning, finally, away from the outspoken words of White and others in the last days of the post-Reconstruction era; "separate but equal" had become the new byword of the day in race relations. And White, the uncomfortable symbol of the stubborn demand by blacks for social equality and civil justice, faded rapidly from the public eye. Never again would he wield the rhetorical power or personal prestige of those days, particularly in the once-friendly white wing of the Republican Party, or in Washington. His move to Philadelphia in 1906 in search of better opportunities was essentially a final admission of decline from a seat so near the center of power.

White's own words, offered in all sincerity as a caution to Howard University law students just two years earlier, had ironically prophesied that decline: "My advice is to go away [from Washington], which in the end means a far greater degree of success, and grander achievements will come to you than to those who hide their talents here, where they are sure to grow rusty and dormant from non-use."[60]

60. "Cong. Geo. H. White Speaks, The Students and Faculty of Howard Law School Entertained by the Eloquent North Carolinian," WCA, 18 March 1899. White, of course, was explaining here why he left Washington in 1877, not counseling against public service as a vocation.

14

The Dream of Whitesboro

The offerings advertised by George White's new land improvement company
in late 1901 were the culmination of a year of hard labor, much of it undertaken in a solitary quest for fulfillment outside of the political world. The
company was White's most lasting concrete accomplishment: a new town,
dedicated to the belief that self-sufficient blacks could not only survive but
flourish, if simply left alone in a neutral, healthy environment.

It was to be an "interesting experiment," wrote the *Colored American* in
early 1901: the establishment of a "colony of Negroes who will live and work
by themselves" in New Jersey's southernmost county, on land being purchased
by the Afro-American Equitable Association. Each colonist was required to be
of "good character, steady and industrious habits," and was to receive several
acres of land in exchange for a promise to till it and pay for it over a period of
ten years. As an enticement, developers were willing to build both a light industrial plant and an industrial school for the children of the colonists. As envisioned, the town would provide an ethnically homogeneous environment for
utopian pioneers, in much the same fashion as nearby Woodbine, created a
decade earlier for Jewish-American immigrants from Eastern Europe.[1]

1. "Negro Colonists to Work Together," dated 9 February 1901, in *WCA*, 23 February 1901;
Jeffery M. Dorwart, *Cape May County, New Jersey: The Making of an American Resort Community*
(New Brunswick, N.J.: Rutgers University Press, 1992), 151–4. The *Colored American* had previously described a January 8 organizational meeting of the Equitable Association, claiming that "a
wealthy Afro-American has agreed to give the ground" (January 19, 1901). Two other quasi-
utopian communities lay up the nearby Atlantic coast: the Methodist resort of Ocean City and
Sea Isle City, a "sanitary and art city."

About half of Cape May County is a narrow peninsula between the Delaware Bay and the Atlantic Ocean; comparatively underpopulated in 1900, it was home to thirteen thousand residents in its 263 square miles. Only a handful of blacks lived here, but the primary impetus for this black colony transcended demographic considerations. A group of Cape May City blacks had created the Equitable Association (also known as the Colored American Equitable Industrial Association) in January both to establish institutions for the care and welfare of blacks and to purchase land for a town exclusively for black residents, in the face of growing local discrimination against the race. At least one white property owner—*Cape May Herald* editor Marcus Scull— had begun a campaign to rid the town of all African Americans in an effort to return to "the glories of pre–Civil War days" and increase the town's resort appeal to wealthy white tourists. Blacks were soon banned from city-sponsored events, and black students were forced to attend a dilapidated school after a new segregated city high school opened, due to unexplained delays in the opening of its black wing.[2]

This discrimination was not typical of New Jersey, which had abolished slavery in 1846 and which prided itself on fair treatment for all its citizens, including its many foreign-born immigrants. A significant amount of real estate in the area of Cape May City was owned by a few affluent blacks, including local store owner Joseph G. Vance and out-of-state residents such as the renowned poet and novelist Paul Laurence Dunbar of Washington, D.C., and George Henry White. But most of Cape May County's blacks were struggling members of the lower class and owned little land; the county's African American population was about eight percent, or twice the state's overall average, according to the 1900 census, and almost all of its black adults worked as farmers or domestic helpers.[3] Up to now their existence had been untroubled; as the nation's mood shifted against equal rights for black citizens, however, old prejudices were apparently rising to the surface, and black leaders were sensitive to the new tide of local segregation.

2. Dorwart, *Cape May County*, 172.

3. Abstract of Census Returns for the County of Cape May, *Census of 1905, State of New Jersey* (Trenton: New Jersey Secretary of State, 1905); *Negro Population, 1790–1915* (Washington, D.C.: GPO, 1918), 43 (Table 13); Dorwart, *Cape May County*, 151. In 1905, Cape May County had 1,377 black residents out of a total population of 17,390; New Jersey's statewide population was still less than 4 percent black in 1910. Holly Beach's population was 8 percent black in 1895; Dorwart notes that blacks had begun settling the county's barrier islands by the 1880s.

According to local records, there were five trustees of the new Equitable Association: the Reverend James W. Fishburn, pastor of the city's AME Zion Church; merchant Joseph G. Vance; hotel porter William L. Selvy; and two others, Thomas J. Griffin and Charles H. Finaman. All but Fishburn, who had moved from South Carolina in 1900, appear to have been longtime local residents. By January 31, the group had taken an option on 1,400 acres of land about ten miles north of Cape May City in Middle Township, and needed just $400 in capital to finalize the purchase, according to an article in the *Washington Post*. The first colonists were expected to be drawn from New Jersey, Virginia, and North Carolina. The *Post* did not note the irony of the land's history: a century and a half earlier, it had belonged to the largest slaveholders in the county, Aaron Leaming Jr. and Thomas Leaming Jr.[4]

It is not clear precisely when George White and his small group of investors became involved in the Cape May venture, although it was certainly before title was finally transferred from the owner, Robert E. Hand, in August of 1901. Hand also owned the *Star of the Cape* newspaper, and periodically praised the progress of the new colony, which had been named Whitesboro by late 1902 in honor of its most famous investor. White and his syndicate were all well-to-do southern blacks, and the purchase was handled by Reverend Fishburn, who seems to have intended primarily to benefit residents of Cape May City. But it may have come down to a question of sufficient capital to finance the purchase price, which eventually amounted to $14,000. In any event, White's circle apparently included no residents of the county at hand; all his fellow investors lived further south, including Dunbar and music teacher Harriet Aletha Gibbs of Washington, D.C.; businessman Wiley H. Bates of Annapolis, Maryland; and Samuel Hynes Vick, real-estate developer and former postmaster of Wilson, North Carolina.[5]

4. Untitled article datelined Cape May, N.J., *Washington Post*, 1 February 1901; Dorwart, *Cape May County*, 173. The *Post* article apparently formed the basis for the February 23 article in the *Colored American*. The Leamings were both sons of eighteenth-century Quaker settlers in Cape May; their slave holdings were small by southern standards, only "three or more each." Only sixty-three slaves were listed as taxable property in the entire Middle Precinct in 1784, according to Dorwart. Aaron Leaming Jr. died in 1780; Thomas Leaming Jr. lived well into the nineteenth century.

5. Dorwart, *Cape May County*, 172, citing a 15 June 1901 article in the *Cape May Herald*. White had so far not been named in any newspaper article. Fishburn, who became the agent for White and his investors, may not have disclosed the names of the syndicate he represented, in

The purchase was finalized in August 1901, and White's new Washington development company began advertising lots for sale by early December. But comparatively few of the first colonists were from New Jersey, as the Equitable Association had seemed to expect; most settlers came from Virginia and North Carolina, perhaps because White's name was more familiar to potential colonists from those areas. Many of the first group of colonists apparently moved from Columbus County, N.C., as early as 1903, including the family of carpenter Henry Wilson "Willie" Spaulding, a relative of White's stepmother; Spaulding began building homes and streets for White's company almost immediately.[6]

White and his investors may have entered the picture at the last moment, or may simply have used the Equitable Association as a front, perhaps in hopes of keeping the price of the land as low as possible; the association held the option on the land, at any rate. It is possible, of course, that the owners may not have been willing to negotiate with outsiders on the same terms as with local residents, hence the use of Reverend Fishburn as an agent. The size of the parcel purchased in August 1901 was significantly larger than originally announced, apparently as large as 2,000 acres, indicating that serious negotiations had continued since the first public announcement in January.[7]

Once negotiations were finalized in August, however, development began quickly; the first 650 lots had been surveyed and laid out for purchase by the

---

order to avoid undue publicity and any effect on the price Hand was asking. "M. A. White" was also listed as one of the deed holders. This may have been White's daughter Mamie, as claimed by George Reid, "The Post-Congressional Career of George H. White, 1901–1918," *Journal of Negro History* 41 (October 1976): 369. A 1901 Cape May County property record, however, refers to White's stepmother, Mary Anna White, as part owner. Gibbs was a daughter of Arkansas judge and U.S. diplomat Mifflin Wistar Gibbs, and later married Washington lawyer Napoleon B. Marshall. Her sister Ida Gibbs Hunt and brother-in-law William H. Hunt—another U.S. diplomat—were also investors in Whitesboro, according to a 1901 property transaction record.

6. Dorwart, *Cape May County,* 174. Henry Spaulding's father was G. S. Spaulding of Columbus County, N.C., a brother of Mary Anna Spaulding White.

7. White, *Who's Who in Philadelphia,* 88; Reid, "Post-Congressional Career," 369. Charles F. White listed the size at 2,000 acres in his sketch, and claimed George White owned "almost three-fourths" of the firm. The acreage was estimated at "1800 or 2000 acres" in White's company advertisement (see below). Reid gives the size as 1,700 acres, citing the Cape May County Deedbook for 1901.

time the first advertisement for Whitesboro appeared in the *Colored American* on December 7. The lots measured 50 by 150 feet (about one-sixth of an acre) and were priced from $50 upward, with a down payment of $5 minimum and monthly payments afterward of $2 to $5 for up to ten years, depending on the income of the purchaser. Sales and financing were to be handled by White's new firm in Washington, D.C., the George H. White Land and Improvement Company; any profits realized from the sales were to be plowed back into the development itself, and White's company would provide land for certain buildings—either for free or at cost—including the small town's first public school.[8]

Although the colony was clearly George White's personal dream, the need for additional investors was obvious. The company was actually a corporation, with shares issued, but White may have repurchased most of them by 1906, when he moved the company to Philadelphia; he reportedly owned about three-fourths of the stock by that time. Of the initial investors, only Samuel Vick seems to have been involved in the later development of Whitesboro itself, although the others apparently remained stockholders for a time; Vick, a very successful owner of commercial real estate in Wilson, served as president of the company.

Dunbar had almost certainly brought the project to White's attention in the first place; he and his wife, Alice, already owned substantial real estate in Cape May County, based in part on his extraordinary earnings as a poet and writer. But Dunbar was plagued by both poor health and marital problems, and soon moved to his native Dayton, Ohio, where he died in 1906. Vick retained an active interest in Whitesboro, visiting the town as late as 1916, although he never moved there; he, Wiley Bates, and Harriet Gibbs continued to live in their respective home states.[9]

8. "Six Hundred and Fifty Choice Lots for Sale," advertisement, WCA, 7 December 1901, and succeeding issues. George White was listed as "Secretary, Treasurer and General Manager," with Samuel H. Vick as president; title references were listed as Robert E. Hand of Erma, N.J.; Dr. Julius Way, clerk and ex-officio register of deeds, and J. B. Hoffman, Esquire, of Cape May Courthouse, N.J. White's firm sold the lot to the Middle Township Board of Education in 1909, according to Dorwart, *Cape May County*, 174.

9. Dorwart, *Cape May County*, 173. Samuel Vick's visit to Whitesboro is recounted in "Whitesboro Zephyrs," *Philadelphia Tribune*, 19 August 1916. He was accompanied by friends and his young son George White Vick, obviously named for his business partner and friend.

The site itself was located eight miles inland from Cape May City on the West New Jersey Railroad line, its center halfway between the coasts of the Atlantic Ocean and the Delaware Bay; in all, three railroads and two county turnpikes crossed the property. It was a lovely rustic setting "entirely free from malaria," if hardly an ideal one for those—such as White's own family—used to urban amenities, but that had never been the point of the settlement. In any event, the White family would spend many vacations there in a hotel they called the Odessa Inn in memory of the youngest daughter, who had died as an infant a decade earlier.[10]

Getting to Whitesboro from the west and north generally involved transportation from Philadelphia, eastward and then south along the West New Jersey Railroad, or by steamboat around the Delaware Bay coast. A new ferry service from Lewes, Delaware, was inaugurated in 1901, allowing visitors from the south to enter New Jersey at Cape May City, after taking the new Queen Anne's railroad east from Baltimore to Lewes. It may have been easier than migrating west by covered wagon, but it was still no easy route for struggling families with small children.[11]

But getting to the Whitesboro site was only one problem George White faced; by late 1901, when his new company began selling the Whitesboro lots, he had become financially overextended. Nearly a year after leaving Congress, he still relied on the limited income from his new law practice, plus his savings and investments, including his stock in the Coleman Cotton Manufacturing Company of Concord, North Carolina. Even after his efforts to obtain a Treasury auditorship had failed, he remained unwilling to move away from Washington; his younger children were attending school there, daughter Mamie at the Armstrong Manual High School and son George Jr. apparently in a private elementary school. Cora Lena's health had not improved, despite surgery in 1901 and continual treatment, including the services of a private nurse. Although the former congressman's net worth was estimated at $20,000 to $30,000, he had apparently poured most

10. "Six Hundred and Fifty Choice Lots for Sale," advertisement. The Odessa Inn was used as a summer hotel; it was mentioned by the *Washington Bee* in August 1905 as a "popular summer resort" with as many as fifty guests at a time. It was still in use as late as 1915, when White's older daughter, now Mrs. Della Garrett, came to Whitesboro for the summer.

11. Dorwart, *Cape May County*, 167–8, 195. The Queen Anne ferry service folded in 1904, and such service was not revived until the 1920s.

of his savings into the Whitesboro venture, which would keep his principal tied up for at least ten years; his only other known assets consisted of his home in Washington and various real-estate holdings in North Carolina.[12]

A confidential letter from Cora Lena White to Booker T. Washington, dated January 3, 1902, reveals the family's financial distress in delicate but heartrending clarity. George White's penchant for privacy and dignity would have prevented him from asking for such help, but his invalid wife felt herself to be the burden. "My husband does not know that I am writing you," she said at one point. "If so, I fear he would object, not that he does not desire your help—but he is so afraid he might annoy you, knowing that you are importuned by so many."[13]

Her condition was so weak that she was forced to dictate the handwritten five-page letter, certainly to a trusted confidante, perhaps her stepdaughter Della. She recounted her "protracted illness," including "a very serious surgical operation (from which I have not yet recovered)" and the "exhorbitant [sic] price of nurse and doctor's bills" as the primary cause of the family's precarious situation. Her husband had never been extravagant, but her illness and other "necessary expenses" had, she explained, made it impossible for him to save anything during his term in Congress.[14]

Only the secure income of "some federal position . . . would enable him to get his affairs in good shape," Mrs. White lamented, never mentioning the Whitesboro venture, perhaps all too aware of its speculative nature. Her husband's legal practice was his only source of income, and it was "very poor— one barely makes a living after years of hard work." Yet if Washington was not

12. Sandbeck, *The Historic Architecture of New Bern*, 286; Reid, "A Biography," 48; White, *Who's Who in Philadelphia*, 88. White had sold the family home in Tarboro in 1900 and the house on Johnson Street in New Bern in 1903; he continued to own the 18th Street house in Washington and a farm near Tarboro in 1912, as well as the Lombard Street building. "George Henry White," *The Biographical Encyclopedia of the United States, 1901* (n.p.), 408. This is the only mention of White's involvement in the Coleman enterprise, which apparently went out of business before Warren Clay Coleman died in 1904. Coleman, a wealthy black merchant, had opened the nation's first black-owned textile mill in Concord in 1895; see Kenzer, *Enterprising Southerners*, 76, and Crowe et al., *A History of African Americans in North Carolina*, 107.

13. Cora L. White (Mrs. Geo. H.) to BTW, 3 January 1902, BTWP.

14. Ibid. "You no doubt know that I have been an invalid for over three years," Cora Lena White wrote Washington. Her poor health "has made such a drain on my husband's financial resources that he has not yet recovered from it."

a lucrative site for a black lawyer, he could only fare worse in the South by "having to contend with the jurors—most of whom are white—Mr. White being somewhat aggressive, though a good man, of course—you know the consequences." She was puzzled at the Republican Party's lack of support for him after his years of hard work, "without any remuneration whatever, and now when he is so much in need of help."[15]

Mrs. White had opened her letter by asking Washington to "grant my prayer if you can possibly do," then gradually leading up to her real mission a page later. "I know that you have great influence with the President [Theodore Roosevelt], and I want to *beg of you* if you think him worthy to please say a word in his behalf to the President" (emphasis in original). It was a risky matter to raise, since Cora Lena had no way of knowing if Roosevelt would agree to appoint her husband, even with Washington's recommendation. White had been told by the White House in early October that "a letter from you [Washington] would greatly strengthen my chances," but would not seal the appointment.[16]

His wife was obviously unaware that George White had almost certainly discussed the matter with Washington privately three months earlier, during the latter's visit to the White House. Whether she was ignorant or her husband discreet, we cannot be sure. But she was not naïve, in any event; her specific request, two pages later, proved to be a shrewd one, if nearly impossible for the new president to grant: "Do you think the President would give Mr. White Mr. Lyons's place and Mr. Lyons Mr. Rucker's in Atlanta, which pays quite as much—I know neither of the latter are your friends since your 'Atlanta speech.' I know also that when you recommend a man for a place it is not whether he is *friend* or enemy—but how much good he will do or reflect on the race"[17] (emphasis in original).

Georgia native Judson W. Lyons, who had served as register of the U.S. Treasury since 1897, was now up for reappointment by Roosevelt. But Georgia leaders still remembered and resented Lyons's "impertinence" in seeking appointment as postmaster of Augusta, which McKinley had initially agreed to

15. Ibid.

16. Ibid.; George H. White to BTW, 7 October 1901, BTWP.

17. Cora L. White to BTW, 3 January 1902, BTWP. Rucker served as federal collector of internal revenue for the Georgia district. Cora Lena White's reference to salary level evoked the 1901 exchange between the *Colored American* and *Cleveland Gazette* over White's refusal of a deputy auditorship, with half the $5,000 salary of a congressman.

but had ultimately withdrawn under strong protests; no appointment for Lyons in Atlanta would sit well with either Democrats or lily-white Republicans in that state. Rucker, Georgia's most prominent black Republican politician as well as the most popular barber in Atlanta, was certainly not the best choice for a trade.

More interesting than the actual request, perhaps, is Mrs. White's assessment of Booker T. Washington's brand of power politics. As the wife of one of the capital's more astute observers, of course, Cora Lena may simply have been repeating what she had heard, although all educated blacks were familiar with Dr. Washington's emergence as both premier educator and presidential adviser. With this section of her letter, the writer was attempting to answer all the leader's possible objections in advance—all but the one she dared not consider or mention, even to herself: the personal opposition of President Roosevelt himself.[18]

"We were so anxious to stay here to let the children complete their grades," she said in a resigned tone, "but unless Mr. White gets work soon, we will of *necessity* have to go." Her plea had now sunk to its lowest, most pitiable level: "You know human nature so well—you can readily see my anxiety—then knowing that it was *all* for *me*. If I could only *have a little hope*" (emphasis in original). Her sense of self-pity was palpable, bordering on the pathetic. Still, she managed to regain her composure at the end, closing with a brief personal note for Washington's family, for his continued success "and that also of Tuskegee."[19]

Cora Lena White probably did not tell her husband of her letter until she had received a reply. It came the third week of January, and the response was careful but frank: there was, unfortunately, nothing Booker T. Washington could do. The letter itself is not available, but George White's response—on behalf of his wife, who was "quite sick, and unable to write"—made it clear that he had read the letter, that he appreciated Washington's candor, and that he now understood where the obstacle lay: with North Carolina's senior senator, his old colleague Jeter Pritchard.[20]

18. Ibid. No record exists in the massive BTW papers of any response to White's October 1901 letter to Washington; the two probably discussed the matter in person instead, since Washington had been in the city at the White House for the now-notorious dinner a week after receiving White's letter.

19. Ibid.

20. George H. White to BTW, 22 January 1902, BTWP. "I was permitted to read your letter of recent date addressed to Mrs. White," he began. "Had I been advised of her intentions, I would

"Yes, an evil one in no less personage perhaps, than Senator J. C. Pritchard, whom I helped to elevate from obscurity from the mountain crags of western North Carolina to his present-day position, is the one who takes delight in misrepresenting and speaking disparagingly of me," White said in his January 22 reply to Washington's letter, "because I have had the temerity to object to his wholesale slaughter of the rights of our people in North Carolina." Despite Pritchard's loss of a political base in North Carolina, he remained an influential Republican leader, and was a strong supporter of Roosevelt. "*If the President's mind is made up from his* [Pritchard's] *statements against me*, I have no appeal, but will quietly bide my time"[21] (emphasis added).

Jeter Pritchard and George White had served together in the 1885 North Carolina General Assembly, White in the senate and Pritchard in the house, and both had been delegates to the 1896 and 1900 Republican national conventions. But they had apparently never been close friends, and moreover had strong political differences; lately Pritchard had become a leader in the party's lily-white movement, and had expressed strong opposition to blacks' holding political office. Such opposition had never extended, however, to Henry Cheatham, whom Pritchard had continued to support even when a scandal ended Cheatham's career; perhaps being a political ally to both brothers-in-law at once was simply not possible. White's anger at the 1900 invitation to Senator Pritchard to speak at the National Afro-American Council convention—extended over White's strong objections—had contained an element of strong personal distaste, as well, for the man he now characterized as "truly a wolf in sheep's clothing."[22]

White now devoted a lengthy paragraph to his personal admiration of Booker T. Washington. It was a rare moment of vulnerability for the former congressman, who now faced a difficult road on his own, with no support from any quarter in his own party, and with little practical help available from his

---

have persuaded her not to have written you, when your position so well known to me . . . leads your efforts in an entirely different direction from that of politics."

21. Ibid. Pritchard (1857–1921) ended his second Senate term in March 1903, having been reelected in January 1897. White had agreed to support Pritchard for reelection and Daniel Russell for governor in 1896 in exchange for James H. Young's support for the congressional nomination; he continued to support Russell afterward, but fell out with Pritchard by 1900.

22. Ibid. Pritchard spoke at the Indianapolis convention over White's strenuous objections, as recounted earlier; see the *Cleveland Gazette*, 8 September 1900.

few real friends. Whatever their philosophical differences, White seemed genuinely fond of the educator, and sincerely proud of his accomplishments, as he now took respectful pains to say: "I wish you to thoroughly understand that your friendship and good will toward me and mine is heartily reciprocated, and I never lose an opportunity to point with pride to the noble achievements you have made in behalf of our people within the last score of years. I always take my hat off to *the man who has accomplished something,* as in your case"[23] (emphasis in original).

He could not resist, however, taking a tired but pointed dig at a few others who had not been so interested in helping anyone but themselves. "I am heartily sick and tired of that hord [sic] of latter day would be leaders, who are great in windy speeches, preambles and resolutions, and absolute nonentities, when their efforts to accomplish something useful are demanded." He gave no hint of their identities, but one suspects the list would have included more than one black church leader, perhaps a few journalists, and even a handful of those still holding appointive office.[24] He may not have confined his list to black leaders, of course, for he had long felt that white Republicans such as Pritchard had misused blacks as political pawns before unceremoniously dumping them. There was no revenge in his comment, only disgust tinged with relief that he was finally out of politics, on the national level, at least, and could now speak with no fear of recrimination from those who had offered nothing but empty words to a brother in need. Ever the gentleman, he chose only to express his deep feelings of disappointment, rather than any rage or bitterness.

Washington's own alliances within the black community were beginning to fray, under fire as he was from radical left-wing leaders and militant journalists like William Monroe Trotter, editor of the new *Boston Guardian.* Washington's close ties to the National Afro-American Council—some said he controlled it completely through the vaunted "Tuskegee Machine," his nationwide body of disciples—complicated his relationships with some influen-

23. Ibid.

24. Reid, "Post-Congressional Career," 368. Reid believes White meant militant black intellectuals, such as W. E. B. Du Bois and William Monroe Trotter. Among others he might have been referring to were National Afro-American Council president Bishop Walters or Bishop Arnett, both of whom had alienated BTW; editor Harry C. Smith of the *Cleveland Gazette;* and certain Democratic black journalists.

tial members of the black aristocracy, many of whom later were instrumental in forming the National Association for the Advancement of Colored People (NAACP) essentially as a counterweight to Washington's influence.[25]

George White was never part of the fabled "Tuskegee Machine," but he retained a strong degree of personal influence as an independent force. His views on the reduced political circumstances of black citizens were well known, receiving renewed emphasis in the nation's black community at least, in an anthology of black literature published early in 1902. He shared a topic in the book, edited by Daniel W. Culp, with longtime friend T. Thomas Fortune: "What Should Be the Negro's Attitude in Politics?" Their viewpoints, never identical, were nonetheless complementary; although Fortune had never held an elective office, he had been quite active in three national organizations, and had campaigned—however reluctantly—for McKinley's reelection in 1900.[26]

White had never publicly attacked the Republican Party for its inconsistent treatment of blacks, and he chose his words carefully now. It was his first lengthy statement on the subject since leaving Congress in March 1901; a year later, his mood had changed. He now had bitter words for the "great majority" of "those claiming to be our best friends" during Reconstruction: "those who had been instrumental in obtaining our freedom," including both federal army bureaucrats and "many adventurers who followed in the wake of that army."[27]

Some of the "new friends" were sincere, he noted, but most were "wholly unscrupulous and worked upon the ignorance, inexperience, and gullibility of the Negro, overtime," to gain political control in the South before pillaging the conquered states and returning to the North. In their wake, the South's black residents and their white neighbors had inevitably been estranged from each other; "the black man was left in the South to endure disfranchisement,

25. Willard Gatewood gives an illuminating glimpse into the era's social and political divisions within the race in "Aristocrats of Color and Jim Crow," a chapter of his *Aristocrats of Color*, 300–22. The biracial NAACP was formed in 1909–1910; Washington remained hostile to it until his death in 1915, according to Gatewood, 318.

26. "What Should Be the Negro's Attitude in Politics?" Topic 13 in Culp, *Twentieth Century Negro Literature*, 224–7.

27. Ibid. White declined to use the term "carpetbaggers," but minced no words in describing them as "human cormorants [who fled] to live in ease and splendor on the results of their pillage."

torture and murder on account of the malice and hatred begotten from his first political experience."[28]

White showed his clear distaste for the corruption, duplicity, and "Jungoism" that had inevitably flowed from the postwar turbulence. "No fair-minded white man would expect to find complete political perfection among a people thus treated," yet blacks had been unfairly singled out for deprivation of the right to vote. All that black citizens now sought was equal treatment and an honest opportunity to prove themselves worthy. "The negro's political attitude should be a firm stand for the right, the support of honest men for office [and] a complete repudiation of any party . . . who seeks [to] hamper or degrade him politically," White wrote, and he should "identify himself with that political party which proves to be the most friendly towards him. There is very little in a name."[29]

In a word, black citizens should work for practical results, since voting based on historical loyalty to the Republican Party was no longer sensible. Such action "will necessitate a division of the Negro vote"—forcing the two major parties to compete for black votes—because the franchise was too valuable to sell or sacrifice; "no right which man enjoys aside from his household should be guarded more sacredly." The time was "ripe for the colored American *to think and act for himself.*" If blacks were still forced to prove themselves worthy of equal rights, this was not too high a price to pay; they must put themselves in "a position to command respect and proper recognition. He who would have equity must first *do* equity"[30] (emphasis added).

In the meantime, the key to long-term success was perseverance, and White counseled each black citizen to "live as an example to his neighbors, ally himself with the best men in the community . . . and the day must certainly come when his rights—political and civil—will be conceded to him." If his advice sounded "rather Utopian," he said, so be it, for only dedicated idealists could restore the purity of the ballot and preserve the republic, for "right must some day prevail." White had now exchanged the garb of a politician for the mantle of a less worldly leader, if only his people would take notice.[31]

White's life since leaving Congress had fallen into the normal patterns he

28. Ibid., 226.
29. Ibid.
30. Ibid., 227.
31. Ibid.

would generally follow as long as he continued to live in Washington: speeches to local civic and literary groups, trips to New Jersey to oversee the development of Whitesboro, occasional trips to nearby cities for speeches and meetings. Otherwise, his days were consumed by the irregular demands of his law practice and of the land development company; rumors of a year earlier that he might begin a law practice elsewhere—New York, Philadelphia, even Ohio—proved to be groundless. He tended to stay near home whenever possible, since Cora Lena's health was no better than before, and she apparently did not travel at all now. Daughter Della, twenty-two, had taken a position as a clerk in the Census Bureau sometime in 1901; she was ill for two weeks in January 1902, but returned to work by the end of the month. All three children lived at home now, fourteen-year-old Mamie as a high school student, also enrolled at Harriet Gibbs's Washington Conservatory of Music, and eight-year-old George Jr., a budding prodigy, preparing to enter high school quite early.[32]

Their father took an active interest in raising his children, and occasionally gave advice to other parents. He reportedly delivered a "practical address on 'Our Children'" in late January at the People's Lyceum in Washington, emphasizing the "necessity of firm character, thrifty habits and practical education" to a large audience. He next spoke at a religious fund-raising event at Ebenezer Methodist Episcopal Church in the city's southeastern quadrant in early February, where his topic was not listed in newspaper coverage, but his other speeches that month dealt, no doubt, with political matters. He addressed separate groups on two occasions in Brooklyn, N.Y., where a reported "snub," based on Associated Press rumors of a "division within the colored citizens," was quickly dismissed as "without foundation" by the Colored American: "his reception was cordial and unanimous." A second speech delivered to the Fleet Street Church of Brooklyn drew a "big house," the same newspaper noted two weeks later: "Mr. White is deservedly popular in New York."[33]

32. Washington Bee, 25 January 1902; WCA, 1 February 1902. As late as mid-December, the Bee had speculated on White's possible move to Philadelphia. Both the Bee and the Colored American noted Della's leave of absence from the census office and her subsequent return to work. The Colored American continued to mention sales of the Whitesboro lots throughout the winter of 1901–1902.

33. "Mr. White on 'Our Children,'" WCA, 1 February 1902; "A Splendid Showing," ibid., 22 February 1902; "Mr. White Not Snubbed," editorial, ibid., 15 February 1902; "City Paragraphs," ibid., 1 March 1902.

White also continued his association with the Afro-American Council, on both the national and local levels. Having been elected president of the city's local council, he officiated at a celebration of Afro-American Council Day on March 16, delivering a "ringing address" at the Second Baptist Lyceum, one of his favorite speaking sites. (No longer being listed among the officers on the council's official letterhead, he seems to have carried through on his threat to resign from his national vice-presidency, but was again elected third vice-president at the national convention in Minneapolis in 1902.) Two weeks later, he made a short address in the same capacity at a public mass meeting of the National Colored Personal Liberty League, held just a block from the White House; his speech recalled the subjects dear to him while in the Congress, touching upon the "suffrage question" and seeking the league's endorsement of a proposed congressional bill "to investigate the amount of property owned by blacks."[34]

At the end of April, White presented a lengthy paper entitled "What of the Future?" before the Bethel Literary and Historical Association, one of the city's largest and most esteemed black groups. Here he expanded upon several of the interrelated themes he and Booker T. Washington had always favored—such as black economic self-reliance, relevant education, and racial unity in business, among others—but went on to include "sensible action in politics," which Washington would have eschewed. Still, White's paper was a characteristic call for action that was utilitarian, not radical; he counseled "the importance of taking a practical view of our situation and then exercising judgment in the application of our force," advocating "a footing in the soil, investments in the great enterprises of the country, possession of homes, [and] education that can be utilized at once," among other behaviors deemed essential for the race.[35]

It was not his first presentation before the Bethel Association membership, but it was a qualitatively different performance from that given at a joint symposium in January 1900, "The Negro in Politics," along with P. B. S.

34. "City Paragraphs," WCA, 22 March 1902; Alexander Walters to E. J. Scott, 2 April 1902, BTWP; "Personal Liberty League's Meeting," WCA, 5 April 1902. On stationery used by Walters in April 1902, the Reverend Ernest Lyons of Maryland was listed as third vice-president, the post to which White had been elected the previous August.

35. "At Bethel Literary: Hon. George H. White Talks of the Future," WCA, 3 May 1902.

Pinchback and Robert H. Terrell. White's earlier segment had been devoted to "His Present Political Status," and the powerful arguments of the "legislative field general" had drawn warm applause from a distinguished audience. Despite its name, the Bethel Association did not restrict itself to academic or theoretical topics, preferring to focus on themes that "illuminated the 'progress of the race'" or addressed public issues of interest to blacks, sometimes issuing public appeals on critical issues such as lynching and racial discrimination. Its meetings were open to the public at large, while actual membership was not limited to the black aristocracy, but included middle-class blacks as well.[36]

White's speeches and papers indicate his dedication to uplifting his race. But the real proof, in the words of W. Calvin Chase, lay in the strong example he was setting: "Get trades and get land. Washington and White's methods. This is the way to solve the race problem." Chase's *Bee* was not always flattering to Booker T. Washington, or even to George White, in part because of his close association with Edward Cooper, whom Chase disdained. Chase had, however, strongly criticized the National Afro-American Council for refusing to elect the former congressman as its president: "He has the respect and confidence of the [Negro] people and what the Council wants is a strong man like Mr. White at its head."[37]

For the moment, Chase was a White admirer, in large part because of the Whitesboro venture. White was spending a significant amount of his time in Cape May County, supervising the small-scale development under way on the land his company had purchased. He devoted at least one week in March to an on-site inspection, and returned for another visit in April, after which he recounted construction work to a prospective property-buyer: "We have had a surveyor and choppers laying out streets and locating corners for some time." White also met with Booker T. Washington at a groundbreaking ceremony

36. "The Negro in Politics," ibid., 6 January 1900; Gatewood, *Aristocrats of Color*, 214–5. Pinchback had spoken on the Negro's past, while principal Terrell had spoken on the race's future. Bethel was one of the largest such organizations in the nation; other "L&H" groups existed in Baltimore, Kansas City, and St. Louis.

37. "Wither Are We Drifting?" *Washington Bee*, 12 October 1901; "Solving the Problem: Ex-Congressman White Purchases Land," editorial, *Washington Bee*, 2 November 1901. The *Bee* praised White's speech before the Second Baptist Lyceum in early October, when White and others recounted the actions of the council convention.

there during the late spring, where he and Joseph Vance discussed project details at length.[38]

As knowledgeable observers were almost certainly aware, the Whitesboro development was broadly inspired by the Tuskegee leader's philosophy, whose influence on White was steadily growing. At least three other all-black industrial and
agricultural communities of this type also sprang up in southern New Jersey, all
inspired by Washington's widely published thoughts on the subject. The nearby
Woodbine community for Jewish-American immigrants had a strong influence
on the design of Whitesboro, including its lot plans and wide boulevards;
Washington took a characteristic interest in Woodbine, as well, even visiting
that town when it became a separate New Jersey borough in 1903.[39]

The Cape May County development, still unnamed, had personal rele-
vance for George White; he had owned land in the area since at least 1899,
and may have hoped to retire there someday. He planned to build a hotel in
the town, and was actively planning to build homes for those who purchased
land and moved to the community. Cora Lena's younger brother, Earnest
Cherry, was one of the first to purchase land in what would become Whitesboro; members of the extended family of George White's stepmother were also
among the earliest settlers, with at least three Spaulding families listed in the
town's 1910 census. Carpenter Willie Spaulding, a nephew of Mary Anna
White, became the site manager for White's firm after his arrival in late 1902
or early 1903. Spaulding's brother Wiley, also a carpenter, had migrated to
Whitesboro by 1905, and a younger relative, John, came after 1908. Each was
married, with a total by 1910 of eight children among them, including five
born in New Jersey.[40]

38. "City Paragraphs," *WCA*, 29 March 1902; George H. White to Mr. General Askew, 17
April 1902, reprinted in Reid, "A Biography," 175; *Cape May Star*, 21 June 1902.

39. Dorwart, *Cape May County*, 173; Richard R. Wright Jr., "Negro Communities in New
Jersey," *Southern Workman*, July 1908. Dorwart cites editor Robert Hand's comments in the *Cape
May Star*: "It will be an agricultural colony on the same plan as . . . Woodbine." On the view that
Washington visited Woodbine in 1903, Dorwart cites Olive S. Barry's paper, "Woodbine, New
Jersey" (footnote, 314). The other African American communities in southern New Jersey were
Gouldtown, Springtown, and Snowhill, according to Wright.

40. U.S. Census, manuscript on microfilm, Cape May County, N.J., 1910. Willie Spaulding
was thirty-seven years old in 1910; he and Wiley Spaulding, thirty-six, had been born in
Columbus County about the time White left for Howard University. The two sons of G. S.
Spaulding were either uncles or older brothers of John Spaulding, age twenty-three in 1910.

Willie Spaulding was the first permanent resident of the settlement, serving as supervisor for the development firm and also as the town's first postmaster, according to a family history written by his son Daniel. Three other North
Carolina natives had already purchased lots there by the time Spaulding arrived: Henry S. Beaman, General Scott Askew, and Earnest Cherry, White's
brother-in-law. Cherry and Askew were farmers, while Beaman established
the village's first country store. According to one historian, a total of fifty-
seven building lots were sold in the first wave of development, mostly to settlers from North Carolina, although at least one Virginia family was listed in
the state's 1905 census. How fast the town grew is not clear; overall estimates
of the early population vary widely, ranging from one hundred in 1905 to
three hundred in 1908, and as high as eight hundred in 1906; only the lowest
figure, however, seems reasonable. In any event, the population was growing
and social infrastructure was needed; at least two churches (Baptist and
Methodist-Episcopal) and a school had been constructed by 1909, on land
provided by George White's firm.[41]

Appropriately, the small town was soon named in honor of its founder.
The original name of the town appears to have been simply "White," but this
had changed to Whitesboro by March of 1902, according to one newspaper
account. Like most pioneer towns, however, its economic identity took much
longer to develop; only the construction of a railroad spur to the Atlantic
Coast in early 1903, across land sold by White's firm to the Atlantic City
Railroad Company, provided jobs outside the housing construction industry
during the first year. But by 1908, a sawmill was opened by a businessman
named Endicott, providing local laborers with much-needed opportunities for
nonfarm employment in manufacturing fish cages. Cape May County itself
was undergoing an economic boom after a long depression, although much of
the prosperity was felt only in the Cape May City area; still, the county's population increased by almost 50 percent between 1900 and 1910.[42]

Their arrival dates in Whitesboro are approximate, based on the birthplaces and birth dates of
their children from the census.

41. Recollections of Daniel W. Spaulding, Cape May County Library, cited by Dorwart,
Cape May County (footnote, 314). Spaulding, born in Whitesboro in 1909, was the youngest of
four children born to Willie and Hattie Spaulding before the 1910 census; his older brother
Theodore was the only sibling born outside New Jersey.

42. U.S. Census, Cape May County, 1900 and 1910; Dorwart, *Cape May County*, 180. The

Whitesboro proper was crossed by three railroad lines: the West Jersey Railroad and the Reading Seashore Railroad, both of which ran southwest through the center of the narrow Cape May peninsula, and a short eastward spur to Holly Beach and Wildwood on the Atlantic coast. The town's small station was a stop on the West Jersey line, just south of Burleigh; the Reading Seashore line was located just east of the town center, with a station at Wildwood Junction. With a surfeit of rail transport available, normal roads were a lower commercial priority at the turn of the century in this remote, rural setting; Cape May Court House, just a few miles north of Whitesboro, was already linked by two turnpikes to its outlying communities, and the barrier islands, of course, required bridges to the mainland for horse-drawn commerce. But the instant popularity of the automobile fueled a massive road- and bridge-building project in the county during the decade before World War I, as local leaders raced to keep up with the sudden demands of thousands of weekend vacationers. Dirt wagon paths and narrow causeways were replaced and upgraded with nearly one hundred miles of county roadways, improved by the construction of gravel- and hard-surface roads capable of carrying sustained vehicular traffic. The projects may also have provided regular employment for manual laborers in Whitesboro, few of whom owned or even needed automobiles, but those who profited most were contractors, gravel pit operators, and certain local politicians, according to local history.[43]

From his vantage point in Washington, George White could easily reach Whitesboro by train and ferry in less than a day's travel. He spent enough time in Cape May County that the *Colored American* lightly teased him, saying he "might write" a book entitled "Some Reasons Why I Should Be Mayor of Whitesboro, N.J."[44] His law practice was only sporadically demanding, and he seemed more comfortable operating as a real-estate developer, partly because it allowed him to spend more time outdoors.

---

county's population was 19,745 in 1910, up from 13,201 in 1900, or a 49.6 percent increase. Most of the population increase came on the county's barrier islands.

43. Dorwart, *Cape May County*, 111–4, 149, 268. The West Jersey Railroad also had an eastward spur from Burleigh to Anglesea and the Holly Beach/Wildwood area; this line, originally built in 1883 as the Anglesea Railroad, was absorbed by the larger West Jersey line five years later, along with the Cape May and Millville Railroad, the county's first line, built in 1863. The Reading Seashore Railroad merged with the Pennsylvania Railroad in 1933, after which the spur to Wildwood was discontinued.

44. "Books They Might Write," *WCA*, 1 March 1902.

White seems to have been devoting much of his legal time to just one cause: work on the disfranchisement test cases from Alabama and Louisiana, now wending their way toward the U.S. Supreme Court. He had worked on the Louisiana case with four other lawyers—one black and three white—on a preliminary basis since late 1900, although the biracial group seemed to experience much difficulty in agreeing on a course of action; one chronicler of the era says they "spent more of their time squabbling with each other than in prosecuting the case." His black colleague was Frederick L. McGhee of St. Paul, Minnesota, a leader in the Afro-American Council but a Democrat and Catholic, soon to be a founder of the Niagara Movement; McGhee, White, and Jesse Lawson comprised the council's bureau on legislation and legal affairs.[45]

Their white counterparts were a gifted, if eclectic, mix of regional talent: Albert E. Pillsbury, former attorney general of Massachusetts, who had assisted White in designing the strategy for the antilynching bill in early 1901; Arthur A. Birney, a former U.S. attorney for the District of Columbia; and Armand Romain, an experienced lawyer from New Orleans. Birney, now in private practice in Washington, was apparently the lead attorney, and had requested a sizable retainer ($500) as early as October 1900 from the council; Birney "wants the best legal talent associated with him in Louisiana and at Washington," Jesse Lawson wrote Booker T. Washington in late 1900.[46]

Booker T. Washington's involvement in the cases was a highly confidential matter, known only to a "handful of persons who . . . kept it carefully hidden." He had encouraged the Afro-American Council to face the disfranchisement issue in late 1899, and George White and others had begun helping to raise funds for the expected appeals; in the spring of 1900, he had even met privately with the group's lawyers on one occasion in Washington, D.C. Lawson wrote Washington regularly thereafter about the progress of the cases, and the educator occasionally heard directly from the principals; Pillsbury, for instance, notified him in July 1901 that "our Louisiana case is begun."[47]

45. Louis R. Harlan, *Booker T. Washington: The Making of a Black Leader, 1856–1901* (New York: Oxford University Press, 1972), 297–9; Harlan and Smock, *The BTW Papers*, 6:182 (note).

46. Jesse Lawson to BTW, 3 October 1900 and 10 October 1900, in Harlan and Smock, *The BTW Papers*, 5:647–9 and 5:651.

47. Harlan, *Booker T. Washington*, 298; A. E. Pillsbury to BTW, 30 July 1901, Harlan and Smock, *The BTW Papers*, 6:182.

Friction was not confined to the members of the legal team. In October 1902, former council chairman Alexander Walters, now chairman of the executive committee, complained to Booker T. Washington that he and T. Thomas Fortune "find it utterly impossible to work harmoniously with Hon. Geo. H. White and Mr. Lawson, chief factors in our Legal Bureau." Walters suggested that a new ten-member steering committee, to be chaired by Washington, assume control of the test cases. Nothing came of the suggestion, but it did not augur well for the future. Fortune, who had succeeded Walters as council chairman three months earlier, was preparing to leave for lengthy travels abroad, and the council seemed rudderless even before his departure; upon his return, an angry, divided Louisville audience literally booed Washington off the council's convention stage in 1903, despite Fortune's best efforts to contain anti-Bookerite sentiments.[48]

State ex rel *Ryanes v. Gleason* (112 La. 612 [1903]), as the case was known, involved a state challenge to the Louisiana constitution of 1898 by one Jordan Ryanes, a black native of Tennessee who had moved to New Orleans in 1860. In 1903 Ryanes lost at the state level, as expected, but for reasons not entirely clear, the lawyers chose not to appeal it to the federal courts. After four years of wrangling over strategy, it was a disappointing conclusion; the Tuskegeean was "somewhat disillusioned by the long struggle and never used a committee of lawyers again."[49]

Whether this had any effect on George White's relationship with Booker T. Washington is unclear. White corresponded occasionally with Tuskegee, including one curious note in December 1902, written as a recommendation on behalf of Richard W. Thompson, who sought a position on Washington's staff. White obviously wrote the letter at Thompson's request; what is not clear is why Thompson felt he needed White's assistance, since he had served

48. Alexander Walters to BTW, 24 October 1902, Harlan and Smock, *The BTW Papers*, 6:351; "The National Afro-American Council," 1–2. In an open letter to council members in December 1902, Fortune said he planned to be in the Far East for about six months, and would leave first vice-president William A. Pledger of Georgia in charge. Booker T. Washington had engineered Fortune's selection at the council's 1902 convention in St. Paul, Minnesota; Walters was "kicked upstairs" to the less important executive committee, on which Washington himself served.

49. Harlan and Smock, *The BTW Papers*, 6:182 (note); Louis R. Harlan, "The Secret Life of Booker T. Washington," *Journal of Southern History* 37 (August 1971): 393–416.

as a confidant to Washington for years. Still, White respectfully interceded, asking the favor "as a personal kindness to me."[50]

By 1904, White was seeking other opportunities for income. That year, he chose to take in active partners for the first time, joining forces with two of Washington's most enterprising and accomplished brothers, George F. T. Cook and John F. Cook Jr. Sons of a former slave turned minister and educator, both had been educated at Oberlin College in the 1850s and had returned to Washington, where John Cook eventually became District of Columbia tax collector and his younger brother the longtime superintendent of the District's black school system (1874–1900). Both were quite well off financially; John Cook was Washington's wealthiest black resident, reputedly worth more than $200,000 in 1895, while George was said to be worth $50,000 or more. When they became partners with White, both were well past normal retirement age yet still actively pursuing business interests: John, seventy-one, in real estate and George, sixty-nine, in construction.[51]

The firm of Cook, Cook and White manufactured bricks at a plant on the District of Columbia line, near the Chesapeake Railroad Station, with a reported capacity of fifty thousand "salmon, arch and red" bricks per day. White retained his office in the Capital Bank Building, 609 "F" Street, NW, and continued to advertise both his law practice and the Cape May development on his company letterhead. The partnership lasted until it was dissolved in late 1906, when White moved to Philadelphia; George Cook apparently continued to run the brick plant afterward, while John Cook opened a separate real estate office.[52]

It was an unusual alliance for White, who had always preferred to remain independent, particularly from the "colored aristocracy," which the Cook brothers personally exemplified. Both Cooks had drawn sharp criticism from black observers for their apparent snobbishness and lack of concern for the needs of lower-class blacks, and White had never been completely comfortable in the rarefied atmosphere of that essentially closed circle of aristocrats.

50. George H. White to BTW, 30 December 1902, BTWP.

51. "George F. T. Cook" and "John Francis Cook, Jr.," in *Dictionary of American Negro Biography*, 123, 126–7.

52. Cora L. White to BTW, 1 June 1904, BTWP; city directory, Washington, D.C., for 1906 and 1907. Mrs. White's letter was written on stationery using the letterhead of Cook, Cook and White.

But neither of the brothers had lost complete touch with their racial roots, as both continued to support black educational opportunities; John Cook, for instance, was a trustee of Howard University for the last thirty-five years of his life, a member of the District's board of education after 1906, and president of the local Samuel Coleridge-Taylor Choral Association. Although the Cooks' money undoubtedly initiated the partnership, such mutual personal interests may have kept the Cooks and George White on congenial personal terms after business interests brought them together.[53]

White's continuing interest in his own children's education occasioned a series of letters between his wife and Booker T. Washington between April and August of 1904. Mamie was due to graduate from the Manual Training High School that spring, and her parents both wished her to continue her education at a private school out of state; Cora Lena White had apparently raised the topic with Washington during a brief conversation sometime in late March, possibly when he was visiting the Whites' home. In his April 2 letter to Mrs. White, Washington asked for clarifying information: "You did not state whether it is your intention to give her a college course, or a course in a New England seminary—that is, whether you wish her to go to a school which prepares for college or to a seminary at which she might finish." This information would facilitate a recommendation for Mamie at an appropriate school, he assured her.[54]

Cora White had intuitively turned to the most powerful friend she had for assistance regarding such an important subject as her daughter's education. Mamie was a very good student with extensive musical training at the Washington Conservatory; she should attend a New England school if at all possible, preferably a school like the esteemed Bradford Academy in Massachusetts, where Washington's daughter Portia was a student. Gaining admittance to such an exclusive, virtually all-white school was difficult; even Washington could not guarantee it, but he was willing to make every effort to help, he said in a letter dated April 29, 1904, accompanying a copy of the Bradford catalogue: "before making any attempt to get your daughter into

53. Gatewood, *Aristocrats of Color*, 40. Despite their wealth and influence, "there was always 'a little prejudice' against the [Cook] family within the black community," according to Gatewood's 1884 citation from the *Washington Bee*.

54. BTW to Cora L. White, 2 April 1904, BTWP. Washington refers to "our conversation about your daughter."

[Bradford], I want to find out if the conditions laid down in the catalog are satisfactory to you. Of course, I am not sure what the decision of the authorities
will be, but there is no reason why an attempt may not be made. If she were
accepted there, I am sure she would be treated in a very satisfactory manner."[55]

Washington cautioned her against unrealistic hopes for Mamie's success,
however, since prejudice still existed against black students: "Of course, there
are some of those schools that are willing to admit one or two colored persons,
but object when more apply; it is not at all agreeable to have to deal with such
conditions, but we must face the facts." Portia, who was due to graduate in
1905, was "very anxious to have your daughter enter while she is there," and
had told her father that Mamie should try to enter by "next fall" (1904).[56]

While no copy of Mrs. White's intervening letter exists, it was clear from
her next letter that she had always hoped Bradford would be an agreeable
choice. Only a relapse of her chronic illness kept her from replying before
June 1, she now wrote: she and her husband had carefully reviewed the catalogue and "feel pleased with the Bradford Academy . . . [we] would be happy
to have you make further investigations" about the possibility of a fall 1904
admission date. They were also delighted at the prospect of Portia Washington as an on-site mentor.[57]

Washington quickly acted on their request, writing the Bradford principal
on June 10. His exceedingly tactful yet knowledgeable manner dissuaded
Laura Knott from taking his request before the Bradford board just yet, for he
asked for her personal opinion first: "There is a colored girl in Washington
who graduates this year from the Manual Training High School, and her parents are anxious to have her attend Bradford. . . . The family is a very respectable and intelligent one, and the girl . . . of good character and with
common sense. . . . I think Portia would be glad for the girl to share her room
next year."[58]

The eminent educator said he understood the potential "embarrassment in
having too many colored girls in one institution," and assured Miss Knott that
"I shall not misunderstand you" if she were completely frank about the situa-

55. BTW to Cora L. White, 29 April 1904, in Harlan and Smock, *The BTW Papers,* 7:491.
56. Ibid.
57. Cora L. White to BTW, 1 June 1904, BTWP.
58. BTW to Laura A. Knott, 10 June 1904, in Harlan and Smock, *The BTW Papers,* 7:527.

tion. "The parents of the girl view the matter in the same manner that I do, and they have suggested that I write you." Knott's reply, cited in Washington's papers, was candid; the school was "already considering another black girl," of which Washington quickly advised the Whites.[59]

Since Bradford policy discouraged "more than one or two [colored girls] there during the same year," perhaps the Whites might consider a school at Northfield, Massachusetts. Mindful of his previous correspondence with Mrs. White, Washington delicately referred to the expenses of the Moody School, which "would be much less than at any other school in New England, I think." He offered to raise the matter with Mr. Moody if they wished, since he was going to Northfield in the near future from his summer home nearby at South Weymouth. But the Moody School was not acceptable to the mother, who had heard that "the religious influence was almost oppressive," she wrote in mid-July. She regretted the lost opportunity for Bradford, but refused to "despair, however, because I know you will assist me in getting her in some good school."[60]

Mrs. White enclosed advertisements for two other schools, one of which "was very good years ago" according to Miss Mattie Shadd, a friend from the city's black aristocracy, and the other a school for which she had received a catalogue. She wrote that she did not know "whether either of these schools [Bridgewater or Abbot] take colored girls," but she hoped Washington would have a suitable recommendation about one of them "unless you can find something better."[61]

Still in South Weymouth on August 9, Washington countered with one new school and a repeated plea for waiting a year and then once again considering Bradford in 1905. Massachusetts's coeducational Cushing Academy at Ashburnham "has the reputation of being a very good institution," but his own wife had warned him "that you might not like it on account of its being a mixed [gender] school." He felt sure Mamie would be admitted to Cushing, but he still felt that the far better choice, where she "would receive every consideration and would be kindly and sympathetically treated by all," was Bradford, "a school I can recommend without any reservation." If Mamie were

59. BTW to Cora L. White, 8 July 1904, BTWP.

60. Ibid.; Cora L. White to BTW, 12 July 1904, BTWP.

61. Cora L. White to BTW, 12 July 1904, BTWP. Mattie Shadd was a member of the wealthy Shadd family, whose money had come from a highly successful catering business.

willing to study privately or in Washington for a year, he could definitely "arrange now for her admission" in 1905.[62]

Mrs. White's August 13 reply apparently ended her correspondence with the Tuskegee president. The last letter began brightly, and was the longest she had written him since 1902; it would be the last one only due to the rapid decline in her health that soon followed. She very much liked the idea of sending her daughter to Bradford, "but cannot say definitely now that she can go next year." If he could arrange to hold a place open for her at Bradford, Cora Lena would soon give him a decisive answer, she said. In the meantime, she had been in touch with a well-known school in Ohio that had no difficulty admitting black students: Oberlin. Her daughter had recently been accepted at the Oberlin Conservatory of Music, and now she was waiting to hear from the institution's college department.

Mrs. White had misgivings, but felt she had little choice in the matter: "It is not the school that I would like her to attend, but it seemed just then that it was the best we could afford. We get no help. And the reason that it is not decided yet [is] because I cannot consent for Mamie to take music only. She must continue her studies as well. . . . I do not wish to keep her home because she has so much to do that her advantages are not what they should be."[63]

Evidently referring to her own illness and her daughter's domestic responsibilities, Cora Lena betrayed her frustration with her own failing health. Otherwise, Washington's suggestion for a year of private study was a sound one, she said, and they would probably undertake it if Oberlin did not accept Mamie into the academic program. In any event, "I will know in a short while, though, because Miss Harriet A. Gibbs is there" at Oberlin. Cora Lena then apologized for something she had agreed to do but regretted afterwards; the disjointed tale involved referral of a gentleman she did not know ("I think it was Mr. Hodges") to Washington for unspecified assistance, perhaps to have his own child recommended to a school. She abruptly seemed forgetful, nervous—a sign, possibly, of mental confusion as her disease progressed.[64]

---

62. BTW to Cora L. White, 9 August 1904, in Harlan and Smock, *The BTW Papers*, 8:41–2.
63. Cora L. White to BTW, 13 August 1904, BTWP.
64. Ibid. Harriet A. Gibbs, a graduate of Oberlin, was a well-known musician who operated

"I have never mentioned anything contained in our communications," she wrote with evident unease. "The only thing that I have written was a letter to a friend of Dr. Francis Grimké and wife," at their urging; the gentleman "used to be, and is now, so far as I know, a friend of theirs. . . . I inadvertently referred him to you without your permission." The awe in which most of his acquaintances and friends held him rarely made Washington a target for surprise referrals, and he did not take such matters lightly; the awe bordered on fear at times, for his occasionally vindictive nature was well known. Mrs. White's scramble to apologize was curiously pitiful for such a proud and refined woman: "It never occurred to me until the very morning I received your letter. I humbly beg your pardon. It was [a] liberty that I never should have taken and I assure you that nothing of the kind shall ever occur again. It was very thoughtless of me."[65]

Why the Grimkés had not approached Washington themselves, but instead forced the ailing woman to act as their intermediary, is not clear. Grimké, a graduate of Princeton and a member of a fine old Charleston, S.C., family, had been minister of the famous 15th Street Presbyterian Church since 1889; his position as a powerful racial and social leader was unquestioned. The Whites had attended services at Grimké's church, arguably the nation's most prestigious black Presbyterian congregation, and perhaps Mrs. White felt unable to refuse such a harmless request. According to her explanation, "they did not write themselves . . . because this church here is self-supporting and they did not like to be under obligations."

In retrospect, this seems almost implausible, although Washington did expect his favors to create a mutually conducive environment, and the Grimkés may not, in fact, have wished to become beholden to him. The outspoken and politically active Dr. Grimké was certainly not bashful when it came to arguing for the reward of merit regardless of social class; he rarely hesitated to criticize anyone for social pretensions, although outsiders did remark perceptively on the lighter-than-average complexion and disproportionately high social standing of his affluent 15th Street parishioners.[66]

---

the Washington Conservatory as well as an investor in the Whitesboro development project; she was a daughter of Judge Mifflin Wistar Gibbs.

65. Ibid.

66. Gatewood, *Aristocrats of Color*, 286–7. The church had 350 members in 1901, almost all

Whatever the reason for the request, Cora Lena White now feared the consequences of her action, perhaps more for her long-suffering husband than for anyone else. George White now included Booker T. Washington among his legal clients, and any disruption of their regular income was clearly a worry for his wife. As for the immediate situation, she fortunately required no further help from Washington, for her doubts about Oberlin were soon resolved. By early October, Mamie was accepted into the Oberlin Academy, and was slated to "leave soon to continue her musical and dramatic study" in Ohio, according to the *Colored American;* before leaving, she gave a piano recital at the Washington Conservatory, the newspaper wrote on October 15. "She is a young pianist of note-worthy talent. There is in her every performance a refined simplicity which proves an irresistible charm. Her whole program was played with fine intelligence and artistic finish and reflected real credit upon her training."[67]

Still not quite seventeen, Mamie enrolled in due course at Oberlin, and was apparently in the middle of her first winter term in Ohio when she received the sad news of her mother's death. Cora Lena died at home on 18th Street on January 19, 1905, despite the years of "skillful attention of some of the most competent physicians in the city [and] the very best attention from her faithful husband and intimate friends and relatives." She had turned forty a month earlier, and had been married to George for slightly less than eighteen years.

W. Calvin Chase described Cora Lena White as "a lady of refinement and great musical ability" and "one of the most remarkable women in the country," praising her "noble qualities and womanly virtues." Her funeral, held two days later at the Whites' home on 18th Street, was attended by the "leading citizens in the State," presumably North Carolina, or perhaps the District; if the guest list also included Booker T. Washington, there was no mention of it.[68]

---

highly educated, high-ranking government bureaucrats and socialites. "There are probably not a dozen black persons who attend that church. Not that they are unwelcome, but it just happens that way," Gatewood quotes "an old black resident of Washington" as saying in 1907.

67. "Washington Conservatory of Music," *WCA,* 15 October 1904. The spelling "Mammie" was probably a typographical error, not uncommon in this newspaper.

68. "Mrs. Geo. H. White," editorial, *Washington Bee,* 4 February 1905; "What I Saw and Heard," *Washington Bee,* 1 April 1905. "Mr. White has the profound sympathy of THE BEE, who

The *Washington Post* was polite, even gracious to the man it had attacked so derisively four years earlier, reporting Mrs. White's death in a respectful obituary that noted her husband's former status, her two children, and her own father's name. Its only minor error was obviously based on information supplied by the family in haste; both the *Post* and its competitor, the *Evening Star*, said her body would be "taken to the former home at Tarboro, N.C., for burial." Cora Lena White was buried instead in New Bern's Greenwood Cemetery, next to the grave of her infant daughter, Odessa, who had died thirteen years earlier.[69]

---

knows him to be a faithful husband and a kind father," wrote Chase. Booker T. Washington was in town two months later for an unannounced White House meeting; his friends Whitefield McKinlay, E. E. Cooper, and P. B. S. Pinchback all told the *Bee* that they saw BTW.

69. "Death of Mrs. Cora Lena White," *Washington Post*, 21 January 1905; "Death of Mrs. White," *Washington Evening Star*, 20 January 1905; N.C. Graves Index, N.C. Department of Archives and History. Cora Lena's mother still lived in Tarboro at the time, but White chose to bury his wife in the family's plot in New Bern, perhaps at her own request, since their daughter Odessa was buried there.

15

Leaving Washington Behind

Twenty-two years after Nancy White's death, George White had now become a widower for the third time. Losing loved ones had become a familiar experience for him over the years, with the deaths of his daughter and his father. But at fifty-two, White was no longer young, and the loss of his wife was especially painful for him now; her death left him almost completely alone at home, with his eleven-year-old son left to raise. Despite Cora Lena's chronic illness, their shared family life had been the bulwark of George's inner strength; the couple had spent nearly two happy decades together, during the most productive years of his public service, through triumph and defeat. He had been a devoted husband, she a thoughtful and supportive wife; even in the last years, as he nursed her through months of pain and chronic depression, they had made joint plans for their own lives and those of their children. Although her death came as a relief of sorts, the empty spot in his heart would never truly heal.

White's two daughters were young women with separate lives of their own. Mamie, now seventeen, was away at Oberlin, where she would remain until 1908. Della, twenty-five, was working at the Census Bureau; she was apparently married, perhaps even with children, before her stepmother died, and had definitely moved away before Mamie left for college. There was no companion left at the house on 18th Street for young George; his closest cousins, the three Cheathams, had all moved away when their father had remarried and returned to North Carolina in 1902.[1]

---

1. The three cousins were Charles Ernest Cheatham, who was within two years of Mamie

It was hardly surprising, then, that White would now consider moving away from Washington, for there was nothing left to hold him there. Had Cora Lena been able, they might well have moved away after he left Congress in 1901; her death simply erased her husband's last strong emotional tie to the nation's capital. All his other bonds to the city were marginal, at best; his law practice, never terribly lucrative, could easily be transplanted to a more congenial location in the North, while Cook, Cook and White, the brick manufacturing partnership, could be dissolved fairly simply. The Cape May real-estate development appeared to be his strongest financial opportunity, and it would be more easily managed from a city more accessible to the Jersey shore. Philadelphia offered attractive educational opportunities for the gifted George Jr., and White had spent much time there in recent years.

So it was that White chose finally to leave Washington, partly for business opportunities, partly for his son's educational welfare. Young George was an exceptionally bright student; like his older first cousin, Charles Ernest Cheatham, he had easily mastered the school system in the District and needed a stronger challenge. Charles had left for Worcester Academy four years earlier, after graduating from high school at age fourteen, and young George was showing the same aptitude for academic success.[2] His eventual goal was Lincoln University, known as the "black Princeton"; not far from Philadelphia, it accepted talented younger boys of high-school age as "special" students in its baccalaureate program.

Still, George White did not move immediately, but gradually began to wind down his affairs in Washington in cautious preparation. It was the practical thing to do, giving young George one last year in familiar surroundings before uprooting the adolescent from memories of his mother and the home he had known for most of his life. A long vacation at the Odessa Inn in Whitesboro that summer helped make the transition easier; George Jr. seems

White's age; Mamie Cheatham, who was four months older than Mamie White; and Plummer Cheatham (Henry P. Jr.), who was eighteen months older than George White Jr.

2. *Indianapolis Freeman*, 27 July 1901; Gerri Major, with Doris E. Saunders, *Gerri Major's Black Society* (Chicago: Johnson, 1976), 232–4. Charles, fourteen, had left for Worcester Academy as the year's youngest graduate of D.C.'s M Street High School; Plummer attended Shaw University before graduating from Temple Law School in 1925. Mamie attended Spelman College in Atlanta, Ga., then married G. Smith Wormley of Washington; she died in Phoenix, Arizona, in 1976. Major mistakenly lists her as George White's cousin, rather than his niece.

to have spent July and August there with his sister Della, now Mrs. J. W. Garrett, and at least one young child, apparently her daughter Ella. The elder George spent two weeks there, returning to Washington in early August, while the rest of the family returned home at the end of the month.[3]

As a member of the District bar association, George White helped plan a reception and boat excursion for fellow black lawyers to nearby Summersett Beach over the Labor Day weekend of September 1905, and his family undoubtedly accompanied him there. But he had begun to lose interest in practicing law in the District, where it was increasingly competitive; more than two dozen black lawyers were now active in Washington, and most were considerably younger than White. Opportunities for political advancement for blacks had all but disappeared, as well. President Roosevelt's appointment in 1903 of Jeter Pritchard as a justice of the D.C. supreme court had been an especially bitter disappointment to George White, negating the false hopes—fanned by an earlier appointment of black principal Robert H. Terrell as municipal judge—that Roosevelt might consider appointing qualified blacks to even higher seats on the bench. While Pritchard's subsequent elevation in 1904 to the U.S. Fourth Circuit Court of Appeals had removed him from routine legal contact with most black lawyers at the working level, his continued presence in an important federal position still rankled George White.[4]

As the lily-white movement took control of the Republican Party machinery, fewer and fewer blacks were even being considered for appointments in the South or elsewhere, and usually for lesser posts. During his first eighteen months in office, Theodore Roosevelt had appointed just 15 black men to federal posts, most of them reappointments of holdovers from the McKinley era; his only major changes had been the selections of John C. Dancy as the

3. "The Week in Society," *Washington Bee*, 5 August 1905 and 2 September 1905. The family "consisted of Mr. M. A. White, his mother, Mrs. Dollie [Della] G. Garrett, Miss Ella and Master George W. White." "Mr." White was probably George White's stepmother, Mrs. Mary Anna White, who may have come to live with the family to care for George Jr. after Cora Lena White's death. Property records involving the 1901 purchase of the land indicate that Mary Anna White was a shareholder in the Whitesboro venture.

4. Ibid., 5 August 1905. White was a member of the bar association's committee on reception; fellow lawyer L. Melendez King, who also had offices in the Capital Savings Bank building, was treasurer. Roosevelt appointed Terrell to the municipal judgeship in 1901; his later appointments of Pritchard were obvious rewards for political service after the latter's forced retirement from the Senate. Judge Pritchard died in office in April 1921.

District's recorder of deeds and Dr. John R. A. Crossland of Missouri as minister to Liberia, after the resignations from those posts of Henry Cheatham and
Owen L. W. Smith, respectively. By contrast, President McKinley had appointed a record number of blacks to federal office during his first six months;
there had been 179, by one count, including at least 16 black postmasters, and
almost all of them had been recommended by Congressman George White.[5]

And while hundreds of blacks continued to work in both the federal and
District governments at medium-level salaries, the tide of the late 1890s had
receded noticeably from its high-water mark. The city's black school system
had been submerged into the white system, as a separate, segregated arm, and
even predominantly black Howard University continued to have both a predominantly white faculty and a white president.[6]

The demise of the *Colored American* was emblematic of the declining political fortunes of blacks in Washington; victim of a declining readership,
falling advertising revenues, and Edward Cooper's financial troubles, the
newspaper had folded just after Roosevelt's election to a full term in 1904. Its
main competitors were the *Record*, where Alex Manly had once worked, and
W. Calvin Chase's now-venerable *Bee*. The *Bee* would continue to publish as
long as Chase lived, and the *Record* would survive, but there was simply not
enough demand in the city for three black weeklies. Edward Cooper's attempt
to start another newspaper, the *Colored Catholic Herald*, quickly failed without
support from Booker T. Washington, and Cooper soon left journalism for
good, taking a job as a District government clerk.[7] Black professionals gener-

5. "Negroes in Federal Office," *New York Times*, 16 April 1903; "Colored Office Holders,"
New York Times, 27 October 1897. The 1903 article also compared Roosevelt's record of black
appointments to those of every predecessor since U.S. Grant; the 1897 article examined
McKinley's early appointments of blacks in detail.

6. Andrew F. Hilyer, *The Twentieth Century Union League Directory* (Washington, D.C.: The
Union League, 1901); Gatewood, *Aristocrats of Color*, 64. Fewer than a dozen blacks held "prominent" positions in the federal government, not counting black diplomats abroad or posted in the
U.S. Army; another three dozen blacks were employed as "high grade clerks," earning at least
$1,400 annually, according to Hilyer. Gatewood says the percentage of blacks employed by the fed-
eral government dropped 6 percent between 1892 and 1908, when only about 20 percent of those
were clerks or better. The D.C. school system employed more than four hundred black teachers and
three dozen black administrators in 1901, when four black professors served on the faculty at
Howard University. Dr. John Gordon, a white man, became Howard's new president in 1903.

7. "What I Saw and Heard," *Washington Bee*, 25 November 1905; E. E. Cooper to Emmett J.

ally continued to prosper in Washington, but the city was less and less the center of the black nation's focus; as more blacks moved to the North and West, Washington played a shrinking role as a symbol of black opportunity and success.

The local situation was undoubtedly on George White's mind when he spoke to the Second Baptist Lyceum during the last week of November 1905, his only recorded speaking engagement in the city that fall. He was also aware of the continuing turmoil in the National Afro-American Council, whose ranks had been purged during a late-summer convention in Detroit; White was no longer affiliated with the national council, and had apparently stepped down as president of the local body as well. But the inner strife that now plagued the council was not new; it had begun openly in 1903, when its convention had vigorously booed Booker T. Washington in Louisville, Kentucky, for counseling patience and blaming black "idleness and crime" for white hostility toward the race. Washington had lost control of the group; even the new president, T. Thomas Fortune, had been unable to stem its slide into virtual anarchy; and Bishop Walters's reappearance as head after 1905 solved few of its problems.[8] The council was being challenged on all sides, as growing hostility toward Booker T. Washington's powerful influence had led directly in mid-1905 to the formation of the Niagara Movement. This influential group of black intellectuals was spearheaded by the brilliant William E. Burghardt Du Bois and demanded civil and political equality for blacks, including the abolition of all racial discrimination; the Niagara group would eventually become the core of the National Association for the Advancement of Colored People (NAACP).

George White had little contact with the Niagara Movement, having relinquished high-profile political activism and preferring not to alienate the still-powerful Washington, now his ally and occasional legal client. Yet several of White's friends in the city of Washington—including John P.

Scott, 9 February 1905, BTWP. The *Colored American* had ceased publication in late 1904; a year later, former editor Edward Cooper had gone to work as a clerk for the District of Columbia Commission. Cooper had unsuccessfully attempted to found a second black newspaper, the *Colored Catholic Herald*, he told Scott in 1905.

8. *Washington Bee*, 2 December and 9 December 1905; "Negroes Hostile to Washington," *New York Times*, 3 July 1903. "Much of the hostility . . . is due to the charge that he is creating sentiment against the higher education of the negro," wrote the *Times*.

Green, never a radical thinker—had already begun to side with Du Bois and William Monroe Trotter well before the Niagara Movement formally emerged.[9] Maneuvering in the new landscape of black politics was complicated at best, since personal friendship with Washington did not always revolve around or depend upon ideological compatibility; until Du Bois left his teaching position at Tuskegee in 1903, for instance, even he and Washington were on good terms, and the improbable but solid relationship between Washington and T. Thomas Fortune mystified many. Yet the political camps were increasingly divided into Bookerites and anti-Bookerites; those in the middle like George White, who wished to avoid such an overt political choice, became fewer and fewer as the decade waned. It was difficult to remain politically close to the Tuskegean after publicly challenging his philosophy, and White still remembered Washington's past kindnesses to Cora Lena.

The tenor of the times and growing black dissatisfaction with second-class citizenship made some type of large-scale protest inevitable, even for the conservative upper-class blacks, whom Washington had courted assiduously. Growing unhappiness with restrictive Jim Crow laws and political ostracism chafed at the consciousness of even very successful blacks, many of whom had only supported Washington in exchange for political favors and the wistful hope that things would eventually improve if black Americans simply remained patient.

Two related developments during the last two months of 1905 combined to put a truly somber imprint on the year for George White and other Washington-area blacks. In November came an ominous announcement, that the office of the recorder of deeds for the District—long a black sinecure, and currently occupied by John C. Dancy—was to be placed under the Civil Service; this meant that when Dancy stepped down, no black would likely be named to succeed him. In mid-December, it was announced that Judson W. Lyons, register of the Treasury since 1898, was planning to retire "because he was not supported [for reappointment] by Booker T. Washington." Lyons may have ex-

---

9. Gatewood, *Aristocrats of Color*, 305, 309. A dinner given for *Boston Guardian* editor Trotter in Washington in December 1903 revealed the "ideological sympathies" of its participants, including White's business partner John F. Cook, his friend Dr. W. S. Lofton, and his longtime ally John P. Green, among others. Gatewood cites Green's revealing letter to Ohio politician George A. Myers on the subject, dated February 4, 1904.

pected this announcement to force the president's hand, but if so, it was an unsuccessful ploy; on January 13, Roosevelt reportedly informed Lyons personally that he would not be appointed to a third term, and that a nonsouthern successor had been chosen.[10]

"The administration expects to rid itself of all colored men in the South who were put into high office by President McKinley through the influence of Senator Hanna," the *New York Sunday Herald* reported. "The only colored Republicans who have a chance . . . are those who live in northern states, where the colored vote cuts a figure in the elections." Besides Lyons, those slated to be removed reportedly included former congressman Robert Smalls, collector of the U.S. port at Beaufort, South Carolina; Henry A. Rucker, collector of internal revenue for the district of Georgia; and five other regional appointees. The president's policy was influenced by "his own experience with the case of Dr. [William Demos] Crum, whom he made collector of the port of Charleston," and by "the active opposition of Dr. Booker T. Washington to the appointment of southern negroes to office," according to the *Herald*.[11]

That few of these men were actually removed from office during the next decade was irrelevant; the perception was enough, one more depressing reminder of how far down the political ladder black Americans had fallen. If only Washington's approval could now guarantee any black a major appointment, no favors at all were likely for non-Bookerites. Worse were the geographical implications; if the South, where three out of four blacks still lived, was no longer even being considered for selections by a Republican president, what would happen after Roosevelt retired, especially if a Democrat was elected? The first question was more easily answered than the second: under a new Republican president, things would either remain the same or continue

10. *Washington Bee*, 2 December 1905; editorial, *Bee*, 16 December 1905; "Cuts Off Negro Office Holders: President Will Not Re-Appoint Lyons Register of the Treasury, and Will Drop Others From the South," *New York Sunday Herald*, 14 January 1906, reprinted in *Bee*, 27 January 1906. The first article in the *Bee* announced the president's executive order dated October 31; the later editorial dealt with Lyons's plans to retire.

11. "Cuts Off Negro Office Holders"; Gatewood, *Aristocrats of Color*, 305; Sherman, *The Republican Party and Black America*, 38–40. Dr. Crum, a staunch supporter of Booker T. Washington, was confirmed for the Charleston post by the Senate in January 1905, after a stubborn two-year battle by Roosevelt, including three recess appointments. Crum resigned in March 1909 under an agreement with incoming president William Howard Taft.

to decline. In the unlikely event of a Democratic victory in 1908, the past augured no better, since the last Democratic president, Cleveland, had appointed even fewer blacks to office than had Roosevelt. Although Cleveland had courted black voters to some extent, so few blacks had yet joined the Democratic Party that it was fruitless to speculate about a pool of popular possible appointments. The national Democratic Party had stumbled badly in 1904, losing in a landslide with a relative unknown against Roosevelt; it would blunder again in 1908 by selecting two-time loser William Jennings Bryan as its nominee.

The truth was becoming clear: black votes were no longer a national factor in either party, and might remain so for decades to come. Accepting this reality was difficult for proud black Republicans like George White who had served their party so faithfully, but George White now took a characteristically independent, if unpredictable, action, perhaps out of despair over the state of political oblivion facing American blacks. The Constitutional League of the United States—more often called simply the Constitution League—was an interracial protest organization financed largely by white Republican businessman and politician John E. Milholland, who had long been a supporter of Booker T. Washington but was now drifting away. White had come to know Milholland during the days of the Alabama and Louisiana disenfranchisement test cases; both Washington and Milholland had provided financing for the test cases in 1903, essentially paying the legal fees of White and other lawyers through the convenient coffers of the National Afro-American Council.[12]

The Constitution League's noisy and somewhat ineffective tactics were to "attack disfranchisement, peonage and mob violence"—all issues of major concern to black leaders—"by court action, legislation and propaganda," according to one historian. Formed by 1904, the Constitution League made its first major move that year by submitting to the Republican national platform committee some strongly worded planks on the rights of black Americans; the

12. August Meier, "Booker T. Washington and the Rise of the NAACP," in *Along the Color Line: Explorations in the Black Experience,* ed. August Meier and Elliott Rudwick (Urbana: University of Illinois Press, 1976); Carolyn Wedin, *Inheritors of the Spirit: Mary White Ovington and the Founding of the NAACP* (New York: John Wiley & Sons, 1998). Wealthy industrialist Milholland (1860–1925) was an early supporter of Washington's National Negro Business League, and, according to Wedin, underwrote many special projects, including much of Mary Ovington's research. Meier says the Constitution League was one of several precursors of the NAACP, but the league operated separately for some time after 1909.

planks were rejected, but the point was made. For more than a year, Milholland and Washington remained on essentially good terms, until it became apparent to both that the league was heading in a direction Washington could not accept.

The specific obstacle that wrecked the relationship came in the form of a bill proposed by Senator Orville Platt, Republican of Connecticut. The Platt bill sought to reduce southern representation in Congress as a punishment for the disfranchisement of black voters, much as the ill-fated Crumpacker amendment of 1901 had attempted to do, with the avid support of then-congressman George White. Booker T. Washington announced his opposition to the Platt bill on philosophical grounds, arguing that if the bill passed, the South would accept the reduction and could then claim—with suitably diabolical logic—that disfranchisement had been constitutionally sanctioned. Milholland soon found Washington had effectively sabotaged the league's independent efforts on the bill, and he turned for help to Niagara Movement organizers Du Bois and Trotter. Washington quickly began to distrust Milholland, and privately labeled him as a "professional friend" of blacks, or a racial hypocrite.[13]

The Platt bill must have alerted George White both to the new Constitution League and its worthwhile actions, and to Washington's deceptive tactics. Whatever the reason, White quickly became an active participant in a separate Constitution League project, this one aimed at convincing the Senate to amend the railroad-rate bill to forbid discrimination against blacks on interstate trains. At its meeting in Philadelphia in early 1906, the league created a special committee to call upon Senator Joseph Benson Foraker of Ohio, who seemed interested in the issue, and other senators in an effort to have such an amendment introduced. Of the five league members named to the lobbying committee, only two were able to complete the task at hand, writer Archibald Grimké of Boston (brother of the pastor at Washington's Fifteenth Street Presbyterian) and George White.[14]

13. Meier, "Rise of the NAACP," 80–1. Others active in the Constitution League included its secretary, Andrew Humphrey of New York, who attempted at first to bring Booker T. Washington into the group. The later rift between Milholland and Washington seems to have begun over an unrelated slight, when an "unfortunate error" prevented Milholland from addressing the Negro Business League's 1905 national convention.

14. "Ex-Congressman White," letter, *Washington Bee*, 9 June 1906. Neither Gen. Henry E. Tremain nor Andrew Humphrey of New York nor Dr. William A. Sinclair of Philadelphia were

Grimké reportedly joined White for a call upon Senator Foraker in March 1906, and according to White's recollection, the two men "urged that the amendment, which he [Foraker] promised to introduce, should not only forbid discrimination but separation, as well, knowing that whenever there is separation the negro never gets equality of service." The pair then called upon Senator Winthrop Crane of Massachusetts, obtaining his assurance of "hearty cooperation with Senator Foraker" on the matter. White called alone upon two other senators, Ohio's Charles Dick and Missouri's William Warner, and drew a positive response, at least from Senator Dick.[15]

On April 12, Foraker and Warner introduced their amendment to Senator Hepburn's railroad-rate bill, entitled "Equal Accommodations for All Classes." But the Warner-Foraker amendment incorporated one red-flag phrase—"or equally good" accommodations—that White and others at the league believed "would do us more harm than good," as he wrote Foraker two weeks later. ("My surprise and disgust can better be imagined than expressed when I saw the [actual] amendment," White said in June.) This was precisely what the Constitution League did *not* want: to "open a loophole for all the discriminations now practiced in all of the Southern States where the Jim Crow car is in full force." If the offending phrase could not be deleted, the league believed the amendment should simply be withdrawn, he had told Foraker.[16]

In a June 2 editorial, the *Bee* had publicly blamed White, Grimké, and a third activist—Howard University professor Kelly Miller—for the final wording of Foraker's amendment, in the process linking White and Grimké to the wrong group (the Civic League) and criticizing them sharply for "meddling." White's irritation with the *Bee* for its inaccurate reporting of his involvement was emphatic but almost anticlimactic. "I am not a member of the Civic League, nor do I know anything of its purpose or membership," he chided the

---

able to visit Washington at the appointed time. The league preferred wording to forbid "any discrimination to be made against Interstate Passenger Traffic on account of race, color or previous condition of servitude."

15. Ibid.

16. Ibid.; editorial, *Washington Bee*, 2 June 1906. White's letter responded testily to the *Bee* editorial, which had criticized White, Grimké, and Howard University professor Kelly Miller for their alleged intervention with Foraker on behalf of the Civic League. The letter also contained White's own April 27 letter to Senator Foraker on the subject.

newspaper, before going on to explain the facts of his and Grimké's actions and returning to his own defense. "I pass your further criticisms and slurs over without notice. I have done much work and sacrificed much of my time, not only in the instance under consideration in behalf of my people, but have been engaged in similar work all of my life, and do not take kindly to criticisms wholly without warrant in fact," he wrote. "I am neither an officeholder nor an office-seeker, but am trying in an humble way to attend to my own business."[17]

White seemed to care little what the quixotic Chase thought of him personally, but insisted that the next time the *Bee* decided to criticize him, it bother to "seek the truth before rushing my name into print" again. With that, White's once-cordial relationship with the *Bee* and its owner abruptly ended; Chase's halfhearted attempt to rectify the matter, by printing White's letter in full on the front page, was too little and too late for the proud White. (Ever the troublemaker, Chase's sarcastic editorial inside that edition of the *Bee* proved the finishing touch.) Beyond getting the facts out into the open, as he had done, the matter was now of no further consequence to White, whose Washington tenure was almost over.

White continued to devote part of his time to charitable pursuits, even as he made plans to move to Philadelphia. He was elected president of the local chapter of the National League for the Protection of Colored Women, which held its organizational meeting in Washington on August 4, 1906. The new society, organized in New York earlier that year by S. Willie Layten, a black Baptist activist, and white social reformer Frances Kellor, concerned itself "with the predicament of women in domestic labor" in the North; early chapters were also formed in Philadelphia and Baltimore. Members of both races were concerned about the twin dangers of prostitution and confiscatory work-contracts, forced on southern black females migrating to the North by unscrupulous labor agents. "The society will appoint an agent to direct all incoming trains and see that the colored women who are strangers to the city are properly taken care of," wrote the *Washington Bee* two weeks later.[18]

17. Ibid.

18. "Testing the Grandfather," *Washington Bee*, 18 August 1906; "National League for the Protection of Colored Women," in *Encyclopedia of African American Culture and History*, ed. Jack Salzman, David L. Smith, and Cornel West (New York: Macmillan, 1996), 4:1960. The league quickly became one of the founding organizations of the umbrella group later known as the Urban League.

Before White made his move to the north, one last event occurred in the summer of 1906 that would occupy much of his legal thinking in the days ahead. The "Brownsville Affray" involved a group of black U.S. Army soldiers stationed at Fort Brown, Texas, and a night of violence that would haunt all concerned for years to come. A dozen or more armed men, later identified by townspeople as members of the all-black battalion, raided the nearby town during the night of August 13; one citizen was killed and two others wounded in a ten-minute barrage of gunfire. The violence erupted just six weeks after the arrival of the black soldiers, who were immediately transferred to an Oklahoma post. After weeks of investigation failed to identify any specific soldiers involved, the Roosevelt administration took the unprecedented step of dishonorably discharging all 167 members of the black battalion from the Army as punishment for refusing to give up the names of the guilty parties.[19]

Implementation of the order was delayed twice, once to avoid interfering with the 1906 congressional elections, and a second time when the Constitution League sent an intermediary to plead with Secretary of War William Howard Taft. Taft agreed to delay execution of the order at Mary Church Terrell's behest, but only for thirty-six hours, or until President Roosevelt had returned to Washington. As soon as the order was finalized, the Constitution League had immediately seized upon the issue, sponsoring protest meetings in several cities and undertaking its own investigation of the incident; among other actions, it dispatched a Tuskegee graduate named Gilchrist Stewart to Texas and Oklahoma at John Milholland's personal expense. Upon his return, Stewart and Mrs. Terrell then met with Roosevelt personally, but were unable to convince him to rescind the order. The league's hastily prepared final report a month later was incomplete, but significantly more effective; once in Foraker's hands, it almost single-handedly forced the Senate into a political battle with Roosevelt over his treatment of the black soldiers.[20]

19. James A. Tinsley, "Roosevelt, Foraker, and the Brownsville Affray," *Journal of Negro History* 41 (January 1956); Ann J. Lane, *The Brownsville Affair: National Crisis and Black Reaction* (n.p., Port Washington, N.Y., 1971). Thorough accounts of the Brownsville affray and its aftermath are found in both; the summary given here is essentially Tinsley's. Lane's chapter "The Constitution League," 25–31, is especially helpful. Mrs. Terrell, the wife of D.C. judge Robert H. Terrell, was president of the National Association of Colored Women and a respected figure in her own right; she and Milholland were among the NAACP's founders.

20. Tinsley, "Brownsville Affray," 50.

George White played a backstage role in the league's actions, probably assisting in the follow-up investigation, which consumed more than a year of the Senate's time and a good deal of Milholland's money. White almost certainly helped compile the initial report, working closely with Stewart and Napoleon B. Marshall, a league attorney who had recently married Whitesboro investor Harriet Gibbs, but he had moved on to Philadelphia before the committee hearings began; only Stewart and Marshall were publicly named in contemporary accounts. In any event, a behind-the-scenes role was a fitting one for White; once again, the star player here was Senator Foraker, in whom White had little reason to place any trust at all on a crucial matter.

Determined to win the 1908 Republican presidential nomination, and hoping to redeem his poor showing on the railroad-rate bill, Foraker seized the Brownsville issue and proceeded to force the Senate committee on military affairs to investigate it, hoping to embarrass Roosevelt along the way. Foraker even underwrote part of the cost of additional league investigations, although Milholland and other contributors absorbed a far larger share.[21] Roosevelt's hasty action was widely disapproved, but few Republicans would go as far as Foraker to prove the point. Neither the soldiers' guilt nor their innocence was ever truly established during the year-long hearings, and Foraker's main accomplishment was a bill to allow the reenlistment of those who met certain requirements.

The Brownsville saga dragged on until August 1910, when fourteen of the original soldiers were allowed to reenlist under the terms of Foraker's legislation. Roosevelt grudgingly signed the bill during his last week in office in 1909. His actions in the Brownsville affair greatly damaged his short-term public image among blacks, and the indirect fallout from it affected others as well; the Constitution League's involvement in the case, for instance, brought heavy criticism from Booker T. Washington and his Tuskegee machine down upon Milholland and others. The league's primary benefactor was judged to be "dangerous" and a modern-day carpetbagger, his league associates labeled as "Blacklegs" and "schemers." Washington even tried to punish Milholland by

21. Lane, *Brownsville Affair*, 27. Milholland estimated the monthly cost of the league's headquarters at between $400 and $500 by July 1907; he had given about $6,000 by that time, while "the colored contributions do not yet amount to $1,000." The league still owed Foraker $500, Milholland told Foraker in a letter dated July 11, 1907.

informing the U.S. postmaster general of his "subversive" agitation; since Milholland had once sold pneumatic-tube equipment to the Post Office Department, this would have been a cunningly invisible way to cut off the league's major source of funds, had it worked.[22]

Undoubtedly the most compelling attack, however, came on the pages of the *New York Age* late in the 1908 Taft presidential campaign, when Washington enlisted the editorial talents of Ralph Waldo Tyler for an opinion piece entitled "The Brownsville Ghouls." Washington's unnamed opponents had worked against Taft in the race, and were now memorably depicted as "human ghouls, worthless parasites who represent nothing save selfish avarice." Shamelessly using the unfortunate Brownsville soldiers as pawns in a selfish quest for personal advancement, the hunger of these "ghouls" for power had led "the race into ambush," wrote Tyler, himself the appointed auditor of the U.S. Navy and no stranger to patronage or self-promotion. Such tactics may have succeeded in minimizing black defections to Democrat William Jennings Bryan in 1908, but it neither warded off the challenge to Washington's power by his determined opponents nor improved the Tuskegee machine's already tarnished image.[23]

Whether or not George White had actively assisted the Constitution League in the Brownsville case, this macabre attack by a Tuskegee machine puppet like Tyler could only have infuriated him. Even as a bystander, he would have considered such attacks on valiant fighters for black civil rights puzzling and unnecessary. White had certainly lost patience with the enigmatic Booker T. Washington more than once over the years, particularly in 1906 over the Platt bill, which he felt deserved a better fate than death in committee. This was just one more sign, and a distinctly odious one, of the fading leader's desperate fight to retain control of the political soul of the nation's black citizens.

But there would be no angry public break between the two men, simply a

22. Meier, "Rise of the NAACP," 82–3. Some of the "schemers" Washington listed were William A. Sinclair, the league's field secretary; Bishop Alexander Walters, a former ally; Rev. Reverdy C. Ransom, a well-known orator in the Niagara Movement; William Monroe Trotter of the *Boston Guardian*; and J. Max Barber, former editor of the *Voice of the Negro*.

23. Ibid. Tyler, former editor of the *Columbus (Ohio) Daily Dispatch*, had once been due for appointment to a more lucrative post, but was set aside during a Roosevelt-Foraker spat over patronage rights. He was auditor of the navy from 1907 until 1913.

new, polite distance. White held few grudges, reserving his strongest disdain for political allies who had intentionally betrayed him, like Pritchard. As it was, by 1908 White had resumed his old independence, drifting now toward the opposition orbit in a city less known for its support of either the Tuskegee philosophy or the militancy of the Niagara Movement than for its old Quaker motto, the City of Brotherly Love.

16

Philadelphia and the Final Years

It was to be George White's last home: a great, sprawling metropolis of nearly 1.5 million, third-largest in the nation in 1906. Philadelphia was a city he had visited many times, and one where he felt comfortable, yet much had changed in the thirty years since he had last lived here. It now had nearly five times as many residents as Washington, D.C.; its black population was a smaller percentage of the total, but almost as large in actual numbers—85,000, compared to the capital's 95,000. Its history was infinitely more complex than Washington's. It was home to one of America's oldest black urban communities; the group known as the Upper Ten contained distinguished native families whose free lineage dated back to the era of the Revolutionary War, along with descendants of the so-called West Indian group and a third contingent whose families had migrated from the South in antebellum times. One of the nation's first black millionaires, recently deceased, had been a longtime Philadelphian, while social clubs and societies organized by blacks were as much as a century old. Recent arrivals had tended to dwarf the old families, the number of blacks having quadrupled since 1870, but the Upper Ten influence was still felt in all walks of daily life.[1]

It was to this crowded city that George White brought his family and his

1. *Negro Population, 1790–1915*, 93 (Tables 9–11); Gatewood, *Aristocrats of Color*, 96–103. Caterer John McKee of Alexandria, Va., who arrived in Philadelphia in 1821, was reputedly a millionaire at his death in 1902, by virtue of astute real-estate investments, especially in Cape May County, N.J. The Free African Society dated back to 1787, the Philadelphia Library Company of Colored Persons to 1833.

dreams in late 1906, the last stop on a long pilgrimage toward professional fulfillment and personal peace. He was able to acclimate quickly to the new environment by using his previous legal and political connections to make a comfortable transition. He first established temporary new offices for his law firm and the real-estate development firm in the heart of the financial district; by the end of 1907, he was living in a building at 1428 Lombard Street, and by the spring of 1908, he had established a permanent home for his family and his offices a block away, at 1508 Lombard Street. He enrolled George Jr. at Philadelphia's Central High School, then transferred him to the new Downington Industrial School, from which the fourteen-year-old entered nearby Lincoln University as a special student in the fall of 1907. Daughter Mamie continued her musical studies at the Oberlin conservatory, having completed the preparatory academy there in 1906.[2]

Always watchful for good business opportunities, White seems to have noticed immediately that Philadelphia's blacks had no commercial bank of their own. Within a year of his arrival, White and a small group of investors—"a few men of excellent repute"—had taken the first step toward establishing one, obtaining a commonwealth charter for the People's Savings Bank of Philadelphia on September 21, 1907. The bank opened for business in January 1908, under the direction of President George H. White and a board of directors containing some of the city's most prominent black citizens: the Reverend E. W. Moore, pastor of Zion Baptist Church, first vice-president; Bishop Levi J. Coppin; economist and minister Richard R. Wright Jr.; undertaker Joseph T. Seth, second vice-president; and local businessman Walter P. Hall, bank treasurer, among others.[3]

People's Savings Bank would be the first full-service bank owned and operated by blacks for black customers in Philadelphia's history. A succession of

2. *Lincoln University Biographical Catalogue, 1918* (Lancaster, Pa.: New Era Printing, 1918), 101. George Jr. received preparatory training at "Central High School, Philadelphia, and Downington, Pa." before entering Lincoln in 1907 and receiving a bachelor's degree in 1911. Among its other missions, the new Downington School served after 1905 as a special preparatory school for Lincoln University. The family's address in March 1908 comes from Mamie's listing of 1428 Lombard Street as her home address in an Oberlin alumni questionnaire.

3. According to a list published in the *Philadelphia Tribune* (4 May 1912), other bank directors were William H. Jackson, William A. Saunders, Isham Bridges, Robert S. Jackson, E. L. Saunders, and Paul Cobb. Officers included Levi A. Cottman, secretary; Martin J. Lehman, cashier; and E. L. Saunders, assistant cashier.

building and loan associations and societies, the most notably successful of which was the Berean, had long offered local black citizens the economic incentive to purchase their own homes, although many of their larger shareholders had been white. The People's Bank did not attempt to supplant the building and loan associations, but rather offered black businesses their first opportunity to obtain commercial accounts and credit through a bank operated by black professionals. Mindful of the checkered history of black-owned banks elsewhere, White and his board managed the bank's affairs conservatively but fairly; all officers were bonded, for instance. The recent failure of Washington's Capital Savings Bank, the nation's first banking institution created and run by blacks, was still fresh in White's memory; his law offices had been housed in their building, and he had undoubtedly lost some of his own money in that failure.[4]

Within four years, the People's Savings Bank had reached a remarkable milestone, having transacted its first million dollars in business. By 1915, the new bank had reportedly handled more than three million in total deposits. Its business was mostly from small-account holders, some of whom had never trusted banks before; even children were encouraged to open accounts in the "Dime Savings" bank at People's. It paid a very fair return on savings, offering 3 percent interest compounded semiannually, and was open six days a week for business, including two evenings from 6 to 8.

The new building at 1508 Lombard Street was renovated before the bank moved there, "remodelled, repapered and repainted, and put in first-class condition for banking purposes." The first floor contained the bank, a directors' room, and White's law office, while other professional offices were leased out on the floor above; White's family residence occupied the entire third floor of the building.[5]

4. Ex-congressman John R. Lynch served as president of the Capital Savings Bank, which opened in October 1888, and D.C. judge Robert H. Terrell was among its officers. The bank had closed by the middle of 1904, under suspicion of its being looted by an unnamed high official, according to Arnett Lindsay, "The Negro in Banking," and was liquidated by 1906. All People's Savings Bank officers were bonded by a "reliable bonding company," the *Philadelphia Tribune* wrote on 23 January 1915; the bank and its deposits were under the "direct supervision of the Banking Commissioner of the Commonwealth of Pennsylvania." The Berean and other local savings and loan associations are described by Roger Lane in *William Dorsey's Philadelphia and Ours* (New York: Oxford University Press, 1991), 250, 288–90.

5. "Peoples Savings Bank a Grand Success," *Philadelphia Tribune*, 4 May 1912; "The Marvelous Growth of the Peoples Savings Bank," *Philadelphia Tribune*, 23 January 1915; adver-

White continued his law practice, with somewhat less competition for clients in Philadelphia than in his last setting; he was one of just fourteen black lawyers in the city in 1908, compared to as many as twenty-four in the smaller Washington seven years earlier. A period study of Pennsylvania's economic life noted that black lawyers were still subject to misgivings among their potential clientele, unlike the relative advantages accorded to black physicians and clergymen. "The Negro lawyer . . . is still a pioneer and at a disadvantage, in that his practice is not private, or among his own people, but he must plead before a white judge often against a white lawyer and generally, with a white jury," wrote Richard R. Wright Jr., soon to become a trustee of George White's bank. Southern-born blacks would easily remember "how great a handicap the lawyer of his race suffers in that section," and would think twice before hiring a black lawyer anywhere else, Wright claimed.[6]

But White's free time and legendary energy were primarily directed to the development of Whitesboro, at least during his first few years in Philadelphia. The New Jersey village had at least a hundred residents by 1906, and seemed on its way to becoming a prosperous settlement; a 1912 description boasted "a good school, two churches, a railway station, hotel, post-office and telephone service" as its main features. White himself owned about three-fourths of the stock in the real estate company, in addition to land he held outright in Whitesboro, such as the Odessa Inn. How much property his company had actually sold by 1909 is not clear, but it probably amounted to a third of the 650 lots listed in 1901; in addition, about half the town had originally been designated as small farms, and could either be sold off in plots to Whitesboro residents or rented to them. White was still engaged in building houses for the town's new residents, although an innovative early project that would have shipped portable homes to the site had never materialized.[7] Whether the corporation had begun to pay dividends is unclear; perhaps not, since all profits were initially designated for expenses of future development.

tisement for People's Savings Bank, *Philadelphia Tribune*, 27 April 1912; "Philadelphia Notes," *Washington Bee*, 19 February 1916. The bank moved into 1508 Lombard Street in February 1909; the Whites were the only family listed as residing at that address in the 1910 census, and they continued to live there until George White's death in 1918.

6. Richard R. Wright Jr., *The Negro in Pennsylvania: A Study in Economic History* (Philadelphia: The A.M.E. Book Concern, 1912), 80. Black physicians outnumbered black lawyers in Pennsylvania by three to one in 1908.

7. White, *Who's Who in Philadelphia*, 88; Reid, "Post-Congressional Career," 366.

By 1908, when the White firm built a new school on land previously purchased by the Middle Township Board of Education, Whitesboro's future appeared bright. White sold the school building to the board for the sum of one dollar in July 1909, according to local records, and it would be used more or less continuously for the next six decades. His daughter Mamie was among the first teachers at the new school, after she completed her studies at Oberlin in 1908 and returned to live with her father and brother in Philadelphia.[8]

But Whitesboro was not immune to the vagaries of Cape May County's up-and-down resort economy. The destruction by fire of the business section of nearby Cape May Court House in 1905 had been a warning sign of the sudden damage to the fragile economy by unexpected disaster; the unforeseen bankruptcy of the East Cape May development project in 1909 threatened to bring down the whole county. As the local economy soured, no new settlers or businesses came to Whitesboro for years, and the town's unsold acreage became a dumping ground for barrier-island refuse. Adding to the unwholesome atmosphere were railroad boxcars filled with rotting seafood, often left for long periods on the sidings at Wildwood Junction, just east of town.[9]

Still, the small town limped through the recession, which was finally ended by the advent of the Great War. In 1915, the Bethlehem Steel Company established the first of several ordnance-proving grounds in Cape May along the Delaware Bay, just west of Whitesboro, while the federal government constructed a U.S. Navy training station on the Atlantic coast, just east of Cape May City.[10] The naval training station included a giant dirigible hangar, later converted to Coast Guard use; both provided employment for local residents during and after World War I.

George White's interest in Whitesboro and its continued development extended to other parts of the Jersey peninsula, as in the case of Great Egg Harbor at the northeast corner of Cape May. In 1913, he received considerable publicity by representing swindled land buyers in an Egg Harbor City land scam, drawing both a front-page picture and a reprint of his letter to the

---

8. As stated in Daniel Spaulding's "History of Whitesboro," cited by Reid, "Post-Congressional Career," 370. Other teachers included Mrs. Alice K. Jones and Mrs. Inez K. Edmund. Mamie did not teach in Whitesboro for long, becoming a teller in her father's bank by mid-1910, according to the census.

9. Dorwart, *Cape May County*, 182–5.

10. Ibid., 185–8, 194.

"land sharks" in the *Philadelphia Tribune*. There was no separate story, but the letter and a subsequent story in the *Tribune*'s next edition gave most of the details: The Egg Harbor Boom Committee had been engaging in questionable practices since at least 1912, often selling homesites in Egg Harbor City to Philadelphia residents without holding title to the property, sometimes with only a limited option. Even the company's few valid titles were incomplete or contained inaccurate boundary descriptions, White noted in a strongly worded letter to the committee, dated April 17, 1913. At least five buyers had retained White to check the validity of their contracts and titles for land purchased between March and October of 1912; White discovered that four of five contracts were invalid, and all his clients were now demanding the return of their money in full.[11]

"We deem it advisable to let the public know our fate, that others may be warned," wrote three of the victims who had retained White and who signed the letter to the *Tribune*.[12] Whether the letter had the desired effect was not mentioned, but its publication did produce a follow-up story exonerating an unrelated firm—also selling Egg Harbor City lots to Philadelphians—of any wrongdoing. "We only sell properties that we own absolutely, consisting of more than one-third of the home-sites in Egg Harbor City," wrote the nervous officers of the Gibson-Bozarth Corporation, located on Philadelphia's Walnut Street. The firm seemed to have much at stake in the venture; in addition to requesting that both White and the city attorney for Egg Harbor City inspect their properties and titles for authenticity, it went so far as to obtain testimonials to its probity by eight prominent black Philadelphians, including White, three ministers, and even the newspaper's city editor. "To be safe, buy only from Gibson-Bozarth," the article warned its readers, in what appeared to be little more than a front-page commercial advertisement.[13]

Such favorable publicity in a widely read black newspaper was certainly not unwelcome for White in 1913, considering his desire to be appointed

11. "Attorney White Exposes Land Sharks Operating in Philadelphia; He Brands Them as Frauds and Writes a Strong Letter," *Philadelphia Tribune*, 17 May 1913.

12. Ibid.

13. "Gibson-Bozarth Corporation Have No Connection with Any Other Company Selling Egg Harbor Land," *Philadelphia Tribune*, 24 May 1913. The testimonials seem to have helped; two years later, the *Tribune* issued a glowing progress report on the development of Egg Harbor City and Gibson-Bozarth's improvements to its park (23 January 1915).

judge of the Court of Common Pleas in Philadelphia County. According to another front-page *Tribune* story a few weeks earlier, black citizens had petitioned Pennsylvania governor John K. Tener to appoint White to one of five recently created judgeships, after a well-attended meeting at the Zion Baptist Church. Despite blacks' loyal support of the government, no black had ever sat on the judicial bench in the city or county, and the petition read, "we . . . feel that we are, therefore, entitled to representation to a much greater extent than we are now getting at the hands of the officials of our Government." The former congressman possessed the "requisite ability, experience, integrity and moral character, as well as the proper training and learning in the law," to serve as a judge, in their opinion. The Presbyterian White was not a member of the Zion congregation, but his ties to its minister were well known; the Reverend E. W. Moore, also vice-president of People's Savings Bank, "briefly reviewed the public career of Mr. White and his activities here" for the petitioners before they acted.[14]

Philadelphia's black citizens would be disappointed in this instance. White was not appointed to the common-pleas bench, nor did he actively seek a subsequent appointment as judge. Yet the city's black community was not totally without representation in local government, since the Seventh Ward, a wide swath of Philadelphia roughly centering on Lombard Street, had long elected black Republicans as members of the city council. In 1913, Richard A. Cooper was the latest in a line which included, among others, *Tribune* publisher Christopher J. Perry. The city's Fifth and Seventh Wards had elected as many as three black councilmen at once in 1890, although even this was less than their proportion of the voting population (roughly 10 percent) at the time. The city had twice elected black lawyer Harry W. Bass to the Pennsylvania legislature. Bass had sought the seat twice as an independent Republican before winning in 1910 and 1912 as the regular party nominee; his speech to the lawmaking body helped derail a bill prohibiting mixed-race marriages shortly after White was proposed for the judgeship.[15]

The call for greater representation for blacks had grown louder in recent

14. "Citizens Petition Governor Tener to Name Lawyer White, Ex-Congressman's Friends Pleased," *Philadelphia Tribune*, 26 April 1913.

15. Lane, *Dorsey's Philadelphia*, 220–2; "Colored Philadelphians in Political Positions," in White, *Who's Who in Philadelphia*, 150–3; "Colored Orator Wins Legislature, Representative Bass' Speech Precedes Defeat of Intermarriage Law," *Philadelphia Tribune*, 3 May 1913.

years, especially since Bass had entered the legislature. Philadelphia already boasted more black policemen, public schoolteachers, and postal employees than almost any other city in the nation, yet the city's blacks continued to play a secondary role in the Republican Party during the first decade of the twentieth century, at least beyond the limits of the largely black Seventh Ward.

George White had not moved to Philadelphia to seek political office; content to pursue his business and professional interests, he had made little effort to expand his portfolio as an active player in the Republican Party since arriving in Pennsylvania. In 1912, however, he showed renewed signs of the old campaign fervor, briefly seeking the Republican nomination for Congress from Pennsylvania's First District, which included part of Philadelphia. The unexpected death of General Henry H. Bingham, a veteran congressman who had held the post since 1879, created the spot White hoped to fill. In an open letter printed by the *Philadelphia Tribune*, White presented his qualifications for the post: thirty-two years as a practicing attorney, eight years as district solicitor in North Carolina, four years as a state legislator there, and, finally, four years in Congress. "I have been a voter in this district and State for several years and feel that, through me, the great state of brotherly love and a 'square deal' can afford to give my race this one national position."[16]

America's black citizens were "entitled to at least one Representative in Congress," White argued, after having "supported the principles of Republicanism consistently for a period of over 45 years." In Pennsylvania, he noted, black voters held the balance of power in several congressional districts, and had always supported Republican nominees. Somewhat cryptically, he then cited his own service "on the fighting line for the principles of Republicanism in Pennsylvania for the last 13 years, beginning under the leadership of Republican principles," before ending with a polite but oddly Rooseveltian closing: "May I hope for your support? Yours for a 'Square Deal,' Geo. H. White."[17]

16. "Announces His Candidacy for Congress, Has Always Been a Stalwart Party Man," *Philadelphia Tribune*, 30 March 1912. The article appeared on page one of the *Tribune*, next to pictures of both White and Bingham and a shorter obituary entitled "General Bingham's Long Career Ends, Civil War Hero Veteran Legislator and 'Father of the House,' Dies." Bingham had died a week earlier at seventy-one.

17. "Announces His Candidacy."

White appeared to be positioning himself alongside an expected ground-swell of support for the former president, now threatening to take back the White House in his bid for an unprecedented third term. It would have been an odd political couple, of course, since Roosevelt had appointed White's nemesis, Jeter Pritchard, to two judgeships but refused to consider White for any lesser office. Roosevelt also bore the additional stain of Brownsville, but despite this, nearly a hundred black leaders had publicly announced their support for Roosevelt two weeks earlier, in the face of President Taft's refusal to condemn lynching or take any positive actions to end segregation. "Teddy" was "the only man . . . in the Republican Party who will revive the principles of Lincoln," the black leaders declared; never had the American Negro "been so thoroughly ignored . . . as he has since William Howard Taft" became president.[18] Roosevelt's "hasty act" in the Brownsville affair paled in comparison to President Taft's "Southern strategy" in removing virtually all black office-holders in that region, a far more insidious sign of Republican intent. Even Taft's unprecedented choice of William H. Lewis for assistant U.S. attorney general in 1911—the highest federal appointment ever given a black to date—earned him little credit.

Alarmed at the prospect of losing all black support completely, Taft capitulated in an April 9 speech to a black audience in Washington, publicly condemning lynching for the first time since becoming president. The speech satisfied some doubters, and was generally received favorably, but Taft was prepared to go no further. When asked by W. E. B. Du Bois to prepare a longer written piece on the subject for the NAACP's new journal, *The Crisis*, the president demurred, sending Du Bois simply a copy of the speech. His advisers were apparently wary, and wisely so, of appearing to cooperate with an anti-Bookerite group.[19]

George White's announcement stirred little interest in Philadelphia, particularly after Taft's speech; little more was heard from his campaign, and he was apparently not even nominated at the district convention.[20] The chaotic

18. Sherman, *The Republican Party and Black America*, 101–2. The statement was issued on March 12 by a group of 18 bishops, 57 ministers, and several black educators from thirteen northern and five southern states.

19. Ibid.; *Washington Bee*, 13 April 1912.

20. Untitled editorial aside, *Philadelphia Tribune*, 8 May 1912. A month before the national GOP convention, the *Tribune* cryptically referred to White's "sharpening a big knife, preparing

situation in 1912 was generally disheartening to most blacks, who saw no clear, positive choice among the national candidates. A bitter national battle between Roosevelt and Taft at the national Republican convention in June went to Taft on the first ballot; most black Republican delegates voted for Taft, despite extreme pressure from Roosevelt forces. Roosevelt's later nomination by the "Bull Moose" Progressive Party, which had seemed to offer unhappy blacks a non-Democratic alternative to Taft, turned out to be yet another false hope as the Progressives quickly turned lily-white in the South. Militant blacks were disgusted with both Roosevelt and Taft, and vowed to vote for Woodrow Wilson, the Democratic governor of New Jersey, particularly in light of Booker T. Washington's continued support for Taft. But as usual, the black vote was too small to cause concern at the national level; comparatively few black men were able to vote, since most blacks still lived in the disfranchised states of the Deep South.

If White was hurt by the lack of interest in his candidacy, he bore the disappointment stoically and quietly, never mentioning it again. It proved to be his last attempt at elective office; at sixty, he had little energy for the demands of a full-fledged campaign. He did continue to be active as a political speaker during local campaigns, and by 1915 returned to the hustings as a member of the Colored Republican Central Committee, where he performed his duties with vigor. On one occasion, "Enthusiasm ran high . . . and was whipped into a seething foam by such orators as George H. White, Sr." and others, including former legislator Harry Bass.[21]

Philadelphia's blacks were generally unhappy with the performance of the current "reform" administration of Mayor Rudolph Blankenburg, and the Central Committee sought to bring out the black vote in large numbers in the city's predominantly black wards to help defeat reform candidates. White and Bass were just two of many well-known local speakers involved in the intensive one-week push; others included Committee secretary Christopher J. Perry, editor of the *Philadelphia Tribune*; Committee treasurer Amos M. Scott; Seventh Ward common councilman Richard A. Cooper; local lawyer John C.

---

to make a desperate lunge in political circles in the near future," but no further accounts were printed.

21. "Members of the Colored Republican Central Committee Actively Engaged in the Municipal Campaign Just Closed," *Philadelphia Tribune*, 6 November 1915. George H. White (Sr.) was one of five committee members pictured on the front page.

Asbury; and twenty-two-year-old George White Jr., a recent graduate of Western Reserve University's law school.

Young George was gaining experience in speaking to large public gatherings, having represented his father on at least one previous occasion after graduating from Lincoln in 1911; while attending the University of Pennsylvania's law school, he had taken his father's place at a testimonial dinner for the former minister of "Mother Bethel" Church in 1912. George Jr. had then transferred from Penn to Western Reserve's law school in Cleveland, Ohio, in 1913. His extracurricular activities at Lincoln, Penn, and Western Reserve were varied, ranging from football at Lincoln to two fraternities, Delta Eta Sigma and Alpha Phi Alpha. He received a bachelor of laws degree from Western Reserve's Franklin Thomas Backus School of Law in June 1915. Returning home briefly after graduation, he joined the Citizens Republican and La Malta clubs and worked as a cashier at his father's bank. The young lawyer apparently preferred Ohio to Philadelphia, however, and he soon relocated there to practice law.[22]

Sites for the 1915 speeches included the Palm Garden, the Citizens Republican Club House, McLaughlin's Hall, the Knights of Pythias Hall, the Germantown Town Hall, and O'Niel Hall on successive nights; overflow crowds of both races cheered the speakers at each stop, according to the *Tribune* coverage, which often waxed purple. At one speech, for instance, "red lights from hundreds of candles lit up the lurid sky and emitted such a volume of sulphur, as to make one believe the lid had been raised from the domain of his Satanic majesty" to devour reformers. The display had been arranged especially for his fellow club member by Citizens Republican Club president Amos Scott, but George White's old rhetorical skills seemed to need no such props.[23]

Not all of White's activities during this period were so exciting or so exhausting. Much of his time was spent in quieter pursuits, including both professional business and extensive work for various local charities, along with frequent family outings to Whitesboro during the spring and summer seasons. Among his legal clients were the Banner Real Estate Company and the Keystone Aid Society, for which he was listed as solicitor in newspaper adver-

22. Ibid.; "Large Crowd Greets Rev. Dr. Fickland," *Philadelphia Tribune*, 4 May 1912; *Lincoln University Biographical Catalogue, 1918*, 101.

23. "Members of the Colored Republican Central Committee."

tisements. He still served as an honorary trustee of Howard University and re-mained active in its local alumni association, serving as its president on at least two occasions (1911 and 1912) and often leading fund-raising activities for his alma mater. He remained deeply interested in all levels of black educa-tion, serving as a board member of the Berean Manual Training Institute, local successor to the fabled Institute for Colored Youth, and as a trustee of Biddle University in his home state. His diverse activities also included ser-vice as a board member of the Frederick Douglass Hospital, one of two local black medical facilities; as a director of the Home for the Protection of Colored Women; and as a member of the board of *Who's Who in Philadelphia*— the local version, for black audiences, of the national Marquis publication.[24]

White also became an early leader in the new NAACP, serving as a mem-ber of the executive committee of the Philadelphia branch, one of the largest in the early days of the NAACP. His civil-rights activism in Philadelphia had dated from his arrival in 1906, when he helped lead protests against the return showing of *The Clansman*, a racially tinged play particularly unpopular with blacks. Written by Thomas Dixon, the play glorified the Ku Klux Klan's role in the South after the war and largely denigrated blacks. Philadelphia mayor Thomas Weaver was forced to cancel a repeat performance of the play, fearing the possibility of racial riots after thousands of black protesters turned up out-side the Walnut Street theater on October 22. White was one of the local leaders involved in negotiations with Mayor Weaver, although the main spokesman was Dr. Nathan F. Mossell, head of the Frederick Douglass Hos-pital.[25]

Both Mossell and White later became active in the NAACP's Phila-delphia branch, one of the first four branches formed outside New York after 1910. The biracial organization brought together members of various other struggling or failing groups in an attempt to reinvigorate the fight for black civil rights; founding members came from the ranks of the Niagara Move-ment, the Constitution League, and the National Afro-American Council,

---

24. White, *Who's Who in Philadelphia*, 88.

25. Obituary of George H. White, *The Crisis*, April 1919; George W. Reid, "George Henry White," in *Dictionary of American Negro Biography*, 646; Gatewood, *Aristocrats of Color*, 315; *Philadelphia Tribune*, 25 January 1913. The Dixon play formed the basis for D. W. Griffith's highly successful movie, "Birth of a Nation," which sparked similar angry protests from blacks throughout the North.

among others. New leaders included Niagara firebrand William E. Burghardt Du Bois and such highly regarded Washington socialites as Mary Church Terrell, the Reverend Owen M. Waller, and Archibald Grimké, formerly of Boston. Although intended as a nationwide organization, the early NAACP generally confined its early activities to large cities in the North and Midwest. The cities of Washington and Baltimore held the southernmost chapters until 1917, both because of Booker T. Washington's adamant opposition to the organization and the reluctance of many blacks to risk their social standing in the Deep South by joining it. Although criticized as exclusive and a "high-caste" social club for black aristocrats, the NAACP soon became the most active civil-rights organization in the nation's history and would remain the most prestigious biracial group across the United States for decades to come.[26]

George White took a vigorous interest in the prospects for the NAACP, offering an unrestrained endorsement of its goals at the organizational meeting of the Philadelphia branch in January 1913, held at Shiloh Baptist Church. According to news accounts, White "did the arousement act. In closing he said he believed in agitation and when dying would leave a codicil in his will to fight on." Mary White Ovington, a white leader from New York, was the main speaker of the evening, but all ears were still ringing from the former congressman's thunder when she rose to begin.[27]

White's active participation in the Philadelphia NAACP served as the final signal of his inevitable philosophical break with Booker T. Washington. The two men had had little contact since White's departure from the nation's capital, although they remained on cordial terms personally, but Washington's animosity toward Du Bois and the NAACP's militant wing made it problematic for him to deal with even its more moderate members, like White. Not long after White joined the new group, the Tuskegee leader visited Philadelphia for a banquet in his honor, in his capacity as president of the National Negro Business League. Former congressman White agreed to serve as one of

26. Gatewood, *Aristocrats of Color*, 313–22. The first NAACP branches outside New York were opened in Boston, Chicago, Philadelphia, and Washington, D.C.; the Washington NAACP branch was established in 1912, and under Grimké's leadership soon became the largest in the nation. An enthusiastic Cleveland branch was headed by *Gazette* editor Harry Smith; Bishop Alexander Walters was an early NAACP activist in New Jersey. Du Bois was the first director of publicity and research. A branch was finally established in Atlanta, Georgia, in 1917.

27. "Society for Advancement Organized," *Philadelphia Tribune*, 25 January 1913.

the featured speakers; it may have been the first meeting between the two men since the days of the Constitution League and Cora Lena White's death. Although White's welcoming words were not recorded by the *Tribune*, they were probably less hyperbolic than those of Mayor Blankenburg, who came to the banquet late and fawned over Washington as "the greatest man your race has produced since the days of [Frederick] Douglass." The dinner was enthusiastic and Washington left the city with good feelings, but there is no record of any subsequent contact between the two men before Washington's death two years later, in November 1915.[28]

White's belief in Christian responsibility drew him to the Young Men's Christian Association (YMCA), which became one of his favorite charitable causes; he served as chairman of the board of managers of Philadelphia's Southwest YMCA branch as late as 1916. The city's black YMCA had not always been successful, even suspending its operations temporarily in the 1890s, but under White's leadership it seems to have revived significantly. In May of 1916, he traveled to New York City to make the opening address to a gathering of black YMCA leaders at that city's Rush Memorial Church, a trip he clearly enjoyed.[29]

White's ties to the YMCA were more than simply charitable, as it turned out. Six months earlier, in an unusual private ceremony held at the Christian Street YMCA building, he had taken wedding vows for the fourth time. Little is known for certain about Mrs. Ellen Avant Macdonald, presumably a widow; both she and her new husband may have preferred to avoid publicity, since only a few friends were even invited to the ceremony. The ceremony was performed by the Reverend John Wesley Lee, longtime pastor of the First African Presbyterian Church and an active YMCA fund raiser, on Thursday, November 11, 1915; only a brief notice in the *Tribune* served to mark the event locally.[30]

28. "Mayor Blankenburg welcomes Dr. Booker T. Washington," *Philadelphia Tribune*, 3 May 1913. The dinner was held April 30, 1913, at the Musical Fund Hall.

29. "Hon. George H. White Speaks in Interests of YMCA," *Philadelphia Tribune*, 17 May 1916.

30. "Ex-Congressman George H. White Married," *Philadelphia Tribune*, 13 November 1915. The bride's name was spelled as "Mrs. Ella A. McDonald" in this story; the spelling given in White's 1918 obituary, presumably furnished by the family and therefore more accurate, is used here.

John Wesley Lee had been pastor of the local church since 1900. He had recently headed a successful campaign to raise $22,500 for the YMCA building fund, and was apparently White's friend as well as minister. His second wife, Mary Murdock Lee, was a native of North Carolina and an 1890 graduate of Scotia Seminary; Mrs. Lee was a contemporary there of Annie Washington Vick, wife of White's business partner in Wilson, North Carolina. Both may have been friends of Ellen Avant Macdonald's, possibly even her classmates at Scotia.

Ellen Macdonald White was a resident of Greensboro, North Carolina, at the time of her marriage, according to a later notice in the *Washington Bee*. George White's new wife was about thirty-eight years of age, nearly a quarter of a century younger than her husband. Born in 1877 to a large family in North Carolina's Brunswick County, she was the younger sister of two prominent African American professionals in North Carolina: Dr. Frank W. Avant of Wilmington and the Reverend William George Avant of New Bern, pastor of St. Cyprian's Episcopal Church. How long Ellen Macdonald had known George White before their marriage is uncertain, although she may have met him while visiting her brother in New Bern two decades earlier, perhaps even at Wiley White's funeral—held at St. Cyprian's Church in 1893, when she would have been just sixteen years of age. If the two met before the White family moved from New Bern in 1894, however, their paths seemingly did not cross again until long after both had been widowed.[31]

The Whites lived at the Lombard Street apartment, and Ellen White accompanied George on trips to Whitesboro over the next three years. During the summer of 1916 they lived in Whitesboro, along with an unnamed granddaughter (probably Della's daughter Fannie), with George White commuting to Philadelphia daily by train. Their presence in Whitesboro was noted by a

31. U.S. Census, Brunswick County, N.C., 1880; author's telephone interview with Carl Moultrie, 25 March 2000. Frank Avant (1875–1973) and William Avant, born 1867, were two of fifteen children of Wesley and Sarah Julia Avant; three-year-old Ellen was also listed in the 1880 census. William graduated from Howard University before entering the Episcopal priesthood; Frank attended Howard, Lincoln University, and Shaw University's medical school. According to her son Carl, Mrs. Sarah Avant Moultrie (daughter of Frank Avant) remembers visiting her aunt—who remarried after George White's death—in Atlantic City, New Jersey, as a child.

local correspondent of the *Philadelphia Tribune*, perhaps with a touch of jealousy; at any rate, the mention was brief but faintly condescending: "Hon. George H. White, Madame and granddaughter of Philadelphia, are spending their summer here."[32]

There is no mention of the reactions of White's children to his remarriage, only the slightest of hints that they may not have entirely approved, possibly because of the difference in the couple's ages; Della, for instance, was thirty-five at the time, perhaps almost the same age as her new stepmother. George Jr., back in Ohio working as a lawyer (perhaps for the Ohio state government), does not seem to have visited Philadelphia often after 1915. Mamie may have continued working at People's Bank as a teller until it closed, but had probably already moved into her own home elsewhere in Philadelphia.

The family would soon be disrupted by tragedy. Just after turning thirty-six, Della died unexpectedly of heart failure in Washington on February 4, 1916, after a brief bout with scarlet fever. Newlyweds George and Ellen White made the sad journey to Washington to bury Della in Woodlawn Cemetery and bring back his young granddaughter, Fannie, according to the *Bee*. It was a sad blow to the aging George White.[33]

The death of Mary Ann Cherry in Tarboro in early 1917 was a sadly poignant event for White. The stalwart family matriarch, now entering her ninth decade, had remained his closest tie to the beloved Cora Lena; he had dutifully helped his mother-in-law draw up her will in 1914 and served as its executor. Mrs. Cherry had by then outlived all but three of her ten children, and divided most of her modest estate among the survivors—Georgianna Green, 60, and her brothers, Henry, 55, and Clarence, 41—but designated

32. "Whitesboro Zephyrs," *Philadelphia Tribune*, 19 August 1916; "Whitesboro News," *Philadelphia Tribune*, 12 May 1915. During a 1915 visit to Whitesboro before his remarriage, White had been "accompanied by a friend, whose name we unfortunately have missed," undoubtedly his future wife.

33. "The Week in Society," *Washington Bee*, 19 February 1916; "Deaths Reported," *Washington Post*, 6 February 1916. Della Garrett's death certificate, on file with the District of Columbia's Vital Records Division, describes her as married and aged 29 (closer to sister Mamie's age). At the time of her death, Della lived alone with her daughter at 1315 Riggs Street, NW, near her father's former residence; the whereabouts of her husband, J. W. "Oscar" Garrett, are not recorded. Woodlawn was the city's best-known African American cemetery at the time, containing the graves of such notables as Blanche K. Bruce and John Mercer Langston.

part of the proceeds of land sales for the five children of her deceased daughters, Cora Lena and Louisa.[34]

In 1917, two more major changes occurred in White's life; one was traumatic, the other much less so. People's Savings Bank appears to have begun suffering financially, perhaps as a result of competition from the new and rapidly growing Brown and Stevens Bank, located a few blocks away on Lombard Street. The private bank was run by two up-and-coming insurance men with previous banking experience, Edward C. Brown and Andrew W. Stevens. Brown and Stevens had previously run an insurance and real-estate company at the same location; Brown, a Philadelphia native, had also organized savings banks in both Newport News and Norfolk, Virginia, as early as 1908, and was still president of the Norfolk bank in 1929, although his Philadelphia flagship had ceased to exist by then.[35]

Perhaps owing also to external economic factors, since this was the year of America's entry into the Great War, George White's bank soon failed. Although conflicting dates appear in the public record, the People's Savings Bank may have closed its doors in liquidation as early as February 1917, and had definitely been dissolved by April 1918; whether it closed voluntarily, was ordered closed by the state, or was even merged into another bank, is not known. Since it was a state-chartered bank, it was required to go through a bureaucratic dissolution process, which was apparently lengthy but not easily traced.[36]

34. Mary Ann Cherry's will, probated in May of 1917, is on file in the office of the Edgecombe County Clerk of Superior Court, Tarboro. Louisa, Mary Ann, and two of their brothers all died before 1900, followed by Cora Lena in 1905. Mrs. Cherry left son Henry the possessions of his brother William, indicating William may have died just before the will was drawn up in 1914.

35. Armstrong Association, *The Negro in Business in Philadelphia* (Philadelphia, 1918); Reid, "Post-Congressional Career," 372; "New Real Estate and Banking," *Philadelphia Tribune*, 18 January 1913; Lindsay, "The Negro in Banking"; Abram L. Harris, *The Negro as Capitalist: A Study of Banking and Business among American Negroes* (New York: Haskell House, 1970), 124–43. The private Brown and Stevens Bank, formed in January 1916, is almost certainly the unnamed successful example cited by the Armstrong study of 1916–1918. Reid applies the Armstrong description to People's Savings Bank, which had closed by 1918; among other discrepancies, White had no partner and no white tenants lived on the upper floors of his bank building. According to Armstrong, the "new" bank showed a gross business of nearly $180,000 in August 1917, a date when People's Savings Bank was technically still open but soon to be liquidated. The B&S building was located at 427 Broad Street, at the corner of Lombard.

36. Reid, "Post-Congressional Career," 371. Reid lists two dates supplied by the Department of Banking, Commonwealth of Pennsylvania. People's Savings Bank was liquidated on February 21, 1917; and formally dissolved on April 25, 1918.

But two clues offer possible answers to the mystery. For one, Mamie White went to work for Brown and Stevens shortly afterward, indicating at least that her ties to her father's bank were not viewed negatively; had People's Bank failed for reasons of mismanagement, for instance, this might not have been the case. Secondly, the Brown and Stevens Company reported a remarkable increase in its deposits in a very short period, growing from less than $900 upon opening in January 1916 to more than $250,000 just two years later, according to their advertisements, indicating a strong possibility of expansion by acquisition—perhaps of People's Savings Bank assets, almost certainly of its customers—along the way.[37]

Reports of the state of financial health of People's Savings Bank are conflicting. One chronicler says its "resources and liabilities never exceeded $11,000." Local newspaper coverage, admittedly less objective, claimed White's bank had received more than $3 million in aggregate deposits between 1907 and 1915.[38] Much of this, apparently, was loaned out, perhaps never to be recouped; purchasers of land in Whitesboro reputedly formed the bulk of its borrowers. But the bank had never been envisioned primarily as a moneymaking institution on a large scale, and for whatever reason his bank was dissolved, George White now faced the unexpected prospect of free time, if not a sharply reduced income as well, in 1917.

It was sadly ironic that a major municipal appointment would appear at just this time, especially under the circumstances of a good friend's death. Harry W. Bass, fellow lawyer and former state legislator, died on June 9, 1917, at age fifty. He had served as an assistant municipal solicitor since February 1916, when Solicitor John P. Connelly had kept a campaign promise to hire at least one black assistant among the eleven staff members he planned to add. Instead, Connelly had hired two blacks, Bass and local attorney John C. Asbury; both were active Republicans, and both had campaigned with White during the 1915 municipal elections.[39]

37. Obituary for Mary A. White, New York Amsterdam News, 7 December 1974; advertisement, Brown and Stevens Bank, Philadelphia Tribune, 11 January 1919. According to her obituary, Mamie White "worked for many years at Brown and Stevenson [sic] bank, the first Black bank in Philadelphia."

38. Harris, The Negro as Capitalist, 124; "The Marvelous Growth of the Peoples Savings Bank."

39. "Harry W. Bass, Noted Orator and Lawyer Buried," Philadelphia Tribune, 16 June 1917; "Hon. George H. White Appointed Assistant City Solicitor," Philadelphia Tribune, 7 July 1917.

By July 7, 1917, sixty-four-year-old George White was named to succeed Bass as assistant city solicitor, assigned to handle prosecution of cases in the municipal court he had once hoped to serve as judge.[40] It was his first public position since leaving Congress in 1901, and the last in a long and distinguished career. Whether he actively sought the appointment, on whose recommendation he was hired, or precisely how long he remained in the job all remain to be answered. That he received one last opportunity to show his talent, at the end of his career, is perhaps enough.

Seventeen months later, the farmer's son from Bladen County died. The *Philadelphia Tribune*, always friendly to George White, described his passing in a full column on its front page a week later, mixing factual descriptions with metaphoric prose. "After sixty-six years of toil, success, disappointments, worries and cares all incident to human life, former Congressman Geo. H. White died at his late residence early last Saturday morning," the article opened. According to a subheadline, White "retired apparently in good health and buoyant spirit," then died in his sleep in the early morning of December 28, ten days after his sixty-sixth birthday.[41]

The *Tribune's* obituary painted a highly personalized view of "one of the strongest men the race has produced," ranging from his birth through his days as a solicitor, with detailed attention to his two terms as the last black congressman. "To have known Mr. White didn't necessarily mean you would share all his views," said the writer, probably *Tribune* occasional editor T. Thomas Fortune, "but you were compelled to respect him." The writer recalled witnessing a conversation between White and the late President McKinley, in which even the man from Ohio found the congressman's "strong personality" irresistible; hearing that White had been unable "to get the ear of a Department chief in appointing a constituent," the President wrote a few words on a piece of paper, signed his name and handed it to White. "The appointment was made that day."[42]

White "brings a wealth of experience in legal knowledge to the position," the newspaper said; he was listed as "ex-Congressman and banker," indicating the People's Savings Bank was still open at this point.

40. "Sudden Death of George H. White, Esq., Saturday Morning," *Philadelphia Tribune*, 4 January 1919.

41. Ibid. White's luck with McKinley had not lasted into his own second term, when he was told by official letter that the slots for several requested appointments were "already filled."

42. "Sudden Death of George H. White, Esq., Saturday Morning."

The indomitable youth from the rural forests of North Carolina had been "endowed with an exceptionally large amount of native ability," but had sought an education to polish himself, "blaz[ing] his way until he found the open, where his native talent had an opportunity to be strengthened to such proportions that men would call him great." When White served as solicitor, he was "successful in having justice meted out to more criminals than any solicitor preceding him," according to his fellow lawyers. He was a "strong race man," yet never showed favoritism when it came to enforcing the law. In Congress, his maiden speech had caused "members dozing in the cloakrooms [to] rush in to resume their seats" to hear the great orator speak, and it remained that way until his departure; "it was all respectful attention and applause whenever the Speaker had occasion . . . to say, 'The Chair recognizes the gentleman from North Carolina.'"[43]

Yet for all its glowing words, the *Tribune* inexplicably glossed over White's final years in Philadelphia, mentioning only "his successful [law] practice, making himself felt in the courts and in the general affairs of the community" in one brief paragraph. There was no mention of the land development firm, of People's Savings Bank, of his position as assistant solicitor, or of any of the countless charitable and political endeavors in which he had been involved. Not even his beloved Whitesboro drew note. In similar short fashion, the newspaper only cursorily noted his recent marriage to Mrs. Macdonald, "with whom he lived happily," and did not give his children's names; Cora Lena was vaguely referred to only as "his late wife," and his first two marriages, however brief, were not mentioned.

Funeral services had been held "over his remains" at White's Lombard Street home, curiously enough, on New Year's Eve, and he was buried the same day. In the year-end news rush, few mainstream newspapers in other cities noted his death, although the *New York Times* managed to insert a brief notice in its Sunday edition on December 29, albeit misspelling his name and calling him only "a negro member of the Fifty-fifth and Fifty-Sixth Congresses from North Carolina." Neither the *Philadelphia Inquirer* nor the *Washington Post* mentioned his passing; the *Washington Bee* carried a four-line notice in its

43. Ibid. According to the article, White was "survived by a wife, one daughter and a son. These children being the offspring of the union between the deceased and his first [sic] wife, who died some years ago." Elsewhere on the same page, the *Tribune* extended sympathy to "Miss White, in the loss of her father, Ex-Congressman White."

next edition, six days later. Alone among the major newspapers of the East Coast was the *Washington Sunday Star,* which carried the only story of any real length; its wire-service article noted White's previous political offices, the name of his successor in Congress from the Second District—Claude Kitchin, still in the House in 1918—and a brief acknowledgment that White had not returned to North Carolina after leaving Congress.[44]

The longest obituary, ironically, came on the front page of the newspaper still owned by White's old adversary, Josephus Daniels. The Sunday edition of the *Raleigh News and Observer* carried a remarkably neutral and factual version, somewhat amplified, of the wire-service story, with two minor errors: White's birthplace was listed as Columbus County, rather than Bladen, and his home while in Congress as Craven County, not Edgecombe. There was, for once, no mention of the ill-fated 1898 address, or the nasty 1900 quarrel over his antilynching speech. Josephus Daniels's intervening years in Washington, perhaps, had tempered his distaste for an old adversary.[45]

By this time, of course, George White was a man from another era, one whose time in the narrow beam of the public limelight had long since passed. For all the acclaim he had once received from his colleagues in Congress, no one rose to pay tribute to him there; there was no black member of the House to do so, nor would there be for another decade to come. White had outlived many younger and more celebrated black contemporaries, such as Booker T. Washington, Alexander Walters, and even Harry Bass, and none had tried harder to serve his race. "Nobly did he battle for our people," editorialized the hometown *Tribune* a week after printing his obituary. "Against great odds his heart always rang true."[46]

The race of life had ended for George White. Another noble heart stopped shortly afterward, and the *Tribune* paused to honor both at once. Its comparable tribute to the late Theodore Roosevelt, who died during the first week of January, was the lead editorial in that week's edition, and the irony of its placement was bittersweet; the former president had followed White into the

44. "George P. White," obituary, *New York Times,* 29 December 1918; "G. H. White, Last Negro Congressman, Is Dead," *Washington Sunday Star,* 29 December 1918; untitled article, *Washington Bee,* 4 January 1919. The *Times* listed the wrong middle initial ("P.") and the wrong age (sixty) for White.

45. "Geo. White, Last Negro Congressman, Is Dead," *RN&O,* 29 December 1918.

46. "Death Loves a Shining Mark," editorial, *Philadelphia Tribune,* 11 January 1919.

next life by a length, but still led him over the threshold into history by a nose.

Colonel Roosevelt was "the most forceful character on the American stage . . . besides being a great leader of men, and a thorough American, [he] was a refined gentleman," the *Tribune* thought, recalling his impromptu invitation to Booker T. Washington to join him at a White House meal shortly after William McKinley's death and his own assumption of the nation's highest office. By becoming the first U.S. president to share a White House meal with a black guest, his invitation had caused a national scandal. But according to the *Tribune*, Roosevelt "simply believed he was doing what was right. No matter what others thought."[47]

The same might well have been said for the man Roosevelt had later declined to appoint to office. For more than a quarter of a century, the *Tribune* now wrote, George White had answered every call "for his splendid aid, either active or sympathetic," often without notice or praise. "Like other men possessing a strong personality, he had his enemies as well as his friends. He was a splendid orator, a good lawyer and a very congenial companion.

"As an advocate he was clear sighted, pointed and wise, and the way he held audiences spellbound won for him many honors in public life. That he made mistakes in his lifetime may not be denied. But who among us have not made mistakes?"[48] The newspaper did not specify his mistakes, nor did it need to; most readers would have understood them intuitively, as they had seemed to understand the man himself—stubborn, tenacious, outspoken, sometimes naïve, compassionate, principled to a fault. Ultimately, he had not succeeded in politics because he could not compromise when circumstances required it; his pride had been the great stumbling block, the pride of a warrior whose defeat is certain but who fights on for the noble cause.

Ten years after his death, almost to the day, White's prophecy of 1901 was fulfilled as Oscar De Priest was elected to the House from Chicago in November 1928, succeeding White as the "leader of the black phalanx." Gradually the number would begin to increase again; by 1945, two; by the 1960s, a half-dozen at once. Like White, however, De Priest served out his three terms as the single elected black member. On a day in February 1930, his solitary status

47. "The Nation Mourns His Death," editorial, ibid., 11 January 1919.
48. "Death Loves a Shining Mark."

changed momentarily, as he rose in the House to introduce two aging companions from another era: John R. Lynch, eighty-two, who had last served nearly a half-century earlier, and Thomas E. Miller, eighty, who had left the House in 1891, a decade before White's retirement. Both received polite, formal applause as they stood next to their younger companion. "I am glad to have the privilege of presenting these gentlemen to you," De Priest said proudly. "They happen to be gentlemen of the racial group with which I am identified, so I am not the only one left."[49]

The trio stood for another moment, arms linked in solidarity, before the House returned to its business. But for an instant, perhaps, a fourth image might have smiled knowingly from a stance just behind them, into the sea of desks and nodding faces of his successors. Perhaps Oscar De Priest had never been completely alone, after all; perhaps George White had been at his shoulder all along, pointing the way.

49. *Congressional Record*, 71st Cong., 2d Sess. (1930), 1:3382. Lynch had retired from Congress in 1883. Miller (1849–1938) had served part of one term from 1890–1891, after he and John Mercer Langston had won contests for seats in the 1888 election. Former congressman Henry Cheatham, now seventy-three, had served with Miller, but did not attend the ceremony. White would have been seventy-seven in 1930.

Epilogue: Eden at Last

For more than a half century after his death, there was little public interest in George Henry White. While articles about him did appear periodically in various African American journals and magazines, few gave him more than cursory treatment, and none appeared in the mainstream media. After the 1972 election of Andrew Young to Congress from Atlanta, however, a certain amount of regional interest in Young's last predecessor from the South did begin to emerge. In mid-1975, the North Carolina Museum of History in Raleigh opened a temporary exhibit on White, as one of several prominent black North Carolinians past and present. A year later, the state's Division of Archives and History dedicated a new historical highway marker to him on New Bern's Broad Street, two blocks south of his Johnson Street home. The house also bears a plaque in his memory.[1]

The street marker's inscription briefly summarizes his career: "George H. White, 1852–1918. Lawyer; member of N.C. legislature, 1881 & 1885. U.S. Congressman, 1897–1901. Born into slavery. Home stands 2 blocks N." Its June 1976 unveiling drew an appreciative audience of black citizens from across the state. White's home at 519 Johnson Street—soon purchased and restored by its new owners, who erected a smaller private plaque to him—would also draw history-minded sightseers of both races. One group of North

1. "Museum Honors Bladen Native," *Fayetteville (N.C.) Observer*, 19 June 1975; reproduction of invitation to marker-dedication ceremony, 2 June 1976, North Carolina Collection Clipping File, UNC Library, University of North Carolina at Chapel Hill.

Carolina lawyers would make a special trip there in 1994, including among them U.S. representative Melvin Watt, one of two African Americans elected to the House from North Carolina in 1992.[2]

No monuments to George White have been raised either in Washington, D.C., or in Philadelphia, where he spent the last dozen years of his life. His grave lies in Delaware County's Eden Cemetery, near Darby, Pennsylvania. Eden was a relatively new graveyard when White arrived in Pennsylvania in 1906, having been dedicated just four years earlier by Jerome Bacon, a teacher at Philadelphia's Institute for Colored Youth (later Cheyney State College). Two of Bacon's partners, John C. Asbury and Martin Lehman, became associates of George White after he moved to Philadelphia. By the time of White's death, Eden had become the only black-owned cemetery of any size in the area. More than eighty thousand of Philadelphia's citizens were interred there by the end of the twentieth century, including such notable blacks as *Tribune* publisher Christopher J. Perry and Amos Scott, Philadelphia's first black magistrate, both White's close friends; the ashes of world-famous singer Marian Anderson, a Philadelphia native who died in 1993, are also interred there. Eden's fifty-three acres of beautifully wooded, rolling grounds also hold the graves relocated from at least four other black cemeteries in the region, after those cemeteries were closed.[3]

The George H. White Land and Improvement Company continued in

2. *Guide to North Carolina Highway Historical Markers*, 8th ed. (Raleigh: N.C. Department of Cultural Resources, 1990), 21; author's interview with U.S. Representative Melvin Watt (D-N.C.), February 26, 1999, Washington, D.C. Similar highway markers have since been erected to two of the state's three other black congressmen—Henry P. Cheatham (Oxford) and John A. Hyman (Warrenton)—as well as to Alabama congressman Benjamin S. Turner, born in Weldon, and to U.S. senator Hiram R. Revels of Mississippi, a Fayetteville native who lived in Lincolnton during the 1840s.

3. Roberta Hughes Wright and Wilbur B. Hughes III, *Lay Down Body: Living History in African American Cemeteries* (Detroit: Visible Ink Press, 1996), 174–5; Lane, *William Dorsey's Philadelphia*, 110; Wright, *The Philadelphia Colored Directory*, 57. The four other black cemeteries absorbed into Eden included the First African Baptist Church cemetery of Delaware County, dating from 1824–1842, excavated in the 1980s, and the private Lebanon, Olive, and Home cemeteries of Philadelphia. The Lebanon cemetery had been closed in 1903, the Olive cemetery was condemned shortly afterward, and the Home cemetery was condemned in the later twentieth century. In 1908, the Eden Cemetery Company's offices were located on Lombard Street near the People's Savings Bank.

business for a number of years after the death of its founder, at least until the Great Depression hit. Under the leadership of a new president, Gibson T. Harrison, the firm relocated to an address on 15th Street in 1919. By 1923, it had begun marketing residential homesites in Wildwood Junction Heights, east of the town of Whitesboro, New Jersey; this may have consisted of undeveloped land remaining from the original tract purchased in 1901, or may have been converted farmland. According to the *Cape May County Gazette*, the lots were selling rapidly in March 1923, reversing a decade-long decline in interest among buyers. The company apparently closed its doors in the late 1920s.[4]

The town continues to exist; although it never truly prospered, Whitesboro still boasts more than a thousand residents and its own post office, and Spaulding descendants are still active among the town's citizenry. Willie Spaulding's son Daniel, born in 1909, later became the town's historian. A street in the small town was named in honor of George White in the years after his death, although the Odessa Inn—named for his youngest daughter— no longer stands.

Less is known about George White's immediate family after his death. His widow, Ellen, may have remained in Philadelphia for a short time after her husband died, but if so, she no longer lived in the Lombard Street apartment in 1919. Ellen White soon remarried and moved to Atlantic City, New Jersey, where she was widowed once again in the late 1930s. There is no mention after 1916 of George White's one known grandchild, Fannie Garrett, after her summer visit to Whitesboro with her grandparents that year.[5]

Daughter Mamie, who went to work for the black-owned Brown and Stevens Bank as a cashier, apparently remained in the Philadelphia area for another decade or so, then moved to New York City sometime after 1931, purchasing an apartment in the Bronx. Over the next forty years, Mamie worked in various capacities, including as a telephone operator, secretary, and personal assistant, and volunteered in various charitable organizations.

---

4. Philadelphia city directory listings for 1919–1927; Dorwart, *Cape May County*, 197. The George H. White firm was located at 26 S. 15th Street in 1919, and had moved to 23 S. 15th Street by 1921. Dorwart cites the *Cape May County Gazette* of 2 March 1923, which wrote that Whitesboro buyers were "mostly colored and hailing from all parts of the country."

5. Author's telephone interview with Carl Moultrie. Ellen White married Edward Coston, who was a policeman in Atlantic City.

Although she continued to use "Miss White" until her death, she apparently married at one point, but had no known children, and was listed as "divorced" on her 1974 death certificate. She became the longest-lived person in her immediate family, dying of natural causes just three weeks before her eighty-seventh birthday; survivors included a number of cousins from both sides of her family. On her mother's side, cousin Charles Cheatham died shortly afterward in nearby New Rochelle, New York, while Mamie Cheatham Wormley—her childhood playmate—died eighteen months later in Phoenix, Arizona; both were aged eighty-eight. The executor of Mamie's will was a more distant cousin, Dr. Odessa Spaulding of Philadelphia, daughter of Whitesboro postmaster Willie Spaulding, who remained close to Mamie until her death.[6]

George H. White Jr. lived until November 1927, when he died of pulmonary tuberculosis in a Pittsburgh sanitarium. Both he and Mamie are buried beside their father in Eden Cemetery, with a single new headstone—placed there by Dr. Spaulding after Mamie's death—bearing all three names. His last reported address was in Ohio in 1918, where he worked as a lawyer, according to the *Lincoln University Biographical Catalogue, 1918*; the catalogue listed his address as Cincinnati, although he probably lived instead in Cleveland, where he had attended law school. An anecdotal remark cited in George Reid's "Biography" paints the youth as "a fast spender of money and the primary reason why his father died poor," but there is no evidence to corroborate this, and no information on his activities after his father's death.[7]

6. Obituary for Mary A. White, *New York Amsterdam News*, 7 December 1974; Oberlin College records; U.S. Social Security records; personal recollections of Dr. Odessa Spaulding, Philadelphia, Pennsylvania; Last Will and Testament of Mary A. White, dated June 5, 1973; Certificate of Death, Bureau of Vital Records, City of New York, dated December 5, 1974. Mamie White's obituary contained minor historical errors, but correctly noted her father's name and her own attendance at Oberlin College. She was apparently married at least once, to Arthur H. Payne; they were divorced in 1918. The dates and places of death for Charles Cheatham and Mamie Cheatham Wormley are from U.S. Social Security records. Dr. Spaulding attended Mamie's funeral and burial, and later erected the gravestone for Mamie's family at her cousin's request.

7. Records at the Eden Memorial Cemetery, 1434 Springfield Road, Darby, Pa.; *Lincoln University Biographical Catalogue, 1918*, 101; city directories, Cincinnati and Cleveland, Ohio, 1915–1920; Reid, "A Biography," 44. White was buried in the "Celestine" area of the cemetery on December 31, 1918. Son George Jr. was buried there on December 6, 1927, followed by Mamie on December 7, 1974; the headstone, much newer than those around it, lists Mamie

The Spaulding family's branches in North Carolina and New Jersey produced a number of extremely influential citizens in the decades after George White's death. Charles Clinton Spaulding, White's first cousin through his stepmother, became one of the nation's most successful African American businessmen of his generation, heading the North Carolina Mutual Life Insurance Company of Durham for nearly thirty years. C. C. Spaulding also became an ardent supporter of Franklin Delano Roosevelt's New Deal policies, thus breaking historical ranks with the staunch Republicanism of his kinsman and his own family.[8] In Philadelphia, attorney Theodore O. Spaulding—oldest son of Whitesboro postmaster Willie Spaulding—bettered George White's local record on at least two counts by becoming the city's second black to serve as a municipal judge and second black Republican nominee for Congress, although his 1952 campaign was unsuccessful. His younger sister Odessa, a retired physician, still lives in Philadelphia.[9]

Over the decades, the White family name was gradually overshadowed in Philadelphia by that of their more successful Spaulding relatives. But more ironic, perhaps, was the appearance of yet another North Carolina family in Philadelphia. White's nephew Plummer Cheatham moved to Philadelphia after serving in the U.S. military in France during World War I; he attended

White's name first. The *Lincoln* entry characterized George White Jr. as a "lawy[er], state of Ohio," and listed his current address as "217 Am Trust Building, Cincinnati, O."; the American Trust Building, however, was in Cleveland. In any event, George White Jr. was listed in neither city's directory between 1915–1920; perhaps he was not yet in private practice, or not yet licensed in Ohio. The remark about him was attributed by Reid to Cleveland Watson of the Cape May County Planning Department.

8. "Charles Clinton Spaulding," *DNCB*, 5:408. Spaulding (1874–1952) became general manager of North Carolina Mutual Life in 1898 and its president in 1923. He was a son of Benjamin Mclean Spaulding, Mary Anna White's brother.

9. Saunders, *100 Years after Emancipation*, xvii, 116, 118; Odessa Spaulding, "Between the Ocean and the Bay," unpublished manuscript provided to the author; letters from Odessa Spaulding to the author, October 1999–January 2000. Theodore Spaulding (1902–1974) ran for Congress from Pennsylvania's Fourth District in 1952 against incumbent Democrat Earl Chudoff; the first black Republican nominee in the Fourth had been Edward W. Henry in 1940. Spaulding's sister Odessa remained close to Mamie White until her death, and made the arrangements for Mamie's funeral and burial in 1974. Their brother Daniel Spaulding (1909–1998), the town's unofficial historian, spent much of his life as a mortgage officer and real estate broker in Maryland. Their mother, Hattie Spaulding, died in Whitesboro in 1971, at age 91.

law school at Temple University and established a legal practice in that city in 1925, not far from his late uncle's home. He was married with one son in 1929, according to a national directory of prominent black citizens, but appears to have died soon afterward.[10]

Plummer's father, the former congressman, was still active in his late seventies as the superintendent of the state's orphanage for black children in Oxford, North Carolina, when he died there in 1935. The elder Cheatham's obituary in the *New York Times* was significantly longer than that accorded his brother-in-law seventeen years earlier, and more precisely accurate as well. In death, if not in life, Henry Cheatham had finally surpassed George White in public recognition.[11]

10. *Who's Who in Colored America, 1929,* 74; Philadelphia city directory for 1927–28. The entry spelled Plummer Cheatham's last name as "Cheatem," along with that of his father, who had no separate listing; Plummer's office is listed as 501 S. 16th Street. Some confusion arises here over Plummer's full name; the *Who's Who* listing contains no "Jr.," then lists his son's name as "Henry P., Jr., b. March 28, 1918." The city directory shows entries for both Henry P. Cheatham and Henry P. Cheatham Jr.; these include the legal offices (1504 South), a home address at 5330 Girard Avenue for Henry P. Cheatham, and a home listing for Henry P. Cheatham Jr. at 2024 N. 16th Street.

11. Associated Press obituary for Henry P. Cheatham, *New York Times,* 30 November 1935. Technically, the obituary misstated his age as seventy-eight—he actually died a month before his birthday—but his name and the facts of his life were accurate. The glowing description of his accomplishments was certainly longer than that given White, who had drawn just four lines in the *Times* in 1918, with his name misspelled and his age wrong.

Appendix

"Farewell Speech" delivered by Representative George H. White before
the U.S. House of Representatives, January 29, 1901

Source: *Congressional Record*, 56th Cong., 2d sess., 34, pt. 1:1634–8.
(Editor's note: Certain portions of the speech dealing with technical details have
been deleted for brevity.)

The CHAIRMAN. The gentleman from North Carolina is recognized in his own right.

Mr. WHITE. Mr. Chairman, in the consideration of the bill now under debate the Committee on Agriculture has had a wide and very varied experience. We have had the farmers and their interests fully represented, and demand that the present seed list, giving to each Member and Delegate 9,000 packages, shall not be diminished, but rather increased. The beauties of their avocation have been elaborately portrayed. The increase of the agricultural industry has been shown beyond any possible doubt, and a little Department, but a few years ago controlled by a commissioner of agriculture, has now grown to wonderful proportion, and is now presided over by a Cabinet officer, Secretary of Agriculture, if you please, and a very good one he is. And with the present ratio of increase this Department is destined in a few years to be one of the largest, if not surpassing all other departments in the President's Cabinet. But this side of the question, with its heterogeneous interests and growth, is not without opposition. . . .

But, Mr. Chairman, there are others on this committee and in this House who are far better prepared to enlighten the world with their eloquence as to what the agriculturists of this country need than your humble servant. I therefore resign to more competent minds the discussion of this bill. I shall consume the remainder of my time in reverting to measures and facts that have in them more weighty interests to me and mine than that of agriculture—matters of life and existence.

I want to enter a plea for the colored man, the colored woman, the colored boy and the colored girl of this country. I would not thus digress from the question at issue and detain the House in a discussion of the interests of this particular people at this time but for the constant and the persistent efforts of certain gentlemen upon this floor to mold and rivet public sentiment against us as a people and to lose no opportunity to hold up the unfortunate few who commit crimes and depredations and lead lives of infamy and shame, as other races do, as fair specimens of representatives of the entire colored race. And at no time, perhaps, during the Fifty-sixth Congress were these charges and countercharges, containing, as they do, slanderous statements, more persistently magnified and pressed upon the attention of the nation than during the consideration of the recent reapportionment bill, which is now a law. As stated some days ago on this floor by me, I then sought diligently to obtain an opportunity to answer some of the statements made by gentlemen from different States, but the privilege was denied me; and I therefore must embrace this opportunity to say, out of season, perhaps, that which I was not permitted to say in season.

In the catalogue of members of Congress in this House perhaps none have been more persistent in their determination to bring the black man into disrepute and, with a labored effort, to show that he was unworthy of the right of citizenship than my colleague from North Carolina, Mr. KITCHIN. During the first session of this Congress, while the Constitutional amendment was pending in North Carolina, he labored long and hard to show that the white race was at all times and under all circumstances superior to the negro by inheritance if not otherwise, and the excuse for his party supporting that amendment, which has since been adopted, was that an illiterate negro was unfit to participate in making the laws of a sovereign State and the administration and execution of them; but an illiterate white man living by his side, with no more or perhaps not as much property, with no more exalted character, no higher thoughts of civilization, no more knowledge of the handicraft of government, had by birth, because he was white, inherited some peculiar qualification, clear, I presume, only in the mind of the gentleman who endeavored to impress it upon others, that entitled him to vote, though he knew nothing whatever of letters. It is true, in my opinion, that men brood over things at times which they would have exist until they fool themselves and actually, sometimes honestly, believe that such things do exist.

I would like to call the gentleman's attention to the fact that the Constitution of the United States forbids the granting of any title of nobility to any citizen thereof, and while it does not in letters forbid the inheritance of this superior caste, I believe in the fertile imagination of the gentleman promulgating it, his position is at least in conflict with the spirit of that organic law of the land. He insists and, I believe, has introduced a resolution in this House for the repeal of the fifteenth amendment to the Constitution. As an excuse for his peculiar notions about the exercise of the right of franchise by citizens of the United States of different nationality, perhaps it would not be amiss to call the attention of this House to a few facts and figures surrounding his birth and rearing. To begin with, he was born in one of the counties in my district, Halifax, a rather significant name.

I might state as a further general fact that the Democrats of North Carolina got possession of the State and local government since my last election in 1898, and that I bid adieu to these historic walls on the 4th day of next March, and that the brother of Mr. KITCHIN will succeed me. Comment is unnecessary. In the town where this young gentleman was born, at the general election last August for the adoption of the constitutional amendment, and the general election for State and county officers, Scotland Neck had a registered white vote of 395, most of whom of course were Democrats, and a registered colored vote of 534, virtually if not all of whom were Republicans, and so voted. When the count was announced, however, there were 831 Democrats to 75 Republicans; but in the town of Halifax, same county, the result was much more pronounced.

In that town the registered Republican vote was 345, and the total registered vote of the township was 539, but when the count was announced it stood 990 Democrats to 41 Republicans, or 492 more Democratic votes counted than were registered votes in the township. Comment here is unnecessary, nor do I think it necessary for anyone to wonder at the peculiar notion my colleague has with reference to the manner of voting and the method of counting those votes, nor is it to be a wonder that he is a member of this Congress, having been brought up and educated in such wonderful notions of dealing out fair-handed justice to his fellow-man.

It would be unfair, however, for me to leave the inference upon the minds of those who hear me that all of the white people of the State of North Carolina hold views with Mr. KITCHIN and think as he does. Thank God there are many noble exceptions to the example he sets, that, too, in the Democratic party; men who have never been afraid that one uneducated, poor, depressed negro could put to flight and chase into degradation two educated, wealthy, thrifty white men. There never has been, nor ever will be, any negro domination in that State, and no one knows it any better than the Democratic party. It is a convenient howl, however, often resorted to in order to consummate a diabolical purpose by scaring the weak and gullible whites into support of measures and men suitable to the demagogue and the ambitious office seeker, whose crave for office overshadows and puts to flight all other considerations, fair or unfair.

As I stated on a former occasion, this young statesman has ample time to learn better and more useful knowledge than he has exhibited in many of his speeches upon this floor, and I again plead for him the statute of youth for the wild and spasmodic notions which he has endeavored to rivet upon his colleagues and this country. But I regret that Mr. KITCHIN is not alone upon this floor in these peculiar notions advanced. I quote from another young member of Congress, hailing from the State of Alabama [Mr. UN-DERWOOD]:

> Mr. Speaker, in five minutes the issues involved in this case can not be discussed. I was in hopes that this question would not come up at this session of Congress. When the fourteenth amendment was originally adopted it was the intention of the legislative body that enacted it and of the people who ratified it to force the Southern people to give the elective franchise to the negro. That was the real purpose of the fourteenth amendment. It failed in that purpose. The fifteenth amendment was adopted for the same purpose. That was successful for the time being. It has proved a lamentable mistake, not only to the people of the South, but to the people of the World, not only to the Democratic party, but to the Republican Party.
>
> The time has now come when the bitterness of civil strife has passed. The people of the South, with fairness and justice to themselves and fairness to that race that has been forced among them—the negro race—are attempting to work away from those conditions; not to

oppress or to put their foot on the neck of the negro race, but to protect their homes and their property against misgovernment and at the same time give this inferior race a chance to grow up and acquire their civilization. When you bring this resolution before this House and thrust it as a firebrand into the legislation here, you do more injury to the negro race of the South than any man has done since the fifteenth amendment was originally enacted. I tell you, sirs, there is but one way to solve this problem. You gentlemen of the North, who do not live among them and do not know the conditions, can not solve it.

We of the South are trying, as God is our judge, to solve it fairly to both races. It can not be done in a day or a week: and I appeal to you, if you are in favor of the unbuilding of the negro race, if you are in favor of honest governments in the Southern States, if you are willing to let us protect our homes and our property—yes, and the investments that you have brought there among us—then I say to you, let us send this resolution to a committee where it may die and never be heard of again. When we have done that, when we have worked out the problem and put if upon a fair basis, then if we are getting more representation than we are entitled to, five or six or ten years from now come to us with the proposition fairly to repeal both the fourteenth and fifteenth amendments and substitute in their place a constitutional amendment that will put representation on a basis that we can all agree is fair and equitable. Do not let us drive it along party lines.

It is an undisputed fact that the negro vote in the State of Alabama, as well as most of the other Southern States, have been effectively suppressed, either one way or the other—in some instances by constitutional amendment and State legislation, in others by cold-blooded fraud and intimidation, but whatever the method pursued, it is not denied, but frankly admitted in the speeches in this House, that the black vote has been eliminated to a large extent. Then, when some of us insist that the plain letter of the Constitution of the United States, which all of us have sworn to support, should be carried out, as expressed in the second section of the fourteenth amendment thereof, to wit:

Representatives shall be apportioned among the several States according to their respective numbers, counting the whole number of persons in each State, excluding Indians not taxed. But when the right to vote at any election for the choice of electors for President and Vice-President of the United States, Representatives in Congress, the executive and judicial officers of a State, or the members of a legislature thereof, is denied to any of the male inhabitants of such State, being twenty-one years of age, and citizens of the United States, or in any way abridged, except for participation in rebellion, or other crime, the basis of representation therein shall be reduced in proportion which the number of such male citizens shall bear to the whole number of male citizens twenty-one years of age in such State. [end of Mr. UNDERWOOD's statement]

That section makes the duty of every member of Congress plain, and yet the gentleman from Alabama [Mr. UNDERWOOD] says that the attempt to enforce this section of the organic law is the throwing down of firebrands, and notifies the world that this attempt to execute the highest law of the land will be retaliated by the South, and the inference is that the negro will be even more severely punished than the horrors through which he has already come.

Let me make it plain: The divine law, as well as most of the State laws, says in substance: "He that sheddeth man's blood, by man shall his blood be shed." A highwayman commits murder, and when the officers of the law undertake to arrest, try, and punish him commensurate with the enormity of his crime, he straightens himself up to his full height and defiantly says to them: "Let me alone: I will not be arrested, I will not be tried, I'll have none of the execution of your laws, and in the event you attempt to execute your laws upon me, I will see to it that many more men, women, or children are murdered."

Here's the plain letter of the Constitution, the plain, simple, sworn duty of every member of Congress; yet these gentlemen from the South say "Yes, we have violated your Constitution of the nation; we regarded it as a local necessity; and now, if you undertake to punish us as the Constitution prescribes, we will see to it that our former deeds of disloyalty to that instrument, our former acts of disfranchisement and opposition to the highest law of the land will be repeated many fold."

Not content with all that has been done to the black man, not because of any deeds that he has done, Mr. UNDERWOOD advances the startling information that these people have been thrust upon the whites of the South, forgetting, perhaps, the horrors of the slave trade, the unspeakable horrors of the transit from the shores of Africa by means of the middle passage to the American clime; the enforced bondage of the blacks and their descendants for two and a half centuries in the United States, now, for the first time perhaps in the history of our lives, the information comes that these poor, helpless, and in the main inoffensive people were thrust upon our Southern brethren.

Individually, and so far as my race is concerned, I care but little about the reduction of Southern representation, except in so far as it becomes my duty to aid in the proper execution of all the laws of the land in whatever sphere in which I may be placed. Such reduction in representation, it is true, would make more secure the installment of the great Republican party in power for many years to come in all of its branches, and at the same time enable that great party to be able to dispense with the further support of the loyal negro vote: and I might here parenthetically state that there are some members of the Republican party to-day—"lily whites," if you please—who, after receiving the unalloyed support of the negro vote for over thirty years, now feel that they have grown a little too good for association with him politically, and are disposed to dump him overboard. I am glad to observe, however, that this class constitutes a very small percentage of those to whom we have always looked for friendship and protection.

I wish to quote from another Southern gentleman, not so young as my other friends, and who always commands attention in this House by his wit and humor, even though his speeches may not be edifying and instructive. I refer to Mr. OTEY, of Virginia, and quote from him in a recent speech on this floor, as follows:

> Justice is merely relative. It can exist between equals. It can exist among homogeneous people. Among equals—among heterogeneous people—it never has and, in the very nature of things, it never will obtain. It can exist among lions, but between lions and lambs, never. If justice were absolute, lions must of necessity perish. Open his ponderous jaws and find the strong teeth which God has made expressly to chew lamb's flesh! When the Society for the Prevention of Cruelty to Animals shall overcome this difficulty, men may hope to settle the race question along sentimental lines, not sooner.

These thoughts on the negro are from the pen, in the main, of one who has studied the negro question, and it was after I heard the gentle-

man from North Carolina, and after the introduction of the Crumpacker bill, that they occurred to me peculiarly appropriate.

I am wholly at sea as to just what Mr. OTEY had in view in advancing the
thoughts contained in the above quotation, unless he wishes to extend the
simile and apply the lion as a white man and the negro as a lamb. In that case
we will gladly accept the comparison, for of all animals known in God's creation the lamb is the most inoffensive, and has been in all ages held up as a
badge of innocence. But what will my good friend of Virginia do with the
Bible, for God says that He created all men of one flesh and blood? Again, we
insist on having one race—the lion clothed with great strength, vicious, and
with destructive propensities, while the other is weak, good natured, inoffensive, and useful—what will he do with all the heterogeneous intermediate animals, ranging all the way from the pure lion to the pure lamb, found on the
plantations of every Southern State in the Union?

I regard his borrowed thoughts, as he admits they are, as very inaptly applied. However, it has perhaps served the purpose for which he intended it—
the attempt to show the inferiority of the one and the superiority of the other.
I fear I am giving too much time in the consideration of these personal comments of members of Congress, but I trust I will be pardoned for making a
passing reference to one more gentleman—Mr. WILSON of South Carolina—who, in the early part of this month, made a speech some parts of which
did great credit to him, showing, as it did, capacity for collating, arranging,
and advancing thoughts of others and of making a pretty strong argument out
of a very poor case.

If he had stopped there, while not agreeing with him, many of us would
have been forced to admit that he had done well. But his purpose was incomplete until he dragged in the reconstruction days and held up to scorn and
ridicule the few ignorant, gullible, and perhaps purchasable negroes who served
in the State legislature of South Carolina over thirty years ago. Not a word
did he say about the unscrupulous white men, in the main bummers who followed in the wake of the Federal Army and settled themselves in the Southern
States, and preyed upon the ignorant and unskilled minds of the colored
people, looted the States of their wealth, brought into lowest disrepute the ignorant colored people, then hied away to their Northern homes for ease and
comfort the balance of their lives, or joined the Democratic party to obtain so-

cial recognition, and have greatly aided in depressing and further degrading those whom they had used as easy tools to accomplish a diabolical purpose.

These few ignorant men who chanced at that time to hold office are given as a reason why the black man should not be permitted to participate in the affairs of the Government which he is forced to pay taxes to support. He insists that they, the Southern whites, are the black man's best friend, and that they are taking him by the hand and trying to lift him up; that they are educating him. For all that he and all Southern people have done in this regard, I wish in behalf of the colored people of the South to extend our thanks. We are not ungrateful to friends, but feel that our toil has made our friends able to contribute the stinty pittance which we have received at their hands.

I read in a Democratic paper a few days ago, the Washington Times, an extract taken from a South Carolina paper, which was intended to exhibit the eagerness with which the negro is grasping every opportunity for educating himself. The clipping showed that the money for each white child in the State ranged from three to five times as much per capita as was given to each colored child. This is helping us some, but not to the extent that one would infer from the gentleman's speech.

If the gentleman to whom I have referred will pardon me, I would like to advance the statement that the musty records of 1868, filed away in the archives of Southern capitols, as to what the negro was thirty-two years ago, is not a proper standard by which the negro living on the threshold of the twentieth century should be measured. Since that time we have reduced the illiteracy of the race at least 45 per cent. We have written and published near 500 books. We have nearly 300 newspapers, 3 of which are dailies. We have now in practice over 2,000 lawyers and a corresponding number of doctors. We have accumulated over $12,000,000 worth of school property and about $40,000,000 worth of church property. We have about 140,000 farms and homes, valued at in the neighborhood of $750,000,000, and personal property valued at about $170,000,000. We have raised about $11,000,000 for educational purposes, and the property per capita for every colored man, woman, and child in the United States is estimated at $75.

We are operating successfully several banks, commercial enterprises among our people in the Southland, including 1 silk mill and 1 cotton factory. We have 32,000 teachers in the schools of the country; we have built, with the aid of our friends, about 20,000 churches, and support 7 colleges, 17 academies, 50 high schools, 5 law schools, 5 medical schools, and 25 theological seminaries. We have over 600,000 acres of land in the South alone. The cotton produced, mainly by black labor, has increased from 4,669,770 bales in 1860 to 11,235,000 in 1899. All this we have done under the most adverse circumstances. We have done it in the face of lynching, burning at the stake, with the humiliation of "Jim Crow" cars, the disfranchisement of our male citizens, slander and degradation of our Women, with the factories closed against us, no negro permitted to be conductor on the railway cars, whether run through the streets of our cities or across the prairies of our great country, no negro permitted to run as engineer on a locomotive, most of the mines closed against us. Labor unions—carpenters, painters, brick masons, machinists, hackmen, and those supplying nearly every conceivable avocation for livelihood have banded themselves together to better their condition, but, with few exceptions, the black face has been left out. The negroes are seldom employed in our mercantile stores. At this we do not wonder. Some day we hope to have them employed in our own stores. With all these odds against us, we are forging our way ahead, slowly, perhaps, but surely. You may tie us and then taunt us for a lack of bravery, but one day we will break the bonds. You may use our labor for two and a half centuries and then taunt us for our poverty, but let me remind you we will not always remain poor. You may withhold even the knowledge of how to read God's word and learn the way from earth to glory and then taunt us for our ignorance, but we would remind you that there is plenty of room at the top, and we are climbing.

After enforced debauchery, with the many kindred horrors incident to slavery, it comes with ill grace from the perpetrators of these deeds to hold up the shortcomings of some of our race to ridicule and scorn.

The new man, the slave who has grown out of the ashes of thirty-five years ago, is inducted into the political and social system, cast into the arena of manhood where he constitutes a new element and becomes a competitor for all its emoluments. He is put upon trial to test his ability to be counted worthy of freedom, worthy of the elective franchise, and thirty-five years of struggling against almost insurmountable odds, under conditions but little removed from slavery itself, he asks a fair and just judgment, not of those whose prejudice has endeavored to forestall, to frustrate his every forward movement, rather those who have lent a helping hand, that he might demonstrate the truth of "the fatherhood of God and the brotherhood of man."

Mr. Chairman, permit me to digress for a few moments for the purpose of calling the attention of the House to two bills which I regard as important, introduced by me in the early part of the first session of this Congress. The first was to give the United States control and entire jurisdiction over all cases of lynching and death by mob violence. During the last session of this Congress I took occasion to address myself in detail to this particular measure, but with all my efforts the bill still sweetly sleeps in the room of the committee to which it was referred. The necessity of legislation along this line is daily being demonstrated. The arena of the lyncher no longer is confined to Southern climes, but is stretching its hydra head over all parts of the Union.

Sow the seed of a tarnished name—
You sow the seed of eternal shame.

It is needless to ask what the harvest will be. You may dodge this question now; you may defer it to a more seasonable day; you may, as the gentleman from Maine, Mr. LITTLEFIELD, puts it—

Waddle in and waddle out,
Until the mind was left in doubt,
Whether the snake that made the track
Was going south or coming back.

This evil peculiar to America, yes, to the United States, must be met somehow, some day.

The other bill to which I wish to call attention is one introduced by me to appropriate $1,000,000 to reimburse depositors of the late Freedman's Savings and Trust Company.

A bill making appropriation for a similar purpose passed the Senate in the first session of the Fiftieth Congress. It was recommended by President Cleveland, and was urged by the Comptroller of the Currency, Mr. Trenholm, in 1886. I can not press home to your minds this matter more strongly than by reproducing the report of the Committee on Banking and Currency, made by Mr. Wilkins on the Senate bill above referred to, as follows:

"In March, 1865, the Freedman's Savings and Trust Company was incorporated by the Congress of the United States to meet the economic and commercial necessities of 7,000,000 of colored people recently emancipated.

"Its incorporators, 50 in number, were named in the act authorizing its erection, and embraced the names of leading philanthropic citizens of the United States, whose names, as was intended, commended the institution to those inexperienced, simple-minded people, who are today its principal creditors.

"The Freedman's Bank, as it is popularly called, was designed originally to perform for this trustful people the functions, as its name implies, of a savings bank, and none other than those hithertofore held in slavery or their descendants were to become its depositors."

Its purpose was (to quote the paragraph in the original law):

"To receive on deposit such sums of money as may from time to time be offered therefor, by or in behalf of persons hithertofore held in slavery in the United States, or their descendants, and investing the same in the stocks, bonds, and Treasury notes, or other securities of the United States."

The distinction provided in the bill in favor of the payment of "such persons in whole or in part of African descent" rests upon the foregoing paragraph of the original law, and no persons other than those named have the right to make use of this institution in any manner; neither have they the right to acquire by any means any interest in its assets.

For four years after the organization of the Freedman's Savings and Trust Company the laws seemed to have been honestly observed by its officers and the provisions in its charter faithfully recognized. Congress itself, however, seems to have been derelict in its duty. One section of the original grant provided that the books of the institution were to be open at all times to inspection and examination of officers appointed by Congress to conduct the same, yet it does not appear that Congress ever appointed an officer for this purpose, nor has an examination of the character contemplated by Congress ever been made. The officers of the bank were to give bonds. There is nothing in the records to show that any bond was ever executed. Any proper examination would have developed this fact, and probably great loss would have been prevented thereby. In 1870 Congress changed or amended the charter without the knowledge or consent of those who had intrusted their savings to its custody. . . .

To-day I hope that the Committee on Banking and Currency who has charge of this measure will yet see its way clear to do tardy justice, long deferred, to this much wronged and unsuspecting people. If individual sections of the country, individual political parties can afford to commit deeds of wrong against us, certainly a great nation like ours will see to it that a people so loyal to its flag as the black man has shown himself in every war from the birth of the Union to this day, will not permit this obligation to go longer un-canceled.

Now, Mr. Chairman, before concluding my remarks I want to submit a brief recipe for the solution of the so-called American negro problem. He asks no special favors, but simply demands that he be given the same chance for existence, for earning a livelihood, for raising himself in the scales of man-hood and womanhood that are accorded to kindred nationalities. Treat him as a man: go into his home and learn of his social conditions; learn of his cares, his troubles, and his hopes for the future: gain his confidence: open the doors of industry to him; let the word "negro," "colored," and "black" be stricken from all the organizations enumerated in the federation of labor.

Help him to overcome his weaknesses, punish the crime-committing class by the courts of the land, measure the standard of the race by its best material, cease to mold prejudicial and unjust public sentiment against him, and my word for it, he will learn to support, hold up the bands of, and join in with that political party, that institution, whether secular or religious, in every commu-nity where he lives, which is destined to do the greatest good for the greatest number. Obliterate race hatred, party prejudice, and help us to achieve nobler ends, greater results, and become more satisfactory citizens to our brother in white.

This, Mr. Chairman, is perhaps the negroes' temporary farewell to the American Congress; but let me say, Phoenix-like he will rise up some day and come again. These parting words are in behalf of an outraged, heart-broken, bruised, and bleeding, but God-fearing people, faithful, industrious, loyal peo-ple—rising people, full of potential force.

Mr. Chairman, in the trial of Lord Bacon, when the court disturbed the counsel for the defendant, Sir Walter Raleigh raised himself up to his full height and, addressing the court, said:

"Sir, I am pleading for the life of a human being."

The only apology that I have to make for the earnestness with which I have spoken is that I am pleading for the life, the liberty, the future happiness, and manhood suffrage for one-eighth of the entire population of the United States. [Loud applause.]

Bibliography

Primary Sources

MANUSCRIPT COLLECTIONS

Library of Congress, Washington, D.C.

Garfield, James A. Papers.
McKinley, William. Papers.
Washington, Booker T. Papers.

Moorland Spingarn Research Center, Howard University, Washington, D.C.

Hunt, William Henry. Papers.
Washington Conservatory of Music. Papers.

Southern Historical Collection, University of North Carolina, Chapel Hill

Butler, Marion. Papers.
Clarke, William J. Papers.
Dent, Louis A. Papers.
Settle, Thomas R. Papers.

NORTH CAROLINA NEWSPAPERS

Goldsboro Daily Argus (1900)
Kinston Daily Free Press (1878–1900)
Littleton True Reformer and Civil Rights Advocate (1900)
New Bern Daily Journal (1880–1901)
Newbernian (1882–1888)

New Bern People's Advocate (1886)
New Bern Weekly Journal (1879–1886)
Raleigh Gazette (1893–1898)
Raleigh News and Observer (1877–1918)
Raleigh Signal (1884–1892)
Rich Square Patron and Gleaner (1892–1901)
Salisbury Star of Zion (1885–1901)
Scotland Neck Commonwealth (1894–1901)
Tarboro Southerner (1894–1901)
Warrenton Gazette (1892–1901)
Weldon N.C. Republican and Civil Rights Advocate (1900)
Wilmington Morning Star (1897–1900)
Wilmington Post (1879–1884)
Wilson Advance (1883–1900)
Windsor Ledger (1892–1901)

OTHER NEWSPAPERS

Boston Globe (1898)
Brooklyn (N.Y.) Daily Eagle (1901)
Charleston (S.C.) Messenger (1901)
Cleveland Gazette (1898–1901)
Indianapolis Freeman (1898–1901)
Indianapolis World (1898–1901)
New York Age (1887–1901)
New York Freeman (1884–1887)
New York Times (1878–1935)
Philadelphia Inquirer (1876)
Philadelphia Tribune (1912–1920)
Springfield (Ill.) State Capital (1901)
Washington Bee (1882–1919)
Washington Colored American (1898–1904)
Washington Daily Record (1900–1901)
Washington People's Advocate (1876–1884)
Washington Post (1897–1905)
Washington Evening & Sunday Star (1877–1918)

GOVERNMENT PUBLICATIONS

New Jersey Department of State. *Census of 1905.*

North Carolina. *Record of the General Assembly, House Journal, 1881.*

————. *Record of the General Assembly, Senate Journal, 1885.*

————. *Report of the Superintendent of Public Instruction, 1881.*

————. *Report of the Superintendent of Public Instruction, 1882.*

————. *Report of the Superintendent of Public Instruction, 1885.*

————. *Report of the Superintendent of Public Instruction, 1886.*

————. Department of the Secretary of State. *North Carolina Government, 1585–1979: A Narrative History.*

————. Department of Cultural Resources. *Guide to North Carolina Highway Historical Markers.* 8th ed.

U.S. Bureau of Education. *The History of Education in North Carolina*, compiled by Charles Lee Smith. No. 3 in *Contributions to American Educational History*, edited by Herbert B. Adams. Washington, D.C.: GPO, 1888.

U.S. Congress. *A Biographical Congressional Directory, 1774–1903.* Washington, D.C.: GPO, 1903.

————. *Biographical Directory of the American Congress, 1774–1961.* Washington, D.C.: GPO, 1961.

————. *Congressional Record, 55th–56th Cong.*

————. *Congressional Directory, 55th–57th Cong.*

U.S. Department of Commerce, Census Office. *Negro Population, 1790–1915.* GPO: Washington, D.C., 1918.

————. Sixth Census (1840).

————. Seventh Census (1850).

————. Eighth Census (1860).

————. Ninth Census (1870).

————. Tenth Census (1880).

————. Twelfth Census (1900).

————. Thirteenth Census (1910).

————. Fourteenth Census (1920).

Government Printing Office. *Register of Officers and Agents, Civil, Military, and Naval, in the Service of the United States on the Thirtieth of September, 1877.* Washington, D.C., 1878.

————. *Report of the Industrial Commission*, X. Washington, D.C., 1901.

MISCELLANEOUS

Burial Records, Eden Memorial Cemetery, Darby, Pa., 1902–1927. Bound volumes at site.

City directories, Philadelphia, Pa., 1905–1930. Microfilm copies, Library of Congress, Washington, D.C.

City directories, Washington, D.C., 1872–1919. Bound volumes, National Archives, Washington, D.C. Microfilm copies, Library of Congress, Washington, D.C.

County Marriage Registers, 1861–1900, Craven and Edgecombe Counties, N.C. Microfilm copies, N.C. Division of Archives and History, Raleigh.

North Carolina Graves Index. Paper card file, N.C. Division of Archives and History, Raleigh.

Officials' Bonds, 1868–1880, Columbus County, N.C. Bound volumes, N.C. Division of Archives and History, Raleigh.

Personnel Records, U.S. Department of Treasury, 1872–1886. Bound volumes, National Archives, Washington, D.C.

Records of the Bureau of Refugees, Freedmen and Abandoned Lands, North Carolina, Wilmington Sub-District, 1865–1870. Microfilm copies, National Archives, Washington, D.C.

Secondary Sources

BOOKS, PAMPHLETS, DISSERTATIONS

Adams, Cyrus Field (Secretary, National Afro-American Council). "The National Afro-American Council." Washington, D.C.: National Afro-American Council, 1902. Pamphlet (microfilm), Library of Congress.

Anderson, Eric. *Race and Politics in North Carolina, 1872–1901: The Black Second.* Baton Rouge: Louisiana State University Press, 1981.

Armstrong Association. "The Negro in Business in Philadelphia: An Investigation by the Armstrong Association of Philadelphia." Philadelphia, 1918. Pamphlet, Library of Congress.

Assembly Sketch Book, Session 1885: North Carolina. Vol. 3. Raleigh, N.C.: Edwards, Broughton, 1885.

Ayers, Edward L. *The Promise of the New South: Life after Reconstruction.* New York: Oxford University Press, 1992.

Barrett, John G. *The Civil War in North Carolina.* Chapel Hill: University of North Carolina Press, 1963.

Bentley, George R. *A History of the Freedmen's Bureau*. Philadelphia: University of Pennsylvania, 1955.

Black Biographical Sources. Edited by Barbara L. Bell. New Haven: Yale University, 1970.

Black Biography, 1790–1950: A Cumulative Index. 3 vols. Edited by Randall K. Burkett, Nancy H. Burkett, and Henry L. Gates Jr. Alexandria, Va.: Chadwyck-Healey, 1991.

Black History: A Guide to Civilian Records in the National Archives. Compiled by Debra L. Newman. Washington, D.C.: National Archives Trust Board, 1984.

Brief for Contestee: In the House of Representatives, Fifty-Fourth Congress, Henry P. Cheatham (Contestant) vs. Frederick A. Woodard (Contestee) from the Second Congressional District of North Carolina. Wilson, N.C.: Landmark Steam Printing House, 1895.

Brown, Hugh V. *A History of the Education of Negroes in North Carolina*. Goldsboro, N.C.: Irving-Swain Press, 1961.

Bullock, Penelope L. *The Afro-American Periodical Press, 1838–1909*. Baton Rouge: Louisiana State University Press, 1981.

Caldwell, Arthur B. *History of the American Negro and His Institutions*. Georgia edition. Vols. 1, 2. Atlanta, Ga.: A.B. Caldwell, 1917–1920.

———. *History of the American Negro and His Institutions*. North Carolina edition. Vol. 4. Atlanta, Ga.: A. B. Caldwell, 1921.

Centennial Encyclopedia of the African Methodist Episcopal Church. Edited by Richard R. Wright Jr. Philadelphia: The A.M.E. Book Concern, 1916.

Chavers, Pearl W. *Conditions that Confront the Colored Race*. Columbus, Ohio: n.p., 1908.

Christian, Charles M. *Black Saga: The African American Experience*. Boston: Houghton Mifflin, 1995.

Christopher, Maurine. *Black Americans in Congress*. Formerly *America's Black Congressmen*. New York: Thomas Y. Crowell, 1976.

Clarke, Erskine. *Our Southern Zion: A History of Calvinism in the South Carolina Low Country, 1690–1990*. Tuscaloosa: University of Alabama Press, 1996.

Clay, William L. *Just Permanent Interests: Black Americans in Congress, 1870–1991*. New York: Amistad Press, 1992.

Clayton, Edward T. *The Negro Politician*. Chicago: Johnson, 1964.

Contemporary Black Biography. 19 vols. Edited by Mpho L. Mabunda. Detroit: Gale Research, 1995.

Corbitt, David L. *The Formation of North Carolina Counties, 1693–1943*. Raleigh: N.C. Department of Archives and History, 1950.

Cromwell, John W. *The Negro in American History*. 1914. Reprint, Chicago: Johnson Reprint, 1964.

Crow, Jeffrey J., Paul D. Escott, and Flora J. Hatley. *A History of African Americans in North Carolina*. Raleigh: N.C. Division of Archives and History, 1992.

Crow, Jeffrey J., and Flora Hatley, eds. *Black Americans in North Carolina and the South*. Chapel Hill: University of North Carolina Press, 1984.

Crow, Jeffrey J., and Robert E. Winters Jr., eds. *The Black Presence in North Carolina*. Raleigh: N.C. Department of Cultural Resources, 1978.

Culp, Daniel W., ed. *Twentieth Century Negro Literature, or a Cyclopedia of Thought on Vital Topics Relating to the American Negro*. Napierville, Ill.: J. L. Nichols, 1902.

Current, Richard N. *Those Terrible Carpetbaggers: A Reinterpretation*. New York: Oxford University Press, 1988.

Cyclopedia of Eminent and Representative Men of the Carolinas of the Nineteenth Century. Vol. 2: *North Carolina*. Edited by Samuel A. Ashe. Madison, Wisc.: Brant & Fuller, 1892.

Dancy, John C. [Jr.], ed. *The Quarterly Almanac, 1893, edited by John C. Dancy, editor of A.M.E. Zion Quarterly, Wilmington, N.C.* Wilmington, N.C., 1893.

Dancy, John C. [III]. *Sand against the Wind: The Memoirs of John C. Dancy*. Detroit: Wayne State University Press, 1966.

Daniels, Josephus. *Editor in Politics*. Chapel Hill: University of North Carolina Press, 1941.

———. *Tar Heel Editor*. 1939. Reprint, Westport, Conn.: Greenwood Press, 1974.

Daniels, Josephus, and Michael R. Winston, eds. *Dictionary of American Negro Biography*. Edited by Rayford W. Logan and Michael R. Winston. New York: W. W. Norton, 1982.

Dictionary of North Carolina Biography. 6 vols. Edited by William S. Powell. Chapel Hill: University of North Carolina Press, 1979–1997.

Directory of Afro-American Resources. Edited by Wallace Schatz. New York: R. R. Bowker, 1970.

Dorwart, Jeffery M. *Cape May County, New Jersey: The Making of an American Resort Community*. New Brunswick, N.J.: Rutgers University Press, 1992.

Duncan, Kay W. "Marriage Records, Columbus County, Whiteville, N.C." Vol. 1. Whiteville, N.C.: Barfield & Duncan Genealogy Service, 1984.

Duster, Alfreda M., ed. *Crusade for Justice: The Autobiography of Ida B. Wells*. Chicago: University of Chicago Press, 1970.

Dyson, Walter. *Howard University, the Capstone of Negro Education: A History, 1867–1940*. Washington, D.C.: Howard University Press, 1941.

Edmonds, Helen G. *The Negro and Fusion Politics in North Carolina, 1894–1901*. Chapel Hill: University of North Carolina Press, 1951.

Elmore, Joseph E. "North Carolina Negro Congressmen, 1875–1901." Master's thesis, University of North Carolina, 1964.

Encyclopedia of African-American Culture and History. 6 vols. Edited by Jack Salzman, David L. Smith, and Cornel West. New York: Macmillan, 1996.

Encyclopedia of Southern History. Edited by David C. Roller and Robert W. Twyman. Baton Rouge: Louisiana State University Press, 1979.

Escott, Paul D. *Many Excellent People: Power and Privilege in North Carolina, 1850–1900*. Chapel Hill: University of North Carolina Press, 1985.

Fitzpatrick, Sandra, and Maria R. Goodwin. *The Guide to Black Washington: Places and Events of Historical and Cultural Significance in the Nation's Capital*. 2d ed. New York: Hippocrene Books, 1990.

———. *Reconstruction: America's Unfinished Revolution, 1863–1877*. New York: Harper & Row, 1988.

Fortune, T. Thomas. *Black and White: Land, Labor, and Politics in the South*. 1884. Reprint, Chicago: Johnson, 1970.

———. *Dreams of Life*. 1905. Reprint, New York: AMS Press, 1975.

Franklin, John Hope. *From Slavery to Freedom*. New York: Vintage Books, 1969.

———. *The Free Negro in North Carolina, 1790–1860*. New York: W. W. Norton, 1971.

Frazier, E. Franklin. *Black Bourgeoisie*. 1957. Reprint, New York: Free Press Paperbacks, 1997.

Freedom's Lawmakers: A Directory of Black Officeholders during Reconstruction. Rev. ed. Edited by Eric Foner. New York: Oxford University Press, 1995.

Fuller, Thomas O. *Twenty Years in Public Life*. Nashville, Tenn.: National Baptist Publishing Board, 1910.

———. *Pictorial History of the American Negro: A Story of Progress and Development along Social, Political, Economic, Educational, and Spiritual Lines*. Memphis, Tenn.: Pictorial History, 1933.

Gatewood, Willard B. *Aristocrats of Color: The Black Elite, 1880–1920*. Bloomington: Indiana University Press, 1990.

Gibbs, Mifflin Wistar. *Shadow and Light: An Autobiography, with Reminiscences of the Last and Present Century*. 1902; reprint, New York: Arno Press and the New York Times, 1968.

Gilmore, Glenda E. *Gender and Jim Crow: Women and the Politics of White Supremacy in North Carolina, 1860–1920*. Chapel Hill: University of North Carolina Press, 1996.

Gosling, Francis G. *Before Freud: Neurasthenia and the American Medical Community, 1870–1910*. Urbana: University of Illinois Press, 1987.

Green, John B. III. *A New Bern Album: Old Photographs of New Bern, North Carolina, and the Surrounding Countryside*. New Bern, N.C.: Tryon Palace Commission, 1985.

Green, John P. *Recollections of the inhabitants, superstitions and Kuklux outrages of the Carolinas*. (Cleveland, Ohio?), 1880.

———. *Facts Stranger than Fiction: Seventy-Five Years of a Busy Life with Reminiscences of Many Great Men and Women*. Cleveland, Ohio: n.p., 1920.

Grimshaw, William H. *Official History of Freemasonry among the Colored People in North America*. 1903. Reprint, New York: Negro Universities Press, 1969.

Hamilton, J. G. de Roulhac. *History of North Carolina: North Carolina since 1860*. Vol. 3. Chicago: Lewis, 1919.

———. *Reconstruction in North Carolina*. 1914. Reprint, Gloucester, Mass.: Peter Smith, 1964.

Hanna, Charles A. *The Scotch-Irish; or, The Scot in North Britain, Northern Ireland, and North America*. Vol. 2. New York: G. W. Putnam's Sons, 1902.

Harlan, Louis R. *Booker T. Washington: The Making of a Black Leader, 1856–1901*. New York: Oxford University Press, 1972.

Harlan, Louis R., and Raymond W. Smock, eds. *The Booker T. Washington Papers*. Urbana: University of Illinois Press, 1972–1989.

Harris, Abram L. *The Negro as Capitalist: A Study of Banking and Business among American Negroes*. 1936. Reprint, New York: Haskell House, 1970.

Hilyer, Andrew F. *The Twentieth Century Union League Directory of the Colored People of Washington, D.C., 1901*. Washington, D.C.: The Union League, 1901.

Historical and Descriptive Review of the State of North Carolina, Including the Manufacturing and Mercantile Industries of the Towns of Edenton, Elizabeth City, Goldsboro, Greenville, Kinston, Newbern, Tarboro, Washington, and Wilson, and Sketches of Their Leading Men and Business Houses. Vol. 2 of *N.C., The Eastern Section*. Charleston, S.C.: Empire, 1885.

Howard University Directory of Graduates, 1870–1985. White Plains, N.Y.: Bernard Charles, 1986.

Howard University Union Alumni Association. *Alumni Catalogue of Howard University, with List of Alumni, 1870–1896*. Washington, D.C.: Howard University, 1896.

Johnson, Donald B., comp. *National Party Platforms, Volume 1, 1840–1956*. Urbana: University of Illinois Press, 1978.

Jordan, David M. *Winfield Scott Hancock: A Soldier's Life*. Bloomington: Indiana University Press, 1996.

Kay, Marvin L. Michael, and Lorin Lee Cary. *Slavery in North Carolina, 1748–1775*. Chapel Hill: University of North Carolina Press, 1995.

Kenzer, Robert C. *Enterprising Southerners: Black Economic Success in North Carolina, 1865–1915*. Charlottesville: University Press of Virginia, 1997.

King, Henry T. *Sketches of Pitt County, 1804–1910*. Raleigh, N.C.: Edwards & Broughton, 1911.

Knight, Edgar W. *Public School Education in North Carolina*. New York: Houghton Mifflin, 1916.

Lamb, Daniel S., ed. *Howard University Medical Department, Washington, D.C.: A Historical, Biographical, and Statistical Souvenir*. 1900. Reprint, Freeport, N.Y.: Books for Libraries Press, 1971.

Lane, Ann J. *The Brownsville Affair: National Crisis and Black Reaction*. Port Washington, N.Y.: n.p., 1971.

Lane, Roger. *William Dorsey's Philadelphia and Ours: On the Past and Future of the Black City in America*. New York: Oxford University Press, 1991.

Langston, John Mercer. *From the Virginia Plantation to the National Capitol*. 1894. Reprint, New York: Arno Press, 1969.

Leech, Margaret. *In the Days of McKinley*. 1959. Reprint, Westport, Conn.: Greenwood Press, 1975.

Leloudis, James L. *Schooling in the New South: Pedagogy, Self, and Society in North Carolina, 1880–1920*. Chapel Hill: University of North Carolina Press, 1996.

Lefler, Hugh T., and Albert R. Newsome. *North Carolina: The History of a Southern State*. 3d ed. Chapel Hill: University of North Carolina Press, 1973.

Lincoln University. *Lincoln University College and Theological Seminary Biographical Catalogue, 1918*. Lancaster, Pa.: New Era Printing, 1918.

Little, Ann C. W., ed. *Columbus County, North Carolina, Recollections and Records*. Whiteville, N.C.: Fisher-Harrison, 1980.

Litwack, Leon F. *Trouble in Mind: Black Southerners in the Age of Jim Crow*. New York: Alfred A. Knopf, 1998.

Litwack, Leon F., and August Meier, eds. *Black Leaders of the Nineteenth Century*. Urbana: University of Illinois Press, 1988.

Logan, Frenise A. *The Negro in North Carolina, 1876–1894*. Chapel Hill: University of North Carolina Press, 1964.

Logan, Rayford W. *Howard University: The First One Hundred Years, 1867–1967*. New York: New York University Press, 1967.

———. *The Betrayal of the Negro, from Rutherford B. Hayes to Woodrow Wilson*. 1965. Reprint, New York: Da Capo Press, 1997.

Lynch, John R. *The Facts of Reconstruction*. New York: Neal, 1913.

———. *Reminiscences of an Active Life*. Chicago: University of Chicago Press, 1970.

Mabry, William A. *The Negro in North Carolina Politics since Reconstruction*. 1940. Reprint, New York: AMS Press, 1970.

Major, Gerri, with Doris E. Saunders. *Gerri Major's Black Society*. Chicago: Johnson, 1976.

Mast, Greg. *State Troops and Volunteers: A Photographic Record of North Carolina's Civil War Soldiers*. Raleigh: N.C. Department of Cultural Resources, 1995.

Matthews, Donald R., ed. *North Carolina Votes: General Election Returns, by County, for President of the United States, 1868–1960, Governor of North Carolina, 1868–1960, United States Senator from North Carolina, 1914–1960.* Chapel Hill: University of North Carolina Press, 1962.

McMurry, Linda O. *To Keep the Waters Troubled: The Life of Ida B. Wells.* New York: Oxford University Press, 1998.

McPherson, James M., et al. *Blacks in America: Bibliographical Essays.* Garden City, N.Y.: Doubleday, 1971.

Meier, August. *Negro Thought in America, 1880–1915: Racial Ideologies in the Age of Booker T. Washington.* Ann Arbor: University of Michigan Press, 1963.

Mitchell, Louis D. *A Story of the Descendants of Benjamin Spaulding (1773–1862), with Genealogy by John A. Spaulding.* Edited by Kathleen M. Kemmerer. Greensboro, N.C.: Deal Printing, 1989.

Mobley, Joseph A. *James City: A Black Community in North Carolina, 1863–1900.* Raleigh: N.C. Department of Archives and History, 1981.

Morison, Samuel Eliot. *The Oxford History of the American People.* New York: Oxford University Press, 1965.

Murray, Percy E. *History of the North Carolina Teachers Association.* Raleigh: N.C. Association of Educators, 1971

Nieman, Donald G., ed. *Black Southerners and the Law (1865–1900).* New York: Garland, 1994.

Noble, Marcus C. S. *A History of the Public Schools of North Carolina.* Chapel Hill: University of North Carolina Press, 1930.

Official Proceedings of the Twelfth Republican National Convention, Held in the City of Philadelphia, June 19, 20, and 21, 1900. Philadelphia: Dunlap Printing, 1900.

"Official Programme, First Annual Meeting of the Afro-American Council at the Metropolitan Baptist Church, Washington, D.C." Pamphlet, Daniel Murray Pamphlet Collection, Library of Congress.

Paschall, Jerry D., ed. *A Historical View of the Columbus County Schools, 1808–1977.* Whiteville, N.C.: Columbus County Board of Education, 1977.

The Philadelphia Colored Directory: A Handbook of the Religious, Social, Political, Professional, Business, and Other Activities of the Negroes of Philadelphia. Compiled by Richard R. Wright Jr., assisted by Ernest Smith. Philadelphia: The Philadelphia Colored Directory Co., 1908.

Powell, William S. *The North Carolina Gazetteer: A Dictionary of Tar Heel Places.* Chapel Hill: University of North Carolina Press, 1968.

Prather, Henry L. *We Have Taken a City: Wilmington Racial Massacre and Coup of 1898.* Rutherford, N.J.: Associated Universities Press, 1984.

Quick, William H. *Negro Stars in All Ages of the World*. Henderson, N.C.: D. E. Aycock, Printer, 1890. 2d ed., 1898.

Ragsdale, Bruce A., and Joel D. Treese. *Black Americans in Congress, 1870–1989*. Washington, D.C.: GPO, 1990.

Reid, George W. "A Biography of George H. White, 1852–1918." Ph.D. dissertation, Howard University, 1974.

Reuter, Edward B. *The Mulatto in the United States, Including a Study of the Role of Mixed-Blood Races throughout the World*. 1918. Reprint, New York: Haskell House, 1969.

Robinson, Wilhelmena. *Historical Negro Biographies*. New York: Publishers Company, 1969.

Rouse, Jordan K. *The Noble Experiment of Warren C. Coleman*. Charlotte, N.C.: Crabtree Press, 1972.

Salser, Mark R., ed. *Black Americans in Congress*. Vol. 1 of *Black Americans in Politics*. Portland, Ore.: National Book, 1991.

Sandbeck, Peter B. *The Historic Architecture of New Bern and Craven County*. New Bern, N.C.: Tryon Palace Commission, 1988.

Saunders, John A. *100 Years after Emancipation: History of the Philadelphia Negro, 1787–1963*. Philadelphia: Philadelphia Tribune Press, 1968.

Schweninger, Loren. *Black Property Owners in the South, 1790–1915*. Urbana: University of Illinois Press, 1997.

Sharpe, Bill. *A New Geography of North Carolina*. 4 vols. Raleigh, N.C.: Sharpe, 1958–1965.

Sherman, Richard B. *The Republican Party and Black America: From McKinley to Hoover, 1896–1933*. Charlottesville: University Press of Virginia, 1973.

Simmons, William J. *Men of Mark: Eminent, Progressive and Rising*. 1887. Reprint, Chicago: Johnson, 1970.

Smith, Samuel D. *The Negro in Congress, 1870–1901*. Chapel Hill: University of North Carolina Press, 1940.

Spaulding, Odessa. "Between the Ocean and the Bay." Photocopy of unpublished, undated manuscript held by the author.

Stover, John F. *The Railroads of the South, 1865–1900: A Study in Finance and Control*. Chapel Hill: University of North Carolina Press, 1955.

Suggs, Henry L., ed. *The Black Press in the Middle West, 1865–1985*. Westport, Conn.: Greenwood Press, 1996.

———, ed. *The Black Press in the South, 1865–1979*. Westport, Conn.: Greenwood Press, 1983.

Swain, Carol M. *Black Faces, Black Interests: The Representation of African Americans in Congress*. Cambridge: Harvard University Press, 1993.

Terrell, Mary C. *A Colored Woman in a White World.* 1940. Reprint, New York: G. K. Hall, 1970.

Tetterton, Beverly, ed. *North Carolina Freedman's Savings & Trust Company Records,* abstracted by Bill Reaves. Raleigh: N.C. Genealogical Society, 1992.

Turner, J. Kelly, and John L. Bridgers Jr. *History of Edgecombe County, North Carolina.* Raleigh, N.C.: Edwards and Broughton Printing, 1920.

Vass, Lachlan C. *History of the Presbyterian Church in New Bern, N.C., with a Resume of Early Ecclesiastical Affairs in Eastern North Carolina and a Sketch of the Early Days of New Bern, N.C.* Richmond, Va.: Whittet and Shepperson Printers, 1886.

Walters, Alexander. *My Life and Work.* New York: Fleming H. Revell, 1917.

Watson, Alan D. *A History of New Bern and Craven County.* New Bern, N.C.: Tryon Palace Commission, 1987.

Wedin, Carolyn. *Inheritors of the Spirit: Mary White Ovington and the Founding of the NAACP.* New York: John Wiley & Sons, 1998.

Who's Who Among African Americans. 11th ed. Edited by Shirelle Phelps. Detroit: Gale Research, 1998.

Who's Who in America. Editions of 1899, 1901–1902, 1906–1907. Chicago: A. N. Marquis, 1899–1907.

Who's Who in Colored America: A Biographical Dictionary of Notable Living Persons of Negro Descent in America. Editions of 1927, 1929, 1933, 1937, 1940, 1944. Edited by Thomas Yenser. New York: Who's Who in Colored America Corp., 1927–1944.

Who's Who in Philadelphia. Edited by Charles F. White. Philadelphia: The A. M. E. Book Concern, 1912.

Who's Who of the Colored Race: General Biographical Dictionary of Men and Women of African Descent. Edited by Frank L. Mather. Chicago: F. L. Mather, 1915.

Who Was Who in America, 1897–1942. Chicago: A. N. Marquis, 1943.

Williams, George W. *History of the Negro Race in America, 1619–1880.* 1883. Reprint, New York: Arno Press, 1968.

Williamson, Joel. *The Crucible of Race: Black-White Relations in the American South since Emancipation.* New York: Oxford University Press, 1984.

Winston, Robert W. *It's a Far Cry.* New York: Henry Holt, 1937.

Wright, Richard R., Jr. *The Negro in Pennsylvania: A Study in Economic History.* Philadelphia: The A. M. E. Book Concern, 1912.

Wright, Roberta Hughes, and Wilbur B. Hughes III. *Lay Down Body: Living History in African American Cemeteries.* Detroit: Visible Ink Press, 1996.

Yearns, W. Buck, ed. *The Papers of Thomas Jordan Jarvis: Vol. I, 1869–1882.* Raleigh: N.C. Department of Archives and History, 1969.

Zangrande, Robert L. *The NAACP Crusade against Lynching, 1909–1950.* Philadelphia: Temple University Press, 1980.

Zopf, Paul E. *North Carolina: A Demographic Profile*. Chapel Hill: Carolina Population Center, 1965.

ARTICLES AND ESSAYS

Adkins, S. G. "History and Status of Education among the Colored People." In *The History of Education in North Carolina*, compiled by Charles L. Smith, for U.S. Bureau of Education. Washington, D.C.: GPO, 1888.

Anderson, Eric. "George Henry White." In *American National Biography*, edited by John A. Garraty and Mark C. Carnes. New York: Oxford University Press, 1999.

————. "James O'Hara of North Carolina: Black Leadership and Local Government." In *Southern Black Leaders of the Reconstruction Era*, ed. Howard N. Rabinowitz. Urbana: University of Illinois Press, 1972.

Balanoff, Elizabeth. "Negro Legislators in the North Carolina General Assembly, July 1868–February 1872." *North Carolina Historical Review* 49 (1972): 21–55.

Cheek, William, and Aimee Lee Cheek. "John Mercer Langston: Principle and Politics." In *Black Leaders of the Nineteenth Century*, ed. Leon Litwack and August Meier. Urbana: University of Illinois Press, 1988.

Christopher, Maurine. "George Henry White." In *Black Americans in Congress*. New York: Thomas Y. Crowell, 1976.

Crow, Jeffrey J. "'Fusion, Confusion, and Negroism': Schisms among Negro Republicans in the North Carolina Election of 1896." *North Carolina Historical Review* 53 (October 1976): 364–84.

Culp, Daniel W. "Hon. George H. White, LL.D." In *Twentieth Century Negro Literature, or a Cyclopedia of Thought on Vital Topics Relating to the American Negro*, ed. Daniel W. Culp, Napierville, Ill.: J. L. Nichols, 1902.

Du Bois, William E. B. "The Freedmen's Bureau." *Atlantic Monthly*, January 1901, 354–65.

Dunning, William A. "The Undoing of Reconstruction." *Atlantic Monthly*, October 1901, 433–49.

Franklin, John Hope. "The Free Negro in the Economic Life of Ante-Bellum North Carolina." In *Free Blacks in America, 1800–1860*, ed. John H. Bracey Jr., August Meier, and Elliott Rudwick. Belmont, Calif.: Wadsworth, 1971.

"George Henry White." In *The Biographical Encyclopedia of the United States*. Chicago: American Biographical Publishing, 1901 (microfilm, Library of Congress).

Harlan, Louis R. "The Secret Life of Booker T. Washington." *Journal of Southern History* 37 (August 1971): 393–416.

Harris, A. H. "George H. White." *Negro History Bulletin* 5, no. 1 (1942): 105–6.

Ingle, H. Larry. "George Henry White." In *Encyclopedia of Southern History*, ed. David

C. Roller and Robert W. Twyman. Baton Rouge: Louisiana State University Press, 1979.

Katz, William L. "George Henry White: A Militant Negro Congressman in the Age of Booker T. Washington." *Negro History Bulletin* 29, no. 6 (1966): 125–6, 134–9.

———. "George Henry White: Militant Congressman." In *Proudly Red and Black: Stories of African and Native Americans*, by William L. Katz and Paula A. Franklin. New York: Atheneum, 1993.

Lindsay, Arnett G. "The Negro in Banking." In *The Negro as a Business Man*, by John H. Harmon Jr., Arnett G. Lindsay, and Carter G. Woodson. Washington, D.C.: Association for the Study of Negro Life and History, 1929.

Logan, Frenise A. "The Colored Industrial Association of North Carolina and Its Fair of 1886." *North Carolina Historical Review* 34 (1957): 58–67.

———. "Influences which Determined the Race Consciousness of George H. White." *Negro History Bulletin* 14, no. 3 (1950): 63–5.

Mabry, William A. "'White Supremacy' and the North Carolina Suffrage Amendment." *North Carolina Historical Review* 13 (1936), 1–24.

Meier, August. "Booker T. Washington and the Rise of the NAACP." In *Along the Color Line: Explorations in the Black Experience*, by August Meier and Elliott Rudwick. Urbana: University of Illinois Press, 1976.

Miller, Allison X. "George Henry White." In *Encyclopedia of African American Culture and History*, ed. Jack Salzman, David L. Smith, and Cornel West, 5:2821–2. New York: Macmillan, 1996.

Mobley, Joe A. "In the Shadow of White Society: Princeville, A Black Town in North Carolina, 1865–1915." *North Carolina Historical Review* 63 (1986): 340–84.

Padgett, James A. "From Slavery to Prominence in North Carolina." *Journal of Negro History* 22 (October 1937): 433–87.

Ragsdale, Bruce A., and Joel D. Treese. "George Henry White." In *Black Americans in Congress, 1870–1989*. Washington, D.C.: GPO, 1990.

Reid, George W. "Congressman George Henry White: His Major Power Base." *Negro History Bulletin* 39, no. 3 (1976): 554–5.

———. "Four in Black: North Carolina's Black Congressmen, 1874–1901." *Journal of Negro History* 44 (1979): 229–43.

———. "George Henry White." In *Dictionary of American Negro Biography*, ed. Rayford W. Logan and Michael R. Winston, 645–6. New York: W. W. Norton, 1982.

———. "The Post-Congressional Career of George H. White, 1901–1918." *Journal of Negro History* 41 (1976): 362–73.

Salser, Mark R. "George Henry White." In *Black Americans in Congress*, by Mark R. Salser. Portland, Ore.: National Book, 1991.

Schenck, William Z. "George Henry White." In *Dictionary of North Carolina Biography*, ed. William S. Powell, 6:174–5. Chapel Hill: University of North Carolina Press, 1996.

Simmons, William J. "Hon. George H. White." In *Men of Mark: Eminent, Progressive, and Rising*. 1887. Reprint, Chicago: Johnson, 1970.

Spragens, William G. "Contributions of the Negro Press to American Culture." In *The Negro Impact on Western Civilization*, ed. Joseph S. Roucek and Thomas Kiernan. New York: Philosophical Library, 1970.

Taylor, Alrutheus A. "Negro Congressmen a Generation After." *Journal of Negro History* 7 (1922): 127–71.

Tinsley, James A. "Roosevelt, Foraker, and the Brownsville Affair." *Journal of Negro History* 41 (1956): 43–65.

Walton, Lester A. "The Negro Comes Back to the United States Congress." *Current History* 30 (1929): 461–3.

White, Charles F. "Hon. George H. White, LL.D." In *Who's Who in Philadelphia*, ed. Charles F. White, 88–90. Philadelphia: The A.M.E. Book Concern, 1912.

White, George H. "Congressman White's Address." *The Southern Workman and Hampton Institute Record* 38 (1899): 244–5.

———. "Injustice to the Colored Voter." *The Independent* 52, January 18, 1900, 176–7.

———. "What Should Be the Negro's Attitude in Politics?" In *Twentieth Century Negro Literature, or a Cyclopedia of Thought on Vital Topics Relating to the American Negro*, ed. Daniel W. Culp, 224–7. Napierville, Ill.: J. L. Nichols, 1902.

Work, Monroe N. "Some Negro Members of Congress." *Journal of Negro History* 5 (1920), 63–119.

Wright, Richard R., Jr. "Negro Communities in New Jersey." *Southern Workman and Hampton Institute Record* 47 (July 1908): 385–93.

Index

Abbott, Israel B., 60–2, 62n, 68n, 69, 92n, 125–6, 128–9, 130, 132–3, 149, 151
Adams, Cyrus Field, 250, 301, 344, 347
Afro-American Equitable Association, 356, 357, 359
Afro-American League, 250
Afro-American Presbyterian, 205
Agricultural and Mechanical College of Alabama, 231n
Alabama and Louisiana test cases. *See State* ex rel *Ryanes v. Gleason*
Aldrich, William F., 325, 329, 336
Allen, David P., 20, 20n, 25
Allen, George, 56n
Allen, John M., 261
Alston, Albert, 147n
Arnett, Benjamin, 315n, 352
Arnett, Henry Y., 315n, 352
Asbury, John C., 409–10, 424
Askew, General Scott, 373
Avant, Ellen. *See* White, Ellen Avant Macdonald
Avant, Frank W., 414
Avant, William George, 414
Aycock, Charles Brantley, 294, 295, 303

Baker, Frazier P., 220–1
Banner Real Estate Company, Philadelphia, Pa., 410
Barrett, Adam M., 30
Bascom, W. F., 34n, 231
Bass, Harry W., 406, 417, 419
Bassett, Ebenezer, 30
Bassett, John Spencer, 295
Bates, Wiley H., 358, 360
Battle, Clinton W., 66, 73, 74n, 88–9, 132, 218n
Beaman, Henry S., 343
Beaufort, N.C., 63
Beaufort County, N.C., 113, 122n
Bertie County, N.C., 48, 104–5, 114, 212, 247
Bee, Washington, D.C., 339, 340, 348, 349, 371, 394, 415, 419
Berean Manual Training Institute, Philadelphia, 411
Bethel Literary & Historical Association, Washington, D.C., 353, 370, 371
Biddle University, 77, 78n, 205, 231n, 274, 411
Billows, Walter E., 285
Bingham, Henry H., 407

Birney, Arthur A., 375
"Black Second" Congressional District, N.C., 38, 47, 66, 104, 106, 112, 127n, 154, 179, 303
Bladen County, N.C., 1, 3–5, 7, 21, 418, 420
Blankenburg, Rudolph, 413
Blount, S. A., 63
Boston Globe, 254
Bradford Academy, 378–9, 380, 381
Bridges, Isham, 401n
Brogden, Curtis H., 72, 101n, 213
Brooklyn (N.Y.) Eagle, 17n
Brown, Edward C., 416
Brown, Edward Everett, 279, 322, 347
Brown, Tom, 219
Brown & Stevens Bank, Philadelphia, 416–7, 425
Brownsville (Texas) Affray, 396–7, 408
Bruce, Blanche K., 31, 31n, 137n, 208, 312, 415n
Bruce, John Edward "Grit," 233
Brunswick County, N.C., 5, 23n, 414
Bryan, Henry R., 100, 101
Bryan, William Jennings, 204, 212, 303, 392, 398
Burke, Robert, 280
Burleigh reapportionment bill, 306, 342
Butler, J. P., 207
Butler, Marion C., 204, 241
Buxton, Ralph P., 23n, 71, 72

Cale, Hugh, 147n, 206n
Canaday, William P., 85, 95n, 105n, 176–7
Cape Fear Indians, 21
Cape Fear River, 4
Cape May County, N.J., 357, 404
Capital Savings Bank, 402
Carmack-Patterson contest (Congress): GHW remarks on, 226
Carr, Elias, 149, 177
Carter, Hawkins W., 66, 73

Chapman, John, 147n
Charles Street A.M.E. Zion Church, Boston, Mass., 254
Charleston (S.C.) Messenger, 340
Charlotte, N.C., 21, 81, 175n
Chase, W. Calvin, 208, 353, 371, 382–3, 388, 394–5
Cheatham, Charles E., 258, 385n, 386, 426
Cheatham, Henry Plummer: active in N.C. Republican Party, 173; background and education, 152, 156; career after Congress, 218n, 250, 265, 312, 314, 354, 422n; death, 428; elections to office, 147, 156, 162–5, 169, 170, 177; career as educator, 138, 152; family members, 168n, 258, 314, 385n; as GHW's opponent in 1894 campaign, 180–97; as recorder of deeds, District of Columbia, 352, 388; relationship with GHW, 144–5, 151–61, 198–204
Cheatham, Henry P., Jr., 258, 386n, 427–8
Cheatham, Laura Joyner, 314
Cheatham, Louisa Cherry, 138, 139, 140, 258, 264–5, 315, 416
Cheatham, Mamie. *See* Wormley, Mamie Cheatham
Cherry, Cora Lena. *See* White, Cora Lena Cherry
Cherry, Earnest, 140, 372, 373
Cherry, Georgianna. *See* Green, Georgianna Cherry
Cherry, Henry C., 132, 138–40, 264
Cherry, Mary Ann Jones, 138–40, 272, 415–6
Christmas, Lewis T., 58n
The Clansman, 411
Clark, Charles C., 135n
Clark, Peter H., 32
Clark, W. W., 99
Clarke, Mary Bayard Devereux, 46–7, 137n
Clarke, William Edwards: active in North Carolina Republican Party, 43; career as educator and lawyer, 42n, 47; death, 137;

education, 39, 43; elections to office, 47,
66, 68, 73, 94, 101; as GHW's opponent in
1882, 97, 100–1; letter to president-elect
Garfield, 71, 86; as postmaster of New Bern,
47n, 104, 164
Clarke, William John: active in N.C. Republican Party, 43; background and education,
43; death, 137; Democratic candidate for
Congress, 137n; career as educator and
lawyer, 23, 39, 43n, 51; career as journalist,
23, 44n, 46; elections to office, 2, 23; mili-
tary career, 2, 23, 46, 46n; proposed for fed-
eral appointment by Garfield, 85–6; serves as
GHW's mentor, 24, 39, 95, 157; Superior
Court judge and clerk, 23, 44n, 46, 261n
Cleveland, Grover, 72, 110, 163
Cleveland (Ohio) Gazette, 318, 333, 340x
"Coalition Mongrel" (1886), 129
Cobb, Paul, 401n
Cottman, Levi A., 401n
Coleman, Warren, 361n
Coleman Cotton Manufacturing Company,
Concord, N.C., 361
Collins, John Henry: as Second District solici-
tor, 50, 94–7, 101, 118, 120, 121, 123–5,
132–4, 172, 302; as candidate for N.C.
house, 135n
Colored American (Washington, D.C.), 224,
225, 231, 232, 267, 270, 318, 319, 331–9,
360, 388
Colored Republican Council, 92
Columbus County, N.C., 2, 3–4, 5, 10, 12, 17,
25, 359, 420
Columbus (Ohio) Daily Dispatch, 318, 333, 340
Constitution(al) League of the United States,
392, 393–4, 396–7,398, 411
Cook, Charles A., 154, 174, 236n
Cook, Cook and White, Washington, D.C.,
377–8, 377n, 386
Cook, George F. T., 377–8
Cook, George W., 35

Cook, John F., Jr., 377–8
Cooper, Edward Elder: background and educa-
tion: 30, 319–20; career as journalist, 30n,
320, 342, 354; career after leaving journal-
ism, 344, 288; as editor of *Colored
American*, 258, 371; relationship with
Booker T. Washington, 231
Cooper, Richard A., 406, 409
Coppin, Levi J., 401
Cornwallis Street Baptist Church, Halifax,
N.S., 254
Cortelyou, George B., 330, 354n
Coston, Ellen W. *See* White, Ellen Avant
Macdonald
Council of Colored Men of the State, 252–4,
256, 264, 276
Courtney, S. E., 208
Covington, D. C., 321–2, 322n
Craven County, N.C., 42, 45, 46, 66–9, 71,
96–7, 111–2, 124, 167, 420
Crawford, Virgil A., 40n
Crews, William H., 178n, 198n, 206n
Croatan Indians, 21, 22
Cromwell, John W., 33
Crossland, John R. A., 315n, 388
Crum, William Demos, 391
Crumpacker, Edgar D., 272, 306, 307
Culp, Daniel W., 17, 367
Cunningham, J. C., 335–7

Daily Record (Washington, D.C.), 258n
Daily Record (Wilmington, N.C.), 281
Dancy, John C.: active in N.C. Republican
Party, 64, 95n, 203, 236, 237; career as fed-
eral appointee, 170; career as journalist, 64,
128n; early life, 63–4; as recorder of deeds,
District of Columbia, 315, 352, 387–8, 390;
relationship with GHW, 63, 137n
Daniels, Charles, 159n
Daniels, Josephus: early career as journalist,
130n, 159; criticizes GHW speech, 237–41;

opinions on lynching, 277, 283; opposes GHW as solicitor, 144–5, 225; opposes GHW's election to Congress, 245–6, 276; opposes GHW's antilynching remarks, 272, 284–5; relationship with GHW during 1899, 270, 276; recalls GHW in memoirs, 277, 304
Dare, Virginia, 21n
Day, William H., 89, 92, 142n
Dent, Louis Addison, 289
De Priest, Oscar S., 421–2
Dingley Tariff, 214, 215, 217
Disfranchisement amendment, N.C., 253, 285, 289, 294–5, 296–7
Dixon, Major, 100
Dockery, Oliver H,. 13, 203
Dolliver, Jonathan, 329
Dortch Act, 58, 59, 108
Dortch, William T., 59n
Douglass, Frederick, 30, 32, 32n, 237n
Douglass Hospital, Philadelphia, 411
DuBois, W. E. Burghardt, 389, 390, 393, 408, 412
Dudley, Edward R., 40, 54, 66n, 69, 83n, 95n, 155n
Dunbar, Paul Laurence, 351n, 357, 358, 360
Dunbar-Nelson, Alice, 360
Duncan, W. B., 18–9
Dunn, William A., 133, 134

Eaves, John B., 169, 171, 172
Ebenezer Presbyterian Church, New Bern, N.C., 44, 52–3, 54, 65, 84, 103
Eden Cemetery, Delaware County, Pa., 424
Edgecombe County, N.C., 48, 66, 67, 69, 122, 247, 420
Edmund, Inez K., 404n
Egg Harbor City, N.J., 404–5
Emancipation Day, 50, 63
Enfield, N.C., 24

"Farewell speech" in Congress by GHW, 309–11. See Appendix for text

Farmers Alliance, 147–8, 161, 164, 190
Fayetteville, N.C., 3, 23n, 55, 77, 79, 81, 115
Fayetteville normal school, 55, 77–9, 81, 150
Fields, John, Jr., 186, 188, 192–7, 201–2
Fifteenth Street Presbyterian Church, Washington, D.C., 382, 393
Finaman, Charles H., 358
First Presbyterian Church, New Bern, N.C., 40, 51–2
Fishburn, James W., 358, 359
Fisher, George T., 56n
Fitzgerald, John, 306, 307
Foraker, Joseph B., 393–4, 396
Fort Fisher, Battle of, 121
Fortune, T. Thomas: activities in NAAC, 250–1, 349, 376, 389, 390; Afro-American League, 250; early acquaintance with GHW, 33, 136; journalistic career, 25n, 33, 33n, 136, 208, 334, 342; later career, 349n, 353, 367, 418
Fountain, W. E., 243, 246, 247
Franklin County, N.C., 15, 16, 80
Freedmen's Bureau, 14, 19, 26, 44, 45
Freeman, Howard F., 197
Freeman, Sarah Spaulding, 8
Freeman, W. S., 11, 13
Fuller, Thomas O., 248n, 253
Furches, David, 174
Fusion politics in N.C., 170, 172–4, 177, 185, 197–8, 209–12, 241–4, 246–8

Garfield, James A., 70, 71, 85, 86, 92, 95
Garrett, Della White (daughter of GHW): attacked in 1898 campaign, 245; birth and early life, 53, 64, 101, 137; children, 385, 387n, 415; death and burial, 415; education, 219; career as educator, 14n, 245, 264, 316; career at U.S. Census Bureau, 369; marriage, 356n, 385, 387, 415n
Garrett, Fannie (granddaughter of GHW), 414, 415
Garrett, James W. Oscar, 387, 415n

Garrett, York D., 140

Gay, Benjamin Stancell, 50

Geer, Solomon, 87–9

Gibbs, Harriet Aletha. *See* Marshall, Harriet Gibbs

Goldsboro, N.C., 58, 78n, 95, 95n, 217n, 243

Goldsboro Daily Argus, 205

Good Samaritan (New Bern, N.C.), 60

Goode, John R., 66n, 69

Grady, Luke, 114n

Grant, Hiram L., 100, 184n, 187, 202, 290, 291, 302

Grant, J. W., 106n

Grant, Ulysses S., 23, 30n

Granville County, N.C., 89

Green, Charles F., 274

Green, Eustace Edward, 57, 57n, 138, 289, 219, 415

Green, George, Jr., 65, 73, 135n

Green, Georgianna Cherry, 57, 57n, 138, 189, 219, 415

Green, John Paterson, 208, 250–1, 301, 337, 340–1, 345, 347, 353, 354

Greene County, N.C., 48, 67

Greensboro, N.C., 78n, 81, 252, 414

Greenville (N.C.) Reflector, 244

Greenwood Cemetery, New Bern, N.C., 54, 166, 180, 384

Greer, David H., 269

Griffin, Thomas J., 358

Griggs, James M., 286

Griggs, John W., 279

Grimké, Archibald, 393, 412

Grimké, Francis J., 382, 393

Grizzard, James M., 146

Grosvenor, Charles S., 306, 207, 208

Hagans, Henry E., 289, 292

Hagans, W. S., 206n, 272

Hahn, Mayer, 99, 129, 135

Halifax County, N.C., 24, 48, 66, 67, 69, 89, 97, 116, 122, 217, 247

Hall, Walter P., 401

Hampton Institute, 230, 268–9

Hancock, Winfield S., 70, 71

Hand, Robert E., 358

Hannon, John H., 202n, 207

Hargett, Israel D., 217n

Harmer, Alfred C.: GHW eulogy for, 271, 304–5

Harris, James H., 68n, 72, 92, 100n, 126

Harris, John C. L., 94, 121n, 123, 131

Harris, Robert, 77, 78n

Harrison, Benjamin, 47n, 110, 163, 217

Harrison, Gibson T., 425

Hatteras Indians, 21

Hayes, Rutherford B., 31–2, 38, 70

Hayley, Paul F., 66, 74, 81

Hays, John, 73, 89

Heath, J. F., 100

Henderson, David B., 271

Henderson, William B., 178, 212

Herritage, William B., 55, 56

Hicks, Alexander B., Jr., 55, 73, 74n, 81–3, 89–90, 91–2

Hill, Edward H., 66n, 69

Hill, James, 207, 208

Holden, William W., 2, 13, 23, 24, 92

Holley, Henry C., 186, 194, 195

Home for Protection of Colored Women, Philadelphia, 411

Hopkins, Moses A., 58n

Howard, General Oliver O., 26

Howard University: founding and history, 24, 25–7, 29, 33; GHW attends, 15, 22, 25, 26–9, 33; GHW's later relationship with, 230, 231n, 411; GHW speaks at, 267–8

Hubbs, Ethelbert, 72

Hubbs, Orlando, 66, 72, 83n, 98, 100, 129

Humphrey, Andrew, 393n

Humphrey, Lotte W., 73, 92, 98, 100, 130

Hunt, Ida Gibbs, 359n

Hunt, William Henry, 359n

Hussey, John E., 106, 135n

Hyman, Dilsey Ann, 148
Hyman, John Adams, 31n, 38, 47, 101

Indianapolis Freeman, 338, 339, 343
Indianapolis World, 338
Independent, 271, 278
"The Injustice to the Colored Voter" (GHW article), 271–2

Jackson, Fanny, 19, 20
Jackson, Robert S., 401n
Jackson, William H., 401n
James City, N.C., 45, 56, 120, 149–50
James City Ferry Company, 120
Jammison, George D., 55
Jarvis, Thomas J., 71, 72, 86, 100, 246
Johnson, Daniel R., 66, 74, 74n, 83, 134
Johnson, Van, 148
Johnson, William H., 97, 99, 101
Jones, Alice K., 404n
Jones, Charity, 140
Jones County, N.C., 48, 67, 113, 167
Jones, "Gen," 53
Jones, John P., 191n
Jones, Mary. *See* Parker, Mary Jones
Jones, Mary Ann. *See* Cherry, Mary Ann Jones

Kellor, Frances, 395
Keystone Aid Society, Philadelphia, 410
King, George H., 66, 74n, 89
Kinston, N.C., 217n, 243
Kinston (N.C.) Free Press, 242, 244, 245
Kirk-Holden "War," 23
Kitchin, Claude, 291, 302
Kitchin, W. H. "Buck," 47, 72, 73, 171n, 210, 291
Kitchin, William W., 25n, 212, 214, 263n, 292, 309
Knott, Laura, 379
Knox, George, 208, 320, 342
Ku Klux Klan, 24, 211

Lane, William B., 100, 135n, 150
Langston, John Mercer, 27, 32, 33, 95, 208, 415n, 422n
Lasker (N.C.) Patron and Gleaner, 184
Lawrence, N.C., 217
Lawson, Isaac, 99, 101
Lawson, Jesse A., 35n, 265, 347, 375, 376
Layten, S. Willie, 395
Leach, John P., 218
Leaming family, New Jersey, 358
Leary, John S., 24, 24n, 50, 137n, 174n, 176n, 322
Lee, John Wesley, 413–4
Lee, Mary Murdock, 414
Lehman, Martin J., 401n, 424
Lehman, R. F., 66, 99
Lenoir County, N.C., 48, 67, 113
Liberal (Anti-Prohibition) Party, N.C., 100, 101, 105, 127
Liliuokalani, Queen, 222, 235
Lincoln (Pa.) University, 52, 57n, 386, 401, 425
Linney, Romulus Z., 213, 215, 236n, 249, 280, 281, 284–5
Littleton, N.C., 168
Livingstone College, 78n, 231n
Lloyd, Henry, 139
Lloyd, James B., 210, 241, 243
Long, John S., 56
Long, W. W., 163n, 169, 171n
Lorimer, William, 221
Lost Colony of Roanoke, 21
Lowry, Henry Berry, 22, 23
Lumbee Indians, 21
Lumberton, N.C., 20, 21, 24, 40
Lynch, John Roy, 208, 293, 317, 354, 422
Lyons, Judson W., 208, 258, 265, 312, 347, 363, 390–1

Mabson, George L., 24, 24n, 50
Macdonald, Ellen. *See* White, Ellen Avant Macdonald

McDougald, George C., 1n

Mackie, Sylvester, 53

McGhee, Frederick L., 375

McKinlay, Whitefield, 352, 353, 384n

McKinley, William, 206, 213, 218, 231–2, 238, 250–2, 267, 276, 279, 293, 301, 303, 349–50, 388, 418, 421

Manly, Alexander L., 248, 251, 258n, 388

Manly, B. C., 90–1

Manly, Matthias, 150

Mann, Joseph, 53

Marshall, Harriet Gibbs, 358, 360, 381, 397

Marshall, Napoleon B., 359n, 397

Martin, James Bryan, 50

Martin, Joseph J., 164n, 184n, 193, 202, 302–3

Martin County, N.C., 122n

Mason, Thomas, 114–5, 133

Mason, William, 329

Mebane, George Allen, 154–5, 160

Metropolitan AME Zion Church, Washington, D.C., 321

Metropolitan Baptist Church, Washington, D.C., 250

Mewboorne, James M., 164, 190

Middleton, Abe, 236, 237

Milholland, John E., 252, 392–3, 396–7

Miller, Kelly, 394

Miller, Thomas E., 422

Miner Fund of Howard University, 33

Mitchell Field Cemetery, Welches Creek, N.C., 7

Money, Hernando D., 292

Montgomery, Jacob H., 106, 108, 131

Moore, E. W., 401, 406

Moore, Leonidas J., 42n, 66n, 98, 154–5

Moore, W. H., 114n

Moore, W. R., 57

Morgan, John T., 286

Morris, Benjamin W., 69

Moseley, Robert G., 40n

Moss, D. Schuyler, 204, 241, 247

Mossell, Nathan F., 411

Mott, John J., 169n, 171, 172

Moye, Gilbert, 53

Mozingo, John I., 205

Murray, Daniel A. P., 279, 347n

Murray, George W., 250, 265

National Afro-American Council: final years of, 389, 411; formation, 250; GHW active in, 250, 258, 265, 291, 337, 347, 370; GHW defeated for presidency of, 348; elected vice-president of, 348; legal bureau of, 375–6, 392; meetings of, 250, 251n, 264, 293, 297, 300, 341, 345, 347, 389; Washington, D.C., chapter of, 370

NAACP (National Association for the Advancement of Colored People): formation, 367, 389; Philadelphia branch formed, 411; GHW active in, 411

National League for the Protection of Colored Women, 395, 411

Naval stores (turpentine), 3, 5, 17, 20n, 50

Neuse River, 37

New Bern, N.C., 34, 37–45, 50–6, 58–60, 75, 78, 120, 199, 213, 219, 384

New Bern Academy, 47, 58

New Bern Daily Journal, 101, 135, 175, 181, 242

New Bern State Colored Normal School, 55–8, 80, 81, 328

Newbernian, 99

New Hanover County, N.C., 92n, 107n, 115n

Newell, John, 73, 87–91

News and Observer, Raleigh, N.C.: cartoons, 291; Josephus Daniels purchases, 159n; opposition to GHW, 237–41, 280–1; mentioned in text, 49, 84, 86, 90, 91, 111, 188, 189, 192, 194, 197, 198, 207, 236, 237, 239, 248, 252, 300, 420

Newsom, J. W., 114–6

Newsom, Samuel G., 66

Newton, Thomas, 40

New York Freeman, 79, 135–6, 137

New York Times, 90, 91, 113, 149, 203, 297–9

Niagara Movement, 389, 411

N.C. Agricultural and Mechanical College, 252

N.C. Colored Conference, 82

N.C. General Assembly: actions of 1881 legislature, 74–9, 81–5, 68–90; actions of 1883 legislature, 58–9, 104–5; actions of 1885 legislature, 106–17; election results for, 73–4, 102, 106, 135, 147, 162–3, 178, 197–8, 212, 246–8, 303

Northampton County, N.C., 48, 67, 97, 97n, 114, 247

Oberlin College and Academy, 377, 383, 404

Oberlin Conservatory, 383

Odessa Inn, 361, 386, 403, 425

O'Hara, James E., 24, 24n, 42, 47, 50, 67, 68n, 72, 73, 92, 98, 100–1, 106, 118–9, 125–7, 133, 149–51, 172–3, 176n, 179

Old Dominion Steamship Company, 120

Otey, Peter, 310

Ovington, Mary White, 392n, 412

Page, E. R., 90, 91

Palmer, Benjamin Boswell, 52

Parker, Mary Jones, 139

Patton, William W., 32

Peabody Fund, 44, 55, 78

Pearson, Richmond, 213, 291

Pembroke, N.C., 21

Pennsylvania, University of, 410

People's Advocate, New Bern, N.C., 118–20, 129, 136

People's Advocate, Washington, D.C., 33

People's Savings Bank, Philadelphia, 401–2, 416–7, 419

Perry, Christopher J., 342, 406, 409, 424

Person, W. Lee, 163n, 164n, 202n, 212, 218n

Pettipher, Willis B., 40n, 65–6, 68, 69

Philadelphia, 30, 31, 139, 292–3, 349, 358, 386, 393, 400

Philadelphia Tribune, 342, 418

Pillsbury, Albert E., 287, 375

Pinchback, Pinckney B. S., 250, 265, 333, 337, 345, 347, 371

Pitt County, N.C., 9, 10, 16, 113

Platt, Orville, 393, 398

Plymouth State Colored Normal School (N.C.), 55, 80n, 81, 138, 156

Powell, William Frank, 312

Price, George W., 92

Price, Joseph C., 82n, 83n, 109, 137n

Pritchard, Jeter Conley, 170, 211, 238, 299, 301, 317, 329, 352, 365, 387

Purnell, Thomas R., 174

Quay, Matthew, 329

Raleigh, N.C., 1, 42, 78n, 86, 90, 92, 95, 106, 112, 115n, 121n, 122, 175n

Raleigh Gazette, 79, 213, 217, 224

Raleigh Morning Post, 225, 239, 243

Raleigh Signal, 23, 170, 175

Randolph, Fannie B. *See* White, Fannie Randolph

Randolph, Henry, 53, 55n

Randolph, John, 53

Randolph, John, Jr., 53, 92n, 101

Randolph, Kate Green, 53, 54n, 101

Randolph, Lewis, 53, 54

Ransom, Matthew Whitaker, 141

Ransom, Reverdy C., 398n

Raymond, J. B., 322

"Red Shirts," 295

Red Springs, N.C., 21

Reed, Thomas B.,

Rehobeth Church and school, Columbus County, N.C., 19

Reid, George W., 15, 28

Republican League, 241

Republican National Convention: of 1892,

170; of 1896, 205–9; of 1900, 292–4; of 1912, 409

Rice, F. B., 175

Rich Square, N.C., 243

Richland Branch, 1

Ridgeway, N.C., 217

Robbins, Augustus, 73, 74n, 164n

Robeson County, N.C., 21–2, 23, 40

Robinson, J. Francis, 254

Rocky Mount, N.C., 217

Rogers, William J., 164, 171n

Romain, Armand, 375

Roosevelt, Theodore, 294, 350, 387, 407–9, 420–1

Roseville, N.C., 15

Rosindale, N.C., 1

Roulhac, Leslie, 106n

Rucker, Henry A., 363–4, 391

Russell, Daniel Lindsay, 23n, 169, 172, 202, 211, 212, 238, 281

Rutherford, Allan M., 14, 14n, 19–20, 29

Rutherford, Della, 19n

Ryanes, Jordan, 376

Saint Augustine's College, 78n, 139

Salisbury, N.C., 80n, 71

Sanders, D. J., 53

Sandy Plains, N.C., 7, 8

Saunders, E. L., 401n

Saunders, William A., 401n

Savage, J. A., 58n

Schenck, John, 173

Scotia Seminary, 14n, 78n, 219

Scott, Allen A., 52, 55, 84, 101

Scott, Amos M., 409, 410, 424

Scott, Emmett J., 348, 350

Scott, Nancy J. See White, Nancy Scott

Scott, Nathan B., 328

Scull, Marcus, 357

Scurlock, George C., 191

Second Baptist Lyceum, Washington, D.C., 345, 349, 370, 389

Second Judicial District, N.C., 111–4, 122, 167, 249

Selvy, William L., 358

Sessions, William and Mary, 10

Seth, Joseph T., 401

Settle, Thomas, 147, 168, 181, 187, 189n, 211, 212

Shadd, Mattie, 380

Sharpe, John T., 100

Shaw, Victoria D., 35

Shaw University, 24n, 77

Shepard, James E., 203

Simmons, Furnifold, 112n, 129, 130, 152, 153, 160, 161–2, 171n, 241–2, 294, 302, 303

Simmons, Henry H., 69

Simpson, Joshua, 90–1

Slap Swamp, 1, 1n, 8n

Smalls, Robert, 208, 215, 215n, 391

Smallwood, Anna L., 35

Smith, Ezra E., 149–50

Smith, Harry C., 319, 341, 342, 344

Smith, Isaac H., 248n

Smith, Owen Lun West, 312, 388

Somerville, Ella W., 58

Southwick, George N., 233–4

Spalding, Benjamin. See Spaulding, Benjamin

Sparks's Circus, Tarboro, N.C., 244–5

Spaulding, Benjamin, 4–7, 7n, 11; children of, 7n, 8, 8n

Spaulding, Benjamin, Jr., 8, 11

Spaulding, Benjamin McLean, 8

Spaulding, Charles C., 427

Spaulding, Daniel, 373n, 425

Spaulding, David, 7

Spaulding, Edith Delphia Jacobs, 7–8

Spaulding, Emmanuel, 7–9, 11; children of, 8, 8n

Spaulding, Guy S., 8, 359n

Spaulding, Hattie Moore, 373n, 427n

Spaulding, Henry, 8

Spaulding, Henry Wilson "Willie," 359, 372, 373, 426

Spaulding, Iver, 7, 7n, 8
Spaulding, John W., 8, 92n, 372
Spaulding, Mariah, 11
Spaulding, Mary Anna. *See* White, Mary
  Anna Spaulding
Spaulding, Odessa, xvi, 426, 427
Spaulding, Sarah Jane. *See* Freeman, Sarah
  Spaulding
Spaulding, Susannah Gumby, 8
Spaulding, Theodore O., 427
Spears, Oscar J., 170, 172
Sprague, Charles F., 271, 329, 332–3
Spraulding, Benjamin. *See* Spaulding,
  Benjamin
Sprawling, Benjamin. *See* Spaulding,
  Benjamin
Stanly, John C., 40
Star of Zion, Salisbury, N.C., 64, 128n
State ex rel *Ryanes v. Gleason,* 375, 376, 392
Stevens, Andrew W., 416
Stewart, Gilchrist, 396
Stimson, Daniel, 99, 129, 135
Strivers' Section, Washington, D.C., 257
Swindell, Samuel, 6
Swindell, Samuel, Jr., 6

Taft, William Howard, 396, 408
Tarboro, N.C., 58, 96, 217n, 219, 243, 289
Tarboro (N.C.) Southerner, 185, 218, 219,
  226, 240, 243, 292, 299–300, 303
Taylor, Robert S., 106n, 108, 110, 114
Terrell, Mary Church, 396, 412
Terrell, Robert H., 371, 387
Thomas, Charles Randolph, 112n
Thomas, Robert, 210
Thompson, Carey P., 35
Thompson, Cyrus, 295
Thompson, Richard W., 347n
Thorne, Edward A., 171, 177
Thornton, Edward L., 120, 121n, 136, 137,
  191

Thornton, Mansfield, 67n
Thorpe, Bryant W., 106n, 114n
Tourgée, Albion W., 23n, 82, 183n
Trotter, William Monroe, 366, 390, 393,
  398n
Tryon Palace, New Bern, N.C., 37
Tucker, Richard, 66n, 69
Turner, J. Milton, 301
Turpentine. *See* Naval stores
Tuskegee Institute, 228, 229, 230, 251, 268,
  364, 397
Tyler, Ralph Waldo, 342, 398, 398n

Union League, 24
U.S. Centennial Exposition, 29–30, 33, 33n
U.S. Civil Service Commission: GHW remarks on, 221–2
U.S. Coast Survey, 29, 31, 328
U.S. Congress, 55th: GHW sworn in as member, 213; bills introduced by GHW, 215,
  220, 224; GHW addressess, 215–7, 221–4,
  226–7, 259–63, 265–6; GHW's activities
  in, 213–4, 215–9, 220–7, 231–2, 233–5,
  256, 259–63; major legislation of, 226,
  234–5
U.S. Congress, 56th: bills introduced by
  GHW, 278, 288, 307; GHW addresses,
  280–1, 282–5, 304–7, 308–11; GHW's
  activities in, 270–5, 278–81, 282–4, 285–8,
  304–11; major legislation of, 306–7
U.S. Industrial Commission: GHW testifies
  before, 273–5

Vance, Joseph G., 357, 358, 372
Vance, Zebulon B., 71, 80n, 110
Vance County, N.C., 48, 104, 167
Vass, Lachlan C., 52n, 56n, 57, 83n
Vick, Annie W., 414
Vick, George White, 360n
Vick, Samuel Hynes, 164n, 358, 360, 414
Vogell, H. C., 45

Waccamaw Indians, 21
Waddell, William H., 73, 74
Wake County, N.C., 97, 113, 121n, 122, 175n
Walters, Alexander: active in NAACP, 412n; death, 420; serves as chairman of National Afro-American Council, 250, 265, 347, 349, 376; defeats GHW for Council chairmanship, 348; supports GHW as successor, 347; relationship with Booker T. Washington, 398n
Ward, Richard C., 106n
Waring, Charles S., 35
Warner-Foraker amendment to Hepburn railroad bill, 394
Warren County, N.C., 48, 67, 69, 96, 97, 122, 247
Warrick, Charles B., 50n
Washington, Booker Taliaferro: correspondence with Cora Lena White, 362–4, 378–83; death, 420; early relationship with GHW, 228–31; aid sought by GHW in obtaining Treasury appointment, 350–1; ideological differences with GHW, 229, 336, 371, 398; relationship with GHW in later years, 372, 398, 412–3; relationship with Theodore Roosevelt, 350–2, 421
Washington Conservatory of Music, 369, 381n, 383
Washington Evening Star, 26, 32, 214n, 384, 420
Washington Post, 214n, 323–6, 358, 384
Wassom, George T., 50n, 95
Watson, James M., 147, 178n
Watson, William W., 66, 73, 76, 86–91, 128, 132, 186, 193
Watt, Melvin, 424
Watts, Samuel W., 237n
Wayne County, N.C., 48, 66, 67, 71, 104–5, 167
Weaver, James B., 70

Weaver, Thomas, 413
Welches Creek Township, 4, 7, 10, 15, 18, 39, 40
Weldon, N.C., 201, 218, 232
Wells-Barnett, Ida B., 220–1
Western Reserve University, 410
"What Should Be the Negro's Attitude in Politics?": GHW article in anthology, 367–8
Whitaker, Spier, 142n
White, Beatrice Odessa (daughter of GHW), 166, 180, 425
White, Charles Henry Clay, 15, 15n
White, Cora Lena Cherry: attacked in 1898 campaign, 245, 246; children of, 166, 416; death and burial, 383–4; early life, 138, 140; family members, 137–40; health, 214, 257–8, 265, 270–1, 272, 288, 298, 315, 361, 362, 369; marriage to GHW, 57n, 132, 137, 156, 385, 415–6. See also Booker Taliaferro Washington, correspondence with
White, Della M. See Garrett, Della White
White, Ellen, 14n
White, Ellen Avant Macdonald (wife of GHW), 413–5, 419, 425
White, Fannie Randolph (wife of GHW), 53–4, 65
White, Flora (sister of GHW), 12n, 13
White, George Elon, 213, 271
White, George Henry: active in N.C. Republican Party, 166, 171–5; articles and letters published, 136, 272, 326–30, 394–5; burial, 424; business and real estate investments, 51, 60, 357, 372; campaign activities for National GOP, 301, 328; campaigns for Congress, xxi, 232, 241–7, 291–2, 298–300, 301–2, 407–9; campaigns for district solicitor, 4–96, 118–25; campaigns for N.C. General Assembly, 65, 94–103, 104–106; candidacy for N.C. attorney general, 174–6; career as educator, 15, 34, 43n, 44, 55, 59,

81, 94; childhood and early life, xiv, 17, 18, 419; early education, xx, 17, 18; family members, 8–10, 13–4, 53–4, 55, 166, 359, 413–5; honorary degrees held, 231n; homes owned, 146, 180, 257, 314, 401; involvement in Philadelphia Republican politics, 407, 409–10; legal career, 24, 42, 42n, 49, 59, 103–4, 120, 288, 319, 403–5, 410; introduces federal antilynching bill, 270; Masonic and fraternal activities, 60, 60n, 166n; memorial plaque to, New Bern, N.C., 423; physical appearance, 25, 25n, 121, 233, 234n, 277, 299; racial heritage, 2, 10–1, 11n, 21, 2n; possible origin of name, 16–7; possible slave status, 10, 18; religious activities, 51, 52, 82, 158, 166n; Prohibition activities as legislator, 75, 82; seeks appointment as municipal judge, 406; seeks appointment as U.S. Treasury auditor, 351; serves as solicitor, 140–5; works as turpentine farmer, 15. *See also* U.S. Congress, 55th and 56th; Constitutional League of the United States; Howard University; N.C. General Assembly; People's Savings Bank; Washington, Booker Taliaferro; White Land & Improvement Company.

White Land & Improvement Company, George H.: develops Whitesboro, N.J., 350, 356, 360, 371, 386; operations after GHW's death, 424–5; shareholders in, 358–60, 359n

White, George Henry, Jr. (son of GHW): birth and early life, 166, 219, 264, 385; career, 410, 415; death and burial, 426; education of, 316, 361, 369, 386, 401, 410

White, John, 21n

White, John W. (brother of GHW), 10, 13

White, Mary Adelyne "Mamie" (daughter of GHW): birth and early life, 166, 219, 264; career, 415, 417, 425; death and burial, xv,

416; education of, 316, 361, 369, 378–81, 383, 385, 401; moves to New York, 425; teaches in Whitesboro, N.J., 404

White, Mary Anna Spaulding (stepmother of GHW), 8, 14, 14n, 359, 35n, 372, 386n

White, Nancy Scott (wife of GHW), 55, 56, 56n, 57, 84n, 103, 385

White, Penelope (sister of GHW), 12n, 13

White, W. F., 11, 13

White, Wesley, 13, 16

White, "White," 13

White, Wiley F. (nephew of GHW), 13, 14n

White, Wiley Franklin (father of GHW): career at U.S. Department of Treasury, 14, 14n, 29; death and burial, 180–1; early life, 9; marriage to Mary Anna Spaulding, 9; moves to Washington, D.C., 15, 15n, 20; political career in Columbus County, 13; property owned, 9–10, 12

White Government Union, 241

Whitesboro, N.J.: founding, 358; development and early history of, 358, 372–4, 403–4, 425; GHW's property in, 403

White supremacy movement, N.C., 240–7

Whiteville, N.C., 5, 12

Whitin (Whitten) School, N.C., 20, 22, 23, 5, 77

Whitten School. *See* Whitin School

Who's Who in America, 9n

Who's Who in Philadelphia, 411

Williams, Alice D. Johnson, 35

Williams, Daniel Hale, 35

Williams, John S., 259, 261

Williamson, John H., 145, 147n, 206n

Williamson, Robert W., 147n, 178n, 243, 249

Williamson, Walter P., 66n, 96, 122

Willis, George B., 66n, 69

Willis, Junius, 53

Wilmington, N.C., 19, 21, 37, 29, 248–9, 281

Wilmington Messenger, 245

Wilmington Morning Star, 240, 242, 248

Wilmington Post, 95, 121

Wilmington racial riot (1898), 248–9, 255–6, 274, 281, 286

Wilson, N.C., 78n, 99, 218, 243

Wilson Advance, 144, 225

Windsor, N.C., 217, 243

Winston, Duncan C., 101

Winston, Francis Donnell, 125, 133, 241, 303

Winston, Robert Watson, 107, 113, 141

Woodard, Frederick A., 106, 127, 171, 177, 179, 183, 197, 204, 211, 291

Woodbine, N.J., 356, 372

Woodbridge, N.C., 75

Woodlawn Cemetery, Washington, D.C., 415

Wormley, Mamie Cheatham, 258, 386n, 426

Wright, John H., 147n, 178, 248n

Wright, Richard R., Jr., 401, 403

YMCA, Philadelphia, 413

Young, James Hunter, 170, 175, 192n, 202, 203, 209, 213, 236

Young, Robert E. "Q," 128

Youngblood, William, 316

Zion Baptist Church, Philadelphia, 401, 406

Zion Wesley College, 108–10